African Music and Oral Data

A Catalog of Field Recordings, 1902-1975

African Field Recordings Survey
Archives of Traditional Music
Indiana University

African Music and Oral Data

A Catalog of Field
Recordings, 1902-1975

Ruth M. Stone

Frank J. Gillis

Indiana University Press
Bloomington & London

Published in Canada by Fitzhenry & Whiteside Limited, Don
Mills, Ontario

Manufactured in the United States of America

Library of Congress Cataloging in Publication Data

Stone, Ruth M., 1945-
    African music and oral data.

1. Music, African--Discography. 2. Oral tradition--Africa--
Discography. I. Gillis, Frank J., 1914- joint author. II.
Title.
ML156.4.P7S8 016.7899'12 75-31419
ISBN 0-253-30262-5   2 3 4 5 80 79 78

Contents

Foreword

The past two decades have witnessed an extraordinary increase in Western man's knowledge of Africa, Africans, and the forms of their unique human expression. This information has been made available to us in an equally extraordinary variety of sources--books, articles, cinema, film strips, phonograph records, tapes, and other means. For most of us, however, the most pressing problem in dealing with this material is of retrieving precisely what we want from the mass that is available.

In some areas, the problem has been alleviated through the compilation of bibliographies, and thus we have some control, at least, over the retrieval of pieces of written literature concerning Africa. Bibliographies abound--of anthropological materials, and pieces of anthropological materials; of politics and pieces of politics; of economics, education, social organization, language, the arts. In short, there are numerous compilations of the various facets of African man's existence and of his comments on them. The totality or adequacy of these compilations is not the question here--the point is that at least beginnings have been made, and we need no longer search all the literature to find the single piece of information we require.

In the field of visual expression, too, a remarkable amount of material is available. Several movie and slide-band collecting points have been established, primarily at academic institutions, along with printed bibliographies and filmographies of the holdings. The number of photographs of pieces of African visual art available in books and magazines is staggering, and while I am not aware of compilations of such materials, some information is available through bibliographies of the media in which they appear.

We have some control, then, over the printed output itself, and through it various other kinds of material, but the same cannot be said for recorded sound. Indeed, we are not even sure when the first recordings were made in Africa, though the Ethnomusicological Section of the Museum für Völkerkunde in Berlin lists as its earliest materials the collections made by Carl Meinhof in East Africa in 1902-1903. Yet this hardly seems reasonable as a first date when we recall that J. Walter Fewkes was recording among the Passamaquoddy Indians in the United States in 1890--surely some earlier recordings exist

for Africa, but if so, we do not know what, or where, they are.
     Yet the flood of materials that started around the turn
of the century has never ceased to flow; indeed, it has multi-
plied without surcease--and probably more geometrically than
arithmetically. No one knows how many recordings of African
songs exist. It does not seem unreasonable to suppose that
at least 100,000 separate 10" 78 rpm records were issued for
commercial sale on the African and international markets.
The record arena today is glutted with 45 rpm recordings, but
again in how many tens or hundreds of thousands we have no
idea, and no one is attempting to keep systematic track of the
production. Probably several thousand early 10" and contempo-
rary 12" LP recordings of African music could now be listed,
but only three systematic attempts have been made to gather
information on these discs; together they cover 600 recordings
comprising approximately 5,700 individual items of African
music. Discographies of the other forms, i.e., 10" 78 rpm
and 7" 45 rpm recordings, have been undertaken sporadically,
but I know of no unified compilation of such attempts.
     This brings us to the present catalog, which is unique
in its listing of noncommercial collections of African music.
The project, as noted in the Preface, was begun eleven years
ago by Willard Rhodes, and has only relatively recently been
brought forward systematically by the present compilers. That
they were able to assemble and contact a list of 3,000 individuals and institutions indicates the enormity of the task;
that some 1,500 responded, and close to 550 provided pertinent
information, is remarkable and also shows how badly the compilation was needed. Now, suddenly, we have a new and detailed
source for the retrieval of information about African music
and oral data, and it has probably at least doubled our available knowledge. How we use that knowledge is, of course,
another matter--let us hope wisely and well--but it is here
for the taking now.
     We all know that the compilation of data is never-ending--
every bibliography (and discography) is out of date on the day
it is published, and of course the present work is no excep-
tion. But the materials presented here are computer-program-
med, so that continual updating and correcting are possible.
And more important, the compilers visualize this project as
never-ending. Thus, we can look forward to a continuing and
continuous stream of information on African music and oral
data recorded in the field. We have not previously been in
a position which allowed us so much optimism.

Indiana University   Alan P. Merriam
Bloomington, Indiana

Preface

The present catalog, based on the African Field Recordings Survey, provides concise summaries of collections of
phonorecordings of music and oral data held by individuals
and institutions throughout the world. The catalog contains
references to primary source data which should be of value to
individuals working with historical materials or planning
future research in the humanities or social sciences.

The catalog is based almost entirely on data supplied
through questionnaires (see Fig. 1), which were sent to nearly
3,000 individuals and institutions. One thousand five hundred
responded to the questionnaires, and some 550 supplied useful
information. Data received were transferred to summary sheets
(see Fig. 2) and subsequently to keypunched computer cards
(see Fig. 3).

Through the use of a computer program entitled GLIB-
SELIND, designed by Jean Nakhnikian, programer-consultant at
the Marshal H. Wrubel Computing Center at Indiana University,
the data were organized into fifteen fields, or categories,
of which thirteen are utilized in the Survey. The program
will index, match, and select within any of these fields/cate-
gories and will print all of the input or only selected parts
of it in any order specified.

The catalog proper, which is followed by three indexes,
is arranged alphabetically by collector or repository, with
data concerning the collection separated into thirteen categories or fields, each of which (except the last) is terminated
by the symbol   , whether there is or is not information within
the category. The thirteen categories within the CATALOG OF
COLLECTORS AND REPOSITORIES are given in the following order
(see Fig. 4):

1. Collector or repository
2. Address of collector or repository
3. Country
4. Town and/or province
5. Culture group
6. Size of collection
7. Year of recording
8. Quality
9. Repository
10. Accession or collection number
11. ATL (Indiana University Archives Tape Library) number
12. Access (degree of restriction placed on use)
13. Subjects

The INDEX TO COUNTRIES includes four categories, given in the following order:

1. Country
2. Collector or repository
3. Culture group
4. Year of recording

The INDEX TO CULTURE GROUPS includes four categories, given in the following order:

1. Culture group
2. Collector or repository
3. Country
4. Year of recording

The INDEX TO SUBJECTS includes five categories, given in the following order:

1. Subject
2. Collector or repository
3. Country
4. Culture group
5. Year of recording

<u>Notes concerning the organization of information within each field</u>:

1. <u>Collector or repository</u>

   * Names of collectors and repositories are listed alphabetically.

   * Multiple collectors are separated by a plus (+) sign, and each collector is listed individually within the catalog.

   * A dash after a surname indicates that the first name of the collector is not known to the compilers.

   * If data regarding a collection follow the name of a repository, the collection is held by that repository and the name of the collector is not known to the compilers.

2. Address of collector or repository

   * Addresses of multiple collectors are separated

by a plus (+) sign and listed in the order
corresponding to the listing of collectors'
names in the first field/category.

* Names of countries are given as a part of the
  address except for U.S.A.

* If a collector is deceased, the designation
  in this category is DECEASED.

3. Country

* The designation for data which have been collected
  from an informant in a country other than the
  home country includes 1) the name of the
  country to which the data pertain and 2)
  the country in which the actual recording
  was made (e.g., NIGERIA-U.S.).

4. Town and/or province

* Towns and/or provinces have been listed when
  available, separated by a comma and appearing
  in alphabetical order.

5. Culture group

* Names of culture groups are given primarily as
  supplied by contributors. A listing of groups
  referred to in the catalog, with cross references to variant spellings and alternate
  names, appears at the end of the INDEX TO
  CULTURE GROUPS. Two sources have been used to
  standardize entries: George P. Murdock, Outline
  of World Cultures, 3d ed., rev. (New Haven:
  Human Relations Area Files, 1969) and Charles F.
  and Florence M. Voegelin, Index of the World's
  Languages (Bloomington: Indiana University,
  1973).

6. Size of collection

* The size of the collection is given in the number
  of hours of recorded time.

7. Year of recording

* The date of recording is given by year, consecu-
  tive years, or various years in which recordings

were made.

8. Quality of recording

   * The quality of the recorded sound is given as
     supplied by contributors or the compilers.

   * Four categories have been used in designating
     quality: EXCELLENT, GOOD, FAIR, and POOR.

9. Repository

   * Names of multiple repositories are separated
     by a plus (+) sign, and each repository is
     listed individually, with address, within
     the catalog.

   * The Archives of Traditional Music is listed as
     a repository when originals and/or copies
     of a collection are housed in the Archives.

10. Accession or collection number

    * The accession number is the key reference number
      assigned to the collection by the various
      repositories.

11. ATL number

    * The ATL number is the reference number of the
      listening copy in the Archives Tape Library
      of the Archives of Traditional Music or its
      Center for African Oral Data.

12. Access

    * This category/field shows the type of restriction
      placed on the outside use of the collection.
      When the category/field is blank, it indicates
      that 1) there are no restrictions placed on
      use, or 2) information on use is not available.
      If RESTRICTED is given, it indicates that per-
      mission of the collector is needed before
      copies can be made and supplied.

13. Subjects

    * Subject headings refer to social activities,

genres, musical instruments, and other
data found within the corpus of the recorded
collection.

* The specificity of subject headings assigned is
  variable, depending upon information supplied
  by the collector or inferred by the compilers
  from the data at hand. The most specific term
  applicable has been chosen. General terms,
  such as "music" and "folklore," have been
  avoided except where no other information is
  available. Indigenous terms which are well
  known among scholars, such as <u>mbira</u> or <u>likembe</u>,
  have been retained.

* The subject heading "WORK-FIELD" refers to songs
  associated with agricultural activity; "LECTURE"
  is used when the recorded collection includes
  an oral presentation on a particular subject.

The African Field Recordings Survey has been conceived as
a continuing project in two respects. First, through a com-
puterization of the data, continual updating and correcting
are possible. We would thus welcome corrections and information regarding other collections which might be included in
the Survey. Second, special printouts covering a particular
period, country, culture group, or subject area are available
for purchase. All correspondence should be directed to:

> African Field Recordings Survey
> 057 Maxwell Hall
> Indiana University
> Bloomington, Indiana 47401

* * * * *

The African Field Recordings Survey represents the ful-
fillment of a project originally organized under the aegis of
the Committee of Fine Arts and the Humanities of the African
Studies Association. In 1964 the Committee received funds from
the Ford Foundation through the Association which enabled it
to undertake five research projects of a bibliographic nature:
an inventory of African visual art in American collections, a
survey of field-recorded African music, a census of noncommercial films on Africa, a survey of commercially issued
films devoted to African subjects, and a discography of African
music on commercially issued longplay disc recordings. The
last two projects have been completed and the results published.

The survey of field-recorded African music was begun by
Professor Willard Rhodes, who in 1964 and again in 1967 sent
out questionnaires requesting information on existing collections of phonorecordings to several hundred individuals and
institutions. Because of the press of other duties, Professor
Rhodes was unable to continue with the project, and we took it
over in 1973 and organized it under the title of African Field
Recordings Survey. We would especially like to recognize the
initial work carried out by Willard Rhodes. His questionnaire
served as a basis for the survey made by the present compilers.

A revised questionnaire was prepared and sent to individuals and institutions during the period 1974-75. The com-
puterized compilation of data gathered was carried out with
financial assistance provided by the Oral Data Committee of
the African Studies Association, again through a Ford Foundation grant, and the Indiana University African Studies Program,
Archives of Traditional Music, Learning Resources Center, and
the Marshal H. Wrubel Computing Center. We are grateful to
the Ford Foundation and those named above for providing funds
and assistance which made it possible to complete this portion
of the Survey.

The present catalog would not have been possible without
the cooperation of many individuals who supplied data on their
own collections and/or offered names of other collectors who
might be contacted. We would like to acknowledge their con-
tributions here.

Our sincere thanks go, as well, to members of the staff of
the Archives of Traditional Music--Louise Spear, Marilyn Graf,
Robert Fogal, Jan Henshaw, Barbara Whaley, and Caroline Card--
for their valuable assistance in research, typing, filing, and
other work related to the compilation. Special mention needs
to be made of editing and research done by Cathy Atkinson.
Finally, the project was assisted by Jean Nakhnikian, computer
programer and consultant, who redesigned portions of her
program for this project.

Grateful acknowledgment is also made here of assistance
provided by advisors to the project and readers who made
critical comments on the form and content of the indexes. They
include Jean Gosebrink, Dorothy S. Lee, Alan P. Merriam, and
Florence M. Voegelin. The ultimate responsibility for the
catalog rests, of course, with us; as compilers we have at-
tempted to summarize as precisely and accurately as possible
the information provided by the contributors.

Indiana University   Ruth M. Stone
Bloomington, Indiana
                                                      Frank J. Gillis

FIGURE 1. QUESTIONNAIRE

INFORMATION REGARDING RECORDINGS OF AFRICAN MUSIC AND ORAL DATA--INDIVIDUALS

Surname _____ First name _____ Middle name _____

Please give names and addresses of individuals you know who have collected in Africa. Use reverse side of form if necessary.

Address _____

_____

_____

Institutional affiliation _____

Please give the following information on all recordings of indigenous African music and oral data which you have, excluding commercial recordings.

Country	Group/ People	Region/ Town	Number of units (discs, tapes)	Hours	Dates Recorded	Types of music or oral data (folklore, oral history, ritual, social, praise, poetry: please specify)

1. Quality of recordings _____ Excellent _____ Good _____ Fair _____ Poor _____ not transferable

2. Brand of recorder _____   3. Rating of performance _____ Excellent _____ Good _____ Fair _____ Poor

4. Would you be willing to make your collection available to an archive of African music for archival use with the rights of the collector reserved? _____

Is your collection already deposited in an archive? _____ If so, where? _____

Additional information:

FIGURE 2. SUMMARY

1. Name of collector(s)   _____

2. Culture group(s)   _____

                                 _____

3. Country   _____

4. Town(s) or province(s)   _____

5. Number of hours   _____hours

6. Dates recorded   _____

7. Earliest date   _____

8. Quality of recordings   excellent   good   fair   poor

9. Place of deposit   _____

10. Accession number _____

11. Degree of restriction _____

12. Year of accession _____

13. Collector's address: _____

                         _____

14. ATL _ _ _ _

15. Major subject headings (including instruments)_____

    _____

    _____

FIGURE 3. SAMPLE COMPUTER CARDS

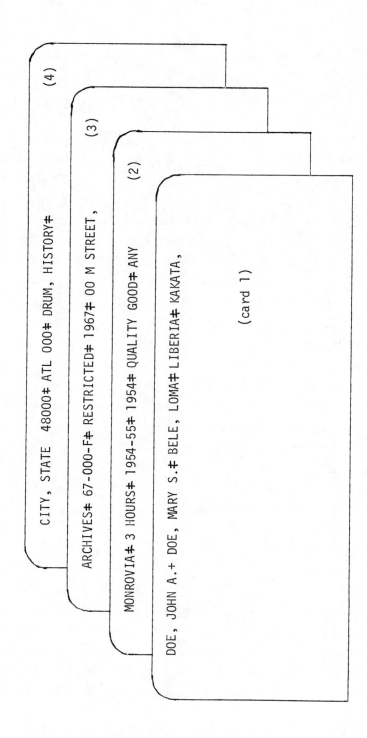

(4)

CITY, STATE 48000≠ ATL 000≠ DRUM, HISTORY≠

(3)

ARCHIVES≠ 67-000-F≠ RESTRICTED≠ 1967≠ 00 M STREET,

(2)

MONROVIA≠ 3 HOURS≠ 1954-55≠ 1954≠ QUALITY GOOD≠ ANY

DOE, JOHN A.+ DOE, MARY S.≠ BELE, LOMA≠ LIBERIA≠ KAKATA,

(card 1)

FIGURE 4. CATEGORIES/FIELDS FOR EACH ENTRY

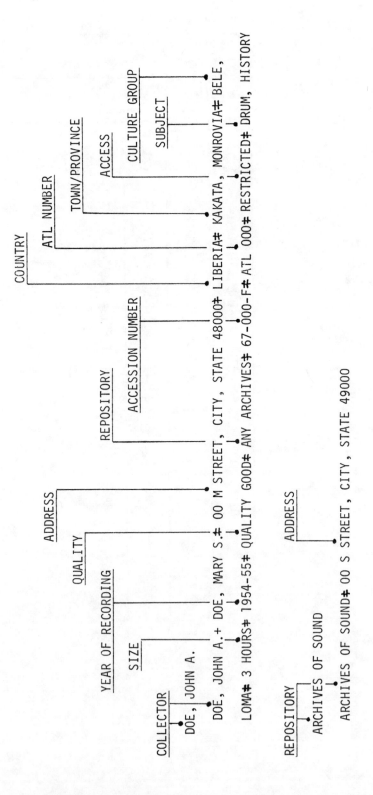

COLLECTOR
DOE, JOHN A.

SIZE

YEAR OF RECORDING

QUALITY

ADDRESS

REPOSITORY

ACCESSION NUMBER

COUNTRY

ATL NUMBER

TOWN/PROVINCE

ACCESS

CULTURE GROUP

SUBJECT

DOE, JOHN A.+ DOE, MARY S.‡ OO M STREET, CITY, STATE 48000‡ LIBERIA‡ KAKATA, MONROVIA≠ BELE,
LOMA‡ 3 HOURS‡ 1954-55‡ QUALITY GOOD≠ ANY ARCHIVES‡ 67-000-F≠ ATL 000≠ RESTRICTED‡ DRUM, HISTORY

REPOSITORY
ARCHIVES OF SOUND

ADDRESS

ARCHIVES OF SOUND‡ OO S STREET, CITY, STATE 49000

African Music
and Oral Data

A Catalog of Field
Recordings, 1902-1975

Catalog of
Collectors and
Repositories

Catalog of Collectors and Repositories

ABDELSAYED, FR. GABRIEL H
  ABDELSAYED, FR. GABRIEL H.A.‡ 97-15 HORACE
  HARDING EXPRESSWAY, APT.10K, CORONA, NEW YORK
  11368‡ EGYPT‡ CAIRO‡ COPT‡ 10 HOURS‡ 1965-69‡
  QUALITY EXCELLENT‡ ‡ ‡ ‡ ‡ CHOIR-COPTIC,
  RITUAL-COPTIC

ABDULKADIR, DATTI
  ABDULKADIR, DATTI‡ ABDULLAHI BAYERO COLLEGE,
  AHMADU BELLO UNIVERSITY, KANO, NIGERIA‡ NIGERIA‡
  NORTHERN NIGERIA‡ HAUSA-FULANI‡ 40 HOURS‡ 1973‡
  QUALITY GOOD‡ ‡ ‡ ‡ ‡ PRAISE, SATIRE

ABIMBOLA, WANDE
  ABIMBOLA, WANDE‡ UNIVERSITY OF IFE, ILE-IFE,
  WESTERN STATE, NIGERIA‡ NIGERIA‡ OYO‡ YORUBA‡ 2
  HOURS‡ 1971‡ QUALITY EXCELLENT‡ ARCHIVES OF
  TRADITIONAL MUSIC‡ 71-302-F‡ ATL 4838-39‡
  RESTRICTED‡ PRAISE-DIVINITY-ESHU,
  PRAISE-DIVINITY-IJALA, RELIGIOUS-PRAISE

ABUZAHRA, NADIA
  ABUZAHRA, NADIA‡ DEPARTMENT OF ANTHROPOLOGY,
  UNIVERSITY OF BRITISH COLUMBIA, VANCOUVER 8,
  BRITISH COLUMBIA, CANADA‡ TUNISIA‡ SIDI AMEUR‡
  SAHEL‡ 4 HOURS‡ 1966‡ QUALITY GOOD‡ ‡ ‡ ‡
  CONVERSATION, RELIGIOUS, RHYME

ADAMS, CHARLES R.
  ADAMS, CHARLES R.‡ DEPARTMENT OF ANTHROPOLOGY,
  UNIVERSITY OF KANSAS, LAWRENCE, KANSAS 66044‡
  LESOTHO‡ PITSENG‡ BASOTHO‡ 30 HOURS‡ 1969-70‡
  QUALITY EXCELLENT‡ ‡ ‡ ‡ ‡ CEREMONY, PRAISE,
  SOCIAL

  ADAMS, CHARLES R.‡ DEPARTMENT OF ANTHROPOLOGY,
  UNIVERSITY OF KANSAS, LAWRENCE, KANSAS 66044‡
  SWAZILAND‡ NORTHEAST‡ SWAZI‡ 3 HOURS‡ 1969-70‡
  QUALITY GOOD‡ ‡ ‡ ‡ ‡ DANCE-SOCIAL, SOCIAL-DANCE

ADLER, -
  ADLER, -‡ ‡ CHAD‡ ‡ MBAYE‡ ‡ ‡ ‡ MUSEE DE L'HOMME‡
  ‡ ‡ ‡

ADUAMAH, E.Y.
  ADUAMAH, E.Y.‡ P.O. BOX 21, LEGON, GHANA‡
  GHANA-TOGO‡ LOWER VOLTA BASIN‡ EWE‡ 13 HOURS‡
  1968-71‡ QUALITY GOOD‡ ARCHIVES OF TRADITIONAL
  MUSIC‡ 73-096-F‡ ‡ RESTRICTED‡ BELL, CHILDREN,
  CHILDREN-GAME, DANCE-ADAVU, DANCE-AFOVU,
  DANCE-GABADA, DANCE-SOGBADZA, DEATH-FUNERAL-YEVE,
  DRUM, DRUM-FRAME, ENTERTAINMENT,
  FESTIVAL-PUBERTY-WOMEN, FESTIVAL-YEVE, GREETING,
  HANDCLAPPING, IDIOPHONE-IRON, PRAYER-LIBATION,
  RATTLE-GOURD, RATTLE-IRON, WAR

AFRICAN STUDIES-I.U.
  DALBY, DAVID+ AFRICAN STUDIES-I.U.‡ SCHOOL OF
  ORIENTAL AND AFRICAN STUDIES, UNIVERSITY OF
  LONDON, LONDON W.C.1, ENGLAND+ INDIANA UNIVERSITY,
  BLOOMINGTON, INDIANA 47401‡ AFRICA-U.S.‡
  BLOOMINGTON, INDIANA‡ ‡ 2 HOURS‡ 1969‡ QUALITY
  GOOD‡ ARCHIVES OF TRADITIONAL MUSIC‡ 69-018-F‡ ‡
  RESTRICTED‡ LANGUAGE-AFRICA-INFLUENCE,
  LINGUISTICS-LECTURE

  DALBY, DAVID+ AFRICAN STUDIES-I.U.‡ SCHOOL OF
  ORIENTAL AND AFRICAN STUDIES, UNIVERSITY OF
  LONDON, LONDON W.C.1, ENGLAND+ INDIANA UNIVERSITY,
  BLOOMINGTON, INDIANA 47401‡ AFRICA-U.S.‡ BERKELEY,
  CALIFORNIA‡ ‡ 1.5 HOURS‡ 1969‡ QUALITY GOOD‡
  ARCHIVES OF TRADITIONAL MUSIC‡ 69-019-F‡ ‡
  RESTRICTED‡ HISTORY, LINGUISTICS-LECTURE

  MPHAHLELE, EZEKIEL+ AFRICAN STUDIES-I.U.‡ -+
  INDIANA UNIVERSITY, BLOOMINGTON, INDIANA 47401‡ ‡
  ‡ ‡ 2 HOURS‡ 1968‡ QUALITY GOOD‡ ARCHIVES OF

AFRICAN STUDIES-I.U.
  TRADITIONAL MUSIC‡ 69-011-F‡ ATL 4382-83‡
  RESTRICTED‡ LECTURE

AFRICANA MUSEUM
  AFRICANA MUSEUM‡ PUBLIC LIBRARY BUILDING, MARKET
  SQUARE, JOHANNESBURG, REPUBLIC OF SOUTH AFRICA‡ ‡
  ‡ ‡ ‡ ‡ ‡ ‡ ‡ ‡

  AFRICANA MUSEUM‡ PUBLIC LIBRARY BUILDING, MARKET
  SQUARE, JOHANNESBURG, SOUTH AFRICA‡ SOUTH AFRICA‡
  ‡ HOTTENTOT, SOTHO, SWAZI, TSWANA, ZULU‡ ‡; ‡ ‡
  AFRICANA MUSEUM‡ ‡ ‡ ‡ BOW-MUSICAL, FLUTE,
  GONG-ROCK, HARP-JAW'S, PRAISE-POETRY

AFRIKA-STUDIECENTRUM
  AFRIKA-STUDIECENTRUM‡ STATIONSPEIN 10, LEIDEN,
  NETHERLANDS‡ ‡ ‡ ‡ ‡ ‡ ‡ ‡ ‡

  AFRIKA-STUDIECENTRUM‡ STATIONSPEIN 10, LEIDEN,
  NETHERLANDS‡ TOGO‡ SANSAMME-MANGO‡ TYOKOSSI‡ 35
  HOURS‡ ‡ ‡ AFRIKA-STUDIECENTRUM‡ ‡ ‡ ‡ FOLKLORE,
  HISTORY, MUSIC, PRAISE-POETRY, PRAYER,
  PRAYER-ISLAMIC, RITUAL, SOCIAL

AGINSKY, ETHEL G.
  AGINSKY, ETHEL G.‡ ‡ SIERRA LEONE-U.S.‡ NEW YORK,
  NEW YORK‡ MENDE‡ .5 HOUR‡ 1933‡ QUALITY FAIR‡
  ARCHIVES OF TRADITIONAL MUSIC‡ PRE'54-006-F‡ ATL
  940‡ RESTRICTED‡ CANTE-FABLE, DRUM

AGUDZE, BERNARD
  AGUDZE, BERNARD‡ B.P. 1401, LOME, TOGO‡ TOGO‡
  AKLAKU, TSIVIEPE‡ EWE‡ 3.5 HOURS‡ 1965-67‡
  QUALITY GOOD‡ ARCHIVES OF TRADITIONAL MUSIC‡
  68-248-F‡ ATL 5088-91‡ RESTRICTED‡ DEATH-MOURNING,
  DRUM-ATUMPAN, DRUM-LANGUAGE, ENTERTAINMENT, WAR

AKPABOT, SAMUEL EKPE
  AKPABOT, SAMUEL EKPE‡ DEPARTMENT OF MUSIC,
  MICHIGAN STATE UNIVERSITY, EAST LANSING, MICHIGAN
  48823‡ NIGERIA‡ SOUTHEAST NIGERIA‡ BIROM, HAUSA,
  IBIBIO, IBO‡ 30 HOURS‡ 1964-73‡ QUALITY GOOD‡ ‡ ‡
  ‡ ‡ CHORDOPHONE, DRUM, FLUTE-ENSEMBLE, HORN,
  RITUAL, SOCIAL, XYLOPHONE

AKYEA, E. OFORI
  AKYEA, E. OFORI‡ INSTITUTE OF AFRICAN STUDIES,
  UNIVERSITY OF GHANA, BOX 73, LEGON, GHANA‡ GHANA‡

AKYEA, E. OFORI
  JUABEN‡ ASANTE‡ 1 HOUR‡ 1967‡ QUALITY FAIR‡
  ARCHIVES OF TRADITIONAL MUSIC‡ 67-215-F‡ ATL
  3307-08‡ RESTRICTED‡ ORAL-DATA-ART

ALBERTS, ARTHUR S.
  ALBERTS, ARTHUR S.‡ 1842 POST ROAD, DARIEN,
  CONNECTICUT 06820‡ AFRICA-WEST‡ 2.5 HOURS‡ BAULE,
  MANO, MOSSI‡ 1949-51‡ 1949‡ ARCHIVES OF
  TRADITIONAL MUSIC‡ BOUAKE(IVORY COAST),
  GANTA(LIBERIA), OUAGADOUGOU(UPPER VOLTA)‡
  68-061-F‡ ‡ RESTRICTED‡ CHILDREN,
  RELIGIOUS-CHRISTIAN

  ALBERTS, ARTHUR S.‡ 1842 POST ROAD, DARIEN,
  CONNECTICUT 06820‡ GHANA‡ ACCRA, ADABRAKA, KUMASI,
  NANWA‡ EWE, GA, IBO, TWI‡ 5.5 HOURS‡ 1949-51‡
  QUALITY GOOD‡ ARCHIVES OF TRADITIONAL MUSIC‡
  68-214-F‡ ATL 3557-77‡ RESTRICTED‡ AEROPHONE,
  CHILDREN, DRUM, GUITAR, XYLOPHONE

  ALBERTS, ARTHUR S.‡ 1842 POST ROAD, DARIEN,
  CONNECTICUT 06820‡ GUINEA‡ KANKAN, KISSIDOUGOU,
  SIDI-DJELLI‡ KISSI, MALINKE‡ 6.5 HOURS‡ 1949-51‡
  QUALITY GOOD‡ ARCHIVES OF TRADITIONAL MUSIC‡
  68-214-F‡ ATL 3557-77‡ RESTRICTED‡ FLUTE, GUITAR,
  HARP-LUTE-KORA, XYLOPHONE

  ALBERTS, ARTHUR S.‡ 1842 POST ROAD, DARIEN,
  CONNECTICUT 06820‡ IVORY COAST‡ BOUAKE‡ BAULE‡ 2
  HOURS‡ 1949-51‡ QUALITY GOOD‡ ARCHIVES OF
  TRADITIONAL MUSIC‡ 68-214-F‡ ATL 3557-77‡
  RESTRICTED‡ DRUM

  ALBERTS, ARTHUR S.‡ 1842 POST ROAD, DARIEN,
  CONNECTICUT 06820‡ LIBERIA‡ MONROVIA‡ ‡ 1 HOUR‡
  1949-51‡ QUALITY EXCELLENT‡ ARCHIVES OF
  TRADITIONAL MUSIC‡ 68-060-F‡ ‡ RESTRICTED‡
  MUSIC-POPULAR

  ALBERTS, ARTHUR S.‡ 1842 POST ROAD, DARIEN,
  CONNECTICUT 06820‡ LIBERIA‡ GANTA, MARSHALL
  ISLAND‡ FANTI, LOMA, MANO‡ 4 HOURS‡ 1949-51‡
  QUALITY GOOD‡ ARCHIVES OF TRADITIONAL MUSIC‡
  68-214-F‡ ATL 3557-77‡ RESTRICTED‡ DRUM, CHISEL,
  HAMMER, STONE-CUTTING

  ALBERTS, ARTHUR S.‡ 1842 POST ROAD, DARIEN,
  CONNECTICUT 06820‡ MALI‡ BAMAKO‡ BAMBARA‡ 1 HOUR‡

ALBERTS, ARTHUR S.
  1949-51‡ QUALITY GOOD‡ ARCHIVES OF TRADITIONAL
  MUSIC‡ 68-214-F‡ ATL 3557-77‡ RESTRICTED‡
  XYLOPHONE

  ALBERTS, ARTHUR S.‡ 1842 POST ROAD, DARIEN,
  CONNECTICUT 06820‡ UPPER VOLTA‡ BOBO-DIOULASSO,
  OUAGADOUGOU‡ BAMBARA, MOSSI‡ 2 HOURS‡ 1949-51‡
  QUALITY GOOD‡ ARCHIVES OF TRADITIONAL MUSIC‡
  68-214-F‡ ATL 3557-77‡ RESTRICTED‡ LUTE-BOWED,
  XYLOPHONE

  ALBERTS, ARTHUR S.‡ 1842 POST ROAD, DARIEN,
  CONNECTICUT 06820‡ ZAIRE‡ ALBERTVILLE, BINDENDELA,
  KASONGO, LEOPOLDVILLE, LWIRO‡ ‡ 4.5 HOURS‡
  1952-54‡ QUALITY EXCELLENT‡ ARCHIVES OF
  TRADITIONAL MUSIC‡ 68-059-F‡ ATL 3557-77‡
  RESTRICTED‡ DRUM-WATER

ALIGWEKWE, EVALYN R.
  ALIGWEKWE, EVALYN R.‡ MARIETTA COLLEGE, MARIETTA,
  OHIO 45750‡ NIGERIA‡ UMUAHIA‡ IBO‡ 1.5 HOURS‡
  1960‡ QUALITY GOOD‡ ‡ ‡ ‡ PRAISE-POETRY

ALLEN, LEONARD E.
  ALLEN, LEONARD E.‡ ‡ SIERRA LEONE‡ ‡ ‡ .5 HOUR‡
  1950‡ ‡ ARCHIVES OF TRADITIONAL MUSIC‡ 73-059-F‡ ‡
  ‡ FOLKTALE

ALPERS, EDWARD ALTER
  ALPERS, EDWARD ALTER‡ DEPARTMENT OF HISTORY,
  UNIVERSITY OF CALIFORNIA, LOS ANGELES, CALIFORNIA
  90024‡ TANZANIA‡ BAGAMOYO, MOROGORO‡ DOE, KAMI,
  KWERE, LUGURU, ZARAMO‡ 80 HOURS‡ 1972-73‡ QUALITY
  GOOD‡ ‡ ‡ ‡ ‡ HISTORY

AMES, DAVID W.
  AMES, DAVID W.‡ ANTHROPOLOGY DEPARTMENT,
  CALIFORNIA STATE UNIVERSITY, SAN FRANCISCO,
  CALIFORNIA 94132‡ GAMBIA, THE‡ BALLANGHAR, NJAU,
  UPPER AND LOWER SALOUM DISTRICTS‡ WOLOF‡ 7 HOURS‡
  1951‡ QUALITY EXCELLENT‡ ARCHIVES OF TRADITIONAL
  MUSIC‡ 66-205-F/C‡ ‡ RESTRICTED‡ CHILDREN-NAMING,
  DANCE, DANCE-MARRIAGE, DRUM-HOURGLASS,
  DRUM-KETTLE, FOLKTALE, HUMOROUS, MARABOUT,
  MARRIAGE, PRAISE, RIDDLE, WORK, WORK-FIELD,
  WRESTLING

  AMES, DAVID W.‡ ANTHROPOLOGY DEPARTMENT,

AMES, DAVID W.
  CALIFORNIA STATE UNIVERSITY, SAN FRANCISCO,
  CALIFORNIA 94132‡ NIGERIA‡ KANO, KATSINA, ZARIA‡
  HAUSA‡ 4 HOURS‡ 1963‡ QUALITY EXCELLENT‡ ARCHIVES
  OF TRADITIONAL MUSIC‡ 66-052-F‡ ATL 4996-99‡
  RESTRICTED‡ AEROPHONE, BELL-DOUBLE,
  BLACKSMITH-PRAISE, BUTCHER, CHILDREN,
  COMMENT-SOCIAL, DANCE, DRUM-BARREL, DRUM-CONICAL,
  DRUM-HOURGLASS, DRUM-KETTLE, DRUM-LANGUAGE,
  DRUM-SNARE, FARMER-PRAISE, HORN-LANGUAGE,
  HORN-VERTICAL, IDIOPHONE-STRUCK, LUTE, MARRIAGE,
  PRAISE-RULER

AMES, DAVID W.‡ ANTHROPOLOGY DEPARTMENT,
  CALIFORNIA STATE UNIVERSITY, SAN FRANCISCO,
  CALIFORNIA 94132‡ NIGERIA‡ ABUJA, BARNAUWA SABUWA,
  BOMO, DAKACE, GIWA, KAJURU, KANO, KARAUKARAU,
  KATSINA‡ FULBE, HAUSA, YORUBA‡ 150 HOURS‡ 1963-64‡
  QUALITY EXCELLENT‡ CENTER FOR AFRICAN ORAL DATA‡
  71-258-F‡ ATL 4676-767‡ RESTRICTED‡
  BLACKSMITH-PRAISE, DANCE-MEN,
  DRUM-CYLINDRICAL-SNARE, DRUM-GOURD,
  DRUM-HOURGLASS, DRUM-KETTLE, FEAST-FARMER,
  FEAST-WOMEN, FLUTE, HUNTER-PRAISE, LUTE-BOWED,
  PRAISE-POETRY, PRAISE-RULER, TATOOING, WORK-FIELD,
  WORK-GRINDING, WRESTLING

AMES, DAVID W.‡ ANTHROPOLOGY DEPARTMENT,
  CALIFORNIA STATE UNIVERSITY, SAN FRANCISCO,
  CALIFORNIA 94132‡ NIGERIA‡ OBIMO, NSUKKA‡ IGBO‡
  12 HOURS‡ 1963-64‡ QUALITY EXCELLENT‡ ARCHIVES OF
  TRADITIONAL MUSIC‡ 68-245-F‡ ‡ RESTRICTED‡
  BELL-DOUBLE, DANCE, DANCE-MASKED, DEATH-FUNERAL,
  DRUM-CLAY-POT, DRUM-CYLINDRICAL, DRUM-FRAME,
  DRUM-SLIT, FLUTE-NOTCHED, HARP-LUTE, HIGHLIFE,
  HORN-TRANSVERSE, IDIOPHONE-WOODEN, LOVE,
  PRAISE-RULER, RATTLE-ANKLE, RATTLE-BASKET,
  RATTLE-GOURD, RELIGIOUS, RELIGIOUS-CHRISTIAN,
  WRESTLING, XYLOPHONE, ZITHER-RAFT

AMES, DAVID W.‡ ANTHROPOLOGY DEPARTMENT,
  CALIFORNIA STATE UNIVERSITY, SAN FRANCISCO,
  CALIFORNIA 94132‡ SENEGAL‡ KER UDESI YASIN,
  MEDINA‡ WOLOF‡ 2 HOURS‡ 1950-51‡ QUALITY GOOD‡
  ARCHIVES OF TRADITIONAL MUSIC‡ 66-205-F/C‡ ‡
  RESTRICTED‡ IDIOPHONE-STRUCK, MARABOUT, MARRIAGE,
  MUSICIAN-GRIOT, PRAISE

ANDERSON, LOIS ANN
    ANDERSON, LOIS ANN‡ 4521 HUMANITIES, SCHOOL OF
    MUSIC, UNIVERSITY OF WISCONSIN, MADISON,
    WISCONSIN 53706‡ MOROCCO‡ MIDDLE ATLAS‡ BERBER‡
    75 HOURS‡ 1971‡ QUALITY EXCELLENT‡ UCLA‡ ‡ ‡ ‡
    POETRY, RIDDLE

    ANDERSON, LOIS ANN‡ 4521 HUMANITIES, SCHOOL OF
    MUSIC, UNIVERSITY OF WISCONSIN, MADISON,
    WISCONSIN 53706‡ UGANDA‡ ‡ ‡ 100 HOURS‡ 1964-66+
    1969‡ QUALITY EXCELLENT‡ UCLA‡ ‡ ‡ ‡ XYLOPHONE

ANDRADE, MANUEL
    ANDRADE, MANUEL+ HERZOG, GEORGE‡ -+ 7001 HOOVER
    ROAD, INDIANAPOLIS, INDIANA 46260‡ ‡ ‡ JABO‡ 2
    HOURS‡ 1931‡ QUALITY FAIR‡ ARCHIVES OF LANGUAGES
    OF THE WORLD‡ ‡ ‡ ‡ GRAMMATICAL-DATA, PROVERB

ANDREWS, LORETTA K.
    ANDREWS, LORETTA K.‡ 343 ROSEBANK AVENUE,
    BALTIMORE, MARYLAND 21212‡ ZAMBIA‡ ZAMBIAN COPPER
    BELT‡ ‡ ‡ 1971‡ ‡ MINDOLO ECUMENICAL FOUNDATION‡ ‡
    ‡ ‡ RELIGIOUS

ANIAKOR, CYRIL CHIKE
    ANIAKOR, CYRIL CHIKE‡ DEPARTMENT OF FINE ARTS,
    ART HISTORY, INDIANA UNIVERSITY, BLOOMINGTON,
    INDIANA 47401‡ NIGERIA‡ IKWERE‡ IKWERE‡ .5 HOUR‡
    1965‡ QUALITY GOOD‡ ‡ ‡ ‡ ‡ FOLKTALE

ANKERMANN, BERNHARD
    ANKERMANN, BERNHARD‡ ‡ CAMEROON‡ ‡ BAMUM‡ .3 HOUR‡
    1909‡ QUALITY FAIR‡ ARCHIVES OF TRADITIONAL MUSIC‡
    59-002-F‡ ATL 1755‡ RESTRICTED‡ DRUM, FLUTE,
    RATTLE

ANSTEY, ROGER THOMAS
    ANSTEY, ROGER THOMAS‡ ELIOT COLLEGE, UNIVERSITY
    OF KENT, CANTERBURY, KENT, ENGLAND‡ ZAIRE‡ BOLOBO,
    LAC LEOPOLD II‡ BABOMA, BASENGELE, BATENDE, BOLIA‡
    2.5 HOURS‡ 1963‡ QUALITY GOOD‡ ‡ ‡ ‡ ‡ HISTORY

ANTHROPOS-INSTITUT
    ANTHROPOS-INSTITUT‡ D 5204 ST. AUGUSTIN, 1 UBER
    SIEBURG, FEDERAL REPUBLIC OF GERMANY‡ ‡ ‡ ‡ ‡ ‡
    ‡ ‡ ‡ ‡

APTHORPE, RAYMOND JAMES
    APTHORPE, RAYMOND JAMES‡ FACULTY OF DEVELOPMENT

APTHORPE, RAYMOND JAMES
  STUDIES, UNIVERSITY OF EAST ANGLIA, NORWICH 88C,
  UNITED KINGDOM‡ ZAMBIA‡ PETAUKE DISTRICT‡ NSENGA‡
  4 HOURS‡ 1961‡ QUALITY EXCELLENT‡ ‡ ‡ ‡

ARCHIVE OF FOLK SONG, LIB
  ARCHIVE OF FOLK SONG, LIBRARY OF CONGRESS‡ 10
  FIRST STREET S.E., WASHINGTON, D.C. 20540‡ ‡ ‡ ‡
  ‡ ‡ ‡ ‡ ‡ ‡

ARCHIVES CULTURELLES DU S
  ARCHIVES CULTURELLES DU SENEGAL‡ 77 AVENUE
  PEYTAVIN, B.P. 11033, DAKAR, SENEGAL‡ ‡ ‡ ‡ ‡ ‡
  ‡ ‡ ‡

ARCHIVES OF ETHNIC MUSIC
  ARCHIVES OF ETHNIC MUSIC AND DANCE‡ SCHOOL OF
  MUSIC, UNIVERSITY OF WASHINGTON, SEATTLE,
  WASHINGTON 98195‡ ‡ ‡ ‡ ‡ ‡ ‡ ‡ ‡ ‡

  ARCHIVES OF ETHNIC MUSIC AND DANCE‡ SCHOOL OF
  MUSIC, UNIVERSITY OF WASHINGTON, SEATTLE,
  WASHINGTON 98195‡ ANGOLA‡ ‡ ‡ ‡ ‡ ‡ ARCHIVES OF
  ETHNIC MUSIC AND DANCE‡ ‡ ‡ RELIGIOUS

  ARCHIVES OF ETHNIC MUSIC AND DANCE‡ SCHOOL OF
  MUSIC, UNIVERSITY OF WASHINGTON, SEATTLE,
  WASHINGTON 98195‡ CAMEROON‡ ‡ ‡ ‡ ‡ ‡ ARCHIVES OF
  ETHNIC MUSIC AND DANCE‡ ‡ ‡ ‡ DRUM,
  HARP-ZITHER-MVET, XYLOPHONE

  ARCHIVES OF ETHNIC MUSIC AND DANCE‡ SCHOOL OF
  MUSIC, UNIVERSITY OF WASHINGTON, SEATTLE,
  WASHINGTON 98195‡ ETHIOPIA‡ ERITREA‡ AMHARA,
  TIGRINYA‡ ‡ ‡ ‡ ARCHIVES OF ETHNIC MUSIC AND
  DANCE‡ ‡ ‡ ‡ DRUM, MARRIAGE, TRUMPET

  ARCHIVES OF ETHNIC MUSIC AND DANCE‡ SCHOOL OF
  MUSIC, UNIVERSITY OF WASHINGTON, SEATTLE,
  WASHINGTON 98195‡ GAMBIA, THE‡ ‡ MANDINKA‡ ‡ ‡ ‡
  ARCHIVES OF ETHNIC MUSIC AND DANCE‡ ‡ ‡ ‡
  HARP-LUTE-KORA

  ARCHIVES OF ETHNIC MUSIC AND DANCE‡ SCHOOL OF
  MUSIC, UNIVERSITY OF WASHINGTON, SEATTLE,
  WASHINGTON 98195‡ GHANA‡ ACCRA, LEGON‡ DAGARTI,
  CAGOMBA, DONNO, EWE, GA, KONKOMBA, LOBI‡ ‡ ‡ ‡
  ARCHIVES OF ETHNIC MUSIC AND DANCE‡ ‡ ‡ ‡
  BAND-BRASS, BELL-DOUBLE, DANCE-ADINKUM,

ARCHIVES OF ETHNIC MUSIC
  DANCE-ADOWA, DANCE-BAWAA, DANCE-GAME-AGBEKOR,
  DANCE-MARRIAGE-BENE, DEATH-FUNERAL, DRUM,
  HIGHLIFE, HORN, LECTURE-ADDY-MUSTAPHA, WORK,
  XYLOPHONE, XYLOPHONE-DUET

  ARCHIVES OF ETHNIC MUSIC AND DANCE‡ SCHOOL OF
  MUSIC, UNIVERSITY OF WASHINGTON, SEATTLE,
  WASHINGTON 98195‡ GUINEA‡ ‡ ‡ ‡ ‡ ARCHIVES OF
  ETHNIC MUSIC AND DANCE‡ ‡ ‡ ‡ HARP-LUTE-KORA,
  XYLOPHONE

  ARCHIVES OF ETHNIC MUSIC AND DANCE‡ SCHOOL OF
  MUSIC, UNIVERSITY OF WASHINGTON, SEATTLE,
  WASHINGTON 98195‡ MOZAMBIQUE‡ ‡ ‡ ‡ ‡ ARCHIVES
  OF ETHNIC MUSIC AND DANCE‡ ‡ ‡ ‡ MARIMBA

  ARCHIVES OF ETHNIC MUSIC AND DANCE‡ SCHOOL OF
  MUSIC, UNIVERSITY OF WASHINGTON, SEATTLE,
  WASHINGTON 98195‡ MOROCCO‡ ‡ ARAB‡ ‡ ‡ ‡ ARCHIVES
  OF ETHNIC MUSIC AND DANCE‡ ‡ ‡ CHILDREN,
  MUSIC-ART-ANDALUSIAN

  ARCHIVES OF ETHNIC MUSIC AND DANCE‡ SCHOOL OF
  MUSIC, UNIVERSITY OF WASHINGTON, SEATTLE,
  WASHINGTON 98195‡ NIGERIA‡ ‡ IGBO‡ ‡ ‡ ‡ ARCHIVES
  OF ETHNIC MUSIC AND DANCE‡ ‡ ‡ ‡ BAND,
  DANCE-MASKED, DRUM

  ARCHIVES OF ETHNIC MUSIC AND DANCE‡ SCHOOL OF
  MUSIC, UNIVERSITY OF WASHINGTON, SEATTLE,
  WASHINGTON 98195‡ RHODESIA‡ SALISBURY‡ ‡ ‡ ‡ ‡
  ARCHIVES OF ETHNIC MUSIC AND DANCE‡ ‡ ‡ ‡
  BAND-TRIBAL-TRUST, BANJO, BELL, CLAPPER-WOODEN,
  DANCE-MONBHONO, DEATH-FUNERAL, DRUM, GUITAR,
  HUNTING, MBIRA, PANPIPES, RATTLE,
  SPIRIT-POSSESSION

  ARCHIVES OF ETHNIC MUSIC AND DANCE‡ SCHOOL OF
  MUSIC, UNIVERSITY OF WASHINGTON, SEATTLE,
  WASHINGTON 98195‡ SENEGAL‡ ‡ ‡ ‡ ‡ ‡ ARCHIVES OF
  ETHNIC MUSIC AND DANCE‡ ‡ ‡ ‡ DRUM,
  HARP-LUTE-KORA, INTERVIEW, KORAN-CHANT

  ARCHIVES OF ETHNIC MUSIC AND DANCE‡ SCHOOL OF
  MUSIC, UNIVERSITY OF WASHINGTON, SEATTLE,
  WASHINGTON 98195‡ UGANDA‡ ‡ BASOGA‡ ‡ ‡ ‡
  ARCHIVES OF ETHNIC MUSIC AND DANCE‡ ‡ ‡ ‡
  NDONGO-ENSEMBLE

ARCHIVES OF ETHNIC MUSIC
    ARCHIVES OF ETHNIC MUSIC AND DANCE‡ SCHOOL OF
    MUSIC, UNIVERSITY OF WASHINGTON, SEATTLE,
    WASHINGTON 98195‡ UPPER VOLTA‡ ‡ BOBO, BWABA,
    DYULA, FULANI, FULBE, GOUIN, GOURMANTCHE, LOBI,
    MINIANKA, MOSSI, SENUFO, YARDSE‡ ‡ ‡ ‡ ARCHIVES
    OF ETHNIC MUSIC AND DANCE‡ ‡ ‡ ‡ AEROPHONE-REED,
    BOW-MUSICAL, CHILDREN, CIRCUMCISION, DRUM,
    DRUM-CYLINDRICAL, DRUM-GOURD, DRUM-HOURGLASS,
    FEAST-HARVEST, FLUTE, GUITAR, HARP-LUTE,
    LUTE-BOWED, MARRIAGE, PRAYER-CHANT-ISLAMIC,
    RATTLE, WHISTLE, WORK-HARVEST,
    WORK-THRESHING-MILLET, XYLOPHONE,
    XYLOPHONE-BIRIFOR, XYLOPHONE-ENSEMBLE

    ARCHIVES OF ETHNIC MUSIC AND DANCE‡ SCHOOL OF
    MUSIC, UNIVERSITY OF WASHINGTON, SEATTLE,
    WASHINGTON 98195‡ ZAMBIA‡ ‡ LOZI, LUCHAZI‡ ‡ ‡ ‡
    ARCHIVES OF ETHNIC MUSIC AND DANCE‡ ‡ ‡ ‡
    XYLOPHONE

ARCHIVES OF LANGUAGES OF
    ARCHIVES OF LANGUAGES OF THE WORLD‡ INDIANA
    UNIVERSITY, RAWLES HALL, BLOOMINGTON, INDIANA
    47401‡ ‡ ‡ ‡ ‡ ‡ ‡ ‡ ‡

    ARCHIVES OF LANGUAGES OF THE WORLD‡ RAWLES HALL,
    INDIANA UNIVERSITY, BLOOMINGTON, INDIANA 47401‡
    LIBERIA‡ ‡ SUSU‡ .5 HOUR‡ ‡ QUALITY GOOD‡
    ARCHIVES OF LANGUAGES OF THE WORLD‡ ‡ ‡ ‡
    INTERVIEW

    ARCHIVES OF LANGUAGES OF THE WORLD‡ RAWLES HALL,
    INDIANA UNIVERSITY, BLOOMINGTON, INDIANA 47401‡
    SOUTH AFRICA‡ ‡ DUMA-KARANGA‡ .5 HOUR‡ 1954‡
    QUALITY GOOD‡ ARCHIVES OF LANGUAGES OF THE WORLD‡
    ‡ ‡ ‡ MUSIC

    ARCHIVES OF LANGUAGES OF THE WORLD‡ RAWLES HALL,
    INDIANA UNIVERSITY, BLOOMINGTON, INDIANA 47401‡ ‡
    ‡ KWA‡ .25 HOUR‡ ‡ QUALITY EXCELLENT‡ ARCHIVES OF
    LANGUAGES OF THE WORLD‡ ‡ ‡ ‡ DRUM-LANGUAGE,
    GRAMMATICAL-DATA-LOKELE

  ARCHIVES OF TRADITIONAL M
    ARCHIVES OF TRADITIONAL MUSIC‡ INDIANA UNIVERSITY,
    MAXWELL HALL 057, BLOOMINGTON, INDIANA 47401‡ ‡ ‡
    ‡ ‡ ‡ ‡ ‡ ‡

ARCHIVES OF TRADITIONAL M
  ARCHIVES OF TRADITIONAL MUSIC‡ ‡ ‡ ‡ YORUBA‡ 1
  HOUR‡ CA1940‡ QUALITY FAIR‡ ARCHIVES OF
  TRADITIONAL MUSIC‡ 60-019-F‡ ATL 1515-16‡ ‡ DANCE,
  DEATH, HUNTING, LOVE, LULLABY, VICTORY, WAR

  ARCHIVES OF TRADITIONAL MUSIC‡ ‡ GHANA‡ ‡ ‡ 2
  HOURS‡ 1950‡ ‡ ARCHIVES OF TRADITIONAL MUSIC‡
  73-057-F‡ ‡ ‡

ARCHIVES SONORES
  ARCHIVES SONORES‡ C.V.R.S., B.P. 7047,
  OUAGADOUGOU, UPPER VOLTA‡ ‡ ‡ ‡ ‡ ‡ ‡ ‡ ‡ ‡

ARGYLE, WILLIAM JOHNSON
  ARGYLE, WILLIAM JOHNSON‡ DEPARTMENT OF AFRICAN
  STUDIES, UNIVERSITY OF NATAL, KING GEORGE V
  AVENUE, DURBAN, SOUTH AFRICA‡ ZAMBIA‡ ‡ SOLI‡ 5
  HOURS‡ 1957-59‡ QUALITY FAIR‡ ‡ ‡ ‡ ‡ COURT-CASE,
  FOLKTALE, RITUAL, SOCIAL

ARMISTEAD, SAMUEL G.
  ARMISTEAD, SAMUEL G. + KATZ, ISRAEL J. +
  SILVERMAN, JOSEPH H.‡ 4524 SPRUCE STREET,
  PHILADELPHIA, PENNSYLVANIA 19139 + 415 WEST 115TH
  STREET, NEW YORK, NEW YORK 10025 + ADLAI
  STEVENSON COLLEGE, UNIVERSITY OF CALIFORNIA,
  SANTA CRUZ, CALIFORNIA 95060‡ MOROCCO‡ SPANISH
  ZONE‡ SEPHARDIC-JEW‡ 60 HOURS‡ 1962‡ QUALITY
  EXCELLENT‡ ‡ ‡ ‡ ‡ BALLAD-SPANISH,
  CIRCUMCISION-CEREMONY, DEATH-DIRGE, FOLKTALE,
  HYMN-HEBREW-METRICAL, MARRIAGE

ARMSTRONG, ROBERT G.
  ARMSTRONG, ROBERT G.‡ INSTITUTE OF AFRICAN
  STUDIES, UNIVERSITY OF IBADAN, NIGERIA‡ NIGERIA‡
  IBADAN‡ YORUBA‡ 1.5 HOURS‡ ‡ QUALITY GOOD‡
  ARCHIVES OF TRADITIONAL MUSIC‡ 72-238-F‡ ATL 5454‡
  ‡ DRAMA-MUSICAL

  ARMSTRONG, ROBERT G.‡ INSTITUTE OF AFRICAN
  STUDIES, UNIVERSITY OF IBADAN, IBADAN, NIGERIA‡
  NIGERIA‡ ‡ YORUBA‡ 1.5 HOURS‡ ‡ QUALITY POOR‡
  ARCHIVES OF TRADITIONAL MUSIC‡ 72-243-F‡ ATL 5461‡
  ‡ DIVINING-ODU-IFA

  ARMSTRONG, ROBERT G. + UNODGWU, PATRICK‡ INSTITUTE
  OF AFRICAN STUDIES, UNIVERSITY OF IBADAN, IBADAN,
  NIGERIA‡ NIGERIA‡ AGILA‡ IDOMA‡ 2 HOURS‡ 1961‡

ARMSTRONG, ROBERT G.
  QUALITY GOOD‡ ARCHIVES OF TRADITIONAL MUSIC‡
  72-245-F‡ ATL 5463-65‡ ‡ DANCE-MASKED-AREKWU,
  DRUM, DRUM-CLAY-POT, PRAISE

  ARMSTRONG, ROBERT G.‡ INSTITUTE OF AFRICAN
  STUDIES, UNIVERSITY OF IBADAN, IBADAN, NIGERIA‡
  NIGERIA‡ IBADAN‡ YORUBA‡ 2 HOURS‡ 1962‡ QUALITY
  GOOD‡ ARCHIVES OF TRADITIONAL MUSIC‡ 72-240-F‡
  ATL 5456‡ ‡ DRAMA-MUSICAL

  ARMSTRONG, ROBERT G.‡ INSTITUTE OF AFRICAN
  STUDIES, UNIVERSITY OF IBADAN, IBADAN, NIGERIA‡
  NIGERIA‡ OTURKPO‡ IDOMA‡ 2 HOURS‡ 1964‡ QUALITY
  GOOD‡ ARCHIVES OF TRADITIONAL MUSIC‡ 72-242-F‡
  ATL 5460‡ ‡ CHILDREN, HANDCLAPPING

  ARMSTRONG, ROBERT G. +WITTIG, R. CURT‡ INSTITUTE
  OF AFRICAN STUDIES, UNIVERSITY OF IBADAN, IBADAN,
  NIGERIA+ 3740 KANAWHA STREET N.W., WASHINGTON,
  D.C. 20015‡ NIGERIA‡ AGILA‡ IDOMA‡ 1 HOUR‡ 1964‡
  QUALITY GOOD‡ ARCHIVES OF TRADITIONAL MUSIC‡
  72-244-F‡ ATL 5462‡ ‡ DANCE-MASKED-ABILE,
  VOICE-DISGUISE

ARNOTT, D.
  ARNOTT, D.‡ SCHOOL OF ORIENTAL AND AFRICAN
  STUDIES, LONDON W.C.1, ENGLAND‡ UPPER VOLTA‡ DORI‡
  MALINKE‡ ‡ 1956‡ ‡ MUSEE DE L'HOMME‡ ‡ ‡ ‡
  XYLOPHONE

AROM, SIMHA
  AROM, SIMHA‡ 6 RUE MALAR, 75007 PARIS, FRANCE‡
  CENTRAL AFRICAN REPUBLIC‡ IPPY, MONGOUMBA,
  SOUTHWEST‡ AKA-PYGMIES, LINDA-BANDA, NGBAKA-MABO‡
  93 HOURS‡ 1964-67+ 1971-73‡ ‡ MUSEE DE L'HOMME‡ ‡
  ‡ ‡ HISTORY, RITUAL, SOCIAL

AWE, BOLANLE ALAKE
  AWE, BOLANLE ALAKE‡ INSTITUTE OF AFRICAN STUDIES,
  UNIVERSITY OF IBADAN, IBADAN, NIGERIA‡ NIGERIA‡
  ILESA-IBADAN, ILESA-MUGBARA‡ YORUBA‡ 3 HOURS‡
  1972-74‡ QUALITY FAIR‡ INSTITUTE OF AFRICAN
  STUDIES, UNIVERSITY OF IBADAN‡ ‡ ‡ ‡ DANCE-OSUN,
  DRUM- OSUN, FESTIVAL-EGUNGUN, HISTORY,
  PRAISE-POETRY, RITUAL

BABALOLA, ADEBOYE
  BABALOLA, ADEBOYE‡ DEPARTMENT OF AFRICAN

BABALOLA, ADEBOYE
  LANGUAGES AND LITERATURE, UNIVERSITY OF LAGOS,
  LAGOS, NIGERIA≠ NIGERIA≠ WEST≠ YORUBA≠ 183 HOURS≠
  1962-74≠ QUALITY FAIR≠ ≠ ≠ ≠ FOLKTALE, POETRY

BACHMANN, FR.
  BACHMANN, FR.≠ ≠ TANZANIA≠ ≠ ≠ .1 HOUR≠ 1908≠
  QUALITY FAIR≠ ARCHIVES OF TRADITIONAL MUSIC≠
  59-002-F≠ ATL 1758≠ RESTRICTED≠ CHILDREN

BAHMAN, GARY
  BAHMAN, GARY≠ 116 W. GRANT, APT. 8, MINNEAPOLIS,
  MINNESOTA 55403≠ SIERRA LEONE≠ KAMABAI,
  KATANTA-BIRIWA CHIEFDOM≠ LIMBA, MANDINGO, TEMNE≠
  12 HOURS≠ 1971≠ QUALITY GOOD≠ ARCHIVES OF
  TRADITIONAL MUSIC≠ 72-231-F≠ ATL 5648-52≠ ≠
  CHILDREN, DEATH-MOURNING, DRUM-BAN, DRUM-CONICAL,
  DRUM-HOURGLASS, DRUM-SLIT, ENTERTAINMENT, FLUTE,
  FOLKTALE, GUITAR, KONGOMA, WAR, WORK-FIELD,
  XYLOPHONE

BAIER, STEPHEN B.
  BAIER, STEPHEN B.≠ DEPARTMENT OF HISTORY,
  UNIVERSITY OF WISCONSIN, MADISON, WISCONSIN 53705≠
  NIGER≠ ZINDER≠ HAUSA, KANURI, TUAREG≠ 71.5 HOURS≠
  1972≠ QUALITY GOOD≠ ARCHIVES OF TRADITIONAL
  MUSIC+ CENTRE REGIONAL DE DOCUMENTATION POUR LA
  TRADITION ORALE≠ 73-053-F≠ ≠ RESTRICTED≠
  HISTORY-ECONOMIC, HISTORY-FAMILY-MERCHANT,
  MERCHANT-INTERVIEW, PRAISE-MERCHANT

BAIRU, TAFLA
  BAIRU, TAFLA≠ INSTITUTE OF ETHIOPIAN STUDIES,
  HAILE SELASSIE UNIVERSITY, P.O. BOX 1176, ADDIS
  ABABA, ETHIOPIA≠ ETHIOPIA≠ GIBI VALLEY≠ GALLA,
  OROMO≠ 120 HOURS≠ 1973-74≠ QUALITY GOOD≠
  INSTITUTE OF ETHIOPIAN STUDIES, HAILE SELASSIE
  UNIVERSITY≠ ≠ ≠ ≠ HISTORY

BAISSAC, -
  BAISSAC, -≠ ≠ UGANDA≠ ≠ GANDA≠ ≠ 1967≠ ≠ MUSEE DE
  L'HOMME≠ ≠ ≠ ≠

BAKER, CATHRYN ANITA
  BAKER, CATHRYN ANITA≠ 10456 SOUTH SEELEY AVENUE,
  CHICAGO, ILLINOIS 60643≠ TUNISIA≠ GABES, GAFSA,
  MEDENINE, SFAX≠ ≠ 150 HOURS≠ 1972-73≠ QUALITY
  EXCELLENT≠ ≠ ≠ ≠ ≠ POETRY, PROSE

BALOGUN, ADISA
  BALOGUN, ADISA‡ MUSIC RESEARCH UNIT, NIGERIAN
  BROADCASTING CORPORATION, IBADAN, NIGERIA‡
  NIGERIA‡ ERIPA‡ YORUBA‡ 1.5 HOURS‡ 1964+ 1970‡
  QUALITY GOOD‡ ‡ ‡ ‡ ‡ DRUM-HOURGLASS,
  FESTIVAL-OGUN, PRAISE-DIVINITY-IJALA

  BALOGUN, ADISA‡ MUSIC RESEARCH UNIT, NIGERIAN
  BROADCASTING CORPORATION, IBADAN, NIGERIA‡
  NIGERIA‡ IBADAN‡ YORUBA‡ 1.5 HOURS‡ 1967‡ QUALITY
  GOOD‡ ARCHIVES OF TRADITIONAL MUSIC‡ 72-239-F‡
  ATL 5455‡ RESTRICTED‡ DEATH-FUNERAL-STATE,
  DEATH-DIRGE, PRAISE-ORIKI

BARNES, SANDRA THEIS
  BARNES, SANDRA THEIS‡ C/O DEPARTMENT OF
  ANTHROPOLOGY, UNIVERSITY MUSEUM, UNIVERSITY OF
  PENNSYLVANIA, PHILADELPHIA, PENNSYLVANIA 19104‡
  NIGERIA‡ LAGOS‡ YORUBA‡ 20 HOURS‡ 1972‡ QUALITY
  FAIR‡ ‡ ‡ ‡ POLITICAL, SOCIAL

BAY, EDNA GRACE
  BAY, EDNA GRACE‡ AFRICAN STUDIES CENTER, 10 LENOX
  STREET, BROOKLINE, MASSACHUSETTS 02146‡ DAHOMEY‡
  ABOMEY‡ FON‡ 1 HOUR‡ 1972‡ QUALITY GOOD‡ ‡ ‡ ‡
  ROYAL

BEIER, ULLI
  BEIER, ULLI+ ROUGET, GILBERT‡ INSTITUTE OF
  AFRICAN STUDIES, UNIVERSITY OF IFE, ILE-IFE,
  NIGERIA+ 1 RUE DES DEUX-PONTS, 75004 PARIS,
  FRANCE‡ NIGERIA‡ ‡ YORUBA‡ ‡ ‡ ‡ MUSEE DE L'HOMME‡
  ‡ ‡ ‡

BELLMAN, BERYL LARRY
  BELLMAN, BERYL LARRY‡ SCHOOL OF SPECIAL STUDIES,
  CALIFORNIA INSTITUTE OF THE ARTS, VALENCIA,
  CALIFORNIA 91356‡ LIBERIA‡ SUCRUMU, ZORZOR
  DISTRICT‡ KPELLE, LOMA‡ 20 HOURS‡ 1969‡ QUALITY
  FAIR‡ ‡ ‡ ‡ CONVERSATION, HISTORY, RELIGIOUS,
  RITUAL, SOCIAL, WORK

BEN-AMOS, DAN
  BEN-AMOS, DAN‡ DEPARTMENT OF FOLKLORE AND
  FOLKLIFE, BOX 13, LOGAN HALL, UNIVERSITY OF
  PENNSYLVANIA, PHILADELPHIA, PENNSYLVANIA 19104‡
  NIGERIA‡ BENIN CITY‡ EDO‡ 130 HOURS‡ 1966‡
  QUALITY EXCELLENT‡ CENTER FOR AFRICAN ORAL DATA‡
  70-092-F‡ ‡ RESTRICTED‡ CANTE-FABLE,

BEN-AMOS, DAN
  CHILDREN-FOLKTALE, CHILDREN-GAME, DANCE,
  FESTIVAL-OLOKUN, FOLKTALE, HISTORY, PRAISE,
  PRAISE-DIVINITY, PROVERB, RIDDLE

  BEN-AMOS, DAN‡ DEPARTMENT OF FOLKLORE AND
  FOLKLIFE, BOX 13, LOGAN HALL, UNIVERSITY OF
  PENNSYLVANIA, PHILADELPHIA, PENNSYLVANIA 19104‡
  NIGERIA‡ ZARIA‡ HAUSA‡ 3 HOURS‡ 1966‡ QUALITY
  EXCELLENT‡ CENTER FOR AFRICAN ORAL DATA‡ 70-105-F‡
  ‡ RESTRICTED‡ NARRATIVE, PROVERB, RIDDLE

BENDER, MARVIN LIONEL
  BENDER, MARVIN LIONEL‡ WESTERN ETHIOPIA LANGUAGE
  SURVEY, P.O. BOX 30705, ADDIS ABABA, ETHIOPIA‡
  ETHIOPIA‡ ‡ BERTA, BODI, MAO, MUSUJI, SAI, TSAMAY‡
  ‡ 1964-74‡ QUALITY GOOD‡ ARCHIVES OF LANGUAGES OF
  THE WORLD‡ ‡ ‡ GRAMMATICAL-DATA

BENTHIEN, CLAUS
  BENTHIEN, CLAUS+ LILLIEBJERG, HANNE+ WICHMANN,
  ERIK‡ ‡ MOROCCO‡ KENITRA, MARRAKECH, MOULAY IDRIS‡
  ‡ ‡ 1967‡ ‡ DANSK FOLKEMINDESAMLING‡ 67/1A-13A‡ ‡
  ‡

  BENTHIEN, CLAUS+ LILLIEBJERG, HANNE+ WICHMANN,
  ERIK‡ ‡ TUNISIA‡ BIZERTE, NEFTA‡ ‡ ‡ 1967‡ ‡
  DANSK FOLKEMINDESAMLING‡ 67/13A-16A‡ ‡ ‡

BERLIN PHONOGRAMM-ARCHIV
  BERLIN PHONOGRAMM-ARCHIV‡ ‡ AFRICA-GERMANY‡
  BERLIN‡ BULE‡ .2 HOUR‡ 1909‡ QUALITY FAIR‡
  ARCHIVES OF TRADITIONAL MUSIC‡ 59-002-F‡ ATL
  1755-56‡ RESTRICTED‡ CLARINET-DOUBLE, DANCE, WAR

BERLINER, PAUL FRANKLIN
  BERLINER, PAUL FRANKLIN‡ 3 COMPTON CIRCLE,
  LEXINGTON, MASSACHUSETTS 02173‡ RHODESIA‡ ‡ SHONA‡
  50 HOURS‡ 1972‡ QUALITY EXCELLENT‡ WESLEYAN
  UNIVERSITY‡ ‡ ‡ ‡ POETRY, SOCIAL

BERNUS, S.
  BERNUS, S.+ ROUCH, JEAN‡ -+ CENTRE DE RECHERCHES
  AFRICAINES, RUE D'ALSACE, 75 PARIS 6E, FRANCE‡
  NIGER‡ ‡ SONRAI‡ ‡ 1960‡ ‡ MUSEE DE L'HOMME‡ ‡ ‡ ‡
  CHORDOPHONE

BESMER, FREMONT E.
  BESMER, FREMONT E.‡ C/O REV. L. ROSE, FULLER MT.

BESMER, FREMONT E.
  ROAD, KENT, CONNECTICUT 06757‡ NIGERIA‡ KANO‡
  HAUSA‡ 60 HOURS‡ 1968-70‡ QUALITY GOOD‡ ARCHIVES
  OF TRADITIONAL MUSIC‡ 70-091-F‡ ‡ ‡ PRAISE,
  PRAISE-RULER

  BESMER, FREMONT E.‡ C/O REV. L. ROSE, FULLER MT.
  ROAD, KENT, CONNECTICUT 06757‡ NIGERIA‡ KANO,
  MAIDUGURI‡ HAUSA‡ 90 HOURS‡ 1972-73‡ QUALITY
  EXCELLENT‡ ‡ ‡ ‡ ‡ CULT-POSSESSION

BIEBUYCK, DANIEL P.
  BIEBUYCK, DANIEL P.‡ DEPARTMENT OF ANTHROPOLOGY,
  UNIVERSITY OF DELAWARE, NEWARK, DELAWARE 19711‡
  ZAIRE‡ EASTERN‡ LEGA, LUBA, LUNDA, MANGBETU,
  MAYOGO, NANDE, NYANGA, ZAMBE‡ 36 HOURS‡ 1952-61‡
  QUALITY EXCELLENT‡ MUSEE ROYAL DE L'AFRIQUE
  CENTRALE‡ ‡ ‡ ‡ DRUM-SLIT, EPIC, HARP, MIRLITON,
  STICK-PERCUSSION, ZITHER

BIRD, CHARLES S.
  BIRD, CHARLES S.‡ LINGUISTICS DEPARTMENT, INDIANA
  UNIVERSITY, BLOOMINGTON, INDIANA 47401‡ MALI‡
  BAMAKO‡ BAMBARA‡ 4 HOURS‡ 1967-68‡ QUALITY
  EXCELLENT‡ CENTER FOR AFRICAN ORAL DATA‡ 71-124-F‡
  ‡ RESTRICTED‡ MUSICIAN-GRIOT, HARP-LUTE-KORA,
  PRAISE, PRAISE-RULER, XYLOPHONE

  BIRD, CHARLES S.‡ LINGUISTICS DEPARTMENT, INDIANA
  UNIVERSITY, BLOOMINGTON, INDIANA 47401‡ MALI‡
  KABAYA‡ BAMBARA‡ 2.5 HOURS‡ 1968‡ QUALITY
  EXCELLENT‡ CENTER FOR AFRICAN ORAL DATA‡ 71-259-F‡
  ATL 4877-78‡ RESTRICTED‡ EPIC-KAMBILI

  BIRD, CHARLES S.‡ LINGUISTICS DEPARTMENT, INDIANA
  UNIVERSITY, BLOOMINGTON, INDIANA 47401‡ MALI‡
  KITA‡ BAMBARA‡ 1.5 HOURS‡ 1968‡ QUALITY EXCELLENT‡
  CENTER FOR AFRICAN ORAL DATA‡ 71-260-F‡ ATL 4876‡
  RESTRICTED‡ EPIC-SUNJATA

  BIRD, CHARLES S.+ KEIM, KAREN R.‡ LINGUISTICS
  DEPARTMENT, INDIANA UNIVERSITY, BLOOMINGTON,
  INDIANA 47401+ AFRICAN STUDIES, INDIANA
  UNIVERSITY, BLOOMINGTON, INDIANA 47401‡ MALI-U.S.‡
  ‡ BAMBARA‡ 2 HOURS‡ 1975‡ QUALITY GOOD‡ ARCHIVES
  OF TRADITIONAL MUSIC‡ 75-043-F‡ ‡ RESTRICTED‡
  EPIC-LECTURE, HERO-EPIC-LECTURE

BISELE, MARGUERITE A.
  BISELE, MARGUERITE A.‡ 2500 GREAT OAKS PARKWAY,
  AUSTIN, TEXAS 78756‡ BOTSWANA‡ GHANZI DISTRICT,
  NGAMILAND‡ KUNG-BUSHMEN‡ 86 HOURS‡ 1971-72‡
  QUALITY GOOD‡ HARVARD UNIVERSITY‡ ‡ ‡ ‡ DANCE,
  FOLKTALE, GAME, WORD-LIST

BLACKING, JOHN A.R.
  BLACKING, JOHN A.R.‡ DEPARTMENT OF SOCIAL
  ANTHROPOLOGY, QUEEN'S UNIVERSITY OF BELFAST,
  BELFAST BT7 1NN, NORTHERN IRELAND‡ SOUTH AFRICA‡
  NORTHERN TRANSVAAL‡ VENDA‡ 60 HOURS‡ 1956-59‡
  QUALITY GOOD‡ BRITISH BROADCASTING CORPORATION+
  INTERNATIONAL LIBRARY OF AFRICAN MUSIC+ QUEEN'S
  UNIVERSITY+ UNIVERSITY OF WITWATERSRAND‡ ‡ ‡ ‡
  DANCE, RITUAL

  BLACKING, JOHN A.R.‡ DEPARTMENT OF SOCIAL
  ANTHROPOLOGY, QUEEN'S UNIVERSITY OF BELFAST,
  BELFAST BT7 1NN, NORTHERN IRELAND‡ UGANDA‡ ‡
  BAGANDA, BATORO, KARAMOJONG‡ 14 HOURS‡ 1965‡
  QUALITY GOOD‡ BRITISH BROADCASTING CORPORATION+
  INTERNATIONAL LIBRARY OF AFRICAN MUSIC+ QUEEN'S
  UNIVERSITY+ UNIVERSITY OF WITWATERSRAND‡ ‡ ‡ ‡
  CEREMONY-PUBERTY, PUBERTY-CEREMONY, SOCIAL

  BLACKING, JOHN A.R.‡ DEPARTMENT OF SOCIAL
  ANTHROPOLOGY, QUEEN'S UNIVERSITY OF BELFAST,
  BELFAST BT7 1NN, NORTHERN IRELAND‡ ZAMBIA‡
  PETAUKE, ZAMBEZI VALLEY‡ TONGA-GWEMBE, NSENGA‡ 30
  HOURS‡ 1957-61‡ QUALITY GOOD‡ BRITISH
  BROADCASTING CORPORATION+ INTERNATIONAL LIBRARY
  OF AFRICAN MUSIC+ QUEEN'S UNIVERSITY+ UNIVERSITY
  OF WITWATERSRAND‡ ‡ ‡ ‡

BLAIR, BOB
  BLAIR, BOB‡ ‡ GHANA‡ ‡ ASANTE‡ 1 HOUR‡ 1958‡
  QUALITY GOOD‡ ARCHIVES OF LANGUAGES OF THE WORLD‡
  ‡ ‡ ‡ CONVERSATION, GRAMMATICAL-DATA-TWI,
  NARRATIVE

BLANK, ARTHUR S., JR.
  BLANK, ARTHUR S., JR.+ BLANK, DONNA H.‡ 31 EVERIT
  STREET, NEW HAVEN, CONNECTICUT 06511‡ IVORY COAST‡
  FACOBLIS, MAN‡ GUERE, WOBE‡ 3 HOURS‡ 1973‡
  QUALITY GOOD‡ ‡ ‡ ‡ ‡ DANCE, DEATH-FUNERAL

BLANK, DONNA H.
  BLANK, ARTHUR S., JR.+ BLANK, DONNA H.‡ 31 EVERIT

BLANK, DONNA H.
  STREET, NEW HAVEN, CONNECTICUT 06511‡ IVORY COAST‡
  FACOBLIS, MAN‡ GUERE, WOBE‡ 3 HOURS‡ 1973‡
  QUALITY GOOD‡ ‡ ‡ ‡ ‡ DANCE, DEATH-FUNERAL

BLOCH, MONICA E.
  BLOCH, MONICA E.‡ LONDON SCHOOL OF ECONOMICS,
  HOUGHTON ST., ALDWYCH, LONDON W.C.1, ENGLAND‡
  MALAGASY REPUBLIC‡ ‡ MERINA, TANALA‡ 9 HOURS‡
  1964-71‡ QUALITY FAIR‡ ‡ ‡ ‡ ‡ HISTORY, RITUAL,
  SOCIAL

BLOUNT, BEN G.
  BLOUNT, BEN G.‡ DEPARTMENT OF ANTHROPOLOGY,
  UNIVERSITY OF TEXAS, AUSTIN, TEXAS 28712‡ KENYA‡
  SOUTH NYANZA‡ LUO‡ .8 HOUR‡ 1971‡ QUALITY GOOD‡ ‡
  ‡ ‡ ‡ DRINKING, SOCIAL

BOAS, FRANZ
  BOAS, FRANZ‡ DECEASED‡ ‡ ‡ IGANDA-LUGANDA‡ ‡
  PRE-1935‡ QUALITY FAIR‡ ARCHIVES OF LANGUAGES OF
  THE WORLD‡ ‡ ‡ ‡ GRAMMATICAL-DATA

  BOAS, FRANZ‡ DECEASED‡ ‡ ‡ KRU‡ ‡ PRE-1935‡
  QUALITY FAIR‡ ARCHIVES OF LANGUAGES OF THE WORLD‡
  ‡ ‡ ‡ FOLKTALE, GRAMMATICAL-DATA

  BOAS, FRANZ‡ DECEASED‡ GHANA‡ ‡ AKWAPIM‡ ‡
  PRE-1935‡ QUALITY FAIR‡ ARCHIVES OF LANGUAGES OF
  THE WORLD‡ ‡ ‡ ‡ GRAMMATICAL-DATA-TWI

  BOAS, FRANZ‡ DECEASED‡ NIGERIA-U.S.‡ ‡ YORUBA‡ .5
  HOUR‡ 1933‡ QUALITY FAIR‡ ARCHIVES OF TRADITIONAL
  MUSIC‡ PRE'54-085-F‡ ATL 943‡ ‡ FOLKTALE

  BOAS, FRANZ‡ DECEASED‡ SIERRA LEONE‡ ‡ BOLUM‡ ‡
  PRE-1935‡ QUALITY FAIR‡ ARCHIVES OF LANGUAGES OF
  THE WORLD‡ ‡ ‡ ‡ RIDDLE

BORGATTI, JEAN M.
  BORGATTI, JEAN M.‡ 5 BEVERLY ROAD, SHREWSBURY,
  MASSACHUSETTS 01545‡ NIGERIA‡ ETSAKO DIVISION,
  OWAN DIVISION, MIDWEST STATE‡ EDO‡ 24 HOURS‡
  1972-73‡ QUALITY GOOD‡ DEPARTMENT OF LINGUISTICS
  AND NIGERIAN LANGUAGES, UNIVERSITY OF IBADAN‡ ‡ ‡
  ‡ DANCE-MASKED, HISTORICAL-TEXT,
  RITUAL-TITLE-TAKING, RITUAL-SHRINE, SOCIAL,
  TITLE-TAKING-RITUAL

BOUQUIAUX, LUC
   BOUQUIAUX, LUC‡ 5 RUE DE MARSEILLE, 75010 PARIS,
   FRANCE‡ CENTRAL AFRICAN REPUBLIC‡ ‡ BANDA, ISONGO,
   MONZOMBO, NGBAKA-MABO‡ 181.5 HOURS‡ ‡ QUALITY
   GOOD‡ ‡ ‡ ‡ ‡ FOLKLORE, MUSIC

BOURGEOT, A.
   BOURGEOT, A.‡ ‡ ALGERIA‡ AHAGGAR‡ TUAREG‡ ‡ 1970‡
   ‡ MUSEE DE L'HOMME‡ ‡ ‡ ‡ DRUM-MORTAR-TINDI,
   POSSESSION

BOWLES, PAUL
   BOWLES, PAUL+ WANKLYN, CHRISTOPHER‡ 2117 TANGER
   SOCCO, TANGIER, MOROCCO+ B.P. 471, MARRAKECH,
   MOROCCO‡ MOROCCO‡ EINZOREN, ESSAOUIRA, GOULIMINE,
   MARRAKECH, MEKNES, TAFRAOUTE, TANGIER, TETUAN,
   TIMQUIRCHT, ZAGORA‡ ‡ 2 HOURS‡ CA1959-62‡ QUALITY
   GOOD‡ ARCHIVES OF TRADITIONAL MUSIC‡ 62-017-F‡
   ATL 2457-60‡ RESTRICTED‡ BEGGAR, CYMBAL, DANCE,
   DRUM-CLAY, DRUM-DERBUKA, DRUM-FRAME,
   FEET-STAMPING, FLUTE, HANDCLAPPING, LUTE-BOWED,
   LUTE-PLUCKED, OBOE, PRAYER-CALL, PROCESSION,
   SLAVE, TAMBOURINE, ULULATION

BRANDILY, MONIQUE
   BRANDILY, MONIQUE‡ 117 RUE N.D. DES CHAMPS, 75006
   PARIS, FRANCE‡ CHAD‡ KANEM, MAYO KEBBI, TIBESTI‡
   KANEMBU, KOTOKO, TEDA‡ 36 HOURS‡ 1961+ 1963+ 1965‡
   QUALITY GOOD‡ MUSEE DE L'HOMME+ MUSEE ROYAL DE
   L'AFRIQUE CENTRALE‡ ‡ ‡ ‡ DRUM, DRUM-WATER,
   EXORCISM, HARP-ARCHED, HORN, MARRIAGE, RITUAL,
   SOCIAL

   BRANDILY, MONIQUE‡ 117 RUE N.D. DES CHAMPS, 75006
   PARIS, FRANCE‡ CHAD‡ ‡ FEZZANAIS, TEDA‡ ‡ 1969‡ ‡
   MUSEE DE L'HOMME‡ ‡ ‡ ‡ CIRCUMCISION,
   CLARINET-DOUBLE, DRUM, DRUM-FRAME, LUTE,
   LUTE-BOWED, MARRIAGE

   BRANDILY, MONIQUE‡ 117 RUE N.D. DES CHAMPS, 75006
   PARIS, FRANCE‡ LIBYA‡ FEZZAN‡ FEZZANAIS, TEDA‡ 8
   HOURS‡ 1969‡ QUALITY GOOD‡ MUSEE DE L'HOMME+
   MUSEE ROYAL DE L'AFRIQUE CENTRALE‡ ‡ ‡ ‡ RITUAL,
   SOCIAL

BRANTLEY, CYNTHIA
   BRANTLEY, CYNTHIA‡ 1011 5TH STREET, 4, DAVIS,
   CALIFORNIA 95616‡ KENYA‡ COAST‡ GIRYAMA‡ 300
   HOURS‡ 1970-71‡ QUALITY FAIR‡ ‡ ‡ ‡ ‡ HISTORY

BRASSEUR, G.
  BRASSEUR, G.+ DI DIO, FRANCOIS+ DIETERLEN,
  GERMAINE+ ROUGET, GILBERT‡ -+ -+ CENTRE DE
  RECHERCHES AFRICAINES, RUE D'ALSACE, 75 PARIS 6E,
  FRANCE+ 1 RUE DES DEUX-PONTS, 75004 PARIS, FRANCE‡
  MALI‡ ‡ BAMBARA, BOZO, DOGON, MALINKE, MARKA,
  MINIANKA, PEUL, RYMAYBE, SARAKOLE, SOMONO,
  SONGHAY‡ ‡ ‡ ‡ MUSEE DE L'HOMME‡ ‡ ‡ ‡

BRAVMANN, RENE A.
  BRAVMANN, RENE A.‡ SCHOOL OF ART, UNIVERSITY OF
  WASHINGTON, SEATTLE, WASHINGTON 98195‡ UPPER
  VOLTA‡ BOBO-DIOULONS, WEST VOLTA‡ BOBO, DYULA‡ 18
  HOURS‡ 1972-74‡ QUALITY EXCELLENT‡ SCHOOL OF ART,
  UNIVERSITY OF WASHINGTON‡ ‡ ‡ ‡ DANCE-MASKED,
  URBAN-BAR, URBAN-NIGHTCLUB

BRITISH BROADCASTING CORP
  BRITISH BROADCASTING CORPORATION‡ SOUND ARCHIVES,
  PORTLAND PLACE, LONDON W1A 1AA, ENGLAND‡ ‡ ‡ ‡ ‡
  ‡ ‡ ‡ ‡ ‡

BROADCASTING CORPORATION
  BROADCASTING CORPORATION OF CHINA‡ 53 JEN AI ROAD,
  SECTION 3, TAIPEI, REPUBLIC OF CHINA‡ ‡ ‡ ‡ ‡ ‡
  ‡ ‡ ‡ ‡

  BROADCASTING CORPORATION OF CHINA‡ 53 JEN AI ROAD,
  SECTION 3, TAIPEI, REPUBLIC OF CHINA‡ ETHIOPIA‡ ‡
  ‡ 2 HOURS‡ ‡ ‡ BROADCASTING CORPORATION OF CHINA‡
  ‡ ‡ ‡ HARVEST, HUNTING, LOVE, WAR

BROEKHUYSE, JAN T.
  BROEKHUYSE, JAN T.‡ KONINKLIJK INSTITUUT VOOR DE
  TROPEN, LINNAEUSTRAAT 2A, AMSTERDAM, NETHERLANDS‡
  UPPER VOLTA‡ TOMA‡ SAMO‡ 21 HOURS‡ 1969‡ QUALITY
  GOOD‡ KONINKLIJK INSTITUUT VOOR DE TROPEN‡ ‡ ‡ ‡
  MUSIC

BROGGER, JAN C.
  BROGGER, JAN C.‡ UNIVERSITETS ETNOGRAFISKE MUSEUM,
  FREDERIKSGATE 2, OSLO, NORWAY‡ ETHIOPIA‡ ‡ SIDAMO‡
  3 HOURS‡ ‡ QUALITY FAIR‡ UNIVERSITETS
  ETNOGRAFISKE MUSEUM‡ ‡ ‡ ‡ DEATH-FUNERAL,
  SPIRIT-POSSESSION

BROOKS, GEORGE
  BROOKS, GEORGE+ DALBY, DAVID+ VAUGHAN, JAMES H.‡
  DEPARTMENT OF HISTORY, INDIANA UNIVERSITY,

BROOKS, GEORGE
  BLOOMINGTON, INDIANA 47401+ SCHOOL OF ORIENTAL
  AND AFRICAN STUDIES, UNIVERSITY OF LONDON, LONDON
  W.C.1, ENGLAND+ DEPARTMENT OF ANTHROPOLOGY,
  INDIANA UNIVERSITY, BLOOMINGTON, INDIANA 47401‡
  AFRICA-U.S.‡ BLOOMINGTON, INDIANA‡ MALINKE‡ 2
  HOURS‡ 1969‡ QUALITY GOOD‡ ARCHIVES OF
  TRADITIONAL MUSIC‡ 69-012-F‡ ‡ RESTRICTED‡
  MALINKE-LECTURE

BROWN, HERBERT
  BROWN, HERBERT‡ ‡ ‡ ‡ FANTI‡ .5 HOUR‡ 1954-57‡
  QUALITY GOOD‡ ARCHIVES OF LANGUAGES OF THE WORLD‡
  ‡ ‡ ‡ GRAMMATICAL-DATA

BROWN, JAMES W.
  BROWN, JAMES W.‡ 3 MERRIMON AVENUE, INMAN, SOUTH
  CAROLINA 29349‡ GHANA‡ KUMASI‡ ASANTE‡ 1 HOUR‡
  1970‡ QUALITY FAIR‡ ‡ ‡ ‡ HISTORY

BRUTUS, DENNIS
  BRUTUS, DENNIS+ SNYDER, EMILE‡ -+ AFRICAN STUDIES,
  INDIANA UNIVERSITY, BLOOMINGTON, INDIANA 47401‡
  SOUTH AFRICA-U.S.‡ MADISON, WISCONSIN‡ ‡ 2 HOURS‡
  1966‡ QUALITY GOOD‡ ARCHIVES OF TRADITIONAL MUSIC‡
  71-015-F‡ ATL 4421-22‡ RESTRICTED‡ POETRY,
  POETRY-INTERVIEW, POLITICS-SPEECH

BRYAN, SAM
  BRYAN, SAM‡ C/O INTERNATIONAL FILM FOUNDATION,
  INC., 475 FIFTH AVENUE, NEW YORK, NEW YORK 10017‡
  MALI‡ ‡ DOGON‡ 1 HOUR‡ 1960‡ QUALITY GOOD‡ ‡ ‡ ‡ ‡
  DANCE

  BRYAN, SAM‡ C/O INTERNATIONAL FILM FOUNDATION,
  INC., 475 FIFTH AVENUE, NEW YORK, NEW YORK 10017‡
  SENEGAL‡ DAKAR‡ ‡ .5 HOUR‡ 1969‡ QUALITY GOOD‡ ‡ ‡
  ‡ ‡ MUSIC

BUCHANAN, CAROLE
  BUCHANAN, CAROLE‡ DEPARTMENT OF HISTORY, SOUTHERN
  METHODIST UNIVERSITY, HILCREST AND UNIVERSITY
  STREETS, DALLAS, TEXAS 75222‡ UGANDA‡ BUNYORO,
  TORO‡ BANYORO, BATORO‡ 7 HOURS‡ 1968-69‡ QUALITY
  GOOD‡ CENTER FOR AFRICAN ORAL DATA‡ 71-163-F‡ ATL
  4550-56‡ RESTRICTED‡ BELL, CATTLE, CHORDOPHONE,
  CULT-POSSESSION, DANCE, DRUM, HISTORY,
  MARKET-INTERVIEW, MARRIAGE, POTTER-INTERVIEW,
  PRAISE-CULT, RATTLE-GOURD

BUNGER, ROBERT LOUIS
  BUNGER, ROBERT LOUIS≠ DEPARTMENT OF SOCIOLOGY AND
  ANTHROPOLOGY, EAST CAROLINA UNIVERSITY,
  GREENVILLE, NORTH CAROLINA 27834≠ KENYA≠ TANA
  RIVER≠ OROMA, POKOMO≠ 8 HOURS≠ 1969-70≠ QUALITY
  GOOD≠ ≠ ≠ ≠ ≠ COURTING, DANCE, INITIATION, LOVE,
  PRAISE-POETRY, PRAISE-GERES, PRAISE-NESE

BYRD, ROBERT OAKES
  BYRD, ROBERT OAKES≠ NORTH PARK COLLEGE, CHICAGO,
  ILLINOIS 60625≠ UGANDA≠ ≠ ALUR, BAGANDA, BAGWERE,
  BAKONJO, BANYANKOLE, BANYOLE, KAKWA, TESO≠ ≠ ≠ ≠
  UGANDA MUSEUM≠ ≠ ≠ ≠ BOW-MUSICAL, DANCE,
  DANCE-CHORAL, DRUM, FLUTE, HARP-BOW-ADEUDEU,
  HARP-BOW-ENANGA, LYRE-BOWL-ENDONGO,
  LYRE-BOWL-ENTONGOLI, SANZA, XYLOPHONE-AMADINDA,
  XYLOPHONE-EMBAIRE, XYLOPHONE-ENDIGA,
  XYLOPHONE-MIRULI

CALAME, B.
  CALAME, B.≠ ≠ MALI≠ ≠ BAMBARA, BOZO, DOGON, MARKA,
  MINIANKA, PEUL, RYMAYBE, SARAKOLE, SOMONO,
  SONGHAY≠ ≠ 1956-57≠ 1960≠ ≠ MUSEE DE L'HOMME≠ ≠ ≠
  ≠ CURING, DANCE, DEATH-FUNERAL, DRUM, FLUTE,
  GONG-ROCK, HORN, LUTE, LUTE-BOWED, RATTLE, WAR,
  WORK, XYLOPHONE

CALKINS, HOWARD W.
  CALKINS, HOWARD W.≠ RADIO DAHOMEY≠ CENTRE
  CULTUREL AMERICAIN, RUE CAPORAL ANANI BERNARD,
  COTONOU, DAHOMEY≠ RADIODIFFUSION DU DAHOMEY,
  COTONOU, DAHOMEY≠ DAHOMEY≠ ≠ DENDI, DOMPAGO, FON,
  MAHI, YORUBA≠ 1 HOUR≠ CA1967≠ QUALITY GOOD≠
  ARCHIVES OF TRADITIONAL MUSIC≠ 67-165-F≠ ATL 5104≠
  ≠ CHORDOPHONE, DANCE, DRUM, FLUTE

CAMARA, S.
  CAMARA, S.≠ ≠ SENEGAL≠ ≠ MALINKE≠ ≠ 1970≠ 1971≠ ≠
  MUSEE DE L'HOMME≠ ≠ ≠ ≠ DRUM-JEMBE, FOLKTALE,
  HARP-LUTE-KORA, HARP-SIMBINGO, HUNTING,
  MUSICIAN-GRIOT

CAMP, CHARLES M.
  CAMP, CHARLES M.≠ TRACEY, HUGH≠ 186 CORA STREET,
  SAN FRANCISCO, CALIFORNIA 94134≠ INTERNATIONAL
  LIBRARY OF AFRICAN MUSIC, BOX 138, ROODEPORT,
  TRANSVAAL, SOUTH AFRICA≠ RHODESIA≠ BIKITA,
  BULAWAYO, GUNDAS, HUZI, MREWA, MTOKO, SALISBURY,
  UMTALI, ZAKA, ZIMBABWE≠ BUDJA, CHIKUNDA, FUNGWE,

CAMP, CHARLES M.
  HERA, HUNGWE, KARANGA, NDAU, NDEBELE, NYANJA,
  NYASA, PEDI, RAMBA, WEMBA, YAO‡ 6 HOURS‡ 1948‡
  QUALITY GOOD‡ ARCHIVES OF TRADITIONAL MUSIC‡
  PRE'54-171-F‡ ATL 303-22‡ ‡ ANCESTOR-CEREMONY,
  BOW-MUSICAL, CANTE-FABLE, CHILDREN, DANCE,
  DEATH-FUNERAL, DIVINING, DRINKING, DRUM,
  DRUM-CYLINDRICAL, FLUTE, FOLKTALE, GUITAR, HORN,
  LAMENT, LULLABY, MBIRA, PANPIPES, RATTLE,
  ULULATION, WAR, WHISTLE-LANGUAGE, WORK-THRESHING,
  YODEL

  CAMP, CHARLES M.+ TRACEY, HUGH‡ 186 CORA STREET,
  SAN FRANCISCO, CALIFORNIA 94134+ INTERNATIONAL
  LIBRARY OF AFRICAN MUSIC, BOX 138, ROODEPORT,
  TRANSVAAL, SOUTH AFRICA‡ SOUTH AFRICA‡ DURBAN
  DEEP MINE, JOHANNESBURG, MESINA COPPER MINE, RAND
  LEASE MINE, ROSE DEEP MINE‡ BHACA, CHOPI, HLUBI,
  NDAU, NYASA, PONDO, SHANGAAN, SOTHO, SWAZI,
  TSWANA, VENDA, XHOSA‡ 2 HOURS‡ 1947-48‡ QUALITY
  FAIR‡ ARCHIVES OF TRADITIONAL MUSIC‡ PRE'54-171-F‡
  ATL 303-22‡ ‡ BOW-MUSICAL, CHILDREN, CONCERTINA,
  DANCE, DRINKING, GUITAR, HARP-ZITHER, LOVE,
  MARRIAGE, MBIRA, XYLOPHONE, ZITHER

  CAMP, CHARLES M.+ TRACEY, HUGH‡ 186 CORA STREET,
  SAN FRANCISCO, CALIFORNIA 94134+ INTERNATIONAL
  LIBRARY OF AFRICAN MUSIC, BOX 138, ROODEPORT,
  TRANSVAAL, SOUTH AFRICA‡ ZAMBIA‡ LIVINGSTONE,
  MAPANZA‡ BEMBA, LALA, LOZI, TONGA, ZINZA‡ 2 HOURS‡
  1947-48‡ QUALITY GOOD‡ ARCHIVES OF TRADITIONAL
  MUSIC‡ PRE'54-171-F‡ ATL 303-22‡ ‡ BOW-MUSICAL,
  CANOE, CANTE-FABLE, DANCE, DEATH-FUNERAL,
  DRINKING, DRUM, DRUM-FRICTION, DRUM-GOBLET,
  GUITAR, HANDCLAPPING, HERDING, HORN, HUNTING,
  LOVE, MBIRA, POSSESSION, PRAISE, RATTLE, WHISTLE,
  WORK, XYLOPHONE

CAMPBELL, CAROL
  CAMPBELL, CAROL‡ 6119 LATONA N.E., SEATTLE,
  WASHINGTON 98195‡ KENYA‡ LAMU, MALINDI, MOMBASA‡
  BAJUN, SWAHILI‡ 12 HOURS‡ 1972‡ QUALITY GOOD‡
  ARCHIVES OF ETHNIC MUSIC AND DANCE‡ ‡ ‡ ‡
  CHILDREN, MARRIAGE, POETRY

CARD, CAROLINE E.
  CARD, CAROLINE E.‡ BOX 256, RD 2, DOVER, NEW
  JERSEY 07801‡ ALGERIA‡ AHAGGAR, TAMANRASSET‡
  TUAREG‡ 1.5 HOURS‡ 1972‡ QUALITY GOOD‡ ARCHIVES

CARD, CAROLINE E.
  OF TRADITIONAL MUSIC‡ 73-056-F‡ ‡ RESTRICTED‡
  LUTE-BOWED-IMZAD

CARLISLE, ROXANE C.
  CARLISLE, ROXANE C.‡ TRENT UNIVERSITY,
  PETERBOROUGH, ONTARIO, CANADA‡ SUDAN‡ AKOBO,
  AKURA, EQUATORIA, FARIANG-RIANGNAM, NORTHERN
  SUDAN, UPPER NILE‡ ANUAK, DINKA, GAALIIN, NUER,
  SHILLUK‡ .5 HOUR‡ 1963‡ QUALITY EXCELLENT‡
  ARCHIVES OF TRADITIONAL MUSIC‡ 66-185-F‡ ATL 5146‡
  RESTRICTED‡ ANCESTOR-RITUAL, CATTLE, DANCE,
  DANCE-AGUUGA, DRUM-BUL, DRUM-DALUKA,
  DRUM-FRAME-RIGG, HORN-GOURD, LUTE-PLUCKED-UD,
  LYRE, MARRIAGE, POETRY, POSSESSION, PRAISE-CATTLE,
  PRAISE-RULER, RITUAL-EXORCISM, WAR

  CARLISLE, ROXANE C.‡ TRENT UNIVERSITY,
  PETERBOROUGH, ONTARIO, CANADA‡ SUDAN‡ ‡ ANUAK,
  DINKA, NUER, SHILLUK‡ ‡ ‡ ‡ MUSEE DE L'HOMME‡ ‡ ‡
  ‡

CARRINGTON, JOHN F.
  CARRINGTON, JOHN F.+ GORDON, MERYL‡ UNIVERSITY
  LIBRE DE LA REPUBLIQUE DE ZAIRE, KINSANGANI,
  ZAIRE+ 100-4 ALDRICH STREET, BRONX, NEW YORK
  10475‡ ZAIRE-U.S.‡ BLOOMINGTON, INDIANA‡ ‡ 2
  HOURS‡ 1975‡ QUALITY FAIR‡ ARCHIVES OF
  TRADITIONAL MUSIC‡ 75-032-F‡ ‡ RESTRICTED‡
  DRUM-LANGUAGE-LECTURE, DRUM-SLIT-LECTURE

CAZDEN, NORMAN
  CAZDEN, NORMAN‡ DEPARTMENT OF MUSIC, UNIVERSITY
  OF MAINE, ORONO, MAINE 04473‡ NIGERIA-U.S.‡ CAMP
  WOODLAND‡ ‡ .5 HOUR‡ 1960‡ QUALITY GOOD‡ ARCHIVES
  OF TRADITIONAL MUSIC‡ 64-015-F‡ ‡ RESTRICTED‡
  OLATUNJI-B.-PERFORMANCE

CENTER FOR AFRICAN ORAL D
  CENTER FOR AFRICAN ORAL DATA‡ INDIANA UNIVERSITY,
  MAXWELL HALL 057, BLOOMINGTON, INDIANA 47401‡ ‡ ‡
  ‡ ‡ ‡ ‡ ‡ ‡ ‡

CENTER FOR THE STUDY OF O
  CENTER FOR THE STUDY OF ORAL LITERATURE‡ HARVARD
  UNIVERSITY, CAMBRIDGE, MASSACHUSETTS 02138‡ ‡ ‡
  ‡ ‡ ‡ ‡ ‡ ‡

CENTRE D'ETUDE ET DE DOCU
   CENTRE D'ETUDE ET DE DOCUMENTATION AFRICAINES
   (CEDAF)‡ PLACE ROYALE 7, 1000 BRUXELLES, BELGIUM‡
   ‡ ‡ ‡ ‡ ‡ ‡ ‡ ‡ ‡

CENTRE D'ETUDES DES TRADI
   CENTRE D'ETUDES DES TRADITIONS ORALES‡ ORSTOM,
   70-74 RUE D'AULNAY, 93140 BONDY, PARIS, FRANCE‡ ‡
   ‡ ‡ ‡ ‡ ‡ ‡ ‡ ‡

CENTRE DE RECHERCHES ANTH
   CENTRE DE RECHERCHES ANTHROPOLOGIQUES‡ MUSÉE DE
   L'HOMME, PLACE DU TROCADERO, 75 PARIS 16E,
   FRANCE‡ ‡ ‡ ‡ ‡ ‡ ‡ ‡ ‡ ‡

   CENTRE DE RECHERCHES ANTHROPOLOGIQUES‡ MUSEE DE
   L'HOMME, PLACE DU TROCADERO, 75 PARIS 16E, FRANCE‡
   SENEGAL‡ ‡ BASSARI, BEDIK, CONIAGUI, MALINKE,
   TENDA‡ 50 HOURS‡ ‡ ‡ CENTRE DE RECHERCHES
   ANTHROPOLOGIQUES‡ ‡ ‡ CEREMONY, DANCE,
   ORAL-DATA

   CENTRE DE RECHERCHES ANTHROPOLOGIQUES
   PREHISTORIQUES ET ETHNOGRAPHIQUES (CRAPE)‡ 3 RUE
   F.D. ROOSEVELT, ALGER, ALGERIA‡ ‡ ‡ ‡ ‡ ‡ ‡ ‡
   ‡

   CENTRE DE RECHERCHES ANTHROPOLOGIQUES
   PREHISTORIQUES ET ETHNOGRAPHIQUES‡ 3 RUE F.D.
   ROOSEVELT, ALGER, ALGERIA‡ ALGERIA‡ ‡ ARAB,
   BERBER, MAGHREB‡ 1500 HOURS‡ ‡ ‡ CENTRE DE
   RECHERCHES ANTHROPOLOGIQUES PREHISTORIQUES ET
   ETHNOGRAPHIQUES‡ ‡ ‡ RESTRICTED‡ FOLKLORE,
   HISTORY, MUSIC, POETRY

CENTRE DE RECHERCHES INTE
   CENTRE DE RECHERCHES INTERDISCIPLINAIRES POUR LE
   DEVELOPPEMENT DE L'EDUCATION, UNIVERSITY
   NATIONALE DU ZAIRE‡ CAMPUS DE KISANGANI,
   KISANGANI, ZAIRE‡ ‡ ‡ ‡ ‡ ‡ ‡ ‡ ‡ ‡

CENTRE FOR NIGERIAN CULTU
   CENTRE FOR NIGERIAN CULTURAL STUDIES, AHMADU
   BELLO UNIVERSITY‡ P.O. BOX 75, KANO, NIGERIA‡ ‡ ‡
   ‡ ‡ ‡ ‡ ‡ ‡

CENTRE FOR THE STUDY OF N
   CENTRE FOR THE STUDY OF NIGERIAN LANGUAGES,
   ABDULLAHI BAYERO COLLEGE‡ AHMADU BELLO UNIVERSITY,

CENTRE FOR THE STUDY OF N
  P.M.B. 3011, KANO, NIGERIA‡ ‡ ‡ ‡ ‡ ‡ ‡ ‡ ‡ ‡

  CENTRE FOR THE STUDY OF NIGERIAN LANGUAGES‡
  ABDULLAHI BAYERO COLLEGE, AHMADU BELLO UNIVERSITY,
  P.M.B. 3011, KANO, NIGERIA‡ NIGERIA‡ NORTHERN
  NIGERIA‡ HAUSA‡ 100 HOURS‡ ‡ ‡ CENTRE FOR THE
  STUDY OF NIGERIAN LANGUAGES‡ ‡ ‡ ‡ FOLKTALE,
  MUSIC, PRAISE

CENTRE OF INTERNATIONAL A
  CENTRE OF INTERNATIONAL AND AREA STUDIES,
  UNIVERSITY OF LONDON‡ 15 WOBURN SQUARE, LONDON
  WC1H ONS, ENGLAND‡ ‡ ‡ ‡ ‡ ‡ ‡ ‡ ‡

CENTRE REGIONAL DE RECHER
  CENTRE REGIONAL DE RECHERCHE ET DE DOCUMENTATION
  POUR LA TRADITION ORALE‡ B.P. 369, NIAMEY, NIGER‡
  ‡ ‡ ‡ ‡ ‡ ‡ ‡ ‡ ‡

CENTRO DE ESTUDOS DE ANTR
  CENTRO DE ESTUDOS DE ANTROPOLOGIA CULTURAL‡ RUA
  JAU 54, LISBON 3, PORTUGAL‡ ‡ ‡ ‡ ‡ ‡ ‡ ‡ ‡ ‡

CHARLES, EUNICE A.
  CHARLES, EUNICE A.‡ HISTORY DEPARTMENT, SOUTHERN
  ILLINOIS UNIVERSITY, CARBONDALE, ILLINOIS 62901‡
  SENEGAL‡ LINGUERE‡ WOLOF‡ 24 HOURS‡ 1970-71‡
  QUALITY EXCELLENT‡ CENTER FOR AFRICAN ORAL DATA‡
  73-004-F‡ ‡ ‡ HISTORY-KINGDOM-JOLOF

CHERKI, SALAH
  CHERKI, SALAH‡ 3, PLATEAU BETANA, VILLA 3, SALA,
  MOROCCO‡ MOROCCO‡ RABAT, SALE‡ ARAB‡ 9 HOURS‡
  CA1960‡ QUALITY GOOD‡ ARCHIVES OF TRADITIONAL
  MUSIC‡ 69-023-F‡ ‡ RESTRICTED‡ MUSIC-ART

CHILDS, GLADWYN
  CHILDS, GLADWYN‡ 1005 TERRACE STREET, SEATTLE,
  WASHINGTON 98104‡ ANGOLA‡ HORAMBC DISTRICT‡
  OVIMBUNDU‡ 2 HOURS‡ 1962‡ QUALITY FAIR‡ ‡ ‡ ‡
  FOLKLORE, HYMN

CHRISTIAN, VALERIE
  CHRISTIAN, VALERIE‡ DEPARTMENT OF ANTHROPOLOGY,
  INDIANA UNIVERSITY, BLOOMINGTON, INDIANA 47401‡
  UPPER VOLTA‡ BOROMO, BOUNOUNA, BOUSSOUMA, DANGO,
  DIEBOUGOU, FADA-NGOURMA, KANTCHARI, KIUMA,
  KOUPELA, MOURDENI, NAMOUNOU, NOUNA, OUAGADOUGOU,

CHRISTIAN, VALERIE
   RAMESSOUM, SIENANA, TOMA‡ BISSA, BOBO, BWABA,
   DAGARA, DYULA, FULANI, FULBE, GOUIN, GOURMANTCHE,
   HAUSA, KASSENA, KWO, LOBI, MARKA, MOSSI, NONDOM,
   POUGOULIS, SAMO-DU-SUD, YARDSE‡ 17 HOURS‡ 1973-74‡
   QUALITY EXCELLENT‡ ARCHIVES OF TRADITIONAL MUSIC+
   ARCHIVES SONORES, C.V.R.S.‡ 74-069-F‡ ‡
   RESTRICTED‡ BAPTISM, CURING-CELEBRATION, CHILDREN,
   DANCE, DANCE-MASKED, DEATH-FUNERAL, DRUM, FLUTE,
   FOLKTALE, GOURD, GUITAR, HARP-LUTE, HISTORY,
   MARRIAGE, PRAISE, RATTLE,SOCIAL

   CHRISTIAN, VALERIE+ ROSELLINI, JAMES N.‡
   DEPARTMENT OF ANTHROPOLOGY, INDIANA UNIVERSITY,
   BLOOMINGTON, INDIANA 47401+ C.V.R.S., B.P. 7047,
   OUAGADOUGOU, UPPER VOLTA‡ UPPER VOLTA‡ KOUPE-LA,
   NOUNA‡ FULBE, KASSENA, MARKA, MOSSI‡ 2 HOURS‡
   1973‡ QUALITY EXCELLENT‡ ARCHIVES OF TRADITIONAL
   MUSIC+ ARCHIVES SONORES, C.V.R.S.‡ 74-068-F‡ ‡
   RESTRICTED‡ DRUM-CYLINDRICAL, GOURD, LUTE-BOWED,
   PRAISE, RATTLE

CIPARISSE, GERARD JEAN
   CIPARISSE, GERARD JEAN‡ 34, RUE JEAN CIPARISSE,
   5000 NAMUR, BELGIQUE‡ ZAIRE‡ BAS CONGO, KWANGO‡
   BAKONGO, BASUKU, BAYAKA‡ 14 HOURS‡ 1970-71‡
   QUALITY EXCELLENT‡ MUSEE ROYAL DE L'AFRIQUE
   CENTRALE‡ ‡ ‡ HISTORY, PRAISE, RITUAL, SOCIAL

CLAUSS, BERNHARD PETER
   CLAUSS, BERNHARD PETER‡ 205 HAMBURG 80,
   SCHLEBUSCHWEG 20, WEST GERMANY‡ ANGOLA‡ HUILA‡
   HIMBA-MUGAMBO‡ .5 HOUR‡ 1970-72‡ QUALITY GOOD‡ ‡ ‡
   ‡ ‡ BOW-MUSICAL, FOLKLORE

   CLAUSS, BERNHARD PETER‡ 205 HAMBURG 80,
   SCHLEBUSCHWEG 20, WEST GERMANY‡ BOTSWANA‡ CENTRAL
   KALAHARI‡ BUSHMEN‡ 1 HOUR‡ 1971-72‡ QUALITY GOOD‡
   ‡ ‡ ‡ ‡ DANCE, GAMBLING, IDIOPHONE-PLUCKED

   CLAUSS, BERNHARD PETER‡ 205 HAMBURG 80,
   SCHLEBUSCHWEG 20, WEST GERMANY‡ CHAD‡ KYABE‡
   SARAKABA‡ .3 HOUR‡ 1973‡ QUALITY GOOD‡ ‡ ‡ ‡ ‡
   CHORDOPHONE

   CLAUSS, BERNHARD PETER‡ 205 HAMBURG 80,
   SCHLEBUSCHWEG 20, WEST GERMANY‡ MALI‡ GAO,
   SIKASSOU‡ BAMBARA, TAMACHECK‡ .5 HOUR‡ 1973‡
   QUALITY GOOD‡ ‡ ‡ ‡ ‡ CHORDOPHONE, DRUM,

CLAUSS, BERNHARD PETER
  XYLOPHONE

  CLAUSS, BERNHARD PETER‡ 205 HAMBURG 80,
  SCHLEBUSCHWEG 20, WEST GERMANY‡ ZAIRE‡ BENI-OICHA‡
  PYGMIES‡ 1 HOUR‡ 1973‡ QUALITY GOOD‡ ‡ ‡ ‡
  CHOIR, CHORDOPHONE, FLUTE, IDIOPHONE

COHEN, DAVID WILLIAM
  COHEN, DAVID WILLIAM‡ DEPARTMENT OF HISTORY, THE
  JOHNS HOPKINS UNIVERSITY, BALTIMORE, MARYLAND
  21218‡ UGANDA‡ BUSOGA‡ BASOGA‡ 100 HOURS‡ 1966-67‡
  QUALITY FAIR‡ MAKERERE UNIVERSITY LIBRARY‡ ‡ ‡ ‡
  DRUM, DRUM-LANGUAGE, HISTORY

  COHEN, DAVID WILLIAM‡ DEPARTMENT OF HISTORY, THE
  JOHNS HOPKINS UNIVERSITY, BALTIMORE, MARYLAND
  21218‡ UGANDA‡ BUSOGA‡ BASOGA‡ 40 HOURS‡ 1971-72‡
  QUALITY FAIR‡ MAKERERE UNIVERSITY LIBRARY‡ ‡ ‡ ‡
  HISTORY, PRAISE

COHEN, RONALD
  COHEN, RONALD‡ ANTHROPOLOGY DEPARTMENT,
  NORTHWESTERN UNIVERSITY, EVANSTON, ILLINOIS 60201‡
  NIGERIA‡ ‡ KANURI‡ 2 HOURS‡ 1956‡ ‡ ARCHIVES OF
  TRADITIONAL MUSIC‡ 60-035-F‡ ‡ RESTRICTED‡ DANCE,
  PRAISE

COLEMAN, MILTON
  COLEMAN, MILTON‡ ‡ UGANDA‡ ‡ KARAMOJONG‡ 2 HOURS‡
  1967‡ ‡ ARCHIVES OF TRADITIONAL MUSIC‡ 68-290-F‡ ‡
  ‡ INTERVIEW, MUSIC

COLLEGE OF MUSIC, UNIVERS
  COLLEGE OF MUSIC, UNIVERSITY OF NIGERIA‡ LAGOS,
  NIGERIA‡ ‡ ‡ ‡ ‡ ‡ ‡ ‡ ‡ ‡

  COLLEGE OF MUSIC, UNIVERSITY OF NIGERIA‡ LAGOS,
  NIGERIA‡ NIGERIA‡ ‡ BINI, BOKI, DAKARAWA,
  EFIK-IBIBIO, EKOI, FULANI, HAUSA, IBO, IDOMA,
  IJAW, JABA, MADA, YALA, YORUBA, ZABEBMAWA‡ ‡ ‡ ‡
  COLLEGE OF MUSIC, UNIVERSITY OF NIGERIA‡ ‡ ‡ ‡
  BIRTH, CHIEF-INSTALLATION, CHILDREN, DRUM,
  ENTERTAINMENT, FESTIVAL-PUBERTY, FLUTE, FOLKTALE,
  HARP, INSULT, LOVE, NAMING-CEREMONY, PRAISE,
  PROVERB, RELIGIOUS-CULT

CONDOMINAS, G.
  CONDOMINAS, G.‡ ‡ MALAGASY REPUBLIC‡ ‡ ‡ ‡ 1959‡ ‡

CONDOMINAS, G.
  MUSEE DE L'HOMME‡ ‡ ‡ ‡ LUTE

COOKE, PETER R.
  COOKE, PETER R.‡ 26 CRAMOND GARDENS, EDINBURGH,
  EH 46 PU SCOTLAND, UNITED KINGDOM‡ UGANDA‡ ‡
  BAGANDA‡ 1 HOUR‡ 1965-68‡ QUALITY EXCELLENT‡
  CENTER FOR AFRICAN ORAL DATA‡ 71-256-F‡ ATL 3533‡
  RESTRICTED‡ DRUM, FLUTE-ENSEMBLE-ROYAL,
  FLUTE-NDERE, FLUTE-NOTCHED, LUTE-BOWED, LYRE,
  PANPIPES, XYLOPHONE, ZITHER

COOPERATIVE AFRICANA MICR
  COOPERATIVE AFRICANA MICROFILM PROJECT (CAMP)‡
  CENTER FOR RESEARCH LIBRARIES, 5721 COTTAGE GROVE
  AVENUE, CHICAGO, ILLINOIS 60637‡ ‡ ‡ ‡ ‡ ‡ ‡ ‡ ‡
  ‡

COPE, TREVOR ANTHONY
  COPE, TREVOR ANTHONY‡ DEPARTMENT OF BANTU
  LANGUAGES, UNIVERSITY OF NATAL, DURBAN, SOUTH
  AFRICA‡ SOUTH AFRICA‡ NATAL, ZULULAND‡ ZULU‡ 15
  HOURS‡ 1965-72‡ QUALITY FAIR‡ ‡ ‡ ‡
  DANCE-BUTHELEZI, DEATH-FUNERAL,
  FIRST-FRUIT-CEREMONY, INSTALLATION-CEREMONY,
  PRAISE

COPLAN, DAVID
  COPLAN, DAVID+ THOMASON, LEE‡ ANTHROPOLOGY
  DEPARTMENT, INDIANA UNIVERSITY, BLOOMINGTON,
  INDIANA 47401+ 10112 SPRING LAKE TERRACE, FAIRFAX,
  VIRGINIA 22030‡ GHANA‡ ABESRE, KUMASI, SOMANYA‡
  ASANTE, EWE, KROBO+ 5 HOURS‡ 1974‡ QUALITY
  EXCELLENT‡ ARCHIVES OF TRADITIONAL MUSIC‡
  74-103-F‡ ‡ RESTRICTED‡ DEATH-FUNERAL, DRUM,
  ENTERTAINMENT, GUITAR, HIGHLIFE,
  STAMPING-TUBE-BAMBOO

COURLANDER, HAROLD
  COURLANDER, HAROLD‡ 5512 BRITE DRIVE, BETHESDA,
  MARYLAND 20034‡ ETHIOPIA‡ ERITREA, GURA‡ TIGRINYA‡
  2 HOURS‡ 1943‡ QUALITY FAIR‡ ARCHIVES OF
  TRADITIONAL MUSIC‡ PRE'54-001-F‡ ATL 452-55‡
  RESTRICTED‡ DRUM, FLUTE, FLUTE-DOUBLE, HARP, WORK

COX, WILLIAM L.
  COX, WILLIAM L.‡ B.P. 1420, BUJUMBURA, BURUNDI‡
  BURUNDI‡ ‡ ‡ 1 HOUR‡ 1962‡ QUALITY GOOD‡ ARCHIVES
  OF TRADITIONAL MUSIC‡ 74-002-F‡ ‡ ‡

COX, WILLIAM L.
  CELEBRATION-INDEPENDENCE,
  INDEPENDENCE-CELEBRATION

CRABB, DAVID
  CRABB, DAVID‡ DEPARTMENT OF SOCIOLOGY AND
  ANTHROPOLOGY, PRINCETON UNIVERSITY, PRINCETON,
  NEW JERSEY 08540‡ NIGERIA‡ EASTERN NIGERIA, OGOJA
  PROVINCE‡ IBO‡ 6 HOURS‡ ‡ QUALITY FAIR‡ ‡ ‡ ‡

CRAVEN, ANNA
  CRAVEN, ANNA‡ NATIONAL MUSEUM, P.M.B. 2127,
  KADUNA, NIGERIA‡ NIGERIA‡ GWARGWADA, NASARAWA
  EMIRATE‡ AFO, GEDE‡ 1.75 HOURS‡ 1969-70‡ QUALITY
  GOOD‡ FEDERAL DEPARTMENT OF ANTIQUITIES, NATIONAL
  MUSEUM, KADUNA‡ ‡ ‡ CEREMONY, PRAISE

CROWLEY, DANIEL J.
  CROWLEY, DANIEL J.‡ ANTHROPOLOGY DEPARTMENT,
  UNIVERSITY OF CALIFORNIA, DAVIS, CALIFORNIA 95616‡
  ZAIRE-U.S.‡ DAVIS, CALIFORNIA‡ ‡ 1 HOUR‡ 1961‡
  QUALITY GOOD‡ ARCHIVES OF TRADITIONAL MUSIC‡
  73-069-F‡ ‡ RESTRICTED‡ FOLKTALE

CURTIN, PHILIP D.
  CURTIN, PHILIP D.‡ 3211 HUMANITIES BUILDING, 435
  NORTH PARK STREET, UNIVERSITY OF WISCONSIN,
  MADISON, WISCONSIN 53706‡ SENEGAL‡ BAKEL, BANI
  ISRAILA, BOKOLAKO, DAKAR, DALAFI, DIANA DIARRE,
  DIDE, DIELANI, GABOU, GOUDIRY, GOUTA, KOUSSAN,
  MADINA DIAKA, SENOUDEBOU, SOUTOUTA, TOMBOURA‡
  ARAB, DIAKHANKE, MALINKE, PULAR, SONINKE‡ 60
  HOURS‡ 1966‡ QUALITY GOOD‡ ARCHIVES OF
  TRADITIONAL MUSIC‡ 67-096-F‡ ‡ ‡ GENEALOGY,
  HISTORY, LUTE-BOWED, MUSICIAN-GRIOT

  CURTIN, PHILIP D.‡ 3211 HUMANITIES BUILDING, 435
  NORTH PARK STREET, UNIVERSITY OF WISCONSIN,
  MADISON, WISCONSIN 53706‡ SENEGAL‡ BANI, DAKAR,
  DIAKA, DIANA, DIANKA MAKAM, DIELANI, GOUDIRY,
  ISRAILA, KIDINA, KOUSSAN‡ ARAB, DIAKHANKE,
  MALINKE, PULAR‡ 13 HOURS‡ 1966‡ QUALITY GOOD‡
  ARCHIVES OF TRADITIONAL MUSIC‡ 68-228-F‡ ‡ ‡
  CHORDPHONE-HOUDOU, DRUM, ENTERTAINMENT,
  EPIC-SUNJATA, FOLKTALE, GENEALOGY, HARP-LUTE-KORA,
  HISTORY, IDIOPHONE-STRUCK, LUTE-BOWED, MARRIAGE,
  PRAISE, PRAISE-RULER, RELIGIOUS-ISLAMIC, WAR

CURTIS, NATALIE
  CURTIS, NATALIE‡ DECEASED‡ AFRICA-EAST‡ ‡ ‡ .2
  HOUR‡ CA1919‡ QUALITY FAIR‡ ARCHIVES OF
  TRADITIONAL MUSIC‡ PRE'54-065-F‡ ATL 1546‡ ‡
  DANCE, HUNTING

  CURTIS, NATALIE‡ DECEASED‡ MOZAMBIQUE‡ ‡ NDAU‡ .2
  HOUR‡ CA1919‡ QUALITY FAIR‡ ARCHIVES OF
  TRADITIONAL MUSIC‡ PRE'54-065-F‡ ATL 1546‡
  RESTRICTED‡ RAIN, WORK-GRINDING

  CURTIS, NATALIE‡ DECEASED‡ SOUTH AFRICA‡ ‡ ZULU‡
  .3 HOUR‡ CA1919‡ QUALITY FAIR‡ ARCHIVES OF
  TRADITIONAL MUSIC‡ PRE'54-065-F‡ ATL 1546‡ ‡
  LAMENT, LOVE

CUTTINGTON COLLEGE
  CUTTINGTON COLLEGE‡ BOX 277, MONROVIA, LIBERIA‡ ‡
  ‡ ‡ ‡ ‡ ‡ ‡ ‡

D'AZEVEDO, WARREN L.
  D'AZEVEDO, WARREN L.‡ ANTHROPOLOGY DEPARTMENT,
  UNIVERSITY OF NEVADA, RENO, NEVADA 89507‡ LIBERIA‡
  MONROVIA‡ AMERICO-LIBERIAN, GOLA, KPELLE, VAI‡ 4
  HOURS‡ 1956-58+ 1966‡ QUALITY GOOD‡ ‡ ‡ ‡ ‡
  CHILDREN, CHILDREN-GAME-RING, HYMN

  D'AZEVEDO, WARREN L.‡ ANTHROPOLOGY DEPARTMENT,
  UNIVERSITY OF NEVADA, RENO, NEVADA 89507‡ LIBERIA‡
  WESTERN‡ GOLA, KPELLE, VAI‡ 1 HOUR‡ 1960‡ QUALITY
  EXCELLENT‡ ‡ ‡ ‡ ‡ ENTERTAINMENT, FESTIVAL

  D'AZEVEDO, WARREN L.‡ ANTHROPOLOGY DEPARTMENT,
  UNIVERSITY OF NEVADA, RENO, NEVADA 89507‡ LIBERIA‡
  ‡ GOLA‡ 1 HOUR‡ 1967‡ QUALITY EXCELLENT‡ ‡ ‡ ‡ ‡
  INSTALLATION, SECRET-SOCIETY-LEADER

D'HERTEFELT, MARUL
  D'HERTEFELT, MARUL‡ P.O. BOX 218, BUTARE, RWANDA‡
  RWANDA‡ ‡ ‡ 200 HOURS‡ 1953-73‡ QUALITY GOOD‡
  INSTITUT NATIONAL DE RECHERCHE SCIENTIFIQUE+
  MUSEE ROYAL DE L'AFRIQUE CENTRALE‡ ‡ ‡ ‡ FOLKLORE,
  HISTORY, POETRY, PROSE

DALBY, DAVID
  BROOKS, GEORGE+ DALBY, DAVID+ VAUGHAN, JAMES H.‡
  DEPARTMENT OF HISTORY, INDIANA UNIVERSITY,
  BLOOMINGTON, INDIANA 47401+ SCHOOL OF ORIENTAL
  AND AFRICAN STUDIES, UNIVERSITY OF LONDON, LONDON

DALBY, DAVID
  W.C.1, ENGLAND+ DEPARTMENT OF ANTHROPOLOGY,
  INDIANA UNIVERSITY, BLOOMINGTON, INDIANA 47401‡
  AFRICA-U.S.‡ BLOOMINGTON, INDIANA‡ MALINKE‡ 2
  HOURS‡ 1969‡ QUALITY GOOD‡ ARCHIVES OF
  TRADITIONAL MUSIC‡ 69-012-F‡ ‡ RESTRICTED‡
  MALINKE-LECTURE

DALBY, DAVID+ AFRICAN STUDIES-I.U.‡ SCHOOL OF
  ORIENTAL AND AFRICAN STUDIES, UNIVERSITY OF
  LONDON, LONDON W.C.1, ENGLAND+ INDIANA UNIVERSITY,
  BLOOMINGTON, INDIANA 47401‡ AFRICA-U.S.‡
  BLOOMINGTON, INDIANA‡ ‡ 2 HOURS‡ 1969‡ QUALITY
  GOOD‡ ARCHIVES OF TRADITIONAL MUSIC‡ 69-018-F‡ ‡
  RESTRICTED‡ LANGUAGE-AFRICA-INFLUENCE,
  LINGUISTICS-LECTURE

DALBY, DAVID+ AFRICAN STUDIES-I.U.‡ SCHOOL OF
  ORIENTAL AND AFRICAN STUDIES, UNIVERSITY OF
  LONDON, LONDON W.C.1, ENGLAND+ INDIANA UNIVERSITY,
  BLOOMINGTON, INDIANA 47401‡ AFRICA-U.S.‡ BERKELEY,
  CALIFORNIA‡ ‡ 1.5 HOURS‡ 1969‡ QUALITY GOOD‡
  ARCHIVES OF TRADITIONAL MUSIC‡ 69-019-F‡ ‡
  RESTRICTED‡ HISTORY, LINGUISTICS-LECTURE

DANSK FOLKEMINDESAMLING
  DANSK FOLKEMINDESAMLING‡ BIRKETINGET 6, 2300
  COPENHAGEN S, DENMARK‡ ‡ ‡ ‡ ‡ ‡ ‡ ‡ ‡ ‡

DAVIDSON, MARJORY
  DAVIDSON, MARJORY‡ 5 THE MINT MILL LANE,
  GODALMING, SURREY GU7 1HB, ENGLAND‡ ZAMBIA‡
  EASTERN REGION‡ NGONI‡ ‡ 1967-71‡ QUALITY GOOD‡ ‡
  ‡ ‡ ‡ FOLKTALE, KALIMBA, PRAISE

DAVIS, GORDON
  DAVIS, GORDON‡ 1738 N. PINECREST, WICHITA, KANSAS
  67208‡ ETHIOPIA‡ ADUWA‡ COPT‡ .5 HOUR‡ 1968‡
  QUALITY GOOD‡ ARCHIVES OF TRADITIONAL MUSIC‡
  71-180-F‡ ATL 4349‡ RESTRICTED‡ BAPTISM,
  CEREMONY-BAPTISM, RELIGIOUS-COPTIC

DE HEN, FERDINAND JOSEPH
  DE HEN, FERDINAND JOSEPH‡ RONSEN HEIRWEG 32,
  DUDENAARDE, BELGIUM‡ MOROCCO‡ ATLAS, CENTRAL,
  HIGH‡ AIT-ATTA, AIT-BU-SUEMMEZ, IHANSALEN‡ 5
  HOURS‡ 1960-61‡ QUALITY GOOD‡ MUSEE ROYAL DE
  L'AFRIQUE CENTRALE‡ ‡ ‡ ‡ DANCE, FOLKLORE,
  PRAISE-POETRY

DEMPWOLFF, OTTO
  DEMPWOLFF, OTTO‡ ‡ TANZANIA‡ ‡ SANDAWE, ZARAMO‡
  .2 HOUR‡ 1910‡ QUALITY FAIR‡ ARCHIVES OF
  TRADITIONAL MUSIC‡ 59-002-F‡ ATL 1757‡ RESTRICTED‡
  DANCE

DENG, FRANCIS
  DENG, FRANCIS‡ EMBASSY OF THE DEMOCRATIC REPUBLIC
  OF THE SUDAN, BANERGATEN 10, 115 22 STOCKHOLM,
  SWEDEN‡ SUDAN‡ ‡ DINKA‡ 23 HOURS‡ 1971‡ ‡
  ARCHIVES OF TRADITIONAL MUSIC‡ 73-051-F‡ ‡ ‡
  CHILDREN, INITIATION, INSULT-AGE-SET,
  PRAISE-HUSBAND, PRAISE-OXEN, RELIGIOUS, SCHOOL,
  WAR

DEPARTMENT D'ETHNOMUSICOL
  DEPARTMENT D'ETHNOMUSICOLOGIE, MUSEE DE L'HOMME‡
  PALAIS DE CHAILLOT, PLACE DU TROCADERO, 75-PARIS
  16E, FRANCE‡ ‡ ‡ ‡ ‡ ‡ ‡ ‡ ‡

DEPARTMENT OF AFRICAN LAN
  DEPARTMENT OF AFRICAN LANGUAGES, UNIVERSITY OF
  CAPE TOWN‡ P.O.B. 594, CAPE TOWN 7700, REPUBLIC
  OF SOUTH AFRICA‡ ‡ ‡ ‡ ‡ ‡ ‡ ‡ ‡ ‡

  DEPARTMENT OF AFRICAN LANGUAGES, UNIVERSITY OF
  RHODESIA‡ P.B. MP 167, MT. PLEASANT, SALISBURY,
  RHODESIA‡ ‡ ‡ ‡ ‡ ‡ ‡ ‡ ‡ ‡

  DEPARTMENT OF AFRICAN LANGUAGES, UNIVERSITY OF
  RHODESIA‡ P.B. MP 167, MT. PLEASANT, SALISBURY,
  RHODESIA‡ RHODESIA‡ ‡ NDEBELE, SHONA‡ 100 HOURS‡ ‡
  ‡ DEPARTMENT OF AFRICAN LANGUAGES, UNIVERSITY OF
  RHODESIA‡ ‡ ‡ ‡ HISTORY, NARRATIVE, PRAISE-POETRY

DEPARTMENT OF ANTHROPOLOG
  DEPARTMENT OF ANTHROPOLOGY, UNIVERSITY OF BRITISH
  COLUMBIA‡ VANCOUVER 8, BRITISH COLUMBIA, CANADA‡ ‡
  ‡ ‡ ‡ ‡ ‡ ‡ ‡

  DEPARTMENT OF ANTHROPOLOGY, UNIVERSITY OF BRITISH
  COLUMBIA‡ DEPARTMENT OF ANTHROPOLOGY, UNIVERSITY
  OF BRITISH COLUMBIA, VANCOUVER 8, BRITISH
  COLUMBIA‡ TUNISIA‡ ‡ ‡ ‡ ‡ DEPARTMENT OF
  ANTHROPOLOGY, UNIVERSITY OF BRITISH COLUMBIA‡ ‡ ‡
  RESTRICTED‡ DRUM, RELIGIOUS, TAMBOURINE

DEPARTMENT OF ANTIQUITIES
  DEPARTMENT OF ANTIQUITIES, NATIONAL ARCHIVES OF

DEPARTMENT OF ANTIQUITIES
  MALAWI‡ P.O.B. 62, ZOMBA, MALAWI‡ ‡ ‡ ‡ ‡ ‡ ‡ ‡
  ‡ ‡

DEPARTMENT OF LINGUISTICS
  DEPARTMENT OF LINGUISTICS AND NIGERIAN LANGUAGES,
  UNIVERSITY OF IBADAN‡ IBADAN, NIGERIA‡ ‡ ‡ ‡ ‡ ‡
  ‡ ‡ ‡

  DEPARTMENT OF LINGUISTICS AND NIGERIAN LANGUAGES,
  UNIVERSITY OF IBADAN‡ IBADAN, NIGERIA‡ NIGERIA‡
  BENIN-PROVINCE, DELTA, IBADAN, IFE, IJEBU, ILESHA,
  RIVERS-STATE‡ EDO, IJO, ISOKO, ITSEKIRI, OWAN,
  YORUBA‡ 33 HOURS‡ 1967-73‡ ‡ DEPARTMENT OF
  LINGUISTICS AND NIGERIAN LANGUAGES, UNIVERSITY OF
  IBADAN‡ ‡ ‡ ‡ FESTIVAL-ESA-ODE, FESTIVAL-IFE,
  FOLKTALE-EDO, FOLKTALE-OTUO, HISTORY-ITSEKIRI,
  HISTORY-KOLOKUMA, HISTORY-NEMBE, NARRATIVE-IFE,
  NARRATIVE-IJEBU, NARRATIVE-IKALE, PRAISE-IJALA,
  PRAISE-POETRY-ESA-EGUN, PRAISE-POETRY-ESA-ODE,
  PRAISE-POETRY-IGEDE-IBI, PRAISE-POETRY-IGEDE-IRE,
  PRAISE-POETRY-OFO

DEPARTMENT OF THEATRE ART
  DEPARTMENT OF THEATRE ARTS, UNIVERSITY OF DAR ES
  SALAAM‡ P.O. BOX 35091, UNIVERSITY HILL, DAR ES
  SALAAM, TANZANIA‡ ‡ ‡ ‡ ‡ ‡ ‡ ‡ ‡ ‡

  DEPARTMENT OF THEATRE ARTS, UNIVERSITY OF DAR ES
  SALAAM‡ P.O. BOX 35091, UNIVERSITY HILL, DAR ES
  SALAAM, TANZANIA‡ TANZANIA‡ ‡ ‡ 3.5 HOURS‡ ‡ ‡
  DEPARTMENT OF THEATRE ARTS, UNIVERSITY OF DAR ES
  SALAAM‡ ‡ ‡ ‡ DRUM-TUNED, XYLOPHONE

DEPLAEN, GUY
  DEPLAEN, GUY‡ BP 23 75, LUBUMBASHI, ZAIRE‡ ZAIRE‡
  SHABA‡ LUBA, YEKE‡ 20 HOURS‡ 1973-74‡ QUALITY
  GOOD‡ INSTITUT DES MUSEES NATIONAUX DU ZAIRE‡ ‡ ‡
  ‡ HISTORY, RITUAL

DES FORGES, ALISON LIEBHA
  DES FORGES, ALISON LIEBHAFSKY‡ 591 LAFAYETTE
  AVENUE, BUFFALO, NEW YORK 14222‡ RWANDA‡ BUTARE,
  MUYAGA‡ BATUTSI‡ 1 HOUR‡ 1968‡ QUALITY GOOD‡ ‡ ‡ ‡
  ‡ SONG-IBIRIIMBO, PRAISE-POETRY,
  ZITHER-TROUGH-INANGA

DEVITT, PAUL C.S.
  DEVITT, PAUL C.S.‡ 49 CHELINSFORD ROAD, LONDON

DEVITT, PAUL C.S.
  E18 2PW, ENGLAND‡ BOTSWANA‡ KALAHARI‡ ‡ 2 HOURS‡
  1971-72‡ QUALITY GOOD‡ ‡ ‡ ‡ ‡
  CHILDREN-CONVERSATION, MUSIC

DI DIO, FRANCOIS
  BRASSEUR, G.+ DI DIO, FRANCOIS+ DIETERLEN,
  GERMAINE+ ROUGET, GILBERT‡ -+ -+ CENTRE DE
  RECHERCHES AFRICAINES, RUE D'ALSACE, 75 PARIS 6E,
  FRANCE+ 1 RUE DES DEUX-PONTS, 75004 PARIS, FRANCE‡
  MALI‡ ‡ BAMBARA, BOZO, DOGON, MALINKE, MARKA,
  MINIANKA, PEUL, RYMAYBE, SARAKOLE, SOMONO,
  SONGHAY‡ ‡ ‡ ‡ MUSEE DE L'HOMME‡ ‡ ‡ ‡

DIAMANG, C.
  DIAMANG, C.‡ ‡ ANGOLA‡ ‡ ‡ ‡ ‡ ‡ MUSEE DE L'HOMME‡
  ‡ ‡ ‡

DIAS, MARGOT
  DIAS, MARGOT‡ CENTRO DE ESTUDOS DE ANTROPOLOGIA
  CULTURAL, RUA JAU 54, LISBON 3, LISBON 3,
  PORTUGAL‡ ANGOLA‡ LUANDA‡ MUSSEQUES‡ .75 HOUR‡
  1960‡ QUALITY FAIR‡ CENTRO DE ESTUDOS DE
  ANTROPOLOGIA CULTURAL‡ ‡ ‡ ‡ MUSIC

  DIAS, MARGOT‡ CENTRO DE ESTUDOS DE ANTROPOLOGIA
  CULTURAL, RUA JAU 54, LISBON 3, PORTUGAL‡
  MOZAMBIQUE‡ PLANALTO‡ MAKONDE‡ 8.5 HOURS‡ 1957-58‡
  QUALITY FAIR‡ CENTRO DE ESTUDOS DE ANTROPOLOGIA
  CULTURAL‡ ‡ ‡ ‡ FOLKTALE, HISTORY, MUSIC

  DIAS, MARGOT‡ CENTRO DE ESTUDOS DE ANTROPOLOGIA
  CULTURAL, RUA JAU 54, LISBON 3, PORTUGAL‡
  MOZAMBIQUE‡ SOUTHERN‡ CHOKWE, CHOPI‡ 2 HOURS‡
  1959‡ QUALITY FAIR‡ CENTRO DE ESTUDOS DE
  ANTROPOLOGIA CULTURAL‡ ‡ ‡ ‡ FOLKTALE, MUSIC

DIETERLEN, GERMAINE
  BRASSEUR, G.+ DI DIO, FRANCOIS+ DIETERLEN,
  GERMAINE+ ROUGET, GILBERT‡ -+ -+ CENTRE DE
  RECHERCHES AFRICAINES, RUE D'ALSACE, 75 PARIS 6E,
  FRANCE+ 1 RUE DES DEUX-PONTS, 75004 PARIS, FRANCE‡
  MALI‡ ‡ BAMBARA, BOZO, DOGON, MALINKE, MARKA,
  MINIANKA, PEUL, RYMAYBE, SARAKOLE, SOMONO,
  SONGHAY‡ ‡ ‡ ‡ MUSEE DE L'HOMME‡ ‡ ‡ ‡

  DIETERLEN, GERMAINE‡ CENTRE DE RECHERCHES
  AFRICAINES, RUE D'ALSACE, 75 PARIS 6E, FRANCE‡
  MALI‡ ‡ DOGON‡ ‡ 1953‡ ‡ MUSEE DE L'HOMME‡ ‡ ‡ ‡

DIETERLEN, GERMAINE
  DEATH, DRUM, FESTIVAL-PLANTING

  DIETERLEN, GERMAINE‡ CENTRE DE RECHERCHES
  AFRICAINES, RUE D'ALSACE, 75 PARIS 6E, FRANCE‡
  MALI‡ ‡ PEUL‡ ‡ 1960‡ ‡ MUSEE DE L'HOMME‡ ‡ ‡ ‡
  POETRY

  DIETERLEN, GERMAINE‡ CENTRE DE RECHERCHES
  AFRICAINES, RUE D'ALSACE, 75 PARIS 6E, FRANCE‡
  MALI‡ ‡ DOGON‡ ‡ 1967‡ ‡ MUSEE DE L'HOMME‡ ‡ ‡ ‡
  CEREMONY-SIGI

  DIETERLEN, GERMAINE‡ CENTRE DE RECHERCHES
  AFRICAINES, RUE D'ALSACE, 75 PARIS 6E, FRANCE‡
  MALI‡ ‡ DOGON‡ ‡ 1969‡ ‡ MUSEE DE L'HOMME‡ ‡ ‡ ‡
  CEREMONY-SIGUI, LANGUAGE-SECRET

DIHOFF, IVAN R.
  DIHOFF, IVAN R.‡ DEPARTMENT OF AFRICAN LANGUAGES
  AND LITERATURE, UNIVERSITY OF WISCONSIN, MADISON,
  WISCONSIN 53706‡ NIGERIA‡ CHORI, KATSINA‡ CHORI,
  HAUSA‡ 7 HOURS‡ 1972‡ QUALITY GOOD‡ ‡ ‡ ‡
  FOLKTALE

DOBRIN, ARTHUR
  DOBRIN, ARTHUR‡ 613 DARTMOUTH STREET, WESTBURY,
  NEW YORK 11590‡ KENYA‡ NYARIBARI‡ GUSII‡ 1.5
  HOURS‡ 1966‡ QUALITY GOOD‡ ARCHIVES OF
  TRADITIONAL MUSIC‡ 67-039-F‡ ‡ RESTRICTED‡
  CEREMONY-CIRCUMCISION, CIRCUMCISION

  DOBRIN, ARTHUR‡ 613 DARTMOUTH STREET, WESTBURY,
  NEW YORK 11590‡ KENYA‡ NYANZA‡ GUSII‡ 1.5 HOURS‡
  1966‡ QUALITY GOOD‡ ARCHIVES OF TRADITONAL MUSIC‡
  66-148-F‡ ‡ RESTRICTED‡ CHILDREN, DEATH-FUNERAL,
  DRINKING, DRUM, GUITAR, LUTE-BOWED, PRAISE, RAIN,
  WAR, WORK-HARVEST

DOHERTY, DEBORAH
  DOHERTY, DEBORAH‡ 2234 HARVARD AVENUE, MONTREAL,
  QUEBEC, CANADA‡ KENYA‡ MARALAL‡ SAMBURU‡ 1 HOUR‡
  1973‡ QUALITY POOR‡ ‡ ‡ ‡ FOLKLORE

DORSON, RICHARD M.
  DORSON, RICHARD M.‡ FOLKLORE INSTITUTE, INDIANA
  UNIVERSITY, BLOOMINGTON, INDIANA 47401‡
  NIGERIA-U.S.‡ BLOOMINGTON, INDIANA‡ BRITISH,
  HAUSA‡ 1 HOUR‡ 1967‡ QUALITY GOOD‡ ARCHIVES OF

DORSON, RICHARD M.
  TRADITIONAL MUSIC‡ 67-220-F‡ ATL 4141‡ ‡
  ORAL-DATA-COLONIAL, ORAL-DATA-INTERVIEW

DRAKE, H. MAX
  DRAKE, H. MAX‡ PACIFIC LUTHERAN UNIVERSITY,
  DEPARTMENT OF SOCIOLOGY, TACOMA, WASHINGTON 98447‡
  MALAWI‡ CHIRADZULU, MZIMBA‡ TUMBUKA, YAO‡ 7 HOURS‡
  1967‡ QUALITY FAIR‡ ‡ ‡ ‡ AUTOBIOGRAPHY,
  HISTORY, WOMEN, WORK

DREWAL, HENRY JOHN
  DREWAL, HENRY JOHN‡ ART DEPARTMENT, CLEVELAND
  STATE UNIVERSITY, CLEVELAND, OHIO 44115‡ DAHOMEY‡
  ANAGO-POBE‡ YORUBA‡ 3 HOURS‡ 1973‡ QUALITY POOR‡ ‡
  ‡ ‡ ‡ CEREMONY-ONDO, RITUAL-ONDO

  DREWAL, HENRY JOHN‡ ART DEPARTMENT, CLEVELAND
  STATE UNIVERSITY, CLEVELAND, OHIO 44115‡ NIGERIA‡
  EGBADA, IGBOMINA‡ YORUBA‡ 10 HOURS‡ 1970-71‡
  QUALITY FAIR‡ ‡ ‡ ‡ ‡ CEREMONY-EFE-GELEDE,
  DANCE-MASKED-EFE-GELEDE, DRUM

DUMONT, LILLIAN E.
  DUMONT, LILLIAN E.‡ 145 4TH AVENUE, NEW YORK, NEW
  YORK 10003‡ DAHOMEY‡ COTONOU‡ FON, YORUBA‡ 2
  HOURS‡ 1973‡ QUALITY GOOD‡ ‡ ‡ ‡ ‡ RITUAL

  DUMONT, LILLIAN E.‡ 145 4TH AVENUE, NEW YORK, NEW
  YORK 10003‡ GHANA‡ NKROFRO‡ ‡ 1 HOUR‡ 1973‡
  QUALITY GOOD‡ ‡ ‡ ‡ ‡ CHILDREN

  DUMONT, LILLIAN E.‡ 145 4TH AVENUE, NEW YORK, NEW
  YORK 10003‡ IVORY COAST‡ ABIDJAN‡ ‡ 1 HOUR‡ 1973‡
  QUALITY GOOD‡ ‡ ‡ ‡ ‡ INTERVIEW-DADIE-BERNARD,
  POETRY

  DUMONT, LILLIAN E.‡ 145 4TH AVENUE, NEW YORK, NEW
  YORK 10003‡ SENEGAL‡ DAKAR, GOREE‡ WOLOF, PEUL‡ 3
  HOURS‡ 1973‡ QUALITY GOOD‡ ‡ ‡ ‡
  INTERVIEW-LAYE-CAMARA, INTERVIEW-SEMBENE-OUSMANE,
  RITUAL

DUNGER, GEORGE A.
  DUNGER, GEORGE A.‡ 1605 S. EUCLID AVENUE, SIOUX
  FALLS, SOUTH DAKOTA 57105‡ CAMEROON‡ ‡ BEKOM,
  DUALA, KAKA, NSUNGLI‡ ‡ ‡ QUALITY FAIR‡ ‡ ‡ ‡
  HISTORY, MUSIC, RELIGIOUS

DURAN, JAMES JOSEPH
  DURAN, JAMES JOSEPH‡ DEPARTMENT OF LINGUISTICS,
  STANFORD UNIVERSITY, STANFORD, CALIFORNIA 94305‡
  KENYA‡ KABIANGA, KERICHO, LUMBWA‡ KIPSIGI‡ ‡ 1971‡
  QUALITY EXCELLENT‡ STANFORD UNIVERSITY LANGUAGE
  LABORATORY‡ ‡ ‡ ‡ CEREMONY-FEMALE, CIRCUMCISION,
  HISTORY, LANGUAGE

ECHENBERG, MYRON J.
  ECHENBERG, MYRON J.‡ DEPARTMENT OF HISTORY,
  MCGILL UNIVERSITY, B.P. 6070, MONTREAL, QUEBEC,
  CANADA‡ UPPER VOLTA‡ LEO, TOUGAN‡ GURUNSI, MARKA,
  SAMO‡ 16.5 HOURS‡ 1967‡ QUALITY GOOD‡ ‡ ‡ ‡ ‡
  HISTORY

ECHEZONA, WILLIAM WILBERF
  ECHEZONA, WILLIAM WILBERFORCE CHUKUDINKA‡
  DEPARTMENT OF MUSIC, UNIVERSITY OF NIGERIA,
  NSUKKA, EAST CENTRAL STATE, NIGERIA‡ NIGERIA‡ ‡
  EFIK, HAUSA, IBO, YORUBA‡ 400 HOURS‡ 1950-75‡
  QUALITY EXCELLENT‡ ‡ ‡ ‡ ‡

EDWARDS, BETTY
  EDWARDS, BETTY‡ ‡ SIERRA LEONE‡ FREETOWN‡ ‡ 1
  HOUR‡ 1969‡ QUALITY GOOD‡ ARCHIVES OF TRADITIONAL
  MUSIC‡ 70-046-F‡ ‡ RESTRICTED‡ RELIGIOUS

EKECHI, FELIX K.
  EKECHI, FELIX K.‡ DEPARTMENT OF HISTORY, KENT
  STATE UNIVERSITY, KENT, OHIO 44242‡ NIGERIA‡
  OWERRI‡ IGBO‡ 1 HOUR‡ 1973‡ QUALITY FAIR‡ ‡ ‡ ‡ ‡
  HISTORY

EL-SHAMY, HASAN M.
  EL-SHAMY, HASAN M.‡ FOLKLORE INSTITUTE, INDIANA
  UNIVERSITY, BLOOMINGTON, INDIANA 47401‡ EGYPT‡
  CAIRO, KAFR AL ZAYTUN‡ ARAB, DINKA, NUBIAN‡ 28
  HOURS‡ 1968-71‡ QUALITY FAIR‡ ARCHIVES OF
  TRADITIONAL MUSIC‡ 71-303-F‡ ATL 5209-20, 5248-49‡
  RESTRICTED‡ CHILDREN-RHYME, FOLKTALE, LEGEND,
  MARRIAGE, RELIGIOUS, RIDDLE

  EL-SHAMY, HASAN M.‡ FOLKLORE INSTITUTE, INDIANA
  UNIVERSITY, BLOOMINGTON, INDIANA 47401‡
  EGYPT-U.S.‡ BROOKLYN, NEW YORK‡ ARAB‡ 5.5 HOURS‡
  1961‡ QUALITY GOOD‡ ARCHIVES OF TRADITIONAL MUSIC‡
  061-040-F‡ FTL 119-42‡ RESTRICTED‡ BELIEF, CUSTOM,
  FOLKTALE

ELLENBERGER, D.F.
  ELLENBERGER, D.F.‡ ‡ SOUTH AFRICA‡ ‡ BASUTO‡ ‡ ‡ ‡
  MUSEE DE L'HOMME‡ ‡ ‡ ‡

ELLOVICH, RISA SUE
  ELLOVICH, RISA SUE‡ DEPARTMENT OF ANTHROPOLOGY,
  INDIANA UNIVERSITY, BLOOMINGTON, INDIANA 47401‡
  IVORY COAST‡ GAGNOA‡ DYULA, MALINKE, VOLTAIC‡ 5
  HOURS‡ 1973-74‡ QUALITY FAIR‡ ARCHIVES OF
  TRADITIONAL MUSIC‡ 75-029-F‡ ‡ RESTRICTED‡
  CHILDREN, DANCE, DRUM, MARRIAGE,
  NARRATIVE-MIGRATION, WOMEN, XYLOPHONE

ELWA RADIO STATION, LIBER
  ELWA RADIO STATION, LIBERIA‡ P.O. BOX 192,
  MONROVIA, LIBERIA‡ ‡ ‡ ‡ ‡ ‡ ‡ ‡ ‡ ‡

  ELWA RADIO STATION, LIBERIA‡ P.O. BOX 192,
  MONROVIA, LIBERIA‡ LIBERIA‡ ‡ ‡ ‡ CA1960-1975‡ ‡
  ELWA RADIO STATION, LIBERIA‡ ‡ ‡ ‡ FOLKTALE,
  HISTORY, MUSIC, RELIGIOUS

ELWA STUDIO, NIGERIA
  ELWA STUDIO, NIGERIA‡ P.O. BOX 40, IGBAJA, ILORIN,
  KWARA STATE, NIGERIA‡ ‡ ‡ ‡ ‡ ‡ ‡ ‡ ‡ ‡

  ELWA STUDIO, NIGERIA‡ P.O. BOX 40, IGBAJA, ILORIN,
  KWARA STATE, NIGERIA‡ NIGERIA‡ ‡ IBO, NUPE,
  YORUBA‡ ‡ ‡ ‡ ELWA STUDIO, NIGERIA‡ ‡ ‡ ‡
  FOLKTALE, HISTORY, MUSIC, PRAISE-POETRY, SOCIAL

ENGLAND, NICHOLAS M.
  ENGLAND, NICHOLAS M.‡ CALIFORNIA INSTITUTE OF THE
  ARTS, VALENCIA, CALIFORNIA 91355‡ ANGOLA‡ ‡
  GANGULA‡ 75 HOURS‡ 1957-61‡ QUALITY EXCELLENT‡ ‡ ‡
  ‡ ‡ BOW-MUSICAL, CEREMONY, CURING-RITUAL

  ENGLAND, NICHOLAS M.‡ CALIFORNIA INSTITUTE OF THE
  ARTS, VALENCIA, CALIFORNIA 91355‡ BOTSWANA‡ ‡
  TSWANA‡ 75 HOURS‡ 1957-61‡ QUALITY EXCELLENT‡ ‡ ‡
  ‡ ‡ BOW-MUSICAL, CEREMONY-INITIATION,
  CURING-RITUAL, INITIATION-CEREMONY

  ENGLAND, NICHOLAS M.‡ CALIFORNIA INSTITUTE OF THE
  ARTS, VALENCIA, CALIFORNIA 91355‡ GHANA‡ ‡ EWE‡
  50 HOURS‡ 1969-70‡ 1972‡ QUALITY EXCELLENT‡ ‡ ‡ ‡
  ‡ DIVINING-AFA-CULT, DRUM

  ENGLAND, NICHOLAS M.‡ CALIFORNIA INSTITUTE OF THE

ENGLAND, NICHOLAS M.
  ARTS, VALENCIA, CALIFORNIA 91355‡ NAMIBIA‡ ‡
  HERERO‡ 75 HOURS‡ 1957-61‡ QUALITY EXCELLENT‡ ‡ ‡
  ‡ ‡ BOW-MUSICAL, CEREMONY-INITIATION,
  CURING-RITUAL, INITIATION-CEREMONY

  ENGLAND, NICHOLAS M.‡ CALIFORNIA INSTITUTE OF THE
  ARTS, VALENCIA, CALIFORNIA 91355‡ NIGERIA‡ ‡
  YORUBA‡ 50 HOURS‡ 1969-70‡ 1972‡ QUALITY
  EXCELLENT‡ ‡ ‡ ‡ RITUAL-SHANGO

  ENGLAND, NICHOLAS M.‡ CALIFORNIA INSTITUTE OF THE
  ARTS, VALENCIA, CALIFORNIA 91355‡ SENEGAL‡ ‡ ‡ 6
  HOURS‡ 1969-70‡ QUALITY EXCELLENT‡ ‡ ‡ ‡
  HARP-LUTE-KORA, XYLOPHONE

ENGLISH FOLK DANCE AND SO
  ENGLISH FOLK DANCE AND SONG SOCIETY ‡ 2 REGENTS
  PARK ROAD, LONDON NW1, ENGLAND‡ ‡ ‡ ‡ ‡ ‡ ‡ ‡
  ‡

ERNOULT, CLAUDE
  ERNOULT, CLAUDE‡ ROUGET, GILBERT‡ -‡ 1 RUE DES
  DEUX-PONTS, 75004 PARIS, FRANCE‡ MAURITANIA‡ ‡ ‡
  ‡ ‡ MUSEE DE L'HOMME‡ ‡ ‡ ‡ MUSICIAN-GRIOT

ESTES, RICHARD D.
  ESTES, RICHARD D.‡ ACADEMY OF NATURAL SCIENCES,
  19TH AND PARKWAY, PHILADELPHIA, PENNSYLVANIA
  19103‡ ANGOLA‡ ZVIMBANGO‡ SONGO‡ .5 HOUR‡ 1970‡
  QUALITY GOOD‡ ‡ ‡ ‡ GUITAR

ETHNOMUSICOLOGY CENTRE JA
  ETHNOMUSICOLOGY CENTRE JAAP KUNST, UNIVERSITY OF
  AMSTERDAM‡ KLOVENIERSBURGWAL 103, AMSTERDAM,
  NETHERLANDS‡ ‡ ‡ ‡ ‡ ‡ ‡ ‡ ‡

  ETHNOMUSICOLOGY CENTRE JAAP KUNST‡ UNIVERSITY OF
  AMSTERDAM, KLOVENIERSBURGWAL 103, AMSTERDAM,
  NETHERLANDS‡ GAMBIA, THE‡ KIANG-EAST, KIANG-WEST,
  KWINELLA‡ MANDINKA‡ 1 HOUR‡ 1958‡ QUALITY GOOD‡
  ETHNOMUSICOLOGY CENTRE JAAP KUNST‡ ‡ ‡ ‡ DANCE,
  MARRIAGE, RITUAL, WORK-HOEING

  ETHNOMUSICOLOGY CENTRE JAAP KUNST‡ UNIVERSITY OF
  AMSTERDAM, KLOVENIERSBURGWAL 103, AMSTERDAM,
  NETHERLANDS‡ MALAWI‡ NSANJE-BOMA‡ LOMWE, MANGANJA‡
  13 HOURS‡ 1971‡ QUALITY GOOD‡ ETHNOMUSICOLOGY
  CENTRE JAAP KUNST‡ ‡ ‡ ‡ FOLKLORE, HISTORY,

ETHNOMUSICOLOGY CENTRE JA
  PRAISE-POETRY, RITUAL, SOCIAL

  ETHNOMUSICOLOGY CENTRE JAAP KUNST‡ UNIVERSITY OF
  AMSTERDAM, KLOVENIERSBURGWAL 103, AMSTERDAM,
  NETHERLANDS‡ SIERRA LEONE‡ ALIKALIA‡ ‡ 1 HOUR‡
  1974‡ QUALITY GOOD‡ ETHNOMUSICOLOGY CENTRE JAAP
  KUNST‡ ‡ ‡ ‡ DANCE, SOCIAL

EULENBERG, JOHN BRYSON
  EULENBERG, JOHN BRYSON‡ P.O. BOX 845, EAST
  LANSING, MICHIGAN 48823‡ NIGERIA‡ KANO‡ HAUSA‡
  1.5 HOURS‡ 1972‡ QUALITY FAIR‡ ‡ ‡ ‡ ‡ CHILDREN,
  SOCIAL

EVERGREEN STATE COLLEGE,
  EVERGREEN STATE COLLEGE, THE, UNIVERSITY OF
  WASHINGTON‡ OLYMPIA, WASHINGTON 98505‡ ‡ ‡ ‡ ‡ ‡
  ‡ ‡ ‡

FACULTE DE THEOLOGIE PROT
  FACULTE DE THEOLOGIE PROTESTANTE‡ B.P. 4011,
  YAOUNDE NLONGKOK, CAMEROON‡ ‡ ‡ ‡ ‡ ‡ ‡ ‡ ‡

FAIK-NZUJI, MADIYA
  FAIK-NZUJI, MADIYA‡ B.P. 1607 LUBUMBASHI, REGION
  DU SHABA, ZAIRE‡ ZAIRE‡ EASTERN KASAI‡ LUBA‡ 50
  HOURS‡ 1974‡ QUALITY GOOD‡ MUSEE ROYAL DE
  L'AFRIQUE CENTRALE‡ ‡ ‡ ‡ BELIEF-INTERVIEW,
  CONVERSATION, CUSTOM-INTERVIEW, DIVINING,
  DRUM-LANGUAGE, RITUAL, SPIRIT, WHISTLE-LANGUAGE

FARSY, MUHAMMED S.
  FARSY, MUHAMMED S.‡ INFORMATION OFFICE, P.O. BOX
  222, ZANZIBAR, TANZANIA‡ TANZANIA-ZANZIBAR‡ ‡ ‡ 1
  HOUR‡ CA1958‡ QUALITY GOOD‡ ARCHIVES OF
  TRADITIONAL MUSIC‡ 59-016-F‡ ‡ ‡ CURING, DANCE,
  DANCE-EXORCISM, DANCE-MARRIAGE, DRUM,
  DRUM-CONICAL, MARRIAGE, TAMBOURINE

FEDERAL DEPARTMENT OF ANT
  FEDERAL DEPARTMENT OF ANTIQUITIES, NATIONAL
  MUSEUM‡ P.M.B. 2127, ALI AKILU ROAD, KADUNA,
  NIGERIA‡ ‡ ‡ ‡ ‡ ‡ ‡ ‡ ‡ ‡

  FEDERAL DEPARTMENT OF ANTIQUITIES, NATIONAL
  MUSEUM, KADUNA‡ P.M.B. 2127, ALI AKILU ROAD,
  KADUNA, NIGERIA‡ NIGERIA‡ NORTHERN STATES‡ ELOYI,
  GEDE‡ ‡ ‡ ‡ FEDERAL DEPARTMENT OF ANTIQUITIES,

FEDERAL DEPARTMENT OF ANT
  NATIONAL MUSEUM, KADUNA‡ ‡ ‡ ‡ AEROPHONE,
  CEREMONY, ENTERTAINMENT, HISTORY, MEMBRANOPHONE

FEDRY, J.
  FEDRY, J.‡ ‡ CHAD‡ ‡ HADJERAI‡ ‡ 1966-67‡ ‡ MUSEE
  DE L'HOMME‡ ‡ ‡ ‡ CEREMONY-MARGAI

FEINBERG, HARVEY
  FEINBERG, HARVEY‡ DEPARTMENT OF HISTORY, SOUTHERN
  CONNECTICUT STATE COLLEGE, NEW HAVEN, CONNECTICUT
  06515‡ GHANA‡ ELMINA‡ FANTI‡ 1 HOUR‡ 1967-68‡
  QUALITY GOOD‡ ‡ ‡ ‡ ‡ CEREMONY, HISTORY

FERCHIOU, SOPHIE
  FERCHIOU, SOPHIE‡ ‡ TUNISIA‡ ‡ ‡ ‡ 1969‡ ‡ MUSEE
  DE L'HOMME‡ ‡ ‡ ‡ DANCE, MARABOUT

FERNANDEZ, JAMES W.
  FERNANDEZ, JAMES W.‡ DEPARTMENT OF ANTHROPOLOGY,
  DARTMOUTH COLLEGE, HANOVER, NEW HAMPSHIRE 03755‡
  GABON‡ KANGO, KOUGOULOU, OYEM-SOUGOUDZAP‡ FANG‡
  18 HOURS‡ 1960‡ QUALITY EXCELLENT‡ ARCHIVES OF
  TRADITIONAL MUSIC‡ 71-255-F‡ ATL 4589-607‡ ‡
  CULT-BWITI, DANCE, DEATH, DRUM-LANGUAGE, GUITAR,
  LULLABY, PRAYER, XYLOPHONE

FERRY, M.P.
  FERRY, M.P.‡ ‡ SENEGAL‡ ‡ BEDIK‡ ‡ ‡ ‡ MUSEE DE
  L'HOMME‡ ‡ ‡ ‡

FETTER, BRUCE
  FETTER, BRUCE‡ BOX 824, UNIVERSITY OF
  WISCONSIN-MADISON, MADISON, WISCONSIN 53201‡
  ZAIRE‡ LUBUMBASHI‡ SETTLERS-AFRICAN‡ 3 HOURS‡
  1972-73‡ QUALITY POOR‡ ‡ ‡ ‡ ‡
  INTERVIEW-WORLD-WAR-I

FIKRY, MONA
  FIKRY, MONA‡ FACULTY OF LAW, BENGHAZI, LIBYA‡
  GHANA‡ WA‡ WALA‡ 120 HOURS‡ 1966-67‡ QUALITY GOOD‡
  CENTER FOR AFRICAN ORAL DATA‡ 69-129-F‡ ATL 5069‡
  RESTRICTED‡ CANTE-FABLE, DANCE, DEATH-FUNERAL,
  DRINKING, DRUM-HOURGLASS, DRUM-LANGUAGE, FOLKTALE,
  FLUTE, GENEALOGY, HISTORY, MARRIAGE, PRAISE-RULER,
  PRAYER, RELIGIOUS-ISLAMIC, RIDDLE, XYLOPHONE

FLORIDA STATE UNIVERSITY,
  FLORIDA STATE UNIVERSITY, ORAL HISTORY‡

FLORIDA STATE UNIVERSITY,
 TALLAHASSE, FLORIDA 32306‡ ‡ ‡ ‡ ‡ ‡ ‡ ‡ ‡ ‡

FOSS, PERKINS
 FOSS, PERKINS‡ DEPARTMENT OF ART, DARTMOUTH
 COLLEGE, HANOVER, NEW HAMPSHIRE 03755‡ NIGERIA‡
 MID-WEST STATE‡ URHOBO‡ 20 HOURS‡ 1971-72‡
 QUALITY GOOD‡ ‡ ‡ ‡ HISTORY, PRAISE-POETRY,
 RITUAL

FRANKEL, GERD
 FRANKEL, GERD‡ DECEASED‡ ‡ ‡ LUHYA‡ 2 HOURS‡ 1959‡
 QUALITY GOOD‡ ARCHIVES OF LANGUAGES OF THE WORLD‡
 ‡ ‡ ‡ GRAMMATICAL-DATA

FROBENIUS INSTITUTE
 FROBENIUS INSTITUTE‡ 6 FRANKFURT AM MAIN,
 LIEBIGSTRASSE 41, FEDERAL REPUBLIC OF GERMANY‡ ‡ ‡
 ‡ ‡ ‡ ‡ ‡ ‡ ‡

FRY, GLADYS M.
 FRY, GLADYS M.‡ DEPARTMENT OF ENGLISH, UNIVERSITY
 OF MARYLAND, COLLEGE PARK, MARYLAND 20742‡
 EGYPT-U.S.‡ BLOOMINGTON, INDIANA‡ ‡ 2 HOURS‡ 1963‡
 QUALITY GOOD‡ ARCHIVES OF TRADITIONAL MUSIC‡
 064-003-F‡ ‡ RESTRICTED‡ FOLKTALE,
 FOLKTALE-INTERVIEW

 FRY, GLADYS M.‡ DEPARTMENT OF ENGLISH, UNIVERSITY
 OF MARYLAND, COLLEGE PARK, MARYLAND 20742‡
 ETHIOPIA-U.S.‡ BLOOMINGTON, INDIANA‡ ‡ 1 HOUR‡
 1963‡ QUALITY GOOD‡ ARCHIVES OF TRADITIONAL MUSIC‡
 064-003-F‡ ‡ RESTRICTED‡ FOLKTALE,
 FOLKTALE-INTERVIEW

 FRY, GLADYS M.‡ DEPARTMENT OF ENGLISH, UNIVERSITY
 OF MARYLAND, COLLEGE PARK, MARYLAND 20742‡
 GHANA-U.S.‡ BLOOMINGTON, INDIANA‡ ‡ 2 HOURS‡ 1963‡
 QUALITY GOOD‡ ARCHIVES OF TRADITIONAL MUSIC‡
 064-003-F‡ ‡ RESTRICTED‡ FOLKTALE,
 FOLKTALE-INTERVIEW

 FRY, GLADYS M.‡ DEPARTMENT OF ENGLISH, UNIVERSITY
 OF MARYLAND, COLLEGE PARK, MARYLAND 20742‡
 KENYA-U.S.‡ BLOOMINGTON, INDIANA‡ ‡ 2 HOURS‡ 1963‡
 QUALITY GOOD‡ ARCHIVES OF TRADITIONAL MUSIC‡
 064-003-F‡ ‡ RESTRICTED‡ FOLKTALE,
 FOLKTALE-INTERVIEW

FRY, GLADYS M.
  FRY, GLADYS M.‡ DEPARTMENT OF ENGLISH, UNIVERSITY
OF MARYLAND, COLLEGE PARK, MARYLAND 20742‡
MALI-U.S.‡ BLOOMINGTON, INDIANA‡ ‡ 2 HOURS‡ 1963‡
QUALITY GOOD‡ ARCHIVES OF TRADITIONAL MUSIC‡
064-003-F‡ ‡ RESTRICTED‡ FOLKTALE,
FOLKTALE-INTERVIEW

  FRY, GLADYS M.‡ DEPARTMENT OF ENGLISH, UNIVERSITY
OF MARYLAND, COLLEGE PARK, MARYLAND 20742‡
NIGERIA-U.S.‡ BLOOMINGTON, INDIANA‡ ‡ 6 HOURS‡
1963‡ QUALITY GOOD‡ ARCHIVES OF TRADITIONAL MUSIC‡
064-003-F‡ ‡ RESTRICTED‡ FOLKTALE,
FOLKTALE-INTERVIEW

  FRY, GLADYS M.‡ DEPARTMENT OF ENGLISH, UNIVERSITY
OF MARYLAND, COLLEGE PARK, MARYLAND 20742‡
RHODESIA-U.S.‡ BLOOMINGTON, INDIANA‡ ‡ 2 HOURS‡
1963‡ QUALITY GOOD‡ ARCHIVES OF TRADITIONAL MUSIC‡
064-003-F‡ ‡ RESTRICTED‡ FOLKTALE,
FOLKTALE-INTERVIEW

  FRY, GLADYS M.‡ DEPARTMENT OF ENGLISH, UNIVERSITY
OF MARYLAND, COLLEGE PARK, MARYLAND 20742‡ SOUTH
AFRICA-U.S.‡ BLOOMINGTON, INDIANA‡ ‡ 2 HOURS‡
1963‡ QUALITY GOOD‡ ARCHIVES OF TRADITIONAL MUSIC‡
064-003-F‡ ‡ RESTRICTED‡ FOLKTALE,
FOLKTALE-INTERVIEW

  FRY, GLADYS M.‡ DEPARTMENT OF ENGLISH, UNIVERSITY
OF MARYLAND, COLLEGE PARK, MARYLAND 20742‡
SUDAN-U.S.‡ BLOOMINGTON, INDIANA‡ ‡ 1 HOUR‡ 1963‡
QUALITY GOOD‡ ARCHIVES OF TRADITIONAL MUSIC‡
064-003-F‡ ‡ RESTRICTED‡ FOLKTALE,
FOLKTALE-INTERVIEW

  FRY, GLADYS M.‡ DEPARTMENT OF ENGLISH, UNIVERSITY
OF MARYLAND, COLLEGE PARK, MARYLAND 20742‡
TUNISIA-U.S.‡ BLOOMINGTON, INDIANA‡ ‡ 1 HOUR‡
1963‡ QUALITY GOOD‡ ARCHIVES OF TRADITIONAL MUSIC‡
064-003-F‡ ‡ RESTRICTED‡ FOLKTALE,
FOLKTALE-INTERVIEW

 GAISSEAU, PIERRE-DOMINIQU
  GAISSEAU, PIERRE-DOMINIQUE‡ ‡ GUINEA‡ ‡ TOMA‡ ‡
1953‡ ‡ MUSEE DE L'HOMME‡ ‡ ‡ ‡

 GALAND, -
  GALAND, -‡ ROUGET, GILBERT‡ -‡ 1 RUE DES

GALAND, —
DEUX-PONTS, 75004 PARIS, FRANCE‡ MOROCCO‡ ‡
BERBER‡ ‡ ‡ ‡ MUSEE DE L'HOMME‡ ‡ ‡ ‡

GAMBIA CULTURAL ARCHIVES
GAMBIA CULTURAL ARCHIVES‡ PRESIDENT'S OFFICE,
QUADRANGLE, BANJUL, THE GAMBIA‡ ‡ ‡ ‡ ‡ ‡ ‡ ‡ ‡
‡

GANSEMANS, JOS
GANSEMANS, JOS‡ STEENWEG OP BRUSSEL, 66, TERVUREN,
BELGIUM‡ RWANDA‡ BYUMBA, CYANGUGU, GISENJI,·
KIBUNGU, KIBUYE, KIGALI, RUHENGERI‡ HUTU, TUTSI,
TWA‡ 105 HOURS‡ 1973-74‡ QUALITY EXCELLENT‡ MUSEE
ROYAL DE L'AFRIQUE CENTRALE‡ ‡ ‡ ‡ DANCE,
INSTRUMENTAL

GANSEMANS, JOS‡ STEENWEG OP BRUSSEL, 66, TERVUREN,
BELGIUM‡ ZAIRE‡ KATANGA‡ LUBA‡ 13.5 HOURS‡ 1970‡
QUALITY EXCELLENT‡ ARCHIVES OF TRADITIONAL MUSIC‡
71-408-F‡ ‡ ‡ BIRTH, BIRTH-TWINS, DANCE, DEATH,
DRUM-LANGUAGE, DRUM-SLIT, ENTERTAINMENT, FLUTE,
GAME, HUNTING, INITIATION, LULLABY, MARRIAGE,
PRAISE, PRAISE-RULER, RATTLE-GOURD, XYLOPHONE

GANSEMANS, JOS‡ STEENWEG OP BRUSSEL, 66, TERVUREN,
BELGIUM‡ ZAIRE‡ SHABA‡ LUBA, LUNDA, SALAMPASU‡ 45
HOURS‡ 1970-73‡ QUALITY EXCELLENT‡ MUSEE ROYAL DE
L'AFRIQUE CENTRALE‡ ‡ ‡ ‡ DANCE, INSTRUMENTAL

GARINE, I. DE
GARINE, I. DE‡ INSTITUT NATIONAL TCHADIEN POUR
LES SCIENCES HUMAINES, B.P. 503, FORT-LAMY, CHAD‡
CHAD‡ ‡ KERA, MUSEY‡ ‡ 1962-63‡ 1965‡ ‡ MUSEE DE
L'HOMME‡ ‡ ‡ ‡ DEATH-FUNERAL, FLUTE, HARP-LUTE,
INITIATION, POSSESSION, WHISTLE

GARLAND, WILLIAM
GARLAND, WILLIAM‡ DEPARTMENT OF ANTHROPOLOGY,
WESTERN MICHIGAN UNIVERSITY, KALAMAZOO, MICHIGAN‡
TANZANIA‡ MATAMBA TOWN, NJOMBE REGION‡ WANJI‡ 20
HOURS‡ 1963-65‡ QUALITY EXCELLENT‡ ‡ ‡ ‡ ‡
DANCE-SOCIAL, RITUAL

GAY, JUDITH S.
GAY, JUDITH S.‡ CLARE HALL, UNIVERSITY OF
CAMBRIDGE, CAMBRIDGE, ENGLAND‡ LIBERIA‡ BONG
COUNTY‡ KPELLE‡ 30 HOURS‡ 1971-73‡ QUALITY GOOD‡
ARCHIVES OF TRADITIONAL MUSIC‡ 74-063-F‡ ‡

GAY, JUDITH S.
  RESTRICTED‡ EPIC, FOLKTALE, HISTORY, RIDDLE

GELZER, DAVID G.
  GELZER, DAVID G.‡ FACULTE DE THEOLOGIE
  PROTESTANTE, B.P. 4011, YAOUNDE NLONGKAK,
  CAMEROON‡ CAMEROON‡ ‡ ‡ ‡ QUALITY FAIR‡ FACULTE
  DE THEOLOGIE PROTESTANTE‡ ‡ ‡ ‡
  RELIGIOUS-CHRISTIAN

GEOFFRION, CHARLES A.
  GEOFFRION, CHARLES A.‡ RURAL ROUTE 4,
  EDWARDSVILLE, ILLINOIS 62025‡ MALAWI‡ MZIMBA,
  NCHEU, NSANJE‡ ACHEWA, MANGANJA, NGONI‡ 3 HOURS‡
  1971-72‡ QUALITY GOOD‡ ‡ ‡ ‡ DANCE,
  DANCE-MALIPENGA, DEATH-FUNERAL, ENTERTAINMENT,
  INITIATION, SECRET-SOCIETY-NJAU

  GEOFFRION, CHARLES A.‡ RURAL ROUTE 4,
  EDWARDSVILLE, ILLINOIS 62025‡ SIERRA LEONE‡
  BONKALOW, KAMBIA, MANGE‡ TEMNE, MANDINGO‡ 2 HOURS‡
  1966-67‡ QUALITY GOOD‡ ARCHIVES OF TRADITIONAL
  MUSIC‡ 70-150-F‡ ATL 5654-55‡ RESTRICTED‡
  DEATH-FUNERAL, ENTERTAINMENT, POLITICAL,
  RELIGIOUS-ISLAMIC, SECRET-SOCIETY

GERHART, GAIL M.
  GERHART, GAIL M.‡ 395 RIVERSIDE DRIVE, NEW YORK,
  NEW YORK 10025‡ SOUTH AFRICA‡ ‡ ‡ .8 HOUR‡ 1964‡
  QUALITY GOOD‡ ‡ ‡ ‡ ‡ CHOIR-NATIONAL-CONGRESS,
  POLITICAL

GERLACH, LUTHER PAUL
  GERLACH, LUTHER PAUL‡ DEPARTMENT OF ANTHROPOLOGY,
  215 FORD HALL, UNIVERSITY OF MINNESOTA,
  MINNEAPOLIS, MINNESOTA 55455‡ KENYA-TANZANIA‡
  KWALE, LUNGA-LUNGA‡ ARAB, DIGO, DURUMA‡ 12 HOURS‡
  1958-60‡ QUALITY GOOD‡ ‡ ‡ ‡ ‡ DANCE,
  ENTERTAINMENT, RITUAL, SPIRIT-POSSESSION

GERSON-KIWI, EDITH
  GERSON-KIWI, EDITH‡ 33 RAEUBAN STREET, JERUSALEM,
  ISRAEL‡ ETHIOPIA‡ ‡ ‡ 1 HOUR‡ 1972‡ QUALITY FAIR‡
  ‡ ‡ ‡ ‡

  GERSON-KIWI, EDITH‡ 33 RAEUBAN STREET, JERUSALEM,
  ISRAEL‡ NAMIBIA‡ ‡ OVAMBO‡ 2 HOURS‡ 1955‡ QUALITY
  FAIR‡ ‡ ‡ ‡ ‡

GESSAIN, M.
   ROUGET, GILBERT+ GESSAIN, R.+ GESSAIN, M.‡ 1 RUE
   DES DEUX-PONTS, 75004 PARIS, FRANCE+ -+ -‡
   SENEGAL‡ ‡ BASSARI, BEDIK‡ ‡ 1967‡ ‡ MUSEE DE
   L'HOMME‡ ‡ ‡ ‡ FLUTE, LULLABY, MASK-VOICE,
   WORK-FIELD

GESSAIN, R.
   ROUGET, GILBERT+ GESSAIN, R.+ GESSAIN, M.‡ 1 RUE
   DES DEUX-PONTS, 75004 PARIS, FRANCE+ -+ -‡
   SENEGAL‡ ‡ BASSARI, BEDIK‡ ‡ 1967‡ ‡ MUSEE DE
   L'HOMME‡ ‡ ‡ ‡ FLUTE, LULLABY, MASK-VOICE,
   WORK-FIELD

GIBSON, GORDON D.
   GIBSON, GORDON D.‡ DEPARTMENT OF ANTHROPOLOGY,
   SMITHSONIAN INSTITUTION, WASHINGTON D.C. 20560‡
   ANGOLA‡ SOUTHWESTERN PROVINCE‡ CHAVIKWA, HAKAWONA,
   HIMBA, KEPE, KUVALE, VATWA, ZIMBA‡ 20 HOURS‡
   1971-73‡ QUALITY GOOD‡ ‡ ‡ ‡ ‡ PRAISE, VOCABULARY

   GIBSON, GORDON D.‡ DEPARTMENT OF ANTHROPOLOGY,
   SMITHSONIAN INSTITUTION, WASHINGTON, D.C. 20560‡
   BOTSWANA‡ NGAMILAND‡ GCIRIKU, HERERO‡ 5 HOURS‡
   1953‡ QUALITY GOOD‡ ‡ ‡ ‡ ‡ FOLKLORE, SOCIAL

   GIBSON, GORDON D.‡ DEPARTMENT OF ANTHROPOLOGY,
   SMITHSONIAN INSTITUTION, WASHINGTON D.C. 20560‡
   NAMIBIA‡ KAOKOVELD‡ HERERO, HIMBA, KUVALE‡ 7
   HOURS‡ 1960-61‡ QUALITY GOOD‡ ‡ ‡ ‡ ‡ FOLKLORE,
   PRAISE

GILLIS, FRANK J.
   GILLIS, FRANK J.+ TRACEY, HUGH‡ ARCHIVES OF
   TRADITIONAL MUSIC, INDIANA UNIVERSITY,
   BLOOMINGTON, INDIANA 47401+ INTERNATIONAL LIBRARY
   OF AFRICAN MUSIC, BOX 138, ROODEPOORT, TRANSVAAL,
   SOUTH AFRICA‡ SOUTH AFRICA-U.S.‡ BLOOMINGTON,
   INDIANA‡ ‡ 1 HOUR‡ 1971‡ QUALITY GOOD‡ ARCHIVES
   OF TRADITIONAL MUSIC‡ 71-308-F‡ ‡ RESTRICTED‡
   INTERVIEW-TRACEY-H.

   MENSAH, ATTAH+ GILLIS, FRANK J.‡ UNIVERSITY OF
   GHANA, LEGON, GHANA+ ARCHIVES OF TRADITIONAL
   MUSIC, INDIANA UNIVERSITY, BLOOMINGTON, INDIANA
   47401‡ ZAMBIA-U.S.‡ BLOOMINGTON, INDIANA‡ ‡ 2
   HOURS‡ 1970‡ QUALITY EXCELLENT‡ ARCHIVES OF
   TRADITIONAL MUSIC‡ 70-087-F‡ ATL 4273-74‡
   RESTRICTED‡ MUSIC-LECTURE

GLAZE, ANITA
  GLAZE, ANITA‡ DEPARTMENT OF ART AND DESIGN, 143
  FINE ARTS BUILDING, UNIVERSITY OF ILLINOIS,
  CHAMPAIGN, ILLINOIS 61820‡ IVORY COAST‡
  DIKODOUGOU‡ SENUFO‡ 18 HOURS‡ 1969-70‡ QUALITY
  GOOD‡ ARCHIVES OF TRADITIONAL MUSIC‡ 71-307-F‡ ‡
  RESTRICTED‡ CANTE-FABLE, DANCE, DANCE-MASKED,
  DEATH-FUNERAL, DRUM-CLAY, DRUM-CYLINDRICAL,
  GREETING, HISTORY, IDIOPHONE-STRUCK, PRAISE,
  RATTLE-GOURD, SECRET-SOCIETY, WORK-FIELD,
  WORK-HOUSE-BUILDING, XYLOPHONE

GLEASON, JUDITH
  GLEASON, JUDITH+ OGUNDIPE, JOHN‡ 26 EAST 91
  STREET, NEW YORK, NEW YORK 10028+ 119 WEST 106
  STREET, NEW YORK, NEW YORK 10025‡ NIGERIA‡
  OSHOGBO‡ YORUBA‡ 12 HOURS‡ 1970‡ QUALITY GOOD‡
  CENTER FOR AFRICAN ORAL DATA‡ 73-002-F‡ ‡ ‡
  DIVINING-ODU-IFA

GORDON, MERYL
  CARRINGTON, JOHN F.+ GORDON, MERYL‡ UNIVERSITY
  LIBRE DE LA REPUBLIQUE DE ZAIRE, KINSANGANI,
  ZAIRE+ 100-4 ALDRICH STREET, BRONX, NEW YORK
  10475‡ ZAIRE-U.S.‡ BLOOMINGTON, INDIANA‡ ‡ 2
  HOURS‡ 1975‡ QUALITY FAIR‡ ARCHIVES OF
  TRADITIONAL MUSIC‡ 75-032-F‡ ‡ RESTRICTED‡
  DRUM-LANGUAGE-LECTURE, DRUM-SLIT-LECTURE

  HANNA, JUDITH LYNNE+ GORDON, MERYL‡ P.O. BOX 1062,
  ENGLEWOOD CLIFFS, NEW JERSEY 07632+ 100-4 ALDRICH
  STREET, BRONX, NEW YORK 10475‡ AFRICA-U.S.‡
  BLOOMINGTON, INDIANA‡ ‡ 2 HOURS‡ 1975‡ QUALITY
  GOOD‡ ARCHIVES OF TRADITIONAL MUSIC‡ 75-045-F‡ ‡
  RESTRICTED‡ DANCE-LECTURE

GRAESSER, MARK W.
  GRAESSER, MARK W.‡ DEPARTMENT OF POLITICAL
  SCIENCE, MEMORIAL UNIVERSITY OF NEWFOUNDLAND, ST.
  JOHN'S, NEWFOUNDLAND, CANADA‡ GHANA‡ EJURA,
  MAMPONG‡ ASANTE, FRAFRA, HAUSA, KANJAGA, KONKOMBA‡
  2 HOURS‡ 1968-69‡ QUALITY GOOD‡ ‡ ‡ ‡ ‡
  COURT-FESTIVAL, DANCE-ADOWA, DANCE-KETE,
  DRUM-ATUMPAN, DRUM-DONNO, DRUM-LANGUAGE,
  FESTIVAL-DURBAR, FLUTE, GOURD, PRAISE

GREENSTEIN, ROBERT CARL
  GREENSTEIN, ROBERT CARL‡ P.O. BOX 30034, CAPITAL
  HILL, LILONGWE 3, MALAWI‡ MALAWI‡ CENTRAL REGION,

GREENSTEIN, ROBERT CARL
  NORTHERN REGION, SOUTHERN REGION‡ AMBO, CHEWA,
  LOMWE, MANGANJA, NGONI, TUMBUKA, YAO‡ 300 HOURS‡
  1971-75‡ QUALITY GOOD‡ DEPARTMENT OF ANTIQUITIES,
  NATIONAL ARCHIVES OF MALAWI, UNIVERSITY OF MALAWI‡
  ‡ ‡ ‡ FOLKLORE, HISTORY

GROHS, ELISABETH
  GROHS, ELISABETH‡ 1 BERLIN 33, MIQUEL STRASSE 75,
  GERMANY‡ TANZANIA‡ HANDENI‡ NDOROBO, NGURU, ZIGUA‡
  6.5 HOURS‡ 1970‡ QUALITY FAIR‡ ‡ ‡ ‡ ‡
  ANCESTOR-WORSHIP, HUNTING,
  PUBERTY-CEREMONY-FEMALE, RITUAL-HUNTING

GUIGNARD, AUDE
  GUIGNARD, AUDE‡ ‡ SENEGAL‡ KEDOUGOU‡ BEDIK,
  MALINKE, PEUL‡ ‡ 1968‡ ‡ MUSEE DE L'HOMME‡ ‡ ‡ ‡
  MUSIC

HAIGHT, BRUCE MARVIN
  HAIGHT, BRUCE MARVIN‡ 314 MOORE HALL, SOCIAL
  SCIENCE AREA, COLLEGE OF GENERAL STUDIES, WESTERN
  MICHIGAN UNIVERSITY, KALAMAZOO, MICHIGAN 49001‡
  GHANA‡ ACCRA, BOLE, TAMALE‡ DYULA, GONJA‡ 50
  HOURS‡ 1972-73‡ QUALITY FAIR‡ ‡ ‡ ‡ HISTORY

  HAIGHT, BRUCE MARVIN‡ 314 MOORE HALL, SOCIAL
  SCIENCE AREA, COLLEGE OF GENERAL STUDIES, WESTERN
  MICHIGAN UNIVERSITY, KALAMAZOO, MICHIGAN 49001‡
  SIERRA LEONE‡ GBENDENBU‡ LOKO‡ 10 HOURS‡ 1967‡
  QUALITY FAIR‡ ‡ ‡ ‡ HISTORY

HALE, KEN
  HALE, KEN‡ ‡ EGYPT‡ CAIRO‡ ARAB‡ .5 HOUR‡ ‡
  QUALITY GOOD‡ ARCHIVES OF LANGUAGES OF THE WORLD‡
  ‡ ‡ ‡ READING-ARABIC-CLASSICAL

HALL, JOHN F.
  HALL, JOHN F.‡ ‡ UPPER VOLTA‡ OUAGADOUGOU‡ MOSSI‡
  4 HOURS‡ 1962‡ QUALITY GOOD‡ ARCHIVES OF
  LANGUAGES OF THE WORLD‡ ‡ ‡ ‡ GRAMMATICAL-DATA

HAMBLY, WILFRED D.
  HAMBLY, WILFRED D.‡ ‡ ANGOLA‡ ‡ OVIMBUNDU‡ 4.5
  HOURS‡ 1929-30‡ QUALITY FAIR‡ ARCHIVES OF
  TRADITIONAL MUSIC‡ PRE'54-007-F‡ ATL 1154-62‡ ‡
  CARRYING, CHILDREN-GAME, DRUM, FOLKTALE,
  RELIGIOUS-CHRISTIAN, WORD-LIST

HANLEY, -
    HANLEY, -‡ ‡ SOUTH AFRICA‡ ‡ ZULU‡ .5 HOUR‡ ‡
    QUALITY GOOD‡ ARCHIVES OF LANGUAGES OF THE WORLD‡
    ‡ ‡ ‡ GRAMMATICAL-DATA

HANLEY, MARY ANN CSJ
    HANLEY, MARY ANN CSJ‡ COLLEGE OF ST. CATHERINE,
    ST. PAUL, MINNESOTA‡ GHANA‡ ACCRA, BOLGATANGA,
    DAFIEMA, KOKOLUGU, NANDOM, NAVRONGO, SIRIGU, TEMA,
    WIAGA‡ BUILSA, DAGARI, EWE, FANTI, FRAFRA, GA,
    KASSENA, NANKANI, TWI‡ 13.5 HOURS‡ 1972‡ QUALITY
    GOOD‡ ARCHIVES OF TRADITIONAL MUSIC‡ 74-094-F‡ ‡
    RESTRICTED‡ BASS-STRING, BELL, DANCE,
    DRUM-ATUMPAN, DRUM-CYLINDRICAL, DRUM-FRAME,
    DRUM-GOURD, DRUM-HOURGLASS, FESTIVAL,
    FLUTE-NOTCHED, GUITAR-ELECTRIC, HANDCLAPPING,
    HIGHLIFE, IDIOPHONE-STRUCK, LUTE-BOWED-GOGE,
    MARRIAGE, MASS-CATHOLIC, MUSIC-ART, ORGAN,
    PREACHING, RATTLE, RELIGIOUS-CHRISTIAN, ULULATION,
    WORK-FIELD, XYLOPHONE

    HANLEY, MARY ANN CSJ‡ COLLEGE OF ST. CATHERINE,
    ST. PAUL, MINNESOTA‡ GHANA‡ ACCRA, KUMASI‡ AKAN,
    EWE, TWI‡ 1 HOUR‡ 1973‡ QUALITY GOOD‡ ARCHIVES OF
    TRADITIONAL MUSIC‡ 74-095-F‡ ‡ RESTRICTED‡
    BELL-DOUBLE, MARRIAGE, RATTLE-GOURD,
    RELIGIOUS-CHRISTIAN, TAMBOURINE

    HANLEY, MARY ANN CSJ‡ COLLEGE OF ST. CATHERINE,
    ST. PAUL, MINNESOTA‡ NIGERIA‡ ABONNEMA, CALABAR,
    EMEKUKU, ENUGU, ESSIAN, IBADAN, ILE-IFE, LAGOS,
    MALLUMFASHI‡ ANGAS, BACHAMA, CHAMBA, EFIK,
    GWANDARA, HAUSA, IBIBIO, IBO, JABA, KERI-KERI,
    YORUBA‡ 12 HOURS‡ 1973‡ QUALITY GOOD‡ ARCHIVES OF
    TRADITIONAL MUSIC‡ 74-095-F‡ ‡ RESTRICTED‡
    BELL-DOUBLE, DRUM, GUITAR, HANDCLAPPING,
    IDIOPHONE-PLUCKED, MASS-CATHOLIC, ORGAN, POT-CLAY,
    PRAISE, RATTLE-GOURD, RELIGIOUS-CHRISTIAN

    HANLEY, MARY ANN CSJ‡ COLLEGE OF ST. CATHERINE,
    ST. PAUL, MINNESOTA‡ UPPER VOLTA‡ OUAGADOUGOU‡ ‡
    .3 HOUR‡ 1972‡ QUALITY GOOD‡ ARCHIVES OF
    TRADITIONAL MUSIC‡ 74-094-F‡ ‡ RESTRICTED‡ BELL,
    DRUM-GOURD, DRUM-HOURGLASS, MASS-CATHOLIC,
    RELIGIOUS-CHRISTIAN

HANNA, JUDITH LYNNE
    HANNA, JUDITH LYNNE+ GORDON, MERYL‡ P.O. BOX 1062,
    ENGLEWOOD CLIFFS, NEW JERSEY 07632+ 100-4 ALDRICH

HANNA, JUDITH LYNNE
  STREET, BRONX, NEW YORK 10475‡ AFRICA-U.S.‡
  BLOOMINGTON, INDIANA‡ ‡ 2 HOURS‡ 1975‡ QUALITY
  GOOD‡ ARCHIVES OF TRADITIONAL MUSIC‡ 75-045-F‡ ‡
  RESTRICTED‡ DANCE-LECTURE

  HANNA, JUDITH LYNNE+ HANNA, WILLIAM J.‡ P.O. BOX
  1062, ENGLEWOOD CLIFFS, NEW JERSEY 07632‡
  ETHIOPIA‡ ‡ ‡ 2 HOURS‡ 1963‡ QUALITY GOOD‡ ‡ ‡ ‡
  DANCE

  HANNA, JUDITH LYNNE+ HANNA, WILLIAM J.‡ P.O. BOX
  1062, ENGLEWOOD CLIFFS, NEW JERSEY 07632‡ NIGERIA‡
  UMUAHIA‡ IBO‡ 8 HOURS‡ 1963‡ QUALITY GOOD‡ ‡ ‡ ‡
  DANCE

  HANNA, JUDITH LYNNE+ HANNA, WILLIAM J.‡ P.O. BOX
  1062, ENGLEWOOD CLIFFS, NEW JERSEY 07632‡ UGANDA‡
  ‡ ACHOLI, BANYOLE‡ 5 HOURS‡ 1963‡ QUALITY GOOD‡ ‡
  ‡ ‡ ‡ DANCE

HANNA, WILLIAM J.
  HANNA, JUDITH LYNNE+ HANNA, WILLIAM J.‡ P.O. BOX
  1062, ENGLEWOOD CLIFFS, NEW JERSEY 07632‡
  ETHIOPIA‡ ‡ ‡ 2 HOURS‡ 1963‡ QUALITY GOOD‡ ‡ ‡ ‡ ‡
  DANCE

  HANNA, JUDITH LYNNE+ HANNA, WILLIAM J.‡ P.O. BOX
  1062, ENGLEWOOD CLIFFS, NEW JERSEY 07632‡ NIGERIA‡
  UMUAHIA‡ IBO‡ 8 HOURS‡ 1963‡ QUALITY GOOD‡ ‡ ‡ ‡
  DANCE

  HANNA, JUDITH LYNNE+ HANNA, WILLIAM J.‡ P.O. BOX
  1062, ENGLEWOOD CLIFFS, NEW JERSEY 07632‡ UGANDA‡
  ‡ ACHOLI, BANYOLE‡ 5 HOURS‡ 1963‡ QUALITY GOOD‡ ‡
  ‡ ‡ ‡ DANCE

HARING, LEE
  HARING, LEE‡ DEPARTMENT OF ENGLISH, BROOKLYN
  COLLEGE, BROOKLYN, NEW YORK 11210‡ KENYA‡
  MACHAKOS‡ AKAMBA‡ 3 HOURS‡ 1967-68‡ QUALITY GOOD‡
  ‡ ‡ ‡ ‡ DANCE-EXHIBITION-TEAM, DANCE-WOMEN,
  FOLKTALE

HARRIES, JEANETTE
  HARRIES, JEANETTE‡ DEPARTMENT OF LINGUISTICS,
  UNIVERSITY OF WISCONSIN, MADISON, WISCONSIN 53706‡
  MOROCCO‡ KHEMISSET‡ BERBER‡ 100 HOURS‡ 1964-65‡
  QUALITY GOOD‡ ‡ ‡ ‡ ‡ DRAMA, FOLKTALE,

HARRIES, JEANETTE
  LINGUISTIC-DATA, RIDDLE, WORK-WOMEN

  HARRIES, JEANETTE≢ DEPARTMENT OF LINGUISTICS,
  UNIVERSITY OF WISCONSIN, MADISON, WISCONSIN 53706≢
  MOROCCO≢ MIDDLE ATLAS≢ BERBER≢ 100 HOURS≢ 1971-72≢
  QUALITY EXCELLENT≢ ≢ ≢ ≢ ≢ MARRIAGE, POETRY

HARRIS, JOHN REES
  HARRIS, JOHN REES≢ 132C SEWALL AVENUE, BROOKLINE,
  MASSACHUSETTS≢ NIGERIA≢ EDE, JESSE, MIDWEST≢
  URHOBO, YORUBA≢ 1.5 HOURS≢ 1965≢ QUALITY FAIR≢ ≢ ≢
  ≢ ≢ DRUM-ROYAL-TIMI-OF-EDE

HARTWIG, GERALD W.
  HARTWIG, GERALD W.≢ DEPARTMENT OF HISTORY, DUKE
  UNIVERSITY, DURHAM, NORTH CAROLINA 27708≢
  TANZANIA≢ KAZILANKANDA, KIHUNGULA, KILIMABUYE,
  MUSOZI, MWIGOYE, NAMAGONDO≢ KEREWE≢ 8 HOURS≢
  1968-69≢ QUALITY GOOD≢ ARCHIVES OF TRADITIONAL
  MUSIC≢ 69-017-F≢ ≢ RESTRICTED≢ BOW-MUSICAL,
  LUTE-BOWED, ZITHER-TROUGH

HARVARD UNIVERSITY
  HARVARD UNIVERSITY≢ CAMBRIDGE, MASSACHUSETTS
  02138≢ ≢ ≢ ≢ ≢ ≢ ≢ ≢ ≢

HASSENPFLUG, EARL C.
  HASSENPFLUG, EARL C.≢ 89 WEST COLLEGE AVENUE,
  WESTERVILLE, OHIO 43081≢ MALI≢ MOPTI, SANGA≢ BOZO,
  DOGON≢ .7 HOUR≢ 1970≢ QUALITY GOOD≢ ≢ ≢ ≢ ≢ DANCE,
  DRUM, XYLOPHONE

HATFIELD, COLBY R.
  HATFIELD, COLBY R.≢ DEPARTMENT OF ANTHROPOLOGY,
  UNIVERSITY OF COLORADO, BOULDER, COLORADO 80302≢
  TANZANIA≢ MWANZA≢ SUKUMA≢ 1 HOUR≢ 1971≢ QUALITY
  GOOD≢ ≢ ≢ ≢ ≢ DRUM, SOCIAL

HAWTHORNE, RICHARD
  HAWTHORNE, RICHARD≢ ≢ LIBERIA≢ SANIQUELLIE≢ MANO≢
  1.5 HOURS≢ 1970≢ QUALITY GOOD≢ ARCHIVES OF
  TRADITIONAL MUSIC≢ 70-149-F≢ ≢ RESTRICTED≢
  MEDICAL-PRACTICE

HAY, MARGARET JEAN
  HAY, MARGARET JEAN≢ DEPARTMENT OF HISTORY,
  WELLESLEY COLLEGE, WELLESLEY, MASSACHUSETTS 02181≢
  KENYA≢ CENTRAL NYANZA, NORTHERN SEME≢ LUO≢ 50

HAY, MARGARET JEAN
  HOURS‡ 1968-70+ 1973‡ QUALITY FAIR‡ ‡ ‡ ‡ ‡
  CHORDOPHONE-NYARTITI, ECONOMIC, HISTORY

HEAD, SYDNEY W.
  HEAD, SYDNEY W.‡ SCHOOL OF COMMUNICATIONS AND
  THEATER, TEMPLE UNIVERSITY, PHILADELPHIA,
  PENNSYLVANIA 19122‡ ETHIOPIA‡ SICAMO‡ ‡ 1 HOUR‡
  1964‡ QUALITY GOOD‡ ‡ ‡ ‡ AGE-GRADE-CEREMONY,
  CEREMONY-AGE-GRADE

  HEAD, SYDNEY W.‡ SCHOOL OF COMMUNICATIONS AND
  THEATER, TEMPLE UNIVERSITY, PHILADELPHIA,
  PENNSYLVANIA 19122‡ SUDAN‡ OMDURMAN‡ DERVISH‡ 1
  HOUR‡ 1962‡ QUALITY GOOD‡ ‡ ‡ ‡ SECT-DERVISH

HEALD, SWETTE SCOTT
  HEALD, SWETTE SCOTT‡ DEPARTMENT OF SOCIOLOGY,
  UNIVERSITY OF LANCASTER, LANCASTER, ENGLAND‡
  UGANDA‡ SOUTHERN BUGISU‡ GISU‡ 30 HOURS‡ 1966-69‡
  QUALITY POOR‡ ‡ ‡ ‡ CIRCUMCISION, HISTORY,
  RITUAL-OBJECT-INTERVIEW

HENDERSON, LAWRENCE
  HENDERSON, LAWRENCE‡ 14 HARLOW CRESCENT, FAIRLAWN,
  NEW JERSEY 07410‡ ANGOLA‡ HUAMBO‡ OVIMBUNDU‡ 1.5
  HOURS‡ 1972‡ QUALITY POOR‡ ‡ ‡ ‡ AUTOBIOGRAPHY

HENRY, JULES
  HENRY, JULES‡ ‡ SOUTH AFRICA-U.S.‡ NEW YORK, NEW
  YORK‡ ZULU‡ .5 HOUR‡ 1935‡ QUALITY FAIR‡ ARCHIVES
  OF TRADITIONAL MUSIC‡ PRE*54-008-F‡ ATL 937‡ ‡

HERBIN, -
  HERBIN, -‡ ‡ SENEGAL‡ ‡ BALANTA, DIOLA, SARAKOLE,
  SERER‡ ‡ ‡ ‡ MUSEE DE L'HOMME‡ ‡ ‡ ‡

HERSKOVITS, FRANCES S.
  HERSKOVITS, MELVILLE J.+ HERSKOVITS, FRANCES S.‡
  DECEASED‡ DAHOMEY‡ ABOMEY, ALLADA, WHYDAH‡ FON‡ 7
  HOURS‡ 1931‡ QUALITY GOOD‡ ARCHIVES OF
  TRADITIONAL MUSIC‡ 67-152-F‡ ATL 4460-69‡ ‡
  CANTE-FABLE, CEREMONY, CHILDREN-TWINS,
  CLOTH-WORKER, CULT-ANCESTRAL, DANCE, DEATH,
  DEATH-FUNERAL, DIVINING, FLUTE, LULLABY, MARRIAGE,
  PRAISE-RULER, RELIGIOUS-PRAISE, RIDICULE,
  SECRET-SOCIETY, WAR, WEAVER, WORK, WORK-FIELD

  HERSKOVITS, MELVILLE J.+ HERSKOVITS, FRANCES S.‡

HERSKOVITS, FRANCES S.
  DECEASED‡ GHANA‡ ASOKORE‡ ASANTE‡ 2.5 HOURS‡ 1931‡
  QUALITY GOOD‡ ARCHIVES OF TRADITIONAL MUSIC‡
  67-152-F‡ ATL 4460-69‡ ‡ CHILDREN-TWINS, COURTING,
  DANCE, DEATH, DEATH-FUNERAL, DEATH-MOURNING,
  HUNTING, LULLABY, PRAISE-RULER, RELIGIOUS-PRAISE,
  SOCIAL-MEN, SOCIAL-WOMEN-INSULT, TOTEM, WORK

  HERSKOVITS, MELVILLE J.+ HERSKOVITS, FRANCES S.‡
  DECEASED‡ NIGERIA‡ ABEOKUTA, IBADAN, LAGOS‡
  YORUBA‡ .5 HOUR‡ 1931‡ QUALITY GOOD‡ ARCHIVES OF
  TRADITIONAL MUSIC‡ 67-152-F‡ ATL 4460-69‡ ‡
  CANTE-FABLE, PROVERB, RELIGIOUS, SECRET-SOCIETY

HERSKOVITS, MELVILLE J.
  HERSKOVITS, MELVILLE J.+ HERSKOVITS, FRANCES S.‡
  DECEASED‡ DAHOMEY‡ ABOMEY, ALLADA, WHYDAH‡ FON‡ 7
  HOURS‡ 1931‡ QUALITY GOOD‡ ARCHIVES OF
  TRADITIONAL MUSIC‡ 67-152-F‡ ATL 4460-69‡ ‡
  CANTE-FABLE, CEREMONY, CHILDREN-TWINS,
  CLOTH-WORKER, CULT-ANCESTRAL, DANCE, DEATH,
  DEATH-FUNERAL, DIVINING, FLUTE, LULLABY, MARRIAGE,
  PRAISE-RULER, RELIGIOUS-PRAISE, RIDICULE,
  SECRET-SOCIETY, WAR, WEAVER, WORK, WORK-FIELD

  HERSKOVITS, MELVILLE J.+ HERSKOVITS, FRANCES S.‡
  DECEASED‡ GHANA‡ ASOKORE‡ ASANTE‡ 2.5 HOURS‡ 1931‡
  QUALITY GOOD‡ ARCHIVES OF TRADITIONAL MUSIC‡
  67-152-F‡ ATL 4460-69‡ ‡ CHILDREN-TWINS, COURTING,
  DANCE, DEATH, DEATH-FUNERAL, DEATH-MOURNING,
  HUNTING, LULLABY, PRAISE-RULER, RELIGIOUS-PRAISE,
  SOCIAL-MEN, SOCIAL-WOMEN-INSULT, TOTEM, WORK

  HERSKOVITS, MELVILLE J.+ HERSKOVITS, FRANCES S.‡
  DECEASED‡ NIGERIA‡ ABEOKUTA, IBADAN, LAGOS‡
  YORUBA‡ .5 HOUR‡ 1931‡ QUALITY GOOD‡ ARCHIVES OF
  TRADITIONAL MUSIC‡ 67-152-F‡ ATL 4460-69‡ ‡
  CANTE-FABLE, PROVERB, RELIGIOUS, SECRET-SOCIETY

HERZOG, GEORGE
  ANDRADE, MANUEL+ HERZOG, GEORGE‡ -+ 7001 HOOVER
  ROAD, INDIANAPOLIS, INDIANA 46260‡ ‡ ‡ JABO‡ 2
  HOURS‡ 1931‡ QUALITY FAIR‡ ARCHIVES OF LANGUAGES
  OF THE WORLD‡ ‡ ‡ ‡ GRAMMATICAL-DATA, PROVERB

  HERZOG, GEORGE‡ 7001 HOOVER ROAD, INDIANAPOLIS,
  INDIANA 46260‡ LIBERIA‡ NIMIAH‡ GREBO, JABO, KRU‡
  8 HOURS‡ 1930‡ ‡ ARCHIVES OF TRADITIONAL MUSIC‡ ‡
  ‡ RESTRICTED‡ DRUM-LANGUAGE, DRUM-SLIT,

HERZOG, GEORGE
  HORN-LANGUAGE, HORN-TRANSVERSE, PROVERB,
  SOCIAL-MEN, SOCIAL-WOMEN, SPIRIT-SOCIETY, WAR,
  XYLOPHONE

HESS, ROBERT A.
  HESS, ROBERT A.‡ MESSIAH COLLEGE, GRANTHAM,
  PENNSYLVANIA 17027‡ NIGERIA‡ NORTHEAST STATE‡
  BURA‡ 1 HOUR‡ 1969‡ QUALITY FAIR‡ ‡ ‡ ‡ ‡
  DEATH-FUNERAL, MARRIAGE

HICKERSON, NANCY
  HICKERSON, NANCY+ HYMES, VIRGINIA+ KELLER, JAMES‡
  ‡ -U.S.‡ ‡ TIGRINYA‡ 8 HOURS‡ 1954‡ QUALITY GOOD‡
  ARCHIVES OF LANGUAGES OF THE WORLD‡ ‡ ‡ ‡
  GRAMMATICAL-DATA

HIMMELHEBER, HANS G.
  HIMMELHEBER, HANS G.‡ 32 WILCKENSTRASSE, 69
  HEIDELBERG, WEST GERMANY‡ IVORY COAST‡ ‡ BAULE,
  DAN, GUERE, GURO, SENUFO‡ ‡ 1952-65‡ QUALITY GOOD‡
  ‡ ‡ ‡ RESTRICTED‡

  HIMMELHEBER, HANS G.‡ 32 WILCKENSSTRASSE, 69
  HEIDELBERG, WEST GERMANY‡ LIBERIA‡ ‡ DAN, KRAHN,
  MANO‡ ‡ 1950-60‡ QUALITY GOOD‡ ‡ ‡ ‡ RESTRICTED‡

  HIMMELHEBER, HANS G.‡ 32 WILCKENSTRASSE, 69
  HEIDELBERG, WEST GERMANY‡ MALI‡ ‡ BAMBARA‡ ‡ 1953‡
  QUALITY GOOD‡ ‡ ‡ ‡ RESTRICTED‡ FOLKLORE, HISTORY,
  PRAISE, RITUAL, SOCIAL

HOHENWART-GERLACHSTEIN, A
  HOHENWART-GERLACHSTEIN, ANNA‡ PYRKERGASSE 10,
  A-1190 VIENNA, AUSTRIA‡ EGYPT‡ ED-DERR, LUXOR
  DISTRICT, MISHZALZ, GENA DISTRICT, TANTA, TOSHKA‡
  ABABDA, BEJA, FADIDJA, FELLAHIN‡ 34 HOURS‡ 1960+
  1962-63‡ QUALITY GOOD‡ PHONOGRAMMARCHIV DER
  OESTERREICHISCHEN‡ ‡ ‡ ‡ MUSIC, ORAL-DATA

HOLIDAY, GEOFFREY D.
  HOLIDAY, GEOFFREY D.‡ ‡ ALGERIA‡ ARAK‡ TUAREG‡ .1
  HOUR‡ CA1958‡ QUALITY GOOD‡ ARCHIVES OF
  TRADITIONAL MUSIC‡ 58-008-F‡ ‡ RESTRICTED‡ LOVE

  HOLIDAY, GEOFFREY D.‡ ‡ NIGER‡ AGADES, TANOUT‡
  TUAREG‡ .9 HOUR‡ CA1958‡ QUALITY GOOD‡ ARCHIVES
  OF TRADITIONAL MUSIC‡ 58-008-F‡ ‡ RESTRICTED‡
  CARAVAN, DRUM, DRUM-WATER, HUNTING,

HOLIDAY, GEOFFREY D.
  LUTE-BOWED-IMZAD

HOLSOE, SVEND E.
  HOLSOE, SVEND E.‡ DEPARTMENT OF ANTHROPOLOGY,
  UNIVERSITY OF DELAWARE, NEWARK, DELAWARE 19711‡
  LIBERIA‡ ‡ DEI, GBANDE, GOLA, KPELLE, MANDINGO,
  VAI‡ 180 HOURS‡ 1965-70‡ QUALITY GOOD‡ ‡ ‡ ‡ ‡
  FOLKTALE, HISTORY, MUSIC, SCRIPT-VAI

HOOVER, JAMES JEFFREY
  HOOVER, JAMES JEFFREY‡ RUDD, IOWA 50471‡ ZAIRE‡
  KAPANGA, MUSUMB, NKALANY RIVER, SHABA‡ LUNDA‡ 20
  HOURS‡ 1973-75‡ QUALITY FAIR‡ ‡ ‡ ‡ DANCE,
  HISTORY, PRAISE-NAME, RITUAL

HOPKINS, JERRY
  HOPKINS, JERRY‡ ‡ ‡ ‡ YORUBA‡ .5 HOUR‡ 1956‡
  QUALITY GOOD‡ ARCHIVES OF LANGUAGES OF THE WORLD‡
  ‡ ‡ ‡ GRAMMATICAL-DATA

HRBEK, IVAN
  HRBEK, IVAN‡ PRAHA 6, SVERDLOVA 2, CZECHOSLOVAKIA‡
  SENEGAL‡ EASTERN‡ SONINKE‡ 30 HOURS‡ ‡ QUALITY
  GOOD‡ ‡ ‡ ‡ ‡ HISTORY-MAHMADU-LAMINE

HURAULT, -
  HURAULT, -‡ ‡ CAMEROON‡ ‡ DOUROU, HAUSA, MBUM‡ ‡ ‡
  ‡ MUSEE DE L'HOMME‡ ‡ ‡ ‡

HURREIZ, SAYED H.
  HURREIZ, SAYED H.‡ SUDAN RESEARCH UNIT,
  UNIVERSITY OF KHARTOUM, KHARTOUM, SUDAN‡ SUDAN‡
  AL AALYB, AL DAMAR, AL DOSHEN, AL KUMUR, HAJAR AL
  TER, KALI, KINNUR‡ GAALIIN‡ 9 HOURS‡ 1970-71‡
  QUALITY GOOD‡ ARCHIVES OF TRADITIONAL MUSIC‡
  71-012-F‡ ATL 4295-307‡ ‡ FOLKTALE,
  FOLKTALE-CYCLE, FOLKTALE-INTERVIEW, GENEALOGY,
  HISTORY, ISLAM-INTERVIEW, ISLAMIC-ORDER-INTERVIEW,
  LEGEND, PRAISE, WELLERISM

HYMES, VIRGINIA
  HICKERSON, NANCY+ HYMES, VIRGINIA+ KELLER, JAMES‡
  ‡ -U.S.‡ ‡ TIGRINYA‡ 8 HOURS‡ 1954‡ QUALITY GOOD‡
  ARCHIVES OF LANGUAGES OF THE WORLD‡ ‡ ‡ ‡
  GRAMMATICAL-DATA

IJAGBEMI, ELIJAH A.
  IJAGBEMI, ELIJAH A.‡ DEPARTMENT OF HISTORY,

IJAGBEMI, ELIJAH A.
  AHMADU BELLO UNIVERSITY, ZARIA, NIGERIA‡ SIERRA
  LEONE‡ NORTHERN PROVINCE‡ TEMNE‡ ‡ 1965-67‡
  QUALITY GOOD‡ ‡ ‡ ‡ ‡ HISTORY, RITUAL

INNES, GORDON
  INNES, GORDON‡ SCHOOL OF ORIENTAL AND AFRICAN
  STUDIES, MALET STREET, LONDON WC1E 7HP, ENGLAND‡
  GAMBIA, THE‡ THE KOMBOS, MACCARTHY ISLAND‡
  MANDINKA‡ 35 HOURS‡ 1968-69‡ QUALITY GOOD‡ GAMBIA
  CULTURAL ARCHIVES‡ ‡ ‡ ‡ FOLKTALE, HISTORY

  INNES, GORDON‡ SCHOOL OF ORIENTAL AND AFRICAN
  STUDIES, MALET STREET, LONDON, WC1E 7HP, ENGLAND‡
  SIERRA LEONE‡ SEGBWEMA‡ MENDE‡ 3 HOURS‡ 1963‡
  QUALITY GOOD‡ ‡ ‡ ‡ ‡ FOLKTALE

INSTITUT D'ETHNOLOGIE DE
  INSTITUT D'ETHNOLOGIE DE L'UNIVERSITE DE
  STRASBOURG‡ 3 RUE DE ROME, 67-STRASBOURG, FRANCE‡
  ‡ ‡ ‡ ‡ ‡ ‡ ‡ ‡ ‡

  INSTITUT D'ETHNOLOGIE DE L'UNIVERSITE DE
  STRASBOURG‡ 3 RUE DE ROME, 67-STRASBOURG, FRANCE‡
  MALI‡ ‡ BAMBARA‡ ‡ ‡ ‡ INSTITUT D'ETHNOLOGIE DE
  L'UNIVERSITE DE STRASBOURG‡ ‡ ‡ ‡ MUSIC, RITUAL

  INSTITUT D'ETHNOLOGIE DE L'UNIVERSITE DE
  STRASBOURG‡ 3 RUE DE ROME, 67-STRASBOURG, FRANCE‡
  MOROCCO‡ MARRAKECH, TAMESLOHT‡ GNAWA‡ ‡ ‡ ‡
  INSTITUT D'ETHNOLOGIE DE L'UNIVERSITE DE
  STRASBOURG‡ ‡ ‡ ‡ DANCE-POSSESSION

  INSTITUT D'ETHNOLOGIE DE L'UNIVERSITE DE
  STRASBOURG‡ 3 RUE DE ROME, 67-STRASBOURG, FRANCE‡
  MOROCCO‡ ‡ GNAWA‡ ‡ ‡ ‡ INSTITUT D'ETHNOLOGIE DE
  L'UNIVERSITE DE STRASBOURG‡ ‡ ‡ ‡ MUSIC, RITUAL

INSTITUT DES MUSEES NATIO
  INSTITUT DES MUSEES NATIONAUX DU ZAIRE‡ B.P. 4249,
  KINSHASA 2, ZAIRE‡ ‡ ‡ ‡ ‡ ‡ ‡ ‡ ‡ ‡

INSTITUT FUR DEN WISSENSC
  INSTITUT FUR DEN WISSENSCHAFTLICHEN FILM‡
  NONNENSTEIG 72, GOTTINGEN, WEST GERMANY‡ ‡ ‡ ‡ ‡
  ‡ ‡ ‡ ‡ ‡

INSTITUT FUR VOLKERKUNDE
  INSTITUT FUR VOLKERKUNDE DER UNIVERSITAT‡ 78

INSTITUT FUR VOLKERKUNDE
  FREIBURG IM BREISGAU, WERDERRING 4, FEDERAL
  REPUBLIC OF GERMANY‡ ‡ ‡ ‡ ‡ ‡ ‡ ‡ ‡ ‡

INSTITUT NATIONAL DE RECH
  INSTITUT NATIONAL DE RECHERCHE SCIENTIFIQUE‡ B.P.
  218, BUTARE, RWANDA‡ ‡ ‡ ‡ ‡ ‡ ‡ ‡ ‡ ‡

INSTITUTE OF AFRICAN STUD
  INSTITUTE OF AFRICAN STUDIES, UNIVERSITY OF GHANA‡
  LEGON, GHANA‡ ‡ ‡ ‡ ‡ ‡ ‡ ‡ ‡ ‡

  INSTITUTE OF AFRICAN STUDIES, UNIVERSITY OF
  IBADAN‡ IBADAN, NIGERIA‡ ‡ ‡ ‡ ‡ ‡ ‡ ‡ ‡ ‡

  INSTITUTE OF AFRICAN STUDIES, UNIVERSITY OF IFE‡
  ILE-IFE, WESTERN STATE, NIGERIA‡ ‡ ‡ ‡ ‡ ‡ ‡ ‡ ‡
  ‡

  INSTITUTE OF AFRICAN STUDIES, UNIVERSITY OF IFE‡
  ILE-IFE, WESTERN STATE, NIGERIA‡ NIGERIA‡ ‡ IBO,
  TIV, YORUBA‡ 700 HOURS‡ ‡ ‡ INSTITUTE OF AFRICAN
  STUDIES, UNIVERSITY OF IFE‡ ‡ ‡ ‡ FOLKTALE,
  HISTORY, PRAISE-POETRY, RITUAL, SOCIAL

INSTITUTE OF ETHIOPIAN ST
  INSTITUTE OF ETHIOPIAN STUDIES‡ HAILE SELASSIE
  UNIVERSITY, P.O. BOX 1176, ADDIS ABABA, ETHIOPIA‡
  ‡ ‡ ‡ ‡ ‡ ‡ ‡ ‡ ‡

INSTITUTE OF ETHNOMUSICOL
  INSTITUTE OF ETHNOMUSICOLOGY, UCLA‡ 405 HILGARD
  AVENUE, LOS ANGELES, CALIFORNIA 90024‡ ‡ ‡ ‡ ‡ ‡ ‡
  ‡ ‡ ‡

INSTITUTO NACIONAL DE FOL
  INSTITUTO NACIONAL DE FOLKLORE‡ APARTADO 6238,
  CARACAS, VENEZUELA‡ ‡ ‡ ‡ ‡ ‡ ‡ ‡ ‡ ‡

  INSTITUTO NACIONAL DE FOLKLORE, VENEZUELA‡
  APARTADO 6238, CARACAS, VENEZUELA‡ BURUNDI‡ ‡ ‡ 1
 • HOUR‡ 1961‡ ‡ INSTITUTO NACIONAL DE FOLKLORE,
  VENEZUELA‡ 189-190‡ ‡ ‡ MUSIC

  INSTITUTO NACIONAL DE FOLKLORE, VENEZUELA‡
  APARTADO 6238, CARACAS, VENEZUELA‡ GHANA‡ ‡ ‡ ‡
  1966‡ ‡ INSTITUTO NACIONAL DE FOLKLORE, VENEZUELA‡
  3426-3482‡ ‡ ‡
  CONGRESS-OF-INTERNATIONAL-FOLK-MUSIC

INSTITUTO NACIONAL DE FOL
    INSTITUTO NACIONAL DE FOLKLORE, VENEZUELA‡
    APARTADO 6238, CARACAS, VENEZUELA‡ TANZANIA‡ ‡ ‡
    1 HOUR‡ 1961‡ ‡ INSTITUTO NACIONAL DE FOLKLORE,
    VENEZUELA‡ 189-190‡ ‡ ‡ MUSIC

INTERNATIONAL LIBRARY OF
    INTERNATIONAL LIBRARY OF AFRICAN MUSIC (ILAM)‡
    P.O. BOX 138, ROODEPOORT, TRANSVAAL, REPUBLIC OF
    SOUTH AFRICA‡ ‡ ‡ ‡ ‡ ‡ ‡ ‡ ‡ ‡

IRVINE, JUDITH TEMKIN
    IRVINE, JUDITH TEMKIN‡ DEPARTMENT OF ANTHROPOLOGY,
    BRANDEIS UNIVERSITY, WALTHAM, MASSACHUSETTS 02154‡
    SENEGAL‡ TAIBA, N'DIAYE‡ WOLOF‡ 8.5 HOURS‡
    1970-71‡ QUALITY GOOD‡ ‡ ‡ ‡ ‡ DRUM, HISTORY,
    POETRY-INSULT, PRAISE-POETRY, RITUAL, SOCIAL

IRWIN, GRAHAM
    OFONAGURO, W. IBEKWE+ IRWIN, GRAHAM‡ DEPARTMENT
    OF HISTORY, BROOKLYN COLLEGE, BEDFORD AVENUE AND
    AVENUE H, NEW YORK, NEW YORK 11210+ 435 W. 119
    ST., APT. 5B, NEW YORK, NEW YORK 10027‡
    NIGERIA-U.S.‡ NEW YORK‡ ‡ .5 HOUR‡ 1967‡ QUALITY
    GOOD‡ ARCHIVES OF TRADITIONAL MUSIC‡ 69-132-F‡
    ATL 3686‡ RESTRICTED‡ SPEECH-OJUNWU-C.O.,
    POLITICS-SPEECH

ISOLA, AKINWUMI
    ISOLA, AKINWUMI‡ INSTITUTE OF AFRICAN STUDIES,
    UNIVERSITY OF IFE, ILE-IFE, NIGERIA‡ NIGERIA‡
    WESTERN STATE‡ YORUBA‡ 25 HOURS‡ 1968-74‡ QUALITY
    FAIR‡ ‡ ‡ ‡ ‡ POETRY-SOCIAL-ETIYERI,
    PRAISE-DIVINITY-SHANGO

JARGY, SIMON
    JARGY, SIMON+ OLSEN, POUL ROVSING‡ - +
    BIRKETINGET 6, 2300 COPENHAGEN S., DENMARK‡ EGYPT‡
    CAIRO‡ ‡ ‡ 1969‡ ‡ DANSK FOLKEMINDESAMLING‡ 69/44‡
    ‡ ‡

JAULIN, -
    JAULIN, -‡ ‡ CHAD‡ ‡ SARA-DEME‡ ‡ ‡ ‡ MUSEE DE
    L'HOMME‡ ‡ ‡ ‡

JENKINS, JEAN
    JENKINS, JEAN‡ 36 PACKINGTON STREET, LONDON N. 1,
    ENGLAND‡ AFRICA-WEST‡ ‡ ‡ ‡ 1960-69‡ QUALITY
    EXCELLENT‡ ‡ ‡ ‡ ‡

JENKINS, JEAN
  JENKINS, JEAN‡ 36 PACKINGTON STREET, LONDON N. 1,
  ENGLAND‡ ETHIOPIA‡ ‡ ‡ ‡ 1962-70‡ QUALITY
  EXCELLENT‡ ‡ ‡ ‡ MUSIC

  JENKINS, JEAN‡ 36 PACKINGTON STREET, LONDON N. 1,
  ENGLAND‡ TANZANIA‡ ‡ ‡ ‡ 1960-61‡ QUALITY
  EXCELLENT‡ ‡ ‡ ‡

  JENKINS, JEAN‡ 36 PACKINGTON STREET, LONDON N. 1,
  ENGLAND‡ UGANDA‡ ‡ ‡ ‡ 1966 + 1970‡ QUALITY
  EXCELLENT‡ ‡ ‡ ‡

JERUSALEM PHONOARCHIVES O
  JERUSALEM PHONOARCHIVES OF ORIENTAL MUSIC‡ HEBREW
  UNIVERSITY, JERUSALEM, ISRAEL‡ ‡ ‡ ‡ ‡ ‡ ‡ ‡ ‡ ‡

JOHNSON, GERALD T.
  JOHNSON, GERALD T.‡ LOGAN MUSEUM, BELOIT COLLEGE,
  BELOIT, WISCONSIN 53511‡ SIERRA LEONE‡ FREETOWN,
  KORI CHIEFDOM‡ MENDE, TEMNE‡ 125 HOURS‡ 1967-68‡
  QUALITY GOOD‡ ARCHIVES OF TRADITIONAL MUSIC‡
  73-055-F‡ ‡ RESTRICTED‡ CANTE-FABLE,
  CHILDREN-GAME, DANCE, FOLKTALE, RELIGIOUS, SCHOOL,
  SECRET-SOCIETY-SANDE

JOHNSON, JOHN W.
  JOHNSON, JOHN W. ‡ 804 WEST ANNIE, AUSTIN, TEXAS
  78704‡ SOMALIA‡ ‡ SOMALI‡ 3 HOURS‡ 1966-69‡
  QUALITY GOOD‡ ARCHIVES OF TRADITIONAL MUSIC‡
  70-151-F‡ ATL 5155-60‡ RESTRICTED‡ POETRY,
  POETRY-HEELLO, POETRY-INTERVIEW, POETRY-WIGLO

JOHNSTON, THOMAS FREDERIC
  JOHNSTON, THOMAS FREDERICK‡ DEPARTMENT OF
  ANTHROPOLOGY, UNIVERSITY OF ALASKA, FAIRBANKS,
  ALASKA 99701‡ MOZAMBIQUE‡ SOUTHWEST MOZAMBIQUE‡
  TSONGA‡ 2 HOURS‡ 1968-70‡ QUALITY GOOD‡
  UNIVERSITY OF WITWATERSRAND‡ ‡ ‡ ‡ MUSIC

  JOHNSTON, THOMAS FREDERICK‡ DEPARTMENT OF
  ANTHROPOLOGY, UNIVERSITY OF ALASKA, FAIRBANKS,
  ALASKA 99701‡ SOUTH AFRICA‡ NORTHEAST TRANSVAAL‡
  TSONGA‡ 2 HOURS‡ 1968-70‡ QUALITY GOOD‡
  UNIVERSITY OF WITWATERSRAND‡ ‡ ‡ ‡ MUSIC

JONES, ARTHUR M.
  JONES, ARTHUR M.‡ 52 WARWICK ROAD, ST. ALBANS,
  HERTS, ENGLAND‡ GHANA-ENGLAND‡ LONDON‡ EWE‡ 3

JONES, ARTHUR M.
  HOURS‡ 1956‡ QUALITY EXCELLENT‡ ARCHIVES OF
  TRADITIONAL MUSIC‡ 71-309-F‡ ATL 5145-46‡
  RESTRICTED‡ BELL-DOUBLE, DANCE-AZIDA,
  DANCE-AGBADZA, DANCE-HUSAGO, DANCE-NYAYITO,
  DANCE-SOGBA, DANCE-SOVU, DRUM-ATSIMEVU,
  DRUM-KAGAN, DRUM-SOGO, HANDCLAPPING,
  IDIOPHONE-ATOKE, RATTLE-GOURD

  JONES, ARTHUR M.‡ 52 WARWICK ROAD, ST. ALBANS,
  HERTS, ENGLAND‡ ZAMBIA‡ ‡ LALA‡ ‡ 1944‡ QUALITY
  GOOD‡ ‡ ‡ ‡ ‡ DANCE-ICILA, DANCE-ICILILI,
  DRUM-AKACHE, DRUM-ICIBITIKU, DRUM-IKULU,
  HANDCLAPPING

JUILLERAT, B.
  JUILLERAT, B.‡ ‡ CAMEROON‡ ‡ KIRDI‡ ‡ 1966+
  1967-68‡ ‡ MUSEE DE L'HOMME‡ ‡ ‡ ‡ DEATH-FUNERAL,
  DRUM, FLUTE, FLUTE-NOTCHED, HARP-LUTE, LOVE,
  PRAISE, WHISTLE, WORK

JUWAYEYI, YUSUF MCDADDLY
  JUWAYEYI, YUSUF MCDADDLY‡ DEPARTMENT OF
  ANTIQUITIES, P.O. BOX 30312, CAPITAL CITY,
  LILONGWE 3, MALAWI‡ MALAWI‡ SOUTHERN‡ ‡ 100 HOURS‡
  1972-75‡ QUALITY EXCELLENT‡ ‡ ‡ ‡ ‡ HISTORY

KABEMBA, MUFUTA KABANDANY
  KABEMBA, MUFUTA KABANDANYI‡ B.P. 3252, LUBUMBASHI,
  ZAIRE‡ ZAIRE‡ KASAYI‡ KUBA, LUBA‡ 83 HOURS‡ 1965+
  1972‡ QUALITY EXCELLENT‡ ‡ ‡ ‡ ‡ DRUM-LANGUAGE,
  POETRY-HEROIC, PRAISE-POETRY, RITUAL

KAEMMER, JOHN E.
  KAEMMER, JOHN E.‡ ANTHROPOLOGY DEPARTMENT,
  INDIANA UNIVERSITY, BLOOMINGTON, INDIANA 47401‡
  RHODESIA‡ MARANKE‡ GARWE, MANYIKA‡ 8 HOURS‡ 1971‡
  QUALITY GOOD‡ ‡ ‡ ‡ RESTRICTED‡ MUSIC

  KAEMMER, JOHN E.‡ DEPARTMENT OF ANTHROPOLOGY,
  INDIANA UNIVERSITY, BLOOMINGTON, INDIANA 47401‡
  RHODESIA‡ MADZIWA‡ KOREKORE, SHONA, ZEZURU‡ 50
  HOURS‡ 1972-73‡ QUALITY EXCELLENT‡ ARCHIVES OF
  TRADITIONAL MUSIC‡ 74-061-F‡ ‡ RESTRICTED‡
  BOW-MUSICAL, CANTE-FABLE, ENTERTAINMENT, FOLKTALE,
  MBIRA, PIPE-ENSEMBLE, RITUAL, SOCIAL

KAPTER, JOHN D.
  KAPTER, JOHN D.‡ GEOGRAPHY DEPARTMENT, UNIVERSITY

KAPTER, JOHN D.
  OF WISCONSIN-STEVENS POINT, STEVENS POINT,
  WISCONSIN 54481‡ ZAIRE‡ WESTERN ZAIRE‡ BAPELENDE,
  BAYAKA‡ .5 HOUR‡ 1970‡ QUALITY EXCELLENT‡ ‡ ‡ ‡ ‡

KATZ, ISRAEL J.
  ARMISTEAD, SAMUEL G. + KATZ, ISRAEL J. +
  SILVERMAN, JOSEPH H.‡ 4524 SPRUCE STREET,
  PHILADELPHIA, PENNSYLVANIA 19139 + 415 WEST 115TH
  STREET, NEW YORK, NEW YORK 10025 + ADLAI
  STEVENSON COLLEGE, UNIVERSITY OF CALIFORNIA,
  SANTA CRUZ, CALIFORNIA 95060‡ MOROCCO‡ SPANISH
  ZONE‡ SEPHARDIC-JEW‡ 60 HOURS‡ 1962‡ QUALITY
  EXCELLENT‡ ‡ ‡ ‡ ‡ BALLAD-SPANISH,
  CIRCUMCISION-CEREMONY, DEATH-DIRGE, FOLKTALE,
  HYMN-HEBREW-METRICAL, MARRIAGE

KATZ, RICHARD
  KATZ, RICHARD‡ 12 WHITTIER STREET, CAMBRIDGE,
  MASSACHUSETTS 02140‡ BOTSWANA‡ DOBE, /GAI/GAI‡
  KUNG-BUSHMEN‡ 30 HOURS‡ 1968‡ QUALITY GOOD‡ ‡ ‡ ‡
  ‡ DANCE-TRANCE, HISTORY, MYTH, RELIGIOUS, RITUAL

KAUFFMAN, ROBERT A.
  KAUFFMAN, ROBERT A.‡ SCHOOL OF MUSIC,
  ETHNOMUSICOLOGY, UNIVERSITY OF WASHINGTON,
  SEATTLE, WASHINGTON 98195‡ RHODESIA‡ ‡ SHONA‡ 25
  HOURS‡ 1960-65, 1971‡ QUALITY EXCELLENT‡
  UNIVERSITY OF WASHINGTON‡ ‡ ‡ ‡ MUSIC,
  MUSIC-URBAN

KAYE, ALAN S.
  KAYE, ALAN S.‡ DEPARTMENT OF LINGUISTICS,
  CALIFORNIA STATE UNIVERSITY, FULLERTON,
  CALIFORNIA 92634‡ CHAD‡ ABECHE, FORT LAMY‡ ARAB‡
  4.5 HOURS‡ 1970‡ QUALITY EXCELLENT‡ ‡ ‡ ‡ ‡ MYTH,
  NARRATIVE, SOCIAL

  KAYE, ALAN S.‡ DEPARTMENT OF LINGUISTICS,
  CALIFORNIA STATE UNIVERSITY, FULLERTON,
  CALIFORNIA 92634‡ NIGERIA‡ MAIDUGURI‡ ARAB-SHUWA‡
  8 HOURS‡ 1974‡ QUALITY EXCELLENT‡ ‡ ‡ ‡ ‡ HISTORY,
  POETRY, SOCIAL

  KAYE, ALAN S.‡ DEPARTMENT OF LINGUISTICS,
  CALIFORNIA STATE UNIVERSITY, FULLERTON,
  CALIFORNIA 92634‡ SUDAN‡ KHARTOUM, OMDURMAN‡ ARAB‡
  4 HOURS‡ 1970‡ QUALITY EXCELLENT‡ ‡ ‡ ‡
  NARRATIVE

KEALIINOHOMOKU, JOANN W.
  KEALIINOHOMOKU, JOANN W.‡ 664 GARCIA STREET,
  SANTA FE, NEW MEXICO 87501‡ GHANA‡ LEGON‡ ‡ 3
  HOURS‡ 1970‡ QUALITY GOOD‡ ARCHIVES OF
  TRADITIONAL MUSIC‡ 74-050-F‡ ‡ ‡
  DANCE-UNIVERSITY-OF-GHANA

KEIL, CHARLES
  KEIL, CHARLES‡ PROGRAM IN AMERICAN STUDIES, SUNY,
  124 WINSPEAR AVENUE, BUFFALO, NEW YORK 14214‡
  NIGERIA‡ IBADAN, JOS-PLATEAU, NORTHERN-REGION,
  OGOJA-PROVINCE, TIVLAND‡ TIV, YORUBA‡ 50 HOURS‡ ‡
  QUALITY FAIR‡ INSTITUTE OF AFRICAN STUDIES,
  UNIVERSITY OF IBADAN‡ ‡ ‡ ‡ FOLKTALE, MUSIC

KEIM, KAREN R.
  BIRD, CHARLES S.+ KEIM, KAREN R.‡ LINGUISTICS
  DEPARTMENT, INDIANA UNIVERSITY, BLOOMINGTON,
  INDIANA 47401+ AFRICAN STUDIES, INDIANA
  UNIVERSITY, BLOOMINGTON, INDIANA 47401‡ MALI-U.S.‡
  ‡ BAMBARA‡ 2 HOURS‡ 1975‡ QUALITY GOOD‡ ARCHIVES
  OF TRADITIONAL MUSIC‡ 75-043-F‡ ‡ RESTRICTED‡
  EPIC-LECTURE, HERO-EPIC-LECTURE

KELLER, JAMES
  HICKERSON, NANCY+ HYMES, VIRGINIA+ KELLER, JAMES‡
  ‡ -U.S.‡ ‡ TIGRINYA‡ 8 HOURS‡ 1954‡ QUALITY GOOD‡
  ARCHIVES OF LANGUAGES OF THE WORLD‡ ‡ ‡ ‡
  GRAMMATICAL-DATA

KILSON, MARION D. DE B.
  KILSON, MARION D. DE B.‡ NEWTON COLLEGE, NEWTON,
  MASSACHUSETTS 02159‡ GHANA‡ ACCRA‡ GA‡ 10 HOURS‡
  1964-65+ 1968‡ QUALITY GOOD‡ ‡ ‡ ‡ ‡ RITUAL

  KILSON, MARION D. DE B.‡ NEWTON COLLEGE, NEWTON,
  MASSACHUSETTS 02159‡ SIERRA LEONE‡ BO, FREETOWN,
  KAILAHUN‡ MENDE‡ 10 HOURS‡ 1960‡ QUALITY GOOD‡ ‡ ‡
  ‡ ‡ FOLKTALE

KINBADE, M. DALE
  KINBADE, M. DALE‡ ‡ ‡ ‡ TONGA‡ ‡ 1960‡ QUALITY
  GOOD‡ ARCHIVES OF LANGUAGES OF THE WORLD‡ ‡ ‡ ‡
  GRAMMATICAL-DATA

KIRK-GREENE, ANTHONY H.M.
  KIRK-GREENE, ANTHONY H.M.‡ ST. ANTHONY'S COLLEGE,
  OXFORD UNIVERSITY, OXFORD, ENGLAND‡ NIGERIA‡
  GBOKO, KAGORO, ZARIA‡ HAUSA, KAGORO, TIV‡ 27.5

KIRK-GREENE, ANTHONY H.M.
  HOURS‡ 1962-65‡ QUALITY FAIR‡ SCHOOL OF ORIENTAL
  AND AFRICAN STUDIES‡ ‡ ‡ ‡ DANCE-TSWANGE,
  FOLKTALE, POETRY-NARRATIVE, SOCIAL

KIRWEN, MICHAEL CARL
  KIRWEN, MICHAEL CARL‡ DIOCESE OF MUSOMA, P.O. BOX
  93, MUSOMA, TANZANIA‡ TANZANIA‡ KISERU, NORTH
  MARA‡ SUBA‡ ‡ 1963-69‡ QUALITY GOOD‡ ‡ ‡ ‡
  DRINKING, LANGUAGE-LUO-CONVERSATION, MARRIAGE

KLEIN, MARTIN A.
  KLEIN, MARTIN A.‡ DEPARTMENT OF HISTORY,
  UNIVERSITY OF TORONTO, TORONTO, ONTARIO, CANADA‡
  SENEGAL‡ SINE-SALOUM‡ WOLOF, SERER‡ ‡ 1963-64‡
  QUALITY POOR‡ ARCHIVES OF TRADITIONAL MUSIC+
  ARCHIVES CULTURELLES, DAKAR‡ 74-099-B/F‡ ‡ ‡
  HISTORY

KLEIS, GERALD W.
  KLEIS, GERALD W.‡ DEPARTMENT OF ANTHROPOLOGY,
  WESTERN MICHIGAN UNIVERSITY, KALAMAZOO, MICHIGAN‡
  CAMEROON‡ KUMBA, SOUTHWEST PROVINCE‡ AROCHUKU,
  BAKUNDU, IGBO, META, NKAMBE, WIDEKUM‡ 2.5 HOURS‡
  1971‡ QUALITY FAIR‡ ‡ ‡ ‡ DANCE, DANCE-WOMEN

KNAPPERT, JAN D.
  KNAPPERT, JAN D.‡ 2 SAINT ANDREWS AVENUE,
  HARPENDEN, HERTS, ENGLAND‡ KENYA‡ MOMBASA‡
  SWAHILI‡ 12 HOURS‡ 1969+ 1973‡ QUALITY FAIR‡ ‡ ‡
  ‡ HYMN, LITURGY

KNIGHT, RODERIC COPLEY
  KNIGHT, RODERIC COPLEY‡ SCHOOL OF MUSIC,
  UNIVERSITY OF WASHINGTON, SEATTLE, WASHINGTON
  98195‡ GAMBIA, THE‡ LOWER RIVER DIVISION,
  MACCARTHY ISLAND DIVISION, UPPER RIVER DIVISION,
  WESTERN DIVISION‡ BALANTA, BAMBARA, FULA, JOLA,
  MANDINKA, TEMNE, WOLOF‡ 141.5 HOURS‡ 1970-71‡
  QUALITY EXCELLENT‡ INSTITUTE OF ETHNOMUSICOLOGY,
  UCLA‡ ‡ ‡ ‡ AUTOBIOGRAPHY-MUSICIAN,
  CHILDREN-NAMING-CEREMONY, DANCE-BUKARABO, DRUM,
  FLUTE, FOLKTALE, GOURD, GUITAR, HARP-LUTE-BOLON,
  HARP-LUTE-KORA, HARP-SIMBINGO, HUNTING,
  INITIATION, KORAN-CHANT, LUTE-PLUCKED-KONTINGO,
  MARRIAGE, MBIRA-BONGO, MONOCHORD,
  MUSIC-MANINKA-ORIGIN, SOCIAL-RALLY,
  XYLOPHONE-BALO

KNIGHT, RODERIC COPLEY
  KNIGHT, RODERIC COPLEY‡ SCHOOL OF MUSIC,
  UNIVERSITY OF WASHINGTON, SEATTLE, WASHINGTON
  98195‡ SENEGAL‡ CASAMANCE, DAKAR‡ FULA, JOLA,
  MANDINKA, WOLOF‡ 8.5 HOURS‡ 1970-71‡ QUALITY
  EXCELLENT‡ UCLA‡ ‡ ‡ ‡ HARP-LUTE-KORA,
  SOCIAL-CELEBRATION

  KNIGHT, RODERIC COPLEY‡ SCHOOL OF MUSIC,
  UNIVERSITY OF WASHINGTON, SEATTLE, WASHINGTON
  98195‡ ZAIRE‡ ‡ ‡ 1.5 HOURS‡ 1970-71‡ QUALITY
  EXCELLENT‡ UCLA‡ ‡ ‡ ‡ DANCE-POPULAR-CONGOLESE,
  MUSIC-POPULAR-CONGOLESE

KOECHLIN, B.
  KOECHLIN, B.‡ ‡ MALAGASY REPUBLIC‡ ‡ MAHAFALY,
  MASIKORO, VEZO‡ ‡ 1967-69‡ ‡ MUSEE DE L'HOMME‡ ‡ ‡
  ‡ ACCORDION, CANTE-FABLE, ETHNOGRAPHY, POSSESSION,
  XYLOPHONE, ZITHER

KOIZUMI, FUMIO
  KOIZUMI, FUMIO‡ SAKURADAI 1-43, NERIMA, TOKYO,
  JAPAN‡ ETHIOPIA‡ ADDIS ABABA‡ AMHARA‡ 8 HOURS‡
  1971‡ QUALITY GOOD‡ ‡ ‡ ‡ ‡ HISTORY, ORAL-DATA,
  RITUAL

  KOIZUMI, FUMIO‡ SAKURADAI 1-43, NERIMA, TOKYO,
  JAPAN‡ NIGERIA‡ IKORODU‡ YORUBA‡ 1 HOUR‡ 1971‡
  QUALITY GOOD‡ ‡ ‡ ‡ ‡ ORAL-DATA, RITUAL, SOCIAL

  KOIZUMI, FUMIO‡ SAKURADAI 1-43, NERIMA, TOKYO,
  JAPAN‡ SENEGAL‡ DAKAR‡ ‡ 2 HOURS‡ 1971‡ QUALITY
  GOOD‡ ‡ ‡ ‡ ‡ GAME, HISTORY, ORAL-DATA

  KOIZUMI, FUMIO‡ SAKURADAI 1-43, NERIMA, TOKYO,
  JAPAN‡ TANZANIA‡ DAR-ES-SALAAM‡ ‡ 3 HOURS‡ 1971‡
  QUALITY GOOD‡ ‡ ‡ ‡ ‡ GAME, ORAL-DATA, SOCIAL

KONINKLIJK INSTITUUT
  KONINKLIJK INSTITUUT‡ KONINKLIJK INSTITUUT VOOR
  DE TROPEN AFDELING CULTURELE EN PHYSISCHE
  ANTHROPOLOGIE, LINNAEUSSTRAAT 2A, AMSTERDAM,
  NETHERLANDS‡ UPPER VOLTA‡ TOMA‡ SAMO‡ 20 HOURS‡ ‡
  ‡ KONINKLIJK INSTITUUT‡ ‡ ‡ ‡

KONINKLIJK INSTITUUT VOOR
  KONINKLIJK INSTITUUT VOOR DE TROPEN AFDELING
  CULTURELE EN PHYSISCHE ANTHROPOLOGIE‡
  LINNAEUSSTRAAT 2A, AMSTERDAM, NETHERLANDS‡ ‡ ‡ ‡ ‡

KONINKLIJK INSTITUUT VOOR
  ‡ ‡ ‡ ‡ ‡

KRAJEWSKI, F. JOSEPH
  KRAJEWSKI, F. JOSEPH‡ 22 BROOKSIDE AVENUE,
  WINCHESTER, MASSACHUSETTS 01890‡ MALAWI‡ MCHINJI
  DISTRICT‡ NYANJA‡ .5 HOUR‡ 1967‡ QUALITY GOOD‡ ‡ ‡
  ‡ ‡ KALIMBA

KRIEL, A.P.
  KRIEL, A.P.‡ DEPARTMENT OF BANTU LANGUAGES,
  FACULTY OF ARTS, UNIVERSITY OF FORT HARE, PRIVATE
  BAG 314, ALICE, CAPE PROVINCE, SOUTH AFRICA‡
  RHODESIA‡ MORGENSTER MISSION‡ KARANGA, SHONA‡ 40
  HOURS‡ 1966‡ QUALITY GOOD‡ DEPARTMENT OF AFRICAN
  LANGUAGES, UNIVERSITY OF CAPE TOWN‡ ‡ ‡ ‡
  FOLKTALE

  KRIEL, A.P.‡ DEPARTMENT OF BANTU LANGUAGES,
  FACULTY OF ARTS, UNIVERSITY OF FORT HARE, PRIVATE
  BAG 314, ALICE, CAPE PROVINCE, SOUTH AFRICA‡
  SOUTH AFRICA‡ DURBAN‡ XHOSA, ZULU‡ 70 HOURS‡ 1973‡
  QUALITY GOOD‡ ‡ ‡ ‡ ‡ FOLKTALE

KROTKI, KAROL JOSEF
  KROTKI, KAROL JOSEF‡ DEPARTMENT OF SOCIOLOGY,
  UNIVERSITY OF ALBERTA, EDMONTON, ALBERTA, CANADA
  T6G 2E‡ MOROCCO‡ ‡ ‡ 200 HOURS‡ 1971‡ QUALITY
  FAIR‡ ‡ ‡ ‡ ‡ CENSUS-INTERVIEW

KUBIK, GERHARD
  KUBIK, GERHARD‡ THALHAIMERGASSE 48/40, A-1160
  VIENNA, AUSTRIA‡ AFRICA-ANGOLA, CAMEROON, CENTRAL
  AFRICAN REPUBLIC, CONGO-PEOPLE'S REPUBLIC OF THE,
  EGYPT, GABON, KENYA, MALAWI, MOZAMBIQUE, NIGERIA,
  SUDAN, TANZANIA, TOGO, UGANDA, ZAIRE, ZAMBIA‡ ‡ ‡
  800 HOURS‡ 1959-73‡ QUALITY GOOD‡
  PHONOGRAMMARCHIV DER OESTERREICHISCHEN‡ ‡ ‡ ‡
  DANCE, HISTORY, RIDDLE, SOCIAL

  KUBIK, GERHARD‡ THALHAIMERGASSE 48/40, VIENNA,
  AUSTRIA‡ CENTRAL AFRICAN REPUBLIC‡ ‡ NZAKARA,
  ZANDE‡ ‡ ‡ ‡ MUSEE DE L'HOMME‡ ‡ ‡ ‡

KULP, PHILIP M.
  KULP, PHILIP M.‡ DEPARTMENT OF SOCIOLOGY, BOX 277,
  SHIPPENSBURG STATE COLLEGE, SHIPPENSBURG,
  PENNSYLVANIA 17257‡ NIGERIA‡ NORTHEAST‡ BURA‡ 2
  HOURS‡ 1973‡ QUALITY FAIR‡ ‡ ‡ ‡ ‡

KULP, PHILIP M.
  CHILDREN-SCHOOL, DANCE, DRUM-LANGUAGE, RELIGIOUS

LA PIN, DIERDRE A.
  LA PIN, DIERDRE A.‡ INSTITUTE OF AFRICAN STUDIES,
  UNIVERSITY OF IBADAN, IBADAN, NIGERIA‡ NIGERIA‡
  IBADAN, ILESHA, LAGOS‡ YORUBA‡ 3 HOURS‡ 1972-73‡
  QUALITY GOOD‡ ‡ ‡ ‡ ‡ FOLKTALE, HISTORY

LAADE, WOLFGANG KARL
  LAADE, WOLFGANG KARL‡ HOLZMOOSRUTISTRASSE 11,
  CH-8820 WADENSWIL, SWITZERLAND‡ TUNISIA‡ ‡ ARAB,
  BERBER, JEW‡ 70 HOURS‡ 1960‡ QUALITY GOOD‡
  MUSIKETHNOLOGISCHE ABTEILUNG, VOLKERKUNDEMUSEUM
  BERLIN‡ ‡ ‡ ‡ KORAN-RECITATION, MARRIAGE,
  MUSIC-ART-ARAB-ANDALUSIAN, POETRY,
  RELIGIOUS-ISLAMIC, RELIGIOUS-JEWISH

LAMAN, K.E.
  LAMAN, K.E.‡ ‡ ZAIRE‡ MADZIA‡ BAKONGO‡ .5 HOUR‡
  1911‡ QUALITY FAIR‡ ARCHIVES OF TRADITIONAL MUSIC‡
  59-002-F‡ ATL 1756‡ RESTRICTED‡ CURING, DANCE,
  DEATH-MOURNING, WORK-FIELD

LAMBRECHT, DORA J.M.
  LAMBRECHT, FRANK L.+ LAMBRECHT, DORA J.M.‡ WORLD
  HEALTH ORGANIZATION, P.O. BOX 104, ENUGU, NIGERIA‡
  BOTSWANA‡ NGAMILAND‡ KUNG-BUSHMEN, YEI‡ 5 HOURS‡
  1967-68‡ QUALITY GOOD‡ ARCHIVES OF TRADITIONAL
  MUSIC‡ 68-209-F‡ ‡ ‡ CHILDREN, CHILDREN-SCHOOL,
  LIKEMBE, STICK-SCRAPED

LAMBRECHT, FRANK L.
  LAMBRECHT, FRANK L.+ LAMBRECHT, DORA J.M.‡ WORLD
  HEALTH ORGANIZATION, P.O. BOX 104, ENUGU, NIGERIA‡
  BOTSWANA‡ NGAMILAND‡ KUNG-BUSHMEN, YEI‡ 5 HOURS‡
  1967-68‡ QUALITY GOOD‡ ARCHIVES OF TRADITIONAL
  MUSIC‡ 68-209-F‡ ‡ ‡ CHILDREN, CHILDREN-SCHOOL,
  LIKEMBE, STICK-SCRAPED

LANGE, WERNER
  LANGE, WERNER‡ 6 FRANKFURT/MAIN, LIEBIGSTRASSE 41,
  FEDERAL REPUBLIC OF GERMANY‡ ETHIOPIA‡ SOUTHWEST
  ETHIOPIA‡ BENS, BOSA, CARA, HINNARIO, KAFA, MERU,
  NA'O, SE, SEKA, SHE, ZARAS‡ 4 HOURS‡ 1972-73‡
  QUALITY FAIR‡ FROBENIUS INSTITUTE‡ ‡ ‡ ‡
  DEATH-FUNERAL, HISTORY, MARRIAGE, WORK

LANGUAGE LABORATORY, UNIV
  LANGUAGE LABORATORY, UNIVERSITY OF WISCONSIN‡
  MADISON, WISCONSIN, USA 53705‡ ‡ ‡ ‡ ‡ ‡ ‡ ‡ ‡ ‡

LANGWORTHY, HARRY W.
  LANGWORTHY, HARRY W.‡ HISTORY DEPARTMENT,
  CLEVELAND STATE UNIVERSITY, CLEVELAND, OHIO 44115‡
  ZAMBIA‡ EASTERN PROVINCE‡ CHEWA‡ 30 HOURS‡ 1964‡
  QUALITY FAIR‡ ‡ ‡ ‡ HISTORY

LARSON, THOMAS J.
  LARSON, THOMAS J.‡ 6315 CAVALIER CORRIDOR, FALLS
  CHURCH, VIRGINIA 22044‡ BOTSWANA‡ OKAVANGO‡
  HAMBUKUSU‡ 9 HOURS‡ 1972‡ QUALITY EXCELLENT‡ ‡ ‡ ‡
  ‡ RITUAL, SOCIAL

LAUER, JOSEPH JEROME
  LAUER, JOSEPH JEROME‡ 3001 WEST BELTLINE HIGHWAY,
  APT. 11, MADISON, WISCONSIN 53713‡ IVORY COAST‡
  GUIGLO‡ GUERE‡ 5 HOURS‡ 1971‡ QUALITY FAIR‡ ‡ ‡ ‡
  ‡ HISTORY

LEMMA, TESFAYE
  LEMMA, TESFAYE‡ ORCHESTRA ETHIOPIA, BOX 30186,
  ADDIS ABABA, ETHIOPIA‡ ETHIOPIA‡ ADDIS ABABA‡ ‡ 2
  HOURS‡ 1970‡ QUALITY GOOD‡ ARCHIVES OF
  TRADITIONAL MUSIC‡ 72-085-F‡ ATL 4649‡ RESTRICTED‡
  LUTE-BOWED-MASENQO, LYRE-KRAR, MARRIAGE, WORK

LESLAU, WOLF
  LESLAU, WOLF‡ DEPARTMENT OF NEAR EASTERN
  LANGUAGES, UCLA, 405 HILGARD AVENUE, LOS ANGELES,
  CALIFORNIA 90024‡ ETHIOPIA‡ ASMARA, DIREDSA‡
  AMHARA, GURAGE, HARARI, SHOA-GALLA, SOMALI,
  TIGRINYA‡ 3.5 HOURS‡ 1947‡ QUALITY FAIR‡ ARCHIVES
  OF TRADITIONAL MUSIC‡ PRE'54-002-F‡ ATL 362-69‡
  RESTRICTED‡ AEROPHONE, CHORDOPHONE,
  DANCE-MARRIAGE, DRUM, FLUTE, FOLKTALE,
  HANDCLAPPING, LITURGY, PRAISE, RELIGIOUS-ISLAMIC,
  WAR, WORD-LIST-AMHARIC, WORD-LIST-HARARI,
  XYLOPHONE

  LESLAU, WOLF‡ DEPARTMENT OF NEAR EASTERN
  LANGUAGES, UCLA, 405 HILGARD AVENUE, LOS ANGELES,
  CALIFORNIA 90024‡ ETHIOPIA‡ ‡ FALASHA‡ .5 HOUR‡
  CA1947‡ QUALITY FAIR‡ ARCHIVES OF TRADITIONAL
  MUSIC‡ PRE'54-214-F‡ ATL 399‡ RESTRICTED‡
  RELIGIOUS

LESTRANGE, M. DE
  LESTRANGE, M. DE‡ ‡ GUINEA‡ ‡ CONIAGUI‡ ‡ ‡ ‡
  MUSEE DE L'HOMME‡ ‡ ‡ ‡

LEUSCHEL, DON
  LEUSCHEL, DON‡ ‡ ‡ ‡ NDEBELE, ZULU‡ 3 HOURS‡
  1957-58‡ QUALITY GOOD‡ ARCHIVES OF LANGUAGES OF
  THE WORLD‡ ‡ ‡ ‡ GRAMMATICAL-DATA

LEVINE, WILLIAM J.
  LEVINE, WILLIAM J.‡ 354 HAMILTON HALL, UNIVERSITY
  OF NORTH CAROLINA, CHAPEL HILL, NORTH CAROLINA
  27514‡ SOMALIA‡ BURAO‡ SOMALI‡ 1 HOUR‡ 1962‡
  QUALITY POOR‡ ‡ ‡ ‡ POLITICAL

LEWIS, HERBERT S.
  LEWIS, HERBERT S.‡ DEPARTMENT OF ANTHROPOLOGY,
  UNIVERSITY OF WISCONSIN, MADISON, WISCONSIN 53706‡
  ETHIOPIA‡ SHOA‡ GALLA‡ 15 HOURS‡ 1965-66‡ QUALITY
  GOOD‡ ‡ ‡ ‡ PRAISE, PRAYER, RELIGIOUS, RITUAL,
  WORK

LHOTE, HENRI JACQUES
  LHOTE, HENRI JACQUES‡ 11 RUE DE L'ARC DE TRIOMPHE,
  75017 PARIS, FRANCE‡ ‡ HAGGAR‡ TUAREG‡ ‡ ‡
  QUALITY GOOD‡ MUSEE DE L'HOMME‡ ‡ ‡ ‡

LILLIEBJERG, HANNE
  BENTHIEN, CLAUS+ LILLIEBJERG, HANNE+ WICHMANN,
  ERIK‡ ‡ MOROCCO‡ KENITRA, MARRAKECH, MOULAY IDRIS‡
  ‡ ‡ 1967‡ ‡ DANSK FOLKEMINDESAMLING‡ 67/1A-13A‡ ‡
  ‡

  BENTHIEN, CLAUS+ LILLIEBJERG, HANNE+ WICHMANN,
  ERIK‡ ‡ TUNISIA‡ BIZERTE, NEFTA‡ ‡ ‡ 1967‡ ‡
  DANSK FOLKEMINDESAMLING‡ 67/13A-16A‡ ‡ ‡

LIMA, AUGUSTO GUILHERME M
  LIMA, AUGUSTO GUILHERME MESQUITELA‡ P.B. 1267
  MUSEUM DE ANGOLA, LUANDA, ANGOLA‡ ANGOLA‡
  CUANDO-CUBANGO, LUNDA‡ BUSHMEN, CHOKWE, NGANGELA‡
  25 HOURS‡ 1963-70‡ QUALITY GOOD‡ ‡ ‡ ‡ ‡ HISTORY,
  RITUAL, SOCIAL

LINENBRUEGGE, GERTRUDE R.
  LINENBRUEGGE, GERTRUDE R.I.‡ OHIO UNIVERSITY
  LIBRARY, ATHENS, OHIO 45701‡ NIGERIA‡ IBADAN‡ IBO‡
  .5 HOUR‡ 1966‡ QUALITY POOR‡ ‡ ‡ ‡ ‡ NAMING

LINGUISTICS AND AFRICAN L
  LINGUISTICS AND AFRICAN LANGUAGES, MAKERERE
  UNIVERSITY‡ P.O. BOX 7062, KAMPALA, UGANDA‡ ‡ ‡ ‡
  ‡ ‡ ‡ ‡ ‡ ‡ ‡

LISZKA, STANLEY WALTER, J
  LISZKA, STANLEY WALTER, JR.‡ DEPARTMENT OF
  HISTORY, ST. CLOUD STATE COLLEGE, ST. CLOUD,
  MINNESOTA 56301‡ KENYA‡ TAITA DISTRICT‡ TAITA‡
  144 HOURS‡ 1972-74‡ QUALITY EXCELLENT‡ ‡ ‡ ‡ ‡
  HISTORY

LIVINGSTONE MUSEUM
  LIVINGSTONE MUSEUM‡ P.O. BOX 498, LIVINGSTON,
  ZAMBIA‡ ‡ ‡ ‡ ‡ ‡ ‡ ‡ ‡ ‡

  LIVINGSTONE MUSEUM‡ P.O. BOX 498, LIVINGSTONE,
  ZAMBIA‡ ZAMBIA‡ ‡ LEYA-SUBIYA‡ 2 HOURS‡ ‡ ‡
  LIVINGSTONE MUSEUM‡ ‡ ‡ ‡ HISTORY

LLOYD, DAVID TYRRELL
  LLOYD, DAVID TYRRELL‡ DEPARTMENT OF HISTORY, UCLA,
  LOS ANGELES, CALIFORNIA‡ ZAIRE‡ REGION DU
  HAUT-ZAIRE‡ AZANDE‡ 150 HOURS‡ 1973‡ QUALITY
  EXCELLENT‡ CENTRE DE RECHERCHES
  INTERDISCIPLINAIRES, DEVELOPPEMENT DE L'EDUCATION,
  UNIVERSITE NATIONALE DU ZAIRE‡ ‡ ‡ ‡ HISTORY,
  HISTORY-ECONOMIC

LOMBARD, JACQUES
  LOMBARD, JACQUES‡ 122 RUE ST. CHARLES, 75015
  PARIS, FRANCE‡ MALAGASY REPUBLIC‡ COTE OUEST‡
  SAKALAVA‡ 200 HOURS‡ 1969-74‡ QUALITY GOOD‡
  CENTRE D'ETUDES DE TRADITION ORAL‡ ‡ ‡ ‡ FOLKLORE,
  HISTORY, POETRY, RITUAL

LONG, RONALD W.
  LONG, RONALD W.‡ 515-36TH STREET, WEST PALM BEACH,
  FLORIDA 33407‡ GHANA‡ ‡ MANDE‡ 40 HOURS‡ 1968‡
  QUALITY FAIR‡ SCHOOL OF ORIENTAL AND AFRICAN
  STUDIES‡ ‡ ‡ ‡ WORD-LIST

  LONG, RONALD W.‡ 515-36TH STREET, WEST PALM BEACH,
  FLORIDA 33407‡ UPPER VOLTA‡ ‡ MANDE‡ 40 HOURS‡
  1968‡ QUALITY FAIR‡ SCHOOL OF ORIENTAL AND
  AFRICAN STUDIES‡ ‡ ‡ ‡ WORD-LIST

LORELLE, -
  LORELLE, -‡ ‡ NIGER‡ ‡ MADURI‡ ‡ ‡ ‡ MUSEE DE

LORELLE, -
  L'HOMME‡ ‡ ‡ ‡

LORTAT-JACOB, BERNARD
  LORTAT-JACOB, BERNARD‡ PALAIS DE CHAILLOT, PLACE
  DU TROCADERO, 75116 PARIS, FRANCE‡ ETHIOPIA‡
  GAMO-GOFA‡ DORZE‡ 7 HOURS‡ 1974-75‡ QUALITY
  EXCELLENT‡ MUSEE DE L'HOMME‡ ‡ ‡ ‡ ENTERTAINMENT,
  HISTORY, LULLABY, LYRE, RITUAL, WORK

  LORTAT-JACOB, BERNARD‡ PALAIS DE CHAILLOT, PLACE
  DU TROCADERO, 75116 PARIS, FRANCE‡ MOROCCO‡ HIGH
  ATLAS‡ AIT-MGOUN‡ ‡ 1969‡ ‡ MUSEE DE L'HOMME‡ ‡ ‡
  ‡ CIRCUMCISION, MARRIAGE

  LORTAT-JACOB, BERNARD‡ PALAIS DE CHAILLOT, PLACE
  DU TROCADERO, 75116 PARIS, FRANCE‡ MOROCCO‡ ‡
  AIT-MGOUN‡ ‡ 1970‡ ‡ MUSEE DE L'HOMME‡ ‡ ‡ ‡
  DANCE-MARRIAGE, FESTIVAL, SHEEP-SHEARING, WORK,
  WORK-GRINDING, WORK-HARVEST

  LORTAT-JACOB, BERNARD‡ PALAIS DE CHAILLOT, PLACE
  DU TROCADERO, 75116 PARIS, FRANCE‡ MOROCCO‡ ‡
  BERBER, TAMAZIGT, TASLHIT‡ 35 HOURS‡ 1969-73‡
  QUALITY EXCELLENT‡ MUSEE DE L'HOMME+ INSTITUTE OF
  ETHNOMUSICOLOGY, UCLA‡ ‡ ‡ ‡ MUSIC-ART, SOCIAL

  LORTAT-JACOB, BERNARD‡ PALAIS DE CHAILLOT, PLACE
  DU TROCADERO, 75116 PARIS, FRANCE‡ MOROCCO‡
  CENTRAL HIGH ATLAS‡ AIT-BOUGMEZ, FTOUKA‡ 40 HOURS‡
  1971‡ ‡ MUSEE DE L'HOMME‡ ‡ ‡ ‡ DANCE, DRUM,
  MUSICIAN, POETRY

LOUDON, JOSEPH BUIST
  LOUDON, JOSEPH BUIST‡ DEPARTMENT OF
  SOCIOLOGY/ANTHROPOLOGY, UNIVERSITY COLLEGE OF
  SWANSEA, SWANSEA SA2 8PP, WALES‡ SOUTH AFRICA‡
  NATAL‡ ZULU‡ 1.5 HOURS‡ 1952‡ QUALITY FAIR‡ ‡ ‡ ‡
  ‡ SOCIAL

  LOUDON, JOSEPH BUIST‡ DEPARTMENT OF
  SOCIOLOGY/ANTHROPOLOGY, UNIVERSITY COLLEGE OF
  SWANSEA, SWANSEA SA2 8PP, WALES‡ TRISTAN DA CUNHA‡
  ‡ ‡ 2.5 HOURS‡ 1963-64‡ QUALITY FAIR‡ ‡ ‡ ‡ ‡
  SOCIAL

LOWIE MUSEUM OF ANTHROPOL
  LOWIE MUSEUM OF ANTHROPOLOGY, UNIVERSITY OF
  CALIFORNIA, BERKELEY‡ KROEBER HALL, BERKELEY,

LOWIE MUSEUM OF ANTHROPOL
  CALIFORNIA 94720‡ ‡ ‡ ‡ ‡ ‡ ‡ ‡ ‡ ‡

LUCKAU, STEPHEN R.
  LUCKAU, STEPHEN R.‡ 1066 EAST SEVENTH SOUTH, SALT
  LAKE CITY, UTAH 84102‡ LIBERIA‡ FISHTOWN, NIMIAH‡
  GREBO, JABO‡ 2 HOURS‡ 1971‡ QUALITY EXCELLENT‡ ‡ ‡
  ‡ ‡ HISTORY, HYMN, PROVERB, SPEECH

MAALU-BUNGI
  MAALU-BUNGI‡ UNIVERSITE NATIONALE DU ZAIRE, B.P.
  1025, LUBUMBASHI, ZAIRE‡ ZAIRE‡ LUBUMBASHI,
  MIKALAYI‡ LULUA‡ 12.5 HOURS‡ 1969‡ 1972‡ 1973‡
  QUALITY GOOD‡ ‡ ‡ ‡ ‡ FOLKTALE

MACDONALD, RODERICK JAMES
  MACDONALD, RODERICK JAMES‡ PROGRAM OF EASTERN
  AFRICAN STUDIES, SYRACUSE UNIVERSITY, 119 COLLEGE
  PLACE, SYRACUSE, NEW YORK 13210‡ MALAWI‡ ‡ ‡ 20
  HOURS‡ 1966-67‡ QUALITY GOOD‡ ‡ ‡ ‡ ‡
  HISTORY-COLONIAL, HISTORY-EDUCATION,
  HISTORY-NATIONALISM

MACGAFFEY, WYATT
  MACGAFFEY, WYATT‡ HAVERFORD COLLEGE, HAVERFORD,
  PENNSYLVANIA 19041‡ ZAIRE‡ LOWER ZAIRE‡ KONGO‡ 10
  HOURS‡ 1970‡ QUALITY GOOD‡ ‡ ‡ ‡ ‡ RELIGIOUS

MADIGAN, BOB
  MADIGAN, BOB‡ ‡ KENYA‡ MACHAKOS‡ KAMBA‡ 7 HOURS‡
  1957-58‡ QUALITY GOOD‡ ARCHIVES OF LANGUAGES OF
  THE WORLD‡ ‡ ‡ ‡ GRAMMATICAL-DATA, HERDING,
  SOCIAL-FAMILY-LIFE, TRADE-VILLAGE

MAGYAR TUDOMANYOS AKADEMI
  MAGYAR TUDOMANYOS AKADEMIA NEPZENEKUTATO CSOPORT‡
  1014 BUDAPEST I, URI U. 49, HUNGARY‡ ‡ ‡ ‡.‡ ‡ ‡ ‡
  ‡ ‡ ‡

  MAGYAR TUDOMANYOS AKADEMIA NEPZENEKUTATO CSOPORT‡
  1014 BUDAPEST 1, URI U. 49, HUNGARY‡ EGYPT‡ ‡
  COPT, FELLAHIN, NUBIAN‡ 50 HOURS‡ 1966-67 ‡ 1969‡
  ‡ MAGYAR TUDOMANYOS AKADEMIA NEPZENEKUTATO
  CSOPORT‡ ‡ ‡ ‡ DRUM, FLUTE, RELIGIOUS-COPTIC,
  RITUAL

  MAGYAR TUDOMANYOS AKADEMIA NEPZENEKUTATO CSOPORT‡
  1014 BUDAPEST 1, URI U. 49, HUNGARY‡ ETHIOPIA‡ ‡
  AMHARA, GALLA, KAFFICHO, KULLO, TIGRE‡ 10 HOURS‡ ‡

MAGYAR TUDOMANYOS AKADEMI
  ‡ MAGYAR TUDOMANYOS AKADEMIA NEPZENEKUTATO
  CSOPORT‡ ‡ ‡ ‡ FOLKLORE

MAKERERE UNIVERSITY
  MAKERERE UNIVERSITY‡ P.O. BOX 7062, KAMPALA,
  UGANDA‡ ‡ ‡ ‡ ‡ ‡ ‡ ‡ ‡ ‡

MAKERERE UNIVERSITY LIBRA
  MAKERERE UNIVERSITY LIBRARY‡ P.O. BOX 7062,
  KAMPALA, UGANDA‡ ‡ ‡ ‡ ‡ ‡ ‡ ‡ ‡ ‡

MALER, THOMAS A.
  MALER, THOMAS A.‡ 2401 REINSBEK, EICHENWEG 8,
  FEDERAL REPUBLIC OF GERMANY‡ TANZANIA‡ MBULU,
  TANGA/BWITI, TANGA/GOMBERO, TANGA/MARAMBA‡ DIGO,
  GIRYAMA, MAKONDE, TINDIGA‡ 28 HOURS‡ 1967-68‡
  QUALITY EXCELLENT‡ ‡ ‡ ‡ ‡ HISTORY, INITIATION,
  LOVE, RITUAL-HEALING-HYPNOSIS

MANN, WILLIAM MICHAEL
  MANN, WILLIAM MICHAEL‡ SCHOOL OF ORIENTAL AND
  AFRICAN STUDIES, MALET STREET, LONDON WC1E 7HP,
  ENGLAND‡ ZAMBIA‡ LUANGWA VALLEY, NORTHERN
  PROVINCE‡ BEMBA, BISA‡ 75 HOURS‡ 1967‡ QUALITY
  GOOD‡ ‡ ‡ ‡ ‡ HUNTING, MUSICIAN, SOCIAL

MAPOMA, ISAIAH MWESA
  MAPOMA, ISAIAH MWESA‡ INSTITUTE OF AFRICAN
  STUDIES, UNIVERSITY OF ZAMBIA, P.O. BOX 900,
  LUSAKA, ZAMBIA‡ ZAMBIA‡ LUAPULA, NORTHERN
  PROVINCES‡ BEMBA‡ 45 HOURS‡ 1968-70+ 1973‡
  QUALITY EXCELLENT‡ ‡ ‡ ‡ ‡ DEATH-FUNERAL, HISTORY,
  PRAISE, RITUAL, ROYAL, SOCIAL

MARAIRE, DUMISANI ABRAHAM
  MARAIRE, DUMISANI ABRAHAM‡ THE EVERGREEN STATE
  COLLEGE, UNIVERSITY OF WASHINGTON, OLYMPIA,
  WASHINGTON 98505‡ RHODESIA‡ MANYIKA, NDAU, ZEZURU‡
  SHONA‡ 10 HOURS‡ 1971+ 1974‡ QUALITY GOOD‡ THE
  EVERGREEN STATE COLLEGE, UNIVERSITY OF WASHINGTON‡
  ‡ ‡ ‡ HISTORY, PRAISE-POETRY, RITUAL, SOCIAL

MARING, JOEL
  MARING, JOEL‡ LINGUISTICS DEPARTMENT, SOUTHERN
  ILLINOIS UNIVERSITY, CARBONDALE, ILLINOIS 62901‡
  LIBERIA‡ ‡ EBURNEO-LIBERIEN, GREBO‡ 3 HOURS‡ 1958‡
  QUALITY GOOD‡ ARCHIVES OF LANGUAGES OF THE WORLD‡
  ‡ ‡ ‡ GRAMMATICAL-DATA

MARING, JOEL
  MARING, JOEL‡ LINGUISTICS DEPARTMENT, SOUTHERN
  ILLINOIS UNIVERSITY, CARBONDALE, ILLINOIS 62901‡
  SOMALIA‡ MOGADISHU‡ SOMALI‡ 1 HOUR‡ 1959‡ QUALITY
  GOOD‡ ARCHIVES OF LANGUAGES OF THE WORLD‡ ‡ ‡ ‡
  GRAMMATICAL-DATA-SOMALI

MARSHALL EXPEDITION PANHA
  MARSHALL EXPEDITION PANHARD-CAPRICORNE‡ ‡ SOUTH
  AFRICA‡ ‡ BUSHMEN‡ ‡ ‡ ‡ MUSEE DE L'HOMME‡ ‡ ‡ ‡

MARTIN, JANE JACKSON
  MARTIN, JANE JACKSON‡ COLLEGE OF LIBERAL AND FINE
  ARTS, UNIVERSITY OF LIBERIA, MONROVIA, LIBERIA‡
  LIBERIA‡ CAVALLA‡ GREBO‡ 6 HOURS‡ 1968‡ 1972-75‡
  QUALITY GOOD‡ ‡ ‡ ‡ ‡ BIOGRAPHY, DRUM, HISTORY,
  MUSIC

MASSING, ANDREAS
  MASSING, ANDREAS‡ 6078 NEU-ISENBERG, 152
  FRIEDENSALLEE, WEST GERMANY‡ LIBERIA‡ DODWIEKEN,
  JOANYE, KABADA, KELO TOWN, KITATUSON, KUNWEA,
  MONROVIA, PANAMA, TUBMANVILLE, WCLEWONKEN‡ KRU‡
  10 HOURS‡ 1971-72‡ QUALITY GOOD‡ CENTER FOR
  AFRICAN ORAL DATA‡ 72-079-F‡ ATL 5282-91‡
  RESTRICTED‡ ENTERTAINMENT, HISTORY,
  RELIGIOUS-CHRISTIAN, WORD-LIST, WORK-FIELD

MATTNER, -
  MATTNER, -‡ ‡ TANZANIA‡ ‡ ‡ .1 HOUR‡ 1909‡
  QUALITY FAIR‡ ARCHIVES OF TRADITIONAL MUSIC‡
  59-002-F‡ ATL 1758‡ RESTRICTED‡ DANCE

MCLEAN, DAVID A.
  MCLEAN, DAVID A.‡ ST. ANDREWS COLLEGE, LAURINBURG,
  NORTH CAROLINA 28352‡ ZAIRE‡ KANANGA, KASAI‡ LUBA‡
  5 HOURS‡ 1954-61‡ QUALITY FAIR‡ ‡ ‡ ‡ ‡
  DIVINING-INTERVIEW

MCLEOD, NORMA
  MCLEOD, NORMA‡ 2619 PEMBROOK TRAIL, AUSTIN, TEXAS‡
  MALAGASY REPUBLIC‡ ‡ ‡ 56 HOURS‡ 1962-63‡ QUALITY
  EXCELLENT‡ ‡ ‡ ‡ ‡ FOLKLORE, HISTORY,
  PRAISE-POETRY, RITUAL, SOCIAL

MEINHOF, CARL
  MEINHOF, CARL‡ ‡ TANZANIA‡ ‡ BONDEI‡ .1 HOUR‡
  1902-03‡ QUALITY FAIR‡ ARCHIVES OF TRADITIONAL
  MUSIC‡ 59-002-F‡ ATL 1757‡ RESTRICTED‡ XYLOPHONE

MENSAH, ATTAH
  MENSAH, ATTAH+ GILLIS, FRANK J.‡ UNIVERSITY OF
  GHANA, LEGON, GHANA+ ARCHIVES OF TRADITIONAL
  MUSIC, INDIANA UNIVERSITY, BLOOMINGTON, INDIANA
  47401‡ ZAMBIA-U.S.‡ BLOOMINGTON, INDIANA‡ ‡ 2
  HOURS‡ 1970‡ QUALITY EXCELLENT‡ ARCHIVES OF
  TRADITIONAL MUSIC‡ 70-087-F‡ ATL 4273-74‡
  RESTRICTED‡ MUSIC-LECTURE

MERRIAM, ALAN P.
  MERRIAM, ALAN P.+ MERRIAM, BARBARA W.‡
  ANTHROPOLOGY DEPARTMENT, INDIANA UNIVERSITY,
  BLOOMINGTON, INDIANA 47401‡ BURUNDI ‡ KAYANZA,
  KITEGA, KIVIMBA, NYANKANDO, RUBURA‡ ABATUTSI,
  BARUNDI, BATWA‡ 6 HOURS‡ 1951-52‡ QUALITY
  EXCELLENT‡ ARCHIVES OF TRADITIONAL MUSIC‡
  66-127-F‡ ATL 4490-527‡ RESTRICTED‡ BOASTING,
  BOW-MUSICAL, DRINKING, DRUM-NGOMA, FLUTE-VERTICAL,
  GREETING, HERDING, HORN-ANTELOPE, HORN-GOURD,
  LUTE-BOWED, MARRIAGE, PRAISE, SOCIAL,
  ZITHER-TROUGH

  MERRIAM, ALAN P.+ MERRIAM, BARBARA W.‡
  ANTHROPOLOGY DEPARTMENT, INDIANA UNIVERSITY,
  BLOOMINGTON, INDIANA 47401‡ RWANDA‡ BUGESERA,
  GITWE, KABGAYE, KIGALI, KANSI, KAYANZA,
  KIBUGABUGA, KIDAHO, KISENYI, KIVIMBA, LAKE
  MUGESERA, MUGOTE, NKURI, NYAGATARE, NYAMATA,
  NYANZA, NYARUBUYE, RUBURA, RUHENGERI‡ ABAGOGWE,
  ABAGOYI, ABAHORORO, ABANYAMBO, ABATUTSI, ABAYOVU,
  BAHIMA, BAHUTU, BAKIGA, BATWA‡ 17 HOURS‡ 1951-52‡
  QUALITY EXCELLENT‡ ARCHIVES OF TRADITIONAL MUSIC‡
  66-127-F‡ ATL 4490-527‡ RESTRICTED‡ BOASTING,
  BOW-MUSICAL, DRUM-NGOMA, FLUTE-VERTICAL, GREETING,
  HERDING, HORN-TRANSVERSE, HOUSE-NEW, MARRIAGE,
  PRAISE, SOCIAL, ZITHER-TROUGH

  MERRIAM, ALAN P.+ MERRIAM, BARBARA W.‡
  ANTHROPOLOGY DEPARTMENT, INDIANA UNIVERSITY,
  BLOOMINGTON, INDIANA 47401‡ ZAIRE‡ BOGORO, CAMP
  PUTNAM, KASHEKE, KADJUJU, IBOKO, LWIRO, MABINZA
  BAY, MOHELI, MPAPOLI‡ BAHIMA, BAKOGA, BAKONGO,
  BAMBUTI, BANGALA, BASHI, BATWA, EKONDA‡ 15 HOURS‡
  1951-52‡ QUALITY EXCELLENT‡ ARCHIVES OF
  TRADITIONAL MUSIC‡ 66-127-F‡ ATL 4490-527‡
  RESTRICTED‡ AEROPHONE-POT, BELL, BOASTING,
  BOW-MUSICAL, CARRYING-GOODS, CEREMONY, CHILDREN,
  CHILDREN-TWINS, DANCE, DEATH, DRINKING,
  DRUM-LOMONDA, DRUM-NGOMA, DRUM-SINGLE-HEADED,

MERRIAM, ALAN P.
  DRUM-SLIT, DRUM-TAMBU, FLUTE-VERTICAL, GUITAR,
  HARP, HERDING, HERDING-MILKING, HORN-TRANSVERSE,
  IDIOPHONE-PLUCKED-KASAYI, LIKEMBE, LULLABY, LUTE,
  LUTE-BOWED, LUTE-PLUCKED, LYRE-BOWL, MARKET,
  MARRIAGE, PADDLING, POLITICAL, RATTLE, SERENADE,
  SOCIAL, SORCERER, SPIRIT-SUPPLICATION,
  STICK-SCRAPED, WAR, WORK, ZITHER-STICK,
  ZITHER-TROUGH

  MERRIAM, ALAN P.+ MERRIAM, BARBARA W.‡
  ANTHROPOLOGY DEPARTMENT, INDIANA UNIVERSITY,
  BLOOMINGTON, INDIANA 47401‡ ZAIRE‡ LUPUPA‡
  BASONGYE‡ 7.5 HOURS‡ 1959-60‡ QUALITY EXCELLENT‡
  ARCHIVES OF TRADITIONAL MUSIC‡ 66-128-F‡ ATL
  4399-405‡ RESTRICTED‡ CHILDREN-GAME,
  DEATH-FUNERAL, DRUM-GOBLET, DRUM-SLIT, FERTILITY,
  FOLKTALE, HUNTING, IDIOPHONE-STRUCK, LIKEMBE,
  MUSICIAN, OCARINA, PRAISE-NAME, RATTLE-BASKET,
  SOCIAL, XYLOPHONE

  MERRIAM, ALAN P.‡ DEPARTMENT OF ANTHROPOLOGY,
  INDIANA UNIVERSITY, BLOOMINGTON, INDIANA 47401‡
  ZAIRE‡ LUPUPA‡ BASONGYE‡ 1.5 HOURS‡ 1973‡ QUALITY
  GOOD‡ ARCHIVES OF TRADITIONAL MUSIC‡ 73-054-F‡ ‡
  RESTRICTED‡ ANTHEM-NATIONAL-ZAIRE, CHILDREN,
  DANCE-SOCIAL, DEATH-MOURNING, DRUM-FRICTION,
  DRUM-SLIT-KIYONDO, DRUM-SLIT-LUNKUFI,
  GONG-METAL-DOUBLE, GREETING, HANDCLAPPING,
  IDIOPHONE-IRON, POLITICAL, RATTLE-BASKET,
  RATTLE-CONTAINER, RELIGIOUS-CHRISTIAN, WHISTLE,
  XYLOPHONE, XYLOPHONE-TUNING

MERRIAM, BARBARA W.
  MERRIAM, ALAN P.+ MERRIAM, BARBARA W.‡
  ANTHROPOLOGY DEPARTMENT, INDIANA UNIVERSITY,
  BLOOMINGTON, INDIANA 47401‡ BURUNDI‡ KAYANZA,
  KITEGA, KIVIMBA, NYANKANDO, RUBURA‡ ABATUTSI,
  BARUNDI, BATWA‡ 6 HOURS‡ 1951-52‡ QUALITY
  EXCELLENT‡ ARCHIVES OF TRADITIONAL MUSIC‡
  66-127-F‡ ATL 4490-527‡ RESTRICTED‡ BOASTING,
  BOW-MUSICAL, DRINKING, DRUM-NGOMA, FLUTE-VERTICAL,
  GREETING, HERDING, HORN-ANTELOPE, HORN-GOURD,
  LUTE-BOWED, MARRIAGE, PRAISE, SOCIAL,
  ZITHER-TROUGH

  MERRIAM, ALAN P.+ MERRIAM, BARBARA W.‡
  ANTHROPOLOGY DEPARTMENT, INDIANA UNIVERSITY,
  BLOOMINGTON, INDIANA 47401‡ RWANDA‡ BUGESERA,

MERRIAM, BARBARA W.
GITWE, KABGAYE, KIGALI, KANSI, KAYANZA,
KIBUGABUGA, KIDAHO, KISENYI, KIVIMBA, LAKE
MUGESERA, MUGOTE, NKURI, NYAGATARE, NYAMATA,
NYANZA, NYARUBUYE, RUBURA, RUHENGERI‡ ABAGOGWE,
ABAGOYI, ABAHORORO, ABANYAMBO, ABATUTSI, ABAYOVU,
BAHIMA, BAHUTU, BAKIGA, BATWA‡ 17 HOURS‡ 1951-52‡
QUALITY EXCELLENT‡ ARCHIVES OF TRADITIONAL MUSIC‡
66-127-F‡ ATL 4490-527‡ RESTRICTED‡ BOASTING,
BOW-MUSICAL, DRUM-NGOMA, FLUTE-VERTICAL, GREETING,
HERDING, HORN-TRANSVERSE, HOUSE-NEW, MARRIAGE,
PRAISE, SOCIAL, ZITHER-TROUGH

MERRIAM, ALAN P.+ MERRIAM, BARBARA W.‡
ANTHROPOLOGY DEPARTMENT, INDIANA UNIVERSITY,
BLOOMINGTON, INDIANA 47401‡ ZAIRE‡ BOGORO, CAMP
PUTNAM, KASHEKE, KADJUJU, IBOKO, LWIRO, MABINZA
BAY, MOHELI, MPAPOLI‡ BAHIMA, BAKOGA, BAKONGO,
BAMBUTI, BANGALA, BASHI, BATWA, EKONDA‡ 15 HOURS‡
1951-52‡ QUALITY EXCELLENT‡ ARCHIVES OF
TRADITIONAL MUSIC‡ 66-127-F‡ ATL 4490-527‡
RESTRICTED‡ AEROPHONE-POT, BELL, BOASTING,
BOW-MUSICAL, CARRYING-GOODS, CEREMONY, CHILDREN,
CHILDREN-TWINS, DANCE, DEATH, DRINKING,
DRUM-LOMONDA, DRUM-NGOMA, DRUM-SINGLE-HEADED,
DRUM-SLIT, DRUM-TAMBU, FLUTE-VERTICAL, GUITAR,
HARP, HERDING, HERDING-MILKING, HORN-TRANSVERSE,
IDIOPHONE-PLUCKED-KASAYI, LIKEMBE, LULLABY, LUTE,
LUTE-BOWED, LUTE-PLUCKED, LYRE-BOWL, MARKET,
MARRIAGE, PADDLING, POLITICAL, RATTLE, SERENADE,
SOCIAL, SORCERER, SPIRIT-SUPPLICATION,
STICK-SCRAPED, WAR, WORK, ZITHER-STICK,
ZITHER-TROUGH

MERRIAM, ALAN P.+ MERRIAM, BARBARA W.‡
ANTHROPOLOGY DEPARTMENT, INDIANA UNIVERSITY,
BLOOMINGTON, INDIANA 47401‡ ZAIRE‡ LUPUPA‡
BASONGYE‡ 7.5 HOURS‡ 1959-60‡ QUALITY EXCELLENT‡
ARCHIVES OF TRADITIONAL MUSIC‡ 66-128-F‡ ATL
4399-405‡ RESTRICTED‡ CHILDREN-GAME,
DEATH-FUNERAL, DRUM-GOBLET, DRUM-SLIT, FERTILITY,
FOLKTALE, HUNTING, IDIOPHONE-STRUCK, LIKEMBE,
MUSICIAN, OCARINA, PRAISE-NAME, RATTLE-BASKET,
SOCIAL, XYLOPHONE

MESSING, SIMON D.
MESSING, SIMON D.‡ DEPARTMENT OF ANTHROPOLOGY,
SOUTHERN CONNECTICUT STATE COLLEGE, NEW HAVEN,
CONNECTICUT 06515‡ ETHIOPIA‡ ‡ AMHARA, GALLA,

MESSING, SIMON D.
  TIGRE‡ 15 HOURS‡ 1961-67‡ QUALITY FAIR‡ ‡ ‡ ‡
  ETHNOGRAPHY-SOCIAL

MILLER, JOSEPH C.
  MILLER, JOSEPH C.‡ DEPARTMENT OF HISTORY,
  UNIVERSITY OF VIRGINIA, CHARLOTTESVILLE, VIRGINIA
  22903‡ ANGOLA‡ MALANJE‡ IMBANGALA‡ 21 HOURS‡ 1969‡
  QUALITY GOOD‡ ‡ ‡ ‡ HISTORY-KASANJE

MILWAUKEE PUBLIC MUSEUM
  MILWAUKEE PUBLIC MUSEUM‡ 800 W. WELLS STREET,
  MILWAUKEE, WISCONSIN 53233‡ ‡ ‡ ‡ ‡ ‡ ‡ ‡ ‡

MISHLER, ROBERT E.
  MISHLER, ROBERT E.‡ DEPARTMENT OF BEHAVIORAL
  SCIENCES, NEW MEXICO HIGHLANDS UNIVERSITY, LAS
  VEGAS, NEW MEXICO 87701‡ NIGERIA‡ NORTHEAST STATE‡
  MARGI‡ 14 HOURS‡ 1971-72‡ QUALITY FAIR‡ ‡ ‡ ‡
  RELIGIOUS-CHRISTIAN

MISJONSSKOLEN
  MISJONSSKOLEN‡ A.-V. DEPARTMENT, BOX 226, 4000
  STAVANGER, NORWAY‡ ‡ ‡ ‡ ‡ ‡ ‡ ‡ ‡

  MISJONSSKOLEN‡ A.-V. DEPARTMENT, BOX 226,
  STAVANGER 4000, NORWAY‡ CAMEROON‡ ‡ ‡ ‡ ‡
  MISJONSSKOLEN‡ ‡ ‡ ‡ FOLKTALE, MUSIC, RELIGIOUS

  MISJONSSKOLEN‡ A.-V. DEPARTMENT, BOX 226,
  STAVANGER 4000, NORWAY‡ MALAGASY REPUBLIC‡ ‡ ‡ ‡
  ‡ MISJONSSKOLEN‡ ‡ ‡ ‡ FOLKTALE, MUSIC, RELIGIOUS

  MISJONSSKOLEN‡ A.-V. DEPARTMENT, BOX 226,
  STAVANGER 4000, NORWAY‡ SOUTH AFRICA‡ ZULULAND‡
  ZULU‡ ‡ ‡ ‡ MISJONSSKOLEN‡ ‡ ‡ ‡ FOLKTALE, MUSIC,
  RELIGIOUS

MISSION SOCIOLOGIQUE DU H
  MISSION SOCIOLOGIQUE DU HAUTE-OUBANGUI‡ B.P. 68,
  BANGASSOU, CENTRAL AFRICAN REPUBLIC‡ ‡ ‡ ‡ ‡ ‡ ‡
  ‡ ‡ ‡

  MISSION SOCIOLOGIQUE DU HAUTE-OUBANGUI‡ B.P. 68,
  BANGASSOU, CENTRAL AFRICAN REPUBLIC‡ CENTRAL
  AFRICAN REPUBLIC‡ HAUT-OUBANGUI‡ NZAKARA, ZANDE‡
  60 HOURS‡ ‡ ‡ MISSION SOCIOLOGIQUE DU
  HAUTE-OUBANGUI‡ ‡ ‡ ‡ FOLKTALE, HARP, HISTORY,
  PRAISE-POETRY, RITUAL

MONDOLANE, EDUARDO
  MORGENTHAU, HENRY+ MONDOLANE, EDUARDO‡ WGBH, 125
  WESTERN AVENUE, BOSTON, MASSACHUSETTS 02134+ -‡
  MOZAMBIQUE‡ ‡ ‡ 1.5 HOURS‡ 1965‡ QUALITY GOOD‡
  ARCHIVES OF TRADITIONAL MUSIC‡ 69-204-F‡ ATL
  3776-77‡ RESTRICTED‡ POLITICAL-INTERVIEW

MOORE, BAI T.
  MOORE, BAI T.‡ DEPARTMENT OF INFORMATION AND
  CULTURAL AFFAIRS, MONROVIA, LIBERIA‡ LIBERIA‡ ‡
  BASSA, DEI, GBANDE, GIO, GOLA, KISSI, KPELLE,
  LOMA, MANDINGO, MANO, MENDE, VAI‡ ‡ 1962-73‡ ‡ ‡ ‡
  ‡ ‡ MUSIC, ORAL-DATA

MOREY, ROBERT H.
  MOREY, ROBERT H.‡ THE SCIENCE OF MAN FOUNDATION,
  AT MOREY HOUSE, 75 PARK AVENUE, CANANDAIGUA, NEW
  YORK 14424‡ LIBERIA‡ ZEALUA, ZIGIDA‡ GBANDE, LOMA,
  MANDINGO‡ .5 HOUR‡ 1935‡ QUALITY FAIR‡ ARCHIVES
  OF TRADITIONAL MUSIC‡ PRE'54-003-F‡ ATL 1087‡
  RESTRICTED‡ DANCE, ENTERTAINMENT, LOVE, WAR

MORGENTHAU, HENRY
  MORGENTHAU, HENRY‡ WGBH, 125 WESTERN AVENUE,
  BOSTON, MASSACHUSETTS 02134‡ KENYA‡ NAIROBI‡ ‡ 3
  HOURS‡ 1961‡ QUALITY GOOD‡ ARCHIVES OF
  TRADITIONAL MUSIC‡ 71-018-F‡ ATL 4327-32‡
  RESTRICTED‡ INTERVIEW-KENYATTA-J.,
  INTERVIEW-MBOYA-T., POLITICS-DISCUSSION

  MORGENTHAU, HENRY+ MONDOLANE, EDUARDO‡ WGBH, 125
  WESTERN AVENUE, BOSTON, MASSACHUSETTS 02134+ -‡
  MOZAMBIQUE‡ ‡ ‡ 1.5 HOURS‡ 1965‡ QUALITY GOOD‡
  ARCHIVES OF TRADITIONAL MUSIC‡ 69-204-F‡ ATL
  3776-77‡ RESTRICTED‡ POLITICAL-INTERVIEW

  MORGENTHAU, HENRY‡ WGBH, 125 WESTERN AVENUE,
  BOSTON, MASSACHUSETTS 02134‡ SOUTH AFRICA‡ ‡ ‡ 1
  HOUR‡ CA1961‡ QUALITY GOOD‡ ARCHIVES OF
  TRADITIONAL MUSIC‡ 71-018-F‡ ATL 4327-32‡
  RESTRICTED‡ ECONOMIC-ORAL-DATA,
  POLITICAL-ORAL-DATA, SOCIAL-ORAL-DATA

  MORGENTHAU, HENRY‡ WGBH, 125 WESTERN AVENUE,
  BOSTON, MASSACHUSETTS 02134‡ TANZANIA‡ ‡ ‡ 7.5
  HOURS‡ 1965‡ QUALITY GOOD‡ ARCHIVES OF
  TRADITIONAL MUSIC‡ 71-017-F‡ ATL 4312-26‡
  RESTRICTED‡ ECONOMIC-INTERVIEW,
  POLITICS-INTERVIEW, NYERERE-PRESIDENT-SPEECH

MOSES, RAE A.
  MOSES, RAE A.‡ 114 4TH STREET, WILMETTE, ILLINOIS‡
  TANZANIA‡ DAR ES SALAAM‡ ‡ 15 HOURS‡ 1966‡
  QUALITY FAIR‡ ‡ ‡ ‡ ‡ SWAHILI-ORAL-CLASSROOM

MOULOUD, MAMMERI
  MOULOUD, MAMMERI‡ 82 RUE LAPERLIER, EL-BIAR,
  ALGERIA‡ ALGERIA‡ GOURARA, KABYLIA, TUAREG‡
  BERBER‡ ‡ ‡ ‡ CENTRE DE RECHERCHES
  ANTHROPOLOGIQUES PREHISTORIQUES ET
  ETHNOGRAPHIQUES‡ ‡ ‡ ‡ HISTORY, POETRY

MPHAHLELE, EZEKIEL
  MPHAHLELE, EZEKIEL+ AFRICAN STUDIES-I.U.‡ -+
  INDIANA UNIVERSITY, BLOOMINGTON, INDIANA 47401‡ ‡
  ‡ ‡ 2 HOURS‡ 1968‡ QUALITY GOOD‡ ARCHIVES OF
  TRADITIONAL MUSIC‡ 69-011-F‡ ATL 4382-83‡
  RESTRICTED‡ LECTURE

MULDROW, ELIZABETH
  MULDROW, WILLIAM+ MULDROW, ELIZABETH‡ C/O
  SPAUGLER, 3894 SOUTH ELM, DENVER, COLORADO 80237‡
  ETHIOPIA‡ KEFFA PROVINCE‡ TESHENNA‡ 4 HOURS‡
  1964-65‡ QUALITY GOOD‡ ARCHIVES CF TRADITIONAL
  MUSIC‡ 74-072-F‡ ‡ RESTRICTED‡ BELLS-LEG,
  DEATH-FUNERAL, FLUTE, HARVEST, HORN-ANIMAL,
  HORN-WOODEN, XYLOPHONE

MULDROW, WILLIAM
  MULDROW, WILLIAM+ MULDROW, ELIZABETH‡ C/O
  SPAUGLER, 3894 SOUTH ELM, DENVER, COLORADO 80237‡
  ETHIOPIA‡ KEFFA PROVINCE‡ TESHENNA‡ 4 HOURS‡
  1964-65‡ QUALITY GOOD‡ ARCHIVES OF TRADITIONAL
  MUSIC‡ 74-072-F‡ ‡ RESTRICTED‡ BELLS-LEG,
  DEATH-FUNERAL, FLUTE, HARVEST, HORN-ANIMAL,
  HORN-WOODEN, XYLOPHONE

MURPHY, ROBERT
  MURPHY, ROBERT‡ DEPARTMENT OF ANTHROPOLOGY,
  COLUMBIA UNIVERSITY, NEW YORK, NEW YORK 10027‡
  NIGER‡ ‡ TUAREG‡ ‡ 1959-60‡ ‡ LOWIE MUSEUM OF
  ANTHROPOLOGY‡ ‡ ‡ ‡ MUSIC, NARRATIVE

  MURPHY, ROBERT‡ DEPARTMENT OF ANTHROPOLOGY,
  COLUMBIA UNIVERSITY, NEW YORK, NEW YORK 10027‡
  NIGERIA‡ ‡ TUAREG‡ ‡ 1959-60‡ ‡ LOWIE MUSEUM OF
  ANTHROPOLOGY‡ ‡ ‡ ‡ MUSIC, NARRATIVE

MURYAR BISHARA, RADIO VOI
  MURYAR BISHARA, RADIO VOICE OF THE GOSPEL
  RECORDING STUDIO‡ P.O. BOX 287, JOS, NIGERIA‡ ‡ ‡
  ‡ ‡ ‡ ‡ ‡ ‡ ‡

MUSEE DE L'HOMME
  MUSEE DE L'HOMME‡ PLACE DU TROCADERO, 75-PARIS
  16E, FRANCE‡ ‡ ‡ ‡ ‡ ‡ ‡ ‡ ‡

MUSEE ROYAL DE L'AFRIQUE
  MUSEE ROYAL DE L'AFRIQUE CENTRALE/KONINGLIJK
  MUSEUM VOOR MIDDEN-AFRIKA‡ STEENWEG OP LEUVEN 13,
  1980 TERVUREN, BELGIUM‡ ‡ ‡ ‡ ‡ ‡ ‡ ‡ ‡ ‡

  MUSEE ROYAL DE L'AFRIQUE CENTRALE‡ STEENWEG OP
  LEUVEN, B-1980, TERVUREN, BELGIUM‡ ‡ ‡ BIROM,
  BOLIA, HOLOHOLO, KANEMBU, KONDA, KONGO, LEGA,
  MBALA, MBUUN, MONGO, NANDE, PENDE, RUNDI, RWANDA,
  SANGA, SHI, SUKU, TETELA, YEKE‡ 800 HOURS‡ ‡ ‡
  MUSEE ROYAL DE L'AFRIQUE CENTRALE‡ ‡ ‡ ‡ EPIC,
  HISTORY, JUDICIAL, RELIGIOUS

MUSEU DO DUNDO
  MUSEU DO DUNDO‡ DUNDO, LUANDA, ANGOLA‡ ‡ ‡ ‡ ‡ ‡
  ‡ ‡ ‡ ‡

  MUSEU DO DUNDO‡ DUNDO, LUANDA, ANGOLA‡ ANGOLA‡
  ALTO-ZAMBEZE, LUANDA‡ LUBA, LUNDA, LWENA, CHOKWE‡
  ‡ ‡ ‡ MUSEU DO DUNDO‡ ‡ ‡ ‡ FOLKLORE, MUSIC

MUSEUM FUR VOLKERKUNDE LE
  MUSEUM FUR VOLKERKUNDE LEIPZIG STAATLICHE
  FORSCHUNGSSTELLE‡ DDR-701 LEIPZIG, TAUBCHENWEG 2,
  GERMAN DEMOCRATIC REPUBLIC‡ ‡ ‡ ‡ ‡ ‡ ‡ ‡ ‡

MUSEUM FUR VOLKERKUNDE, A
  MUSEUM FUR VOLKERKUNDE, AUSTRIA‡ A-1014 VIENNA,
  HELDENPLATZ, AUSTRIA‡ ‡ ‡ ‡ ‡ ‡ ‡ ‡ ‡

MUSEUM OF MALAWI
  MUSEUM OF MALAWI‡ P.O. BOX 30360, CHICHIRI,
  BLANTYRE 3, MALAWI‡ ‡ ‡ ‡ ‡ ‡ ‡ ‡ ‡

MUSIKETHNOLOGISCHE ABTEIL
  MUSIKETHNOLOGISCHE ABTEILUNG, VOLKERKUNDEMUSEUM
  BERLIN‡ 1 BERLIN 33-DAHLEM, FEDERAL REPUBLIC OF
  GERMANY‡ ‡ ‡ ‡ ‡ ‡ ‡ ‡ ‡

MUSIKWISSENSCHAFTLICHES I
  MUSIKWISSENSCHAFTLICHES INSTITUT DER FREIEN
  UNIVERSITAT BERLIN‡ PETER LENNE-STRASSE 22,
  BERLIN-DAHLEM, FEDERAL REPUBLIC OF GERMANY‡ ‡ ‡ ‡
  ‡ ‡ ‡ ‡ ‡ ‡

MYKLEBUST, ROLF
  MYKLEBUST, ROLF‡ NORSK RIKSKRINGKASTING, OSLO 3,
  NORWAY‡ GHANA‡ AKUM, KODZIDAN, KUMASI, LEGON‡ ‡
  2.5 HOURS‡ 1966‡ QUALITY GOOD‡ NORSK
  RIKSKRINGKASTING‡ ‡ ‡ ‡

NANCARROW, OWEN T.
  NANCARROW, OWEN T.‡ UNIVERSITY OF RHODESIA, P.B.
  MP 167, MT. PLEASANT, SALISBURY, RHODESIA‡
  RHODESIA‡ MATABELELAND‡ NDEBELE‡ 15 HOURS‡
  1970-71‡ QUALITY FAIR‡ ‡ ‡ ‡ ‡ NARRATIVE

NATIONAL MUSEUM OF TANZAN
  NATIONAL MUSEUM OF TANZANIA‡ P.O. BOX 511, DAR ES
  SALAAM, TANZANIA‡ ‡ ‡ ‡ ‡ ‡ ‡ ‡ ‡ ‡

  NATIONAL MUSEUM OF TANZANIA‡ P.O. BOX 511, DAR ES
  SALAAM, TANZANIA‡ TANZANIA‡ MBEYA DISTRICT‡
  MAKONDE, MALILA, MWERA, YAO‡ 3 HOURS‡ ‡ ‡
  NATIONAL MUSEUM OF TANZANIA‡ ‡ ‡ ‡ DRUM, HISTORY,
  RATTLE, RITUAL

NETTL, BRUNO
  NETTL, BRUNO +RABEN, JOSEPH‡ SCHOOL OF MUSIC,
  UNIVERSITY OF ILLINOIS, URBANA, ILLINOIS 61801
  +DEPARTMENT OF ENGLISH, QUEEN'S COLLEGE, FLUSHING,
  NEW YORK 11367‡ NIGERIA-U.S.‡ BLOOMINGTON,
  INDIANA‡ IBO‡ 1 HOUR‡ 1950-51‡ QUALITY GOOD‡
  ARCHIVES OF TRADITIONAL MUSIC‡ PRE'54-182-F‡ ATL
  296-97‡ RESTRICTED‡ CHILDREN-GAME,
  CHILDREN-SCHOOL, DANCE, DRUM, RATTLE-BASKET, WAR

NEWBURY, DAVID S.
  NEWBURY, DAVID S.‡ IRSAC, LWIRO, D.S. BUKAVU,
  ZAIRE‡ ZAIRE‡ KIVU PROVINCE‡ BAHAVU‡ 25 HOURS‡
  1972-74‡ QUALITY GOOD‡ ARCHIVES OF TRADITIONAL
  MUSIC‡ ‡ ‡ ‡ HISTORY-ROYAL, RELIGIOUS

NEWBURY, DOROTHY J.
  NEWBURY, DOROTHY J.‡ 316 COLLEGE BOULEVARD, MOUNT
  VERNON, IOWA 52314‡ LIBERIA‡ MONROVIA, NIMBA,
  ZIGGIDA‡ BASSA, LOMA‡ 6.5 HOURS‡ 1969-70+ 1972‡
  QUALITY GOOD‡ ‡ ‡ ‡ ‡ CELEBRATION-CENTENNIAL,

NEWBURY, DOROTHY J.
  CONVERSATION, INAUGURATION-PRESIDENT, INTERVIEW,
  PRAYER, RATTLE-GOURD, TRUE-WHIG-PARTY

NEWBURY, M. CATHARINE
  NEWBURY, M. CATHARINE‡ IRSAC, LWIRO, D.S. BUKAVU,
  ZAIRE‡ RWANDA‡ KINYAGA‡ BANYARWANDA‡ 25 HOURS‡
  1970-72‡ QUALITY GOOD‡ ARCHIVES CF TRADITIONAL
  MUSIC‡ ‡ ‡ HISTORY-FAMILY, HISTORY-POLITICAL

NICOLAISEN, IDA
  NICOLAISEN, IDA‡ ‡ NIGER‡ IN ATES, TA N FIFANEN‡
  TUAREG‡ ‡ 1966‡ ‡ DANSK FOLKEMINDESAMLING‡
  66/1A-8A‡ ‡ ‡

NJAKA, MAZI E.N.
  NJAKA, MAZI E.N.‡ 3805 CEDAR DRIVE, BALTIMORE,
  MARYLAND 21207‡ NIGERIA‡ AKAOKWA‡ ‡ .5 HOUR‡ 1972‡
  QUALITY FAIR‡ ‡ ‡ ‡ ‡ RELIGIOUS-CATHOLIC

NKETIA, J.H. KWABENA
  NKETIA, J.H. KWABENA+ WARE, NAOMI‡ INSTITUTE OF
  AFRICAN STUDIES, P.O. BOX 25, LEGON, GHANA+
  DEPARTMENT OF SOCIOLOGY, ANTHROPOLOGY, AND SOCIAL
  WORK, UNIVERSITY OF WISCONSIN, OSHKOSH, WISCONSIN
  54901‡ GHANA-U.S.‡ BLOOMINGTON, INDIANA‡ AKAN‡ 1
  HOUR‡ 1965‡ QUALITY GOOD‡ ARCHIVES OF TRADITIONAL
  MUSIC‡ 65-145-F‡ ‡ RESTRICTED‡
  MUSICIANS-AKAN-LECTURE

NORSK RIKSKRINGKASTING
  NORSK RIKSKRINGKASTING‡ BJORNSTJERNE BJORNSONS
  PLASS 1, OSLO, NORWAY‡ ‡ ‡ ‡ ‡ ‡ ‡ ‡ ‡ ‡

  NORSK RIKSKRINGKASTING‡ BJORNSTJERNE BJORNSONS
  PLASS 1, OSLO, NORWAY‡ GHANA‡ KUMASI, LEGON‡ ‡ 3
  HOURS‡ 1966‡ ‡ NORSK RIKSKRINGKASTING‡ ‡ ‡ ‡ BELL,
  DRUM, FLUTE, HORN, HORN-ELEPHANT,
  INTERNATIONAL-FOLK-MUSIC-COUNCIL, RATTLE, STICK

NOSS, PHILIP A.
  NOSS, PHILIP A.‡ DEPARTMENT OF AFRICAN LANGUAGES
  AND LITERATURE, UNIVERSITY OF WISCONSIN, MADISON,
  WISCONSIN 53706‡ CAMEROON‡ BETARE OYA, BOULI,
  GAROUA BOULAI, KALALDI, MEIGANGA‡ GBAYA‡ 20 HOURS‡
  1966-67‡ QUALITY EXCELLENT‡ CENTER FOR AFRICAN
  ORAL DATA‡ 71-003-F‡ ATL 4912-39‡ RESTRICTED‡
  DIVINING, FOLKTALE, FOLKTALE-HUNTING, HISTORY,
  HUNTING, INITIATION, PARABLE, PROVERB, RIDDLE,

NOSS, PHILIP A.
  TRAPPING

ODED, ARYE
  ODED, ARYE‡ 5 NEVE-GRANOT, JERUSALEM, ISRAEL‡
  UGANDA‡ BUGANDA, MBALE‡ BAGANDA, BAYUDAYA‡ 25
  HOURS‡ 1967-68‡ QUALITY GOOD‡ MAKERERE UNIVERSITY‡
  ‡ ‡ ‡ HISTORY, PRAYER-SABBATH,
  RELIGIOUS-AFRICAN-JEWISH, RELIGIOUS-ISLAMIC

OERTLI, PEO
  OERTLI, PEO‡ MUNSTERGASSE 25, 8001 ZURICH,
  SWITZERLAND‡ DAHOMEY‡ ALLADA‡ AIZO‡ 5.5 HOURS‡
  1973-74‡ QUALITY EXCELLENT‡ ‡ ‡ ‡ CEREMONY,
  IMPROVISATION, PROVERB, RELIGIOUS, RITUAL

OFFICE DE LA RECHERCHE SC
  OFFICE DE LA RECHERCHE SCIENTIFIQUE ET TECHNIQUE
  D'OUTRE-MER (ORSTOM)‡ 24 RUE BAYARD, 75008 PARIS,
  FRANCE‡ ‡ ‡ ‡ ‡ ‡ ‡ ‡ ‡

OFONAGURO, W. IBEKWE
  OFONAGURO, W. IBEKWE+ IRWIN, GRAHAM‡ DEPARTMENT
  OF HISTORY, BROOKLYN COLLEGE, BEDFORD AVENUE AND
  AVENUE H, NEW YORK, NEW YORK 11210+ 435 W. 119
  ST., APT. 5B, NEW YORK, NEW YORK 10027‡
  NIGERIA-U.S.‡ NEW YORK‡ ‡ .5 HOUR‡ 1967‡ QUALITY
  GOOD‡ ARCHIVES OF TRADITIONAL MUSIC‡ 69-132-F‡
  ATL 3686‡ RESTRICTED‡ SPEECH-OJUNWU-C.O.,
  POLITICS-SPEECH

OFRI, DORITH
  OFRI, DORITH‡ 38, ATHENEE, 1206 GENEVE,
  SWITZERLAND‡ LIBERIA‡ GAWULA, MONROVIA, SOWOLO‡
  VAI‡ 30 HOURS‡ 1965-72‡ QUALITY GOOD‡ ‡ ‡ ‡
  CHILDREN, DANCE, HISTORY, PRAISE-POETRY,
  RITUAL-ISLAMIC-FEAST, WORK-COOPERATIVE

OGBU, JOHN U.
  OGBU, JOHN U.‡ ANTHROPOLOGY DEPARTMENT,
  UNIVERSITY OF CALIFORNIA, BERKELEY, CALIFORNIA
  94720‡ NIGERIA‡ AFIKPO DIVISION‡ IBO‡ 1 HOUR‡
  1972‡ QUALITY FAIR‡ ‡ ‡ ‡ POETRY-ELEGIAC,
  POETRY-ITU-AFA, POETRY-RITUAL, PRAISE-POETRY

  OGBU, JOHN U.+ PEEK, PHILIP M.‡ ANTHROPOLOGY
  DEPARTMENT, UNIVERSITY OF CALIFORNIA, BERKELEY,
  CALIFORNIA 94720+ DEPARTMENT OF ANTHROPOLOGY,
  DREW UNIVERSITY, MADISON, NEW JERSEY 07940‡

OGBU, JOHN U.
  NIGERIA-U.S.‡ BERKELEY, CALIFORNIA‡ IGBO‡ 1 HOUR‡
  1968‡ QUALITY GOOD‡ ARCHIVES OF TRADITIONAL MUSIC‡
  69-195-F‡ ‡ RESTRICTED‡ FOLKTALE,
  FOLKTALE-INTERVIEW

OGIERIRIAIXI, EVINMA
  OGIERIRIAIXI, EVINMA‡ SCHOOL OF AFRICAN AND ASIAN
  STUDIES, UNIVERSITY OF LAGOS, LAGOS, NIGERIA‡
  NIGERIA‡ BENIN CITY‡ EDO‡ 24 HOURS‡ 1970-73‡
  QUALITY GOOD‡ ‡ ‡ ‡ ‡ FOLKLORE

OGUNDIPE, JOHN
  GLEASON, JUDITH‡ OGUNDIPE, JOHN‡ 26 EAST 91
  STREET, NEW YORK, NEW YORK 10028‡ 119 WEST 106
  STREET, NEW YORK, NEW YORK 10025‡ NIGERIA‡
  OSHOGBO‡ YORUBA‡ 12 HOURS‡ 1970‡ QUALITY GOOD‡
  CENTER FOR AFRICAN ORAL DATA‡ 73-002-F‡ ‡ ‡
  DIVINING-ODU-IFA

OKIE, PACKARD L.
  OKIE, PACKARD L.‡ ST. MARGARET'S EPISCOPAL CHURCH,
  150 ELM STREET, EMMAUS, PENNSYLVANIA 18049‡
  LIBERIA‡ CAPE MOUNT, ROBERTSPORT‡ BASSA, GBANDE,
  GOLA, KISSI, LOMA, MENDE, VAI‡ 1.5 HOURS‡ 1947-54‡
  QUALITY GOOD‡ ARCHIVES OF TRADITIONAL MUSIC‡
  PRE'54-004-F‡ ATL 1173-75‡ ‡ DANCE-WESTERN,
  ENTERTAINMENT, GUITAR, SECRET-SOCIETY

  OKIE, PACKARD L.‡ ST. MARGARET'S EPISCOPAL CHURCH,
  150 ELM STREET, EMMAUS, PENNSYLVANIA 18049‡
  LIBERIA‡ ROBERTSPORT‡ BASSA, KRU‡ .5 HOUR‡
  1947-54‡ QUALITY GOOD‡ ARCHIVES OF TRADITIONAL
  MUSIC‡ PRE'54-005-F‡ ATL 1272‡ ‡
  RELIGIOUS-CHRISTIAN

  OKIE, PACKARD L.‡ ST. MARGARET'S EPISCOPAL CHURCH,
  150 ELM STREET, EMMAUS, PENNSYLVANIA 18049‡
  LIBERIA‡ BROMLEY, CUTTINGTON, GBANGA‡ BASSA, BELE,
  GIO, KPELLE, KRU, MANDINGO, VAI‡ 8 HOURS‡ 1947-54‡
  QUALITY GOOD‡ ARCHIVES OF TRADITIONAL MUSIC‡
  57-001-F‡ ATL 1247-71‡ ‡ CANTE-FABLE, DRUM,
  DRUM-HOURGLASS, ENTERTAINMENT, GUITAR,
  HORN-WOODEN, RATTLE-GOURD, RELIGIOUS-ISLAMIC,
  SECRET-SOCIETY, WORK-FIELD, XYLOPHONE,
  ZITHER-TRIANGULAR-FRAME

OLMSTEAD, JUDITH VIRGINIA
  OLMSTEAD, JUDITH VIRGINIA‡ DEPARTMENT OF

OLMSTEAD, JUDITH VIRGINIA
  ANTHROPOLOGY, UNIVERSITY OF MASSACHUSETTS-BOSTON,
  BOSTON, MASSACHUSETTS 02125‡ ETHIOPIA‡ GAMU
  HIGHLAND, GEMU GAFA PROVINCE‡ DITA, DORZE‡ 22.5
  HOURS‡ 1969-71+ 1973‡ QUALITY GOOD‡ ‡ ‡ ‡ ‡
  HISTORY, LYRE

OLSEN, POUL ROVSING
  JARGY, SIMON+ OLSEN, POUL ROVSING‡ - +
  BIRKETINGET 6, 2300 COPENHAGEN S., DENMARK‡ EGYPT‡
  CAIRO‡ ‡ ‡ 1969‡ ‡ DANSK FOLKEMINDESAMLING‡ 69/44‡
  ‡ ‡

ONWUKA, RALPH I.
  ONWUKA, RALPH I.‡ P.O. BOX 229, UNIVERSITY OF
  ALBERTA, EDMONTON, ALBERTA, CANADA‡ NIGERIA‡ ‡
  IBO‡ ‡ ‡ QUALITY GOOD‡ ‡ ‡ ‡ ‡ SOCIAL

OPLAND, JEFFREY
  OPLAND, JEFFREY‡ 57 DUNKELD ROAD, WESTVILLE NORTH,
  NATAL 3630, SOUTH AFRICA‡ SOUTH AFRICA‡ CISKEI,
  KWAZULU, TRANSKEI‡ XHOSA, ZULU‡ 100 HOURS‡
  1969-73‡ QUALITY GOOD‡ CENTER FOR THE STUDY OF
  ORAL LITERATURE, HARVARD UNIVERSITY‡ ‡ ‡ ‡
  FOLKTALE, POETRY

ORENT, AMNON
  ORENT, AMNON‡ 28 HANADIV STREET, HERZLIYA, ISRAEL‡
  ETHIOPIA‡ BONGA‡ KAFA‡ 10 HOURS‡ 1966-67‡ QUALITY
  GOOD‡ ‡ ‡ ‡ ‡ GRAMMATICAL-DATA, HISTORY, PRAISE,
  WORK

ORI, R.
  UPADHYAYA, HARI S.+ ORI, R.‡ DIRECTOR, INDIAN
  FOLK CULTURE RESEARCH INSTITUTE, DEPARTMENT OF
  HINDI, BENARES HINDU UNIVERSITY, VARANSI, INDIA+
  -‡ MAURITIUS‡ MAURITIUS ISLAND‡ UTTAR-PRADESH‡ 1
  HOUR‡ 1961‡ QUALITY GOOD‡ ARCHIVES OF TRADITIONAL
  MUSIC‡ 65-279-F‡ ‡ RESTRICTED‡ DRUM,
  LUTE-BOWED-SARANGI,RELIGIOUS, SOCIAL-CONDITIONS

OTTENHEIMER, HARRIET
  OTTENHEIMER, HARRIET+ OTTENHEIMER, MARTIN‡
  DEPARTMENT OF SOCIOLOGY AND ANTHROPOLOGY, KANSAS
  STATE UNIVERSITY, MANHATTAN, KANSAS‡ COMORO
  ISLANDS‡ ANJOUAN, DOMONI, GRANDE COMORE‡ ‡ 30
  HOURS‡ 1967-68‡ QUALITY GOOD‡ ‡ ‡ ‡ ‡ FOLKTALE,
  HISTORY, MARRIAGE, RELIGIOUS

OTTENHEIMER, MARTIN
OTTENHEIMER, HARRIET+ OTTENHEIMER, MARTIN‡
DEPARTMENT OF SOCIOLOGY AND ANTHROPOLOGY, KANSAS
STATE UNIVERSITY, MANHATTAN, KANSAS‡ COMORO
ISLANDS‡ ANJOUAN, DOMONI, GRANDE COMORE‡ ‡ 30
HOURS‡ 1967-68‡ QUALITY GOOD‡ ‡ ‡ ‡ FOLKTALE,
HISTORY, MARRIAGE, RELIGIOUS

OWEN, WILFRED, JR.
OWEN, WILFRED, JR.‡ 1570 OAK AVENUE, DRYDEN HALL
705, NORTHWESTERN UNIVERSITY, EVANSTON, ILLINOIS
60201‡ GHANA‡ NKORANZA‡ ASANTE, BRONG, EWE, FANTI,
GA, TWI‡ 38 HOURS‡ 1970-71‡ QUALITY EXCELLENT‡
CENTER FOR AFRICAN ORAL DATA‡ 72-237-F‡ ATL
5474-507‡ RESTRICTED‡ FESTIVAL, FOLKTALE,
GREETING, HISTORY, PRAISE-RULER, SPORTS

PAASCHE, -
PAASCHE, -‡ ‡ TANZANIA‡ ‡ KIZIBA‡ .1 HOUR‡ 1910‡
QUALITY FAIR‡ ARCHIVES OF TRADITIONAL MUSIC‡
59-002-F‡ ATL 1757‡ RESTRICTED‡ DRUM, HORN

PAGE, MELVIN E.
PAGE, MELVIN E.‡ 415 ORCHARD, EAST LANSING,
MICHIGAN 48823‡ MALAWI‡ ‡ ‡ 80 HOURS‡ 1972-74‡
QUALITY FAIR‡ ‡ ‡ ‡ ‡ HISTORY-TWENTIETH-CENTURY,
MILITARY

PAIRAULT, CLAUDE ALBERT
PAIRAULT, CLAUDE ALBERT‡ B.P. 8008, ABIDJAN,
IVORY COAST‡ CHAD‡ LAKE IRO‡ GULA-IRO‡ 30 HOURS‡
1959-64‡ QUALITY EXCELLENT‡ 117 RUE NOTRE DAME
DES CHAMPS, 75006 PARIS, FRANCE‡ ‡ ‡ ‡ HISTORY,
MUSIC, RITUAL

PANTALEONI, HEWITT
PANTALEONI, HEWITT‡ STATE UNIVERSITY COLLEGE, 81
ELM STREET, ONEONTA, NEW YORK‡ GHANA‡ ANYAKO‡ EWE‡
14 HOURS‡ 1969-71‡ QUALITY GOOD‡ ‡ ‡ ‡ ‡ DANCE,
DRUM, HISTORY

PARE, -
PARE, -+ TARDITS, CLAUDE‡ -+ 33 RUE CROULEBARBE,
75013 PARIS, FRANCE‡ CAMEROON‡ ‡ BAMUM‡ ‡ ‡ ‡
MUSEE DE L'HOMME‡ ‡ ‡ ‡ HISTORY-DYNASTIC-BAMUM

PARKER, CAROLYN ANN
PARKER, CAROLYN ANN‡ UNIVERSITY OF TEXAS AT
AUSTIN, 2601 UNIVERSITY, AUSTIN, TEXAS 78712‡

PARKER, CAROLYN ANN
  KENYA‡ COAST‡ BAJUN, SWAHILI‡ ‡ 1971-72‡ QUALITY
  FAIR‡ ‡ ‡ ‡ ‡ CONVERSATION, INTERVIEW-ENGLISH,
  INTERVIEW-SWAHILI, FOLKLORE, MUSIC

PEEK, PHILIP M.
  OGBU, JOHN U.+ PEEK, PHILIP M.‡ ANTHROPOLOGY
  DEPARTMENT, UNIVERSITY OF CALIFORNIA, BERKELEY,
  CALIFORNIA 94720+ DEPARTMENT OF ANTHROPOLOGY,
  DREW UNIVERSITY, MADISON, NEW JERSEY C7940‡
  NIGERIA-U.S.‡ BERKELEY, CALIFORNIA‡ IGBO‡ 1 HOUR‡
  1968‡ QUALITY GOOD‡ ARCHIVES OF TRADITIONAL MUSIC‡
  69-195-F‡ ‡ RESTRICTED‡ FOLKTALE,
  FOLKTALE-INTERVIEW

  PEEK, PHILIP M.‡ DEPARTMENT OF ANTHROPOLOGY, DREW
  UNIVERSITY, MADISON, NEW JERSEY 07940‡ NIGERIA‡
  ISOKO DIVISION‡ IGBO-WESTERN, ISOKO‡ 100 HOURS‡
  1970-71‡ QUALITY GOOD‡ ARCHIVES OF TRADITIONAL
  MUSIC‡ ‡ ‡ ‡ CEREMONY-RELIGIOUS, DIVINING,
  FESTIVAL, HISTORY, RELIGIOUS, WORD-LIST

PELLIGRA, D.
  PELLIGRA, D.‡ ‡ ALGERIA‡ ‡ TUAREG‡ ‡ 1970‡ ‡
  MUSEE DE L'HOMME‡ ‡ ‡ ‡ DRUM, LUTE-BOWED-IMZAD

PENCHOEN, THOMAS GOODENOU
  PENCHOEN, THOMAS GOODENOUGH‡ NEAR EASTERN
  LANGUAGES, 302 ROYCE HALL, UCLA, LOS ANGELES
  CALIFORNIA 90024‡ ALGERIA‡ AIN ZAATOUT‡
  BERBER-AURES‡ 2 HOURS‡ 1973‡ QUALITY GOOD‡ ‡ ‡ ‡ ‡

  PENCHOEN, THOMAS GOODENOUGH‡ NEAR EASTERN
  LANGUAGES, 302 ROYCE HALL, UCLA, LOS ANGELES,
  CALIFORNIA 90024‡ MOROCCO‡ MEKIIES‡
  BERBER-AYT-NDIR‡ 10 HOURS‡ 1969-74‡ QUALITY GOOD‡
  ‡ ‡ ‡ ‡ ORAL-DATA

  PENCHOEN, THOMAS GOODENOUGH‡ NEAR EASTERN
  LANGUAGES, 302 ROYCE HALL, UCLA, LOS ANGELES,
  CALIFORNIA 90024‡ TUNISIA‡ GUELLALA‡
  BERBER-DJERBA‡ 4 HOURS‡ 1969‡ QUALITY GOOD‡ ‡ ‡ ‡
  ‡ ORAL-DATA

PEPPER, HERBERT
  PEPPER, HERBERT‡ B.P. 11033, DAKAR, SENEGAL‡
  GABON‡ ‡ FANG‡ ‡ 1960‡ ‡ MUSEE DE L'HOMME‡ ‡ ‡ ‡
  EPIC, HARP-ZITHER-MVET

PEVAR, MARC DAVID
  PEVAR, MARC DAVID‡ BOX 129, KENNETT SQUARE,
  PENNSYLVANIA‡ GAMBIA, THE‡ KOMBO‡ MANDINKA‡ 20
  HOURS‡ 1972‡ QUALITY EXCELLENT‡ LIBRARY OF
  CONGRESS+ UNIVERSITY OF PENNSYLVANIA‡ ‡ ‡ ‡
  HARP-LUTE-KORA, PRAISE

PHONOGRAMMARCHIV DER OEST
  PHONOGRAMMARCHIV DER OESTERREICHISCHEN AKADEMIE
  DER WISSENSCHAFTEN‡ LIEBIGGASSE 5, VIENNA 1,
  AUSTRIA‡ ‡ ‡ ‡ ‡ ‡ ‡ ‡ ‡ ‡

PHONOTHEQUE NATIONALE
  PHONOTHEQUE NATIONALE‡ 19, RUE DES BERNARDINS,
  75-PARIS 5E, FRANCE‡ ‡ ‡ ‡ ‡ ‡ ‡ ‡ ‡ ‡

PIA, JOSEPH J.
  PIA, JOSEPH J.‡ DEPARTMENT OF LINGUISTICS,
  SYRACUSE UNIVERSITY, SYRACUSE, NEW YORK 13210‡
  SOMALIA‡ MOGADISCIO‡ SOMALI‡ 20 HOURS‡ 1962‡
  QUALITY GOOD‡ ‡ ‡ ‡ NARRATIVE-PROSE

PIRRO, ELLEN B.
  PIRRO, ELLEN B.‡ 6024 WATERBURY CIRCLE, DES
  MOINES, IOWA 50312‡ KENYA‡ NAIROBI‡ ‡ 1 HOUR‡
  1969‡ QUALITY FAIR‡ ‡ ‡ ‡ ‡ FESTIVAL

PLANCK, EBBE
  PLANCK, EBBE‡ ‡ ALGERIA‡ BEL ABBES, EL OUED‡ ‡ ‡
  1969‡ ‡ DANSK FOLKEMINDESAMLING‡ 69/3A-5A‡ ‡ ‡

PLOTNICOV, LEONARD
  PLOTNICOV, LEONARD‡ DEPARTMENT OF ANTHROPOLOGY,
  UNIVERSITY OF PITTSBURGH, PITTSBURGH,
  PENNSYLVANIA 15260‡ NIGERIA‡ EKET, GBOKO, JOS,
  OPOBO, UYO‡ BIROM, EFIK, HAUSA, IBIBIO, IBO, IJAW,
  KAGORO, KATAM, TIV‡ ‡ 1961-62‡ ‡ LOWIE MUSEUM OF
  ANTHROPOLOGY‡ ‡ ‡ ‡ BELL-DOUBLE, DRUM-EKOMAH,
  FLUTE, GOURD, PROVERB, RATTLE,
  SECRET-SOCIETY-MALE-IDIONG,
  SECRET-SOCIETY-MALE-OGBON, STICK, SOCIAL, WAR,
  XYLOPHONE, ZITHER

PREMPEH, KOFI
  PREMPEH, KOFI‡ ‡ GHANA‡ ‡ ASANTE‡ 1 HOUR‡ 1950‡ ‡
  ARCHIVES OF TRADITIONAL MUSIC‡ 73-058-F‡ ‡ ‡

PRESTON, JEROME, JR.
  PRESTON, JEROME, JR.‡ 10 VANE STREET, WELLESLEY,

PRESTON, JEROME, JR.
  MASSACHUSETTS 02181‡ KENYA‡ KAMOGAMBO LOCATION‡
  LUO‡ .5 HOUR‡ 1966‡ QUALITY POOR‡ ‡ ‡ ‡ ‡
  GREETING, PRAYER

PRINCE, RAYMOND HAROLD
  PRINCE, RAYMOND HAROLD‡ 1266 PINE AVENUE WEST,
  MONTREAL, CANADA‡ NIGERIA‡ NORTHERN REGION,
  WESTERN REGION‡ ‡ 1.5 HOURS‡ ‡ QUALITY POOR‡ ‡ ‡ ‡
  ‡

PRUITT, WILLIAM F., JR.
  PRUITT, WILLIAM F., JR.‡ AFRICAN STUDIES PROGRAM,
  KALAMAZOO COLLEGE, KALAMAZOO, MICHIGAN 49001‡
  ZAIRE‡ KASAI‡ KETE, PYGMIES, SALAMPASU‡ 61 HOURS‡
  1966-67‡ QUALITY GOOD‡ ‡ ‡ ‡ DANCE,
  DEATH-FUNERAL, FOLKTALE, HISTORY, PRAISE-POETRY

PRUITT, WILLIAM F., SR.
  PRUITT, WILLIAM F., SR.‡ C/O WILLIAM F. PRUITT,
  JR., KALAMAZOO COLLEGE, KALAMAZOO, MICHIGAN 49001‡
  ZAIRE‡ LUEBO‡ LUBA, LULUA‡ 2 HOURS‡ 1945-49‡
  QUALITY GOOD‡ ARCHIVES OF TRADITIONAL MUSIC‡
  74-101-F‡ ‡ RESTRICTED‡ MISSION-PRESBYTERIAN

QUEEN'S UNIVERSITY OF BEL
  QUEEN'S UNIVERSITY OF BELFAST, THE‡ BELFAST BT7
  1NN, NORTHERN IRELAND‡ ‡ ‡ ‡ ‡ ‡ ‡ ‡ ‡ ‡

QUERSIN, BENOIT J.
  QUERSIN, BENOIT J.+ QUERSIN, CHRISTINE M.‡ MUSEE
  ROYAL DE L'AFRIQUE CENTRALE, CH. DE LOUVAIN, 1980
  TERVUREN, BELGIUM‡ CAMEROON‡ BAFEMBEU-BANEKANE,
  BAFIA, BANYO, FUMBAN, GOUFAN, KIMI, KRIBI, LEVEM,
  MESANGSANG, NGOLNGOK, SAA, TALA, YAOUNDE‡ BAFIA,
  BALLOM, BAMILEKE, BAMUM, BULU ETCN, PEUL, PYGMIES,
  SANAGA, TIKAR, VUTE‡ 20 HOURS‡ 1967‡ QUALITY GOOD‡
  ARCHIVES OF TRADITIONAL MUSIC+ MUSEE ROYAL DE
  L'AFRIQUE CENTRALE‡ 72-233-F‡ ‡ RESTRICTED‡
  BELL-DOUBLE, DANCE, CANCE-WAR, DRUM, DRUM-FRAME,
  DRUM-SINGLE-HEADED, DRUM-SLIT, ENTERTAINMENT,
  FLUTE, HARP-ZITHER, HORN, PRAISE-RULER, RATTLE,
  STICK-SCRAPED, TOPICAL

  QUERSIN, BENOIT J.+ QUERSIN, CHRISTINE M.‡ MUSEE
  ROYAL DE L'AFRIQUE CENTRALE, CH. DE LOUVAIN, 1980
  TERVUREN, BELGIUM‡ NIGERIA‡ ABUKU, AKWANGA,
  BUGUMA, BWARAT, DENGI, EDE, GANI, GBOKO, IFE,
  IKERE, JOS, KATSINA-ALA, KEFFI, KURU, LAFIA,

QUERSIN, BENOIT J.
  LANGTANG, LOKO, MAKURDI, MANGU, NASSARAWA,
  OSHOGBO, OTURKPO, PANKSHIN, SHENCAM, WASE, WUKARI,
  ZAWAN‡ ABAKPA-RIGA, AFO, ALAGO, ANGAS, ANKWAI,
  BIROM, BUROM, CHAMBA, EGGON, FULANI, HAUSA, ICHEN,
  IDOMA, JARAWA, JUKUN, KALABARI, KANTANA, KUTEP,
  KWALLA, NUPE, PYEM, RINDRE, TIV, YERGAM, YORUBA‡
  60 HOURS‡ 1972-73‡ QUALITY EXCELLENT‡ UNIVERSITY
  OF IFE‡ ‡ ‡ BOW-MUSICAL, CULT-SHANGO,
  DANCE-HARVEST, DANCE-MASKED, DANCE-WAR,
  DEATH-FUNERAL, DRUM-APINTI, DRUM-BATA,
  DRUM-HOURGLASS, DRUM-POT, DRUM-SLIT,
  ENTERTAINMENT, FLUTE, GOURD-STRUCK, HORN,
  LUTE-BOWED, MARRIAGE, OBOE, ORCHESTRA-ROYAL,
  PRAISE-RULER, RATTLE-GOURD, ROYAL-ORCHESTRA,
  SANZA, SHRINE-OSHUN, SOCIAL, XYLOPHONE, ZITHER,
  ZITHER-RAFT

  QUERSIN, BENOIT J.‡ MUSEE ROYAL DE L'AFRIQUE
  CENTRALE, CH. DE LOUVAIN, 1980 TERVUREN, BELGIUM‡
  ZAIRE‡ BUALELE, BULOMBO, KAKENGE, MBEEMBI, MBELO,
  MOMONA, MUSHENGE, POMBO‡ BUSHOONG, COOFA, IBAAM,
  NGEENDE, PYAANG, SHOOWA‡ 10 HOURS‡ 1970‡ QUALITY
  EXCELLENT‡ MUSEE ROYAL DE L'AFRIQUE CENTRALE‡ ‡ ‡
  ‡ BELL, DANCE, DANCE-SHAMAN, DEATH-FUNERAL,
  DRUM-SINGLE-HEADED, GOURD-STRUCK, HISTORY,
  INITIATION, LUTE-MULTIPLE-BOW, PRAISE-RULER,
  RULER, SANZA, SOCIAL

  QUERSIN, BENOIT J.‡ MUSEE ROYAL DE L'AFRIQUE
  CENTRALE, CH. DE LOUVAIN, 1980 TERVUREN, BELGIUM‡
  ZAIRE‡ BANGOKUNGU, BOYEKA, BUTELA, IKONGO, ITIPO,
  LOONGO, MAPEKE, MOMBOYO, MPAHA, PENDA, TONDO‡
  BATWA, EKONDA, NTOMBA‡ 4.5 HOURS‡ 1970‡ QUALITY
  EXCELLENT‡ ARCHIVES OF TRADITIONAL MUSIC‡
  72-248-F‡ ‡ RESTRICTED‡ DANCE, DANCE-ACROBATIC,
  DANCE-WAR, DRUM, DRUM-LANGUAGE, DRUM-SLIT,
  LUTE-MULTIPLE-BOW, INITIATION-FEMALE, SANZA,
  STICK-SCRAPED, ZITHER

  QUERSIN, BENOIT J.+ QUERSIN, CHRISTINE M.‡ MUSEE
  ROYAL DE L'AFRIQUE CENTRALE, CH. DE LOUVAIN, 1980
  TERVUREN, BELGIUM‡ ZAIRE‡ BIKORO, BOBULAMO,
  BONGILA, BOYEKA, BUTELA, ELINGOLA, IBEKE-BOLIA,
  IBOKO, ITIPO, LIESE, LOONGO, LOPANZO, LOYILE,
  MBANGA ILONGO, MBANGA NKOTESE, MBOLO, MPOTIA,
  NSAW, WENGA‡ BATWA, BOLIA, EKONDA‡ 20 HOURS‡ 1971‡
  QUALITY EXCELLENT‡ ARCHIVES OF TRADITIONAL MUSIC,
  MUSEE ROYAL DE L'AFRIQUE CENTRALE‡ 72-235-F‡ ‡

QUERSIN, BENOIT J.
  RESTRICTED‡ ANCESTOR-INVOCATION, DANCE,
  DANCE-ACROBATIC, DANCE-WAR, DEATH-FUNERAL, DRUM,
  DRUM-SLIT, ENTERTAINMENT, HORN-ANTELOPE,
  HORN-GOURD, HUNTING, IDIOPHONE-STRUCK, LIKEMBE,
  LULLABY, LUTE-MULTIPLE-BOW, PRAISE, PROVERB,
  RATTLE, SHAMAN, SONG-CYCLE-BOBONGO, STICK-SCRAPED,
  TOPICAL, WORK

  QUERSIN, BENOIT J.+ QUERSIN, CHRISTINE M.‡ MUSEE
  ROYAL DE L'AFRIQUE CENTRALE, CH. DE LOUVAIN, 1980
  TERVUREN, BELGIUM‡ ZAIRE‡ BASANKUSU, BEFALE,
  BOFOKA, BOKATOLA, BOLOMBA, BOLONDO, BONGILI, BOSO
  DJAFO, BOTEKA, IKELA, ISAKA, LONGO, MAKAKO,
  MOPANGA, NTOMA, WAKA, WATSI, WEMA, YA, YALIFAFU‡
  BAKUTU, BOKOTE, BONGANDO, BOSAKA, BOYELA, NKUNDU,
  PYGMIES-BATWA, PYGMIES-NGOMBE‡ 50 HOURS‡ 1972‡
  QUALITY EXCELLENT‡ MUSEE ROYAL DE L'AFRIQUE
  CENTRALE‡ ‡ ‡ ‡ AGE-SET, DANCE, DANCE-ANCESTOR,
  DANCE-HEALER, DANCE-WAR, DEATH-FUNERAL, DRUM,
  ENTERTAINMENT, FLUTE-GLOBULAR, HISTORY,
  HORN-ANTELOPE, HORN-ELEPHANT, HUNTING,
  LUTE-MULTIPLE-BOW, PADDLING, SANZA, WORK,
  WRESTLING

QUERSIN, CHRISTINE M.
  QUERSIN, BENOIT J.+ QUERSIN, CHRISTINE M.‡ MUSEE
  ROYAL DE L'AFRIQUE CENTRALE, CH. DE LOUVAIN, 1980
  TERVUREN, BELGIUM‡ CAMEROON‡ BAFEMBEU-BANEKANE,
  BAFIA, BANYO, FUMBAN, GOUFAN, KIMI, KRIBI, LEVEM,
  MESANGSANG, NGOLNGOK, SAA, TALA, YAOUNDE‡ BAFIA,
  BALLOM, BAMILEKE, BAMUM, BULU ETON, PEUL, PYGMIES,
  SANAGA, TIKAR, VUTE‡ 20 HOURS‡ 1967‡ QUALITY GOOD‡
  ARCHIVES OF TRADITIONAL MUSIC+ MUSEE ROYAL DE
  L'AFRIQUE CENTRALE‡ 72-233-F‡ ‡ RESTRICTED‡
  BELL-DOUBLE, DANCE, DANCE-WAR, DRUM, DRUM-FRAME,
  DRUM-SINGLE-HEADED, DRUM-SLIT, ENTERTAINMENT,
  FLUTE, HARP-ZITHER, HORN, PRAISE-RULER, RATTLE,
  STICK-SCRAPED, TOPICAL

  QUERSIN, BENOIT J.+ QUERSIN, CHRISTINE M.‡ MUSEE
  ROYAL DE L'AFRIQUE CENTRALE, CH. DE LOUVAIN, 1980
  TERVUREN, BELGIUM‡ NIGERIA‡ ABUKU, AKWANGA,
  BUGUMA, BWARAT, DENGI, EDE, GANI, GBOKO, IFE,
  IKERE, JOS, KATSINA-ALA, KEFFI, KURU, LAFIA,
  LANGTANG, LOKO, MAKURDI, MANGU, NASSARAWA,
  OSHOGBO, OTURKPO, PANKSHIN, SHENDAM, WASE, WUKARI,
  ZAWAN‡ ABAKPA-RIGA, AFO, ALAGO, ANGAS, ANKWAI,
  BIROM, BUROM, CHAMBA, EGGON, FULANI, HAUSA, ICHEN,

QUERSIN, CHRISTINE M.
  IDOMA, JARAWA, JUKUN, KALABARI, KANTANA, KUTEP,
  KWALLA, NUPE, PYEM, RINDRE, TIV, YERGAM, YORUBA‡
  60 HOURS‡ 1972-73‡ QUALITY EXCELLENT‡ UNIVERSITY
  OF IFE‡ ‡ ‡ ‡ BOW-MUSICAL, CULT-SHANGO,
  DANCE-HARVEST, DANCE-MASKED, DANCE-WAR,
  DEATH-FUNERAL, DRUM-APINTI, DRUM-BATA,
  DRUM-HOURGLASS, DRUM-POT, DRUM-SLIT,
  ENTERTAINMENT, FLUTE, GOURD-STRUCK, HORN,
  LUTE-BOWED, MARRIAGE, OBOE, ORCHESTRA-ROYAL,
  PRAISE-RULER, RATTLE-GOURD, ROYAL-ORCHESTRA,
  SANZA, SHRINE-OSHUN, SOCIAL, XYLOPHONE, ZITHER,
  ZITHER-RAFT

  QUERSIN, BENOIT J.+ QUERSIN, CHRISTINE M.‡ MUSEE
  ROYAL DE L'AFRIQUE CENTRALE, CH. DE LOUVAIN, 1980
  TERVUREN, BELGIUM‡ ZAIRE‡ BIKORO, BOBULAMO,
  BONGILA, BOYEKA, BUTELA, ELINGOLA, IBEKE-BOLIA,
  IBOKO, ITIPO, LIESE, LOONGO, LOPANZO, LOYILE,
  MBANGA ILONGO, MBANGA NKOTESE, MBOLO, MPOTIA,
  NSAW, WENGA‡ BATWA, BOLIA, EKONDA‡ 20 HOURS‡ 1971‡
  QUALITY EXCELLENT‡ ARCHIVES OF TRADITIONAL MUSIC,
  MUSEE ROYAL DE L'AFRIQUE CENTRALE‡ 72-235-F‡ ‡
  RESTRICTED‡ ANCESTOR-INVOCATION, DANCE,
  DANCE-ACROBATIC, DANCE-WAR, DEATH-FUNERAL, DRUM,
  DRUM-SLIT, ENTERTAINMENT, HORN-ANTELOPE,
  HORN-GOURD, HUNTING, IDIOPHONE-STRUCK, LIKEMBE,
  LULLABY, LUTE-MULTIPLE-BOW, PRAISE, PROVERB,
  RATTLE, SHAMAN, SONG-CYCLE-BOBONGO, STICK-SCRAPED,
  TOPICAL, WORK

  QUERSIN, BENOIT J.+ QUERSIN, CHRISTINE M.‡ MUSEE
  ROYAL DE L'AFRIQUE CENTRALE, CH. DE LOUVAIN, 1980
  TERVUREN, BELGIUM‡ ZAIRE‡ BASANKUSU, BEFALE,
  BOFOKA, BOKATOLA, BOLOMBA, BOLONDO, BONGILI, BOSO
  DJAFO, BOTEKA, IKELA, ISAKA, LONGO, MAKAKO,
  MOPANGA, NTOMA, WAKA, WATSI, WEMA, YA, YALIFAFU‡
  BAKUTU, BOKOTE, BONGANDO, BOSAKA, BOYELA, NKUNDU,
  PYGMIES-BATWA, PYGMIES-NGOMBE‡ 50 HOURS‡ 1972‡
  QUALITY EXCELLENT‡ MUSEE ROYAL DE L'AFRIQUE
  CENTRALE‡ ‡ ‡ ‡ AGE-SET, DANCE, DANCE-ANCESTOR,
  DANCE-HEALER, DANCE-WAR, DEATH-FUNERAL, DRUM,
  ENTERTAINMENT, FLUTE-GLOBULAR, HISTORY,
  HORN-ANTELOPE, HORN-ELEPHANT, HUNTING,
  LUTE-MULTIPLE-BOW, PADDLING, SANZA, WORK,
  WRESTLING

RABEN, JOSEPH
  NETTL, BRUNO +RABEN, JOSEPH‡ SCHOOL OF MUSIC,

RABEN, JOSEPH
  UNIVERSITY OF ILLINOIS, URBANA, ILLINOIS 61801
  +DEPARTMENT OF ENGLISH, QUEEN'S COLLEGE, FLUSHING,
  NEW YORK 11367‡ NIGERIA-U.S.‡ BLOOMINGTON,
  INDIANA‡ IBO‡ 1 HOUR‡ 1950-51‡ QUALITY GOOD‡
  ARCHIVES OF TRADITIONAL MUSIC‡ PRE'54-182-F‡ ATL
  296-97‡ RESTRICTED‡ CHILDREN-GAME,
  CHILDREN-SCHOOL, DANCE, DRUM, RATTLE-BASKET, WAR

  RABEN, JOSEPH‡ DEPARTMENT OF ENGLISH, QUEEN'S
  COLLEGE, FLUSHING, NEW YORK 11367‡ NIGERIA-U.S.‡
  BLOOMINGTON, INDIANA‡ IBO‡ .5 HOUR‡ 1950‡ QUALITY
  GOOD‡ ARCHIVES OF TRADITIONAL MUSIC‡ 061-029-F‡ ‡
  RESTRICTED‡ FOLKTALE

  RABEN, JOSEPH‡ DEPARTMENT OF ENGLISH, QUEEN'S
  COLLEGE, FLUSHING, NEW YORK 11367‡ NIGERIA-U.S.‡
  BLOOMINGTON, INDIANA‡ IBO‡ .2 HOUR‡ 1950‡ QUALITY
  GOOD‡ ARCHIVES OF TRADITIONAL MUSIC‡ 061-042-F‡ ‡
  RESTRICTED‡ CHILDREN-GAME

RADIO CLUBE DE MOCAMBIQUE
  RADIO CLUBE DE MOCAMBIQUE‡ P.O. BOX 594, LOURENCO
  MARQUES, MOZAMBIQUE‡ ‡ ‡ ‡ ‡ ‡ ‡ ‡ ‡

  RADIO CLUBE DE MOCAMBIQUE‡ P.O. BOX 594, LOURENCO
  MARQUES, MOZAMBIQUE‡ MOZAMBIQUE‡ CHIBUTO, GUIJA,
  MAPUTO, MARRACUENE, MOCAMBIQUE ISLAND, MORRUMBENE,
  MOSSURIZE, NAMPULA, NANGOLOLO, SABIE, ZAVALA‡
  CHANGANE, CHENGUE, CHOPI, LUBA, MAKONDE, MAKUA,
  RONGA, SWAZI, VADANDA, VANDAU, VATSUA‡ 135 HOURS‡
  ‡ ‡ RADIO CLUBE DE MOCAMBIQUE‡ ‡ ‡ ‡ FOLKLORE,
  RELIGIOUS, RITUAL

RADIO DAHOMEY
  CALKINS, HOWARD W.+ RADIO DAHOMEY‡ CENTRE
  CULTUREL AMERICAIN, RUE CAPORAL ANANI BERNARD,
  COTONOU, DAHOMEY+ RADIODIFFUSION DU DAHOMEY,
  COTONOU, DAHOMEY‡ DAHOMEY‡ ‡ DENDI, DOMPAGO, FON,
  MAHI, YORUBA‡ 1 HOUR‡ CA1967‡ QUALITY GOOD‡
  ARCHIVES OF TRADITIONAL MUSIC‡ 67-165-F‡ ATL 5104‡
  ‡ CHORDOPHONE, DANCE, DRUM, FLUTE

RADIODIFFUSION DU DAHOMEY
  RADIODIFFUSION DU DAHOMEY‡ COTONOU, DAHOMEY‡ ‡ ‡ ‡
  ‡ ‡ ‡ ‡ ‡ ‡

RANSBOTYN DE DECKER, DANI
  RANSBOTYN DE DECKER, DANIEL‡ 111 AVENUE DU HARAS,

RANSBOTYN DE DECKER, DANI
  1150 BRUXELLES, BELGIQUE‡ TOGO‡ AGOU, DAYES‡ BOGO,
  EWE‡ 14 HOURS‡ 1972-74‡ QUALITY GOOD‡ ‡ ‡ ‡ ‡
  GAME, HISTORY, PROVERB, RITUAL, SOCIAL

  RANSBOTYN DE DECKER, DANIEL‡ 111 AVENUE DU HARAS,
  1150 BRUXELLES, BELGIQUE‡ ZAIRE‡ BUCONGO‡ BAKONGO‡
  2 HOURS‡ 1968‡ QUALITY GOOD‡ ‡ ‡ ‡ ‡ HISTORY

RANUNG, BJORN L.C.
  RANUNG, BJORN L.C.‡ INSTITUTE OF SOCIAL
  ANTHROPOLOGY, UNIVERSITY OF STOCKHOLM, STOCKHOLM,
  SWEDEN‡ NIGERIA‡ OTURKPO‡ IGEDE‡ 8 HOURS‡ 1971-72‡
  QUALITY EXCELLENT‡ ‡ ‡ ‡ ‡ PRAISE-ANCESTOR,
  DEATH-FUNERAL, HISTORY, PRAISE, SECRET-SOCIETY

RAPHAEL, RONALD P.
  RAPHAEL, RONALD P.‡ 701 NORTH LINCOLN STREET,
  BLOOMINGTON, INDIANA 47401‡ CAMEROON‡ BANYO‡
  FULBE, KONDJA, VUTE, WAWA‡ ‡ 1974‡ QUALITY
  EXCELLENT‡ ‡ ‡ ‡ ‡ HISTORY

  RAPHAEL, RONALD P.‡ 701 NORTH LINCOLN STREET,
  BLOOMINGTON, INDIANA 47401‡ NIGERIA‡ GEMBU, YOLA,
  NORTHEASTERN STATE‡ FULBE, MAMBILA‡ ‡ 1974‡
  QUALITY EXCELLENT‡ ‡ ‡ ‡ HISTORY

RAYFIELD, JOAN R.
  RAYFIELD, JOAN R.‡ DEPARTMENT OF SOCIOLOGY, YORK
  UNIVERSITY, 4700 KEELE STREET, DOWNSVIEW M3J 1P3
  ONTARIO, CANADA‡ IVORY COAST‡ ABIDJAN‡ BAULE,
  MALINKE, SENUFO‡ 20 HOURS‡ 1972-73‡ QUALITY FAIR‡
  ‡ ‡ ‡ ‡ CEREMONY, DANCE

REDDEN, JAMES ERSKINE
  REDDEN, JAMES ERSKINE‡ DEPARTMENT OF LINGUISTICS,
  SOUTHERN ILLINOIS UNIVERSITY, CARBONDALE,
  ILLINOIS 62901‡ CAMEROON‡ ‡ BANTU‡ 40 HOURS‡
  1971‡ QUALITY GOOD‡ ‡ ‡ ‡ ‡ SENTENCE, WORD-LIST

  REDDEN, JAMES ERSKINE‡ DEPARTMENT OF LINGUISTICS,
  SOUTHERN ILLINOIS UNIVERSITY, CARBONDALE,
  ILLINOIS 62901‡ GHANA‡ ‡ AKIM, AKWAPIM, ASANTE,
  EWE‡ 20 HOURS‡ 1958-63‡ QUALITY GOOD‡ ARCHIVES OF
  LANGUAGES OF THE WORLD‡ ‡ ‡ ‡
  GRAMMATICAL-DATA-EWE, GRAMMATICAL-DATA-TWI

  REDDEN, JAMES ERSKINE‡ DEPARTMENT OF LINGUISTICS,
  SOUTHERN ILLINOIS UNIVERSITY, CARBONDALE,

REDDEN, JAMES ERSKINE
  ILLINOIS 62901‡ KENYA‡ KISUMU‡ LUO‡ 4 HOURS‡ 1959‡
  QUALITY GOOD‡ ARCHIVES OF LANGUAGES OF THE WORLD‡
  ‡ ‡ ‡ GRAMMATICAL-DATA

  REDDEN, JAMES ERSKINE‡ DEPARTMENT OF LINGUISTICS,
  SOUTHERN ILLINOIS UNIVERSITY, CARBONDALE,
  ILLINOIS 62901‡ KENYA‡ SUKUMU‡ LUO‡ 10 HOURS‡
  1960-65‡ QUALITY GOOD‡ ARCHIVES OF LANGUAGES OF
  THE WORLD‡ ‡ ‡ ‡ SENTENCE, WORD-LIST

  REDDEN, JAMES ERSKINE‡ DEPARTMENT OF LINGUISTICS,
  SOUTHERN ILLINOIS UNIVERSITY, CARBONDALE,
  ILLINOIS 62901‡ UPPER VOLTA‡ OUAGADOUGOU‡ MOSSI‡
  10 HOURS‡ 1962-63‡ QUALITY GOOD‡ ARCHIVES OF
  LANGUAGES OF THE WORLD‡ ‡ ‡ ‡ SENTENCE, WORD-LIST

  REDDEN, JAMES ERSKINE‡ DEPARTMENT OF LINGUISTICS,
  SOUTHERN ILLINOIS UNIVERSITY, CARBONDALE,
  ILLINOIS 62901‡ -U.S.‡ ‡ BAMBARA‡ 1.5 HOURS‡ 1962‡
  QUALITY GOOD‡ ARCHIVES OF LANGUAGES OF THE WORLD‡
  ‡ ‡ ‡ GRAMMATICAL-DATA

  REDDEN, JAMES ERSKINE‡ DEPARTMENT OF LINGUISTICS,
  SOUTHERN ILLINOIS UNIVERSITY, CARBONDALE,
  ILLINOIS 62901‡ ZAIRE‡ KINSHASA‡ LINGALA‡ 10
  HOURS‡ 1962‡ QUALITY FAIR‡ ARCHIVES OF LANGUAGES
  OF THE WORLD‡ ‡ ‡ ‡ GRAMMATICAL-DATA

  REDDEN, JAMES ERSKINE‡ DEPARTMENT OF LINGUISTICS,
  SOUTHERN ILLINOIS UNIVERSITY, CARBONDALE,
  ILLINOIS 62901‡ ‡ ‡ ITSEKIRI‡ .75 HOUR‡ 1958‡
  QUALITY POOR‡ ARCHIVES OF LANGUAGES OF THE WORLD‡
  ‡ ‡ ‡ GRAMMATICAL-DATA

  REDDEN, JAMES ERSKINE‡ DEPARTMENT OF LINGUISTICS,
  SOUTHERN ILLINOIS UNIVERSITY, CARBONDALE,
  ILLINOIS 62901‡ ‡ ‡ TONGA‡ ‡ 1959-60‡ QUALITY
  GOOD‡ ARCHIVES OF LANGUAGES OF THE WORLD‡ ‡ ‡ ‡
  GRAMMATICAL-DATA

REEFE, THOMAS Q.
  REEFE, THOMAS Q.‡ 114 SEA VIEW DRIVE, EL CERRITO,
  CALIFORNIA 94530‡ ZAIRE‡ ‡ LUBA‡ 20 HOURS‡
  1972-73‡ QUALITY EXCELLENT‡ ‡ ‡ ‡ ‡ HISTORY,
  MUSIC

REID, MARLENE B.
  REID, MARLENE B.‡ 3811 O'HARA STREET, PITTSBURGH,

REID, MARLENE B.
  PENNSYLVANIA 15206‡ TANZANIA‡ ‡ BASUKUMA‡ ‡ 1966+
  1969‡ QUALITY GOOD‡ ‡ ‡ ‡ ‡ PRAISE, RITUAL,
  SOCIAL

REINING, PRISCILLA
  REINING, PRISCILLA‡ DEPARTMENT OF ANTHROPOLOGY,
  CATHOLIC UNIVERSITY OF AMERICA, WASHINGTON D.C.
  20017‡ TANZANIA‡ BUKOBA DISTRICT, LAKE PROVINCE‡
  HAYA‡ 1 HOUR‡ ‡ ‡ ‡ ‡ ‡
  TRANSLATION-HAYA-HAYA-DICTIONARY,
  TRANSLATION-KU-KW-VERBS,
  TRANSLATION-MU-BA-CLASS-NOUNS

RHODES, WILLARD
  RHODES, WILLARD‡ 445 RIVERSIDE DRIVE, NEW YORK,
  NEW YORK 10027‡ NIGERIA‡ KANO‡ FULANI, HAUSA, TIV,
  TUAREG, YORUBA‡ 25 HOURS‡ 1973-74‡ QUALITY
  EXCELLENT‡ ARCHIVES OF TRADITIONAL MUSIC‡
  75-020-F‡ ‡ ‡ AEROPHONE-DOUBLE-REED,
  BUTCHER-PRAISE, CHILDREN, CHILDREN-GAME, DANCE,
  DRUM-KALANGU, DRUM-KAZAGI, FARMER, FESTIVAL-STATE,
  FLUTE, GONG-ROCK, GOURD, HUNTING, LUTE-BOWED-GOGE,
  LUTE-PLUCKED-GARAYA, MARRIAGE, RATTLE-GOURD,
  XYLOPHONE, ZITHER-RAFT

  RHODES, WILLARD‡ 445 RIVERSIDE DRIVE, NEW YORK,
  NEW YORK 10027‡ RHODESIA‡ MTOKO‡ SHONA‡ 25 HOURS‡
  1958-59‡ QUALITY GOOD‡ ‡ ‡ ‡ ‡ SOCIAL

  RHODES, WILLARD‡ 445 RIVERSIDE DRIVE, NEW YORK,
  NEW YORK 10027‡ ZAMBIA‡ LUSAKA‡ SHONA‡ 1 HOUR‡
  1958-59‡ QUALITY GOOD‡ ‡ ‡ ‡ ‡ POLITICAL

RICARD, ALAIN J.
  RICARD, ALAIN J.‡ 112 AVENUE GRAL LECLERC, 33200
  BORDEAUX, FRANCE‡ TOGO‡ LOME‡ EWE‡ 40 HOURS‡ 1973‡
  QUALITY GOOD‡ ‡ ‡ ‡ ‡ DRAMA, ENTERTAINMENT

RIGGS, VENDA
  RIGGS, VENDA‡ ‡ NIGERIA‡ ‡ YORUBA‡ 1 HOUR‡ 1949‡
  QUALITY FAIR‡ ARCHIVES OF LANGUAGES OF THE WORLD‡
  ‡ ‡ ‡ GRAMMATICAL-DATA

RITZENTHALER, PAT
  RITZENTHALER, ROBERT + RITZENTHALER, PAT‡ 5631
  SOUTH KURTZ ROAD, HALES CORNERS, WISCONSIN 53130‡
  CAMEROON‡ BAFUT‡ BAFUT‡ ‡ 1959‡ QUALITY GOOD‡
  MILWAUKEE PUBLIC MUSEUM‡ ‡ ‡ ‡ DEATH-FUNERAL,

RITZENTHALER, PAT
  LULLABY, PRAISE, SOCIAL, WORK

RITZENTHALER, ROBERT
  RITZENTHALER, ROBERT + RITZENTHALER, PAT‡ 5631
  SOUTH KURTZ ROAD, HALES CORNERS, WISCONSIN 53130‡
  CAMEROON‡ BAFUT‡ BAFUT‡ ‡ 1959‡ QUALITY GOOD‡
  MILWAUKEE PUBLIC MUSEUM‡ ‡ ‡ ‡ DEATH-FUNERAL,
  LULLABY, PRAISE, SOCIAL, WORK

ROBBIN, LAWRENCE H.
  ROBBIN, LAWRENCE H.‡ DEPARTMENT OF ANTHROPOLOGY,
  MICHIGAN STATE UNIVERSITY, EAST LANSING, MICHIGAN‡
  KENYA‡ CENTRAL, SOUTH‡ TURKANA‡ 2 HOURS‡ 1965-66‡
  QUALITY GOOD‡ ‡ ‡ ‡ ‡ BOASTING

  ROBBIN, LAWRENCE H.‡ DEPARTMENT OF ANTHROPOLOGY,
  MICHIGAN STATE UNIVERSITY, EAST LANSING, MICHIGAN‡
  UGANDA‡ KATOBCK‡ POKOT‡ 2 HOURS‡ 1970‡ QUALITY
  GOOD‡ ‡ ‡ ‡ ‡ BOASTING, CEREMONY-COMET-SIGHTING

ROBBINS, MICHAEL COOK
  ROBBINS, MICHAEL COOK‡ DEPARTMENT OF ANTHROPOLOGY,
  UNIVERSITY OF MISSOURI, COLUMBIA, MISSOURI 65201‡
  UGANDA‡ ‡ BAGANDA‡ 5 HOURS‡ 1967-72‡ QUALITY
  EXCELLENT‡ ‡ ‡ ‡ ‡ SOCIAL

ROBERTSON, CLAIRE C.
  ROBERTSON, CLAIRE C.‡ 1336 LINN STREET, STATE
  COLLEGE, PENNSYLVANIA 16801‡ GHANA‡ ACCRA‡ GA‡
  120 HOURS‡ 1972‡ QUALITY FAIR‡ ARCHIVES OF
  TRADITIONAL MUSIC‡ 74-098-F‡ ‡ RESTRICTED‡
  HISTORY-LIFE, MARKET-TRADER-INTERVIEW,
  MARRIAGE-INTERVIEW, WOMEN-INTERVIEW

ROBINSON, DAVID W.
  ROBINSON, DAVID W.‡ HISTORY DEPARTMENT, 237 HALL
  OF GRADUATE STUDIES, YALE UNIVERSITY, NEW HAVEN,
  CONNECTICUT 06520‡ SENEGAL‡ DAKAR, FUTA TORO‡
  PULAR‡ 100 HOURS‡ 1968-69‡ QUALITY GOOD‡ ARCHIVES
  OF TRADITIONAL MUSIC‡ 70-094-F‡ ‡ ‡ HISTORY

ROGERS, HENRY EDWIN
  ROGERS, HENRY EDWIN‡ DEPARTMENT OF LINGUISTIC
  STUDIES, UNIVERSITY OF TORONTO, TORONTO, ONTARIO,
  CANADA M55 1A1‡ SIERRA LEONE‡ SHENGI‡ SHERBRO‡ .5
  HOUR‡ 1966‡ QUALITY POOR‡ ‡ ‡ ‡ ‡ FOLKTALE

ROMERO, PATRICIA
  ROMERO, PATRICIA‡ ‡ GHANA‡ KUMASI‡ ASANTE‡ 1 HOUR‡
  1972‡ QUALITY GOOD‡ ‡ ‡ ‡ RITUAL

  ROMERO, PATRICIA‡ ‡ KENYA‡ NAIROBI‡ ‡ 1.25 HOURS‡
  1973‡ QUALITY GOOD‡ ‡ ‡ ‡ ‡
  INTERVIEW-MAKANNEU-RAS, MANCHESTER-CONFERENCE

  ROMERO, PATRICIA‡ ‡ NIGERIA‡ EASTERN REGION‡ IBO‡
  1.5 HOURS‡ 1973‡ QUALITY GOOD‡ ‡ ‡ ‡ ‡
  BIAFRAN-WAR-INTERVIEW, INTERVIEW-NKEM-NWANKO,
  INTERVIEW-OKO-WONODA

ROSELLINI, JAMES N.
  CHRISTIAN, VALERIE+ ROSELLINI, JAMES N.‡
  DEPARTMENT OF ANTHROPOLOGY, INDIANA UNIVERSITY,
  BLOOMINGTON, INDIANA 47401+ C.V.R.S., B.P. 7047,
  OUAGADOUGOU, UPPER VOLTA‡ UPPER VOLTA‡ KOUPE-LA,
  NOUNA‡ FULBE, KASSENA, MARKA, MOSSI‡ 2 HOURS‡
  1973‡ QUALITY EXCELLENT‡ ARCHIVES OF TRADITIONAL
  MUSIC+ ARCHIVES SONORES, C.V.R.S.‡ 74-068-F‡ ‡
  RESTRICTED‡ DRUM-CYLINDRICAL, GOURD, LUTE-BOWED,
  PRAISE, RATTLE

ROSEN, -
  ROSEN, -‡ ‡ ETHIOPIA‡ ‡ ‡ .1 HOUR‡ 1905‡ QUALITY
  FAIR‡ ARCHIVES OF TRADITIONAL MUSIC‡ 59-002-F‡
  ATL 1757‡ RESTRICTED‡ WAR

ROSS, MARC HOWARD
  ROSS, MARC HOWARD‡ DEPARTMENT OF POLITICAL
  SCIENCE, BRYN MAWR COLLEGE, BRYN MAWR,
  PENNSYLVANIA 19010‡ KENYA‡ KIAMBU‡ KIKUYU‡ 1.5
  HOURS‡ 1967‡ QUALITY FAIR‡ ‡ ‡ ‡ ‡ DRINKING,
  POLITICAL-EMERGENCY

ROTBERG, ROBERT I.
  ROTBERG, ROBERT I.‡ DEPARTMENT OF POLITICAL
  SCIENCE, MASSACHUSETTS INSTITUTE OF TECHNOLOGY,
  CAMBRIDGE, MASSACHUSETTS 02139‡ ZAMBIA‡ NORTHERN‡
  BISA‡ ‡ 1967‡ QUALITY GOOD‡ ‡ ‡ ‡ ‡ HISTORY,
  INTERVIEW

ROUCH, JEAN
  BERNUS, S.+ ROUCH, JEAN‡ -+ CENTRE DE RECHERCHES
  AFRICAINES, RUE D'ALSACE, 75 PARIS 6E, FRANCE‡
  NIGER‡ ‡ SONRAI‡ ‡ 1960‡ ‡ MUSEE DE L'HOMME‡ ‡ ‡ ‡
  CHORDOPHONE

ROUCH, JEAN
  ROUCH, JEAN‡ CENTRE DE RECHERCHES AFRICAINES, RUE
  D'ALSACE, 75 PARIS 6E, FRANCE‡ NIGER‡ ‡ SONGHAY‡ ‡
  ‡ ‡ MUSEE DE L'HOMME‡ ‡ ‡ ‡

ROUGET, GILBERT
  BEIER, ULLI+ ROUGET, GILBERT‡ INSTITUTE OF
  AFRICAN STUDIES, UNIVERSITY OF IFE, ILE-IFE,
  NIGERIA+ 1 RUE DES DEUX-PONTS, 75004 PARIS,
  FRANCE‡ NIGERIA‡ ‡ YORUBA‡ ‡ ‡ ‡ MUSEE DE L'HOMME‡
  ‡ ‡

  BRASSEUR, G.+ DI DIO, FRANCOIS+ DIETERLEN,
  GERMAINE+ ROUGET, GILBERT‡ -+ -+ CENTRE DE
  RECHERCHES AFRICAINES, RUE D'ALSACE, 75 PARIS 6E,
  FRANCE+ 1 RUE DES DEUX-PONTS, 75004 PARIS, FRANCE‡
  MALI‡ ‡ BAMBARA, BOZO, DOGON, MALINKE, MARKA,
  MINIANKA, PEUL, RYMAYBE, SARAKOLE, SOMONO,
  SONGHAY‡ ‡ ‡ ‡ MUSEE DE L'HOMME‡ ‡ ‡ ‡

  ERNOULT, CLAUDE+ ROUGET, GILBERT‡ -+ 1 RUE DES
  DEUX-PONTS, 75004 PARIS, FRANCE‡ MAURITANIA‡ ‡ ‡ ‡
  ‡ ‡ MUSEE DE L'HOMME‡ ‡ ‡ ‡ MUSICIAN-GRIOT

  GALAND, -+ ROUGET, GILBERT‡ -+ 1 RUE DES
  DEUX-PONTS, 75004 PARIS, FRANCE‡ MOROCCO‡ ‡
  BERBER‡ ‡ ‡ MUSEE DE L'HOMME‡ ‡ ‡ ‡

  ROUGET, GILBERT‡ 1 RUE DES DEUX-PONTS, 75004
  PARIS, FRANCE‡ CONGO, PEOPLE'S REPUBLIC OF THE‡
  OUESSO‡ PYGMIES-NGOUNDI‡ 25 HOURS‡ 1948‡ QUALITY
  GOOD‡ MUSEE DE L'HOMME‡ ‡ ‡ ‡ MUSIC

  ROUGET, GILBERT‡ 1 RUE DE DEUX-PONTS, 75004 PARIS,
  FRANCE‡ DAHOMEY‡ ‡ FON, GUN, HOLI, NAGO‡ ‡ 1952‡ ‡
  MUSEE DE L'HOMME‡ ‡ ‡ ‡ DANCE-MASKED-GELEDE,
  DIVINING, FESTIVAL-SHANGO, FESTIVAL-TOHOSSOU,
  FLUTE, ROYAL, SANZA, SECRET-SOCIETY, SPIRIT,
  ZITHER

  ROUGET, GILBERT‡ 1, RUE DES DEUX-PONTS, 75004
  PARIS, FRANCE‡ DAHOMEY‡ SOUTH DAHOMEY‡ FON, GUN,
  YORUBA‡ 30 HOURS‡ 1952-71‡ QUALITY GOOD‡ MUSEE DE
  L'HOMME‡ ‡ ‡ ‡ MUSIC

  ROUGET, GILBERT‡ 1 RUE DES DEUX-PONTS, 75004
  PARIS, FRANCE‡ GUINEA‡ ‡ KONON, MALINKE, MANON,
  PEUL‡ ‡ ‡ MUSEE DE L'HOMME‡ ‡ ‡ ‡

ROUGET, GILBERT
  ROUGET, GILBERT‡ 1, RUE DES DEUX-PONTS, 75004
  PARIS, FRANCE‡ GUINEA‡ KANKAN‡ MALINKE‡ 15 HOURS‡
  1952‡ QUALITY GOOD‡ MUSEE DE L'HOMME‡ ‡ ‡ ‡ MUSIC

  ROUGET, GILBERT‡ 1 RUE DES DEUX-PONTS, 75004
  PARIS, FRANCE‡ GUINEA‡ KANKAN, KARALA‡ MALINKE‡ ‡
  1952‡ ‡ MUSEE DE L'HOMME‡ ‡ ‡ ‡ CHILDREN,
  CHORDOPHONE-DOZO-KONU, CIRCUMCISION, DRUM-WATER,
  FESTIVAL, FLUTE-TRANSVERSE, GAME, HARP-BURUNUBA,
  HARP-LUTE-BOLON, HARP-LUTE-KOGBELENU,
  HARP-LUTE-KORA, LUTE-DYELI-KONU, LULLABY,
  MUSICIAN-GRIOT, PURIFICATION, XYLOPHONE-BALA

  ROUGET, GILBERT‡ 1 RUE DES DEUX-PONTS, 75004
  PARIS, FRANCE‡ IVORY COAST‡ ‡ ADIOUKROU, BAULE,
  EBRIE‡ ‡ ‡ ‡ MUSEE DE L'HOMME‡ ‡ ‡ ‡

  ROUGET, GILBERT‡ 1 RUE DE DEUX-PONTS, 75004 PARIS,
  FRANCE‡ IVORY COAST‡ ‡ ADIOUKROU, EBRIE‡ ‡ 1952‡ ‡
  MUSEE DE L'HOMME‡ ‡ ‡ ‡ DRUM, WAR

  ROUGET, GILBERT‡ 1 RUE DE DEUX-PONTS, 75004 PARIS,
  FRANCE‡ MAURITANIA‡ ‡ ‡ ‡ 1952‡ ‡ MUSEE DE
  L'HOMME‡ ‡ ‡ ‡ HARP, LUTE

  ROUGET, GILBERT‡ 1 RUE DES DEUX-PONTS, 75004
  PARIS, FRANCE‡ SENEGAL‡ ‡ LEBOU, PEUL, WOLOF‡ ‡ ‡
  ‡ MUSEE DE L'HOMME‡ ‡ ‡ ‡

  ROUGET, GILBERT‡ 1 RUE DES DEUX-PONTS, 75004
  PARIS, FRANCE‡ SENEGAL‡ ‡ LEBOU, PEUL, SARAKOLE,
  SOCE, TUKULOR, WOLOF‡ ‡ 1952‡ ‡ MUSEE DE L'HOMME‡
  ‡ ‡ ‡ BOW-MUSICAL, CIRCUMCISION, DANCE-POSSESSION,
  DEATH-MOURNING, GAME, MARRIAGE, MUSICIAN-GRIOT,
  WORK

  ROUGET, GILBERT+ GESSAIN, R.+ GESSAIN, M.‡ 1 RUE
  DES DEUX-PONTS, 75004 PARIS, FRANCE+ -+ -‡
  SENEGAL‡ ‡ BASSARI, BEDIK‡ ‡ 1967‡ ‡ MUSEE DE
  L'HOMME‡ ‡ ‡ ‡ FLUTE, LULLABY, MASK-VOICE,
  WORK-FIELD

  ROUGET, GILBERT+ TARDITS, CLAUDE+ VERGER, PIERRE‡
  1 RUE DES DEUX-PONTS, 75004 PARIS, FRANCE+ 33 RUE
  CROULEBARBE, 75013 PARIS, FRANCE+ -‡ DAHOMEY‡ ‡
  ADJA, FON, GUN, ITCHA, MINA, NAGO‡ ‡ ‡ ‡ MUSEE DE
  L'HOMME‡ ‡ ‡ ‡

RUBIN, ARNOLD G.
   RUBIN, ARNOLD G.‡ DEPARTMENT OF ART, UNIVERSITY
   OF CALIFORNIA, 405 HILGARD AVENUE, LOS ANGELES,
   CALIFORNIA 90024‡ NIGERIA‡ AKWANA, DONGA,
   LANGTANG, RAFIN KADA, TAKUM, WUKARI‡ CHAMBA,
   HAUSA, IBO, JUKUN, KUTEP, TIKARI, TIV‡ 10 HOURS‡
   1964-65‡ QUALITY GOOD‡ ARCHIVES OF TRADITIONAL
   MUSIC‡ 67-122-F‡ ATL 3406-30‡ ‡ BELL-DOUBLE,
   BLACKSMITH, COMMENT-SOCIAL, CURING-SOCIETY,
   DANCE-MASKED, DANCE-SOCIAL, DEATH-FUNERAL, DRUM,
   ENTERTAINMENT, FLUTE, FLUTE-VERTICAL, FOLKTALE,
   HORN-ANTELOPE, LUTE-PLUCKED, MARRIAGE,
   RATTLE-GOURD, SOCIETY-CURING, WARM-UP,
   WORK-GRINDING, XYLOPHONE, ZITHER-RAFT

RUTHERFORD, DOUGLAS I.
   RUTHERFORD, DOUGLAS I.‡ 1009 CHURCH STREET, ANN
   ARBOR, MICHIGAN 48103‡ MALI‡ BAMAKO‡ BAMBARA‡ 2.5
   HOURS‡ 1972‡ QUALITY EXCELLENT‡ ‡ ‡ ‡ ‡
   HARP-LUTE-KORA, HARP-LUTE-INSTRUCTION

SANDGREN, DAVID PETER
   SANDGREN, DAVID PETER‡ 426 SOUTH 5TH STREET,
   MOORHEAD, MINNESOTA 56560‡ KENYA‡ CENTRAL
   PROVINCE, KIAMBU DISTRICT, MURUNGA DISTRICT‡
   KIKUYU‡ 140 HOURS‡ 1970-71‡ QUALITY GOOD‡ ‡ ‡ ‡ ‡
   HISTORY-KIKUYU, HISTORY-POLITICAL, HISTORY-SOCIAL

SAPIR, J. DAVID
   SAPIR, J. DAVID‡ DEPARTMENT OF ANTHROPOLOGY AND
   SOCIOLOGY, UNIVERSITY OF VIRGINIA,
   CHARLOTTESVILLE, VIRGINIA 22903‡ SENEGAL‡ LOWER
   CASAMANCE‡ DIOLA-FOGNY, DIOLA-KASA‡ 48 HOURS‡
   1960-65‡ QUALITY EXCELLENT‡ CENTER FOR AFRICAN
   ORAL DATA‡ 70-103, 104-F‡ ATL 4153-235, 4238-43‡
   RESTRICTED‡ BOW-MUSICAL, DEATH-FUNERAL, DRUM-SLIT,
   FOLKTALE, HISTORY, HARP-LUTE-KORA, HORN-LANGUAGE,
   MARRIAGE-ISLAMIC, PRAISE, WORD-LIST, WORK-FIELD,
   WORK-HARVEST, WRESTLING

SARDAN, J.-P. OLIVIER DE
   SARDAN, J.-P. OLIVIER DE‡ ‡ NIGER‡ TILLABERI‡
   SONGHAY‡ ‡ 1969‡ ‡ MUSEE DE L'HOMME‡ ‡ ‡ ‡ DANCE,
   LUTE, WOMEN, WORK-POUNDING

SAVARY, CLAUDE
   SAVARY, CLAUDE‡ 65 BOULEVARD CARL-VOGT, 1205
   GENEVE, SWITZERLAND‡ DAHOMEY‡ ABOMEY‡ FON‡ 19
   HOURS‡ 1966-67‡ QUALITY GOOD‡ ‡ ‡ ‡ ‡ FOLKLORE,

SAVARY, CLAUDE
  RITUAL-VODUN

SAYAD, ALI
  SAYAD, ALI‡ C.R.A.P.E.(MUSEE DU BARDO), 3 AVENUE
  F.D. ROOSEVELT, ALGIERS, ALGERIA‡ ALGERIA‡
  KABYLIE‡ KABYLE‡ 20 HOURS‡ 1968-70‡ QUALITY FAIR‡
  ‡ ‡ ‡ ‡ ENTERTAINMENT, FOLKLORE, HISTORY, SOCIAL

  SAYAD, ALI‡ C.R.A.P.E. (MUSEE DU BARDO), 3 AVENUE
  F.D. ROOSEVELT, ALGIERS, ALGERIA‡ ALGERIA‡
  L'AURES‡ CHAOUI‡ 3 HOURS‡ 1971-72‡ QUALITY FAIR‡ ‡
  ‡ ‡ ‡ FOLKLORE

SCANDANAVIAN INSTITUTE OF
  SCANDANAVIAN INSTITUTE OF AFRICAN STUDIES‡ BOX
  345, 751 06 UPPSALA, SWEDEN‡ ‡ ‡ ‡ ‡ ‡ ‡ ‡ ‡ ‡

SCHAEFFNER, ANDRE
  SCHAEFFNER, ANDRE‡ CENTRE NATIONAL DE LA
  RECHERCHE SCIENTIFIQUE, 35 RUE FONTAINE-A-MULARD,
  PARIS, 13E, FRANCE‡ GUINEA‡ ‡ BASA‡ ‡ ‡ ‡ MUSEE
  DE L'HOMME‡ ‡ ‡ ‡

SCHEUB, HAROLD
  SCHEUB, HAROLD‡ DEPARTMENT OF AFRICAN LANGUAGES
  AND LITERATURE, UNIVERSITY OF WISCONSIN, MADISON,
  WISCONSIN 53706‡ SOUTH AFRICA‡ KWAZULU, TRANSKEI‡
  XHOSA, ZULU‡ 550 HOURS‡ 1967-68‡ QUALITY
  EXCELLENT‡ ‡ ‡ ‡ ‡ HISTORY, NARRATIVE-IINTSOMI,
  NARRATIVE-IZINGANEKWANE, PRAISE-IZIBONGO

  SCHEUB, HAROLD‡ DEPARTMENT OF AFRICAN LANGUAGES
  AND LITERATURE, UNIVERSITY OF WISCONSIN, MADISON,
  WISCONSIN 53706‡ SOUTH AFRICA‡ KWAZULU, NDEBELE,
  TRANSKEI‡ NDEBELE, XHOSA, ZULU‡ 230 HOURS‡
  1972-73‡ QUALITY EXCELLENT‡ ‡ ‡ ‡ ‡
  NARRATIVE-IINTSOMI, NARRATIVE-IZINGANEKWANE,
  NARRATIVE-IZINGANU

  SCHEUB, HAROLD‡ DEPARTMENT OF AFRICAN LANGUAGES
  AND LITERATURE, UNIVERSITY OF WISCONSIN, MADISON,
  WISCONSIN 53706‡ SWAZILAND‡ ‡ SWAZI‡ 120 HOURS‡
  1972-73‡ QUALITY EXCELLENT‡ ‡ ‡ ‡
  NARRATIVE-TINSIMU

SCHOOL OF ORIENTAL AND AF
  SCHOOL OF ORIENTAL AND AFRICAN STUDIES (SOAS)‡
  UNIVERSITY OF LONDON, LONDON, WC1, ENGLAND‡ ‡ ‡ ‡

SCHOOL OF ORIENTAL AND AF
‡ ‡ ‡ ‡ ‡ ‡

SCHWARTZ, -
  SCHWARTZ, -‡ ‡ TANZANIA‡ ‡ ZINZA‡ .1 HOUR‡ 1906‡
  QUALITY FAIR‡ ARCHIVES OF TRADITIONAL MUSIC‡
  59-002-F‡ ATL 1757‡ RESTRICTED‡

SCHWARZ, JEAN
  SCHWARZ, JEAN‡ PALAIS DE CHAILLOT, PARIS 16E,
  FRANCE‡ CAMEROON‡ ‡ BANEN‡ ‡ 1968‡ ‡ MUSEE DE
  L'HOMME‡ ‡ ‡ ‡ DRUM-LANGUAGE

SCHWEEGER-HEFEL, ANNEMARI
  SCHWEEGER-HEFEL, ANNEMARIE‡ 1010 WIEN I,
  STEPHAUSPLATZ 6, AUSTRIA‡ UPPER VOLTA‡ ‡ DOGON,
  KURUMBA, PEUL‡ 56 HOURS‡ ‡ QUALITY EXCELLENT‡
  PHONOGRAMMARCHIV DER OESTERREICHISCHEN‡ ‡ ‡ ‡
  FOLKLORE, MUSIC

  SCHWEEGER-HEFEL, ANNEMARIE‡ 1010 WEIN I,
  STEPHAUSPLATZ 6, AUSTRIA‡ UPPER VOLTA‡ DJELGEDJI‡
  KURUMBA, PEUL, RIWAIBE‡ 50 HOURS‡ 1961-69‡
  QUALITY GOOD‡ PHONOGRAMMARCHIV DER
  OESTERREICHISCHEN‡ ‡ ‡ ‡

SEDLAK, PHILIP A.S.
  SEDLAK, PHILIP A.S.‡ OFFICE OF INTERNATIONAL
  PROGRAMS, UNIVERSITY OF SOUTHERN CALIFORNIA, LOS
  ANGELES, CALIFORNIA 90007‡ KENYA‡ GEDE, LAMU,
  MARIAKANI‡ DURUMA, GIRYAMA, SWAHILI‡ 10 HOURS‡
  1971‡ QUALITY GOOD‡ ‡ ‡ ‡ ‡ BALLAD,
  CURING-ANTI-WITCHCRAFT, LOVE, SOCIAL-CRITICISM

SELIGMAN, THOMAS KNOWLES
  SELIGMAN, THOMAS KNOWLES‡ 34 WOODLAND AVENUE, SAN
  FRANCISCO, CALIFORNIA 94117‡ LIBERIA‡ SUCRUMU‡
  KPELLE‡ 1 HOUR‡ 1970‡ QUALITY GOOD‡ ‡ ‡ ‡ ‡ DANCE,
  ENTERTAINMENT

SEYFRIED, CAPTAIN
  SEYFRIED, CAPTAIN‡ ‡ TANZANIA‡ ‡ ‡ .2 HOUR‡
  1906-09‡ QUALITY FAIR‡ ARCHIVES OF TRADITIONAL
  MUSIC‡ 59-002-F‡ ATL 1757-58‡ RESTRICTED‡ DANCE,
  RATTLE

SHAMAY, M.
  SHAMAY, M.‡ ‡ ALGERIA‡ GRANDE KABYLIE‡ ‡ ‡ 1968‡ ‡
  MUSEE DE L'HOMME‡ ‡ ‡ ‡ WOMEN

SHEFFIELD, JAMES
  SHEFFIELD, JAMES‡ TEACHERS COLLEGE, COLUMBIA
  UNIVERSITY, BOX 218, 525 WEST 120TH STREET, NEW
  YORK, NEW YORK 10027‡ DAHOMEY‡ KETU, OHORI, POBE‡
  YORUBA‡ 23 HOURS‡ 1971+ 1973‡ QUALITY GOOD‡ ‡ ‡
  ‡ ARTIST, BIOGRAPHY-ARTIST, HISTORY, RITUAL

  SHEFFIELD, JAMES‡ TEACHERS COLLEGE, COLUMBIA
  UNIVERSITY, BOX 218, 525 WEST 120TH STREET, NEW
  YORK, NEW YORK 10027‡ NIGERIA‡ EGBADO‡ YORUBA‡ 20
  HOURS‡ 1971‡ QUALITY GOOD‡ ‡ ‡ ‡ HISTORY,
  RITUAL

SHELEMAY, KAY KAUFMAN
  SHELEMAY, KAY KAUFMAN‡ 6356-C BANDERA, DALLAS,
  TEXAS 75225‡ ETHIOPIA‡ AMBOBER, TADDA, WOLLEKA‡
  FALASHA-JEW‡ 55 HOURS‡ 1973‡ QUALITY GOOD‡
  ARCHIVES OF TRADITIONAL MUSIC‡ 73-031-F‡ ‡
  RESTRICTED‡ CEREMONY-FALASHA, FLUTE-EMBILTA,
  LITURGY-FALASHA, LUTE-BOWED-MASENQO, MILIKIT,
  PRIEST-FALASHA-INTERVIEW, WASHINT

SHOSTAK, MARJORIE JANET
  SHOSTAK, MARJORIE JANET‡ HARVARD UNIVERSITY,
  WILLIAM JAMES HALL, ROOM 320, CAMBRIDGE,
  MASSACHUSETTS 02138‡ BOTSWANA‡ NGAMILAND‡ HERERO,
  KUNG-BUSHMEN‡ 260 HOURS‡ 1969-71‡ QUALITY GOOD‡ ‡
  ‡ ‡ ‡ HISTORY-LIFE, HYMN, LANGUAGE

SIEBER, ROY
  SIEBER, ROY‡ FINE ARTS DEPARTMENT, INDIANA
  UNIVERSITY, BLOOMINGTON, INDIANA 47401‡ NIGERIA‡
  EDE‡ YORUBA‡ 3 HOURS‡ 1971‡ QUALITY EXCELLENT‡ ‡
  ‡ ‡ HISTORY-EDE

SIEGMANN, WILLIAM CHARLES
  SIEGMANN, WILLIAM CHARLES‡ AFRICAN STUDIES
  PROGRAM, INDIANA UNIVERSITY, BLOOMINGTON, INDIANA
  47401‡ LIBERIA‡ GRAND BASSA COUNTY, LOFFA COUNTY‡
  BASSA, GBANDE‡ 34 HOURS‡ 1973-74‡ QUALITY GOOD‡ ‡
  ‡ ‡ ‡ HISTORY, RITUAL, SOCIAL

SIGWALT, RICHARD
  SIGWALT, RICHARD+ SOSNE, ELINOR‡ DEPARTMENT OF
  SOCIOLOGY, OLD DOMINION UNIVERSITY, NORFOLK,
  VIRGINIA 23508‡ ZAIRE‡ KIVU‡ SHI‡ 60 HOURS‡
  1971-73‡ QUALITY POOR‡ ‡ ‡ ‡ ‡ DANCE, FOLKTALE,
  HISTORY, MARRIAGE, MUSIC

SILVERMAN, JOSEPH H.
  ARMISTEAD, SAMUEL G. + KATZ, ISRAEL J. +
  SILVERMAN, JOSEPH H.‡ 4524 SPRUCE STREET,
  PHILADELPHIA, PENNSYLVANIA 19139 + 415 WEST 115TH
  STREET, NEW YORK, NEW YORK 10025 + ADLAI
  STEVENSON COLLEGE, UNIVERSITY OF CALIFORNIA,
  SANTA CRUZ, CALIFORNIA 95060‡ MOROCCO‡ SPANISH
  ZONE‡ SEPHARDIC-JEW‡ 60 HOURS‡ 1962‡ QUALITY
  EXCELLENT‡ ‡ ‡ ‡ BALLAD-SPANISH,
  CIRCUMCISION-CEREMONY, DEATH-DIRGE, FOLKTALE,
  HYMN-HEBREW-METRICAL, MARRIAGE

SIMMONS, W.S.
  SIMMONS, W.S.‡ DEPARTMENT OF ANTHROPOLOGY,
  UNIVERSITY OF CALIFORNIA, BERKELEY, CALIFORNIA
  94720‡ SENEGAL‡ CASAMANCE‡ BADYARANKE‡ 1 HOUR‡
  1964-66‡ QUALITY GOOD‡ ‡ ‡ ‡ INITIATION

SIMPSON, AL
  SIMPSON, AL‡ ‡ ‡ ‡ BULU‡ 1 HOUR‡ 1958‡ QUALITY
  GOOD‡ ARCHIVES OF LANGUAGES OF THE WORLD‡ ‡ ‡ ‡
  GRAMMATICAL-DATA

SKINNER, A. NEIL
  SKINNER, A. NEIL+ SKINNER, MARGARET G.‡ 2215 ETON
  RIDGE, MADISON, WISCONSIN 53705‡ NIGERIA‡
  NORTHERN STATES‡ ANGAS, FULA, HAUSA, KABBA,
  YORUBA‡ ‡ 1967-74‡ QUALITY FAIR‡ LANGUAGE
  LABORATORY, UNIVERSITY OF WISCONSIN‡ ‡ ‡ ‡
  FOLKTALE, INTERVIEW, MUSIC, POETRY

SKINNER, ELLIOTT P.
  SKINNER, ELLIOTT P.‡ DEPARTMENT OF ANTHROPOLOGY,
  COLUMBIA UNIVERSITY, NEW YORK 10027‡ UPPER VOLTA‡
  OUAGADOUGOU‡ MOSSI‡ 10 HOURS‡ 1955-65‡ QUALITY
  GOOD‡ ‡ ‡ ‡ RESTRICTED‡ HISTORY, RITUAL, SOCIAL

SKINNER, MARGARET G.
  SKINNER, A. NEIL+ SKINNER, MARGARET G.‡ 2215 ETON
  RIDGE, MADISON, WISCONSIN 53705‡ NIGERIA‡
  NORTHERN STATES‡ ANGAS, FULA, HAUSA, KABBA,
  YORUBA‡ ‡ 1967-74‡ QUALITY FAIR‡ LANGUAGE
  LABORATORY, UNIVERSITY OF WISCONSIN‡ ‡ ‡ ‡
  FOLKTALE, INTERVIEW, MUSIC, POETRY

SMEND, W.A.
  SMEND, W.A.‡ ‡ TOGO‡ ‡ HAUSA‡ .4 HOUR‡ 1905‡
  QUALITY FAIR‡ ARCHIVES OF TRADITIONAL MUSIC‡
  59-002-F‡ ATL 1755‡ RESTRICTED‡ AEROPHONE,

SMEND, W.A.
    DRUM-LANGUAGE, DRUM-PROVERB, FLUTE, HUNTING,
    PROVERB-DRUM, RATTLE

SMITS, LUCAS GERARDUS ALF
    SMITS, LUCAS GERARDUS ALFONSUS‡ UNIVERSITY OF
    BOTSWANA, LESOTHO AND SWAZILAND, ROMA, LESOTHO‡
    ALGERIA‡ DJANET/TASSILI, TAMANRASSET‡ TUAREG‡ 1.5
    HOURS‡ 1968-69‡ QUALITY POOR‡ ‡ ‡ ‡ ‡ DANCE, DRUM,
    FLUTE, SOCIAL

    SMITS, LUCAS GERARDUS ALFONSUS‡ UNIVERSITY OF
    BOTSWANA, LESOTHO AND SWAZILAND, ROMA, LESOTHO‡
    BOTSWANA‡ KANGWA REGION, NORTHERN KALAHARI‡
    KUNG-BUSHMEN, SAN‡ 2 HOURS‡ 1972‡ QUALITY FAIR‡ ‡
    ‡ ‡ ‡ IDIOPHONE-PLUCKED, SOCIAL

    SMITS, LUCAS GERARDUS ALFONSUS‡ UNIVERSITY OF
    BOTSWANA, LESOTHO AND SWAZILAND, ROMA, LESOTHO‡
    LESOTHO‡ HA BAROANA, HA KTOBA, MATELA‡ BASOTHO‡ 3
    HOURS‡ 1969‡ 1974-75‡ QUALITY GOOD‡ ‡ ‡ ‡ ‡
    SOCIAL

SMOCK, DAVID R.
    SMOCK, DAVID R.‡ 100 VERNON DRIVE, SCARSDALE, NEW
    YORK‡ NIGERIA‡ EASTERN REGION‡ IBO‡ 2 HOURS‡
    1962-63‡ QUALITY GOOD‡ ‡ ‡ ‡ ‡ AUTOBIOGRAPHY,
    SOCIAL

SMOLEY, R.A.
    SMOLEY, R.A.‡ 301 ELM STREET, WEST MIFFLIN,
    PENNSYLVANIA 15122‡ DAHOMEY-U.S.‡ PITTSBURGH,
    PENNSYLVANIA‡ ‡ 1.5 HOURS‡ 1970‡ QUALITY GOOD‡
    ARCHIVES OF TRADITIONAL MUSIC‡ 70-127-F‡ ‡ ‡
    FESTIVAL

SNYDER, EMILE
    BRUTUS, DENNIS‡ SNYDER, EMILE‡ -‡ AFRICAN STUDIES,
    INDIANA UNIVERSITY, BLOOMINGTON, INDIANA 47401‡
    SOUTH AFRICA-U.S.‡ MADISON, WISCONSIN‡ ‡ 2 HOURS‡
    1966‡ QUALITY GOOD‡ ARCHIVES OF TRADITIONAL MUSIC‡
    71-015-F‡ ATL 4421-22‡ RESTRICTED‡ POETRY,
    POETRY-INTERVIEW, POLITICS-SPEECH

SNYDER, FRANCIS GREGORY
    SNYDER, FRANCIS GREGORY‡ OSGOODE HALE LAW SCHOOL,
    YORK UNIVERSITY, 4700 KEELE STREET, DOWNSVIEW,
    ONTARIO M3J1P3 CANADA‡ SENEGAL‡ CASAMANCE‡ DIOLA‡
    40 HOURS‡ 1970‡ QUALITY GOOD‡ ARCHIVES

SNYDER, FRANCIS GREGORY
  CULTURELLES DU SENEGAL‡ ‡ ‡ ‡ LAND-TRANSFER,
  LAND-USE, LEGAL, SOCIAL

  SNYDER, FRANCIS GREGORY‡ OSGOODE HALL LAW SCHOOL,
  YORK UNIVERSITY, 4700 KEELE STREET, DOWNSVIEW,
  ONTARIO M3J1P3, CANADA‡ SENEGAL‡ CASAMANCE‡ DIOLA‡
  30 HOURS‡ 1973‡ QUALITY GOOD‡ ARCHIVES
  CULTURELLES DU SENEGAL‡ ‡ ‡ ‡ INHERITANCE,
  LAND-USE, SOCIAL

SOCIETE DE RADIODIFFUSION
  SOCIETE DE RADIODIFFUSION DE LA FRANCE D'OUTRE
  MER‡ ‡ UPPER VOLTA‡ ‡ MOSSI‡ ‡ ‡ ‡ MUSEE DE
  L'HOMME‡ ‡ ‡ ‡ DEATH-FUNERAL

SOLANO, ROBERT P.
  SOLANO, ROBERT P.‡ 4 RICHMOND AVENUE, ONEONTA,
  NEW YORK‡ GHANA‡ KUMASI, TAMALI‡ ‡ 82 HOURS‡
  1970-71‡ QUALITY GOOD‡ ‡ ‡ ‡ ‡ MUSIC

  SOLANO, ROBERT P.‡ 4 RICHMOND AVENUE, ONEONTA,
  NEW YORK‡ UPPER VOLTA‡ ‡ ‡ 6 HOURS‡ 1970-71‡
  QUALITY GOOD‡ ‡ ‡ ‡ ‡ MUSIC

SOSNE, ELINOR
  SIGWALT, RICHARD+ SOSNE, ELINOR‡ DEPARTMENT OF
  SOCIOLOGY, OLD DOMINION UNIVERSITY, NORFOLK,
  VIRGINIA 23508‡ ZAIRE‡ KIVU‡ SHI‡ 60 HOURS‡
  1971-73‡ QUALITY POOR‡ ‡ ‡ ‡ ‡ DANCE, FOLKTALE,
  HISTORY, MARRIAGE, MUSIC

SPAIN, DAVID H.
  SPAIN, DAVID H.‡ 1237 FEDERAL AVENUE E., SEATTLE,
  WASHINGTON 98102‡ NIGERIA‡ MAIDUGURI‡ KANURI‡ 3
  HOURS‡ 1966-67‡ QUALITY GOOD‡ ‡ ‡ ‡ COURT,
  SOCIAL

SPEED, FRANCIS E.
  SPEED, FRANCIS E.‡ INSTITUTE OF AFRICAN STUDIES,
  UNIVERSITY OF IFE, ILE-IFE, NIGERIA‡ NIGERIA‡
  OSHOGBO‡ YORUBA‡ 5 HOURS‡ 1966‡ QUALITY GOOD‡
  ARCHIVES OF TRADITIONAL MUSIC‡ 72-241-F‡ ATL
  5457-59‡ RESTRICTED‡ DIVINING-ODU-IFA

  SPEED, FRANCIS E.+ THIEME, DARIUS L.‡ INSTITUTE
  OF AFRICAN STUDIES, UNIVERSITY OF IFE, ILE-IFE,
  NIGERIA+ BLACK STUDIES IN MUSIC PROJECT, MUSIC
  DEPARTMENT, FISK UNIVERSITY, NASHVILLE, TENNESSEE

SPEED, FRANCIS E.
  37703‡ NIGERIA‡ LANLATE-WESTERN REGION‡ YORUBA‡
  .5 HOUR‡ 1966‡ QUALITY EXCELLENT‡ ARCHIVES OF
  TRADITIONAL MUSIC‡ 66-226-F‡ ‡ RESTRICTED‡
  DANCE-MASKED-ORO, DRUM-AGERE, DRUM-APESIN,
  DRUM-BATA, DRUM-HOURGLASS-DUNDUN, DRUM-LANGUAGE,
  DRUM-PROVERB, HUNTING, PROVERB-DRUM

SPENCER, LEON P.
  SPENCER, LEON P.‡ TALLADEGA COLLEGE, TALLADEGA,
  ALABAMA 35160‡ KENYA‡ ‡ KAMBA, KIKUYU, KISII, LUO‡
  50 HOURS‡ 1968-69‡ QUALITY GOOD‡ ‡ ‡ ‡
  HISTORY-MISSION-CHRISTIAN

SPENCER, WILLIAM
  SPENCER, WILLIAM‡ DEPARTMENT OF HISTORY, FLORIDA
  STATE UNIVERSITY, TALLAHASSEE, FLORIDA 32306‡
  MOROCCO‡ CASABLANCA‡ ‡ 2 HOURS‡ 1969‡ QUALITY
  EXCELLENT‡ FLORIDA STATE UNIVERSITY-ORAL HISTORY‡
  ‡ ‡ ‡ HISTORY, INTERVIEW-IBRAHIM-A.

  SPENCER, WILLIAM‡ DEPARTMENT OF HISTORY, FLORIDA
  STATE UNIVERSITY, TALLAHASSIE, FLORIDA 32306‡
  TUNISIA‡ TESTOUR‡ MALOUF‡ 8 HOURS‡ 1966-67‡
  QUALITY EXCELLENT‡ FLORIDA STATE UNIVERSITY‡ ‡ ‡ ‡
  FESTIVAL-ANDALUSIAN, SOCIAL

STAHLKE, HERBERT F.W.
  STAHLKE, HERBERT F.W.‡ DEPARTMENT OF ENGLISH,
  GEORGIA STATE UNIVERSITY, ATLANTA, GEORGIA 30303‡
  NIGERIA‡ ALIFOKPA, OGOJA‡ YATYE‡ 2 HOURS‡ 1966-67‡
  QUALITY FAIR‡ ‡ ‡ ‡ FOLKLORE

STANFORD UNIVERSITY LANGU
  STANFORD UNIVERSITY LANGUAGE LABORATORY‡
  DEPARTMENT OF LINGUISTICS, STANFORD UNIVERSITY,
  STANFORD, CALIFORNIA 94305‡ ‡ ‡ ‡ ‡ ‡ ‡ ‡ ‡ ‡

STARR, FREDERICK A.
  STARR, FREDERICK A.‡ DECEASED‡ ZAIRE‡ BOLOBO,
  IKOKO, NDOMBE, YAKUSU‡ BAKUBA, BALUBA‡ 1 HOUR‡
  1906‡ QUALITY FAIR‡ ARCHIVES OF TRADITIONAL MUSIC‡
  69-015-F‡ ATL 3617-18‡ ‡ BOW-MUSICAL, OCARINA,
  RATTLE, WHISTLE

STENNES, LESLIE H.
  STENNES, LESLIE H.‡ 3709 24TH AVENUE SOUTH,
  MINNEAPOLIS, MINNESOTA 55406‡ CAMEROON‡ ‡ FULANI,
  GIDDER‡ 10 HOURS‡ 1956-73‡ QUALITY GOOD‡ ‡ ‡ ‡ ‡

STENNES, LESLIE H.
  ORAL-DATA

STONE, RUTH M.
  STONE, RUTH M.+ STONE, VERLON L.≠ ARCHIVES OF
  TRADITIONAL MUSIC, INDIANA UNIVERSITY,
  BLOOMINGTON, INDIANA 47401≠ LIBERIA≠ GBANGA,
  GBEYILATAA, GBOROLA, SANOYEA, TOTOTA≠ KPELLE≠ 8
  HOURS≠ 1970≠ QUALITY EXCELLENT≠ CENTER FOR
  AFRICAN ORAL DATA≠ 73-052-F≠ ATL 5903-07≠
  RESTRICTED≠ BOW-MUSICAL, CANTE-FABLE,
  CHILDREN-GAME, DANCE, DRUM-CYLINDRICAL,
  DRUM-GOBLET, DRUM-HOURGLASS, DRUM-LANGUAGE,
  DRUM-SLIT, ENTERTAINMENT, HORN-TRANSVERSE,
  HORN-WOODEN, IDIOPHONE-METAL, IDIOPHONE-GLASS,
  KONGOMA, LUTE-MULTIPLE-BOW, RATTLE-CONTAINER,
  RATTLE-GOURD, SANZA, SCRIPT-KPELLE-INTERVIEW,
  TOPICAL, VOICE-DISGUISE, WORK-FIELD-CLEARING,
  WORK-PLANTING, XYLOPHONE, ZITHER-TRIANGULAR-FRAME

STONE, VERLON L.
  STONE, RUTH M.+ STONE, VERLON L.≠ ARCHIVES OF
  TRADITIONAL MUSIC, INDIANA UNIVERSITY,
  BLOOMINGTON, INDIANA 47401≠ LIBERIA≠ GBANGA,
  GBEYILATAA, GBOROLA, SANOYEA, TOTOTA≠ KPELLE≠ 8
  HOURS≠ 1970≠ QUALITY EXCELLENT≠ CENTER FOR
  AFRICAN ORAL DATA≠ 73-052-F≠ ATL 5903-07≠
  RESTRICTED≠ BOW-MUSICAL, CANTE-FABLE,
  CHILDREN-GAME, DANCE, DRUM-CYLINDRICAL,
  DRUM-GOBLET, DRUM-HOURGLASS, DRUM-LANGUAGE,
  DRUM-SLIT, ENTERTAINMENT, HORN-TRANSVERSE,
  HORN-WOODEN, IDIOPHONE-METAL, IDIOPHONE-GLASS,
  KONGOMA, LUTE-MULTIPLE-BOW, RATTLE-CONTAINER,
  RATTLE-GOURD, SANZA, SCRIPT-KPELLE-INTERVIEW,
  TOPICAL, VOICE-DISGUISE, WORK-FIELD-CLEARING,
  WORK-PLANTING, XYLOPHONE, ZITHER-TRIANGULAR-FRAME

STRUMPF, MITCHEL
  STRUMPF, MITCHEL≠ 3122A PORTAGE BAY PLACE,
  SEATTLE, WASHINGTON 98102≠ GHANA≠ EAST COAST,
  NANDOM, NORTHEAST≠ DAGARTI, EWE, KONKOMBA≠ 42
  HOURS≠ 1969-72≠ QUALITY GOOD≠ UNIVERSITY OF
  GHANA+ UNIVERSITY OF WASHINGTON≠ ≠ ≠ DANCE,
  DEATH-FUNERAL, PRAISE

STUDSTILL, JOHN D.
  STUDSTILL, JOHN D.≠ ANTHROPOLOGY DEPARTMENT,
  INDIANA UNIVERSITY, BLOOMINGTON, INDIANA 47401≠
  ZAIRE≠ SHABA (KATANGA)≠ LUBA≠ 9.5 HOURS≠ 1972≠

STUDSTILL, JOHN D.
QUALITY GOOD‡ CENTER FOR AFRICAN ORAL DATA‡
73-003-F‡ ‡ RESTRICTED‡ EPIC-LUBA, FOLKTALE,
HISTORY, LEGEND, MYTH, MYTH-ORIGIN

STUTTMAN, LEONARD M.
STUTTMAN, LEONARD M.‡ AMERICAN SOYBEAN
ASSOCIATION, P.O. BOX 150, HUDSON, IOWA 50643‡
LIBERIA‡ BPEAPLE, HARBEL, TAPPITA‡ GREBO, KRAHN‡
5 HOURS‡ 1956‡ QUALITY EXCELLENT‡ ‡ ‡ ‡ DANCE,
DRUM, FOLKTALE, HIGHLIFE, RELIGIOUS-CHRISTIAN

SUDAN NATIONAL MUSEUM
SUDAN NATIONAL MUSEUM‡ P.O. BOX 178, KHARTOUM,
SUDAN‡ ‡ ‡ ‡ ‡ ‡ ‡ ‡ ‡

SUDAN NATIONAL MUSEUM‡ P.O BOX 178, KHARTOUM,
SUDAN‡ SUDAN‡ ‡ BONGO, JALUO, NUBIAN‡ 12 HOURS‡
1959-64‡ QUALITY GOOD‡ SUDAN NATIONAL MUSEUM‡ ‡ ‡
‡ BIRTH, CEREMONY-HUNTING, DEATH-MOURNING,
FOLKTALE, HISTORY, HUNTING-CEREMONY, RITUAL,
SOCIAL

SULZMANN, ERIKA
SULZMANN, ERIKA‡ INSTITUT FUR ETHNOLOGIE DER
UNIVERSITAT MAINZ, 65 MAINZ, SAARSTRASSE 21,
GERMANY‡ CONGO, PEOPLE'S REPUBLIC OF THE‡ BATEKE
PLATEAU‡ ATYO‡ ‡ 1962‡ QUALITY GOOD‡ ‡ ‡ ‡ ‡
DEATH-MOURNING, DRUM, POLITICAL, PRAISE, RITUAL

SULZMANN, ERIKA‡ INSTITUT FUR ETHNOLOGIE DER
UNIVERSITAT MAINZ, 65 MAINZ, SAARSTRASSE 21,
GERMANY‡ ZAIRE‡ BANDUNDU PROVINCE, EQUATOR
PROVINCE, LAKE TUMBA‡ BABOMA, BASENGELE, BOLIA,
EKONDA, NTOMBA‡ ‡ 1953-72‡ QUALITY GOOD‡ ‡ ‡ ‡ ‡
ASSOCIATION-ATEPYA, DRUM, ECONOMIC, EPIC, HISTORY,
LEGAL, POLITICAL, RELIGIOUS, RITUAL-MAGIC, SOCIAL

SURUGUE, BERNARD
SURUGUE, BERNARD‡ ‡ NIGER‡ NIAMEY‡ DJERMA-SONGHAY‡
‡ 1969‡ ‡ MUSEE DE L'HOMME‡ ‡ ‡ ‡ LUTE-BOWED

SZCZESNIAK, ANDREW L.
SZCZESNIAK, ANDREW L.‡ ‡ NIGERIA-U.S.‡
BLOOMINGTON, INDIANA‡ IBO‡ 1 HOUR‡ 1961‡ QUALITY
GOOD‡ ARCHIVES OF TRADITIONAL MUSIC‡ 061-019-F‡
FTL 172-73‡ RESTRICTED‡ FOLKTALE,
FOLKTALE-INTERVIEW

TAPE LIBRARY, DEPARTMENT
  TAPE LIBRARY, DEPARTMENT OF LINGUISTICS AND
  NIGERIAN LANGUAGES, UNIVERSITY OF IBADAN‡ IBADAN,
  NIGERIA‡ ‡ ‡ ‡ ‡ ‡ ‡ ‡ ‡ ‡

TARDITS, CLAUDE
  PARE, -+ TARDITS, CLAUDE‡ -+ 33 RUE CROULEBARBE,
  75013 PARIS, FRANCE‡ CAMEROON‡ ‡ BAMUM‡ ‡ ‡ ‡
  MUSEE DE L'HOMME‡ ‡ ‡ ‡ HISTORY-DYNASTIC-BAMUM

  ROUGET, GILBERT+ TARDITS, CLAUDE+ VERGER, PIERRE‡
  1 RUE DES DEUX-PONTS, 75004 PARIS, FRANCE+ 33 RUE
  CROULEBARBE, 75013 PARIS, FRANCE+ -‡ DAHOMEY‡ ‡
  ADJA, FON, GUN, ITCHA, MINA, NAGO‡ ‡ ‡ ‡ MUSEE DE
  L'HOMME‡ ‡ ‡ ‡

  TARDITS, CLAUDE‡ 33 RUE CROULEBARBE, 75013 PARIS,
  FRANCE‡ DAHOMEY‡ PORTO-NOVO‡ GUN‡ ‡ ‡ QUALITY
  FAIR‡ MUSEE DE L'HOMME‡ ‡ ‡ ‡ RITUAL, SOCIAL

  TARDITS, CLAUDE‡ 33 RUE CROULEBARBE, 75013 PARIS,
  FRANCE‡ DAHOMEY‡ ‡ GUN‡ ‡ 1955‡ ‡ MUSEE DE
  L'HOMME‡ ‡ ‡ ‡ MUSICIAN, ROYAL

TENRAA, ERIC WILLIAM FRED
  TENRAA, ERIC WILLIAM FREDERICK‡ DEPARTMENT OF
  ANTHROPOLOGY, UNIVERSITY OF WESTERN AUSTRALIA,
  NEDLANDS, WESTERN AUSTRALIA‡ TANZANIA‡ CENTRAL
  TANZANIA, DODOMA REGION, KONDOA AREA‡ BURUNGE,
  SANDAWE, SWAHILI‡ 40 HOURS‡ 1958-66‡ QUALITY GOOD‡
  ‡ ‡ ‡ ‡ COMBAT-VERBAL, FOLKTALE, HISTORY,
  MUSICIAN, RIDDLE, RITUAL

TESSMAN, GUNTHER
  TESSMAN, GUNTHER‡ ‡ CAMEROON‡ ‡ FANG-PANGWE‡ .2
  HOUR‡ 1907‡ QUALITY FAIR‡ ARCHIVES OF TRADITIONAL
  MUSIC‡ 59-002-F‡ ATL 1756‡ RESTRICTED‡
  CHORDOPHONE, XYLOPHONE

  TESSMAN, GUNTHER‡ ‡ EQUATORIAL GUINEA‡ BEBAI‡
  FANG‡ .1 HOUR‡ 1907‡ QUALITY FAIR‡ ARCHIVES OF
  TRADITIONAL MUSIC‡ 59-002-F‡ ATL 1756‡ RESTRICTED‡
  DEATH-FUNERAL

THIEL, JOSEF FRANZ
  THIEL, JOSEF FRANZ‡ ANTHROPOS-INSTITUT, D-5205
  ST. AUGUSTIN, 1 UBER SIEBURG, FEDERAL REPUBLIC OF
  GERMANY‡ ZAIRE‡ BANDUNDU‡ MBALA, TEKE, YANSI‡ 200
  HOURS‡ 1961-71‡ QUALITY GOOD‡ ANTHROPOS-INSTITUT‡

THIEL, JOSEF FRANZ
‡ ‡ ‡ FOLKLORE, HISTORY, SOCIAL-REFORM,
LANGUAGE-YANSI

THIEME, DARIUS L.
SPEED, FRANCIS E.+ THIEME, DARIUS L.‡ INSTITUTE
OF AFRICAN STUDIES, UNIVERSITY OF IFE, ILE-IFE,
NIGERIA+ BLACK STUDIES IN MUSIC PROJECT, MUSIC
DEPARTMENT, FISK UNIVERSITY, NASHVILLE, TENNESSEE
37703‡ NIGERIA‡ LANLATE-WESTERN REGION‡ YORUBA‡
.5 HOUR‡ 1966‡ QUALITY EXCELLENT‡ ARCHIVES OF
TRADITIONAL MUSIC‡ 66-226-F‡ ‡ RESTRICTED‡
DANCE-MASKED-ORO, DRUM-AGERE, DRUM-APESIN,
DRUM-BATA, DRUM-HOURGLASS-DUNDUN, DRUM-LANGUAGE,
DRUM-PROVERB, HUNTING, PROVERB-DRUM

THIEME, DARIUS L.‡ BLACK STUDIES IN MUSIC PROJECT,
MUSIC DEPARTMENT, FISK UNIVERSITY, NASHVILLE,
TENNESSEE 37703‡ NIGERIA‡ WESTERN REGION‡ YORUBA‡
42 HOURS‡ 1964-66‡ QUALITY EXCELLENT‡ ARCHIVE OF
FOLK SONG, LIBRARY OF CONGRESS‡ ‡ ‡ ‡ FESTIVAL,
RITUAL

THOMASON, LEE
COPLAN, DAVID+ THOMASON, LEE‡ ANTHROPOLOGY
DEPARTMENT, INDIANA UNIVERSITY, BLOOMINGTON,
INDIANA 47401+ 10112 SPRING LAKE TERRACE, FAIRFAX,
VIRGINIA 22030‡ GHANA‡ ABESRE, KUMASI, SOMANYA‡
ASANTE, EWE, KROBO‡ 5 HOURS‡ 1974‡ QUALITY
EXCELLENT‡ ARCHIVES OF TRADITIONAL MUSIC‡
74-103-F‡ ‡ RESTRICTED‡ DEATH-FUNERAL, DRUM,
ENTERTAINMENT, GUITAR, HIGHLIFE,
STAMPING-TUBE-BAMBOO

TLOU, THOMAS
TLOU, THOMAS‡ DEPARTMENT OF HISTORY, UNIVERSITY
OF BOTSWANA, LESOTHO AND SWAZILAND, PRIVATE BAG
22, GABORONE, BOTSWANA‡ BOTSWANA‡ NORTHWESTERN
BOTSWANA‡ HERERO, LOZI, MBUKUSHU, ROLONG, TSWANA,
YEI‡ 20 HOURS‡ 1970‡ QUALITY GOOD‡ CENTER FOR
AFRICAN ORAL DATA‡ 73-001-F‡ ‡ RESTRICTED‡
HISTORY

TRACEY, HUGH
CAMP, CHARLES M.+ TRACEY, HUGH‡ 186 CORA STREET,
SAN FRANCISCO, CALIFORNIA 94134+ INTERNATIONAL
LIBRARY OF AFRICAN MUSIC, BOX 138, ROODEPORT,
TRANSVAAL, SOUTH AFRICA‡ RHODESIA‡ BIKITA,
BULAWAYO, GUNDAS, HUZI⊙MREWA, MTOKO, SALISBURY,

TRACEY, HUGH
   UMTALI, ZAKA, ZIMBABWE‡ BUDJA, CHIKUNDA, FUNGWE,
   HERA, HUNGWE, KARANGA, NDAU, NDEBELE, NYANJA,
   NYASA, PEDI, RAMBA, WEMBA, YAO‡ 6 HOURS‡ 1948‡
   QUALITY GOOD‡ ARCHIVES OF TRADITIONAL MUSIC‡
   PRE'54-171-F‡ ATL 303-22‡ ‡ ANCESTOR-CEREMONY,
   BOW-MUSICAL, CANTE-FABLE, CHILDREN, DANCE,
   DEATH-FUNERAL, DIVINING, DRINKING, DRUM,
   DRUM-CYLINDRICAL, FLUTE, FOLKTALE, GUITAR, HORN,
   LAMENT, LULLABY, MBIRA, PANPIPES, RATTLE,
   ULULATION, WAR, WHISTLE-LANGUAGE, WORK-THRESHING,
   YODEL

   CAMP, CHARLES M.+ TRACEY, HUGH‡ 186 CORA STREET,
   SAN FRANCISCO, CALIFORNIA 94134+ INTERNATIONAL
   LIBRARY OF AFRICAN MUSIC, BOX 138, ROODEPORT,
   TRANSVAAL, SOUTH AFRICA‡ SOUTH AFRICA‡ DURBAN
   DEEP MINE, JOHANNESBURG, MESINA COPPER MINE, RAND
   LEASE MINE, ROSE DEEP MINE‡ BHACA, CHOPI, HLUBI,
   NDAU, NYASA, PONDO, SHANGAAN, SOTHO, SWAZI,
   TSWANA, VENDA, XHOSA‡ 2 HOURS‡ 1947-48‡ QUALITY
   FAIR‡ ARCHIVES OF TRADITIONAL MUSIC‡ PRE'54-171-F‡
   ATL 303-22‡ ‡ BOW-MUSICAL, CHILDREN, CONCERTINA,
   DANCE, DRINKING, GUITAR, HARP-ZITHER, LOVE,
   MARRIAGE, MBIRA, XYLOPHONE, ZITHER

   CAMP, CHARLES M.+ TRACEY, HUGH‡ 186 CORA STREET,
   SAN FRANCISCO, CALIFORNIA 94134+ INTERNATIONAL
   LIBRARY OF AFRICAN MUSIC, BOX 138, ROODEPORT,
   TRANSVAAL, SOUTH AFRICA‡ ZAMBIA‡ LIVINGSTONE,
   MAPANZA‡ BEMBA, LALA, LOZI, TONGA, ZINZA‡ 2 HOURS‡
   1947-48‡ QUALITY GOOD‡ ARCHIVES OF TRADITIONAL
   MUSIC‡ PRE'54-171-F‡ ATL 303-22‡ ‡ BOW-MUSICAL,
   CANOE, CANTE-FABLE, DANCE, DEATH-FUNERAL,
   DRINKING, DRUM, DRUM-FRICTION, DRUM-GOBLET,
   GUITAR, HANDCLAPPING, HERDING, HORN, HUNTING,
   LOVE, MBIRA, POSSESSION, PRAISE, RATTLE, WHISTLE,
   WORK, XYLOPHONE

   GILLIS, FRANK J.+ TRACEY, HUGH‡ ARCHIVES OF
   TRADITIONAL MUSIC, INDIANA UNIVERSITY,
   BLOOMINGTON, INDIANA 47401+ INTERNATIONAL LIBRARY
   OF AFRICAN MUSIC, BOX 138, ROODEPOORT, TRANSVAAL,
   SOUTH AFRICA‡ SOUTH AFRICA-U.S.‡ BLOOMINGTON,
   INDIANA‡ ‡ 1 HOUR‡ 1971‡ QUALITY GOOD‡ ARCHIVES
   OF TRADITIONAL MUSIC‡ 71-308-F‡ ‡ RESTRICTED‡
   INTERVIEW-TRACEY-H.

TRADITIONAL MUSIC DOCUMEN
  TRADITIONAL MUSIC DOCUMENTATION PROJECT‡ 3740
  KANAWHA STREET N.W., WASHINGTCN, D.C. 20015‡ ‡ ‡
  ‡ ‡ ‡ ‡ ‡ ‡

  TRADITIONAL MUSIC DOCUMENTATION PROJECT‡ 3740
  KANAWHA STREET, N.W., WASHINGTON, D.C. 20015‡
  MOZAMBIQUE‡ ‡ CHOPI‡ ‡ ‡ ‡ TRADITIONAL MUSIC
  DOCUMENTATION PROJECT‡ ‡ ‡ ‡ FOLKLORE, HISTORY,
  PRAISE-POETRY, RITUAL, SOCIAL

  TRADITIONAL MUSIC DOCUMENTATION PROJECT‡ 3740
  KANAWHA STREET, N.W., WASHINGTON, D.C. 20015‡
  NIGERIA‡ ‡ IBIBIO, IBO, KALABARI, TIV, YORUBA‡ ‡ ‡
  ‡ TRADITIONAL MUSIC DOCUMENTATION PROJECT‡ ‡ ‡ ‡
  FOLKLORE, HISTORY, PRAISE-POETRY, RITUAL, SOCIAL

  TRADITIONAL MUSIC DOCUMENTATION PROJECT‡ 3740
  KANAWHA STREET, N.W., WASHINGTON, D.C. 20015‡
  RHODESIA‡ ‡ KARANGA, MANYIKE-BOCHA, NDAU, NJANJA,
  SENA-TONGA, ZEZURU‡ ‡ ‡ ‡ TRADITIONAL MUSIC
  DOCUMENTATION PROJECT‡ ‡ ‡ ‡ MBIRA

  TRADITIONAL MUSIC DOCUMENTATION PROJECT‡ 3740
  KANAWHA STREET, N.W., WASHINGTON, D.C. 20015‡
  UPPER VOLTA‡ ‡ ‡ ‡ ‡ TRADITIONAL MUSIC
  DOCUMENTATION PROJECT‡ ‡ ‡ FOLKLORE, HISTORY,
  PRAISE-POETRY, RITUAL, SOCIAL

TRAEGER, PAUL
  TRAEGER, PAUL‡ ‡ TUNISIA‡ ‡ BERBER‡ .1 HOUR‡ 1903‡
  QUALITY FAIR‡ ARCHIVES OF TRADITIONAL MUSIC‡
  59-002-F‡ ATL 1757‡ RESTRICTED‡

TRAGER, LILLIAN
  TRAGER, LILLIAN‡ DEPARTMENT OF ANTHROPOLOGY,
  UNIVERSITY OF WASHINGTON, SEATTLE, WASHINGTON
  98195‡ NIGERIA‡ IJEBU-JESHA, ILESA‡ YORUBA‡ 1
  HOUR‡ 1974‡ QUALITY FAIR‡ ‡ ‡ ‡
  FESTIVAL-YAM-NEW

TRANSCRIPTION CENTRE, THE
  TRANSCRIPTION CENTRE, THE‡ 6 PADDINGTON STREET,
  LONDON W.1., ENGLAND‡ ‡ ‡ ‡ ‡ ‡ ‡ ‡ ‡ ‡

TSEHAI, BRHANE SILASSIE
  TSEHAI, BRHANE SILASSIE‡ INSTITUTE OF ETHIOPIAN
  STUDIES, HAILE SELASSIE UNIVERSITY, P.O. BOX 1176,
  ADDIS ABABA, ETHIOPIA‡ ETHIOPIA‡ SIDAMO‡ DARASSA,

TSEHAI, BRHANE SILASSIE
  SIDAMO, WOLAMO‡ 105 HOURS‡ 1969-73‡ QUALITY GOOD‡
  INSTITUTE OF ETHIOPIAN STUDIES, HAILE SELASSIE
  UNIVERSITY‡ ‡ ‡ ‡ HISTORY

TUBIANA, -
  TUBIANA, -‡ ‡ ETHIOPIA‡ ‡ ‡ ‡ ‡ ‡ MUSEE DE
  L'HOMME‡ ‡ ‡ ‡

TUCKER, ARCHIBALD NORMAN
  TUCKER, ARCHIBALD NORMAN‡ 76 GRANVILLE ROAD,
  SEVEN OAKS, KENT TN13 1HA, ENGLAND‡ KENYA‡ ‡ LUO‡
  ‡ ‡ QUALITY GOOD‡ ‡ ‡ ‡ ‡ FOLKTALE,
  GRAMMATICAL-DATA

  TUCKER, ARCHIBALD NORMAN‡ 76 GRANVILLE ROAD,
  SEVEN OAKS, KENT TN13 1HA, ENGLAND‡ SOUTH AFRICA‡
  ‡ PEDI, SOTHO, TSWANA, XHOSA, ZULU‡ ‡ ‡ QUALITY
  GOOD‡ ‡ ‡ ‡ PHONETICS

  TUCKER, ARCHIBALD NORMAN‡ 76 GRANVILLE ROAD,
  SEVEN OAKS, KENT TN13 1HA, ENGLAND‡ SUDAN‡ ‡ BARI,
  DINKA, LOTUKO, SHILLUK, ZANDE‡ ‡ ‡ QUALITY GOOD‡ ‡
  ‡ ‡ ‡ GRAMMATICAL-DATA

  TUCKER, ARCHIBALD NORMAN‡ 76 GRANVILLE ROAD,
  SEVEN OAKS, KENT TN13 1HA, ENGLAND‡ TANZANIA‡ ‡
  HADZA, IRAQW, NGAZIJA, SANDAWE, SANYE, SWAHILI‡ ‡
  ‡ QUALITY GOOD‡ ‡ ‡ ‡ ‡ FOLKTALE,
  GRAMMATICAL-DATA

  TUCKER, ARCHIBALD NORMAN‡ 76 GRANVILLE ROAD,
  SEVEN OAKS, KENT TN13 1HA, ENGLAND‡ UGANDA‡ ‡
  ACHOLI, BAGANDA, IK, KARAMOJONG, TEPETH, TESO‡ ‡ ‡
  QUALITY GOOD‡ ‡ ‡ ‡ ‡ FOLKTALE, GRAMMATICAL-DATA

TURNER, VICTOR WITTER
  TURNER, VICTOR WITTER‡ COMMITTEE ON SOCIAL
  THOUGHT, UNIVERSITY OF CHICAGO, CHICAGO, ILLINOIS
  60634‡ UGANDA‡ MBALE‡ BAGISU‡ 5 HOURS‡ 1966‡
  QUALITY FAIR‡ ‡ ‡ ‡ ‡ CEREMONY-CIRCUMCISION,
  CIRCUMCISION, RITUAL

UGANDA MUSEUM
  UGANDA MUSEUM‡ P.O. BOX 365, KAMPALA, UGANDA‡ ‡ ‡
  ‡ ‡ ‡ ‡ ‡ ‡

UHLIG, -
  UHLIG, -‡ ‡ TANZANIA‡ ‡ WANYAMWEZI‡ .1 HOUR‡ 1910‡

UHLIG, -
  QUALITY FAIR‡ ARCHIVES OF TRADITIONAL MUSIC‡
  59-002-F‡ ATL 1757‡ RESTRICTED‡ DRINKING

UNITED CHRISTIAN MISSIONA
  UNITED CHRISTIAN MISSIONARY SOCIETY, DISCIPLES OF
  CHRIST‡ 222 SOUTH DOWNEY AVENUE, BOX 1986,
  INDIANAPOLIS, INDIANA 46206‡ ‡ ‡ ‡ ‡ ‡ ‡ ‡ ‡ ‡

  UNITED CHRISTIAN MISSIONARY SOCIETY, DISCIPLES OF
  CHRIST‡ 222 SOUTH DOWNEY AVENUE, BOX 1986,
  INDIANAPOLIS, INDIANA 46206‡ ZAIRE‡ ‡ LINGÁLA,
  LONKUNDO‡ 20 HOURS‡ ‡ QUALITY FAIR‡ UNITED
  CHRISTIAN MISSIONARY SOCIETY, DISCIPLES OF CHRIST‡
  ‡ ‡ ‡ HYMN, WORK

UNIVERSITETS ETNOGRAFISKE
  UNIVERSITETS ETNOGRAFISKE MUSEUM‡ FREDERIKSGATE 2,
  OSLO, NORWAY‡ ‡ ‡ ‡ ‡ ‡ ‡ ‡ ‡

UNIVERSITY OF GHANA
  UNIVERSITY OF GHANA‡ P.O.B. 25, LEGON, GHANA‡ ‡ ‡
  ‡ ‡ ‡ ‡ ‡ ‡

UNIVERSITY OF IFE
  UNIVERSITY OF IFE‡ ILE-IFE, WESTERN STATE,
  NIGERIA‡ ‡ ‡ ‡ ‡ ‡ ‡ ‡ ‡

UNIVERSITY OF MALAWI
  UNIVERSITY OF MALAWI‡ P.O. BOX 5097, LIMBE,
  MALAWI‡ ‡ ‡ ‡ ‡ ‡ ‡ ‡ ‡ ‡

UNIVERSITY OF PENNSYLVANI
  UNIVERSITY OF PENNSYLVANIA‡ PHILADELPHIA,
  PENNSYLVANIA 19174‡ ‡ ‡ ‡ ‡ ‡ ‡ ‡ ‡ ‡

UNIVERSITY OF WASHINGTON
  UNIVERSITY OF WASHINGTON‡ SEATTLE, WASHINGTON
  98195‡ ‡ ‡ ‡ ‡ ‡ ‡ ‡ ‡ ‡

UNOOGWU, PATRICK
  ARMSTRONG, ROBERT G.+ UNOOGWU, PATRICK‡ INSTITUTE
  OF AFRICAN STUDIES, UNIVERSITY OF IBADAN, IBADAN,
  NIGERIA‡ NIGERIA‡ AGILA‡ IDOMA‡ 2 HOURS‡ 1961‡
  QUALITY GOOD‡ ARCHIVES OF TRADITIONAL MUSIC‡
  72-245-F‡ ATL 5463-65‡ ‡ DANCE-MASKED-AREKWU,
  DRUM, DRUM-CLAY-POT, PRAISE

UPADHYAYA, HARI S.
  UPADHYAYA, HARI S.+ ORI, R.‡ DIRECTOR, INDIAN
  FOLK CULTURE RESEARCH INSTITUTE, DEPARTMENT OF
  HINDI, BENARES HINDU UNIVERSITY, VARANSI, INDIA+
  -‡ MAURITIUS‡ MAURITIUS ISLAND‡ UTTAR-PRADESH‡ 1
  HOUR‡ 1961‡ QUALITY GOOD‡ ARCHIVES OF TRADITIONAL
  MUSIC‡ 65-279-F‡ ‡ RESTRICTED‡ DRUM,
  LUTE-BOWED-SARANGI,RELIGIOUS, SOCIAL-CONDITIONS

VAILLANT, JANET G.
  VAILLANT, JANET G.‡ 276 COLLEGE ROAD, CONCORD,
  MASSACHUSETTS 01742‡ SENEGAL‡ DAKAR, JOAL‡ SERER‡
  10 HOURS‡ 1973‡ QUALITY EXCELLENT‡ ‡ ‡ ‡ ‡
  POLITICS-1930-1950

VALLEE, ROGER P.
  VALLEE, ROGER P.‡ 400 COCHRAN ROAD, PITTSBURGH,
  PENNSYLVANIA 15228‡ CONGO, PEOPLE'S REPUBLIC OF
  THE‡ BRAZZAVILLE‡ ‡ .5 HOUR‡ 1967‡ QUALITY GOOD‡ ‡
  ‡ ‡ ‡ ORAL-DATA-LINGALA

VAN OVEN, JACOBA
  VAN OVEN, JACOBA‡ INSTITUTE OF EDUCATION,
  UNIVERSITY OF SIERRA LEONE, PRIVATE MAIL BAG,
  TOWER HILL, FREETOWN, SIERRA LEONE‡ SIERRA LEONE‡
  BANDAJUMA-PUJEHUN DISTRICT, BLAMA-PUJEHUN
  DISTRICT, BONTHE, BUMBAN, FAIRO, FALABA, FOINDU,
  FREETOWN, JOJOIMA, KAMABAI, KATANTA, KONAKRY DEE,
  LUNGI, MAGBURAKA, MAHERA, MAKAMBI, MAKENI, MANOWA,
  MASINGBI, MATTRU-JONG, MOYAMBA, NYAMBA TANENE,
  PLANTAIN ISLAND, POTORU, ROGBORE, ROKULAN, SAHN
  MALEN, SHENGE, SOKURELA, TUASU, YAGALA, ZIMMI‡
  FULA, GALLINAS, GOLA, LIMBA, LOKO, MANDINGO,
  MENDE, SHERBRO, SUSU, TEMNE, VAI, YALUNKA‡ 8
  HOURS‡ 1964-67‡ QUALITY EXCELLENT‡ ARCHIVES OF
  TRADITIONAL MUSIC‡ 68-215-F‡ ATL 5095-100‡ ‡
  BOW-MUSICAL, DANCE, DANCE-ACROBATIC, DANCE-MASKED,
  DRUM-BAN, DRUM-CONICAL, DRUM-CYLINDRICAL,
  DRUM-FRAME, DRUM-HOURGLASS, DRUM-KETTLE,
  DRUM-LANGUAGE, DRUM-SLIT, FLUTE-TRANSVERSE,
  HARP-BOW-BOLON-BATA, HANDCLAPPING,
  HARP-LUTE-KONDENE, HARP-LUTE-KORA, HORN-ELEPHANT,
  HUNTING, IDIOPHONE-STRUCK, KONGOMA, LUTE,
  LUTE-BOWED, LUTE-MULTIPLE-BOW, MUSICIAN, PRAISE,
  PRAISE-RULER, RATTLE-CONTAINER, RATTLE-GOURD,
  RELIGIOUS-ISLAMIC, SANZA, SECRET-SOCIETY,
  XYLOPHONE, ZITHER-TRIANGULAR-FRAME

VAN ROUVEROY VAN NIEUWAAL
  VAN ROUVEROY VAN NIEUWAAL, EMILE A.B.‡
  AFRIKA-STUDIECENTRUM, STATIONSPLEIN 10, LEIDEN,
  HOLLAND‡ TOGO‡ MANGO, SANSANNE‡ KOSSI‡ 30 HOURS‡
  1969-73‡ QUALITY GOOD‡ ‡ ‡ ‡ ‡ HISTORY, POETRY,
  PRAYER-CHRISTIAN, PRAYER-ISLAMIC

VAN THIEL, PAUL A.H.
  VAN THIEL, PAUL A.H.‡ VEENLANTSTRAAT 2, SCHIEDAM,
  HOLLAND‡ UGANDA‡ WESTERN REGION‡ BANTU,
  BANYANKOLE‡ 13 HOURS‡ 1964-65‡ 1969‡ 1970-72‡
  QUALITY GOOD‡ MUSEE ROYAL DE L'AFRIQUE CENTRALE‡ ‡
  ‡ ‡ DRUM, FLUTE, HEROIC-RECITATION, HISTORY, HORN,
  PIPE, RITUAL, ROYAL, SOCIAL

VANVELSEN, J.
  VANVELSEN, J.‡ DEPARTMENT OF SOCIOLOGY AND SOCIAL
  ANTHROPOLOGY, UNIVERSITY COLLEGE, ABERYSTWYTH,
  WALES, UNITED KINGDOM‡ MALAWI‡ NKATA BAY‡ TONGA‡
  10 HOURS‡ 1960‡ QUALITY FAIR‡ ‡ ‡ ‡ ‡ POLITICAL

  VANVELSEN, J.‡ DEPARTMENT OF SOCIOLOGY AND SOCIAL
  ANTHROPOLOGY, UNIVERSITY COLLEGE, ABERYSTWYTH,
  WALES, UNITED KINGDOM‡ UGANDA‡ KABERAMAIDO‡ KUMAM‡
  15 HOURS‡ 1948-60‡ QUALITY FAIR‡ ‡ ‡ ‡ ‡ DANCE,
  ENTERTAINMENT, LOVE, POSSESSION

VAUGHAN, JAMES H.
  BROOKS, GEORGE‡ DALBY, DAVID‡ VAUGHAN, JAMES H.‡
  DEPARTMENT OF HISTORY, INDIANA UNIVERSITY,
  BLOOMINGTON, INDIANA 47401‡ SCHOOL OF ORIENTAL
  AND AFRICAN STUDIES, UNIVERSITY OF LONDON, LONDON
  W.C.1, ENGLAND‡ DEPARTMENT OF ANTHROPOLOGY,
  INDIANA UNIVERSITY, BLOOMINGTON, INDIANA 47401‡
  AFRICA-U.S.‡ BLOOMINGTON, INDIANA‡ MALINKE‡ 2
  HOURS‡ 1969‡ QUALITY GOOD‡ ARCHIVES OF
  TRADITIONAL MUSIC‡ 69-012-F‡ ‡ RESTRICTED‡
  MALINKE-LECTURE

  VAUGHAN, JAMES H.‡ ANTHROPOLOGY DEPARTMENT,
  INDIANA UNIVERSITY, BLOOMINGTON, INDIANA 47401‡
  NIGERIA‡ MADAGALI DISTRICT‡ MARGI, VENGO‡ 1 HOUR‡
  1960‡ QUALITY FAIR‡ ARCHIVES OF TRADITIONAL MUSIC‡
  75-053-F‡ ‡ RESTRICTED‡ MUSIC

  VAUGHAN, JAMES H.‡ ANTHROPOLOGY DEPARTMENT,
  INDIANA UNIVERSITY, BLOOMINGTON, INDIANA 47401‡
  NIGERIA‡ MADAGALI DISTRICT‡ MARGI‡ .3 HOUR‡ 1960‡
  QUALITY GOOD‡ ARCHIVES OF TRADITIONAL MUSIC‡

VAUGHAN, JAMES H.
  75-052-F‡ ‡ RESTRICTED‡ DEATH-FUNERAL-STAGED

  VAUGHAN, JAMES H.‡ ANTHROPOLOGY DEPARTMENT,
  INDIANA UNIVERSITY, BLOOMINGTON, INDIANA 47401‡
  NIGERIA‡ MADAGALI DISTRICT‡ MARGI‡ 1 HOUR‡ 1974‡
  QUALITY EXCELLENT‡ ARCHIVES OF TRADITIONAL MUSIC‡
  75-054-F‡ ‡ RESTRICTED‡ CHILDREN, CHORDOPHONE,
  DEATH-FUNERAL, LUTE-BOWED, RULER-INTERVIEW,
  ULULATION

  VAUGHAN, JAMES H.‡ ANTHROPOLOGY DEPARTMENT,
  INDIANA UNIVERSITY, BLOOMINGTON, INDIANA 47401‡
  NIGERIA‡ MADAGALI DISTRICT‡ MARGI‡ 3 HOURS‡ 1974‡
  QUALITY GOOD‡ ARCHIVES OF TRADITIONAL MUSIC‡
  75-055-F‡ ‡ RESTRICTED‡ HISTORY-LIFE, WORD-LIST

VELLENGA, DOROTHY DEE
  VELLENGA, DOROTHY DEE‡ DEPARTMENT OF
  SOCIOLOGY/ANTHROPOLOGY, MUSKINGUM COLLEGE, NEW
  CONCORD, OHIO 43762‡ GHANA‡ ACCRA, ASAMANKESE‡ ‡
  1 HOUR‡ 1969‡ QUALITY GOOD‡ ‡ ‡ ‡ HYMN, SOCIAL,
  SPIRITUAL

VERDIER, RAYMOND
  VERDIER, RAYMOND‡ ‡ TOGO‡ ‡ KABRE‡ ‡ ‡ ‡ MUSEE DE
  L'HOMME‡ ‡ ‡ ‡

VERGER, PIERRE
  ROUGET, GILBERT+ TARDITS, CLAUDE+ VERGER, PIERRE‡
  1 RUE DES DEUX-PONTS, 75004 PARIS, FRANCE+ 33 RUE
  CROULEBARBE, 75013 PARIS, FRANCE+ -‡ DAHOMEY‡ ‡
  ADJA, FON, GUN, ITCHA, MINA, NAGO‡ ‡ ‡ ‡ MUSEE DE
  L'HOMME‡ ‡ ‡ ‡

VERMEER, DONALD E.
  VERMEER, DONALD E.‡ DEPARTMENT OF GEOGRAPHY AND
  ANTHROPOLOGY, LOUISIANA STATE UNIVERSITY, BATON
  ROUGE, LOUISIANA 70803‡ GHANA‡ KPANDU, VOLTA
  REGION‡ EWE‡ 1 HOUR‡ 1969‡ QUALITY GOOD‡ ‡ ‡ ‡ ‡
  DRUM, CHIEF-INSTALLATION

VERNIER, -
  VERNIER, -‡ ‡ MALAGASY REPUBLIC‡ ‡ ANTANDROY,
  ANTANOSY, BETSILEO, COMORIENS, MAHAFALY, MERINA,
  SAKALAVA, TANALA‡ ‡ ‡ ‡ MUSEE DE L'HOMME‡ ‡ ‡ ‡

VERSFELD, BARBARA
  VERSFELD, BARBARA‡ 6 CHAPEL ROAD, ROSEBANK, CAPE

VERSFELD, BARBARA
  TOWN, SOUTH AFRICA‡ SOUTH AFRICA‡ ‡ XHOSA‡ 1.5
  HOURS‡ 1965‡ QUALITY GOOD‡ ARCHIVES OF
  TRADITIONAL MUSIC‡ 66-237-F‡ ‡ ‡ FOLKTALE

VIDAL, PIERRE ANTOINE
  VIDAL, PIERRE ANTOINE‡ LABORATOIRE D'ETHNOLOGIE,
  UNIVERSITE DE PARIS X, 92001 NANTERRE, FRANCE‡
  CENTRAL AFRICAN REPUBLIC‡ BOUAR, BOZOUM,
  NORTHWEST‡ GBAYA, KARA‡ 9 HOURS‡ 1961-74‡ QUALITY
  FAIR‡ ‡ ‡ ‡ ‡ INITIATION-MALE, INITIATION-FEMALE,
  RITUAL-BANA, RITUAL-LABI, RITUAL-METALLURGY

VIVELO, FRANK ROBERT
  VIVELO, FRANK ROBERT‡ DEPARTMENT OF SOCIAL
  SCIENCES, UNIVERSITY OF MISSOURI-ROLLA, ROLLA,
  MISSOURI 65401‡ BOTSWANA‡ NGAMILAND‡ HERERO‡ .7
  HOUR‡ 1973‡ QUALITY GOOD‡ ‡ ‡ ‡ ‡ MUSIC

WALLMAN, SANDRA
  WALLMAN, SANDRA‡ 33 DEODAS ROAD, LONDON SW 15,
  ENGLAND‡ LESOTHO‡ LOWLAND, RURAL‡ BASUTO‡ 4 HOURS‡
  1963‡ QUALITY FAIR‡ ‡ ‡ ‡ ‡ MUSIC, POLITICAL

WANKLYN, CHRISTOPHER
  BOWLES, PAUL+ WANKLYN, CHRISTOPHER‡ 2117 TANGER
  SOCCO, TANGIER, MOROCCO+ B.P. 471, MARRAKECH,
  MOROCCO‡ MOROCCO‡ EINZOREN, ESSAOUIRA, GOULIMINE,
  MARRAKECH, MEKNES, TAFRAOUTE, TANGIER, TETUAN,
  TIMQUIRCHT, ZAGORA‡ ‡ 2 HOURS‡ CA1959-62‡ QUALITY
  GOOD‡ ARCHIVES OF TRADITIONAL MUSIC‡ 62-017-F‡
  ATL 2457-60‡ RESTRICTED‡ BEGGAR, CYMBAL, DANCE,
  DRUM-CLAY, DRUM-DERBUKA, DRUM-FRAME,
  FEET-STAMPING, FLUTE, HANDCLAPPING, LUTE-BOWED,
  LUTE-PLUCKED, OBOE, PRAYER-CALL, PROCESSION,
  SLAVE, TAMBOURINE, ULULATION

  WANKLYN, CHRISTOPHER‡ B.P. 471, MARRAKECH,
  MOROCCO‡ MOROCCO‡ ATLAS MOUNTAINS, OURIKA VALLEY,
  TALATENOUSS‡ AIT-SIDI-MERRI, DEGWANA, MISIWA,
  OULED-MTAA‡ 3 HOURS‡ 1963+ 1969‡ QUALITY GOOD‡
  ARCHIVES OF TRADITIONAL MUSIC‡ 74-119-F‡ ‡ ‡ BELL,
  CYMBAL-FINGER, DANCE, DRUM-FRAME, DRUM-POTTERY,
  ENTERTAINMENT, LUTE-BOWED-KAMENJA, MARRIAGE,
  TRANCE-SUFI

WARE, NAOMI
  NKETIA, J.H. KWABENA+ WARE, NAOMI‡ INSTITUTE OF
  AFRICAN STUDIES, P.O. BOX 25, LEGON, GHANA+

WARE, NAOMI
   DEPARTMENT OF SOCIOLOGY, ANTHROPOLOGY, AND SOCIAL
   WORK, UNIVERSITY OF WISCONSIN, OSHKOSH, WISCONSIN
   54901‡ GHANA-U.S.‡ BLOOMINGTON, INDIANA‡ AKAN‡ 1
   HOUR‡ 1965‡ QUALITY GOOD‡ ARCHIVES OF TRADITIONAL
   MUSIC‡ 65-145-F‡ ‡ RESTRICTED‡
   MUSICIANS-AKAN-LECTURE

   WARE, NAOMI‡ DEPARTMENT OF SOCIOLOGY,
   ANTHROPOLOGY, AND SOCIAL WORK, UNIVERSITY OF
   WISCONSIN, OSHKOSH, WISCONSIN 54901‡ SIERRA LEONE‡
   FREETOWN‡ ‡ 5 HOURS‡ 1969‡ QUALITY GOOD‡ ARCHIVES
   OF TRADITIONAL MUSIC‡ 70-045-F‡ ‡ RESTRICTED‡
   FESTIVAL-JAZZ, JAZZ

WARNIER, JEAN-PIERRE
   WARNIER, JEAN-PIERRE‡ DEPARTMENT OF ANTHROPOLOGY,
   UNIVERSITY OF PENNSYLVANIA, PHILADELPHIA,
   PENNSYLVANIA 19104‡ CAMEROON‡ BAMENDA, NORTHWEST
   PROVINCE‡ MANKON‡ 10 HOURS‡ 1972-74‡ QUALITY GOOD‡
   ‡ ‡ ‡ ‡ CHILDREN-TWINS-RITUAL, FOLKTALE, HISTORY,
   RECREATION, SOCIETY-MEN

WARREN, DENNIS M.
   WARREN, DENNIS M.‡ DEPARTMENT OF SOCIOLOGY AND
   ANTHROPOLOGY, IOWA STATE UNIVERSITY, AMES, IOWA
   50010‡ GHANA‡ TECHIMAN‡ BONO‡ 27 HOURS‡ 1969-71‡
   QUALITY GOOD‡ CENTER FOR AFRICAN ORAL DATA‡
   72-249-F‡ ATL 5516-70‡ RESTRICTED‡ DRUM-LANGUAGE,
   FESTIVAL-APOO, FESTIVAL-YAM, FOLKTALE, HIGHLIFE,
   HISTORY-COUNCIL-STOOL, HISTORY-DEITY,
   HISTORY-TOWN, POSSESSION, PRAISE, PUBERTY-FEMALE

WEISS, -
   WEISS, -‡ ‡ SUDAN‡ ‡ FUNG‡ ‡ ‡ ‡ MUSEE DE L'HOMME‡
   ‡ ‡ ‡

WEISSWANGE, KARIN I.S.
   WEISSWANGE, KARIN I.S.‡ D-638 BAD HOMBURG V.D. H.,
   OBERER REISBERG 21, FEDERAL REPUBLIC OF WEST
   GERMANY‡ LIBERIA‡ ‡ LOMA, MANDINGO‡ ‡ 1963-65+
   1972-73‡ ‡ MUSIKWISSENSCHAFTLICHES INSTITUT DER
   FREIEN UNIVERSITAT BERLIN‡ ‡ ‡ ‡ DANCE, DRUM,
   FOLKTALE, HARP, WORK

WELCH, DAVID B.
   WELCH, DAVID B.‡ 26 CORNELIA STREET, APT. 7, NEW
   YORK, NEW YORK 10014‡ NIGERIA‡ EDE, ILA-ORANGUN,
   ISEYIN, OGBOMOSO, OSOGBO, OYO‡ YORUBA‡ 24 HOURS‡

WELCH, DAVID B.
  1970-71‡ QUALITY EXCELLENT‡ ARCHIVES OF
  TRADITIONAL MUSIC‡ 74-003-F‡ ‡ RESTRICTED‡
  DRUM-BATA, DRUM-HOURGLASS-DUNDUN, DRUM-IYALU,
  FESTIVAL-YAM, PRAISE, PRAISE-ORIKI, PRAISE-SHANGO,
  RATTLE

WEMAN, HENRY PAUL
  WEMAN, HENRY PAUL‡ TORSGATAN 2, 75222 UPPSALA,
  SWEDEN‡ RHODESIA‡ BEITBRIDGE-DISTRICT,
  MUSUME-DISTRICT‡ KARANGA, LEMBA, VENDA, ZULU‡ 10
  HOURS‡ 1957‡ ‡ ‡ ‡ ‡ ‡ BOW-MUSICAL, CHILDREN,
  CHILDREN-SCHOOL, DANCE, DRUM, HANDCLAPPING,
  HERDING, HORN, LULLABY, MBIRA, MBIRA-TUNING,
  RATTLE, RELIGIOUS-CHRISTIAN, WORK-FIELD,
  WORK-THRESHING

  WEMAN, HENRY PAUL‡ TORSGATAN 2, 75222 UPPSALA,
  SWEDEN‡ SOUTH AFRICA‡ BEITBRIDGE-DISTRICT,
  MAHLABATINI-DISTRICT‡ VENDA, ZULU‡ 9 HOURS‡
  1956-57‡ ‡ ‡ ‡ ‡ ‡ BOW-MUSICAL, CANTE-FABLE,
  CHILDREN, CONCERTINA, ENTERTAINMENT, HANDCLAPPING,
  HUNTING, LAMENT, LOVE, MARRIAGE, MILITARY, WAR

WEMAN, PAUL HENRY
  WEMAN, PAUL HENRY‡ TORSGATAN 2, 75222 UPPSALA,
  SWEDEN‡ NIGERIA‡ LAGOS‡ YORUBA‡ 1 HOUR‡ 1957‡ ‡ ‡
  ‡ ‡ ‡ DRUM, ORGAN, RELIGIOUS-CHRISTIAN

  WEMAN, PAUL HENRY‡ TORSGATAN 2, 75222 UPPSALA,
  SWEDEN‡ TANZANIA‡ BUKOBA-DISTRICT‡ HAYA, SUKUMA,
  SWAHILI‡ 5 HOURS‡ 1957‡ ‡ ‡ ‡ ‡ BOW-MUSICAL,
  CHILDREN-SCHOOL, DANCE, DRUM, HANDCLAPPING, HORN,
  HUNTING, MARRIAGE, RELIGIOUS-CHRISTIAN,
  WORK-FIELD, ZITHER-TROUGH

  WEMAN, PAUL HENRY‡ TORSGATAN 2, 75222 UPPSALA,
  SWEDEN‡ ZAIRE‡ ELISABETHVILLE‡ LUBA‡ 1 HOUR‡ 1957‡
  ‡ ‡ ‡ ‡ ‡ DRUM, RELIGIOUS-CHRISTIAN, XYLOPHONE

  WEMAN, PAUL HENRY‡ TORSGATAN 2, 75222 UPPSALA,
  SWEDEN‡ ZAMBIA‡ MAPANDA‡ ‡ .2 HOUR‡ 1957‡ ‡ ‡ ‡
  ‡ RELIGIOUS-CHRISTIAN

WESLEYAN UNIVERSITY
  WESLEYAN UNIVERSITY‡ HIGH STREET, MIDDLETOWN,
  CONNECTICUT 06457‡ ‡ ‡ ‡ ‡ ‡ ‡ ‡ ‡ ‡

WEST, MONTY
  WEST, MONTY‡ ‡ ‡ ‡ FANTI‡ ‡ 1957‡ QUALITY GOOD‡
  ARCHIVES OF LANGUAGES OF THE WORLD‡ ‡ ‡ ‡
  GRAMMATICAL-DATA-FANTI

WESTPHAL, ERNST O.J.
  WESTPHAL, ERNST O.J.‡ DEPARTMENT OF AFRICAN
  LANGUAGES, UNIVERSITY OF CAPE TOWN, RONDEBOSCH
  7700, REPUBLIC OF SOUTH AFRICA‡ BOTSWANA‡
  NORTHERN BOTSWANA‡ BUSHMEN, HOTTENTOT, YEI‡ ‡
  1953-74‡ QUALITY GOOD‡ ‡ ‡ ‡ RESTRICTED‡ FOLKLORE,
  HISTORY, LINGUISTIC-DATA, MUSIC

  WESTPHAL, ERNST O.J.‡ DEPARTMENT OF AFRICAN
  LANGUAGES, UNIVERSITY OF CAPE TOWN, RONDEBOSCH
  7700, REPUBLIC OF SOUTH AFRICA‡ NAMIBIA‡ ‡
  BUSHMEN, KUANYAMA‡ ‡ 1953-74‡ QUALITY GOOD‡ ‡ ‡ ‡
  ‡ FOLKLORE, HISTORY, LINGUISTIC-DATA, MUSIC

  WESTPHAL, ERNST O.J.‡ DEPARTMENT OF AFRICAN
  LANGUAGES, UNIVERSITY OF CAPE TOWN, RONDEBOSCH
  7700, REPUBLIC OF SOUTH AFRICA‡ SOUTH AFRICA‡
  CAPE‡ BUSHMEN‡ ‡ 1953-74‡ QUALITY GOOD‡ ‡ ‡ ‡
  FOLKLORE, HISTORY, LINGUISTIC-DATA, MUSIC

WICHMANN, ERICK
  WICHMANN, ERICK‡ ‡ MOROCCO‡ ASRIR, MARRAKECH,
  QUARZAZATE, TANTAN, TINERSHIR, TODRAVALLEY‡
  BERBER-JEBALA, BERBER-REGUIBAT‡ ‡ 1969‡ ‡ DANSK
  FOLKEMINDESAMLING‡ 69/10A-34A‡ ‡ ‡

WICHMANN, ERIK
  BENTHIEN, CLAUS+ LILLIEBJERG, HANNE+ WICHMANN,
  ERIK‡ ‡ MOROCCO‡ KENITRA, MARRAKECH, MOULAY IDRIS‡
  ‡ ‡ 1967‡ ‡ DANSK FOLKEMINDESAMLING‡ 67/1A-13A‡ ‡
  ‡

  BENTHIEN, CLAUS+ LILLIEBJERG, HANNE+ WICHMANN,
  ERIK‡ ‡ TUNISIA‡ BIZERTE, NEFTA‡ ‡ ‡ 1967‡ ‡
  DANSK FOLKEMINDESAMLING‡ 67/13A-16A‡ ‡ ‡

WIDSTRAND, CARL G.
  WIDSTRAND, CARL G.‡ SCANDINAVIAN INSTITUTE OF
  AFRICAN STUDIES, BOX 98 S-750 02, UPPSALA 1,
  SWEDEN‡ ‡ ‡ SWAHILI‡ 15 HOURS‡ ‡ QUALITY GOOD‡
  SCANDINAVIAN INSTITUTE OF AFRICAN STUDIES‡ ‡ ‡ ‡
  MUSIC

WILLETT, FRANK
   WILLETT, FRANK‡ DEPARTMENT OF ART HISTORY,
   NORTHWESTERN UNIVERSITY, EVANSTON, ILLINOIS 60201‡
   NIGERIA‡ MODAKEKE‡ YORUBA‡ 1 HOUR‡ 1972‡ QUALITY
   EXCELLENT‡ ‡ ‡ ‡ BELL, DRUM-FRAME, DRUM-L'BONGO,
   MASS-YORUBA, RATTLE

WILLIAMS, CHESTER S.
   WILLIAMS, CHESTER S.‡ 2807 SAN PAULO, DALLAS,
   TEXAS 75228‡ SOMALIA‡ MOGADISHU‡ ‡ 1 HOUR‡ 1962‡
   QUALITY GOOD‡ ARCHIVES OF TRADITIONAL MUSIC‡
   65-136-F‡ ‡ ‡ DRUM, FLUTE, LUTE, TAMBOURINE

WILLIAMSON, KAY
   WILLIAMSON, KAY‡ DEPARTMENT OF LINGUISTICS AND
   NIGERIAN LANGUAGES, UNIVERSITY OF IBADAN, IBADAN,
   NIGERIA‡ NIGERIA‡ MID-WEST STATE, RIVERS STATE‡
   IJO‡ 25 HOURS‡ 1959‡ QUALITY FAIR‡ TAPE LIBRARY,
   DEPARTMENT OF LINGUISTICS AND NIGERIAN LANGUAGES,
   UNIVERSITY OF IBADAN‡ ‡ ‡ ‡ DRUM, FESTIVAL,
   FOLKLORE, HISTORY

WILLIS, ROY GEOFFREY
   WILLIS, ROY GEOFFREY‡ DEPARTMENT OF SOCIAL
   ANTHROPOLOGY, UNIVERSITY OF EDINBURGH, GEORGE
   SQUARE, EDINBURGH EH8 9U, SCOTLAND‡ TANZANIA‡
   UFIPA‡ FIPA‡ 6 HOURS‡ 1966‡ QUALITY FAIR‡ ‡ ‡ ‡ ‡
   FOLKLORE, MUSIC, MYTH

WILSON, VIVIAN J.
   WILSON, VIVIAN J.‡ NATIONAL MUSEUM, BULAWAYO,
   P.O. BOX 240, BULAWAYO, RHODESIA‡ RHODESIA‡
   ZAMBEZI‡ TONGA‡ .5 HOUR‡ 1970‡ QUALITY EXCELLENT‡
   ‡ ‡ ‡ ‡ MUSIC, ORAL-CATA

WITTIG, R. CURT
   ARMSTRONG, ROBERT G. +WITTIG, R. CURT‡ INSTITUTE
   OF AFRICAN STUDIES, UNIVERSITY OF IBADAN, IBADAN,
   NIGERIA+ 3740 KANAWHA STREET N.W., WASHINGTON,
   D.C. 20015‡ NIGERIA‡ AGILA‡ IDOMA‡ 1 HOUR‡ 1964‡
   QUALITY GOOD‡ ARCHIVES OF TRADITIONAL MUSIC‡
   72-244-F‡ ATL 5462‡ ‡ DANCE-MASKED-ABILE,
   VOICE-DISGUISE

   WITTIG, R. CURT‡ INSTITUTE OF AFRICAN STUDIES,
   UNIVERSITY OF IBADAN, IBADAN, NIGERIA‡ NIGERIA‡
   OYO‡ YORUBA‡ 1 HOUR‡ 1965‡ QUALITY GOOD‡ ARCHIVES
   OF TRADITIONAL MUSIC‡ 72-246-F‡ ATL 5466‡
   RESTRICTED‡ DANCE-MASKED-EGUNGUN, DRUM

WITWATERSRAND, UNIVERSITY
  WITWATERSRAND, UNIVERSITY OF‡ JAN SMUTS AVENUE,
  JOHANNESBURG, REPUBLIC OF SOUTH AFRICA‡ ‡ ‡ ‡ ‡
  ‡ ‡ ‡ ‡ ‡

WOLFF, HANS
  WOLFF, HANS‡ DECEASED‡ NIGERIA‡ DELTA PROVINCE,
  UGHELLI‡ AGBADU, URHOBO‡ ‡ 1953‡ QUALITY GOOD‡
  ARCHIVES OF LANGUAGES OF THE WORLD‡ ‡ ‡ ‡
  CONVERSATION, PROVERB

  WOLFF, HANS‡ DECEASED‡ NIGERIA‡ JOS, PLATEAU
  PROVINCE‡ BIROM‡ ‡ 1953‡ QUALITY GOOD‡ ARCHIVES
  OF LANGUAGES OF THE WORLD‡ ‡ ‡ ‡ FOLKTALE

  WOLFF, HANS‡ DECEASED‡ NIGERIA‡ BENIN CITY, BENIN
  PROVINCE‡ EDO-BINI‡ ‡ 1953‡ QUALITY FAIR‡
  ARCHIVES OF LANGUAGES OF THE WORLD‡ ‡ ‡ ‡ PROVERB

  WOLFF, HANS‡ DECEASED‡ NIGERIA‡ OWERRI PROVINCE‡
  IBO‡ ‡ 1953‡ QUALITY FAIR‡ ARCHIVES OF LANGUAGES
  OF THE WORLD‡ ‡ ‡ ‡ CONVERSATION

  WOLFF, HANS‡ DECEASED‡ NIGERIA‡ KABBA PROVINCE,
  OKENI‡ IGBIRA‡ ‡ 1953‡ QUALITY GOOD‡ ARCHIVES OF
  LANGUAGES OF THE WORLD‡ ‡ ‡ ‡ GRAMMATICAL-DATA

  WOLFF, HANS‡ DECEASED‡ NIGERIA‡ RIVERS PROVINCE‡
  IJO, KALABARI‡ ‡ 1953‡ QUALITY GOOD‡ ARCHIVES OF
  LANGUAGES OF THE WORLD‡ ‡ ‡ ‡
  GRAMMATICAL-DATA-OKRIKA

  WOLFF, HANS‡ DECEASED‡ NIGERIA‡ DELTA PROVINCE,
  WARRI‡ IJO, ITSEKIRI‡ ‡ 1953‡ QUALITY GOOD‡
  ARCHIVES OF LANGUAGES OF THE WORLD‡ ‡ ‡ ‡
  FOLKTALE

  WOLFF, HANS‡ DECEASED‡ NIGERIA‡ DELTA PROVINCE‡
  IJO, IJAW-WESTERN‡ ‡ 1953‡ QUALITY FAIR‡ ARCHIVES
  OF LANGUAGES OF THE WORLD‡ ‡ ‡ ‡
  GRAMMATICAL-DATA-MEIN, GRAMMATICAL-DATA-TARAKIRI

  WOLFF, HANS‡ DECEASED‡ NIGERIA‡ BENUE PROVINCE‡
  JUKUN‡ .5 HOUR‡ 1953‡ QUALITY GOOD‡ ARCHIVES OF
  LANGUAGES OF THE WORLD‡ ‡ ‡ ‡ FOLKTALE,
  GRAMMATICAL-DATA, PROVERB

  WOLFF, HANS‡ DECEASED‡ NIGERIA‡ ZARIA PROVINCE‡
  KAJE‡ .5 HOUR‡ 1953‡ QUALITY GOOD‡ ARCHIVES OF

WOLFF, HANS
  LANGUAGES OF THE WORLD‡ ‡ ‡ ‡ GRAMMATICAL-DATA

  WOLFF, HANS‡ DECEASED‡ NIGERIA‡ BIDA CITY, NIGER
  PROVINCE‡ NUPE‡ ‡ 1953‡ QUALITY GOOD‡ ARCHIVES OF
  LANGUAGES OF THE WORLD‡ ‡ ‡ ‡ PROVERB-BIDA

  WOLFF, HANS‡ DECEASED‡ NIGERIA‡ LAGOS, WARRI,
  ZARIA‡ EFIK, HAUSA, IBIBIO, KAJE, SOBO, PABIR,
  YORUBA‡ 2.5 HOURS‡ 1953-54‡ QUALITY GOOD‡
  ARCHIVES OF TRADITIONAL MUSIC‡ 59-015-F‡ ATL
  1830-35‡ RESTRICTED‡ CANTE-FABLE, DANCE,
  DEATH-FUNERAL, DRUM, LUTE-BOWED, PRAISE,
  RELIGIOUS-CHRISTIAN, RELIGIOUS-ISLAMIC,
  SECRET-SOCIETY

  WOLFF, HANS‡ DECEASED‡ NIGERIA-U.S.‡ MICHIGAN‡
  YORUBA‡ 4 HOURS‡ 1960-64‡ QUALITY EXCELLENT‡
  ARCHIVES OF TRADITIONAL MUSIC‡ 72-236-F‡ ATL
  3937-38‡ RESTRICTED‡ FOLKTALE, PRAISE-NAME,
  PROVERB

WOLLNER, CHAD A.
  WOLLNER, CHAD A.‡ C/O THE PAUL WOLLNER FOUNDATION,
  INC., 266 WEST STREET, NEW YORK, NEW YORK 10013‡
  ETHIOPIA‡ SOUTHWEST‡ ‡ 20 HOURS‡ 1972‡ QUALITY
  EXCELLENT‡ ‡ ‡ ‡ FOLKLORE, HISTORY,
  PRAISE-POETRY, RITUAL, SOCIAL

  WOLLNER, CHAD A.‡ C/O THE PAUL WOLLNER FOUNDATION,
  INC., 266 WEST STREET, NEW YORK, NEW YORK 10013‡
  KENYA‡ ‡ ‡ 3 HOURS‡ 1972‡ QUALITY EXCELLENT‡ ‡ ‡ ‡
  ‡ FOLKLORE, HISTORY, PRAISE-POETRY, RITUAL,
  SOCIAL

WYLIE, KENNETH CHARLES
  WYLIE, KENNETH CHARLES‡ 2796 SEDGWICK, BRONX, NEW
  YORK 10468‡ NIGERIA‡ ABUJA EMIRATE, NORTHEASTERN
  STATE‡ ‡ 15 HOURS‡ 1965-66‡ QUALITY FAIR‡ ‡ ‡ ‡ ‡
  HISTORY

  WYLIE, KENNETH CHARLES‡ 2796 SEDGWICK, BRONX, NEW
  YORK 10468‡ SIERRA LEONE‡ KAILAHUN DISTRICT, PORT
  LOKO DISTRICT‡ MENDE‡ 22 HOURS‡ 1965-66+ 1970‡
  QUALITY FAIR‡ ‡ ‡ ‡ HISTORY

YODER, WALTER D.
  YODER, WALTER D.‡ ‡ SOUTH AFRICA-U.S.‡
  BLOOMINGTON, INDIANA‡ ‡ .5 HOUR‡ 1955‡ QUALITY

YODER, WALTER D.
  GOOD‡ ARCHIVES OF TRADITIONAL MUSIC‡ 060-023-F‡ ‡
  RESTRICTED‡ BELIEF, LEGEND

YOUSSEF, AIT
  YOUSSEF, AIT‡ ‡ MOROCCO‡ MARRAKECH‡ ‡ ‡ ‡ ‡ MUSEE
  DE L'HOMME‡ ‡ ‡ ‡

  YOUSSEF, AIT‡ ‡ MOROCCO‡ MARRAKECH‡ ‡ ‡ 1966‡ ‡
  MUSEE DE L'HOMME‡ ‡ ‡ ‡ CURING, POSSESSION

ZEMP, HUGO
  ZEMP, HUGO‡ DEPARTMENT D'ETHNOMUSICOLOGIE, MUSEE
  DE L'HOMME, PALAIS DE CHAILLOT, PARIS 16E, FRANCE‡
  IVORY COAST‡ ‡ BAULE, DAN, GUERE, MALINKE, SENUFO‡
  28 HOURS‡ 1962‡ 1964-67‡ QUALITY EXCELLENT‡ MUSEE
  DE L'HOMME‡ ‡ ‡ ‡ SOCIAL

  ZEMP, HUGO‡ PALAIS DE CHAILLOT, PARIS 16E, FRANCE‡
  MOROCCO‡ TAZA‡ ‡ ‡ 1960‡ ‡ MUSEE DE L'HOMME‡ ‡ ‡ ‡
  DRUM, MARRIAGE, OBOE

ZEMPLEIVI, ANDRAS
  ZEMPLEIVI, ANDRAS‡ 10, RUE DES TROIS PORTES,
  75005 PARIS, FRANCE‡ CHAD‡ LERE‡ MOUNDANG‡ 2
  HOURS‡ 1969‡ QUALITY GOOD‡ ‡ ‡ ‡ ‡ FOLKTALE,
  RITUAL-SPIRIT-POSSESSION,
  SPIRIT-POSSESSION-SHINKI

  ZEMPLEIVI, ANDRAS‡ 10, RUE DES TROIS PORTES,
  75005 PARIS, FRANCE‡ IVORY COAST‡ SINEMATIALI‡
  SENUFO-NA-FAARA‡ 6 HOURS‡ 1972-74‡ QUALITY GOOD‡ ‡
  ‡ ‡ ‡ CEREMONY-INITIATION-PORO, DANCE-MASKED-PORO,
  DEATH-FUNERAL, FOLKTALE, INITIATION-PORO,
  RITUAL-SACRED-FOREST

Index to
Countries

Index to Countries

-U.S.
   HICKERSON, NANCY+ HYMES, VIRGINIA+ KELLER, JAMES‡
   TIGRINYA‡ 1954

   REDDEN, JAMES ERSKINE‡ BAMBARA‡ 1962

AFRICA-ANGOLA, CAMEROON,
   KUBIK, GERHARD‡ ‡ 1959-73

AFRICA-EAST
   CURTIS, NATALIE‡ ‡ CA1919

AFRICA-GERMANY
   BERLIN PHONOGRAMM-ARCHIV‡ BULE‡ 1909

AFRICA-U.S.
   BROOKS, GEORGE+ DALBY, DAVID+ VAUGHAN, JAMES H.‡
   MALINKE‡ 1969

   DALBY, DAVID+ AFRICAN STUDIES-I.U.‡ ‡ 1969

   DALBY, DAVID+ AFRICAN STUDIES-I.L.‡ ‡ 1969

   HANNA, JUDITH LYNNE+ GORDON, MERYL‡ ‡ 1975

AFRICA-WEST
   ALBERTS, ARTHUR S.‡ BAULE, MANO, MOSSI‡ 1949

   JENKINS, JEAN‡ ‡ 1960-69

ALGERIA
  BOURGEOT, A.‡ TUAREG‡ 1970

  CARD, CAROLINE E.‡ TUAREG‡ 1972

  CENTRE DE RECHERCHES ANTHROPOLOGIQUES
  PREHISTORIQUES ET ETHNOGRAPHIQUES‡ ARAB, BERBER,
  MAGHREB‡

  HOLIDAY, GEOFFREY D.‡ TUAREG‡ CA1958

  MOULOUD, MAMMERI‡ BERBER‡

  PELLIGRA, D.‡ TUAREG‡ 1970

  PENCHOEN, THOMAS GOODENOUGH‡ BERBER-AURES‡ 1973

  PLANCK, EBBE‡ ‡ 1969

  SAYAD, ALI‡ KABYLE‡ 1968-70

  SAYAD, ALI‡ CHAOUI‡ 1971-72

  SHAMAY, M.‡ ‡ 1968

  SMITS, LUCAS GERARDUS ALFONSUS‡ TUAREG‡ 1968-69
ANGOLA
  ARCHIVES OF ETHNIC MUSIC AND DANCE‡ ‡

  CHILDS, GLADWYN‡ OVIMBUNDU‡ 1962

  CLAUSS, BERNHARD PETER‡ HIMBA-MUGAMBO‡ 1970-72

  DIAMANG, C.‡ ‡

  DIAS, MARGOT‡ MUSSEQUES‡ 1960

  ENGLAND, NICHOLAS M.‡ GANGULA‡ 1957-61

  ESTES, RICHARD D.‡ SONGO‡ 1970

  GIBSON, GORDON D.‡ CHAVIKWA, HAKAWONA, HIMBA,
  KEPE, KUVALE, VATWA, ZIMBA‡ 1971-73

  HAMBLY, WILFRED D.‡ OVIMBUNDU‡ 1929-30

  HENDERSON, LAWRENCE‡ OVIMBUNDU‡ 1972

CAMEROON
  ANKERMANN, BERNHARD‡ BAMUM‡ 1909

  ARCHIVES OF ETHNIC MUSIC AND DANCE‡ ‡

  DUNGER, GEORGE A.‡ BEKCM, DUALA, KAKA, NSUNGLI‡

  GELZER, DAVID G.‡ ‡

  HURAULT, -‡ DOUROU, HAUSA, MBUM‡

  JUILLERAT, B.‡ KIRDI‡ 1966+ 1967-68

  KLEIS, GERALD W.‡ AROCHUKU, BAKUNDU, IGBO, META,
  NKAMBE, WIDEKUM‡ 1971

  MISJONSSKOLEN‡ ‡

  NOSS, PHILIP A.‡ GBAYA‡ 1966-67

  PARE, -+ TARDITS, CLAUDE‡ BAMUM‡

  QUERSIN, BENOIT J.+ QUERSIN, CHRISTINE M.‡ BAFIA,
  BALLOM, BAMILEKE, BAMUM, BULU ETON, PEUL, PYGMIES,
  SANAGA, TIKAR, VUTE‡ 1967

  RAPHAEL, RONALD P.‡ FULBE, KONDJA, VUTE, WAWA‡
  1974

  REDDEN, JAMES ERSKINE‡ BANTU‡ 1971

  RITZENTHALER, ROBERT + RITZENTHALER, PAT‡ BAFUT‡
  1959

  SCHWARZ, JEAN‡ BANEN‡ 1968

  STENNES, LESLIE H.‡ FULANI, GIDDER‡ 1956-73

  TESSMAN, GUNTHER‡ FANG-PANGWE‡ 1907

  WARNIER, JEAN-PIERRE‡ MANKON‡ 1972-74

CENTRAL AFRICAN REPUBLIC
  AROM, SIMHA‡ AKA-PYGMIES, LINDA-BANDA,
  NGBAKA-MABO‡ 1964-67+ 1971-73

  BOUQUIAUX, LUC‡ BANDA, ISONGO, MONZOMBO,
  NGBAKA-MABO‡

CENTRAL AFRICAN REPUBLIC
  KUBIK, GERHARD‡ NZAKARA, ZANDE‡

  MISSION SOCIOLOGIQUE DU HAUTE-OUBANGUI‡ NZAKARA,
  ZANDE‡

  VIDAL, PIERRE ANTOINE‡ GBAYA, KARA‡ 1961-74

CHAD
  ADLER, -‡ MBAYE‡

  BRANDILY, MONIQUE‡ KANEMBU, KOTOKO, TEDA‡ 1961+
  1963+ 1965

  BRANDILY, MONIQUE‡ FEZZANAIS, TEDA‡ 1969

  CLAUSS, BERNHARD PETER‡ SARAKABA‡ 1973

  FEDRY, J.‡ HADJERAI‡ 1966-67

  GARINE, I. DE‡ KERA, MUSEY‡ 1962-63+ 1965

  JAULIN, -‡ SARA-DEME‡

  KAYE, ALAN S.‡ ARAB‡ 1970

  PAIRAULT, CLAUDE ALBERT‡ GULA-IRO‡ 1959-64

  ZEMPLEIVI, ANDRAS‡ MOUNDANG‡ 1969

COMORO ISLANDS
  OTTENHEIMER, HARRIET+ OTTENHEIMER, MARTIN‡ ‡
  1967-68

CONGO, PEOPLE'S REPUBLIC
  ROUGET, GILBERT‡ PYGMIES-NGOUNDI‡ 1948

  SULZMANN, ERIKA‡ ATYO‡ 1962

  VALLEE, ROGER P.‡ ‡ 1967

DAHOMEY
  BAY, EDNA GRACE‡ FON‡ 1972

  CALKINS, HOWARD W.+ RADIO DAHOMEY‡ DENDI, DOMPAGO,
  FON, MAHI, YORUBA‡ CA1967

  DREWAL, HENRY JOHN‡ YORUBA‡ 1973

DAHOMEY
  DUMONT, LILLIAN E.‡ FON, YORUBA‡ 1973

  HERSKOVITS, MELVILLE J.+ HERSKOVITS, FRANCES S.‡
  FON‡ 1931

  OERTLI, PEO‡ AIZO‡ 1973-74

  ROUGET, GILBERT‡ FON, GUN, HOLI, NAGO‡ 1952

  ROUGET, GILBERT‡ FON, GUN, YORUBA‡ 1952-71

  ROUGET, GILBERT+ TARDITS, CLAUDE+ VERGER, PIERRE‡
  ADJA, FON, GUN, ITCHA, MINA, NAGO‡

  SAVARY, CLAUDE‡ FON‡ 1966-67

  SHEFFIELD, JAMES‡ YORUBA‡ 1971+ 1973

  TARDITS, CLAUDE‡ GUN‡

  TARDITS, CLAUDE‡ GUN‡ 1955

DAHOMEY-U.S.
  SMOLEY, R.A.‡ ‡ 1970

EGYPT
  ABDELSAYED, FR. GABRIEL H.A.‡ COPT‡ 1965-69

  EL-SHAMY, HASAN M.‡ ARAB, DINKA, NUBIAN‡ 1968-71

  HALE, KEN‡ ARAB‡

  HOHENWART-GERLACHSTEIN, ANNA‡ ABABDA, BEJA,
  FADIDJA, FELLAHIN‡ 1960+ 1962-63

  JARGY, SIMON+ OLSEN, POUL ROVSING‡ ‡ 1969

  MAGYAR TUDOMANYOS AKADEMIA NEPZENEKUTATO CSOPORT‡
  COPT, FELLAHIN, NUBIAN‡ 1966-67 + 1969

EGYPT-U.S.
  EL-SHAMY, HASAN M.‡ ARAB‡ 1961

  FRY, GLADYS M.‡ ‡ 1963

EQUATORIAL GUINEA
  TESSMAN, GUNTHER‡ FANG‡ 1907

ETHIOPIA
  ARCHIVES OF ETHNIC MUSIC AND DANCE‡ AMHARA,
  TIGRINYA‡

  BAIRU, TAFLA‡ GALLA, OROMO‡ 1973-74

  BENDER, MARVIN LIONEL‡ BERTA, BODI, MAO, MUSUJI,
  SAI, TSAMAY‡ 1964-74

  BROADCASTING CORPORATION OF CHINA‡ ‡

  BROGGER, JAN C.‡ SIDAMO‡

  COURLANDER, HAROLD‡ TIGRINYA‡ 1943

  DAVIS, GORDON‡ COPT‡ 1968

  GERSON-KIWI, EDITH‡ ‡ 1972

  HANNA, JUDITH LYNNE+ HANNA, WILLIAM J.‡ ‡ 1963

  HEAD, SYDNEY W.‡ ‡ 1964

  JENKINS, JEAN‡ ‡ 1962-70

  KOIZUMI, FUMIO‡ AMHARA‡ 1971

  LANGE, WERNER‡ BENS, BOSA, CARA, HINNARIO, KAFA,
  MERU, NA'O, SE, SEKA, SHE, ZARAS‡ 1972-73

  LEMMA, TESFAYE‡ ‡ 1970

  LESLAU, WOLF‡ AMHARA, GURAGE, HARARI, SHOA-GALLA,
  SOMALI, TIGRINYA‡ 1947

  LESLAU, WOLF‡ FALASHA‡ CA1947

  LEWIS, HERBERT S.‡ GALLA‡ 1965-66

  LORTAT-JACOB, BERNARD‡ DORZE‡ 1974-75

  MAGYAR TUDOMANYOS AKADEMIA NEPZENEKUTATO CSOPORT‡
  AMHARA, GALLA, KAFFICHO, KULLO, TIGRE‡

  MESSING, SIMON D.‡ AMHARA, GALLA, TIGRE‡ 1961-67

  MULDROW, WILLIAM+ MULDROW, ELIZABETH‡ TESHENNA‡
  1964-65

ETHIOPIA
  OLMSTEAD, JUDITH VIRGINIA‡ DITA, DORZE‡ 1969-71+
  1973

  ORENT, AMNON‡ KAFA‡ 1966-67

  ROSEN, -‡ ‡ 1905

  SHELEMAY, KAY KAUFMAN‡ FALASHA-JEW‡ 1973

  TSEHAI, BRHANE SILASSIE‡ DARASSA, SIDAMO, WOLAMO‡
  1969-73

  TUBIANA, -‡ ‡

  WOLLNER, CHAD A.‡ ‡ 1972

ETHIOPIA-U.S.
  FRY, GLADYS M.‡ ‡ 1963

GABON
  FERNANDEZ, JAMES W.‡ FANG‡ 1960

  PEPPER, HERBERT‡ FANG‡ 1960

GAMBIA, THE
  AMES, DAVID W.‡ WOLOF‡ 1951

  ARCHIVES OF ETHNIC MUSIC AND DANCE‡ MANDINKA‡

  ETHNOMUSICOLOGY CENTRE JAAP KUNST‡ MANDINKA‡ 1958

  INNES, GORDON‡ MANDINKA‡ 1968-69

  KNIGHT, RODERIC COPLEY‡ BALANTA, BAMBARA, FULA,
  JOLA, MANDINKA, TEMNE, WOLOF‡ 1970-71

  PEVAR, MARC DAVID‡ MANDINKA‡ 1972

GHANA
  AKYEA, E. OFORI‡ ASANTE‡ 1967

  ALBERTS, ARTHUR S.‡ EWE, GA, IBO, TWI‡ 1949-51

  ARCHIVES OF ETHNIC MUSIC AND DANCE‡ DAGARTI,
  DAGOMBA, DONNO, EWE, GA, KONKOMBA, LOBI‡

  ARCHIVES OF TRADITIONAL MUSIC‡ ‡ 1950

GHANA

BLAIR, BOB‡ ASANTE‡ 1958

BOAS, FRANZ‡ AKWAPIM‡ PRE-1935

BROWN, JAMES W.‡ ASANTE‡ 1970

COPLAN, DAVID+ THOMASON, LEE‡ ASANTE, EWE, KROBO‡ 1974

DUMONT, LILLIAN E.‡ ‡ 1973

ENGLAND, NICHOLAS M.‡ EWE‡ 1969-70+ 1972

FEINBERG, HARVEY‡ FANTI‡ 1967-68

FIKRY, MONA‡ WALA‡ 1966-67

GRAESSER, MARK W.‡ ASANTE, FRAFRA, HAUSA, KANJAGA, KONKOMBA‡ 1968-69

HAIGHT, BRUCE MARVIN‡ DYULA, GONJA‡ 1972-73

HANLEY, MARY ANN CSJ‡ BUILSA, DAGARI, EWE, FANTI, FRAFRA, GA, KASSENA, NANKANI, TWI‡ 1972

HANLEY, MARY ANN CSJ‡ AKAN, EWE, TWI‡ 1973

HERSKOVITS, MELVILLE J.+ HERSKOVITS, FRANCES S.‡ ASANTE‡ 1931

INSTITUTO NACIONAL DE FOLKLORE, VENEZUELA‡ ‡ 1966

KEALIINOHOMOKU, JOANN W.‡ ‡ 1970

KILSON, MARION D. DE B.‡ GA‡ 1964-65+ 1968

LONG, RONALD W.‡ MANDE‡ 1968

MYKLEBUST, ROLF‡ ‡ 1966

NORSK RIKSKRINGKASTING‡ ‡ 1966

OWEN, WILFRED, JR.‡ ASANTE, BRONG, EWE, FANTI, GA, TWI‡ 1970-71

PANTALEONI, HEWITT‡ EWE‡ 1969-71

PREMPEH, KOFI‡ ASANTE‡ 1950

GHANA
  REDDEN, JAMES ERSKINE‡ AKIM, AKWAPIM, ASANTE, EWE‡
  1958-63

  ROBERTSON, CLAIRE C.‡ GA‡ 1972

  ROMERO, PATRICIA‡ ASANTE‡ 1972

  SOLANO, ROBERT P.‡ ‡ 1970-71

  STRUMPF, MITCHEL‡ DAGARTI, EWE, KONKOMBA‡ 1969-72

  VELLENGA, DOROTHY DEE‡ ‡ 1969

  VERMEER, DONALD E.‡ EWE‡ 1969

  WARREN, DENNIS M.‡ BONO‡ 1969-71

GHANA-ENGLAND
  JONES, ARTHUR M.‡ EWE‡ 1956

GHANA-TOGO
  ADUAMAH, E.Y.‡ EWE‡ 1968-71

GHANA-U.S.
  FRY, GLADYS M.‡ ‡ 1963

  NKETIA, J.H. KWABENA+ WARE, NAOMI‡ AKAN‡ 1965

GUINEA
  ALBERTS, ARTHUR S.‡ KISSI, MALINKE‡ 1949-51

  ARCHIVES OF ETHNIC MUSIC AND DANCE‡ ‡

  GAISSEAU, PIERRE-DOMINIQUE‡ TOMA‡ 1953

  LESTRANGE, M. DE‡ CONIAGUI‡

  ROUGET, GILBERT‡ KONON, MALINKE, MANON, PEUL‡

  ROUGET, GILBERT‡ MALINKE‡ 1952

  ROUGET, GILBERT‡ MALINKE‡ 1952

  SCHAEFFNER, ANDRE‡ BASA‡

IVORY COAST
  ALBERTS, ARTHUR S.‡ BAULE‡ 1949-51

IVORY COAST
  BLANK, ARTHUR S., JR.≢ BLANK, DONNA H.≢ GUERE,
  WOBE≢ 1973

  DUMONT, LILLIAN E.≢ ≢ 1973

  ELLOVICH, RISA SUE≢ DYULA, MALINKE, VOLTAIC≢
  1973-74

  GLAZE, ANITA≢ SENUFO≢ 1969-70

  HIMMELHEBER, HANS G.≢ BAULE, DAN, GUERE, GURO,
  SENUFO≢ 1952-65

  LAUER, JOSEPH JEROME≢ GUERE≢ 1971

  RAYFIELD, JOAN R.≢ BAULE, MALINKE, SENUFO≢
  1972-73

  ROUGET, GILBERT≢ ADIOUKROU, BAULE, EBRIE≢

  ROUGET, GILBERT≢ ADICUKROU, EBRIE≢ 1952

  ZEMP, HUGO≢ BAULE, DAN, GUERE, MALINKE, SENUFO≢
  1962+ 1964-67

  ZEMPLEIVI, ANDRAS≢ SENUFO-NA-FAARA≢ 1972-74

KENYA
  BLOUNT, BEN G.≢ LUO≢ 1971

  BRANTLEY, CYNTHIA≢ GIRYAMA≢ 1970-71

  BUNGER, ROBERT LOUIS≢ OROMA, POKOMO≢ 1969-70

  CAMPBELL, CAROL≢ BAJUN, SWAHILI≢ 1972

  DOBRIN, ARTHUR≢ GUSII≢ 1966

  DOBRIN, ARTHUR≢ GUSII≢ 1966

  DOHERTY, DEBORAH≢ SAMBURU≢ 1973

  DURAN, JAMES JOSEPH≢ KIPSIGI≢ 1971

  HARING, LEE≢ AKAMBA≢ 1967-68

  HAY, MARGARET JEAN≢ LUO≢ 1968-70+ 1973

KENYA
 KNAPPERT, JAN D.‡ SWAHILI‡ 1969+ 1973

 LISZKA, STANLEY WALTER, JR.‡ TAITA‡ 1972-74

 MADIGAN, BOB‡ KAMBA‡ 1957-58

 MORGENTHAU, HENRY‡ ‡ 1961

 PARKER, CAROLYN ANN‡ BAJUN, SWAHILI‡ 1971-72

 PIRRO, ELLEN B.‡ ‡ 1969

 PRESTON, JEROME, JR.‡ LUO‡ 1966

 REDDEN, JAMES ERSKINE‡ LUO‡ 1959

 REDDEN, JAMES ERSKINE‡ LUO‡ 1960-65

 ROBBIN, LAWRENCE H.‡ TURKANA‡ 1965-66

 ROMERO, PATRICIA‡ ‡ 1973

 ROSS, MARC HOWARD‡ KIKUYU‡ 1967

 SANDGREN, DAVID PETER‡ KIKUYU‡ 1970-71

 SEDLAK, PHILIP A.S.‡ DURUMA, GIRYAMA, SWAHILI‡ 1971

 SPENCER, LEON P.‡ KAMBA, KIKUYU, KISII, LUO‡ 1968-69

 TUCKER, ARCHIBALD NORMAN‡ LUO‡

 WOLLNER, CHAD A.‡ ‡ 1972

KENYA-TANZANIA
 GERLACH, LUTHER PAUL‡ ARAB, DIGO, DURUMA‡ 1958-60

KENYA-U.S.
 FRY, GLADYS M.‡ ‡ 1963

LESOTHO
 ADAMS, CHARLES R.‡ BASOTHO‡ 1969-70

 SMITS, LUCAS GERARDUS ALFONSUS‡ BASOTHO‡ 1969+ 1974-75

LESOTHO
  WALLMAN, SANDRA‡ BASUTO‡ 1963

LIBERIA
  ALBERTS, ARTHUR S.‡ ‡ 1949-51

  ALBERTS, ARTHUR S.‡ FANTI, LOMA, MANO‡ 1949-51

  ARCHIVES OF LANGUAGES OF THE WORLD‡ SUSU‡

  BELLMAN, BERYL LARRY‡ KPELLE, LOMA‡ 1969

  D'AZEVEDO, WARREN L.‡ AMERICO-LIBERIAN, GOLA,
  KPELLE, VAI‡ 1956-58+ 1966

  D'AZEVEDO, WARREN L.‡ GOLA, KPELLE, VAI‡ 1960

  D'AZEVEDO, WARREN L.‡ GOLA‡ 1967

  ELWA RADIO STATION, LIBERIA‡ ‡ CA1960-1975

  GAY, JUDITH S.‡ KPELLE‡ 1971-73

  HAWTHORNE, RICHARD‡ MANO‡ 1970

  HERZOG, GEORGE‡ GREBO, JABO, KRU‡ 1930

  HIMMELHEBER, HANS G.‡ DAN, KRAHN, MANO‡ 1950-60

  HOLSOE, SVEND E.‡ DEI, GBANDE, GOLA, KPELLE,
  MANDINGO, VAI‡ 1965-70

  LUCKAU, STEPHEN R.‡ GREBO, JABO‡ 1971

  MAKING, JOEL‡ EBURNEO-LIBERIEN, GREBO‡ 1958

  MARTIN, JANE JACKSON‡ GREBO‡ 1968+ 1972-75

  MASSING, ANDREAS‡ KRU‡ 1971-72

  MOORE, BAI T.‡ BASSA, DEI, GBANDE, GIO, GOLA,
  KISSI, KPELLE, LOMA, MANDINGO, MANO, MENDE, VAI‡
  1962-73

  MOREY, ROBERT H.‡ GBANDE, LOMA, MANDINGO‡ 1935

  NEWBURY, DOROTHY J.‡ BASSA, LOMA‡ 1969-70+ 1972

  OFRI, DORITH‡ VAI‡ 1965-72

LIBERIA
  OKIE, PACKARD L.≠ BASSA, GBANDE, GOLA, KISSI,
  LOMA, MENDE, VAI≠ 1947-54

  OKIE, PACKARD L.≠ BASSA, KRU≠ 1947-54

  OKIE, PACKARD L.≠ BASSA, BELE, GIO, KPELLE, KRU,
  MANDINGO, VAI≠ 1947-54

  SELIGMAN, THOMAS KNOWLES≠ KPELLE≠ 1970

  SIEGMANN, WILLIAM CHARLES≠ BASSA, GBANDE≠ 1973-74

  STONE, RUTH M.+ STONE, VERLON L.≠ KPELLE≠ 1970

  STUTTMAN, LEONARD M.≠ GREBO, KRAHN≠ 1956

  WEISSWANGE, KARIN I.S.≠ LOMA, MANDINGO≠ 1963-65+
  1972-73

LIBYA
  BRANDILY, MONIQUE≠ FEZZANAIS, TEDA≠ 1969

MALAGASY REPUBLIC
  BLOCH, MONICA E.≠ MERINA, TANALA≠ 1964-71

  CONDOMINAS, G.≠ ≠ 1959

  KOECHLIN, B.≠ MAHAFALY, MASIKORO, VEZO≠ 1967-69

  LOMBARD, JACQUES≠ SAKALAVA≠ 1969-74

  MCLEOD, NORMA≠ ≠ 1962-63

  MISJONSSKOLEN≠ ≠

  VERNIER, -≠ ANTANDROY, ANTANOSY, BETSILEO,
  COMORIENS, MAHAFALY, MERINA, SAKALAVA, TANALA≠

MALAWI
  DRAKE, H. MAX≠ TUMBUKA, YAO≠ 1967

  ETHNOMUSICOLOGY CENTRE JAAP KUNST≠ LOMWE,
  MANGANJA≠ 1971

  GEOFFRION, CHARLES A.≠ ACHEWA, MANGANJA, NGONI≠
  1971-72

  GREENSTEIN, ROBERT CARL≠ AMBO, CHEWA, LOMWE,

MALAWI
  MANGANJA, NGONI, TUMBUKA, YAO‡ 1971-75

  JUWAYEYI, YUSUF MCDADDLY‡ ‡ 1972-75

  KRAJEWSKI, F. JOSEPH‡ NYANJA‡ 1967

  MACDONALD, RODERICK JAMES‡ ‡ 1966-67

  PAGE, MELVIN E.‡ ‡ 1972-74

  VANVELSEN, J.‡ TONGA‡ 1960

MALI
  ALBERTS, ARTHUR S.‡ BAMBARA‡ 1949-51

  BIRD, CHARLES S.‡ BAMBARA‡ 1967-68

  BIRD, CHARLES S.‡ BAMBARA‡ 1968

  BIRD, CHARLES S.‡ BAMBARA‡ 1968

  BRASSEUR, G.+ DI DIO, FRANCOIS+ DIETERLEN,
  GERMAINE+ ROUGET, GILBERT‡ BAMBARA, BOZO, DOGON,
  MALINKE, MARKA, MINIANKA, PEUL, RYMAYBE, SARAKOLE,
  SOMONO, SONGHAY‡

  BRYAN, SAM‡ DOGON‡ 1960

  CALAME, B.‡ BAMBARA, BOZO, DOGON, MARKA, MINIANKA,
  PEUL, RYMAYBE, SARAKOLE, SOMONO, SONGHAY‡
  1956-57+ 1960

  CLAUSS, BERNHARD PETER‡ BAMBARA, TAMACHECK‡ 1973

  DIETERLEN, GERMAINE‡ DOGON‡ 1953

  DIETERLEN, GERMAINE‡ PEUL‡ 1960

  DIETERLEN, GERMAINE‡ DOGON‡ 1967

  DIETERLEN, GERMAINE‡ DOGON‡ 1969

  HASSENPFLUG, EARL C.‡ BOZO, DOGON‡ 1970

  HIMMELHEBER, HANS G.‡ BAMBARA‡ 1953

  INSTITUT D'ETHNOLOGIE DE L'UNIVERSITE DE
  STRASBOURG‡ BAMBARA‡

MALI
  RUTHERFORD, DOUGLAS I.‡ BAMBARA‡ 1972

MALI-U.S.
  BIRD, CHARLES S.+ KEIM, KAREN R.‡ BAMBARA‡ 1975

  FRY, GLADYS M.‡ ‡ 1963

MAURITANIA
  ERNOULT, CLAUDE+ ROUGET, GILBERT‡ ‡

  ROUGET, GILBERT‡ ‡ 1952

MAURITIUS
  UPADHYAYA, HARI S.+ ORI, R.‡ UTTAR-PRADESH‡ 1961

MOROCCO
  ANDERSON, LOIS ANN‡ BERBER‡ 1971

  ARCHIVES OF ETHNIC MUSIC AND DANCE‡ ARAB‡

  ARMISTEAD, SAMUEL G. + KATZ, ISRAEL J. +
  SILVERMAN, JOSEPH H.‡ SEPHARDIC-JEW‡ 1962

  BENTHIEN, CLAUS+ LILLIEBJERG, HANNE+ WICHMANN,
  ERIK‡ ‡ 1967

  BOWLES, PAUL+ WANKLYN, CHRISTOPHER‡ ‡ CA1959-62

  CHERKI, SALAH‡ ARAB‡ CA1960

  DE HEN, FERDINAND JOSEPH‡ AIT-ATTA,
  AIT-BU-SUEMMEZ, IHANSALEN‡ 1960-61

  GALAND, -+ ROUGET, GILBERT‡ BERBER‡

  HARRIES, JEANETTE‡ BERBER‡ 1964-65

  HARRIES, JEANETTE‡ BERBER‡ 1971-72

  INSTITUT D'ETHNOLOGIE DE L'UNIVERSITE DE
  STRASBOURG‡ GNAWA‡

  INSTITUT D'ETHNOLOGIE DE L'UNIVERSITE DE
  STRASBOURG‡ GNAWA‡

  KROTKI, KAROL JOSEF‡ ‡ 1971

  LORTAT-JACOB, BERNARD‡ AIT-MGOUN‡ 1969

MOROCCO
  LORTAT-JACOB, BERNARD‡ AIT-MGOUN‡ 1970

  LORTAT-JACOB, BERNARD‡ BERBER, TAMAZIGT, TASLHIT‡
  1969-73

  LORTAT-JACOB, BERNARD‡ AIT-BOUGMEZ, FTOUKA‡ 1971

  PENCHOEN, THOMAS GOODENOUGH‡ BERBER-AYT-NDIR‡
  1969-74

  SPENCER, WILLIAM‡ ‡ 1969

  WANKLYN, CHRISTOPHER‡ AIT-SIDI-MERRI, DEGWANA,
  MISIWA, OULED-MTAA‡ 1963+ 1969

  WICHMANN, ERICK‡ BERBER-JEBALA, BERBER-REGUIBAT‡
  1969

  YOUSSEF, AIT‡ ‡

  YOUSSEF, AIT‡ ‡ 1966

  ZEMP, HUGO‡ ‡ 1960

MOZAMBIQUE
  ARCHIVES OF ETHNIC MUSIC AND DANCE‡ ‡

  CURTIS, NATALIE‡ NDAU‡ CA1919

  DIAS, MARGOT‡ MAKONDE‡ 1957-58

  DIAS, MARGOT‡ CHOKWE, CHOPI‡ 1959

  JOHNSTON, THOMAS FREDERICK‡ TSONGA‡ 1968-70

  MORGENTHAU, HENRY+ MONDOLANE, EDUARDO‡ ‡ 1965

  RADIO CLUBE DE MOCAMBIQUE‡ CHANGANE, CHENGUE,
  CHOPI, LUBA, MAKONDE, MAKUA, RONGA, SWAZI,
  VADANDA, VANDAU, VATSUA‡

  TRADITIONAL MUSIC DOCUMENTATION PROJECT‡ CHOPI‡

NAMIBIA
  ENGLAND, NICHOLAS M.‡ HERERO‡ 1957-61

  GERSON-KIWI, EDITH‡ OVAMBO‡ 1955

NAMIBIA
  GIBSON, GORDON D.‡ HERERO, HIMBA, KUVALE‡ 1960-61

  WESTPHAL, ERNST O.J.‡ BUSHMEN, KUANYAMA‡ 1953-74

NIGER
  BAIER, STEPHEN B.‡ HAUSA, KANURI, TUAREG‡ 1972

  BERNUS, S.+ ROUCH, JEAN‡ SONRAI‡ 1960

  HOLIDAY, GEOFFREY D.‡ TUAREG‡ CA1958

  LORELLE, -‡ MAOURI‡

  MURPHY, ROBERT‡ TUAREG‡ 1959-60

  NICOLAISEN, IDA‡ TUAREG‡ 1966

  ROUCH, JEAN‡ SONGHAY‡

  SARDAN, J.-P. OLIVIER DE‡ SONGHAY‡ 1969

  SURUGUE, BERNARD‡ DJERMA-SONGHAY‡ 1969

NIGERIA
  ABDULKADIR, DATTI‡ HAUSA-FULANI‡ 1973

  ABIMBOLA, WANDE‡ YORUBA‡ 1971

  AKPABOT, SAMUEL EKPE‡ BIROM, HAUSA, IBIBIO, IBO‡
  1964-73

  ALIGWEKWE, EVALYN R.‡ IBO‡ 1960

  AMES, DAVID W.‡ HAUSA‡ 1963

  AMES, DAVID W.‡ FULBE, HAUSA, YORUBA‡ 1963-64

  AMES, DAVID W.‡ IGBO‡ 1963-64

  ANIAKOR, CYRIL CHIKE‡ IKWERE‡ 1965

  ARCHIVES OF ETHNIC MUSIC AND DANCE‡ IGBO‡

  ARMSTRONG, ROBERT G.‡ YORUBA‡

  ARMSTRONG, ROBERT G.‡ YORUBA‡

  ARMSTRONG, ROBERT G.+ UNOOGWU, PATRICK‡ IDOMA‡

NIGERIA
  1961

  ARMSTRONG, ROBERT G.‡ YORUBA‡ 1962

  ARMSTRONG, ROBERT G.‡ IDOMA‡ 1964

  ARMSTRONG, ROBERT G. +WITTIG, R. CURT‡ IDOMA‡
  1964

  AWE, BOLANLE ALAKE‡ YORUBA‡ 1972-74

  BABALOLA, ADEBOYE‡ YORUBA‡ 1962-74

  BALOGUN, ADISA‡ YORUBA‡ 1964+ 1970

  BALOGUN, ADISA‡ YORUBA‡ 1967

  BARNES, SANDRA THEIS‡ YORUBA‡ 1972

  BEIER, ULLI+ ROUGET, GILBERT‡ YORUBA‡

  BEN-AMOS, DAN‡ EDO‡ 1966

  BEN-AMOS, DAN‡ HAUSA‡ 1966

  BESMER, FREMONT E.‡ HAUSA‡ 1968-70

  BESMER, FREMONT E.‡ HAUSA‡ 1972-73

  BORGATTI, JEAN M.‡ EDO‡ 1972-73

  CENTRE FOR THE STUDY OF NIGERIAN LANGUAGES‡ HAUSA‡

  COHEN, RONALD‡ KANURI‡ 1956

  COLLEGE OF MUSIC, UNIVERSITY OF NIGERIA‡ BINI,
  BOKI, DAKARAWA, EFIK-IBIBIO, EKOI, FULANI, HAUSA,
  IBO, IDOMA, IJAW, JABA, MADA, YALA, YORUBA,
  ZABEBMAWA‡

  CRABB, DAVID‡ IBO‡

  CRAVEN, ANNA‡ AFO, GEDE‡ 1969-70

  DEPARTMENT OF LINGUISTICS AND NIGERIAN LANGUAGES,
  UNIVERSITY OF IBADAN‡ EDO, IJO, ISOKO, ITSEKIRI,
  OWAN, YORUBA‡ 1967-73

NIGERIA

DIHOFF, IVAN R.‡ CHORI, HAUSA‡ 1972

DREWAL, HENRY JOHN‡ YORUBA‡ 1970-71

ECHEZONA, WILLIAM WILBERFORCE CHUKUDINKA‡ EFIK, HAUSA, IBO, YORUBA‡ 1950-75

EKECHI, FELIX K.‡ IGBO‡ 1973

ELWA STUDIO, NIGERIA‡ IBO, NUPE, YORUBA‡

ENGLAND, NICHOLAS M.‡ YORUBA‡ 1969-70+ 1972

EULENBERG, JOHN BRYSON‡ HAUSA‡ 1972

FEDERAL DEPARTMENT OF ANTIQUITIES, NATIONAL MUSEUM, KADUNA‡ ELOYI, GEDE‡

FOSS, PERKINS‡ URHOBO‡ 1971-72

GLEASON, JUDITH+ OGUNDIPE, JOHN‡ YORUBA‡ 1970

HANLEY, MARY ANN CSJ‡ ANGAS, BACHAMA, CHAMBA, EFIK, GWANDARA, HAUSA, IBIBIO, IBO, JABA, KERI-KERI, YORUBA‡ 1973

HANNA, JUDITH LYNNE+ HANNA, WILLIAM J.‡ IBO‡ 1963

HARRIS, JOHN REES‡ URHOBO, YORUBA‡ 1965

HERSKOVITS, MELVILLE J.+ HERSKOVITS, FRANCES S.‡ YORUBA‡ 1931

HESS, ROBERT A.‡ BURA‡ 1969

INSTITUTE OF AFRICAN STUDIES, UNIVERSITY OF IFE‡ IBO, TIV, YORUBA‡

ISOLA, AKINWUMI‡ YORUBA‡ 1968-74

KAYE, ALAN S.‡ ARAB-SHUWA‡ 1974

KEIL, CHARLES‡ TIV, YORUBA‡

KIRK-GREENE, ANTHONY H.M.‡ HAUSA, KAGORO, TIV‡ 1962-65

KOIZUMI, FUMIO‡ YORUBA‡ 1971

NIGERIA
  KULP, PHILIP M.‡ BURA‡ 1973

  LA PIN, DIERDRE A.‡ YORUBA‡ 1972-73

  LINENBRUEGGE, GERTRUDE R.I.‡ IBO‡ 1966

  MISHLER, ROBERT E.‡ MARGI‡ 1971-72

  MURPHY, ROBERT‡ TUAREG‡ 1959-60

  NJAKA, MAZI E.N.‡ ‡ 1972

  OGBU, JOHN U.‡ IBO‡ 1972

  OGIERIRIAIXI, EVINMA‡ EDO‡ 1970-73

  ONWUKA, RALPH I.‡ IBO‡

  PEEK, PHILIP M.‡ IGBO-WESTERN, ISOKO‡ 1970-71

  PLOTNICOV, LEONARD‡ BIROM, EFIK, HAUSA, IBIBIO,
  IBO, IJAW, KAGORO, KATAM, TIV‡ 1961-62

  PRINCE, RAYMOND HAROLD‡ ‡

  QUERSIN, BENOIT J.‡ QUERSIN, CHRISTINE M.‡
  ABAKPA-RIGA, AFO, ALAGO, ANGAS, ANKWAI, BIROM,
  BUROM, CHAMBA, EGGON, FULANI, HAUSA, ICHEN, IDOMA,
  JARAWA, JUKUN, KALABARI, KANTANA, KUTEP, KWALLA,
  NUPE, PYEM, RINDRE, TIV, YERGAM, YORUBA‡ 1972-73

  RANUNG, BJORN L.C.‡ IGEDE‡ 1971-72

  RAPHAEL, RONALD P.‡ FULBE, MAMBILA‡ 1974

  RHODES, WILLARD‡ FULANI, HAUSA, TIV, TUAREG,
  YORUBA‡ 1973-74

  RIGGS, VENDA‡ YORUBA‡ 1949

  ROMERO, PATRICIA‡ IBO‡ 1973

  RUBIN, ARNOLD G.‡ CHAMBA, HAUSA, IBO, JUKUN,
  KUTEP, TIKARI, TIV‡ 1964-65

  SHEFFIELD, JAMES‡ YORUBA‡ 1971

  SIEBER, ROY‡ YORUBA‡ 1971

NIGERIA
  SKINNER, A. NEIL+ SKINNER, MARGARET G.≠ ANGAS,
  FULA, HAUSA, KABBA, YORUBA≠ 1967-74

  SMOCK, DAVID R.≠ IBO≠ 1962-63

  SPAIN, DAVID H.≠ KANURI≠ 1966-67

  SPEED, FRANCIS E.≠ YORUBA≠ 1966

  SPEED, FRANCIS E.+ THIEME, DARIUS L.≠ YORUBA≠
  1966

  STAHLKE, HERBERT F.W.≠ YATYE≠ 1966-67

  THIEME, DARIUS L.≠ YORUBA≠ 1964-66

  TRADITIONAL MUSIC DOCUMENTATION PROJECT≠ IBIBIO,
  IBO, KALABARI, TIV, YORUBA≠

  TRAGER, LILLIAN≠ YORUBA≠ 1974

  VAUGHAN, JAMES H.≠ MARGI, VENGO≠ 1960

  VAUGHAN, JAMES H.≠ MARGI≠ 1960

  VAUGHAN, JAMES H.≠ MARGI≠ 1974

  VAUGHAN, JAMES H.≠ MARGI≠ 1974

  WELCH, DAVID B.≠ YORUBA≠ 1970-71

  WEMAN, PAUL HENRY≠ YORUBA≠ 1957

  WILLETT, FRANK≠ YORUBA≠ 1972

  WILLIAMSON, KAY≠ IJO≠ 1959

  WITTIG, R. CURT≠ YORUBA≠ 1965

  WOLFF, HANS≠ AGBADU, URHOBO≠ 1953

  WOLFF, HANS≠ BIROM≠ 1953

  WOLFF, HANS≠ EDO-BINI≠ 1953

  WOLFF, HANS≠ IBO≠ 1953

  WOLFF, HANS≠ IGBIRA≠ 1953

NIGERIA
  WOLFF, HANS‡ IJO, KALABARI‡ 1953

  WOLFF, HANS‡ IJO, ITSEKIRI‡ 1953

  WOLFF, HANS‡ IJO, IJAW-WESTERN‡ 1953

  WOLFF, HANS‡ JUKUN‡ 1953

  WOLFF, HANS‡ KAJE‡ 1953

  WOLFF, HANS‡ NUPE‡ 1953

  WOLFF, HANS‡ EFIK, HAUSA, IBIBIO, KAJE, SOBO,
  PABIR, YORUBA‡ 1953-54

  WYLIE, KENNETH CHARLES‡ ‡ 1965-66

NIGERIA-U.S.
  BOAS, FRANZ‡ YORUBA‡ 1933

  CAZDEN, NORMAN‡ ‡ 1960

  DORSON, RICHARD M.‡ BRITISH, HAUSA‡ 1967

  FRY, GLADYS M.‡ ‡ 1963

  NETTL, BRUNO +RABEN, JOSEPH‡ IBO‡ 1950-51

  OFONAGURO, W. IBEKWE+ IRWIN, GRAHAM‡ ‡ 1967

  OGBU, JOHN U.+ PEEK, PHILIP M.‡ IGBO‡ 1968

  RABEN, JOSEPH‡ IBO‡ 1950

  RABEN, JOSEPH‡ IBO‡ 1950

  SZCZESNIAK, ANDREW L.‡ IBO‡ 1961

  WOLFF, HANS‡ YORUBA‡ 1560-64

RHODESIA
  ARCHIVES OF ETHNIC MUSIC AND DANCE‡ ‡

  BERLINER, PAUL FRANKLIN‡ SHONA‡ 1972

  CAMP, CHARLES M.+ TRACEY, HUGH‡ BUDJA, CHIKUNDA,
  FUNGWE, HERA, HUNGWE, KARANGA, NDAU, NDEBELE,
  NYANJA, NYASA, PEDI, RAMBA, WEMBA, YAO‡ 1948

RHODESIA
  DEPARTMENT OF AFRICAN LANGUAGES, UNIVERSITY OF
  RHODESIA‡ NDEBELE, SHONA‡

  KAEMMER, JOHN E.‡ GARWE, MANYIKA‡ 1971

  KAEMMER, JOHN E.‡ KOREKORE, SHONA, ZEZURU‡
  1972-73

  KAUFFMAN, ROBERT A.‡ SHONA‡ 1960-65, 1971

  KRIEL, A.P.‡ KARANGA, SHONA‡ 1966

  MARAIRE, DUMISANI ABRAHAM‡ SHONA‡ 1971+ 1974

  NANCARROW, GWEN T.‡ NDEBELE‡ 1970-71

  RHODES, WILLARD‡ SHONA‡ 1958-59

  TRADITIONAL MUSIC DOCUMENTATION PROJECT‡ KARANGA,
  MANYIKE-BOCHA, NDAU, NJANJA, SENA-TONGA, ZEZURU‡

  WEMAN, HENRY PAUL‡ KARANGA, LEMBA, VENDA, ZULU‡
  1957

  WILSON, VIVIAN J.‡ TONGA‡ 1970

RHODESIA-U.S.
  FRY, GLADYS M.‡ ‡ 1963

RWANDA
  D'HERTEFELT, MARUL‡ ‡ 1953-73

  DES FORGES, ALISON LIEBHAFSKY‡ BATUTSI‡ 1968

  GANSEMANS, JOS‡ HUTU, TUTSI, TWA‡ 1973-74

  MERRIAM, ALAN P.+ MERRIAM, BARBARA W.‡ ABAGOGWE,
  ABAGOYI, ABAHORORO, ABANYAMBO, ABATUTSI, ABAYOVU,
  BAHIMA, BAHUTU, BAKIGA, BATWA‡ 1951-52

  NEWBURY, M. CATHARINE‡ BANYARWANDA‡ 1970-72

SENEGAL
  AMES, DAVID W.‡ WOLOF‡ 1950-51

  ARCHIVES OF ETHNIC MUSIC AND DANCE‡ ‡

  BRYAN, SAM‡ ‡ 1969

SENEGAL
   SNYDER, FRANCIS GREGORY‡ DIOLA‡ 1970

   SNYDER, FRANCIS GREGORY‡ DIOLA‡ 1973

   VAILLANT, JANET G.‡ SERER‡ 1973

SIERRA LEONE
   ALLEN, LEONARD E.‡ ‡ 1950

   BAHMAN, GARY‡ LIMBA, MANDINGO, TEMNE‡ 1971

   BOAS, FRANZ‡ BOLUM‡ PRE-1935

   EDWARDS, BETTY‡ ‡ 1969

   ETHNOMUSICOLOGY CENTRE JAAP KUNST‡ ‡ 1974

   GEOFFRION, CHARLES A.‡ TEMNE, MANDINGO‡ 1966-67

   HAIGHT, BRUCE MARVIN‡ LOKO‡ 1967

   IJAGBEMI, ELIJAH A.‡ TEMNE‡ 1965-67

   INNES, GORDON‡ MENDE‡ 1963

   JOHNSON, GERALD T.‡ MENDE, TEMNE‡ 1967-68

   KILSON, MARION D. DE B.‡ MENDE‡ 1960

   ROGERS, HENRY EDWIN‡ SHERBRO‡ 1966

   VAN OVEN, JACOBA‡ FULA, GALLINAS, GOLA, LIMBA,
   LOKO, MANDINGO, MENDE, SHERBRO, SUSU, TEMNE, VAI,
   YALUNKA‡ 1964-67

   WARE, NAOMI‡ ‡ 1969

   WYLIE, KENNETH CHARLES‡ MENDE‡ 1965-66+ 1970

SIERRA LEONE-U.S.
   AGINSKY, ETHEL G.‡ MENDE‡ 1933

SOMALIA
   JOHNSON, JOHN W. ‡ SOMALI‡ 1966-69

   LEVINE, WILLIAM J.‡ SOMALI‡ 1962

   MARING, JOEL‡ SOMALI‡ 1959

SOUTH AFRICA
  VERSFELD, BARBARA‡ XHOSA‡ 1965

  WEMAN, HENRY PAUL‡ VENDA, ZULU‡ 1956-57

  WESTPHAL, ERNST O.J.‡ BUSHMEN‡ 1953-74

SOUTH AFRICA-U.S.
  BRUTUS, DENNIS‡ SNYDER, EMILE‡ ‡ 1966

  FRY, GLADYS M.‡ ‡ 1963

  GILLIS, FRANK J.‡ TRACEY, HUGH‡ ‡ 1971

  HENRY, JULES‡ ZULU‡ 1935

  YODER, WALTER D.‡ ‡ 1955

SUDAN
  CARLISLE, ROXANE C.‡ ANUAK, DINKA, GAALIIN, NUER,
  SHILLUK‡ 1963

  CARLISLE, ROXANE C.‡ ANUAK, DINKA, NUER, SHILLUK‡

  DENG, FRANCIS‡ DINKA‡ 1971

  HEAD, SYDNEY W.‡ DERVISH‡ 1962

  HURREIZ, SAYED H.‡ GAALIIN‡ 1970-71

  KAYE, ALAN S.‡ ARAB‡ 1970

  SUDAN NATIONAL MUSEUM‡ BONGO, JALUO, NUBIAN‡
  1959-64

  TUCKER, ARCHIBALD NORMAN‡ BARI, DINKA, LOTUKO,
  SHILLUK, ZANDE‡

  WEISS, -‡ FUNG‡

SUDAN-U.S.
  FRY, GLADYS M.‡ ‡ 1963

SWAZILAND
  ADAMS, CHARLES R.‡ SWAZI‡ 1969-70

  SCHEUB, HAROLD‡ SWAZI‡ 1972-73

TANZANIA
  ALPERS, EDWARD ALTER‡ DOE, KAMI, KWERE, LUGURU,
  ZARAMO‡ 1972-73

  BACHMANN, FR.‡ ‡ 1908

  DEMPWOLFF, OTTO‡ SANDAWE, ZARAMO‡ 1910

  DEPARTMENT OF THEATRE ARTS, UNIVERSITY OF DAR ES
  SALAAM‡ ‡

  GARLAND, WILLIAM‡ WANJI‡ 1963-65

  GROHS, ELISABETH‡ NDCROBO, NGURU, ZIGUA‡ 1970

  HARTWIG, GERALD W.‡ KEREWE‡ 1968-69

  HATFIELD, COLBY R.‡ SUKUMA‡ 1971

  INSTITUTO NACIONAL DE FOLKLORE, VENEZUELA‡ ‡ 1961

  JENKINS, JEAN‡ ‡ 1960-61

  KIRWEN, MICHAEL CARL‡ SUBA‡ 1963-69

  KOIZUMI, FUMIO‡ ‡ 1971

  MALER, THOMAS A.‡ DIGO, GIRYAMA, MAKONDE, TINDIGA‡
  1967-68

  MATTNER, -‡ ‡ 1909

  MEINHOF, CARL‡ BONDEI‡ 1902-03

  MORGENTHAU, HENRY‡ ‡ 1965

  MOSES, RAE A.‡ ‡ 1966

  NATIONAL MUSEUM OF TANZANIA‡ MAKONDE, MALILA,
  MWERA, YAO‡

  PAASCHE, -‡ KIZIBA‡ 1910

  REID, MARLENE B.‡ BASUKUMA‡ 1966+ 1969

  REINING, PRISCILLA‡ HAYA‡

  SCHWARTZ, -‡ ZINZA‡ 1906

TANZANIA
  SEYFRIED, CAPTAIN‡ ‡ 1906-09

  TENRAA, ERIC WILLIAM FREDERICK‡ BURUNGE, SANDAWE,
  SWAHILI‡ 1958-66

  TUCKER, ARCHIBALD NORMAN‡ HADZA, IRAQW, NGAZIJA,
  SANDAWE, SANYE, SWAHILI‡

  UHLIG, -‡ WANYAMWEZI‡ 1910

  WEMAN, PAUL HENRY‡ HAYA, SUKUMA, SWAHILI‡ 1957

  WILLIS, ROY GEOFFREY‡ FIPA‡ 1966

TANZANIA-ZANZIBAR
  FARSY, MUHAMMED S.‡ ‡ CA1958

TOGO
  AFRIKA-STUDIECENTRUM‡ TYOKOSSI‡

  AGUDZE, BERNARD‡ EWE‡ 1965-67

  RANSBOTYN DE DECKER, DANIEL‡ BOGO, EWE‡ 1972-74

  RICARD, ALAIN J.‡ EWE‡ 1973

  SMEND, W.A.‡ HAUSA‡ 1905

  VAN ROUVEROY VAN NIEUWAAL, EMILE A.B.‡ KOSSI‡
  1969-73

  VERDIER, RAYMOND‡ KABRE‡

TRISTAN DA CUNHA
  LOUDON, JOSEPH BUIST‡ ‡ 1963-64

TUNISIA
  ABUZAHRA, NADIA‡ SAHEL‡ 1966

  BAKER, CATHRYN ANITA‡ ‡ 1972-73

  BENTHIEN, CLAUS+ LILLIEBJERG, HANNE+ WICHMANN,
  ERIK‡ ‡ 1967

  DEPARTMENT OF ANTHROPOLOGY, UNIVERSITY OF BRITISH
  COLUMBIA‡ ‡

  FERCHIOU, SOPHIE‡ ‡ 1969

TUNISIA
  LAADE, WOLFGANG KARL‡ ARAB, BERBER, JEW‡ 1960

  PENCHOEN, THOMAS GOODENOUGH‡ BERBER-DJERBA‡ 1969

  SPENCER, WILLIAM‡ MALOUF‡ 1966-67

  TRAEGER, PAUL‡ BERBER‡ 1903

TUNISIA-U.S.
  FRY, GLADYS M.‡ ‡ 1963

UGANDA
  ANDERSON, LOIS ANN‡ ‡ 1964-66+ 1969

  ARCHIVES OF ETHNIC MUSIC AND DANCE‡ BASOGA‡

  BAISSAC, -‡ GANDA‡ 1967

  BLACKING, JOHN A.R.‡ BAGANDA, BATORO, KARAMOJONG‡
  1965

  BUCHANAN, CAROLE‡ BANYORO, BATORO‡ 1968-69

  BYRD, ROBERT OAKES‡ ALUR, BAGANDA, BAGWERE,
  BAKONJO, BANYANKOLE, BANYOLE, KAKWA, TESO‡

  COHEN, DAVID WILLIAM‡ BASOGA‡ 1966-67

  COHEN, DAVID WILLIAM‡ BASOGA‡ 1971-72

  COLEMAN, MILTON‡ KARAMOJONG‡ 1967

  COOKE, PETER R.‡ BAGANDA‡ 1965-68

  HANNA, JUDITH LYNNE+ HANNA, WILLIAM J.‡ ACHOLI,
  BANYOLE‡ 1963

  HEALD, SWETTE SCOTT‡ GISU‡ 1966-69

  JENKINS, JEAN‡ ‡ 1966 + 1970

  ODED, ARYE‡ BAGANDA, BAYUDAYA‡ 1967-68

  ROBBIN, LAWRENCE H.‡ POKOT‡ 1970

  ROBBINS, MICHAEL COOK‡ BAGANDA‡ 1967-72

  TUCKER, ARCHIBALD NORMAN‡ ACHOLI, BAGANDA, IK,

UGANDA
  KARAMOJONG, TEPETH, TESO‡

  TURNER, VICTOR WITTER‡ BAGISU‡ 1966

  VAN THIEL, PAUL A.H.‡ BANTU, BANYANKOLE‡ 1964-65+
  1969+ 1970-72

  VANVELSEN, J.‡ KUMAM‡ 1948-60

UPPER VOLTA
  ALBERTS, ARTHUR S.‡ BAMBARA, MOSSI‡ 1949-51

  ARCHIVES OF ETHNIC MUSIC AND DANCE‡ BOBO, BWABA,
  DYULA, FULANI, FULBE, GOUIN, GOURMANTCHE, LOBI,
  MINIANKA, MOSSI, SENUFO, YARDSE‡

  ARNOTT, D.‡ MALINKE‡ 1956

  BRAVMANN, RENE A.‡ BOBO, DYULA‡ 1972-74

  BROEKHUYSE, JAN T.‡ SAMO‡ 1969

  CHRISTIAN, VALERIE‡ BISSA, BOBO, BWABA, DAGARA,
  DYULA, FULANI, FULBE, GOUIN, GOURMANTCHE, HAUSA,
  KASSENA, KWO, LOBI, MARKA, MOSSI, NONDOM,
  POUGOULIS, SAMO-DU-SUD, YARDSE‡ 1973-74

  CHRISTIAN, VALERIE+ ROSELLINI, JAMES N.‡ FULBE,
  KASSENA, MARKA, MOSSI‡ 1973

  ECHENBERG, MYRON J.‡ GURUNSI, MARKA, SAMO‡ 1967

  HALL, JOHN F.‡ MOSSI‡ 1962

  HANLEY, MARY ANN CSJ‡ ‡ 1972

  KONINKLIJK INSTITUUT‡ SAMO‡

  LONG, RONALD W.‡ MANDE‡ 1968

  REDDEN, JAMES ERSKINE‡ MOSSI‡ 1962-63

  SCHWEEGER-HEFEL, ANNEMARIE‡ DOGON, KURUMBA, PEUL‡

  SCHWEEGER-HEFEL, ANNEMARIE‡ KURUMBA, PEUL,
  RIWAIBE‡ 1961-69

  SKINNER, ELLIOTT P.‡ MOSSI‡ 1955-65

UPPER VOLTA
    SOCIETE DE RADIODIFFUSION DE LA FRANCE D'OUTRE
    MER‡ MOSSI‡

    SOLANO, ROBERT P.‡ ‡ 1970-71

    TRADITIONAL MUSIC DOCUMENTATION PROJECT‡ ‡

ZAIRE
    ALBERTS, ARTHUR S.‡ ‡ 1952-54

    ANSTEY, ROGER THOMAS‡ BABOMA, BASENGELE, BATENDE,
    BOLIA‡ 1963

    BIEBUYCK, DANIEL P.‡ LEGA, LUBA, LUNDA, MANGBETU,
    MAYOGO, NANDE, NYANGA, ZAMBE‡ 1952-61

    CIPARISSE, GERARD JEAN‡ BAKONGO, BASUKU, BAYAKA‡
    1970-71

    CLAUSS, BERNHARD PETER‡ PYGMIES‡ 1973

    DEPLAEN, GUY‡ LUBA, YEKE‡ 1973-74

    FAIK-NZUJI, MADIYA‡ LUBA‡ 1974

    FETTER, BRUCE‡ SETTLERS-AFRICAN‡ 1972-73

    GANSEMANS, JOS‡ LUBA‡ 1970

    GANSEMANS, JOS‡ LUBA, LUNDA, SALAMPASU‡ 1970-73

    HOOVER, JAMES JEFFREY‡ LUNDA‡ 1973-75

    KABEMBA, MUFUTA KABANDANYI‡ KUBA, LUBA‡ 1965+
    1972

    KAPTER, JOHN D.‡ BAPELENDE, BAYAKA‡ 1970

    KNIGHT, RODERIC COPLEY‡ ‡ 1970-71

    LAMAN, K.E.‡ BAKONGO‡ 1911

    LLOYD, DAVID TYRRELL‡ AZANDE‡ 1973

    MAALU-BUNGI‡ LULUA‡ 1969+ 1972+ 1973

    MACGAFFEY, WYATT‡ KONGO‡ 1970

ZAIRE

MCLEAN, DAVID A.‡ LUBA‡ 1954-61

MERRIAM, ALAN P.+ MERRIAM, BARBARA W.‡ BAHIMA, BAKOGA, BAKONGO, BAMBUTI, BANGALA, BASHI, BATWA, EKONDA‡ 1951-52

MERRIAM, ALAN P.+ MERRIAM, BARBARA W.‡ BASONGYE‡ 1959-60

MERRIAM, ALAN P.‡ BASONGYE‡ 1973

NEWBURY, DAVID S.‡ BAHAVU‡ 1972-74

PRUITT, WILLIAM F., JR.‡ KETE, PYGMIES, SALAMPASU‡ 1966-67

PRUITT, WILLIAM F., SR.‡ LUBA, LULUA‡ 1945-49

QUERSIN, BENOIT J.‡ BUSHOONG, COOFA, IBAAM, NGEENDE, PYAANG, SHOOWA‡ 1970

QUERSIN, BENOIT J.‡ BATWA, EKONDA, NTOMBA‡ 1970

QUERSIN, BENOIT J.+ QUERSIN, CHRISTINE M.‡ BATWA, BOLIA, EKONDA‡ 1971

QUERSIN, BENOIT J.+ QUERSIN, CHRISTINE M.‡ BAKUTU, BOKOTE, BONGANDO, BOSAKA, BOYELA, NKUNDU, PYGMIES-BATWA, PYGMIES-NGOMBE‡ 1972

RANSBOTYN DE DECKER, DANIEL‡ BAKONGO‡ 1968

REDDEN, JAMES ERSKINE‡ LINGALA‡ 1962

REEFE, THOMAS Q.‡ LUBA‡ 1972-73

SIGWALT, RICHARD+ SOSNE, ELINOR‡ SHI‡ 1971-73

STARR, FREDERICK A.‡ BAKUBA, BALUBA‡ 1906

STUDSTILL, JOHN D.‡ LUBA‡ 1972

SULZMANN, ERIKA‡ BABOMA, BASENGELE, BOLIA, EKONDA, NTOMBA‡ 1953-72

THIEL, JOSEF FRANZ‡ MBALA, TEKE, YANSI‡ 1961-71

UNITED CHRISTIAN MISSIONARY SOCIETY, DISCIPLES OF

ZAIRE
  CHRIST‡ LINGALA, LONKUNDO‡

  WEMAN, PAUL HENRY‡ LUBA‡ 1957

ZAIRE—U.S.
  CARRINGTON, JOHN F.+ GORDON, MERYL‡ ‡ 1975

  CROWLEY, CANIEL J.‡ ‡ 1961

ZAMBIA
  ANDREWS, LORETTA K.‡ ‡ 1971

  APTHORPE, RAYMOND JAMES‡ NSENGA‡ 1961

  ARCHIVES OF ETHNIC MUSIC AND DANCE‡ LOZI, LUCHAZI‡

  ARGYLE, WILLIAM JOHNSON‡ SOLI‡ 1957-59

  BLACKING, JOHN A.R.‡ TONGA-GWEMBE, NSENGA‡
  1957-61

  CAMP, CHARLES M.+ TRACEY, HUGH‡ BEMBA, LALA, LOZI,
  TONGA, ZINZA‡ 1947-48

  DAVIDSON, MARJORY‡ NGONI‡ 1967-71

  JONES, ARTHUR M.‡ LALA‡ 1944

  LANGWORTHY, HARRY W.‡ CHEWA‡ 1964

  LIVINGSTONE MUSEUM‡ LEYA-SUBIYA‡

  MANN, WILLIAM MICHAEL‡ BEMBA, BISA‡ 1967

  MAPOMA, ISAIAH MWESA‡ BEMBA‡ 1968-70+ 1973

  RHODES, WILLARD‡ SHONA‡ 1958-59

  ROTBERG, ROBERT I.‡ BISA‡ 1967

  WEMAN, PAUL HENRY‡ ‡ 1957

ZAMBIA—U.S.
  MENSAH, ATTAH+ GILLIS, FRANK J.‡ ‡ 1970

Index to
Culture Groups

Index to Culture Groups

ABABDA
  HOHENWART-GERLACHSTEIN, ANNA‡ EGYPT‡ 1960+
  1962-63

ABAGOGWE
  MERRIAM, ALAN P.+ MERRIAM, BARBARA W.‡ RWANDA‡
  1951-52

ABAGOYI
  MERRIAM, ALAN P.+ MERRIAM, BARBARA W.‡ RWANDA‡
  1951-52

ABAHORORO
  MERRIAM, ALAN P.+ MERRIAM, BARBARA W.‡ RWANDA‡
  1951-52

ABAKPA-RIGA
  QUERSIN, BENOIT J.+ QUERSIN, CHRISTINE M.‡
  NIGERIA‡ 1972-73

ABANYAMBO
  MERRIAM, ALAN P.+ MERRIAM, BARBARA W.‡ RWANDA‡
  1951-52

ABATUTSI
  MERRIAM, ALAN P.+ MERRIAM, BARBARA W.‡ BURUNDI‡
  1951-52

  MERRIAM, ALAN P.+ MERRIAM, BARBARA W.‡ RWANDA‡

ABATUTSI
  1951-52

ABAYOVU
  MERRIAM, ALAN P.+ MERRIAM, BARBARA W.‡ RWANDA‡
  1951-52

ACHEWA
  GEOFFRION, CHARLES A.‡ MALAWI‡ 1971-72

ACHOLI
  HANNA, JUDITH LYNNE+ HANNA, WILLIAM J.‡ UGANDA‡
  1963

  TUCKER, ARCHIBALD NORMAN‡ UGANDA‡

ADIOUKROU
  ROUGET, GILBERT‡ IVORY COAST‡

  ROUGET, GILBERT‡ IVORY COAST‡ 1952

ADJA
  ROUGET, GILBERT+ TARDITS, CLAUDE+ VERGER, PIERRE‡
  DAHOMEY‡

AFO
  CRAVEN, ANNA‡ NIGERIA‡ 1969-70

  QUERSIN, BENOIT J.+ QUERSIN, CHRISTINE M.‡
  NIGERIA‡ 1972-73

AGBADU
  WOLFF, HANS‡ NIGERIA‡ 1953

AIT-ATTA
  DE HEN, FERDINAND JOSEPH‡ MOROCCO‡ 1960-61

AIT-BOUGMEZ
  LORTAT-JACOB, BERNARD‡ MOROCCO‡ 1971

AIT-BU-SUEMMEZ
  DE HEN, FERDINAND JOSEPH‡ MOROCCO‡ 1960-61

AIT-MGOUN
  LORTAT-JACOB, BERNARD‡ MOROCCO‡ 1969

  LORTAT-JACOB, BERNARD‡ MOROCCO‡ 1970

AIT-SIDI-MERRI
  WANKLYN, CHRISTOPHER‡ MOROCCO‡ 1963+ 1969

AIZO
  OERTLI, PEO‡ DAHOMEY‡ 1973-74

AKA-PYGMIES
  AROM, SIMHA‡ CENTRAL AFRICAN REPUBLIC‡ 1964-67+
  1971-73

AKAMBA
  HARING, LEE‡ KENYA‡ 1967-68

AKAN
  HANLEY, MARY ANN CSJ‡ GHANA‡ 1973

  NKETIA, J.H. KWABENA+ WARE, NAOMI‡ GHANA-U.S.‡
  1965

AKIM
  REDDEN, JAMES ERSKINE‡ GHANA‡ 1958-63

AKWAPIM
  BOAS, FRANZ‡ GHANA‡ PRE-1935

  REDDEN, JAMES ERSKINE‡ GHANA‡ 1958-63

ALAGO
  QUERSIN, BENOIT J.+ QUERSIN, CHRISTINE M.‡
  NIGERIA‡ 1972-73

ALUR
  BYRD, ROBERT OAKES‡ UGANDA‡

AMBO
  GREENSTEIN, ROBERT CARL‡ MALAWI‡ 1971-75

AMERICO-LIBERIAN
  D'AZEVEDO, WARREN L.‡ LIBERIA‡ 1956-58+ 1966

AMHARA
  ARCHIVES OF ETHNIC MUSIC AND DANCE‡ ETHIOPIA‡

  KOIZUMI, FUMIO‡ ETHIOPIA‡ 1971

  LESLAU, WOLF‡ ETHIOPIA‡ 1947

  MAGYAR TUDOMANYOS AKADEMIA NEPZENEKUTATO CSOPORT‡
  ETHIOPIA‡

AMHARA
  MESSING, SIMON D.‡ ETHIOPIA‡ 1961-67

ANGAS
  HANLEY, MARY ANN CSJ‡ NIGERIA‡ 1973

  QUERSIN, BENOIT J.+ QUERSIN, CHRISTINE M.‡
  NIGERIA‡ 1972-73

  SKINNER, A. NEIL+ SKINNER, MARGARET G.‡ NIGERIA‡
  1967-74

ANKWAI
  QUERSIN, BENOIT J.+ QUERSIN, CHRISTINE M.‡
  NIGERIA‡ 1972-73

ANTANDROY
  VERNIER, -‡ MALAGASY REPUBLIC‡

ANTANOSY
  VERNIER, -‡ MALAGASY REPUBLIC‡

ANUAK
  CARLISLE, ROXANE C.‡ SUDAN‡ 1963

  CARLISLE, ROXANE C.‡ SUDAN‡

ARAB
  ARCHIVES OF ETHNIC MUSIC AND DANCE‡ MOROCCO‡

  CENTRE DE RECHERCHES ANTHROPOLOGIQUES
  PREHISTORIQUES ET ETHNOGRAPHIQUES‡ ALGERIA‡

  CHERKI, SALAH‡ MOROCCO‡ CA1960

  CURTIN, PHILIP D.‡ SENEGAL‡ 1966

  CURTIN, PHILIP D.‡ SENEGAL‡ 1966

  EL-SHAMY, HASAN M.‡ EGYPT‡ 1968-71

  EL-SHAMY, HASAN M.‡ EGYPT-U.S.‡ 1961

  GERLACH, LUTHER PAUL‡ KENYA-TANZANIA‡ 1958-60

  HALE, KEN‡ EGYPT‡

  KAYE, ALAN S.‡ CHAD‡ 1970

BADYARANKE
  SIMMONS, W.S.‡ SENEGAL‡ 1964-66

BAFIA
  QUERSIN, BENOIT J.+ QUERSIN, CHRISTINE M.‡
  CAMEROON‡ 1967

BAFUT
  RITZENTHALER, ROBERT + RITZENTHALER, PAT‡
  CAMEROON‡ 1959

BAGANDA
  BLACKING, JOHN A.R.‡ UGANDA‡ 1965

  BYRD, ROBERT OAKES‡ UGANDA‡

  COOKE, PETER R.‡ UGANDA‡ 1965-68

  ODED, ARYE‡ UGANDA‡ 1967-68

  ROBBINS, MICHAEL COOK‡ UGANDA‡ 1967-72

  TUCKER, ARCHIBALD NORMAN‡ UGANDA‡

BAGISU
  TURNER, VICTOR WITTER‡ UGANDA‡ 1966

BAGWERE
  BYRD, ROBERT OAKES‡ UGANDA‡

BAHAVU
  NEWBURY, DAVID S.‡ ZAIRE‡ 1972-74

BAHIMA
  MERRIAM, ALAN P.+ MERRIAM, BARBARA W.‡ RWANDA‡
  1951-52

  MERRIAM, ALAN P.+ MERRIAM, BARBARA W.‡ ZAIRE‡
  1951-52

BAHUTU
  MERRIAM, ALAN P.+ MERRIAM, BARBARA W.‡ RWANDA‡
  1951-52

BAJUN
  CAMPBELL, CAROL‡ KENYA‡ 1972

  PARKER, CAROLYN ANN‡ KENYA‡ 1971-72

BAKIGA
  MERRIAM, ALAN P.+ MERRIAM, BARBARA W.‡ RWANDA‡
  1951-52

BAKOGA
  MERRIAM, ALAN P.+ MERRIAM, BARBARA W.‡ ZAIRE‡
  1951-52

BAKONGO
  CIPARISSE, GERARD JEAN‡ ZAIRE‡ 1970-71

  LAMAN, K.E.‡ ZAIRE‡ 1911

  MERRIAM, ALAN P.+ MERRIAM, BARBARA W.‡ ZAIRE‡
  1951-52

  RANSBOTYN DE DECKER, DANIEL‡ ZAIRE‡ 1968

BAKONJO
  BYRD, ROBERT OAKES‡ UGANDA‡

BAKUBA
  STARR, FREDERICK A.‡ ZAIRE‡ 1906

BAKUNDU
  KLEIS, GERALD W.‡ CAMEROON‡ 1971

BAKUTU
  QUERSIN, BENOIT J.+ QUERSIN, CHRISTINE M.‡ ZAIRE‡
  1972

BALANTA
  HERBIN, -‡ SENEGAL‡

  KNIGHT, RODERIC COPLEY‡ GAMBIA, THE‡ 1970-71

BALLOM
  QUERSIN, BENOIT J.+ QUERSIN, CHRISTINE M.‡
  CAMEROON‡ 1967

BALUBA
  STARR, FREDERICK A.‡ ZAIRE‡ 1906

BAMBARA
  ALBERTS, ARTHUR S.‡ MALI‡ 1949-51

  ALBERTS, ARTHUR S.‡ UPPER VOLTA‡ 1949-51

  BIRD, CHARLES S.‡ MALI‡ 1967-68

BAMBARA
  BIRD, CHARLES S.‡ MALI‡ 1968

  BIRD, CHARLES S.‡ MALI‡ 1968

  BIRD, CHARLES S.+ KEIM, KAREN R.‡ MALI-U.S.‡ 1975

  BRASSEUR, G.+ DI DIO, FRANCOIS+ DIETERLEN,
  GERMAINE+ ROUGET, GILBERT‡ MALI‡

  CALAME, B.‡ MALI‡ 1956-57+ 1960

  CLAUSS, BERNHARD PETER‡ MALI‡ 1973

  HIMMELHEBER, HANS G.‡ MALI‡ 1953

  INSTITUT D'ETHNOLOGIE DE L'UNIVERSITE DE
  STRASBOURG‡ MALI‡

  KNIGHT, RODERIC COPLEY‡ GAMBIA, THE‡ 1970-71

  REDDEN, JAMES ERSKINE‡ -U.S.‡ 1962

  RUTHERFORD, DOUGLAS I.‡ MALI‡ 1972

BAMBUTI
  MERRIAM, ALAN P.+ MERRIAM, BARBARA W.‡ ZAIRE‡
  1951-52

BAMILEKE
  QUERSIN, BENOIT J.+ QUERSIN, CHRISTINE M.‡
  CAMEROON‡ 1967

BAMUM
  ANKERMANN, BERNHARD‡ CAMEROON‡ 1909

  PARE, -+ TARDITS, CLAUDE‡ CAMEROON‡

  QUERSIN, BENOIT J.+ QUERSIN, CHRISTINE M.‡
  CAMEROON‡ 1967

BANDA
  BOUQUIAUX, LUC‡ CENTRAL AFRICAN REPUBLIC‡

BANEN
  SCHWARZ, JEAN‡ CAMEROON‡ 1968

BANGALA
  MERRIAM, ALAN P.+ MERRIAM, BARBARA W.‡ ZAIRE‡

BANGALA
  1951-52

BANTU
  REDDEN, JAMES ERSKINE‡ CAMEROON‡ 1971

  VAN THIEL, PAUL A.H.‡ UGANDA‡ 1964-65+ 1969+
  1970-72

BANYANKOLE
  BYRD, ROBERT OAKES‡ UGANDA‡

  VAN THIEL, PAUL A.H.‡ UGANDA‡ 1964-65+ 1969+
  1970-72

BANYARWANDA
  NEWBURY, M. CATHARINE‡ RWANDA‡ 1970-72

BANYOLE
  BYRD, ROBERT OAKES‡ UGANDA‡

  HANNA, JUDITH LYNNE+ HANNA, WILLIAM J.‡ UGANDA‡
  1963

BANYORO
  BUCHANAN, CAROLE‡ UGANDA‡ 1968-69

BAPELENDE
  KAPTER, JOHN D.‡ ZAIRE‡ 1970

BARI
  TUCKER, ARCHIBALD NORMAN‡ SUDAN‡

BARUNDI
  MERRIAM, ALAN P.+ MERRIAM, BARBARA W.‡ BURUNDI‡
  1951-52

BASA
  SCHAEFFNER, ANDRE‡ GUINEA‡

BASENGELE
  ANSTEY, ROGER THOMAS‡ ZAIRE‡ 1963

  SULZMANN, ERIKA‡ ZAIRE‡ 1953-72

BASHI
  MERRIAM, ALAN P.+ MERRIAM, BARBARA W.‡ ZAIRE‡
  1951-52

BASOGA
ARCHIVES OF ETHNIC MUSIC AND DANCE‡ UGANDA‡

COHEN, DAVID WILLIAM‡ UGANDA‡ 1966-67

COHEN, DAVID WILLIAM‡ UGANDA‡ 1971-72

BASONGYE
MERRIAM, ALAN P.+ MERRIAM, BARBARA W.‡ ZAIRE‡ 1959-60

MERRIAM, ALAN P.‡ ZAIRE‡ 1973

BASOTHO
ADAMS, CHARLES R.‡ LESOTHO‡ 1969-70

SMITS, LUCAS GERARDUS ALFONSUS‡ LESOTHO‡ 1969+ 1974-75

BASSA
MOORE, BAI T.‡ LIBERIA‡ 1962-73

NEWBURY, DOROTHY J.‡ LIBERIA‡ 1969-70+ 1972

OKIE, PACKARD L.‡ LIBERIA‡ 1947-54

OKIE, PACKARD L.‡ LIBERIA‡ 1947-54

OKIE, PACKARD L.‡ LIBERIA‡ 1947-54

SIEGMANN, WILLIAM CHARLES‡ LIBERIA‡ 1973-74

BASSARI
CENTRE DE RECHERCHES ANTHROPOLOGIQUES‡ SENEGAL‡

ROUGET, GILBERT+ GESSAIN, R.+ GESSAIN, M.‡ SENEGAL‡ 1967

BASUKU
CIPARISSE, GERARD JEAN‡ ZAIRE‡ 1970-71

BASUKUMA
REID, MARLENE B.‡ TANZANIA‡ 1966+ 1969

BASUTO
ELLENBERGER, D.F.‡ SOUTH AFRICA‡

WALLMAN, SANDRA‡ LESOTHO‡ 1963

BATENDE
  ANSTEY, ROGER THOMAS‡ ZAIRE‡ 1963

BATORO
  BLACKING, JOHN A.R.‡ UGANDA‡ 1965

  BUCHANAN, CAROLE‡ UGANDA‡ 1968-69

BATUTSI
  DES FORGES, ALISON LIEBHAFSKY‡ RWANDA‡ 1968

BATWA
  MERRIAM, ALAN P.+ MERRIAM, BARBARA W.‡ BURUNDI‡
  1951-52

  MERRIAM, ALAN P.+ MERRIAM, BARBARA W.‡ RWANDA‡
  1951-52

  MERRIAM, ALAN P.+ MERRIAM, BARBARA W.‡ ZAIRE‡
  1951-52

  QUERSIN, BENOIT J.‡ ZAIRE‡ 1970

  QUERSIN, BENOIT J.+ QUERSIN, CHRISTINE M.‡ ZAIRE‡
  1971

BAULE
  ALBERTS, ARTHUR S.‡ AFRICA-WEST‡ 1949

  ALBERTS, ARTHUR S.‡ IVORY COAST‡ 1949-51

  HIMMELHEBER, HANS G.‡ IVORY COAST‡ 1952-65

  RAYFIELD, JOAN R.‡ IVORY COAST‡ 1972-73

  ROUGET, GILBERT‡ IVORY COAST‡

  ZEMP, HUGO‡ IVORY COAST‡ 1962+ 1964-67

BAYAKA
  CIPARISSE, GERARD JEAN‡ ZAIRE‡ 1970-71

  KAPTER, JOHN D.‡ ZAIRE‡ 1970

BAYUDAYA
  ODED, ARYE‡ UGANDA‡ 1967-68

BEDIK
  CENTRE DE RECHERCHES ANTHROPOLOGIQUES‡ SENEGAL‡

BEDIK
  FERRY, M.P.‡ SENEGAL‡

  GUIGNARD, AUDE‡ SENEGAL‡ 1968

  ROUGET, GILBERT+ GESSAIN, R.+ GESSAIN, M.‡
  SENEGAL‡ 1967

BEJA
  HOHENWART-GERLACHSTEIN, ANNA‡ EGYPT‡ 1960+
  1962-63

BEKOM
  DUNGER, GEORGE A.‡ CAMEROON‡

BELE
  OKIE, PACKARD L.‡ LIBERIA‡ 1947-54

BEMBA
  CAMP, CHARLES M.+ TRACEY, HUGH‡ ZAMBIA‡ 1947-48

  MANN, WILLIAM MICHAEL‡ ZAMBIA‡ 1967

  MAPOMA, ISAIAH MWESA‡ ZAMBIA‡ 1968-70+ 1973

BENS
  LANGE, WERNER‡ ETHIOPIA‡ 1972-73

BERBER
  ANDERSON, LOIS ANN‡ MOROCCO‡ 1971

  CENTRE DE RECHERCHES ANTHROPOLOGIQUES
  PREHISTORIQUES ET ETHNOGRAPHIQUES‡ ALGERIA‡

  GALAND, -+ ROUGET, GILBERT‡ MOROCCO‡

  HARRIES, JEANETTE‡ MOROCCO‡ 1964-65

  HARRIES, JEANETTE‡ MOROCCO‡ 1971-72

  LAADE, WOLFGANG KARL‡ TUNISIA‡ 1960

  LORTAT-JACOB, BERNARD‡ MOROCCO‡ 1969-73

  MOULOUD, MAMMERI‡ ALGERIA‡

  TRAEGER, PAUL‡ TUNISIA‡ 1903

BERBER—AURES
  PENCHOEN, THOMAS GOODENOUGH‡ ALGERIA‡ 1973

BERBER—AYT—NDIR
  PENCHOEN, THOMAS GOODENOUGH‡ MOROCCO‡ 1969-74

BERBER—DJERBA
  PENCHOEN, THOMAS GOODENOUGH‡ TUNISIA‡ 1969

BERBER—JEBALA
  WICHMANN, ERICK‡ MOROCCO‡ 1969

BERBER—REGUIBAT
  WICHMANN, ERICK‡ MOROCCO‡ 1969

BERTA
  BENDER, MARVIN LIONEL‡ ETHIOPIA‡ 1964-74

BETSILEO
  VERNIER, -‡ MALAGASY REPUBLIC‡

BHACA
  CAMP, CHARLES M.+ TRACEY, HUGH‡ SOUTH AFRICA‡
  1947-48

BINI
  COLLEGE OF MUSIC, UNIVERSITY OF NIGERIA‡ NIGERIA‡

BIROM
  AKPABOT, SAMUEL EKPE‡ NIGERIA‡ 1964-73

  MUSEE ROYAL DE L'AFRIQUE CENTRALE‡ ‡

  PLOTNICOV, LEONARD‡ NIGERIA‡ 1961-62

  QUERSIN, BENOIT J.+ QUERSIN, CHRISTINE M.‡
  NIGERIA‡ 1972-73

  WOLFF, HANS‡ NIGERIA‡ 1953

BISA
  MANN, WILLIAM MICHAEL‡ ZAMBIA‡ 1967

  ROTBERG, ROBERT I.‡ ZAMBIA‡ 1967

BISSA
  CHRISTIAN, VALERIE‡ UPPER VOLTA‡ 1973-74

BOBO
  ARCHIVES OF ETHNIC MUSIC AND DANCE‡ UPPER VOLTA‡

  BRAVMANN, RENE A.‡ UPPER VOLTA‡ 1972-74

  CHRISTIAN, VALERIE‡ UPPER VOLTA‡ 1973-74

BODI
  BENDER, MARVIN LIONEL‡ ETHIOPIA‡ 1964-74

BOGO
  RANSBOTYN DE DECKER, DANIEL‡ TOGO‡ 1972-74

BOKI
  COLLEGE OF MUSIC, UNIVERSITY OF NIGERIA‡ NIGERIA‡

BOKOTE
  QUERSIN, BENOIT J.+ QUERSIN, CHRISTINE M.‡ ZAIRE‡
  1972

BOLIA
  ANSTEY, ROGER THOMAS‡ ZAIRE‡ 1963

  MUSEE ROYAL DE L'AFRIQUE CENTRALE‡ ‡

  QUERSIN, BENOIT J.+ QUERSIN, CHRISTINE M.‡ ZAIRE‡
  1971

  SULZMANN, ERIKA‡ ZAIRE‡ 1953-72

BOLUM
  BOAS, FRANZ‡ SIERRA LEONE‡ PRE-1935

BONDEI
  MEINHOF, CARL‡ TANZANIA‡ 1902-03

BONGANDO
  QUERSIN, BENOIT J.+ QUERSIN, CHRISTINE M.‡ ZAIRE‡
  1972

BONGO
  SUDAN NATIONAL MUSEUM‡ SUDAN‡ 1959-64

BONO
  WARREN, DENNIS M.‡ GHANA‡ 1969-71

BOSA
  LANGE, WERNER‡ ETHIOPIA‡ 1972-73

BOSAKA
  QUERSIN, BENOIT J.+ QUERSIN, CHRISTINE M.‡ ZAIRE‡
  1972

BOYELA
  QUERSIN, BENOIT J.+ QUERSIN, CHRISTINE M.‡ ZAIRE‡
  1972

BOZO
  BRASSEUR, G.+ DI DIO, FRANCOIS+ DIETERLEN,
  GERMAINE+ ROUGET, GILBERT‡ MALI‡

  CALAME, B.‡ MALI‡ 1956-57+ 1960

  HASSENPFLUG, EARL C.‡ MALI‡ 1970

BRITISH
  DORSON, RICHARD M.‡ NIGERIA-U.S.‡ 1967

BRONG
  OWEN, WILFRED, JR.‡ GHANA‡ 1970-71

BUDJA
  CAMP, CHARLES M.+ TRACEY, HUGH‡ RHODESIA‡ 1948

BUILSA
  HANLEY, MARY ANN CSJ‡ GHANA‡ 1972

BULE
  BERLIN PHONOGRAMM-ARCHIV‡ AFRICA-GERMANY‡ 1909

BULU
  QUERSIN, BENOIT J.+ QUERSIN, CHRISTINE M.‡
  CAMEROON‡ 1967

  SIMPSON, AL‡ ‡ 1958

BURA
  HESS, ROBERT A.‡ NIGERIA‡ 1969

  KULP, PHILIP M.‡ NIGERIA‡ 1973

BUROM
  QUERSIN, BENOIT J.+ QUERSIN, CHRISTINE M.‡
  NIGERIA‡ 1972-73

BURUNGE
  TENRAA, ERIC WILLIAM FREDERICK‡ TANZANIA‡ 1958-66

BUSHMEN
  CLAUSS, BERNHARD PETER‡ BOTSWANA‡ 1971-72

  LIMA, AUGUSTO GUILHERME MESQUITELA‡ ANGOLA‡
  1963-70

  MARSHALL EXPEDITION PANHARD-CAPRICORNE‡ SOUTH
  AFRICA‡

  WESTPHAL, ERNST O.J.‡ BOTSWANA‡ 1953-74

  WESTPHAL, ERNST O.J.‡ NAMIBIA‡ 1953-74

  WESTPHAL, ERNST O.J.‡ SOUTH AFRICA‡ 1953-74

BUSHOONG
  QUERSIN, BENOIT J.‡ ZAIRE‡ 1970

BWABA
  ARCHIVES OF ETHNIC MUSIC AND DANCE‡ UPPER VOLTA‡

  CHRISTIAN, VALERIE‡ UPPER VOLTA‡ 1973-74

CARA
  LANGE, WERNER‡ ETHIOPIA‡ 1972-73

CHAMBA
  HANLEY, MARY ANN CSJ‡ NIGERIA‡ 1973

  QUERSIN, BENOIT J.+ QUERSIN, CHRISTINE M.‡
  NIGERIA‡ 1972-73

  RUBIN, ARNOLD G.‡ NIGERIA‡ 1964-65

CHANGANE
  RADIO CLUBE DE MOCAMBIQUE‡ MOZAMBIQUE‡

CHAOUI
  SAYAD, ALI‡ ALGERIA‡ 1971-72

CHAVIKWA
  GIBSON, GORDON D.‡ ANGOLA‡ 1971-73

CHENGUE
  RADIO CLUBE DE MOCAMBIQUE‡ MOZAMBIQUE‡

CHEWA
  GREENSTEIN, ROBERT CARL‡ MALAWI‡ 1971-75

CHEWA
  LANGWORTHY, HARRY W.‡ ZAMBIA‡ 1964

CHIKUNDA
  CAMP, CHARLES M.+ TRACEY, HUGH‡ RHODESIA‡ 1948

CHOKWE
  DIAS, MARGOT‡ MOZAMBIQUE‡ 1959

  LIMA, AUGUSTO GUILHERME MESQUITELA‡ ANGOLA‡
  1963-70

  MUSEU DO DUNDO‡ ANGOLA‡

CHOPI
  CAMP, CHARLES M.+ TRACEY, HUGH‡ SOUTH AFRICA‡
  1947-48

  DIAS, MARGOT‡ MOZAMBIQUE‡ 1959

  RADIO CLUBE DE MOCAMBIQUE‡ MOZAMBIQUE‡

  TRADITIONAL MUSIC DOCUMENTATION PROJECT‡
  MOZAMBIQUE‡

CHORI
  DIHOFF, IVAN R.‡ NIGERIA‡ 1972

COMORIENS
  VERNIER, -‡ MALAGASY REPUBLIC‡

CONIAGUI
  CENTRE DE RECHERCHES ANTHROPOLOGIQUES‡ SENEGAL‡

  LESTRANGE, M. DE‡ GUINEA‡

COOFA
  QUERSIN, BENOIT J.‡ ZAIRE‡ 1970

COPT
  ABDELSAYED, FR. GABRIEL H.A.‡ EGYPT‡ 1965-69

  DAVIS, GORDON‡ ETHIOPIA‡ 1968

  MAGYAR TUDOMANYOS AKADEMIA NEPZENEKUTATO CSOPORT‡
  EGYPT‡ 1966-67 + 1969

DAGARA
  CHRISTIAN, VALERIE‡ UPPER VOLTA‡ 1973-74

DAGARI
  HANLEY, MARY ANN CSJ‡ GHANA‡ 1972

DAGARTI
  ARCHIVES OF ETHNIC MUSIC AND DANCE‡ GHANA‡

  STRUMPF, MITCHEL‡ GHANA‡ 1969-72

DAGOMBA
  ARCHIVES OF ETHNIC MUSIC AND DANCE‡ GHANA‡

DAKARAWA
  COLLEGE OF MUSIC, UNIVERSITY OF NIGERIA‡ NIGERIA‡

DAN
  HIMMELHEBER, HANS G.‡ IVORY COAST‡ 1952-65

  HIMMELHEBER, HANS G.‡ LIBERIA‡ 1950-60

  ZEMP, HUGO‡ IVORY COAST‡ 1962+ 1964-67

DARASSA
  TSEHAI, BRHANE SILASSIE‡ ETHIOPIA‡ 1969-73

DEGWANA
  WANKLYN, CHRISTOPHER‡ MOROCCO‡ 1963+ 1969

DEI
  HOLSOE, SVEND E.‡ LIBERIA‡ 1965-70

  MOORE, BAI T.‡ LIBERIA‡ 1962-73

DENDI
  CALKINS, HOWARD W.+ RADIO DAHOMEY‡ DAHOMEY‡
  CA1967

DERVISH
  HEAD, SYDNEY W.‡ SUDAN‡ 1962

DIAKHANKE
  CURTIN, PHILIP D.‡ SENEGAL‡ 1966

  CURTIN, PHILIP D.‡ SENEGAL‡ 1966

DIGO
  GERLACH, LUTHER PAUL‡ KENYA-TANZANIA‡ 1958-60

  MALER, THOMAS A.‡ TANZANIA‡ 1967-68

DOGON
  SCHWEEGER-HEFEL, ANNEMARIE‡ UPPER VOLTA‡

DOMPAGO
  CALKINS, HOWARD W.+ RADIO DAHOMEY‡ DAHOMEY‡
  CA1967

DONNO
  ARCHIVES OF ETHNIC MUSIC AND DANCE‡ GHANA‡

DORZE
  LORTAT-JACOB, BERNARD‡ ETHIOPIA‡ 1974-75

  OLMSTEAD, JUDITH VIRGINIA‡ ETHIOPIA‡ 1969-71+
  1973

DOUROU
  HURAULT, -‡ CAMEROON‡

DUALA
  DUNGER, GEORGE A.‡ CAMEROON‡

DUMA-KARANGA
  ARCHIVES OF LANGUAGES OF THE WORLD‡ SOUTH AFRICA‡
  1954

DURUMA
  GERLACH, LUTHER PAUL‡ KENYA-TANZANIA‡ 1958-60

  SEDLAK, PHILIP A.S.‡ KENYA‡ 1971

DYULA
  ARCHIVES OF ETHNIC MUSIC AND DANCE‡ UPPER VOLTA‡

  BRAVMANN, RENE A.‡ UPPER VOLTA‡ 1972-74

  CHRISTIAN, VALERIE‡ UPPER VOLTA‡ 1973-74

  ELLOVICH, RISA SUE‡ IVORY COAST‡ 1973-74

  HAIGHT, BRUCE MARVIN‡ GHANA‡ 1972-73

EBRIE
  ROUGET, GILBERT‡ IVORY COAST‡

  ROUGET, GILBERT‡ IVORY COAST‡ 1952

EBURNEO-LIBERIEN
  MARING, JOEL‡ LIBERIA‡ 1958

ETON
  QUERSIN, BENOIT J.+ QUERSIN, CHRISTINE M.‡
  CAMEROON‡ 1967

EWE
  ADUAMAH, E.Y.‡ GHANA-TOGO‡ 1968-71

  AGUDZE, BERNARD‡ TOGO‡ 1965-67

  ALBERTS, ARTHUR S.‡ GHANA‡ 1949-51

  ARCHIVES OF ETHNIC MUSIC AND DANCE‡ GHANA‡

  COPLAN, DAVID+ THOMASON, LEE‡ GHANA‡ 1974

  ENGLAND, NICHOLAS M.‡ GHANA‡ 1969-70+ 1972

  HANLEY, MARY ANN CSJ‡ GHANA‡ 1972

  HANLEY, MARY ANN CSJ‡ GHANA‡ 1973

  JONES, ARTHUR M.‡ GHANA-ENGLAND‡ 1956

  OWEN, WILFRED, JR.‡ GHANA‡ 1970-71

  PANTALEONI, HEWITT‡ GHANA‡ 1969-71

  RANSBOTYN DE DECKER, DANIEL‡ TOGO‡ 1972-74

  REDDEN, JAMES ERSKINE‡ GHANA‡ 1958-63

  RICARD, ALAIN J.‡ TOGO‡ 1973

  STRUMPF, MITCHEL‡ GHANA‡ 1969-72

  VERMEER, DONALD E.‡ GHANA‡ 1969

FADIDJA
  HOHENWART-GERLACHSTEIN, ANNA‡ EGYPT‡ 1960+
  1962-63

FALASHA
  LESLAU, WOLF‡ ETHIOPIA‡ CA1947

FALASHA-JEW
  SHELEMAY, KAY KAUFMAN‡ ETHIOPIA‡ 1973

FANG
  FERNANDEZ, JAMES W.‡ GABON‡ 1960

FANG
  PEPPER, HERBERT‡ GABON‡ 1960

  TESSMAN, GUNTHER‡ EQUATORIAL GUINEA‡ 1907

FANG-PANGWE
  TESSMAN, GUNTHER‡ CAMEROON‡ 1907

FANTI
  ALBERTS, ARTHUR S.‡ LIBERIA‡ 1949-51

  BROWN, HERBERT‡ ‡ 1954-57

  FEINBERG, HARVEY‡ GHANA‡ 1967-68

  HANLEY, MARY ANN CSJ‡ GHANA‡ 1972

  OWEN, WILFRED, JR.‡ GHANA‡ 1970-71

  WEST, MONTY‡ ‡ 1957

FELLAHIN
  HOHENWART-GERLACHSTEIN, ANNA‡ EGYPT‡ 1960+
  1962-63

  MAGYAR TUDOMANYOS AKADEMIA NEPZENEKUTATO CSOPORT‡
  EGYPT‡ 1966-67 + 1969

FEZZANAIS
  BRANDILY, MONIQUE‡ CHAD‡ 1969

  BRANDILY, MONIQUE‡ LIBYA‡ 1969

FIPA
  WILLIS, ROY GEOFFREY‡ TANZANIA‡ 1966

FON
  BAY, EDNA GRACE‡ DAHOMEY‡ 1972

  CALKINS, HOWARD W.+ RADIO DAHOMEY‡ DAHOMEY‡
  CA1967

  DUMONT, LILLIAN E.‡ DAHOMEY‡ 1973

  HERSKOVITS, MELVILLE J.+ HERSKOVITS, FRANCES S.‡
  DAHOMEY‡ 1931

  ROUGET, GILBERT‡ DAHOMEY‡ 1952

FON
  ROUGET, GILBERT‡ DAHOMEY‡ 1952-71

  ROUGET, GILBERT+ TARDITS, CLAUDE+ VERGER, PIERRE‡
  DAHOMEY‡

  SAVARY, CLAUDE‡ DAHOMEY‡ 1966-67

FRAFRA
  GRAESSER, MARK W.‡ GHANA‡ 1968-69

  HANLEY, MARY ANN CSJ‡ GHANA‡ 1972

FTOUKA
  LORTAT-JACOB, BERNARD‡ MOROCCO‡ 1971

FULA
  KNIGHT, RODERIC COPLEY‡ GAMBIA, THE‡ 1970-71

  KNIGHT, RODERIC COPLEY‡ SENEGAL‡ 1970-71

  SKINNER, A. NEIL+ SKINNER, MARGARET G.‡ NIGERIA‡
  1967-74

  VAN OVEN, JACOBA‡ SIERRA LEONE‡ 1964-67

FULANI
  ARCHIVES OF ETHNIC MUSIC AND DANCE‡ UPPER VOLTA‡

  CHRISTIAN, VALERIE‡ UPPER VOLTA‡ 1973-74

  COLLEGE OF MUSIC, UNIVERSITY OF NIGERIA‡ NIGERIA‡

  QUERSIN, BENOIT J.+ QUERSIN, CHRISTINE M.‡
  NIGERIA‡ 1972-73

  RHODES, WILLARD‡ NIGERIA‡ 1973-74

  STENNES, LESLIE H.‡ CAMEROON‡ 1956-73

FULBE
  AMES, DAVID W.‡ NIGERIA‡ 1963-64

  ARCHIVES OF ETHNIC MUSIC AND DANCE‡ UPPER VOLTA‡

  CHRISTIAN, VALERIE‡ UPPER VOLTA‡ 1973-74

  CHRISTIAN, VALERIE+ ROSELLINI, JAMES N.‡ UPPER
  VOLTA‡ 1973

FULBE
  RAPHAEL, RONALD P.‡ CAMEROON‡ 1974

  RAPHAEL, RONALD P.‡ NIGERIA‡ 1974

FUNG
  WEISS, -‡ SUDAN‡

FUNGWE
  CAMP, CHARLES M.+ TRACEY, HUGH‡ RHODESIA‡ 1948

GAALIIN
  CARLISLE, ROXANE C.‡ SUDAN‡ 1963

  HURREIZ, SAYED H.‡ SUDAN‡ 1970-71

GALLA
  BAIRU, TAFLA‡ ETHIOPIA‡ 1973-74

  LEWIS, HERBERT S.‡ ETHIOPIA‡ 1965-66

  MAGYAR TUDOMANYOS AKADEMIA NEPZENEKUTATO CSOPORT‡
  ETHIOPIA‡

  MESSING, SIMON D.‡ ETHIOPIA‡ 1961-67

GALLINAS
  VAN OVEN, JACOBA‡ SIERRA LEONE‡ 1964-67

GANDA
  BAISSAC, -‡ UGANDA‡ 1967

GANGULA
  ENGLAND, NICHOLAS M.‡ ANGOLA‡ 1957-61

GARWE
  KAEMMER, JOHN E.‡ RHODESIA‡ 1971

GBANDE
  HOLSOE, SVEND E.‡ LIBERIA‡ 1965-70

  MOORE, BAI T.‡ LIBERIA‡ 1962-73

  MOREY, ROBERT H.‡ LIBERIA‡ 1935

  OKIE, PACKARD L.‡ LIBERIA‡ 1947-54

  SIEGMANN, WILLIAM CHARLES‡ LIBERIA‡ 1973-74

GBAYA
  NOSS, PHILIP A.‡ CAMEROON‡ 1966-67

  VIDAL, PIERRE ANTOINE‡ CENTRAL AFRICAN REPUBLIC‡
  1961-74

GCIRIKU
  GIBSON, GORDON D.‡ BOTSWANA‡ 1953

GEDE
  CRAVEN, ANNA‡ NIGERIA‡ 1969-70

  FEDERAL DEPARTMENT OF ANTIQUITIES, NATIONAL
  MUSEUM, KADUNA‡ NIGERIA‡

GIDDER
  STENNES, LESLIE H.‡ CAMEROON‡ 1956-73

GIO
  MOORE, BAI T.‡ LIBERIA‡ 1962-73

  OKIE, PACKARD L.‡ LIBERIA‡ 1947-54

GIRYAMA
  BRANTLEY, CYNTHIA‡ KENYA‡ 1970-71

  MALER, THOMAS A.‡ TANZANIA‡ 1967-68

  SEDLAK, PHILIP A.S.‡ KENYA‡ 1971

GISU
  HEALD, SWETTE SCOTT‡ UGANDA‡ 1966-69

GNAWA
  INSTITUT D'ETHNOLOGIE DE L'UNIVERSITE DE
  STRASBOURG‡ MOROCCO‡

  INSTITUT D'ETHNOLOGIE DE L'UNIVERSITE DE
  STRASBOURG‡ MOROCCO‡

GOLA
  D'AZEVEDO, WARREN L.‡ LIBERIA‡ 1956-58+ 1966

  D'AZEVEDO, WARREN L.‡ LIBERIA‡ 1960

  D'AZEVEDO, WARREN L.‡ LIBERIA‡ 1967

  HOLSOE, SVEND E.‡ LIBERIA‡ 1965-70

GOLA
  MOORE, BAI T.‡ LIBERIA‡ 1962-73

  OKIE, PACKARD L.‡ LIBERIA‡ 1947-54

  VAN OVEN, JACOBA‡ SIERRA LEONE‡ 1964-67

GONJA
  HAIGHT, BRUCE MARVIN‡ GHANA‡ 1972-73

GOUIN
  ARCHIVES OF ETHNIC MUSIC AND DANCE‡ UPPER VOLTA‡

  CHRISTIAN, VALERIE‡ UPPER VOLTA‡ 1973-74

GOURMANTCHE
  ARCHIVES OF ETHNIC MUSIC AND DANCE‡ UPPER VOLTA‡

  CHRISTIAN, VALERIE‡ UPPER VOLTA‡ 1973-74

GREBO
  HERZOG, GEORGE‡ LIBERIA‡ 1930

  LUCKAU, STEPHEN R.‡ LIBERIA‡ 1971

  MARING, JOEL‡ LIBERIA‡ 1958

  MARTIN, JANE JACKSON‡ LIBERIA‡ 1968+ 1972-75

  STUTTMAN, LEONARD M.‡ LIBERIA‡ 1956

GUERE
  BLANK, ARTHUR S., JR.+ BLANK, DONNA H.‡ IVORY
  COAST‡ 1973

  HIMMELHEBER, HANS G.‡ IVORY COAST‡ 1952-65

  LAUER, JOSEPH JEROME‡ IVORY COAST‡ 1971

  ZEMP, HUGO‡ IVORY COAST‡ 1962+ 1964-67

GULA-IRO
  PAIRAULT, CLAUDE ALBERT‡ CHAD‡ 1959-64

GUN
  ROUGET, GILBERT‡ DAHOMEY‡ 1952

  ROUGET, GILBERT‡ DAHOMEY‡ 1952-71

GUN
  ROUGET, GILBERT‡ TARDITS, CLAUDE‡ VERGER, PIERRE‡
  DAHOMEY‡

  TARDITS, CLAUDE‡ DAHOMEY‡

  TARDITS, CLAUDE‡ DAHOMEY‡ 1955

GURAGE
  LESLAU, WOLF‡ ETHIOPIA‡ 1947

GURO
  HIMMELHEBER, HANS G.‡ IVORY COAST‡ 1952-65

GURUNSI
  ECHENBERG, MYRON J.‡ UPPER VOLTA‡ 1967

GUSII
  DOBRIN, ARTHUR‡ KENYA‡ 1966

  DOBRIN, ARTHUR‡ KENYA‡ 1966

GWANDARA
  HANLEY, MARY ANN CSJ‡ NIGERIA‡ 1973

HADJERAI
  FEDRY, J.‡ CHAD‡ 1966-67

HADZA
  TUCKER, ARCHIBALD NORMAN‡ TANZANIA‡

HAKAWONA
  GIBSON, GORDON D.‡ ANGOLA‡ 1971-73

HAMBUKUSU
  LARSON, THOMAS J.‡ BOTSWANA‡ 1972

HARARI
  LESLAU, WOLF‡ ETHIOPIA‡ 1947

HAUSA
  AKPABOT, SAMUEL EKPE‡ NIGERIA‡ 1964-73

  AMES, DAVID W.‡ NIGERIA‡ 1963

  AMES, DAVID W.‡ NIGERIA‡ 1963-64

  BAIER, STEPHEN B.‡ NIGER‡ 1972

HAUSA
  BEN-AMOS, DAN‡ NIGERIA‡ 1966

  BESMER, FREMONT E.‡ NIGERIA‡ 1968-70

  BESMER, FREMONT E.‡ NIGERIA‡ 1972-73

  CENTRE FOR THE STUDY OF NIGERIAN LANGUAGES‡
  NIGERIA‡

  CHRISTIAN, VALERIE‡ UPPER VOLTA‡ 1973-74

  COLLEGE OF MUSIC, UNIVERSITY OF NIGERIA‡ NIGERIA‡

  DIHOFF, IVAN R.‡ NIGERIA‡ 1972

  DORSON, RICHARD M.‡ NIGERIA-U.S.‡ 1967

  ECHEZONA, WILLIAM WILBERFORCE CHUKUDINKA‡ NIGERIA‡
  1950-75

  EULENBERG, JOHN BRYSON‡ NIGERIA‡ 1972

  GRAESSER, MARK W.‡ GHANA‡ 1968-69

  HANLEY, MARY ANN CSJ‡ NIGERIA‡ 1973

  HURAULT, -‡ CAMEROON‡

  KIRK-GREENE, ANTHONY H.M.‡ NIGERIA‡ 1962-65

  PLOTNICOV, LEONARD‡ NIGERIA‡ 1961-62

  QUERSIN, BENOIT J.‡ QUERSIN, CHRISTINE M.‡
  NIGERIA‡ 1972-73

  RHODES, WILLARD‡ NIGERIA‡ 1973-74

  RUBIN, ARNOLD G.‡ NIGERIA‡ 1964-65

  SKINNER, A. NEIL‡ SKINNER, MARGARET G.‡ NIGERIA‡
  1967-74

  SMEND, W.A.‡ TOGO‡ 1905

  WOLFF, HANS‡ NIGERIA‡ 1953-54

HAUSA-FULANI
  ABDULKADIR, DATTI‡ NIGERIA‡ 1973

HAYA
  REINING, PRISCILLA‡ TANZANIA‡

  WEMAN, PAUL HENRY‡ TANZANIA‡ 1957

HERA
  CAMP, CHARLES M.+ TRACEY, HUGH‡ RHODESIA‡ 1948

HERERO
  ENGLAND, NICHOLAS M.‡ NAMIBIA‡ 1957-61

  GIBSON, GORDON D.‡ BOTSWANA‡ 1953

  GIBSON, GORDON D.‡ NAMIBIA‡ 1960-61

  SHOSTAK, MARJORIE JANET‡ BOTSWANA‡ 1969-71

  TLOU, THOMAS‡ BOTSWANA‡ 1970

  VIVELO, FRANK ROBERT‡ BOTSWANA‡ 1973

HIMBA
  GIBSON, GORDON D.‡ ANGOLA‡ 1971-73

  GIBSON, GORDON D.‡ NAMIBIA‡ 1960-61

HIMBA-MUGAMBO
  CLAUSS, BERNHARD PETER‡ ANGOLA‡ 1970-72

HINNARIO
  LANGE, WERNER‡ ETHIOPIA‡ 1972-73

HLUBI
  CAMP, CHARLES M.+ TRACEY, HUGH‡ SOUTH AFRICA‡
  1947-48

HOLI
  ROUGET, GILBERT‡ DAHOMEY‡ 1952

HOLOHOLO
  MUSEE ROYAL DE L'AFRIQUE CENTRALE‡ ‡

HOTTENTOT
  AFRICANA MUSEUM‡ SOUTH AFRICA‡

  WESTPHAL, ERNST O.J.‡ BOTSWANA‡ 1953-74

HUNGWE
  CAMP, CHARLES M.+ TRACEY, HUGH‡ RHODESIA‡ 1948

HUTU
  GANSEMANS, JOS‡ RWANDA‡ 1973-74

IBAAM
  QUERSIN, BENOIT J.‡ ZAIRE‡ 1970

IBIBIO
  AKPABOT, SAMUEL EKPE‡ NIGERIA‡ 1964-73

  HANLEY, MARY ANN CSJ‡ NIGERIA‡ 1973

  PLOTNICOV, LEONARD‡ NIGERIA‡ 1961-62

  TRADITIONAL MUSIC DOCUMENTATION PROJECT‡ NIGERIA‡

  WOLFF, HANS‡ NIGERIA‡ 1953-54

IBO
  AKPABOT, SAMUEL EKPE‡ NIGERIA‡ 1964-73

  ALBERTS, ARTHUR S.‡ GHANA‡ 1949-51

  ALIGWEKWE, EVALYN R.‡ NIGERIA‡ 1960

  COLLEGE OF MUSIC, UNIVERSITY OF NIGERIA‡ NIGERIA‡

  CRABB, DAVID‡ NIGERIA‡

  ECHEZONA, WILLIAM WILBERFORCE CHUKUDINKA‡ NIGERIA‡
  1950-75

  ELWA STUDIO, NIGERIA‡ NIGERIA‡

  HANLEY, MARY ANN CSJ‡ NIGERIA‡ 1973

  HANNA, JUDITH LYNNE‡ HANNA, WILLIAM J.‡ NIGERIA‡
  1963

  INSTITUTE OF AFRICAN STUDIES, UNIVERSITY OF IFE‡
  NIGERIA‡

  LINENBRUEGGE, GERTRUDE R.I.‡ NIGERIA‡ 1966

  NETTL, BRUNO ‡RABEN, JOSEPH‡ NIGERIA-U.S.‡
  1950-51

  OGBU, JOHN U.‡ NIGERIA‡ 1972

  ONWUKA, RALPH I.‡ NIGERIA‡

IBO
  PLOTNICOV, LEONARD‡ NIGERIA‡ 1961-62

  RABEN, JOSEPH‡ NIGERIA-U.S.‡ 195C

  RABEN, JOSEPH‡ NIGERIA-U.S.‡ 1950

  ROMERO, PATRICIA‡ NIGERIA‡ 1973

  RUBIN, ARNOLD G.‡ NIGERIA‡ 1964-65

  SMOCK, DAVID R.‡ NIGERIA‡ 1962-63

  SZCZESNIAK, ANDREW L.‡ NIGERIA-U.S.‡ 1961

  TRADITIONAL MUSIC DOCUMENTATION PROJECT‡ NIGERIA‡

  WOLFF, HANS‡ NIGERIA‡ 1953

ICHEN
  QUERSIN, BENOIT J.+ QUERSIN, CHRISTINE M.‡
  NIGERIA‡ 1972-73

IDOMA
  ARMSTRONG, ROBERT G.+ UNOOGWU, PATRICK‡ NIGERIA‡
  1961

  ARMSTRONG, ROBERT G.‡ NIGERIA‡ 1964

  ARMSTRONG, ROBERT G. +WITTIG, R. CURT‡ NIGERIA‡
  1964

  COLLEGE OF MUSIC, UNIVERSITY OF NIGERIA‡ NIGERIA‡

  QUERSIN, BENOIT J.+ QUERSIN, CHRISTINE M.‡
  NIGERIA‡ 1972-73

IGANDA-LUGANDA
  BOAS, FRANZ‡ ‡ PRE-1935

IGBIRA
  WOLFF, HANS‡ NIGERIA‡ 1953

IGBO
  AMES, DAVID W.‡ NIGERIA‡ 1963-64

  ARCHIVES OF ETHNIC MUSIC AND DANCE‡ NIGERIA‡

  EKECHI, FELIX K.‡ NIGERIA‡ 1973

ISONGO
  BOUQUIAUX, LUC‡ CENTRAL AFRICAN REPUBLIC‡

ITCHA
  ROUGET, GILBERT+ TARDITS, CLAUDE+ VERGER, PIERRE‡
  DAHOMEY‡

ITSEKIRI
  DEPARTMENT OF LINGUISTICS AND NIGERIAN LANGUAGES,
  UNIVERSITY OF IBADAN‡ NIGERIA‡ 1967-73

  REDDEN, JAMES ERSKINE‡ ‡ 1958

  WOLFF, HANS‡ NIGERIA‡ 1953

JABA
  COLLEGE OF MUSIC, UNIVERSITY OF NIGERIA‡ NIGERIA‡

  HANLEY, MARY ANN CSJ‡ NIGERIA‡ 1973

JABO
  ANDRADE, MANUEL+ HERZOG, GEORGE‡ ‡ 1931

  HERZOG, GEORGE‡ LIBERIA‡ 1930

  LUCKAU, STEPHEN R.‡ LIBERIA‡ 1971

JALUO
  SUDAN NATIONAL MUSEUM‡ SUDAN‡ 1959-64

JARAWA
  QUERSIN, BENOIT J.+ QUERSIN, CHRISTINE M.‡
  NIGERIA‡ 1972-73

JEW
  LAADE, WOLFGANG KARL‡ TUNISIA‡ 1960

JOLA
  KNIGHT, RODERIC COPLEY‡ GAMBIA, THE‡ 1970-71

  KNIGHT, RODERIC COPLEY‡ SENEGAL‡ 1970-71

JUKUN
  QUERSIN, BENOIT J.+ QUERSIN, CHRISTINE M.‡
  NIGERIA‡ 1972-73

  RUBIN, ARNOLD G.‡ NIGERIA‡ 1964-65

  WOLFF, HANS‡ NIGERIA‡ 1953

KABBA
SKINNER, A. NEIL+ SKINNER, MARGARET G.‡ NIGERIA‡
1967-74

KABRE
VERDIER, RAYMOND‡ TOGO‡

KABYLE
SAYAD, ALI‡ ALGERIA‡ 1968-70

KAFA
LANGE, WERNER‡ ETHIOPIA‡ 1972-73

ORENT, AMNON‡ ETHIOPIA‡ 1966-67

KAFFICHO
MAGYAR TUDOMANYOS AKADEMIA NEPZENEKUTATO CSOPORT‡
ETHIOPIA‡

KAGORO
KIRK-GREENE, ANTHONY H.M.‡ NIGERIA‡ 1962-65

PLOTNICOV, LEONARD‡ NIGERIA‡ 1961-62

KAJE
WOLFF, HANS‡ NIGERIA‡ 1953

WOLFF, HANS‡ NIGERIA‡ 1953-54

KAKA
DUNGER, GEORGE A.‡ CAMEROON‡

KAKWA
BYRD, ROBERT OAKES‡ UGANDA‡

KALABARI
QUERSIN, BENOIT J.+ QUERSIN, CHRISTINE M.‡
NIGERIA‡ 1972-73

TRADITIONAL MUSIC DOCUMENTATION PROJECT‡ NIGERIA‡

WOLFF, HANS‡ NIGERIA‡ 1953

KAMBA
MADIGAN, BOB‡ KENYA‡ 1957-58

SPENCER, LEON P.‡ KENYA‡ 1968-69

KAMI
  ALPERS, EDWARD ALTER‡ TANZANIA‡ 1972-73

KANEMBU
  BRANDILY, MONIQUE‡ CHAD‡ 1961+ 1963+ 1965

  MUSEE ROYAL DE L'AFRIQUE CENTRALE‡ ‡

KANJAGA
  GRAESSER, MARK W.‡ GHANA‡ 1968-69

KANTANA
  QUERSIN, BENOIT J.+ QUERSIN, CHRISTINE M.‡
  NIGERIA‡ 1972-73

KANURI
  BAIER, STEPHEN B.‡ NIGER‡ 1972

  COHEN, RONALD‡ NIGERIA‡ 1956

  SPAIN, DAVID H.‡ NIGERIA‡ 1966-67

KARA
  VIDAL, PIERRE ANTOINE‡ CENTRAL AFRICAN REPUBLIC‡
  1961-74

KARAMOJONG
  BLACKING, JOHN A.R.‡ UGANDA‡ 1965

  COLEMAN, MILTON‡ UGANDA‡ 1967

  TUCKER, ARCHIBALD NORMAN‡ UGANDA‡

KARANGA
  CAMP, CHARLES M.+ TRACEY, HUGH‡ RHODESIA‡ 1948

  KRIEL, A.P.‡ RHODESIA‡ 1966

  TRADITIONAL MUSIC DOCUMENTATION PROJECT‡ RHODESIA‡

  WEMAN, HENRY PAUL‡ RHODESIA‡ 1957

KASSENA
  CHRISTIAN, VALERIE‡ UPPER VOLTA‡ 1973-74

  CHRISTIAN, VALERIE+ ROSELLINI, JAMES N.‡ UPPER
  VOLTA‡ 1973

  HANLEY, MARY ANN CSJ‡ GHANA‡ 1972

KONGO
  MACGAFFEY, WYATT‡ ZAIRE‡ 1970

  MUSEE ROYAL DE L'AFRIQUE CENTRALE‡ ‡

KONKOMBA
  ARCHIVES OF ETHNIC MUSIC AND DANCE‡ GHANA‡

  GRAESSER, MARK W.‡ GHANA‡ 1968-69

  STRUMPF, MITCHEL‡ GHANA‡ 1969-72

KONON
  ROUGET, GILBERT‡ GUINEA‡

KOREKORE
  KAEMMER, JOHN E.‡ RHODESIA‡ 1972-73

KOSSI
  VAN ROUVEROY VAN NIEUWAAL, EMILE A.B.‡ TOGO‡
  1969-73

KOTOKO
  BRANDILY, MONIQUE‡ CHAD‡ 1961+ 1963+ 1965

KPELLE
  BELLMAN, BERYL LARRY‡ LIBERIA‡ 1969

  D'AZEVEDO, WARREN L.‡ LIBERIA‡ 1956-58+ 1966

  D'AZEVEDO, WARREN L.‡ LIBERIA‡ 1960

  GAY, JUDITH S.‡ LIBERIA‡ 1971-73

  HOLSOE, SVEND E.‡ LIBERIA‡ 1965-70

  MOORE, BAI T.‡ LIBERIA‡ 1962-73

  OKIE, PACKARD L.‡ LIBERIA‡ 1947-54

  SELIGMAN, THOMAS KNOWLES‡ LIBERIA‡ 1970

  STONE, RUTH M.+ STONE, VERLON L.‡ LIBERIA‡ 1970

KRAHN
  HIMMELHEBER, HANS G.‡ LIBERIA‡ 1950-60

  STUTTMAN, LEONARD M.‡ LIBERIA‡ 1956

KROBO
  COPLAN, DAVID+ THOMASON, LEE‡ GHANA‡ 1974

KRU
  BOAS, FRANZ‡ ‡ PRE-1935

  HERZOG, GEORGE‡ LIBERIA‡ 1930

  MASSING, ANDREAS‡ LIBERIA‡ 1971-72

  OKIE, PACKARD L.‡ LIBERIA‡ 1947-54

  OKIE, PACKARD L.‡ LIBERIA‡ 1947-54

KUANYAMA
  WESTPHAL, ERNST O.J.‡ NAMIBIA‡ 1953-74

KUBA
  KABEMBA, MUFUTA KABANDANYI‡ ZAIRE‡ 1965+ 1972

KULLO
  MAGYAR TUDOMANYOS AKADEMIA NEPZENEKUTATO CSOPORT‡
  ETHIOPIA‡

KUMAM
  VANVELSEN, J.‡ UGANDA‡ 1948-60

KUNG-BUSHMEN
  BISELE, MARGUERITE A.‡ BOTSWANA‡ 1971-72

  KATZ, RICHARD‡ BOTSWANA‡ 1968

  LAMBRECHT, FRANK L.+ LAMBRECHT, DORA J.M.‡
  BOTSWANA‡ 1967-68

  SHOSTAK, MARJORIE JANET‡ BOTSWANA‡ 1969-71

  SMITS, LUCAS GERARDUS ALFONSUS‡ BOTSWANA‡ 1972

KURUMBA
  SCHWEEGER-HEFEL, ANNEMARIE‡ UPPER VOLTA‡

  SCHWEEGER-HEFEL, ANNEMARIE‡ UPPER VOLTA‡ 1961-69

KUTEP
  QUERSIN, BENOIT J.+ QUERSIN, CHRISTINE M.‡
  NIGERIA‡ 1972-73

  RUBIN, ARNOLD G.‡ NIGERIA‡ 1964-65

KUVALE
  GIBSON, GORDON D.‡ ANGOLA‡ 1971-73

  GIBSON, GORDON D.‡ NAMIBIA‡ 1960-61

KWA
  ARCHIVES OF LANGUAGES OF THE WORLD‡ ‡

KWALLA
  QUERSIN, BENOIT J.+ QUERSIN, CHRISTINE M.‡
  NIGERIA‡ 1972-73

KWERE
  ALPERS, EDWARD ALTER‡ TANZANIA‡ 1972-73

KWO
  CHRISTIAN, VALERIE‡ UPPER VOLTA‡ 1973-74

LALA
  CAMP, CHARLES M.+ TRACEY, HUGH‡ ZAMBIA‡ 1947-48

  JONES, ARTHUR M.‡ ZAMBIA‡ 1944

LEBOU
  ROUGET, GILBERT‡ SENEGAL‡

  ROUGET, GILBERT‡ SENEGAL‡ 1952

LEGA
  BIEBUYCK, DANIEL P.‡ ZAIRE‡ 1952-61

  MUSEE ROYAL DE L'AFRIQUE CENTRALE‡ ‡

LEMBA
  WEMAN, HENRY PAUL‡ RHODESIA‡ 1957

LEYA-SUBIYA
  LIVINGSTONE MUSEUM‡ ZAMBIA‡

LIMBA
  BAHMAN, GARY‡ SIERRA LEONE‡ 1971

  VAN OVEN, JACOBA‡ SIERRA LEONE‡ 1964-67

LINDA-BANDA
  AROM, SIMHA‡ CENTRAL AFRICAN REPUBLIC‡ 1964-67+
  1971-73

LINGALA
  REDDEN, JAMES ERSKINE≠ ZAIRE≠ 1962

  UNITED CHRISTIAN MISSIONARY SOCIETY, DISCIPLES OF
  CHRIST≠ ZAIRE≠

LOBI
  ARCHIVES OF ETHNIC MUSIC AND DANCE≠ GHANA≠

  ARCHIVES OF ETHNIC MUSIC AND DANCE≠ UPPER VOLTA≠

  CHRISTIAN, VALERIE≠ UPPER VOLTA≠ 1973-74

LOKO
  HAIGHT, BRUCE MARVIN≠ SIERRA LEONE≠ 1967

  VAN OVEN, JACOBA≠ SIERRA LEONE≠ 1964-67

LOMA
  ALBERTS, ARTHUR S.≠ LIBERIA≠ 1949-51

  BELLMAN, BERYL LARRY≠ LIBERIA≠ 1969

  MOORE, BAI T.≠ LIBERIA≠ 1962-73

  MOREY, ROBERT H.≠ LIBERIA≠ 1935

  NEWBURY, DOROTHY J.≠ LIBERIA≠ 1969-70+ 1972

  OKIE, PACKARD L.≠ LIBERIA≠ 1947-54

  WEISSWANGE, KARIN I.S.≠ LIBERIA≠ 1963-65+ 1972-73

LOMWE
  ETHNOMUSICOLOGY CENTRE JAAP KUNST≠ MALAWI≠ 1971

  GREENSTEIN, ROBERT CARL≠ MALAWI≠ 1971-75

LONKUNDO
  UNITED CHRISTIAN MISSIONARY SOCIETY, DISCIPLES OF
  CHRIST≠ ZAIRE≠

LOTUKO
  TUCKER, ARCHIBALD NORMAN≠ SUDAN≠

LOZI
  ARCHIVES OF ETHNIC MUSIC AND DANCE≠ ZAMBIA≠

  CAMP, CHARLES M.+ TRACEY, HUGH≠ ZAMBIA≠ 1947-48

LOZI
  TLOU, THOMAS‡ BOTSWANA‡ 1970

LUBA
  BIEBUYCK, DANIEL P.‡ ZAIRE‡ 1952-61

  DEPLAEN, GUY‡ ZAIRE‡ 1973-74

  FAIK-NZUJI, MADIYA‡ ZAIRE‡ 1974

  GANSEMANS, JOS‡ ZAIRE‡ 1970

  GANSEMANS, JOS‡ ZAIRE‡ 1970-73

  KABEMBA, MUFUTA KABANDANYI‡ ZAIRE‡ 1965+ 1972

  MCLEAN, DAVID A.‡ ZAIRE‡ 1954-61

  MUSEU DO DUNDO‡ ANGOLA‡

  PRUITT, WILLIAM F., SR.‡ ZAIRE‡ 1945-49

  RADIO CLUBE DE MOCAMBIQUE‡ MOZAMBIQUE‡

  REEFE, THOMAS Q.‡ ZAIRE‡ 1972-73

  STUDSTILL, JOHN D.‡ ZAIRE‡ 1972

  WEMAN, PAUL HENRY‡ ZAIRE‡ 1957

LUCHAZI
  ARCHIVES OF ETHNIC MUSIC AND DANCE‡ ZAMBIA‡

LUGURU
  ALPERS, EDWARD ALTER‡ TANZANIA‡ 1972-73

LUHYA
  FRANKEL, GERD‡ ‡ 1959

LULUA
  MAALU-BUNGI‡ ZAIRE‡ 1969+ 1972+ 1973

  PRUITT, WILLIAM F., SR.‡ ZAIRE‡ 1945-49

LUNDA
  BIEBUYCK, DANIEL P.‡ ZAIRE‡ 1952-61

  GANSEMANS, JOS‡ ZAIRE‡ 1970-73

LUNDA
  HOOVER, JAMES JEFFREY‡ ZAIRE‡ 1973-75

  MUSEU DO DUNDO‡ ANGOLA‡

LUO
  BLOUNT, BEN G.‡ KENYA‡ 1971

  HAY, MARGARET JEAN‡ KENYA‡ 1968-70+ 1973

  PRESTON, JEROME, JR.‡ KENYA‡ 1966

  REDDEN, JAMES ERSKINE‡ KENYA‡ 1959

  REDDEN, JAMES ERSKINE‡ KENYA‡ 1960-65

  SPENCER, LEON P.‡ KENYA‡ 1968-69

  TUCKER, ARCHIBALD NORMAN‡ KENYA‡

LWENA
  MUSEU DO DUNDO‡ ANGOLA‡

MADA
  COLLEGE OF MUSIC, UNIVERSITY OF NIGERIA‡ NIGERIA‡

MAGHREB
  CENTRE DE RECHERCHES ANTHROPOLOGIQUES
  PREHISTORIQUES ET ETHNOGRAPHIQUES‡ ALGERIA‡

MAHAFALY
  KOECHLIN, B.‡ MALAGASY REPUBLIC‡ 1967-69

  VERNIER, -‡ MALAGASY REPUBLIC‡

MAHI
  CALKINS, HOWARD W.+ RADIO DAHOMEY‡ DAHOMEY‡
  CA1967

MAKONDE
  DIAS, MARGOT‡ MOZAMBIQUE‡ 1957-58

  MALER, THOMAS A.‡ TANZANIA‡ 1967-68

  NATIONAL MUSEUM OF TANZANIA‡ TANZANIA‡

  RADIO CLUBE DE MOCAMBIQUE‡ MOZAMBIQUE‡

MAKUA
  RADIO CLUBE DE MOCAMBIQUE‡ MOZAMBIQUE‡

MALILA
  NATIONAL MUSEUM OF TANZANIA‡ TANZANIA‡

MALINKE
  ALBERTS, ARTHUR S.‡ GUINEA‡ 1949-51

  ARNOTT, D.‡ UPPER VOLTA‡ 1956

  BRASSEUR, G.+ DI DIO, FRANCOIS+ DIETERLEN,
  GERMAINE+ ROUGET, GILBERT‡ MALI‡

  BROOKS, GEORGE+ DALBY, DAVID+ VAUGHAN, JAMES H.‡
  AFRICA-U.S.‡ 1969

  CAMARA, S.‡ SENEGAL‡ 1970+ 1971

  CENTRE DE RECHERCHES ANTHROPOLOGIQUES‡ SENEGAL‡

  CURTIN, PHILIP D.‡ SENEGAL‡ 1966

  CURTIN, PHILIP D.‡ SENEGAL‡ 1966

  ELLOVICH, RISA SUE‡ IVORY COAST‡ 1973-74

  GUIGNARD, AUDE‡ SENEGAL‡ 1968

  RAYFIELD, JOAN R.‡ IVORY COAST‡ 1972-73

  ROUGET, GILBERT‡ GUINEA‡

  ROUGET, GILBERT‡ GUINEA‡ 1952

  ROUGET, GILBERT‡ GUINEA‡ 1952

  ZEMP, HUGO‡ IVORY COAST‡ 1962+ 1964-67

MALOUF
  SPENCER, WILLIAM‡ TUNISIA‡ 1966-67

MAMBILA
  RAPHAEL, RONALD P.‡ NIGERIA‡ 1974

MANDE
  LONG, RONALD W.‡ GHANA‡ 1968

  LONG, RONALD W.‡ UPPER VOLTA‡ 1968

MANDINGO
　BAHMAN, GARY‡ SIERRA LEONE‡ 1971

　GEOFFRION, CHARLES A.‡ SIERRA LEONE‡ 1966-67

　HOLSOE, SVEND E.‡ LIBERIA‡ 1965-70

　MOORE, BAI T.‡ LIBERIA‡ 1962-73

　MOREY, ROBERT H.‡ LIBERIA‡ 1935

　OKIE, PACKARD L.‡ LIBERIA‡ 1947-54

　VAN OVEN, JACOBA‡ SIERRA LEONE‡ 1964-67

　WEISSWANGE, KARIN I.S.‡ LIBERIA‡ 1963-65‡ 1972-73

MANDINKA
　ARCHIVES OF ETHNIC MUSIC AND DANCE‡ GAMBIA, THE‡

　ETHNOMUSICOLOGY CENTRE JAAP KUNST‡ GAMBIA, THE‡
　1958

　INNES, GORDON‡ GAMBIA, THE‡ 1968-69

　KNIGHT, RODERIC COPLEY‡ GAMBIA, THE‡ 1970-71

　KNIGHT, RODERIC COPLEY‡ SENEGAL‡ 1970-71

　PEVAR, MARC DAVID‡ GAMBIA, THE‡ 1972

MANGANJA
　ETHNOMUSICOLOGY CENTRE JAAP KUNST‡ MALAWI‡ 1971

　GEOFFRION, CHARLES A.‡ MALAWI‡ 1971-72

　GREENSTEIN, ROBERT CARL‡ MALAWI‡ 1971-75

MANGBETU
　BIEBUYCK, DANIEL P.‡ ZAIRE‡ 1952-61

MANKON
　WARNIER, JEAN-PIERRE‡ CAMEROON‡ 1972-74

MANO
　ALBERTS, ARTHUR S.‡ AFRICA-WEST‡ 1949

　ALBERTS, ARTHUR S.‡ LIBERIA‡ 1949-51

MANO
  HAWTHORNE, RICHARD‡ LIBERIA‡ 1970

  HIMMELHEBER, HANS G.‡ LIBERIA‡ 1950-60

  MOORE, BAI T.‡ LIBERIA‡ 1962-73

MANON
  ROUGET, GILBERT‡ GUINEA‡

MANYIKA
  KAEMMER, JOHN E.‡ RHODESIA‡ 1971

MANYIKE-BOCHA
  TRADITIONAL MUSIC DOCUMENTATION PROJECT‡ RHODESIA‡

MAO
  BENDER, MARVIN LIONEL‡ ETHIOPIA‡ 1964-74

MAOURI
  LORELLE, -‡ NIGER‡

MARGI
  MISHLER, ROBERT E.‡ NIGERIA‡ 1971-72

  VAUGHAN, JAMES H.‡ NIGERIA‡ 1960

  VAUGHAN, JAMES H.‡ NIGERIA‡ 1960

  VAUGHAN, JAMES H.‡ NIGERIA‡ 1974

  VAUGHAN, JAMES H.‡ NIGERIA‡ 1974

MARKA
  BRASSEUR, G.+ DI DIO, FRANCOIS+ DIETERLEN,
  GERMAINE+ ROUGET, GILBERT‡ MALI‡

  CALAME, B.‡ MALI‡ 1956-57+ 1960

  CHRISTIAN, VALERIE‡ UPPER VOLTA‡ 1973-74

  CHRISTIAN, VALERIE+ ROSELLINI, JAMES N.‡ UPPER
  VOLTA‡ 1973

  ECHENBERG, MYRON J.‡ UPPER VOLTA‡ 1967

MASIKORO
  KOECHLIN, B.‡ MALAGASY REPUBLIC‡ 1967-69

MAYOGO
   BIEBUYCK, DANIEL P.‡ ZAIRE‡ 1952-61

MBALA
   MUSEE ROYAL DE L'AFRIQUE CENTRALE‡ ‡

   THIEL, JOSEF FRANZ‡ ZAIRE‡ 1961-71

MBAYE
   ADLER, -‡ CHAD‡

MBUKUSHU
   TLOU, THOMAS‡ BOTSWANA‡ 1970

MBUM
   HURAULT, -‡ CAMEROON‡

MBUUN
   MUSEE ROYAL DE L'AFRIQUE CENTRALE‡ ‡

MENDE
   AGINSKY, ETHEL G.‡ SIERRA LEONE-U.S.‡ 1933

   INNES, GORDON‡ SIERRA LEONE‡ 1963

   JOHNSON, GERALD T.‡ SIERRA LEONE‡ 1967-68

   KILSON, MARION D. DE B.‡ SIERRA LEONE‡ 1960

   MOORE, BAI T.‡ LIBERIA‡ 1962-73

   OKIE, PACKARD L.‡ LIBERIA‡ 1947-54

   VAN OVEN, JACOBA‡ SIERRA LEONE‡ 1964-67

   WYLIE, KENNETH CHARLES‡ SIERRA LEONE‡ 1965-66+
   1970

MERINA
   BLOCH, MONICA E.‡ MALAGASY REPUBLIC‡ 1964-71

   VERNIER, -‡ MALAGASY REPUBLIC‡

MERU
   LANGE, WERNER‡ ETHIOPIA‡ 1972-73

META
   KLEIS, GERALD W.‡ CAMEROON‡ 1971

MINA
    ROUGET, GILBERT+ TARDITS, CLAUDE+ VERGER, PIERRE‡
    DAHOMEY‡

MINIANKA
    ARCHIVES OF ETHNIC MUSIC AND DANCE‡ UPPER VOLTA‡

    BRASSEUR, G.+ DI DIO, FRANCOIS+ DIETERLEN,
    GERMAINE+ ROUGET, GILBERT‡ MALI‡

    CALAME, B.‡ MALI‡ 1956-57+ 1960

MISIWA
    WANKLYN, CHRISTOPHER‡ MOROCCO‡ 1963+ 1969

MONGO
    MUSEE ROYAL DE L'AFRIQUE CENTRALE‡ ‡

MONZOMBO
    BOUQUIAUX, LUC‡ CENTRAL AFRICAN REPUBLIC‡

MOSSI
    ALBERTS, ARTHUR S.‡ AFRICA-WEST‡ 1949

    ALBERTS, ARTHUR S.‡ UPPER VOLTA‡ 1949-51

    ARCHIVES OF ETHNIC MUSIC AND DANCE‡ UPPER VOLTA‡

    CHRISTIAN, VALERIE‡ UPPER VOLTA‡ 1973-74

    CHRISTIAN, VALERIE+ ROSELLINI, JAMES N.‡ UPPER
    VOLTA‡ 1973

    HALL, JOHN F.‡ UPPER VOLTA‡ 1962

    REDDEN, JAMES ERSKINE‡ UPPER VOLTA‡ 1962-63

    SKINNER, ELLIOTT P.‡ UPPER VOLTA‡ 1955-65

    SOCIETE DE RADIODIFFUSION DE LA FRANCE D'OUTRE
    MER‡ UPPER VOLTA‡

MOUNDANG
    ZEMPLEIVI, ANDRAS‡ CHAD‡ 1969

MUSEY
    GARINE, I. DE‡ CHAD‡ 1962-63+ 1965

MUSSEQUES
  DIAS, MARGOT‡ ANGOLA‡ 1960

MUSUJI
  BENDER, MARVIN LIONEL‡ ETHIOPIA‡ 1964-74

MWERA
  NATIONAL MUSEUM OF TANZANIA‡ TANZANIA‡

NAGO
  ROUGET, GILBERT‡ DAHOMEY‡ 1952

  ROUGET, GILBERT+ TARDITS, CLAUDE+ VERGER, PIERRE‡
  DAHOMEY‡

NANDE
  BIEBUYCK, DANIEL P.‡ ZAIRE‡ 1952-61

  MUSEE ROYAL DE L'AFRIQUE CENTRALE‡ ‡

NANKANI
  HANLEY, MARY ANN CSJ‡ GHANA‡ 1972

NDAU
  CAMP, CHARLES M.+ TRACEY, HUGH‡ RHODESIA‡ 1948

  CAMP, CHARLES M.+ TRACEY, HUGH‡ SOUTH AFRICA‡
  1947-48

  CURTIS, NATALIE‡ MOZAMBIQUE‡ CA1919

  TRADITIONAL MUSIC DOCUMENTATION PROJECT‡ RHODESIA‡

NDEBELE
  CAMP, CHARLES M.+ TRACEY, HUGH‡ RHODESIA‡ 1948

  DEPARTMENT OF AFRICAN LANGUAGES, UNIVERSITY OF
  RHODESIA‡ RHODESIA‡

  LEUSCHEL, DON‡ ‡ 1957-58

  NANCARROW, OWEN T.‡ RHODESIA‡ 1970-71

  SCHEUB, HAROLD‡ SOUTH AFRICA‡ 1972-73

NDOROBO
  GROHS, ELISABETH‡ TANZANIA‡ 1970

NGANGELA
   LIMA, AUGUSTO GUILHERME MESQUITELA‡ ANGOLA‡
   1963-70

NGAZIJA
   TUCKER, ARCHIBALD NORMAN‡ TANZANIA‡

NGBAKA-MABO
   AROM, SIMHA‡ CENTRAL AFRICAN REPUBLIC‡ 1964-67+
   1971-73

   BOUQUIAUX, LUC‡ CENTRAL AFRICAN REPUBLIC‡

NGEENDE
   QUERSIN, BENOIT J.‡ ZAIRE‡ 1970

NGONI
   DAVIDSON, MARJORY‡ ZAMBIA‡ 1967-71

   GEOFFRION, CHARLES A.‡ MALAWI‡ 1971-72

   GREENSTEIN, ROBERT CARL‡ MALAWI‡ 1971-75

NGURU
   GROHS, ELISABETH‡ TANZANIA‡ 1970

NJANJA
   TRADITIONAL MUSIC DOCUMENTATION PROJECT‡ RHODESIA‡

NKAMBE
   KLEIS, GERALD W.‡ CAMEROON‡ 1971

NKUNDU
   QUERSIN, BENOIT J.+ QUERSIN, CHRISTINE M.‡ ZAIRE‡
   1972

NONDOM
   CHRISTIAN, VALERIE‡ UPPER VOLTA‡ 1973-74

NSENGA
   APTHORPE, RAYMOND JAMES‡ ZAMBIA‡ 1961

   BLACKING, JOHN A.R.‡ ZAMBIA‡ 1957-61

NSUNGLI
   DUNGER, GEORGE A.‡ CAMEROON‡

NTOMBA
   QUERSIN, BENOIT J.‡ ZAIRE‡ 1970

OULED—MTAA
  WANKLYN, CHRISTOPHER‡ MOROCCO‡ 1963+ 1969

OVAMBO
  GERSON-KIWI, EDITH‡ NAMIBIA‡ 1955

OVIMBUNDU
  CHILDS, GLADWYN‡ ANGOLA‡ 1962

  HAMBLY, WILFRED D.‡ ANGOLA‡ 1929-30

  HENDERSON, LAWRENCE‡ ANGOLA‡ 1972

OWAN
  DEPARTMENT OF LINGUISTICS AND NIGERIAN LANGUAGES,
  UNIVERSITY OF IBADAN‡ NIGERIA‡ 1967-73

PABIR
  WOLFF, HANS‡ NIGERIA‡ 1953-54

PEDI
  CAMP, CHARLES M.+ TRACEY, HUGH‡ RHODESIA‡ 1948

  TUCKER, ARCHIBALD NORMAN‡ SOUTH AFRICA‡

PENDE
  MUSEE ROYAL DE L'AFRIQUE CENTRALE‡ ‡

PEUL
  BRASSEUR, G.+ DI DIO, FRANCOIS+ DIETERLEN,
  GERMAINE+ ROUGET, GILBERT‡ MALI‡

  CALAME, B.‡ MALI‡ 1956-57+ 1960

  DIETERLEN, GERMAINE‡ MALI‡ 1960

  DUMONT, LILLIAN E.‡ SENEGAL‡ 1973

  GUIGNARD, AUDE‡ SENEGAL‡ 1968

  QUERSIN, BENOIT J.+ QUERSIN, CHRISTINE M.‡
  CAMEROON‡ 1967

  ROUGET, GILBERT‡ GUINEA‡

  ROUGET, GILBERT‡ SENEGAL‡

  ROUGET, GILBERT‡ SENEGAL‡ 1952

PEUL
  SCHWEEGER-HEFEL, ANNEMARIE‡ UPPER VOLTA‡

  SCHWEEGER-HEFEL, ANNEMARIE‡ UPPER VOLTA‡ 1961-69

POKOMO
  BUNGER, ROBERT LOUIS‡ KENYA‡ 1969-70

POKOT
  ROBBIN, LAWRENCE H.‡ UGANDA‡ 1970

PONDO
  CAMP, CHARLES M.+ TRACEY, HUGH‡ SOUTH AFRICA‡
  1947-48

POUGOULIS
  CHRISTIAN, VALERIE‡ UPPER VOLTA‡ 1973-74

PULAR
  CURTIN, PHILIP D.‡ SENEGAL‡ 1966

  CURTIN, PHILIP D.‡ SENEGAL‡ 1966

  ROBINSON, DAVID W.‡ SENEGAL‡ 1968-69

PYAANG
  QUERSIN, BENOIT J.‡ ZAIRE‡ 1970

PYEM
  QUERSIN, BENOIT J.+ QUERSIN, CHRISTINE M.‡
  NIGERIA‡ 1972-73

PYGMIES
  CLAUSS, BERNHARD PETER‡ ZAIRE‡ 1973

  PRUITT, WILLIAM F., JR.‡ ZAIRE‡ 1966-67

  QUERSIN, BENOIT J.+ QUERSIN, CHRISTINE M.‡
  CAMEROON‡ 1967

PYGMIES-BATWA
  QUERSIN, BENOIT J.+ QUERSIN, CHRISTINE M.‡ ZAIRE‡
  1972

PYGMIES-NGOMBE
  QUERSIN, BENOIT J.+ QUERSIN, CHRISTINE M.‡ ZAIRE‡
  1972

PYGMIES-NGOUNDI
  ROUGET, GILBERT‡ CONGO, PEOPLE'S REPUBLIC OF THE‡
  1948

RAMBA
  CAMP, CHARLES M.+ TRACEY, HUGH‡ RHODESIA‡ 1948

RINDRE
  QUERSIN, BENOIT J.+ QUERSIN, CHRISTINE M.‡
  NIGERIA‡ 1972-73

RIWAIBE
  SCHWEEGER-HEFEL, ANNEMARIE‡ UPPER VOLTA‡ 1961-69

ROLONG
  TLOU, THOMAS‡ BOTSWANA‡ 1970

RONGA
  RADIO CLUBE DE MOCAMBIQUE‡ MOZAMBIQUE‡

RUNDI
  MUSEE ROYAL DE L'AFRIQUE CENTRALE‡ ‡

RWANDA
  MUSEE ROYAL DE L'AFRIQUE CENTRALE‡ ‡

RYMAYBE
  BRASSEUR, G.+ DI DIO, FRANCOIS+ DIETERLEN,
  GERMAINE+ ROUGET, GILBERT‡ MALI‡

  CALAME, B.‡ MALI‡ 1956-57+ 1960

SAHEL
  ABUZAHRA, NADIA‡ TUNISIA‡ 1966

SAI
  BENDER, MARVIN LIONEL‡ ETHIOPIA‡ 1964-74

SAKALAVA
  LOMBARD, JACQUES‡ MALAGASY REPUBLIC‡ 1969-74

  VERNIER, -‡ MALAGASY REPUBLIC‡

SALAMPASU
  GANSEMANS, JOS‡ ZAIRE‡ 1970-73

  PRUITT, WILLIAM F., JR.‡ ZAIRE‡ 1966-67

SAMBURU
  DOHERTY, DEBORAH‡ KENYA‡ 1973

SAMO
  BROEKHUYSE, JAN T.‡ UPPER VOLTA‡ 1969

  ECHENBERG, MYRON J.‡ UPPER VOLTA‡ 1967

  KONINKLIJK INSTITUUT‡ UPPER VOLTA‡

SAMO-DU-SUD
  CHRISTIAN, VALERIE‡ UPPER VOLTA‡ 1973-74

SAN
  SMITS, LUCAS GERARDUS ALFONSUS‡ BOTSWANA‡ 1972

SANAGA
  QUERSIN, BENOIT J.+ QUERSIN, CHRISTINE M.‡
  CAMEROON‡ 1967

SANDAWE
  DEMPWOLFF, OTTO‡ TANZANIA‡ 1910

  TENRAA, ERIC WILLIAM FREDERICK‡ TANZANIA‡ 1958-66

  TUCKER, ARCHIBALD NORMAN‡ TANZANIA‡

SANGA
  MUSEE ROYAL DE L'AFRIQUE CENTRALE‡ ‡

SANYE
  TUCKER, ARCHIBALD NORMAN‡ TANZANIA‡

SARA-DEME
  JAULIN, -‡ CHAD‡

SARAKABA
  CLAUSS, BERNHARD PETER‡ CHAD‡ 1973

SARAKOLE
  BRASSEUR, G.+ DI DIO, FRANCOIS+ DIETERLEN,
  GERMAINE+ ROUGET, GILBERT‡ MALI‡

  CALAME, B.‡ MALI‡ 1956-57+ 1960

  HERBIN, -‡ SENEGAL‡

  ROUGET, GILBERT‡ SENEGAL‡ 1952

SEKA
  LANGE, WERNER‡ ETHIOPIA‡ 1972-73

SENA-TONGA
  TRADITIONAL MUSIC DOCUMENTATION PROJECT‡ RHODESIA‡

SENUFO
  ARCHIVES OF ETHNIC MUSIC AND DANCE‡ UPPER VOLTA‡

  GLAZE, ANITA‡ IVORY COAST‡ 1969-70

  HIMMELHEBER, HANS G.‡ IVORY COAST‡ 1952-65

  RAYFIELD, JOAN R.‡ IVORY COAST‡ 1972-73

  ZEMP, HUGO‡ IVORY COAST‡ 1962+ 1964-67

SENUFO-NA-FAARA
  ZEMPLEIVI, ANDRAS‡ IVORY COAST‡ 1972-74

SEPHARDIC-JEW
  ARMISTEAD, SAMUEL G. + KATZ, ISRAEL J. +
  SILVERMAN, JOSEPH H.‡ MOROCCO‡ 1962

SERER
  HERBIN, -‡ SENEGAL‡

  KLEIN, MARTIN A.‡ SENEGAL‡ 1963-64

  VAILLANT, JANET G.‡ SENEGAL‡ 1973

SETTLERS-AFRICAN
  FETTER, BRUCE‡ ZAIRE‡ 1972-73

SHANGAAN
  CAMP, CHARLES M.+ TRACEY, HUGH‡ SOUTH AFRICA‡
  1947-48

SHE
  LANGE, WERNER‡ ETHIOPIA‡ 1972-73

SHERBRO
  ROGERS, HENRY EDWIN‡ SIERRA LEONE‡ 1966

  VAN OVEN, JACOBA‡ SIERRA LEONE‡ 1964-67

SHI
  MUSEE ROYAL DE L'AFRIQUE CENTRALE‡ ‡

SHI
  SIGWALT, RICHARD‡ SOSNE, ELINOR‡ ZAIRE‡ 1971-73

SHILLUK
  CARLISLE, ROXANE C.‡ SUDAN‡ 1963

  CARLISLE, ROXANE C.‡ SUDAN‡

  TUCKER, ARCHIBALD NORMAN‡ SUDAN‡

SHOA-GALLA
  LESLAU, WOLF‡ ETHIOPIA‡ 1947

SHONA
  BERLINER, PAUL FRANKLIN‡ RHODESIA‡ 1972

  DEPARTMENT OF AFRICAN LANGUAGES, UNIVERSITY OF
  RHODESIA‡ RHODESIA‡

  KAEMMER, JOHN E.‡ RHODESIA‡ 1972-73

  KAUFFMAN, ROBERT A.‡ RHODESIA‡ 1960-65, 1971

  KRIEL, A.P.‡ RHODESIA‡ 1966

  MARAIRE, DUMISANI ABRAHAM‡ RHODESIA‡ 1971+ 1974

  RHODES, WILLARD‡ RHODESIA‡ 1958-59

  RHODES, WILLARD‡ ZAMBIA‡ 1958-59

SHOOWA
  QUERSIN, BENOIT J.‡ ZAIRE‡ 1970

SIDAMO
  BROGGER, JAN C.‡ ETHIOPIA‡

  TSEHAI, BRHANE SILASSIE‡ ETHIOPIA‡ 1969-73

SOBO
  WOLFF, HANS‡ NIGERIA‡ 1953-54

SOCE
  ROUGET, GILBERT‡ SENEGAL‡ 1952

SOLI
  ARGYLE, WILLIAM JOHNSON‡ ZAMBIA‡ 1957-59

SOMALI
  JOHNSON, JOHN W. ǂ SOMALIAǂ 1966-69

  LESLAU, WOLFǂ ETHIOPIAǂ 1947

  LEVINE, WILLIAM J.ǂ SOMALIAǂ 1962

  MARING, JOELǂ SOMALIAǂ 1959

  PIA, JOSEPH J.ǂ SOMALIAǂ 1962

SOMONO
  BRASSEUR, G.+ DI DIO, FRANCOIS+ DIETERLEN,
  GERMAINE+ ROUGET, GILBERTǂ MALIǂ

  CALAME, B.ǂ MALIǂ 1956-57+ 1960

SONGHAY
  BRASSEUR, G.+ DI DIO, FRANCOIS+ DIETERLEN,
  GERMAINE+ ROUGET, GILBERTǂ MALIǂ

  CALAME, B.ǂ MALIǂ 1956-57+ 1960

  ROUCH, JEANǂ NIGERǂ

  SARDAN, J.-P. OLIVIER DEǂ NIGERǂ 1969

SONGO
  ESTES, RICHARD D.ǂ ANGOLAǂ 1970

SONINKE
  CURTIN, PHILIP D.ǂ SENEGALǂ 1966

  HRBEK, IVANǂ SENEGALǂ

SONRAI
  BERNUS, S.+ ROUCH, JEANǂ NIGERǂ 1960

SOTHO
  AFRICANA MUSEUMǂ SOUTH AFRICAǂ

  CAMP, CHARLES M.+ TRACEY, HUGHǂ SOUTH AFRICAǂ
  1947-48

  TUCKER, ARCHIBALD NORMANǂ SOUTH AFRICAǂ

SUBA
  KIRWEN, MICHAEL CARL ǂ TANZANIAǂ 1963-69

TAMAZIGT
  LORTAT-JACOB, BERNARD‡ MOROCCO‡ 1969-73

TANALA
  BLOCH, MONICA E.‡ MALAGASY REPUBLIC‡ 1964-71

  VERNIER, -‡ MALAGASY REPUBLIC‡

TASLHIT
  LORTAT-JACOB, BERNARD‡ MOROCCO‡ 1969-73

TEDA
  BRANDILY, MONIQUE‡ CHAD‡ 1961+ 1963+ 1965

  BRANDILY, MONIQUE‡ CHAD‡ 1969

  BRANDILY, MONIQUE‡ LIBYA‡ 1969

TEKE
  THIEL, JOSEF FRANZ‡ ZAIRE‡ 1961-71

TEMNE
  BAHMAN, GARY‡ SIERRA LEONE‡ 1971

  GEOFFRION, CHARLES A.‡ SIERRA LEONE‡ 1966-67

  IJAGBEMI, ELIJAH A.‡ SIERRA LEONE‡ 1965-67

  JOHNSON, GERALD T.‡ SIERRA LEONE‡ 1967-68

  KNIGHT, RODERIC COPLEY‡ GAMBIA, THE‡ 1970-71

  VAN OVEN, JACOBA‡ SIERRA LEONE‡ 1964-67

TENDA
  CENTRE DE RECHERCHES ANTHROPOLOGIQUES‡ SENEGAL‡

TEPETH
  TUCKER, ARCHIBALD NORMAN‡ UGANDA‡

TESHENNA
  MULDROW, WILLIAM+ MULDROW, ELIZABETH‡ ETHIOPIA‡
  1964-65

TESO
  BYRD, ROBERT OAKES‡ UGANDA‡

  TUCKER, ARCHIBALD NORMAN‡ UGANDA‡

TETELA
  MUSEE ROYAL DE L'AFRIQUE CENTRALE‡ ‡

TIGRE
  MAGYAR TUDOMANYOS AKADEMIA NEPZENEKUTATO CSOPORT‡
  ETHIOPIA‡

  MESSING, SIMON D.‡ ETHIOPIA‡ 1961-67

TIGRINYA
  ARCHIVES OF ETHNIC MUSIC AND DANCE‡ ETHIOPIA‡

  COURLANDER, HAROLD‡ ETHIOPIA‡ 1943

  HICKERSON, NANCY+ HYMES, VIRGINIA+ KELLER, JAMES‡
  -U.S.‡ 1954

  LESLAU, WOLF‡ ETHIOPIA‡ 1947

TIKAR
  QUERSIN, BENOIT J.+ QUERSIN, CHRISTINE M.‡
  CAMEROON‡ 1967

TIKARI
  RUBIN, ARNOLD G.‡ NIGERIA‡ 1964-65

TINDIGA
  MALER, THOMAS A.‡ TANZANIA‡ 1967-68

TIV
  INSTITUTE OF AFRICAN STUDIES, UNIVERSITY OF IFE‡
  NIGERIA‡

  KEIL, CHARLES‡ NIGERIA‡

  KIRK-GREENE, ANTHONY H.M.‡ NIGERIA‡ 1962-65

  PLOTNICOV, LEONARD‡ NIGERIA‡ 1961-62

  QUERSIN, BENOIT J.+ QUERSIN, CHRISTINE M.‡
  NIGERIA‡ 1972-73

  RHODES, WILLARD‡ NIGERIA‡ 1973-74

  RUBIN, ARNOLD G.‡ NIGERIA‡ 1964-65

  TRADITIONAL MUSIC DOCUMENTATION PROJECT‡ NIGERIA‡

TOMA
  GAISSEAU, PIERRE-DOMINIQUE‡ GUINEA‡ 1953

TONGA
  CAMP, CHARLES M.+ TRACEY, HUGH‡ ZAMBIA‡ 1947-48

  KINBADE, M. DALE‡ ‡ 1960

  REDDEN, JAMES ERSKINE‡ ‡ 1959-60

  VANVELSEN, J.‡ MALAWI‡ 1960

  WILSON, VIVIAN J.‡ RHODESIA‡ 1970

TONGA-GWEMBE
  BLACKING, JOHN A.R.‡ ZAMBIA‡ 1957-61

TSAMAY
  BENDER, MARVIN LIONEL‡ ETHIOPIA‡ 1964-74

TSONGA
  JOHNSTON, THOMAS FREDERICK‡ MOZAMBIQUE‡ 1968-70

  JOHNSTON, THOMAS FREDERICK‡ SOUTH AFRICA‡ 1968-70

TSWANA
  AFRICANA MUSEUM‡ SOUTH AFRICA‡

  CAMP, CHARLES M.+ TRACEY, HUGH‡ SOUTH AFRICA‡
  1947-48

  ENGLAND, NICHOLAS M.‡ BOTSWANA‡ 1957-61

  TLOU, THOMAS‡ BOTSWANA‡ 1970

  TUCKER, ARCHIBALD NORMAN‡ SOUTH AFRICA‡

TUAREG
  BAIER, STEPHEN B.‡ NIGER‡ 1972

  BOURGEOT, A.‡ ALGERIA‡ 1970

  CARD, CAROLINE E.‡ ALGERIA‡ 1972

  HOLIDAY, GEOFFREY D.‡ ALGERIA‡ CA1958

  HOLIDAY, GEOFFREY D.‡ NIGER‡ CA1958

  LHOTE, HENRI JACQUES‡ ‡

UTTAR-PRADESH
  UPADHYAYA, HARI S.+ ORI, R.‡ MAURITIUS‡ 1961

VACANDA
  RADIO CLUBE DE MOCAMBIQUE‡ MOZAMBIQUE‡

VAI
  D'AZEVEDO, WARREN L.‡ LIBERIA‡ 1956-58+ 1966

  D'AZEVEDO, WARREN L.‡ LIBERIA‡ 1960

  HOLSOE, SVEND E.‡ LIBERIA‡ 1965-70

  MOORE, BAI T.‡ LIBERIA‡ 1962-73

  OFRI, DORITH‡ LIBERIA‡ 1965-72

  OKIE, PACKARD L.‡ LIBERIA‡ 1947-54

  OKIE, PACKARD L.‡ LIBERIA‡ 1947-54

  VAN OVEN, JACOBA‡ SIERRA LEONE‡ 1964-67

VANDAU
  RADIO CLUBE DE MOCAMBIQUE‡ MOZAMBIQUE‡

VATSUA
  RADIO CLUBE DE MOCAMBIQUE‡ MOZAMBIQUE‡

VATWA
  GIBSON, GORDON D.‡ ANGOLA‡ 1971-73

VENDA
  BLACKING, JOHN A.R.‡ SOUTH AFRICA‡ 1956-59

  CAMP, CHARLES M.+ TRACEY, HUGH‡ SOUTH AFRICA‡
  1947-48

  WEMAN, HENRY PAUL‡ RHODESIA‡ 1957

  WEMAN, HENRY PAUL‡ SOUTH AFRICA‡ 1956-57

VENGO
  VAUGHAN, JAMES H.‡ NIGERIA‡ 1960

VEZO
  KOECHLIN, B.‡ MALAGASY REPUBLIC‡ 1967-69

VOLTAIC
  ELLOVICH, RISA SUE‡ IVORY COAST‡ 1973-74

VUTE
  QUERSIN, BENOIT J.+ QUERSIN, CHRISTINE M.‡
  CAMEROON‡ 1967

  RAPHAEL, RONALD P.‡ CAMEROON‡ 1974

WALA
  FIKRY, MONA‡ GHANA‡ 1966-67

WANJI
  GARLAND, WILLIAM‡ TANZANIA‡ 1963-65

WANYAMWEZI
  UHLIG, -‡ TANZANIA‡ 1910

WAWA
  RAPHAEL, RONALD P.‡ CAMEROON‡ 1974

WEMBA
  CAMP, CHARLES M.+ TRACEY, HUGH‡ RHODESIA‡ 1948

WIDEKUM
  KLEIS, GERALD W.‡ CAMEROON‡ 1971

WOBE
  BLANK, ARTHUR S., JR.+ BLANK, DONNA H.‡ IVORY
  COAST‡ 1973

WOLAMO
  TSEHAI, BRHANE SILASSIE‡ ETHIOPIA‡ 1969-73

WOLOF
  AMES, DAVID W.‡ GAMBIA, THE‡ 1951

  AMES, DAVID W.‡ SENEGAL‡ 1950-51

  CHARLES, EUNICE A.‡ SENEGAL‡ 1970-71

  DUMONT, LILLIAN E.‡ SENEGAL‡ 1973

  IRVINE, JUDITH TEMKIN‡ SENEGAL‡ 1970-71

  KLEIN, MARTIN A.‡ SENEGAL‡ 1963-64

  KNIGHT, RODERIC COPLEY‡ GAMBIA, THE‡ 1970-71

WOLOF
  KNIGHT, RODERIC COPLEY‡ SENEGAL‡ 1970-71

  ROUGET, GILBERT‡ SENEGAL‡

  ROUGET, GILBERT‡ SENEGAL‡ 1952

XHOSA
  CAMP, CHARLES M.+ TRACEY, HUGH‡ SOUTH AFRICA‡
  1947-48

  KRIEL, A.P.‡ SOUTH AFRICA‡ 1973

  OPLAND, JEFFREY‡ SOUTH AFRICA‡ 1969-73

  SCHEUB, HAROLD‡ SOUTH AFRICA‡ 1967-68

  SCHEUB, HAROLD‡ SOUTH AFRICA‡ 1972-73

  TUCKER, ARCHIBALD NORMAN‡ SOUTH AFRICA‡

  VERSFELD, BARBARA‡ SOUTH AFRICA‡ 1965

YALA
  COLLEGE OF MUSIC, UNIVERSITY OF NIGERIA‡ NIGERIA‡

YALUNKA
  VAN OVEN, JACOBA‡ SIERRA LEONE‡ 1964-67

YANSI
  THIEL, JOSEF FRANZ‡ ZAIRE‡ 1961-71

YAO
  CAMP, CHARLES M.+ TRACEY, HUGH‡ RHODESIA‡ 1948

  DRAKE, H. MAX‡ MALAWI‡ 1967

  GREENSTEIN, ROBERT CARL‡ MALAWI‡ 1971-75

  NATIONAL MUSEUM OF TANZANIA‡ TANZANIA‡

YARDSE
  ARCHIVES OF ETHNIC MUSIC AND DANCE‡ UPPER VOLTA‡

  CHRISTIAN, VALERIE‡ UPPER VOLTA‡ 1973-74

YATYE
  STAHLKE, HERBERT F.W.‡ NIGERIA‡ 1966-67

YEI
  LAMBRECHT, FRANK L.+ LAMBRECHT, DORA J.M.‡
  BOTSWANA‡ 1967-68

  TLOU, THOMAS‡ BOTSWANA‡ 1970

  WESTPHAL, ERNST O.J.‡ BOTSWANA‡ 1953-74

YEKE
  DEPLAEN, GUY‡ ZAIRE‡ 1973-74

  MUSEE ROYAL DE L'AFRIQUE CENTRALE‡ ‡

YERGAM
  QUERSIN, BENOIT J.+ QUERSIN, CHRISTINE M.‡
  NIGERIA‡ 1972-73

YORUBA
  ABIMBOLA, WANDE‡ NIGERIA‡ 1971

  AMES, DAVID W.‡ NIGERIA‡ 1963-64

  ARCHIVES OF TRADITIONAL MUSIC‡ ‡ CA1940

  ARMSTRONG, ROBERT G.‡ NIGERIA‡

  ARMSTRONG, ROBERT G.‡ NIGERIA‡

  ARMSTRONG, ROBERT G.‡ NIGERIA‡ 1962

  AWE, BOLANLE ALAKE‡ NIGERIA‡ 1972-74

  BABALOLA, ADEBOYE‡ NIGERIA‡ 1962-74

  BALOGUN, ADISA‡ NIGERIA‡ 1964+ 1970

  BALOGUN, ADISA‡ NIGERIA‡ 1967

  BARNES, SANDRA THEIS‡ NIGERIA‡ 1972

  BEIER, ULLI+ ROUGET, GILBERT‡ NIGERIA‡

  BOAS, FRANZ‡ NIGERIA-U.S.‡ 1933

  CALKINS, HOWARD W.+ RADIO DAHOMEY‡ DAHOMEY‡
  CA1967

  COLLEGE OF MUSIC, UNIVERSITY OF NIGERIA‡ NIGERIA‡

YORUBA

DEPARTMENT OF LINGUISTICS AND NIGERIAN LANGUAGES,.
UNIVERSITY OF IBADAN‡ NIGERIA‡ 1967-73

DREWAL, HENRY JOHN‡ DAHOMEY‡ 1973

DREWAL, HENRY JOHN‡ NIGERIA‡ 1970-71

DUMONT, LILLIAN E.‡ DAHOMEY‡ 1973

ECHEZONA, WILLIAM WILBERFORCE CHUKUDINKA‡ NIGERIA‡
1950-75

ELWA STUDIO, NIGERIA‡ NIGERIA‡

ENGLAND, NICHOLAS M.‡ NIGERIA‡ 1969-70+ 1972

GLEASON, JUDITH+ OGUNDIPE, JOHN‡ NIGERIA‡ 1970

HANLEY, MARY ANN CSJ‡ NIGERIA‡ 1973

HARRIS, JOHN REES‡ NIGERIA‡ 1965

HERSKOVITS, MELVILLE J.+ HERSKOVITS, FRANCES S.‡
NIGERIA‡ 1931

HOPKINS, JERRY‡ ‡ 1956

INSTITUTE OF AFRICAN STUDIES, UNIVERSITY OF IFE‡
NIGERIA‡

ISOLA, AKINWUMI‡ NIGERIA‡ 1968-74

KEIL, CHARLES‡ NIGERIA‡

KOIZUMI, FUMIO‡ NIGERIA‡ 1971

LA PIN, DIERDRE A.‡ NIGERIA‡ 1972-73

QUERSIN, BENOIT J.+ QUERSIN, CHRISTINE M.‡
NIGERIA‡ 1972-73

RHODES, WILLARD‡ NIGERIA‡ 1973-74

RIGGS, VENDA‡ NIGERIA‡ 1949

ROUGET, GILBERT‡ DAHOMEY‡ 1952-71

SHEFFIELD, JAMES‡ DAHOMEY‡ 1971+ 1973

YORUBA
  SHEFFIELD, JAMES‡ NIGERIA‡ 1971

  SIEBER, ROY‡ NIGERIA‡ 1971

  SKINNER, A. NEIL‡ SKINNER, MARGARET G.‡ NIGERIA‡
  1967-74

  SPEED, FRANCIS E.‡ NIGERIA‡ 1966

  SPEED, FRANCIS E.‡ THIEME, DARIUS L.‡ NIGERIA‡
  1966

  THIEME, DARIUS L.‡ NIGERIA‡ 1964-66

  TRADITIONAL MUSIC DOCUMENTATION PROJECT‡ NIGERIA‡

  TRAGER, LILLIAN‡ NIGERIA‡ 1974

  WELCH, DAVID B.‡ NIGERIA‡ 1970-71

  WEMAN, PAUL HENRY‡ NIGERIA‡ 1957

  WILLETT, FRANK‡ NIGERIA‡ 1972

  WITTIG, R. CURT‡ NIGERIA‡ 1965

  WOLFF, HANS‡ NIGERIA‡ 1953-54

  WOLFF, HANS‡ NIGERIA-U.S.‡ 1960-64

ZABEBMAWA
  COLLEGE OF MUSIC, UNIVERSITY OF NIGERIA‡ NIGERIA‡

ZAMBE
  BIEBUYCK, DANIEL P.‡ ZAIRE‡ 1952-61

ZANDE
  KUBIK, GERHARD‡ CENTRAL AFRICAN REPUBLIC‡

  MISSION SOCIOLOGIQUE DU HAUTE-OUBANGUI‡ CENTRAL
  AFRICAN REPUBLIC‡

  TUCKER, ARCHIBALD NORMAN‡ SUDAN‡

ZARAMO
  ALPERS, EDWARD ALTER‡ TANZANIA‡ 1972-73

  DEMPWOLFF, OTTO‡ TANZANIA‡ 1910

ZARAS
  LANGE, WERNER‡ ETHIOPIA‡ 1972-73

ZEZURU
  KAEMMER, JOHN E.‡ RHODESIA‡ 1972-73

  TRADITIONAL MUSIC DOCUMENTATION PROJECT‡ RHODESIA‡

ZIGUA
  GROHS, ELISABETH‡ TANZANIA‡ 1970

ZIMBA
  GIBSON, GORDON D.‡ ANGOLA‡ 1971-73

ZINZA
  CAMP, CHARLES M.+ TRACEY, HUGH‡ ZAMBIA‡ 1947-48

  SCHWARTZ, -‡ TANZANIA‡ 1906

ZULU
  AFRICANA MUSEUM‡ SOUTH AFRICA‡

  COPE, TREVOR ANTHONY‡ SOUTH AFRICA‡ 1965-72

  CURTIS, NATALIE‡ SOUTH AFRICA‡ CA1919

  HANLEY, -‡ SOUTH AFRICA‡

  HENRY, JULES‡ SOUTH AFRICA-U.S.‡ 1935

  KRIEL, A.P.‡ SOUTH AFRICA‡ 1973

  LEUSCHEL, DON‡ ‡ 1957-58

  LOUDON, JOSEPH BUIST‡ SOUTH AFRICA‡ 1952

  MISJONSSKOLEN‡ SOUTH AFRICA‡

  OPLAND, JEFFREY‡ SOUTH AFRICA‡ 1969-73

  SCHEUB, HAROLD‡ SOUTH AFRICA‡ 1967-68

  SCHEUB, HAROLD‡ SOUTH AFRICA‡ 1972-73

  TUCKER, ARCHIBALD NORMAN‡ SOUTH AFRICA‡

  WEMAN, HENRY PAUL‡ RHODESIA‡ 1957

  WEMAN, HENRY PAUL‡ SOUTH AFRICA‡ 1956-57

Abatutsi	see also	Batutsi, Tutsi
Achewa	see also	Chewa
Adyukru	see	Adioukrou
Aja	see	Adja
Aka	see also	Pygmies
Akamba	see also	Kamba
Ankole	see	Banyankole
Ashanti	see	Asante
Azande	see also	Zande
Baganda	see also	Ganda
Bagisu	see also	Gisu
Bagogwe	see	Abagogwe
Bagoyi	see	Abagoyi
Bahema	see	Bahima
Bahororo	see	Abahororo
Bahutu	see also	Hutu
Bakongo	see also	Kongo
Bakuba	see also	Kuba
Baluba	see also	Luba
Bambara	see also	Dyula, Malinke, Mandingo, Mandinka
Bandi	see	Gbande
Banyambo	see	Abanyambo
Banyarwanda	see also	Rwanda
Baoule	see	Baule
Barundi	see also	Rundi
Bashi	see also	Shi
Basotho	see also	Basuto, Sotho
Basuku	see also	Suku
Basukuma	see also	Sukuma
Basuto	see also	Basotho, Sotho
Batua	see	Batwa
Batutsi	see also	Abatutsi, Tutsi
Batwa	see also	Pygmies, Twa
Bayovu	see	Abayovu
Belle	see	Bele
Boma	see	Baboma
Bushmen	see also	Kung-Bushmen
Cewa	see	Achewa, Chewa
Chewa	see also	Achewa
Dan	see also	Gio
Diola	see also	Jola
Dioula	see	Dyula
Dyola	see	Diola
Dyula	see also	Bambara, Malinke, Mandingo, Mandinka
Foulah	see	Fula
Fula	see also	Fulani, Fulbe, Peul
Fulani	see also	Fula, Fulbe, Peul
Fulbe	see also	Fula, Fulani, Peul

Ganda	see	also	Baganda
Gio	see	also	Dan
Gisu	see	also	Bagisu
Gogwe	see		Abagogwe
Goyi	see		Abagoyi
Gwere	see		Bagwere
Havu	see		Bahavu
Hororo	see		Abahororo
Hutu	see	also	Bahutu
Ibo	see	also	Igbo
Igbo	see	also	Ibo
Ijaw	see	also	Ijo
Ijo	see	also	Ijaw
Jola	see	also	Diola
Kamba	see	also	Akamba
Kiga	see		Bakiga
Koga	see		Bakoga
Kongo	see	also	Bakongo
Konjo	see		Bakonjo
Kuba	see	also	Bakuba
Kundu	see		Bakundu
Kung-Bushmen	see	also	Bushmen
Kutu	see		Bakutu
Loma	see	also	Toma
Luba	see	also	Baluba
Malinke	see	also	Bambara, Dyula, Mandingo, Mandinka
Mandingo	see	also	Bambara, Dyula, Malinke, Mandinka
Mandinka	see	also	Bambara, Dyula, Malinke, Mandingo
Mbuti	see		Bambuti
Ngala	see		Bangala
Nkundo	see		Lonkundo
Nyambo	see		Abanyambo
Nyankole	see		Banyankole
Peul	see	also	Fula, Fulani, Fulbe
Pygmies	see	also	Aka, Batwa, Twa
Rundi	see	also	Barundi
Rwanda	see	also	Banyarwanda
Sengele	see		Basengele
Senoufo	see		Senufo
Shi	see	also	Bashi
Sidama	see		Sidamo
Songe	see		Basongye
Sotho	see	also	Basotho, Basuto
Suku	see	also	Basuku
Sukuma	see	also	Basukuma
Tchokwe	see		Chokwe
Toma	see	also	Loma

Tutsi	see also	Abatutsi, Batutsi
Twa	see also	Batwa, Pygmies
Tyo	see	Atyo
Watutsi	see	Abatutsi, Batutsi, Tutsi
Yovu	see	Abayovu
Zande	see also	Azande

Index to
Subjects

Index to Subjects

ACCORDION
  KOECHLIN, B.‡ MALAGASY REPUBLIC‡ MAHAFALY,
  MASIKORO, VEZO‡ 1967-69

AEROPHONE
  ALBERTS, ARTHUR S.‡ GHANA‡ EWE, GA, IBO, TWI‡
  1949-51

  AMES, DAVID W.‡ NIGERIA‡ HAUSA‡ 1963

  FEDERAL DEPARTMENT OF ANTIQUITIES, NATIONAL
  MUSEUM, KADUNA‡ NIGERIA‡ ELOYI, GEDE‡

  LESLAU, WOLF‡ ETHIOPIA‡ AMHARA, GURAGE, HARARI,
  SHOA-GALLA, SOMALI, TIGRINYA‡ 1947

  SMEND, W.A.‡ TOGO‡ HAUSA‡ 1905

AEROPHONE-DOUBLE-REED
  RHODES, WILLARD‡ NIGERIA‡ FULANI, HAUSA, TIV,
  TUAREG, YORUBA‡ 1973-74

AEROPHONE-POT
  MERRIAM, ALAN P.+ MERRIAM, BARBARA W.‡ ZAIRE‡
  BAHIMA, BAKOGA, BAKONGO, BAMBUTI, BANGALA, BASHI,
  BATWA, EKONDA‡ 1951-52

AEROPHONE-REED
  ARCHIVES OF ETHNIC MUSIC AND DANCE‡ UPPER VOLTA‡

AEROPHONE-REED
  BOBO, BWABA, DYULA, FULANI, FULBE, GOUIN,
  GOURMANTCHE, LOBI, MINIANKA, MOSSI, SENUFO,
  YARDSE‡

AGE-GRADE-CEREMONY
  HEAD, SYDNEY W.‡ ETHIOPIA‡ ‡ 1964

AGE-SET
  QUERSIN, BENOIT J.+ QUERSIN, CHRISTINE M.‡ ZAIRE‡
  BAKUTU, BOKOTE, BONGANDO, BOSAKA, BOYELA, NKUNDU,
  PYGMIES-BATWA, PYGMIES-NGOMBE‡ 1972

ANCESTOR-CEREMONY
  CAMP, CHARLES M.+ TRACEY, HUGH‡ RHODESIA‡ BUDJA,
  CHIKUNDA, FUNGWE, HERA, HUNGWE, KARANGA, NDAU,
  NDEBELE, NYANJA, NYASA, PEDI, RAMBA, WEMBA, YAO‡
  1948

ANCESTOR-INVOCATION
  QUERSIN, BENOIT J.+ QUERSIN, CHRISTINE M.‡ ZAIRE‡
  BATWA, BOLIA, EKONDA‡ 1971

ANCESTOR-RITUAL
  CARLISLE, ROXANE C.‡ SUDAN‡ ANUAK, DINKA, GAALIIN,
  NUER, SHILLUK‡ 1963

ANCESTOR-WORSHIP
  GROHS, ELISABETH‡ TANZANIA‡ NDOROBO, NGURU, ZIGUA‡
  1970

ANTHEM-NATIONAL-ZAIRE
  MERRIAM, ALAN P.‡ ZAIRE‡ BASONGYE‡ 1973

ARTIST
  SHEFFIELD, JAMES‡ DAHOMEY‡ YORUBA‡ 1971+ 1973

ASSOCIATION-ATEPYA
  SULZMANN, ERIKA‡ ZAIRE‡ BABOMA, BASENGELE, BOLIA,
  EKONDA, NTOMBA‡ 1953-72

AUTOBIOGRAPHY
  DRAKE, H. MAX‡ MALAWI‡ TUMBUKA, YAO‡ 1967

  HENDERSON, LAWRENCE‡ ANGOLA‡ OVIMBUNDU‡ 1972

  SMOCK, DAVID R.‡ NIGERIA‡ IBO‡ 1962-63

AUTOBIOGRAPHY-MUSICIAN
  KNIGHT, RODERIC COPLEY‡ GAMBIA, THE‡ BALANTA,
  BAMBARA, FULA, JOLA, MANDINKA, TEMNE, WOLOF‡
  1970-71

BALLAD
  SEDLAK, PHILIP A.S.‡ KENYA‡ DURUMA, GIRYAMA,
  SWAHILI‡ 1971

BALLAD-SPANISH
  ARMISTEAD, SAMUEL G. + KATZ, ISRAEL J. +
  SILVERMAN, JOSEPH H.‡ MOROCCO‡ SEPHARDIC-JEW‡
  1962

BAND
  ARCHIVES OF ETHNIC MUSIC AND DANCE‡ NIGERIA‡ IGBO‡

BAND-BRASS
  ARCHIVES OF ETHNIC MUSIC AND DANCE‡ GHANA‡
  DAGARTI, DAGOMBA, DONNO, EWE, GA, KONKOMBA, LOBI‡

BAND-TRIBAL-TRUST
  ARCHIVES OF ETHNIC MUSIC AND DANCE‡ RHODESIA‡ ‡

BANJO
  ARCHIVES OF ETHNIC MUSIC AND DANCE‡ RHODESIA‡ ‡

BAPTISM
  CHRISTIAN, VALERIE‡ UPPER VOLTA‡ BISSA, BOBO,
  BWABA, DAGARA, DYULA, FULANI, FULBE, GOUIN,
  GOURMANTCHE, HAUSA, KASSENA, KWO, LOBI, MARKA,
  MOSSI, NONDOM, POUGOULIS, SAMO-DU-SUD, YARDSE‡
  1973-74

  DAVIS, GORDON‡ ETHIOPIA‡ COPT‡ 1968

BASS-STRING
  HANLEY, MARY ANN CSJ‡ GHANA‡ BUILSA, DAGARI, EWE,
  FANTI, FRAFRA, GA, KASSENA, NANKANI, TWI‡ 1972

BEGGAR
  BOWLES, PAUL+ WANKLYN, CHRISTOPHER‡ MOROCCO‡ ‡
  CA1959-62

BELIEF
  EL-SHAMY, HASAN M.‡ EGYPT-U.S.‡ ARAB‡ 1961

  YODER, WALTER D.‡ SOUTH AFRICA-U.S.‡ ‡ 1955

BELIEF-INTERVIEW
  FAIK-NZUJI, MADIYA‡ ZAIRE‡ LUBA‡ 1974

BELL
  ADUAMAH, E.Y.‡ GHANA-TOGO‡ EWE‡ 1968-71

  ARCHIVES OF ETHNIC MUSIC AND DANCE‡ RHODESIA‡ ‡

  BUCHANAN, CAROLE‡ UGANDA‡ BANYORO, BATORO‡
  1968-69

  HANLEY, MARY ANN CSJ‡ GHANA‡ BUILSA, DAGARI, EWE,
  FANTI, FRAFRA, GA, KASSENA, NANKANI, TWI‡ 1972

  HANLEY, MARY ANN CSJ‡ UPPER VOLTA‡ ‡ 1972

  MERRIAM, ALAN P.+ MERRIAM, BARBARA W.‡ ZAIRE‡
  BAHIMA, BAKOGA, BAKONGO, BAMBUTI, BANGALA, BASHI,
  BATWA, EKONDA‡ 1951-52

  NORSK RIKSKRINGKASTING‡ GHANA‡ ‡ 1966

  QUERSIN, BENOIT J.‡ ZAIRE‡ BUSHOONG, COOFA, IBAAM,
  NGEENDE, PYAANG, SHOOWA‡ 1970

  WANKLYN, CHRISTOPHER‡ MOROCCO‡ AIT-SIDI-MERRI,
  DEGWANA, MISIWA, OULED-MTAA‡ 1963+ 1969

  WILLETT, FRANK‡ NIGERIA‡ YORUBA‡ 1972

BELL-DOUBLE
  AMES, DAVID W.‡ NIGERIA‡ HAUSA‡ 1963

  AMES, DAVID W.‡ NIGERIA‡ IGBO‡ 1963-64

  ARCHIVES OF ETHNIC MUSIC AND DANCE‡ GHANA‡
  DAGARTI, DAGOMBA, DONNO, EWE, GA, KONKOMBA, LOBI‡

  HANLEY, MARY ANN CSJ‡ GHANA‡ AKAN, EWE, TWI‡ 1973

  HANLEY, MARY ANN CSJ‡ NIGERIA‡ ANGAS, BACHAMA,
  CHAMBA, EFIK, GWANDARA, HAUSA, IBIBIO, IBO, JABA,
  KERI-KERI, YORUBA‡ 1973

  JONES, ARTHUR M.‡ GHANA-ENGLAND‡ EWE‡ 1956

  PLOTNICOV, LEONARD‡ NIGERIA‡ BIROM, EFIK, HAUSA,
  IBIBIO, IBO, IJAW, KAGORO, KATAM, TIV‡ 1961-62

BELL-DOUBLE
  QUERSIN, BENOIT J.+ QUERSIN, CHRISTINE M.‡
  CAMEROON‡ BAFIA, BALLOM, BAMILEKE, BAMUM, BULU
  ETON, PEUL, PYGMIES, SANAGA, TIKAR, VUTE‡ 1967

  RUBIN, ARNOLD G.‡ NIGERIA‡ CHAMBA, HAUSA, IBO,
  JUKUN, KUTEP, TIKARI, TIV‡ 1964-65

BELLS-LEG
  MULDROW, WILLIAM+ MULDROW, ELIZABETH‡ ETHIOPIA‡
  TESHENNA‡ 1964-65

BIAFRAN-WAR-INTERVIEW
  ROMERO, PATRICIA‡ NIGERIA‡ IBO‡ 1973

BIOGRAPHY
  MARTIN, JANE JACKSON‡ LIBERIA‡ GREBO‡ 1968+
  1972-75

BIOGRAPHY-ARTIST
  SHEFFIELD, JAMES‡ DAHOMEY‡ YORUBA‡ 1971+ 1973

BIRTH
  COLLEGE OF MUSIC, UNIVERSITY OF NIGERIA‡ NIGERIA‡
  BINI, BOKI, DAKARAWA, EFIK-IBIBIO, EKOI, FULANI,
  HAUSA, IBO, IDOMA, IJAW, JABA, MADA, YALA, YORUBA,
  ZABEBMAWA‡

  GANSEMANS, JOS‡ ZAIRE‡ LUBA‡ 1970

  SUDAN NATIONAL MUSEUM‡ SUDAN‡ BONGO, JALUO,
  NUBIAN‡ 1959-64

BIRTH-TWINS
  GANSEMANS, JOS‡ ZAIRE‡ LUBA‡ 1970

BLACKSMITH
  RUBIN, ARNOLD G.‡ NIGERIA‡ CHAMBA, HAUSA, IBO,
  JUKUN, KUTEP, TIKARI, TIV‡ 1964-65

BLACKSMITH-PRAISE
  AMES, DAVID W.‡ NIGERIA‡ HAUSA‡ 1963

  AMES, DAVID W.‡ NIGERIA‡ FULBE, HAUSA, YORUBA‡
  1963-64

BOASTING
  MERRIAM, ALAN P.+ MERRIAM, BARBARA W.‡ BURUNDI‡
  ABATUTSI, BARUNDI, BATWA‡ 1951-52

BOASTING
  MERRIAM, ALAN P.+ MERRIAM, BARBARA W.‡ RWANDA‡
  ABAGOGWE, ABAGOYI, ABAHORJRD, ABANYAMBO, ABATUTSI,
  ABAYOVU, BAHIMA, BAHUTU, BAKIGA, BATWA‡ 1951-52

  MERRIAM, ALAN P.+ MERRIAM, BARBARA W.‡ ZAIRE‡
  BAHIMA, BAKOGA, BAKONGO, BAMBUTI, BANGALA, BASHI,
  BATWA, EKONDA‡ 1951-52

  ROBBIN, LAWRENCE H.‡ KENYA‡ TURKANA‡ 1965-66

  ROBBIN, LAWRENCE H.‡ UGANDA‡ POKOT‡ 1970

BOW-MUSICAL
  AFRICANA MUSEUM‡ SOUTH AFRICA‡ HOTTENTOT, SOTHO,
  SWAZI, TSWANA, ZULU‡

  ARCHIVES OF ETHNIC MUSIC AND DANCE‡ UPPER VOLTA‡
  BOBO, BWABA, DYULA, FULANI, FULBE, GOUIN,
  GOURMANTCHE, LOBI, MINIANKA, MOSSI, SENUFO,
  YARDSE‡

  BYRD, ROBERT OAKES‡ UGANDA‡ ALUR, BAGANDA,
  BAGWERE, BAKONJO, BANYANKOLE, BANYOLE, KAKWA,
  TESO‡

  CAMP, CHARLES M.+ TRACEY, HUGH‡ RHODESIA‡ BUDJA,
  CHIKUNDA, FUNGWE, HERA, HUNGWE, KARANGA, NDAU,
  NDEBELE, NYANJA, NYASA, PEDI, RAMBA, WEMBA, YAO‡
  1948

  CAMP, CHARLES M.+ TRACEY, HUGH‡ SOUTH AFRICA‡
  BHACA, CHOPI, HLUBI, NDAU, NYASA, PONDO, SHANGAAN,
  SOTHO, SWAZI, TSWANA, VENDA, XHOSA‡ 1947-48

  CAMP, CHARLES M.+ TRACEY, HUGH‡ ZAMBIA‡ BEMBA,
  LALA, LOZI, TONGA, ZINZA‡ 1947-48

  CLAUSS, BERNHARD PETER‡ ANGOLA‡ HIMBA-MUGAMBO‡
  1970-72

  ENGLAND, NICHOLAS M.‡ ANGOLA‡ GANGULA‡ 1957-61

  ENGLAND, NICHOLAS M.‡ BOTSWANA‡ TSWANA‡ 1957-61

  ENGLAND, NICHOLAS M.‡ NAMIBIA‡ HERERO‡ 1957-61

  HARTWIG, GERALD W.‡ TANZANIA‡ KEREWE‡ 1968-69

BOW-MUSICAL
  KAEMMER, JOHN E.‡ RHODESIA‡ KOREKORE, SHONA,
  ZEZURU‡ 1972-73

  MERRIAM, ALAN P.+ MERRIAM, BARBARA W.‡ BURUNDI‡
  ABATUTSI, BARUNDI, BATWA‡ 1951-52

  MERRIAM, ALAN P.+ MERRIAM, BARBARA W.‡ RWANDA‡
  ABAGOGWE, ABAGOYI, ABAHURORU, ABANYAMBO, ABATUTSI,
  ABAYOVU, BAHIMA, BAHUTU, BAKIGA, BATWA‡ 1951-52

  MERRIAM, ALAN P.+ MERRIAM, BARBARA W.‡ ZAIRE‡
  BAHIMA, BAKOGA, BAKONGO, BAMBUTI, BANGALA, BASHI,
  BATWA, EKONDA‡ 1951-52

  QUERSIN, BENOIT J.+ QUERSIN, CHRISTINE M.‡
  NIGERIA‡ ABAKPA-RIGA, AFO, ALAGO, ANGAS, ANKWAI,
  BIROM, BUROM, CHAMBA, EGGON, FULANI, HAUSA, ICHEN,
  IDOMA, JARAWA, JUKUN, KALABARI, KANTANA, KUTEP,
  KWALLA, NUPE, PYEM, RINDRE, TIV, YERGAM, YORUBA‡
  1972-73

  ROUGET, GILBERT‡ SENEGAL‡ LEBOU, PEUL, SARAKOLE,
  SOCE, TUKULOR, WOLOF‡ 1952

  SAPIR, J. DAVID‡ SENEGAL‡ DIOLA-FOGNY, DIOLA-KASA‡
  1960-65

  STARR, FREDERICK A.‡ ZAIRE‡ BAKUBA, BALUBA‡ 1906

  STONE, RUTH M.+ STONE, VERLON L.‡ LIBERIA‡ KPELLE‡
  1970

  VAN OVEN, JACOBA‡ SIERRA LEONE‡ FULA, GALLINAS,
  GOLA, LIMBA, LOKO, MANDINGO, MENDE, SHERBRO, SUSU,
  TEMNE, VAI, YALUNKA‡ 1964-67

  WEMAN, HENRY PAUL‡ RHODESIA‡ KARANGA, LEMBA,
  VENDA, ZULU‡ 1957

  WEMAN, HENRY PAUL‡ SOUTH AFRICA‡ VENDA, ZULU‡
  1956-57

  WEMAN, PAUL HENRY‡ TANZANIA‡ HAYA, SUKUMA,
  SWAHILI‡ 1957

BUTCHER
  AMES, DAVID W.‡ NIGERIA‡ HAUSA‡ 1963

BUTCHER-PRAISE
  RHODES, WILLARD‡ NIGERIA‡ FULANI, HAUSA, TIV,
  TUAREG, YORUBA‡ 1973-74

CANOE
  CAMP, CHARLES M.+ TRACEY, HUGH‡ ZAMBIA‡ BEMBA,
  LALA, LOZI, TONGA, ZINZA‡ 1947-48

CANTE-FABLE
  AGINSKY, ETHEL G.‡ SIERRA LEONE-U.S.‡ MENDE‡ 1933

  BEN-AMOS, DAN‡ NIGERIA‡ EDO‡ 1966

  CAMP, CHARLES M.+ TRACEY, HUGH‡ RHODESIA‡ BUDJA,
  CHIKUNDA, FUNGWE, HERA, HUNGWE, KARANGA, NDAU,
  NDEBELE, NYANJA, NYASA, PEDI, RAMBA, WEMBA, YAO‡
  1948

  CAMP, CHARLES M.+ TRACEY, HUGH‡ ZAMBIA‡ BEMBA,
  LALA, LOZI, TONGA, ZINZA‡ 1947-48

  FIKRY, MONA‡ GHANA‡ WALA‡ 1966-67

  GLAZE, ANITA‡ IVORY COAST‡ SENUFO‡ 1969-70

  HERSKOVITS, MELVILLE J.+ HERSKOVITS, FRANCES S.‡
  DAHOMEY‡ FON‡ 1931

  HERSKOVITS, MELVILLE J.+ HERSKOVITS, FRANCES S.‡
  NIGERIA‡ YORUBA‡ 1931

  JOHNSON, GERALD T.‡ SIERRA LEONE‡ MENDE, TEMNE‡
  1967-68

  KAEMMER, JOHN E.‡ RHODESIA‡ KOREKORE, SHONA,
  ZEZURU‡ 1972-73

  KOECHLIN, B.‡ MALAGASY REPUBLIC‡ MAHAFALY,
  MASIKORO, VEZO‡ 1967-69

  OKIE, PACKARD L.‡ LIBERIA‡ BASSA, BELE, GIO,
  KPELLE, KRU, MANDINGO, VAI‡ 1947-54

  STONE, RUTH M.+ STONE, VERLON L.‡ LIBERIA‡ KPELLE‡
  1970

  WEMAN, HENRY PAUL‡ SOUTH AFRICA‡ VENDA, ZULU‡
  1956-57

CANTE-FABLE
  WOLFF, HANS‡ NIGERIA‡ EFIK, HAUSA, IBIBIO, KAJE,
  SOBO, PABIR, YORUBA‡ 1953-54

CARAVAN
  HOLIDAY, GEOFFREY D.‡ NIGER‡ TUAREG‡ CA1958

CARRYING
  HAMBLY, WILFRED D.‡ ANGOLA‡ OVIMBUNDU‡ 1929-30

CARRYING-GOODS
  MERRIAM, ALAN P.+ MERRIAM, BARBARA W.‡ ZAIRE‡
  BAHIMA, BAKOGA, BAKONGO, BAMBUTI, BANGALA, BASHI,
  BATWA, EKONDA‡ 1951-52

CATTLE
  BUCHANAN, CAROLE‡ UGANDA‡ BANYORO, BATORO‡
  1968-69

  CARLISLE, ROXANE C.‡ SUDAN‡ ANUAK, DINKA, GAALIIN,
  NUER, SHILLUK‡ 1963

CELEBRATION-CENTENNIAL
  NEWBURY, DOROTHY J.‡ LIBERIA‡ BASSA, LOMA‡
  1969-70+ 1972

CELEBRATION-INDEPENDENCE
  COX, WILLIAM L.‡ BURUNDI‡ ‡ 1962

CENSUS-INTERVIEW
  KROTKI, KAROL JOSEF‡ MOROCCO‡ ‡ 1971

CEREMONY
  ADAMS, CHARLES R.‡ LESOTHO‡ BASOTHO‡ 1969-70

  CENTRE DE RECHERCHES ANTHROPOLOGIQUES‡ SENEGAL‡
  BASSARI, BEDIK, CONIAGUI, MALINKE, TENDA‡

  CRAVEN, ANNA‡ NIGERIA‡ AFO, GEDE‡ 1969-70

  ENGLAND, NICHOLAS M.‡ ANGOLA‡ GANGULA‡ 1957-61

  FEDERAL DEPARTMENT OF ANTIQUITIES, NATIONAL
  MUSEUM, KADUNA‡ NIGERIA‡ ELOYI, GEDE‡

  FEINBERG, HARVEY‡ GHANA‡ FANTI‡ 1967-68

  HERSKOVITS, MELVILLE J.+ HERSKOVITS, FRANCES S.‡
  DAHOMEY‡ FON‡ 1931

CEREMONY
  MERRIAM, ALAN P.+ MERRIAM, BARBARA W.≠ ZAIRE≠
  BAHIMA, BAKOGA, BAKONGO, BAMBUTI, BANGALA, BASHI,
  BATWA, EKONDA≠ 1951-52

  OERTLI, PEO≠ DAHOMEY≠ AIZO≠ 1973-74

  RAYFIELD, JOAN R.≠ IVORY COAST≠ BAULE, MALINKE,
  SENUFO≠ 1972-73

CEREMONY-AGE-GRADE
  HEAD, SYDNEY W.≠ ETHIOPIA≠ ≠ 1964

CEREMONY-BAPTISM
  DAVIS, GORDON≠ ETHIOPIA≠ COPT≠ 1968

CEREMONY-CIRCUMCISION
  DOBRIN, ARTHUR≠ KENYA≠ GUSII≠ 1966

  TURNER, VICTOR WITTER≠ UGANDA≠ BAGISU≠ 1966

CEREMONY-COMET-SIGHTING
  ROBBIN, LAWRENCE H.≠ UGANDA≠ POKOT≠ 1970

CEREMONY-EFE-GELEDE
  DREWAL, HENRY JOHN≠ NIGERIA≠ YORUBA≠ 1970-71

CEREMONY-FALASHA
  SHELEMAY, KAY KAUFMAN≠ ETHIOPIA≠ FALASHA-JEW≠
  1973

CEREMONY-FEMALE
  DURAN, JAMES JOSEPH≠ KENYA≠ KIPSIGI≠ 1971

CEREMONY-HUNTING
  SUDAN NATIONAL MUSEUM≠ SUDAN≠ BONGO, JALUO,
  NUBIAN≠ 1959-64

CEREMONY-INITIATION
  ENGLAND, NICHOLAS M.≠ BOTSWANA≠ TSWANA≠ 1957-61

  ENGLAND, NICHOLAS M.≠ NAMIBIA≠ HERERO≠ 1957-61

CEREMONY-INITIATION-PORO
  ZEMPLEIVI, ANDRAS≠ IVORY COAST≠ SENUFO-NA-FAARA≠
  1972-74

CEREMONY-MARGAI
  FEDRY, J.≠ CHAD≠ HADJERAI≠ 1966-67

CEREMONY-ONDO
  DREWAL, HENRY JOHN‡ DAHOMEY‡ YORUBA‡ 1973

CEREMONY-PUBERTY
  BLACKING, JOHN A.R.‡ UGANDA‡ BAGANDA, BATORO,
  KARAMOJONG‡ 1965

CEREMONY-RELIGIOUS
  PEEK, PHILIP M.‡ NIGERIA‡ IGBO-WESTERN, ISOKO‡
  1970-71

CEREMONY-SIGI
  DIETERLEN, GERMAINE‡ MALI‡ DOGON‡ 1967

CEREMONY-SIGUI
  DIETERLEN, GERMAINE‡ MALI‡ DOGON‡ 1969

CHIEF-INSTALLATION
  COLLEGE OF MUSIC, UNIVERSITY OF NIGERIA‡ NIGERIA‡
  BINI, BOKI, DAKARAWA, EFIK-IBIBIO, EKOI, FULANI,
  HAUSA, IBO, IDOMA, IJAW, JABA, MADA, YALA, YORUBA,
  ZABEBMAWA‡

  VERMEER, DONALD E.‡ GHANA‡ EWE‡ 1969

CHILDREN
  ADUAMAH, E.Y.‡ GHANA-TOGO‡ EWE‡ 1968-71

  ALBERTS, ARTHUR S.‡ AFRICA-WEST‡ BAULE, MANO,
  MOSSI‡ 1949

  ALBERTS, ARTHUR S.‡ GHANA‡ EWE, GA, IBO, TWI‡
  1949-51

  AMES, DAVID W.‡ NIGERIA‡ HAUSA‡ 1963

  ARCHIVES OF ETHNIC MUSIC AND DANCE‡ MOROCCO‡ ARAB‡

  ARCHIVES OF ETHNIC MUSIC AND DANCE‡ UPPER VOLTA‡
  BOBO, BWABA, DYULA, FULANI, FULBE, GOUIN,
  GOURMANTCHE, LOBI, MINIANKA, MOSSI, SENUFO,
  YARDSE‡

  ARMSTRONG, ROBERT G.‡ NIGERIA‡ IDOMA‡ 1964

  BACHMANN, FR.‡ TANZANIA‡ ‡ 1908

  BAHMAN, GARY‡ SIERRA LEONE‡ LIMBA, MANDINGO,
  TEMNE‡ 1971

CHILDREN
  CAMP, CHARLES M.+ TRACEY, HUGH‡ RHODESIA‡ BUDJA,
  CHIKUNDA, FUNGWE, HERA, HUNGWE, KARANGA, NDAU,
  NDEBELE, NYANJA, NYASA, PEDI, RAMBA, WEMBA, YAO‡
  1948

  CAMP, CHARLES M.+ TRACEY, HUGH‡ SOUTH AFRICA‡
  BHACA, CHOPI, HLUBI, NDAU, NYASA, PONDO, SHANGAAN,
  SOTHO, SWAZI, TSWANA, VENDA, XHOSA‡ 1947-48

  CAMPBELL, CAROL‡ KENYA‡ BAJUN, SWAHILI‡ 1972

  CHRISTIAN, VALERIE‡ UPPER VOLTA‡ BISSA, BOBO,
  BWABA, DAGARA, DYULA, FULANI, FULBE, GOUIN,
  GOURMANTCHE, HAUSA, KASSENA, KWO, LOBI, MARKA,
  MOSSI, NONDOM, POUGOULIS, SAMO-DU-SUD, YARDSE‡
  1973-74

  COLLEGE OF MUSIC, UNIVERSITY OF NIGERIA‡ NIGERIA‡
  BINI, BOKI, DAKARAWA, EFIK-IBIBIO, EKOI, FULANI,
  HAUSA, IBO, IDOMA, IJAW, JABA, MADA, YALA, YORUBA,
  ZABEBMAWA‡

  D'AZEVEDO, WARREN L.‡ LIBERIA‡ AMERICO-LIBERIAN,
  GOLA, KPELLE, VAI‡ 1956-58+ 1966

  DENG, FRANCIS‡ SUDAN‡ DINKA‡ 1971

  DOBRIN, ARTHUR‡ KENYA‡ GUSII‡ 1966

  DUMONT, LILLIAN E.‡ GHANA‡ ‡ 1973

  ELLOVICH, RISA SUE‡ IVORY COAST‡ DYULA, MALINKE,
  VOLTAIC‡ 1973-74

  EULENBERG, JOHN BRYSON‡ NIGERIA‡ HAUSA‡ 1972

  LAMBRECHT, FRANK L.+ LAMBRECHT, DORA J.M.‡
  BOTSWANA‡ KUNG-BUSHMEN, YEI‡ 1967-68

  MERRIAM, ALAN P.+ MERRIAM, BARBARA W.‡ ZAIRE‡
  BAHIMA, BAKOGA, BAKONGO, BAMBUTI, BANGALA, BASHI,
  BATWA, EKONDA‡ 1951-52

  MERRIAM, ALAN P.‡ ZAIRE‡ BASONGYE‡ 1973

  OFRI, DORITH‡ LIBERIA‡ VAI‡ 1965-72

  RHODES, WILLARD‡ NIGERIA‡ FULANI, HAUSA, TIV,

CHILDREN
  TUAREG, YORUBA‡ 1973-74

  ROUGET, GILBERT‡ GUINEA‡ MALINKE‡ 1952

  VAUGHAN, JAMES H.‡ NIGERIA‡ MARGI‡ 1974

  WEMAN, HENRY PAUL‡ RHODESIA‡ KARANGA, LEMBA,
  VENDA, ZULU‡ 1957

  WEMAN, HENRY PAUL‡ SOUTH AFRICA‡ VENDA, ZULU‡
  1956-57

CHILDREN-CONVERSATION
  DEVITT, PAUL C.S.‡ BOTSWANA‡ ‡ 1971-72

CHILDREN-FOLKTALE
  BEN-AMOS, DAN‡ NIGERIA‡ EDO‡ 1966

CHILDREN-GAME
  ADUAMAH, E.Y.‡ GHANA-TOGO‡ EWE‡ 1968-71

  BEN-AMOS, DAN‡ NIGERIA‡ EDO‡ 1966

  HAMBLY, WILFRED D.‡ ANGOLA‡ OVIMBUNDU‡ 1929-30

  JOHNSON, GERALD T.‡ SIERRA LEONE‡ MENDE, TEMNE‡
  1967-68

  MERRIAM, ALAN P.+ MERRIAM, BARBARA W.‡ ZAIRE‡
  BASONGYE‡ 1959-60

  NETTL, BRUNO +RABEN, JOSEPH‡ NIGERIA-U.S.‡ IBO‡
  1950-51

  RABEN, JOSEPH‡ NIGERIA-U.S.‡ IBO‡ 1950

  RHODES, WILLARD‡ NIGERIA‡ FULANI, HAUSA, TIV,
  TUAREG, YORUBA‡ 1973-74

  STONE, RUTH M.+ STONE, VERLON L.‡ LIBERIA‡ KPELLE‡
  1970

CHILDREN-GAME-RING
  D'AZEVEDO, WARREN L.‡ LIBERIA‡ AMERICO-LIBERIAN,
  GOLA, KPELLE, VAI‡ 1956-58+ 1966

CHILDREN-NAMING
  AMES, DAVID W.‡ GAMBIA, THE‡ WOLOF‡ 1951

CHILDREN-NAMING-CEREMONY
  KNIGHT, RODERIC COPLEY‡ GAMBIA, THE‡ BALANTA,
  BAMBARA, FULA, JOLA, MANDINKA, TEMNE, WOLOF‡
  1970-71

CHILDREN-RHYME
  EL-SHAMY, HASAN M.‡ EGYPT‡ ARAB, DINKA, NUBIAN‡
  1968-71

CHILDREN-SCHOOL
  KULP, PHILIP M.‡ NIGERIA‡ BURA‡ 1973

  LAMBRECHT, FRANK L.+ LAMBRECHT, DORA J.M.‡
  BOTSWANA‡ KUNG-BUSHMEN, YEI‡ 1967-68

  NETTL, BRUNO +RABEN, JOSEPH‡ NIGERIA-U.S.‡ IBO‡
  1950-51

  WEMAN, HENRY PAUL‡ RHODESIA‡ KARANGA, LEMBA,
  VENDA, ZULU‡ 1957

  WEMAN, PAUL HENRY‡ TANZANIA‡ HAYA, SUKUMA,
  SWAHILI‡ 1957

CHILDREN-TWINS
  HERSKOVITS, MELVILLE J.+ HERSKOVITS, FRANCES S.‡
  DAHOMEY‡ FON‡ 1931

  HERSKOVITS, MELVILLE J.+ HERSKOVITS, FRANCES S.‡
  GHANA‡ ASANTE‡ 1931

  MERRIAM, ALAN P.+ MERRIAM, BARBARA W.‡ ZAIRE‡
  BAHIMA, BAKOGA, BAKONGO, BAMBUTI, BANGALA, BASHI,
  BATWA, EKONDA‡ 1951-52

CHILDREN-TWINS-RITUAL
  WARNIER, JEAN-PIERRE‡ CAMEROON‡ MANKON‡ 1972-74

CHISEL
  ALBERTS, ARTHUR S.‡ LIBERIA‡ FANTI, LOMA, MANO‡
  1949-51

CHOIR
  CLAUSS, BERNHARD PETER‡ ZAIRE‡ PYGMIES‡ 1973

CHOIR-COPTIC
  ABDELSAYED, FR. GABRIEL H.A.‡ EGYPT‡ COPT‡
  1965-69

CHOIR-NATIONAL-CONGRESS
  GERHART, GAIL M.‡ SOUTH AFRICA‡ ‡ 1964

CHORDOPHONE
  AKPABOT, SAMUEL EKPE‡ NIGERIA‡ BIROM, HAUSA,
  IBIBIO, IBO‡ 1964-73

  BERNUS, S.+ ROUCH, JEAN‡ NIGER‡ SONRAI‡ 1960

  BUCHANAN, CAROLE‡ UGANDA‡ BANYORO, BATORO‡
  1968-69

  CALKINS, HOWARD W.+ RADIO DAHOMEY‡ DAHOMEY‡ DENDI,
  DOMPAGO, FON, MAHI, YORUBA‡ CA1967

  CLAUSS, BERNHARD PETER‡ CHAD‡ SARAKABA‡ 1973

  CLAUSS, BERNHARD PETER‡ MALI‡ BAMBARA, TAMACHECK‡
  1973

  CLAUSS, BERNHARD PETER‡ ZAIRE‡ PYGMIES‡ 1973

  LESLAU, WOLF‡ ETHIOPIA‡ AMHARA, GURAGE, HARARI,
  SHOA-GALLA, SOMALI, TIGRINYA‡ 1947

  TESSMAN, GUNTHER‡ CAMEROON‡ FANG-PANGWE‡ 1907

  VAUGHAN, JAMES H.‡ NIGERIA‡ MARGI‡ 1974

CHORDOPHONE-DOZO-KONU
  ROUGET, GILBERT‡ GUINEA‡ MALINKE‡ 1952

CHORDOPHONE-NYARTITI
  HAY, MARGARET JEAN‡ KENYA‡ LUO‡ 1968-70+ 1973

CHORDPHONE-HOUDOU
  CURTIN, PHILIP D.‡ SENEGAL‡ ARAB, DIAKHANKE,
  MALINKE, PULAR‡ 1966

CIRCUMCISION
  ARCHIVES OF ETHNIC MUSIC AND DANCE‡ UPPER VOLTA‡
  BOBO, BWABA, DYULA, FULANI, FULBE, GOUIN,
  GOURMANTCHE, LOBI, MINIANKA, MOSSI, SENUFO,
  YARDSE‡

  BRANDILY, MONIQUE‡ CHAD‡ FEZZANAIS, TEDA‡ 1969

  DOBRIN, ARTHUR‡ KENYA‡ GUSII‡ 1966

CIRCUMCISION
  DURAN, JAMES JOSEPH‡ KENYA‡ KIPSIGI‡ 1971

  HEALD, SWETTE SCOTT‡ UGANDA‡ GISU‡ 1966-69

  LORTAT-JACOB, BERNARD‡ MOROCCO‡ AIT-MGOUN‡ 1969

  ROUGET, GILBERT‡ GUINEA‡ MALINKE‡ 1952

  ROUGET, GILBERT‡ SENEGAL‡ LEBOU, PEUL, SARAKOLE,
  SOCE, TUKULOR, WOLOF‡ 1952

  TURNER, VICTOR WITTER‡ UGANDA‡ BAGISU‡ 1966

CIRCUMCISION-CEREMONY
  ARMISTEAD, SAMUEL G. + KATZ, ISRAEL J. +
  SILVERMAN, JOSEPH H.‡ MOROCCO‡ SEPHARDIC-JEW‡
  1962

CLAPPER-WOODEN
  ARCHIVES OF ETHNIC MUSIC AND DANCE‡ RHODESIA‡ ‡

CLARINET-DOUBLE
  BERLIN PHONOGRAMM-ARCHIV‡ AFRICA-GERMANY‡ BULE‡
  1909

  BRANDILY, MONIQUE‡ CHAD‡ FEZZANAIS, TEDA‡ 1969

CLOTH-WORKER
  HERSKOVITS, MELVILLE J.+ HERSKOVITS, FRANCES S.‡
  DAHOMEY‡ FON‡ 1931

COMBAT-VERBAL
  TENRAA, ERIC WILLIAM FREDERICK‡ TANZANIA‡ BURUNGE,
  SANDAWE, SWAHILI‡ 1958-60

COMMENT-SOCIAL
  AMES, DAVID W.‡ NIGERIA‡ HAUSA‡ 1963

  RUBIN, ARNOLD G.‡ NIGERIA‡ CHAMBA, HAUSA, IBO,
  JUKUN, KUTEP, TIKARI, TIV‡ 1964-65

CONCERTINA
  CAMP, CHARLES M.+ TRACEY, HUGH‡ SOUTH AFRICA‡
  BHACA, CHOPI, HLUBI, NDAU, NYASA, PONDO, SHANGAAN,
  SOTHO, SWAZI, TSWANA, VENDA, XHOSA‡ 1947-48

  WEMAN, HENRY PAUL‡ SOUTH AFRICA‡ VENDA, ZULU‡
  1956-57

CONGRESS-OF-INTERNATIONAL
   INSTITUTO NACIONAL DE FOLKLORE, VENEZUELA‡ GHANA‡
   ‡ 1966

CONVERSATION
   ABUZAHRA, NADIA‡ TUNISIA‡ SAHEL‡ 1966

   BELLMAN, BERYL LARRY‡ LIBERIA‡ KPELLE, LOMA‡ 1969

   BLAIR, BOB‡ GHANA‡ ASANTE‡ 1958

   FAIK-NZUJI, MADIYA‡ ZAIRE‡ LUBA‡ 1974

   NEWBURY, DOROTHY J.‡ LIBERIA‡ BASSA, LOMA‡
   1969-70‡ 1972

   PARKER, CAROLYN ANN‡ KENYA‡ BAJUN, SWAHILI‡
   1971-72

   WOLFF, HANS‡ NIGERIA‡ AGBADU, URHOBO‡ 1953

   WOLFF, HANS‡ NIGERIA‡ IBO‡ 1953

COURT
   SPAIN, DAVID H.‡ NIGERIA‡ KANURI‡ 1966-67

COURT-CASE
   ARGYLE, WILLIAM JOHNSON‡ ZAMBIA‡ SOLI‡ 1957-59

COURT-FESTIVAL
   GRAESSER, MARK W.‡ GHANA‡ ASANTE, FRAFRA, HAUSA,
   KANJAGA, KONKOMBA‡ 1968-69

COURTING
   BUNGER, ROBERT LOUIS‡ KENYA‡ OROMA, POKOMO‡
   1969-70

   HERSKOVITS, MELVILLE J.‡ HERSKOVITS, FRANCES S.‡
   GHANA‡ ASANTE‡ 1931

CULT-ANCESTRAL
   HERSKOVITS, MELVILLE J.‡ HERSKOVITS, FRANCES S.‡
   DAHOMEY‡ FON‡ 1931

CULT-BWITI
   FERNANDEZ, JAMES W.‡ GABON‡ FANG‡ 1960

CULT-POSSESSION
   BESMER, FREMONT E.‡ NIGERIA‡ HAUSA‡ 1972-73

CULT-POSSESSION
  BUCHANAN, CAROLE‡ UGANDA‡ BANYORO, BATORO‡
  1968-69

CULT-SHANGO
  QUERSIN, BENOIT J.+ QUERSIN, CHRISTINE M.‡
  NIGERIA‡ ABAKPA-RIGA, AFO, ALAGO, ANGAS, ANKWAI,
  BIROM, BUROM, CHAMBA, EGGON, FULANI, HAUSA, ICHEN,
  IDOMA, JARAWA, JUKUN, KALABARI, KANTANA, KUTEP,
  KWALLA, NUPE, PYEM, RINDRE, TIV, YERGAM, YORUBA‡
  1972-73

CURING
  CALAME, B.‡ MALI‡ BAMBARA, BOZO, DOGON, MARKA,
  MINIANKA, PEUL, RYMAYBE, SARAKOLE, SOMONO,
  SONGHAY‡ 1956-57+ 1960

  FARSY, MUHAMMED S.‡ TANZANIA-ZANZIBAR‡ ‡ CA1958

  LAMAN, K.E.‡ ZAIRE‡ BAKONGO‡ 1911

  YOUSSEF, AIT‡ MOROCCO‡ ‡ 1966

CURING-ANTI-WITCHCRAFT
  SEDLAK, PHILIP A.S.‡ KENYA‡ DURUMA, GIRYAMA,
  SWAHILI‡ 1971

CURING-CELEBRATION
  CHRISTIAN, VALERIE‡ UPPER VOLTA‡ BISSA, BOBO,
  BWABA, DAGARA, DYULA, FULANI, FULBE, GOUIN,
  GOURMANTCHE, HAUSA, KASSENA, KWO, LOBI, MARKA,
  MOSSI, NONDOM, POUGOULIS, SAMO-DU-SUD, YARDSE‡
  1973-74

CURING-RITUAL
  ENGLAND, NICHOLAS M.‡ ANGOLA‡ GANGULA‡ 1957-61

  ENGLAND, NICHOLAS M.‡ BOTSWANA‡ TSWANA‡ 1957-61

  ENGLAND, NICHOLAS M.‡ NAMIBIA‡ HERERO‡ 1957-61

CURING-SOCIETY
  RUBIN, ARNOLD G.‡ NIGERIA‡ CHAMBA, HAUSA, IBO,
  JUKUN, KUTEP, TIKARI, TIV‡ 1964-65

CUSTOM
  EL-SHAMY, HASAN M.‡ EGYPT-U.S.‡ ARAB‡ 1961

CUSTOM-INTERVIEW
  FAIK-NZUJI, MADIYA‡ ZAIRE‡ LUBA‡ 1974

CYMBAL
  BOWLES, PAUL+ WANKLYN, CHRISTOPHER‡ MOROCCO‡ ‡
  CA1959-62

CYMBAL-FINGER
  WANKLYN, CHRISTOPHER‡ MOROCCO‡ AIT-SIDI-MERRI,
  DEGWANA, MISIWA, OULED-MTAA‡ 1963+ 1969

DANCE
  AMES, DAVID W.‡ GAMBIA, THE‡ WOLOF‡ 1951

  AMES, DAVID W.‡ NIGERIA‡ HAUSA‡ 1963

  AMES, DAVID W.‡ NIGERIA‡ IGBO‡ 1963-64

  ARCHIVES OF TRADITIONAL MUSIC‡ ‡ YORUBA‡ CA1940

  BEN-AMOS, DAN‡ NIGERIA‡ EDO‡ 1966

  BERLIN PHONOGRAMM-ARCHIV‡ AFRICA-GERMANY‡ BULE‡
  1909

  BISELE, MARGUERITE A.‡ BOTSWANA‡ KUNG-BUSHMEN‡
  1971-72

  BLACKING, JOHN A.R.‡ SOUTH AFRICA‡ VENDA‡ 1956-59

  BLANK, ARTHUR S., JR.+ BLANK, DONNA H.‡ IVORY
  COAST‡ GUERE, WOBE‡ 1973

  BOWLES, PAUL+ WANKLYN, CHRISTOPHER‡ MOROCCO‡ ‡
  CA1959-62

  BRYAN, SAM‡ MALI‡ DOGON‡ 1960

  BUCHANAN, CAROLE‡ UGANDA‡ BANYORO, BATORO‡
  1968-69

  BUNGER, ROBERT LOUIS‡ KENYA‡ OROMA, POKOMO‡
  1969-70

  BYRD, ROBERT OAKES‡ UGANDA‡ ALUR, BAGANDA,
  BAGWERE, BAKONJO, BANYANKOLE, BANYOLE, KAKWA,
  TESO‡

  CALAME, B.‡ MALI‡ BAMBARA, BOZO, DOGON, MARKA,

DANCE
   MINIANKA, PEUL, RYMAYBE, SARAKOLE, SOMONO,
   SONGHAY‡ 1956-57+ 1960

   CALKINS, HOWARD W.+ RADIO DAHOMEY‡ DAHOMEY‡ DENDI,
   DOMPAGO, FON, MAHI, YORUBA‡ CA1967

   CAMP, CHARLES M.+ TRACEY, HUGH‡ RHODESIA‡ BUDJA,
   CHIKUNDA, FUNGWE, HERA, HUNGWE, KARANGA, NDAU,
   NDEBELE, NYANJA, NYASA, PEDI, RAMBA, WEMBA, YAO‡
   1948

   CAMP, CHARLES M.+ TRACEY, HUGH‡ SOUTH AFRICA‡
   BHACA, CHOPI, HLUBI, NDAU, NYASA, PONDO, SHANGAAN,
   SOTHO, SWAZI, TSWANA, VENDA, XHOSA‡ 1947-48

   CAMP, CHARLES M.+ TRACEY, HUGH‡ ZAMBIA‡ BEMBA,
   LALA, LOZI, TONGA, ZINZA‡ 1947-48

   CARLISLE, ROXANE C.‡ SUDAN‡ ANUAK, DINKA, GAALIIN,
   NUER, SHILLUK‡ 1963

   CENTRE DE RECHERCHES ANTHROPOLOGIQUES‡ SENEGAL‡
   BASSARI, BEDIK, CONIAGUI, MALINKE, TENDA‡

   CHRISTIAN, VALERIE‡ UPPER VOLTA‡ BISSA, BOBO,
   BWABA, DAGARA, DYULA, FULANI, FULBE, GOUIN,
   GOURMANTCHE, HAUSA, KASSENA, KWO, LOBI, MARKA,
   MOSSI, NONDOM, POUGOULIS, SAMO-DU-SUD, YARDSE‡
   1973-74

   CLAUSS, BERNHARD PETER‡ BOTSWANA‡ BUSHMEN‡
   1971-72

   COHEN, RONALD‡ NIGERIA‡ KANURI‡ 1956

   CURTIS, NATALIE‡ AFRICA-EAST‡ ‡ CA1919

   DE HEN, FERDINAND JOSEPH‡ MOROCCO‡ AIT-ATTA,
   AIT-BU-SUEMMEZ, IHANSALEN‡ 1960-61

   DEMPWOLFF, OTTO‡ TANZANIA‡ SANDAWE, ZARAMO‡ 1910

   ELLOVICH, RISA SUE‡ IVORY COAST‡ DYULA, MALINKE,
   VOLTAIC‡ 1973-74

   ETHNOMUSICOLOGY CENTRE JAAP KUNST‡ GAMBIA, THE‡
   MANDINKA‡ 1958

DANCE
    ETHNOMUSICOLOGY CENTRE JAAP KUNST‡ SIERRA LEONE‡ ‡
    1974

    FARSY, MUHAMMED S.‡ TANZANIA-ZANZIBAR‡ ‡ CA1958

    FERCHIOU, SOPHIE‡ TUNISIA‡ ‡ 1969

    FERNANDEZ, JAMES W.‡ GABON‡ FANG‡ 1960

    FIKRY, MONA‡ GHANA‡ WALA‡ 1966-67

    GANSEMANS, JOS‡ RWANDA‡ HUTU, TUTSI, TWA‡ 1973-74

    GANSEMANS, JOS‡ ZAIRE‡ LUBA‡ 1970

    GANSEMANS, JOS‡ ZAIRE‡ LUBA, LUNDA, SALAMPASU‡
    1970-73

    GEOFFRION, CHARLES A.‡ MALAWI‡ ACHEWA, MANGANJA,
    NGONI‡ 1971-72

    GERLACH, LUTHER PAUL‡ KENYA-TANZANIA‡ ARAB, DIGO,
    DURUMA‡ 1958-60

    GLAZE, ANITA‡ IVORY COAST‡ SENUFO‡ 1969-70

    HANLEY, MARY ANN CSJ‡ GHANA‡ BUILSA, DAGARI, EWE,
    FANTI, FRAFRA, GA, KASSENA, NANKANI, TWI‡ 1972

    HANNA, JUDITH LYNNE+ HANNA, WILLIAM J.‡ ETHIOPIA‡
    ‡ 1963

    HANNA, JUDITH LYNNE+ HANNA, WILLIAM J.‡ NIGERIA‡
    IBO‡ 1963

    HANNA, JUDITH LYNNE+ HANNA, WILLIAM J.‡ UGANDA‡
    ACHOLI, BANYOLE‡ 1963

    HASSENPFLUG, EARL C.‡ MALI‡ BOZO, DOGON‡ 1970

    HERSKOVITS, MELVILLE J.+ HERSKOVITS, FRANCES S.‡
    DAHOMEY‡ FON‡ 1931

    HERSKOVITS, MELVILLE J.+ HERSKOVITS, FRANCES S.‡
    GHANA‡ ASANTE‡ 1931

    HOOVER, JAMES JEFFREY‡ ZAIRE‡ LUNDA‡ 1973-75

DANCE

  JOHNSON, GERALD T.‡ SIERRA LEONE‡ MENDE, TEMNE‡
  1967-68

  KLEIS, GERALD W.‡ CAMEROON‡ AROCHUKU, BAKUNDU,
  IGBO, META, NKAMBE, WIDEKUM‡ 1971

  KUBIK, GERHARD‡ AFRICA-ANGOLA, CAMEROON, CENTRAL
  AFRICAN REPUBLIC, CONGO-PEOPLE'S REPUBLIC OF THE,
  EGYPT, GABON, KENYA, MALAWI, MOZAMBIQUE, NIGERIA,
  SUDAN, TANZANIA, TOGO, UGANDA, ZAIRE, ZAMBIA‡ ‡
  1959-73

  KULP, PHILIP M.‡ NIGERIA‡ BURA‡ 1973

  LAMAN, K.E.‡ ZAIRE‡ BAKONGO‡ 1911

  LORTAT-JACOB, BERNARD‡ MOROCCO‡ AIT-BOUGMEZ,
  FTOUKA‡ 1971

  MATTNER, -‡ TANZANIA‡ ‡ 1909

  MERRIAM, ALAN P.+ MERRIAM, BARBARA W.‡ ZAIRE‡
  BAHIMA, BAKOGA, BAKONGO, BAMBUTI, BANGALA, BASHI,
  BATWA, EKONDA‡ 1951-52

  MOREY, ROBERT H.‡ LIBERIA‡ GBANDE, LOMA, MANDINGO‡
  1935

  NETTL, BRUNO +RABEN, JOSEPH‡ NIGERIA-U.S.‡ IBO‡
  1950-51

  OFRI, DORITH‡ LIBERIA‡ VAI‡ 1965-72

  PANTALEONI, HEWITT‡ GHANA‡ EWE‡ 1969-71

  PRUITT, WILLIAM F., JR.‡ ZAIRE‡ KETE, PYGMIES,
  SALAMPASU‡ 1966-67

  QUERSIN, BENOIT J.+ QUERSIN, CHRISTINE M.‡
  CAMEROON‡ BAFIA, BALLOM, BAMILEKE, BAMUM, BULU
  ETON, PEUL, PYGMIES, SANAGA, TIKAR, VUTE‡ 1967

  QUERSIN, BENOIT J.‡ ZAIRE‡ BUSHOONG, COOFA, IBAAM,
  NGEENDE, PYAANG, SHOOWA‡ 1970

  QUERSIN, BENOIT J.‡ ZAIRE‡ BATWA, EKONDA, NTOMBA‡
  1970

DANCE
  WEMAN, PAUL HENRY‡ TANZANIA‡ HAYA, SUKUMA,
  SWAHILI‡ 1957

  WOLFF, HANS‡ NIGERIA‡ EFIK, HAUSA, IBIBIO, KAJE,
  SOBO, PABIR, YORUBA‡ 1953-54

DANCE-ACROBATIC
  QUERSIN, BENOIT J.‡ ZAIRE‡ BATWA, EKONDA, NTOMBA‡
  1970

  QUERSIN, BENOIT J.+ QUERSIN, CHRISTINE M.‡ ZAIRE‡
  BATWA, BOLIA, EKONDA‡ 1971

  VAN OVEN, JACOBA‡ SIERRA LEONE‡ FULA, GALLINAS,
  GOLA, LIMBA, LOKO, MANDINGO, MENDE, SHERBRO, SUSU,
  TEMNE, VAI, YALUNKA‡ 1964-67

DANCE-ADAVU
  ADUAMAH, E.Y.‡ GHANA-TOGO‡ EWE‡ 1968-71

DANCE-ADINKUM
  ARCHIVES OF ETHNIC MUSIC AND DANCE‡ GHANA‡
  DAGARTI, DAGOMBA, DONNO, EWE, GA, KONKOMBA, LOBI‡

DANCE-ADOWA
  ARCHIVES OF ETHNIC MUSIC AND DANCE‡ GHANA‡
  DAGARTI, DAGOMBA, DONNO, EWE, GA, KONKOMBA, LOBI‡

  GRAESSER, MARK W.‡ GHANA‡ ASANTE, FRAFRA, HAUSA,
  KANJAGA, KONKOMBA‡ 1968-69

DANCE-AFOVU
  ADUAMAH, E.Y.‡ GHANA-TOGO‡ EWE‡ 1968-71

DANCE-AGBADZA
  JONES, ARTHUR M.‡ GHANA-ENGLAND‡ EWE‡ 1956

DANCE-AGUUGA
  CARLISLE, ROXANE C.‡ SUDAN‡ ANUAK, DINKA, GAALIIN,
  NUER, SHILLUK‡ 1963

DANCE-ANCESTOR
  QUERSIN, BENOIT J.+ QUERSIN, CHRISTINE M.‡ ZAIRE‡
  BAKUTU, BOKOTE, BONGANDO, BOSAKA, BOYELA, NKUNDU,
  PYGMIES-BATWA, PYGMIES-NGOMBE‡ 1972

DANCE-AZIDA
  JONES, ARTHUR M.‡ GHANA-ENGLAND‡ EWE‡ 1956

DANCE-BAWAA
   ARCHIVES OF ETHNIC MUSIC AND DANCE‡ GHANA‡
   DAGARTI, DAGOMBA, DONNO, EWE, GA, KONKOMBA, LOBI‡

DANCE-BUKARABO
   KNIGHT, RODERIC COPLEY‡ GAMBIA, THE‡ BALANTA,
   BAMBARA, FULA, JOLA, MANDINKA, TEMNE, WOLOF‡
   1970-71

DANCE-BUTHELEZI
   COPE, TREVOR ANTHONY‡ SOUTH AFRICA‡ ZULU‡ 1965-72

DANCE-CHORAL
   BYRD, ROBERT OAKES‡ UGANDA‡ ALUR, BAGANDA,
   BAGWERE, BAKONJO, BANYANKOLE, BANYOLE, KAKWA,
   TESO‡

DANCE-EXHIBITION-TEAM
   HARING, LEE‡ KENYA‡ AKAMBA‡ 1967-68

DANCE-EXORCISM
   FARSY, MUHAMMED S.‡ TANZANIA-ZANZIBAR‡ ‡ CA1958

DANCE-GABADA
   ADUAMAH, E.Y.‡ GHANA-TOGO‡ EWE‡ 1968-71

DANCE-GAME-AGBEKOR
   ARCHIVES OF ETHNIC MUSIC AND DANCE‡ GHANA‡
   DAGARTI, DAGOMBA, DONNO, EWE, GA, KONKOMBA, LOBI‡

DANCE-HARVEST
   QUERSIN, BENOIT J.+ QUERSIN, CHRISTINE M.‡
   NIGERIA‡ ABAKPA-RIGA, AFO, ALAGO, ANGAS, ANKWAI,
   BIROM, BUROM, CHAMBA, EGGON, FULANI, HAUSA, ICHEN,
   IDOMA, JARAWA, JUKUN, KALABARI, KANTANA, KUTEP,
   KWALLA, NUPE, PYEM, RINDRE, TIV, YERGAM, YORUBA‡
   1972-73

DANCE-HEALER
   QUERSIN, BENOIT J.+ QUERSIN, CHRISTINE M.‡ ZAIRE‡
   BAKUTU, BOKOTE, BONGANDO, BOSAKA, BOYELA, NKUNDU,
   PYGMIES-BATWA, PYGMIES-NGOMBE‡ 1972

DANCE-HUSAGO
   JONES, ARTHUR M.‡ GHANA-ENGLAND‡ EWE‡ 1956

DANCE-ICILA
   JONES, ARTHUR M.‡ ZAMBIA‡ LALA‡ 1944

DANCE-ICILILI
  JONES, ARTHUR M.‡ ZAMBIA‡ LALA‡ 1944

DANCE-KETE
  GRAESSER, MARK W.‡ GHANA‡ ASANTE, FRAFRA, HAUSA,
  KANJAGA, KONKOMBA‡ 1968-69

DANCE-LECTURE
  HANNA, JUDITH LYNNE+ GORDON, MERYL‡ AFRICA-U.S.‡ ‡
  1975

DANCE-MALIPENGA
  GEOFFRION, CHARLES A.‡ MALAWI‡ ACHEWA, MANGANJA,
  NGONI‡ 1971-72

DANCE-MARRIAGE
  AMES, DAVID W.‡ GAMBIA, THE‡ WOLOF‡ 1951

  FARSY, MUHAMMED S.‡ TANZANIA-ZANZIBAR‡ ‡ CA1958

  LESLAU, WOLF‡ ETHIOPIA‡ AMHARA, GURAGE, HARARI,
  SHOA-GALLA, SOMALI, TIGRINYA‡ 1947

  LORTAT-JACOB, BERNARD‡ MOROCCO‡ AIT-MGOUN‡ 1970

DANCE-MARRIAGE-BENE
  ARCHIVES OF ETHNIC MUSIC AND DANCE‡ GHANA‡
  DAGARTI, DAGOMBA, DONNO, EWE, GA, KONKOMBA, LOBI‡

DANCE-MASKED
  AMES, DAVID W.‡ NIGERIA‡ IGBO‡ 1963-64

  ARCHIVES OF ETHNIC MUSIC AND DANCE‡ NIGERIA‡ IGBO‡

  BORGATTI, JEAN M.‡ NIGERIA‡ EDO‡ 1972-73

  BRAVMANN, RENE A.‡ UPPER VOLTA‡ BOBO, DYULA‡
  1972-74

  CHRISTIAN, VALERIE‡ UPPER VOLTA‡ BISSA, BOBO,
  BWABA, DAGARA, DYULA, FULANI, FULBE, GOUIN,
  GOURMANTCHE, HAUSA, KASSENA, KWO, LOBI, MARKA,
  MOSSI, NONDOM, POUGOULIS, SAMO-DU-SUD, YARDSE‡
  1973-74

  GLAZE, ANITA‡ IVORY COAST‡ SENUFO‡ 1969-70

  QUERSIN, BENOIT J.+ QUERSIN, CHRISTINE M.‡
  NIGERIA‡ ABAKPA-RIGA, AFO, ALAGO, ANGAS, ANKWAI,

DANCE-MASKED
  BIROM, BUROM, CHAMBA, EGGON, FULANI, HAUSA, ICHEN,
  IDOMA, JARAWA, JUKUN, KALABARI, KANTANA, KUTEP,
  KWALLA, NUPE, PYEM, RINDRE, TIV, YERGAM, YORUBA‡
  1972-73

  RUBIN, ARNOLD G.‡ NIGERIA‡ CHAMBA, HAUSA, IBO,
  JUKUN, KUTEP, TIKARI, TIV‡ 1964-65

  VAN OVEN, JACOBA‡ SIERRA LEONE‡ FULA, GALLINAS,
  GOLA, LIMBA, LOKO, MANDINGO, MENDE, SHERBRO, SUSU,
  TEMNE, VAI, YALUNKA‡ 1964-67

DANCE-MASKED-ABILE
  ARMSTRONG, ROBERT G. +WITTIG, R. CURT‡ NIGERIA‡
  IDOMA‡ 1964

DANCE-MASKED-AREKWU
  ARMSTRONG, ROBERT G.+ UNOOGWU, PATRICK‡ NIGERIA‡
  IDOMA‡ 1961

DANCE-MASKED-EFE-GELEDE
  DREWAL, HENRY JOHN‡ NIGERIA‡ YORUBA‡ 1970-71

DANCE-MASKED-EGUNGUN
  WITTIG, R. CURT‡ NIGERIA‡ YORUBA‡ 1965

DANCE-MASKED-GELEDE
  ROUGET, GILBERT‡ DAHOMEY‡ FON, GUN, HOLI, NAGO‡
  1952

DANCE-MASKED-ORO
  SPEED, FRANCIS E.+ THIEME, DARIUS L.‡ NIGERIA‡
  YORUBA‡ 1966

DANCE-MASKED-PORO
  ZEMPLEIVI, ANDRAS‡ IVORY COAST‡ SENUFO-NA-FAARA‡
  1972-74

DANCE-MEN
  AMES, DAVID W.‡ NIGERIA‡ FULBE, HAUSA, YORUBA‡
  1963-64

DANCE-MONBHONO
  ARCHIVES OF ETHNIC MUSIC AND DANCE‡ RHODESIA‡ ‡

DANCE-NYAYITO
  JONES, ARTHUR M.‡ GHANA-ENGLAND‡ EWE‡ 1956

DANCE-OSUN
  AWE, BOLANLE ALAKE‡ NIGERIA‡ YORUBA‡ 1972-74

DANCE-POPULAR-CONGOLESE
  KNIGHT, RODERIC COPLEY‡ ZAIRE‡ ‡ 1970-71

DANCE-POSSESSION
  INSTITUT D'ETHNOLOGIE DE L'UNIVERSITE DE
  STRASBOURG‡ MOROCCO‡ GNAWA‡

  ROUGET, GILBERT‡ SENEGAL‡ LEBOU, PEUL, SARAKOLE,
  SOCE, TUKULOR, WOLOF‡ 1952

DANCE-SHAMAN
  QUERSIN, BENOIT J.‡ ZAIRE‡ BUSHOONG, COOFA, IBAAM,
  NGEENDE, PYAANG, SHOOWA‡ 1970

DANCE-SOCIAL
  ADAMS, CHARLES R.‡ SWAZILAND‡ SWAZI‡ 1969-70

  GARLAND, WILLIAM‡ TANZANIA‡ WANJI‡ 1963-65

  MERRIAM, ALAN P.‡ ZAIRE‡ BASONGYE‡ 1973

  RUBIN, ARNOLD G.‡ NIGERIA‡ CHAMBA, HAUSA, IBO,
  JUKUN, KUTEP, TIKARI, TIV‡ 1964-65

DANCE-SOGBA
  JONES, ARTHUR M.‡ GHANA-ENGLAND‡ EWE‡ 1956

DANCE-SOGBADZA
  ADUAMAH, E.Y.‡ GHANA-TOGO‡ EWE‡ 1968-71

DANCE-SOVU
  JONES, ARTHUR M.‡ GHANA-ENGLAND‡ EWE‡ 1956

DANCE-TRANCE
  KATZ, RICHARD‡ BOTSWANA‡ KUNG-BUSHMEN‡ 1968

DANCE-TSWANGE
  KIRK-GREENE, ANTHONY H.M.‡ NIGERIA‡ HAUSA, KAGORO,
  TIV‡ 1962-65

DANCE-UNIVERSITY-OF-GHANA
  KEALIINOHOMOKU, JOANN W.‡ GHANA‡ ‡ 1970

DANCE-WAR
  QUERSIN, BENOIT J.‡ QUERSIN, CHRISTINE M.‡
  CAMEROON‡ BAFIA, BALLOM, BAMILEKE, BAMUM, BULU

DANCE-WAR
  ETON, PEUL, PYGMIES, SANAGA, TIKAR, VUTE≠ 1967

  QUERSIN, BENOIT J.+ QUERSIN, CHRISTINE M.≠
  NIGERIA≠ ABAKPA-RIGA, AFO, ALAGO, ANGAS, ANKWAI,
  BIROM, BUROM, CHAMBA, EGGON, FULANI, HAUSA, ICHEN,
  IDOMA, JARAWA, JUKUN, KALABARI, KANTANA, KUTEP,
  KWALLA, NUPE, PYEM, RINDRE, TIV, YERGAM, YORUBA≠
  1972-73

  QUERSIN, BENOIT J.≠ ZAIRE≠ BATWA, EKONDA, NTOMBA≠
  1970

  QUERSIN, BENOIT J.+ QUERSIN, CHRISTINE M.≠ ZAIRE≠
  BATWA, BOLIA, EKONDA≠ 1971

  QUERSIN, BENOIT J.+ QUERSIN, CHRISTINE M.≠ ZAIRE≠
  BAKUTU, BOKOTE, BONGANDO, BOSAKA, BOYELA, NKUNDU,
  PYGMIES-BATWA, PYGMIES-NGOMBE≠ 1972

DANCE-WESTERN
  OKIE, PACKARD L.≠ LIBERIA≠ BASSA, GBANDE, GOLA,
  KISSI, LOMA, MENDE, VAI≠ 1947-54

DANCE-WOMEN
  HARING, LEE≠ KENYA≠ AKAMBA≠ 1967-68

  KLEIS, GERALD W.≠ CAMEROON≠ AROCHUKU, BAKUNDU,
  IGBO, META, NKAMBE, WIDEKUM≠ 1971

DEATH
  ARCHIVES OF TRADITIONAL MUSIC≠ ≠ YORUBA≠ CA1940

  DIETERLEN, GERMAINE≠ MALI≠ DOGON≠ 1953

  FERNANDEZ, JAMES W.≠ GABON≠ FANG≠ 1960

  GANSEMANS, JOS≠ ZAIRE≠ LUBA≠ 1970

  HERSKOVITS, MELVILLE J.+ HERSKOVITS, FRANCES S.≠
  DAHOMEY≠ FON≠ 1931

  HERSKOVITS, MELVILLE J.+ HERSKOVITS, FRANCES S.≠
  GHANA≠ ASANTE≠ 1931

  MERRIAM, ALAN P.+ MERRIAM, BARBARA W.≠ ZAIRE≠
  BAHIMA, BAKOGA, BAKONGO, BAMBUTI, BANGALA, BASHI,
  BATWA, EKONDA≠ 1951-52

DEATH-DIRGE
  ARMISTEAD, SAMUEL G. + KATZ, ISRAEL J. +
  SILVERMAN, JOSEPH H.‡ MOROCCO‡ SEPHARDIC-JEW‡
  1962

  BALOGUN, ADISA‡ NIGERIA‡ YORUBA‡ 1967

DEATH-FUNERAL
  AMES, DAVID W.‡ NIGERIA‡ IGBO‡ 1963-64

  ARCHIVES OF ETHNIC MUSIC AND DANCE‡ GHANA‡
  DAGARTI, DAGOMBA, DONNO, EWE, GA, KONKOMBA, LOBI‡

  ARCHIVES OF ETHNIC MUSIC AND DANCE‡ RHODESIA‡ ‡

  BLANK, ARTHUR S., JR.+ BLANK, DONNA H.‡ IVORY
  COAST‡ GUERE, WOBE‡ 1973

  BROGGER, JAN C.‡ ETHIOPIA‡ SIDAMO‡

  CALAME, B.‡ MALI‡ BAMBARA, BOZO, DOGON, MARKA,
  MINIANKA, PEUL, RYMAYBE, SARAKOLE, SOMONO,
  SONGHAY‡ 1956-57+ 1960

  CAMP, CHARLES M.+ TRACEY, HUGH‡ RHODESIA‡ BUDJA,
  CHIKUNDA, FUNGWE, HERA, HUNGWE, KARANGA, NDAU,
  NDEBELE, NYANJA, NYASA, PEDI, RAMBA, WEMBA, YAO‡
  1948

  CAMP, CHARLES M.+ TRACEY, HUGH‡ ZAMBIA‡ BEMBA,
  LALA, LOZI, TONGA, ZINZA‡ 1947-48

  CHRISTIAN, VALERIE‡ UPPER VOLTA‡ BISSA, BOBO,
  BWABA, DAGARA, DYULA, FULANI, FULBE, GOUIN,
  GOURMANTCHE, HAUSA, KASSENA, KWO, LOBI, MARKA,
  MOSSI, NONDOM, POUGOULIS, SAMO-DU-SUD, YARDSE‡
  1973-74

  COPE, TREVOR ANTHONY‡ SOUTH AFRICA‡ ZULU‡ 1965-72

  COPLAN, DAVID+ THOMASON, LEE‡ GHANA‡ ASANTE, EWE,
  KRUBU‡ 1974

  DOBRIN, ARTHUR‡ KENYA‡ GUSII‡ 1966

  FIKRY, MONA‡ GHANA‡ WALA‡ 1966-67

  GARINE, I. DE‡ CHAD‡ KERA, MUSEY‡ 1962-63+ 1965

DEATH-FUNERAL
GEOFFRION, CHARLES A.‡ MALAWI‡ ACHEWA, MANGANJA,
NGONI‡ 1971-72

GEOFFRION, CHARLES A.‡ SIERRA LEONE‡ TEMNE,
MANDINGO‡ 1966-67

GLAZE, ANITA‡ IVORY COAST‡ SENUFO‡ 1969-70

HERSKOVITS, MELVILLE J.+ HERSKOVITS, FRANCES S.‡
DAHOMEY‡ FON‡ 1931

HERSKOVITS, MELVILLE J.+ HERSKOVITS, FRANCES S.‡
GHANA‡ ASANTE‡ 1931

HESS, ROBERT A.‡ NIGERIA‡ BURA‡ 1969

JUILLERAT, B.‡ CAMEROON‡ KIRDI‡ 1966+ 1967-68

LANGE, WERNER‡ ETHIOPIA‡ BENS, BOSA, CARA,
HINNARIO, KAFA, MERU, NA'O, SE, SEKA, SHE, ZARAS‡
1972-73

MAPOMA, ISAIAH MWESA‡ ZAMBIA‡ BEMBA‡ 1968-70+
1973

MERRIAM, ALAN P.+ MERRIAM, BARBARA W.‡ ZAIRE‡
BASONGYE‡ 1959-60

MULDROW, WILLIAM+ MULDROW, ELIZABETH‡ ETHIOPIA‡
TESHENNA‡ 1964-65

PRUITT, WILLIAM F., JR.‡ ZAIRE‡ KETE, PYGMIES,
SALAMPASU‡ 1966-67

QUERSIN, BENOIT J.+ QUERSIN, CHRISTINE M.‡
NIGERIA‡ ABAKPA-RIGA, AFO, ALAGO, ANGAS, ANKWAI,
BIROM, BUROM, CHAMBA, EGGON, FULANI, HAUSA, ICHEN,
IDOMA, JARAWA, JUKUN, KALABARI, KANTANA, KUTEP,
KWALLA, NUPE, PYEM, RINDRE, TIV, YERGAM, YORUBA‡
1972-73

QUERSIN, BENOIT J.‡ ZAIRE‡ BUSHOONG, COOFA, IBAAM,
NGEENDE, PYAANG, SHOOWA‡ 1970

QUERSIN, BENOIT J.+ QUERSIN, CHRISTINE M.‡ ZAIRE‡
BATWA, BOLIA, EKONDA‡ 1971

QUERSIN, BENOIT J.+ QUERSIN, CHRISTINE M.‡ ZAIRE‡

DEATH-FUNERAL
  BAKUTU, BOKOTE, BONGANDO, BOSAKA, BOYELA, NKUNDU,
  PYGMIES-BATWA, PYGMIES-NGOMBE‡ 1972

  RANUNG, BJORN L.C.‡ NIGERIA‡ IGEDE‡ 1971-72

  RITZENTHALER, ROBERT + RITZENTHALER, PAT‡
  CAMEROON‡ BAFUT‡ 1959

  RUBIN, ARNOLD G.‡ NIGERIA‡ CHAMBA, HAUSA, IBO,
  JUKUN, KUTEP, TIKARI, TIV‡ 1964-65

  SAPIR, J. DAVID‡ SENEGAL‡ DIOLA-FOGNY, DIOLA-KASA‡
  1960-65

  SOCIETE DE RADIODIFFUSION DE LA FRANCE D'OUTRE
  MER‡ UPPER VOLTA‡ MOSSI‡

  STRUMPF, MITCHEL‡ GHANA‡ DAGARTI, EWE, KONKOMBA‡
  1969-72

  TESSMAN, GUNTHER‡ EQUATORIAL GUINEA‡ FANG‡ 1907

  VAUGHAN, JAMES H.‡ NIGERIA‡ MARGI‡ 1974

  WOLFF, HANS‡ NIGERIA‡ EFIK, HAUSA, IBIBIO, KAJE,
  SOBO, PABIR, YORUBA‡ 1953-54

  ZEMPLEIVI, ANDRAS‡ IVORY COAST‡ SENUFO-NA-FAARA‡
  1972-74

DEATH-FUNERAL-STAGED
  VAUGHAN, JAMES H.‡ NIGERIA‡ MARGI‡ 1960

DEATH-FUNERAL-STATE
  BALOGUN, ADISA‡ NIGERIA‡ YORUBA‡ 1967

DEATH-FUNERAL-YEVE
  ADUAMAH, E.Y.‡ GHANA-TOGO‡ EWE‡ 1968-71

DEATH-MOURNING
  AGUDZE, BERNARD‡ TOGO‡ EWE‡ 1965-67

  BAHMAN, GARY‡ SIERRA LEONE‡ LIMBA, MANDINGO,
  TEMNE‡ 1971

  HERSKOVITS, MELVILLE J.+ HERSKOVITS, FRANCES S.‡
  GHANA‡ ASANTE‡ 1931

DEATH-MOURNING
   LAMAN, K.E.‡ ZAIRE‡ BAKONGO‡ 1911

   MERRIAM, ALAN P.‡ ZAIRE‡ BASONGYE‡ 1973

   ROUGET, GILBERT‡ SENEGAL‡ LEBOU, PEUL, SARAKOLE,
   SOCE, TUKULOR, WOLOF‡ 1952

   SUDAN NATIONAL MUSEUM‡ SUDAN‡ BONGO, JALUO,
   NUBIAN‡ 1959-64

   SULZMANN, ERIKA‡ CONGO, PEOPLE'S REPUBLIC OF THE‡
   ATYO‡ 1962

DIVINING
   CAMP, CHARLES M.+ TRACEY, HUGH‡ RHODESIA‡ BUDJA,
   CHIKUNDA, FUNGWE, HERA, HUNGWE, KARANGA, NDAU,
   NDEBELE, NYANJA, NYASA, PEDI, RAMBA, WEMBA, YAO‡
   1948

   FAIK-NZUJI, MADIYA‡ ZAIRE‡ LUBA‡ 1974

   HERSKOVITS, MELVILLE J.+ HERSKOVITS, FRANCES S.‡
   DAHOMEY‡ FON‡ 1931

   NOSS, PHILIP A.‡ CAMEROON‡ GBAYA‡ 1966-67

   PEEK, PHILIP M.‡ NIGERIA‡ IGBO-WESTERN, ISOKO‡
   1970-71

   ROUGET, GILBERT‡ DAHOMEY‡ FON, GUN, HOLI, NAGO‡
   1952

DIVINING-AFA-CULT
   ENGLAND, NICHOLAS M.‡ GHANA‡ EWE‡ 1969-70+ 1972

DIVINING-INTERVIEW
   MCLEAN, DAVID A.‡ ZAIRE‡ LUBA‡ 1954-61

DIVINING-ODU-IFA
   ARMSTRONG, ROBERT G.‡ NIGERIA‡ YORUBA‡

   GLEASON, JUDITH+ OGUNDIPE, JOHN‡ NIGERIA‡ YORUBA‡
   1970

   SPEED, FRANCIS E.‡ NIGERIA‡ YORUBA‡ 1966

DRAMA
   HARRIES, JEANETTE‡ MOROCCO‡ BERBER‡ 1964-65

DRAMA
  RICARD, ALAIN J.‡ TOGO‡ EWE‡ 1973

DRAMA—MUSICAL
  ARMSTRONG, ROBERT G.‡ NIGERIA‡ YORUBA‡

  ARMSTRONG, ROBERT G.‡ NIGERIA‡ YORUBA‡ 1962

DRINKING
  BLOUNT, BEN G.‡ KENYA‡ LUO‡ 1971

  CAMP, CHARLES M.+ TRACEY, HUGH‡ RHODESIA‡ BUDJA,
  CHIKUNDA, FUNGWE, HERA, HUNGWE, KARANGA, NDAU,
  NDEBELE, NYANJA, NYASA, PEDI, RAMBA, WEMBA, YAO‡
  1948

  CAMP, CHARLES M.+ TRACEY, HUGH‡ SOUTH AFRICA‡
  BHACA, CHOPI, HLUBI, NDAU, NYASA, PONDO, SHANGAAN,
  SOTHO, SWAZI, TSWANA, VENDA, XHOSA‡ 1947-48

  CAMP, CHARLES M.+ TRACEY, HUGH‡ ZAMBIA‡ BEMBA,
  LALA, LOZI, TONGA, ZINZA‡ 1947-48

  DOBRIN, ARTHUR‡ KENYA‡ GUSII‡ 1966

  FIKRY, MONA‡ GHANA‡ WALA‡ 1966-67

  KIRWEN, MICHAEL CARL‡ TANZANIA‡ SUBA‡ 1963-69

  MERRIAM, ALAN P.+ MERRIAM, BARBARA W.‡ BURUNDI‡
  ABATUTSI, BARUNDI, BATWA‡ 1951-52

  MERRIAM, ALAN P.+ MERRIAM, BARBARA W.‡ ZAIRE‡
  BAHIMA, BAKOGA, BAKONGO, BAMBUTI, BANGALA, BASHI,
  BATWA, EKONDA‡ 1951-52

  ROSS, MARC HOWARD‡ KENYA‡ KIKUYU‡ 1967

  UHLIG, -‡ TANZANIA‡ WANYAMWEZI‡ 1910

DRUM
  ADUAMAH, E.Y.‡ GHANA-TOGO‡ EWE‡ 1968-71

  AGINSKY, ETHEL G.‡ SIERRA LEONE-U.S.‡ MENDE‡ 1933

  AKPABOT, SAMUEL EKPE‡ NIGERIA‡ BIROM, HAUSA,
  IBIBIO, IBO‡ 1964-73

  ALBERTS, ARTHUR S.‡ GHANA‡ EWE, GA, IBO, TWI‡

DRUM
  1949-51

  ALBERTS, ARTHUR S.‡ IVORY COAST‡ BAULE‡ 1949-51

  ALBERTS, ARTHUR S.‡ LIBERIA‡ FANTI, LOMA, MANO‡
  1949-51

  ANKERMANN, BERNHARD‡ CAMEROON‡ BAMUM‡ 1909

  ARCHIVES OF ETHNIC MUSIC AND DANCE‡ CAMEROON‡ ‡

  ARCHIVES OF ETHNIC MUSIC AND DANCE‡ ETHIOPIA‡
  AMHARA, TIGRINYA‡

  ARCHIVES OF ETHNIC MUSIC AND DANCE‡ GHANA‡
  DAGARTI, DAGOMBA, DONNO, EWE, GA, KONKOMBA, LOBI‡

  ARCHIVES OF ETHNIC MUSIC AND DANCE‡ NIGERIA‡ IGBO‡

  ARCHIVES OF ETHNIC MUSIC AND DANCE‡ RHODESIA‡ ‡

  ARCHIVES OF ETHNIC MUSIC AND DANCE‡ SENEGAL‡ ‡

  ARCHIVES OF ETHNIC MUSIC AND DANCE‡ UPPER VOLTA‡
  BOBO, BWABA, DYULA, FULANI, FULBE, GOUIN,
  GOURMANTCHE, LOBI, MINIANKA, MOSSI, SENUFO,
  YARDSE‡

  ARMSTRONG, ROBERT G.+ UNODGWU, PATRICK‡ NIGERIA‡
  IDOMA‡ 1961

  BRANDILY, MONIQUE‡ CHAD‡ KANEMBU, KOTOKO, TEDA‡
  1961+ 1963+ 1965

  BRANDILY, MONIQUE‡ CHAD‡ FEZZANAIS, TEDA‡ 1969

  BUCHANAN, CAROLE‡ UGANDA‡ BANYORO, BATORO‡
  1968-69

  BYRD, ROBERT OAKES‡ UGANDA‡ ALUR, BAGANDA,
  BAGWERE, BAKONJO, BANYANKOLE, BANYOLE, KAKWA,
  TESO‡

  CALAME, B.‡ MALI‡ BAMBARA, BOZO, DOGON, MARKA,
  MINIANKA, PEUL, RYMAYBE, SARAKOLE, SOMONO,
  SONGHAY‡ 1956-57+ 1960

  CALKINS, HOWARD W.+ RADIO DAHOMEY‡ DAHOMEY‡ DENDI,

DRUM

DOMPAGO, FON, MAHI, YORUBA‡ CA1967

CAMP, CHARLES M.+ TRACEY, HUGH‡ RHODESIA‡ BUDJA,
CHIKUNDA, FUNGWE, HERA, HUNGWE, KARANGA, NDAU,
NDEBELE, NYANJA, NYASA, PEDI, RAMBA, WEMBA, YAO‡
1948

CAMP, CHARLES M.+ TRACEY, HUGH‡ ZAMBIA‡ BEMBA,
LALA, LOZI, TONGA, ZINZA‡ 1947-48

CHRISTIAN, VALERIE‡ UPPER VOLTA‡ BISSA, BOBO,
BWABA, DAGARA, DYULA, FULANI, FULBE, GOUIN,
GOURMANTCHE, HAUSA, KASSENA, KWO, LOBI, MARKA,
MOSSI, NONDOM, POUGOULIS, SAMO-DU-SUD, YARDSE‡
1973-74

CLAUSS, BERNHARD PETER‡ MALI‡ BAMBARA, TAMACHECK‡
1973

COHEN, DAVID WILLIAM‡ UGANDA‡ BASOGA‡ 1966-67

COLLEGE OF MUSIC, UNIVERSITY OF NIGERIA‡ NIGERIA‡
BINI, BOKI, DAKARAWA, EFIK-IBIBIO, EKOI, FULANI,
HAUSA, IBO, IDOMA, IJAW, JABA, MADA, YALA, YORUBA,
ZABEBMAWA‡

COOKE, PETER R.‡ UGANDA‡ BAGANDA‡ 1965-68

COPLAN, DAVID+ THOMASON, LEE‡ GHANA‡ ASANTE, EWE,
KROBO‡ 1974

COURLANDER, HAROLD‡ ETHIOPIA‡ TIGRINYA‡ 1943

CURTIN, PHILIP D.‡ SENEGAL‡ ARAB, DIAKHANKE,
MALINKE, PULAR‡ 1966

DEPARTMENT OF ANTHROPOLOGY, UNIVERSITY OF BRITISH
COLUMBIA‡ TUNISIA‡ ‡

DIETERLEN, GERMAINE‡ MALI‡ DOGON‡ 1953

DOBRIN, ARTHUR‡ KENYA‡ GUSII‡ 1966

DREWAL, HENRY JOHN‡ NIGERIA‡ YORUBA‡ 1970-71

ELLOVICH, RISA SUE‡ IVORY COAST‡ DYULA, MALINKE,
VOLTAIC‡ 1973-74

DRUM
  ENGLAND, NICHOLAS M.‡ GHANA‡ EWE‡ 1969-70+ 1972

  FARSY, MUHAMMED S.‡ TANZANIA-ZANZIBAR‡ ‡ CA1958

  HAMBLY, WILFRED D.‡ ANGOLA‡ OVIMBUNDU‡ 1929-30

  HANLEY, MARY ANN CSJ‡ NIGERIA‡ ANGAS, BACHAMA,
  CHAMBA, EFIK, GWANDARA, HAUSA, IBIBIO, IBO, JABA,
  KERI-KERI, YORUBA‡ 1973

  HASSENPFLUG, EARL C.‡ MALI‡ BOZO, DOGON‡ 1970

  HATFIELD, COLBY R.‡ TANZANIA‡ SUKUMA‡ 1971

  HOLIDAY, GEOFFREY D.‡ NIGER‡ TUAREG‡ CA1958

  IRVINE, JUDITH TEMKIN‡ SENEGAL‡ WOLOF‡ 1970-71

  JUILLERAT, B.‡ CAMEROON‡ KIRDI‡ 1966+ 1967-68

  KNIGHT, RODERIC COPLEY‡ GAMBIA, THE‡ BALANTA,
  BAMBARA, FULA, JOLA, MANDINKA, TEMNE, WOLOF‡
  1970-71

  LESLAU, WOLF‡ ETHIOPIA‡ AMHARA, GURAGE, HARARI,
  SHOA-GALLA, SOMALI, TIGRINYA‡ 1947

  LORTAT-JACOB, BERNARD‡ MOROCCO‡ AIT-BOUGMEZ,
  FTOUKA‡ 1971

  MAGYAR TUDOMANYOS AKADEMIA NEPZENEKUTATO CSOPORT‡
  EGYPT‡ COPT, FELLAHIN, NUBIAN‡ 1966-67 + 1969

  MARTIN, JANE JACKSON‡ LIBERIA‡ GREBO‡ 1968+
  1972-75

  NATIONAL MUSEUM OF TANZANIA‡ TANZANIA‡ MAKONDE,
  MALILA, MWERA, YAO‡

  NETTL, BRUNO +RABEN, JOSEPH‡ NIGERIA-U.S.‡ IBO‡
  1950-51

  NORSK RIKSKRINGKASTING‡ GHANA‡ ‡ 1966

  OKIE, PACKARD L.‡ LIBERIA‡ BASSA, BELE, GIO,
  KPELLE, KRU, MANDINGO, VAI‡ 1947-54

  PAASCHE, -‡ TANZANIA‡ KIZIBA‡ 1910

DRUM
  PANTALEONI, HEWITT‡ GHANA‡ EWE‡ 1969-71

  PELLIGRA, D.‡ ALGERIA‡ TUAREG‡ 1970

  QUERSIN, BENOIT J.+ QUERSIN, CHRISTINE M.‡
  CAMEROON‡ BAFIA, BALLOM, BAMILEKE, BAMUM, BULU
  ETON, PEUL, PYGMIES, SANAGA, TIKAR, VUTE‡ 1967

  QUERSIN, BENOIT J.‡ ZAIRE‡ BATWA, EKONDA, NTOMBA‡
  1970

  QUERSIN, BENOIT J.+ QUERSIN, CHRISTINE M.‡ ZAIRE‡
  BATWA, BOLIA, EKONDA‡ 1971

  QUERSIN, BENOIT J.+ QUERSIN, CHRISTINE M.‡ ZAIRE‡
  BAKUTU, BOKOTE, BONGANDO, BOSAKA, BOYELA, NKUNDU,
  PYGMIES-BATWA, PYGMIES-NGOMBE‡ 1972

  ROUGET, GILBERT‡ IVORY COAST‡ ADIOUKROU, EBRIE‡
  1952

  RUBIN, ARNOLD G.‡ NIGERIA‡ CHAMBA, HAUSA, IBO,
  JUKUN, KUTEP, TIKARI, TIV‡ 1964-65

  SMITS, LUCAS GERARDUS ALFONSUS‡ ALGERIA‡ TUAREG‡
  1968-69

  STUTTMAN, LEONARD M.‡ LIBERIA‡ GREBO, KRAHN‡ 1956

  SULZMANN, ERIKA‡ CONGO, PEOPLE'S REPUBLIC OF THE‡
  ATYO‡ 1962

  SULZMANN, ERIKA‡ ZAIRE‡ BABOMA, BASENGELE, BOLIA,
  EKONDA, NTOMBA‡ 1953-72

  UPADHYAYA, HARI S.+ ORI, R.‡ MAURITIUS‡
  UTTAR-PRADESH‡ 1961

  VAN THIEL, PAUL A.H.‡ UGANDA‡ BANTU, BANYANKOLE‡
  1964-65+ 1969+ 1970-72

  VERMEER, DONALD E.‡ GHANA‡ EWE‡ 1969

  WEISSWANGE, KARIN I.S.‡ LIBERIA‡ LOMA, MANDINGO‡
  1963-65+ 1972-73

  WEMAN, PAUL HENRY‡ NIGERIA‡ YORUBA‡ 1957

DRUM
  WEMAN, HENRY PAUL‡ RHODESIA‡ KARANGA, LEMBA,
  VENDA, ZULU‡ 1957

  WEMAN, PAUL HENRY‡ TANZANIA‡ HAYA, SUKUMA,
  SWAHILI‡ 1957

  WEMAN, PAUL HENRY‡ ZAIRE‡ LUBA‡ 1957

  WILLIAMS, CHESTER S.‡ SOMALIA‡ ‡ 1962

  WILLIAMSON, KAY‡ NIGERIA‡ IJO‡ 1959

  WITTIG, R. CURT‡ NIGERIA‡ YORUBA‡ 1965

  WOLFF, HANS‡ NIGERIA‡ EFIK, HAUSA, IBIBIO, KAJE,
  SOBO, PABIR, YORUBA‡ 1953-54

  ZEMP, HUGO‡ MOROCCO‡ ‡ 1960

DRUM- OSUN
  AWE, BOLANLE ALAKE‡ NIGERIA‡ YORUBA‡ 1972-74

DRUM-AGERE
  SPEED, FRANCIS E.+ THIEME, DARIUS L.‡ NIGERIA‡
  YORUBA‡ 1966

DRUM-AKACHE
  JONES, ARTHUR M.‡ ZAMBIA‡ LALA‡ 1944

DRUM-APESIN
  SPEED, FRANCIS E.+ THIEME, DARIUS L.‡ NIGERIA‡
  YORUBA‡ 1966

DRUM-APINTI
  QUERSIN, BENOIT J.+ QUERSIN, CHRISTINE M.‡
  NIGERIA‡ ABAKPA-RIGA, AFO, ALAGO, ANGAS, ANKWAI,
  BIROM, BUROM, CHAMBA, EGGON, FULANI, HAUSA, ICHEN,
  IDOMA, JARAWA, JUKUN, KALABARI, KANTANA, KUTEP,
  KWALLA, NUPE, PYEM, RINDRE, TIV, YERGAM, YORUBA‡
  1972-73

DRUM-ATSIMEVU
  JONES, ARTHUR M.‡ GHANA-ENGLAND‡ EWE‡ 1956

DRUM-ATUMPAN
  AGUDZE, BERNARD‡ TOGO‡ EWE‡ 1965-67

  GRAESSER, MARK W.‡ GHANA‡ ASANTE, FRAFRA, HAUSA,

DRUM—ATUMPAN
  KANJAGA, KONKOMBA‡ 1968-69

  HANLEY, MARY ANN CSJ‡ GHANA‡ BUILSA, DAGARI, EWE,
  FANTI, FRAFRA, GA, KASSENA, NANKANI, TWI‡ 1972

DRUM—BAN
  BAHMAN, GARY‡ SIERRA LEONE‡ LIMBA, MANDINGO,
  TEMNE‡ 1971

  VAN OVEN, JACOBA‡ SIERRA LEONE‡ FULA, GALLINAS,
  GOLA, LIMBA, LOKO, MANDINGO, MENDE, SHERBRO, SUSU,
  TEMNE, VAI, YALUNKA‡ 1964-67

DRUM—BARREL
  AMES, DAVID W.‡ NIGERIA‡ HAUSA‡ 1963

DRUM—BATA
  QUERSIN, BENOIT J.+ QUERSIN, CHRISTINE M.‡
  NIGERIA‡ ABAKPA-RIGA, AFO, ALAGO, ANGAS, ANKWAI,
  BIROM, BUROM, CHAMBA, EGGON, FULANI, HAUSA, ICHEN,
  IDOMA, JARAWA, JUKUN, KALABARI, KANTANA, KUTEP,
  KWALLA, NUPE, PYEM, RINDRE, TIV, YERGAM, YORUBA‡
  1972-73

  SPEED, FRANCIS E.+ THIEME, DARIUS L.‡ NIGERIA‡
  YORUBA‡ 1966

  WELCH, DAVID B.‡ NIGERIA‡ YORUBA‡ 1970-71

DRUM—BUL
  CARLISLE, ROXANE C.‡ SUDAN‡ ANUAK, DINKA, GAALIIN,
  NUER, SHILLUK‡ 1963

DRUM—CLAY
  BOWLES, PAUL+ WANKLYN, CHRISTOPHER‡ MOROCCO‡ ‡
  CA1959-62

  GLAZE, ANITA‡ IVORY COAST‡ SENUFO‡ 1969-70

DRUM—CLAY-POT
  AMES, DAVID W.‡ NIGERIA‡ IGBO‡ 1963-64

  ARMSTRONG, ROBERT G.+ UNJUGWU, PATRICK‡ NIGERIA‡
  IDOMA‡ 1961

DRUM—CONICAL
  AMES, DAVID W.‡ NIGERIA‡ HAUSA‡ 1963

DRUM-CONICAL
  BAHMAN, GARY‡ SIERRA LEONE‡ LIMBA, MANDINGO,
  TEMNE‡ 1971

  FARSY, MUHAMMED S.‡ TANZANIA-ZANZIBAR‡ ‡ CA1958

  VAN OVEN, JACOBA‡ SIERRA LEONE‡ FULA, GALLINAS,
  GOLA, LIMBA, LOKO, MANDINGO, MENDE, SHERBRO, SUSU,
  TEMNE, VAI, YALUNKA‡ 1964-67

DRUM-CYLINDRICAL
  AMES, DAVID W.‡ NIGERIA‡ IGBO‡ 1963-64

  ARCHIVES OF ETHNIC MUSIC AND DANCE‡ UPPER VOLTA‡
  BOBO, BWABA, DYULA, FULANI, FULBE, GOUIN,
  GOURMANTCHE, LOBI, MINIANKA, MOSSI, SENUFO,
  YARDSE‡

  CAMP, CHARLES M.+ TRACEY, HUGH‡ RHODESIA‡ BUDJA,
  CHIKUNDA, FUNGWE, HERA, HUNGWE, KARANGA, NDAU,
  NDEBELE, NYANJA, NYASA, PEDI, RAMBA, WEMBA, YAO‡
  1948

  CHRISTIAN, VALERIE+ ROSELLINI, JAMES N.‡ UPPER
  VOLTA‡ FULBE, KASSENA, MARKA, MOSSI‡ 1973

  GLAZE, ANITA‡ IVORY COAST‡ SENUFO‡ 1969-70

  HANLEY, MARY ANN CSJ‡ GHANA‡ BUILSA, DAGARI, EWE,
  FANTI, FRAFRA, GA, KASSENA, NANKANI, TWI‡ 1972

  STONE, RUTH M.+ STONE, VERLON L.‡ LIBERIA‡ KPELLE‡
  1970

  VAN OVEN, JACOBA‡ SIERRA LEONE‡ FULA, GALLINAS,
  GOLA, LIMBA, LOKO, MANDINGO, MENDE, SHERBRO, SUSU,
  TEMNE, VAI, YALUNKA‡ 1964-67

DRUM-CYLINDRICAL-SNARE
  AMES, DAVID W.‡ NIGERIA‡ FULBE, HAUSA, YORUBA‡
  1963-64

DRUM-DALUKA
  CARLISLE, ROXANE C.‡ SUDAN‡ ANUAK, DINKA, GAALIIN,
  NUER, SHILLUK‡ 1963

DRUM-DERBUKA
  BOWLES, PAUL+ WANKLYN, CHRISTOPHER‡ MOROCCO‡ ‡
  CA1959-62

DRUM-DONNO
  GRAESSER, MARK W.‡ GHANA‡ ASANTE, FRAFRA, HAUSA,
  KANJAGA, KONKOMBA‡ 1968-69

DRUM-EKOMAH
  PLOTNICOV, LEONARD‡ NIGERIA‡ BIRCM, EFIK, HAUSA,
  IBIBIO, IBO, IJAW, KAGORO, KATAM, TIV‡ 1961-62

DRUM-FRAME
  ADUAMAH, E.Y.‡ GHANA-TOGO‡ EWE‡ 1968-71

  AMES, DAVID W.‡ NIGERIA‡ IGBO‡ 1963-64

  BOWLES, PAUL+ WANKLYN, CHRISTOPHER‡ MOROCCO‡ ‡
  CA1959-62

  BRANDILY, MONIQUE‡ CHAD‡ FEZZANAIS, TEDA‡ 1969

  HANLEY, MARY ANN CSJ‡ GHANA‡ BUILSA, DAGARI, EWE,
  FANTI, FRAFRA, GA, KASSENA, NANKANI, TWI‡ 1972

  QUERSIN, BENOIT J.+ QUERSIN, CHRISTINE M.‡
  CAMEROON‡ BAFIA, BALLOM, BAMILEKE, BAMUM, BULU
  ETON, PEUL, PYGMIES, SANAGA, TIKAR, VUTE‡ 1967

  VAN OVEN, JACOBA‡ SIERRA LEONE‡ FULA, GALLINAS,
  GOLA, LIMBA, LOKO, MANDINGO, MENDE, SHERBRO, SUSU,
  TEMNE, VAI, YALUNKA‡ 1964-67

  WANKLYN, CHRISTOPHER‡ MOROCCO‡ AIT-SIDI-MERRI,
  DEGWANA, MISIWA, OULED-MTAA‡ 1963+ 1969

  WILLETT, FRANK‡ NIGERIA‡ YORUBA‡ 1972

DRUM-FRAME-RIGG
  CARLISLE, ROXANE C.‡ SUDAN‡ ANUAK, DINKA, GAALIIN,
  NUER, SHILLUK‡ 1963

DRUM-FRICTION
  CAMP, CHARLES M.+ TRACEY, HUGH‡ ZAMBIA‡ BEMBA,
  LALA, LOZI, TONGA, ZINZA‡ 1947-48

  MERRIAM, ALAN P.‡ ZAIRE‡ BASONGYE‡ 1973

DRUM-GOBLET
  CAMP, CHARLES M.+ TRACEY, HUGH‡ ZAMBIA‡ BEMBA,
  LALA, LOZI, TONGA, ZINZA‡ 1947-48

  MERRIAM, ALAN P.+ MERRIAM, BARBARA W.‡ ZAIRE‡

DRUM-GOBLET
  BASONGYE‡ 1959-60

  STONE, RUTH M.+ STONE, VERLON L.‡ LIBERIA‡ KPELLE‡
  1970

DRUM-GOURD
  AMES, DAVID W.‡ NIGERIA‡ FULBE, HAUSA, YORUBA‡
  1963-64

  ARCHIVES OF ETHNIC MUSIC AND DANCE‡ UPPER VOLTA‡
  BOBO, BWABA, DYULA, FULANI, FULBE, GOUIN,
  GOURMANTCHE, LOBI, MINIANKA, MOSSI, SENUFO,
  YARDSE‡

  HANLEY, MARY ANN CSJ‡ GHANA‡ BUILSA, DAGARI, EWE,
  FANTI, FRAFRA, GA, KASSENA, NANKANI, TWI‡ 1972

  HANLEY, MARY ANN CSJ‡ UPPER VOLTA‡ ‡ 1972

DRUM-HOURGLASS
  AMES, DAVID W.‡ GAMBIA, THE‡ WOLOF‡ 1951

  AMES, DAVID W.‡ NIGERIA‡ HAUSA‡ 1963

  AMES, DAVID W.‡ NIGERIA‡ FULBE, HAUSA, YORUBA‡
  1963-64

  ARCHIVES OF ETHNIC MUSIC AND DANCE‡ UPPER VOLTA‡
  BOBO, BWABA, DYULA, FULANI, FULBE, GOUIN,
  GOURMANTCHE, LOBI, MINIANKA, MOSSI, SENUFO,
  YARDSE‡

  BAHMAN, GARY‡ SIERRA LEONE‡ LIMBA, MANDINGO,
  TEMNE‡ 1971

  BALOGUN, ADISA‡ NIGERIA‡ YORUBA‡ 1964+ 1970

  FIKRY, MONA‡ GHANA‡ WALA‡ 1966-67

  HANLEY, MARY ANN CSJ‡ GHANA‡ BUILSA, DAGARI, EWE,
  FANTI, FRAFRA, GA, KASSENA, NANKANI, TWI‡ 1972

  HANLEY, MARY ANN CSJ‡ UPPER VOLTA‡ ‡ 1972

  OKIE, PACKARD L.‡ LIBERIA‡ BASSA, BELE, GIO,
  KPELLE, KRU, MANDINGO, VAI‡ 1947-54

  QUERSIN, BENOIT J.+ QUERSIN, CHRISTINE M.‡

DRUM-HOURGLASS
  NIGERIA‡ ABAKPA-RIGA, AFO, ALAGO, ANGAS, ANKWAI,
  BIROM, BUROM, CHAMBA, EGGON, FULANI, HAUSA, ICHEN,
  IDOMA, JARAWA, JUKUN, KALABARI, KANTANA, KUTEP,
  KWALLA, NUPE, PYEM, RINDRE, TIV, YERGAM, YORUBA‡
  1972-73

  STONE, RUTH M.+ STONE, VERLON L.‡ LIBERIA‡ KPELLE‡
  1970

  VAN OVEN, JACOBA‡ SIERRA LEONE‡ FULA, GALLINAS,
  GOLA, LIMBA, LOKO, MANDINGO, MENDE, SHERBRO, SUSU,
  TEMNE, VAI, YALUNKA‡ 1964-67

DRUM-HOURGLASS-DUNDUN
  SPEED, FRANCIS E.+ THIEME, DARIUS L.‡ NIGERIA‡
  YORUBA‡ 1966

  WELCH, DAVID B.‡ NIGERIA‡ YORUBA‡ 1970-71

DRUM-ICIBITIKU
  JONES, ARTHUR M.‡ ZAMBIA‡ LALA‡ 1944

DRUM-IKULU
  JONES, ARTHUR M.‡ ZAMBIA‡ LALA‡ 1944

DRUM-IYALU
  WELCH, DAVID B.‡ NIGERIA‡ YORUBA‡ 1970-71

DRUM-JEMBE
  CAMARA, S.‡ SENEGAL‡ MALINKE‡ 1970+ 1971

DRUM-KAGAN
  JONES, ARTHUR M.‡ GHANA-ENGLAND‡ EWE‡ 1956

DRUM-KALANGU
  RHODES, WILLARD‡ NIGERIA‡ FULANI, HAUSA, TIV,
  TUAREG, YORUBA‡ 1973-74

DRUM-KAZAGI
  RHODES, WILLARD‡ NIGERIA‡ FULANI, HAUSA, TIV,
  TUAREG, YORUBA‡ 1973-74

DRUM-KETTLE
  AMES, DAVID W.‡ GAMBIA, THE‡ WOLOF‡ 1951

  AMES, DAVID W.‡ NIGERIA‡ HAUSA‡ 1963

  AMES, DAVID W.‡ NIGERIA‡ FULBE, HAUSA, YORUBA‡

DRUM-KETTLE
  1963-64

  VAN OVEN, JACOBA‡ SIERRA LEONE‡ FULA, GALLINAS,
  GOLA, LIMBA, LOKO, MANDINGO, MENDE, SHERBRO, SUSU,
  TEMNE, VAI, YALUNKA‡ 1964-67

DRUM-L'BONGO
  WILLETT, FRANK‡ NIGERIA‡ YORUBA‡ 1972

DRUM-LANGUAGE
  AGUDZE, BERNARD‡ TOGO‡ EWE‡ 1965-67

  AMES, DAVID W.‡ NIGERIA‡ HAUSA‡ 1963

  ARCHIVES OF LANGUAGES OF THE WORLD‡ ‡ KWA‡

  COHEN, DAVID WILLIAM‡ UGANDA‡ BASOGA‡ 1966-67

  FAIK-NZUJI, MADIYA‡ ZAIRE‡ LUBA‡ 1974

  FERNANDEZ, JAMES W.‡ GABON‡ FANG‡ 1960

  FIKRY, MONA‡ GHANA‡ WALA‡ 1966-67

  GANSEMANS, JOS‡ ZAIRE‡ LUBA‡ 1970

  GRAESSER, MARK W.‡ GHANA‡ ASANTE, FRAFRA, HAUSA,
  KANJAGA, KONKOMBA‡ 1968-69

  HERZOG, GEORGE‡ LIBERIA‡ GREBO, JABO, KRU‡ 1930

  KABEMBA, MUFUTA KABANDANYI‡ ZAIRE‡ KUBA, LUBA‡
  1965‡ 1972

  KULP, PHILIP M.‡ NIGERIA‡ BURA‡ 1973

  QUERSIN, BENOIT J.‡ ZAIRE‡ BATWA, EKONDA, NTOMBA‡
  1970

  SCHWARZ, JEAN‡ CAMEROON‡ BANEN‡ 1968

  SMEND, W.A.‡ TOGO‡ HAUSA‡ 1905

  SPEED, FRANCIS E.‡ THIEME, DARIUS L.‡ NIGERIA‡
  YORUBA‡ 1966

  STONE, RUTH M.‡ STONE, VERLON L.‡ LIBERIA‡ KPELLE‡
  1970

DRUM-LANGUAGE
  VAN OVEN, JACOBA‡ SIERRA LEONE‡ FULA, GALLINAS,
  GOLA, LIMBA, LOKO, MANDINGO, MENDE, SHERBRO, SUSU,
  TEMNE, VAI, YALUNKA‡ 1964-67

  WARREN, DENNIS M.‡ GHANA‡ BONO‡ 1969-71

DRUM-LANGUAGE-LECTURE
  CARRINGTON, JOHN F.+ GORDON, MERYL‡ ZAIRE-U.S.‡ ‡
  1975

DRUM-LOMONDA
  MERRIAM, ALAN P.+ MERRIAM, BARBARA W.‡ ZAIRE‡
  BAHIMA, BAKOGA, BAKONGO, BAMBUTI, BANGALA, BASHI,
  BATWA, EKONDA‡ 1951-52

DRUM-MORTAR-TINDI
  BOURGEOT, A.‡ ALGERIA‡ TUAREG‡ 1970

DRUM-NGOMA
  MERRIAM, ALAN P.+ MERRIAM, BARBARA W.‡ BURUNDI‡
  ABATUTSI, BARUNDI, BATWA‡ 1951-52

  MERRIAM, ALAN P.+ MERRIAM, BARBARA W.‡ RWANDA‡
  ABAGOGWE, ABAGOYI, ABAHORORO, ABANYAMBO, ABATUTSI,
  ABAYOVU, BAHIMA, BAHUTU, BAKIGA, BATWA‡ 1951-52

  MERRIAM, ALAN P.+ MERRIAM, BARBARA W.‡ ZAIRE‡
  BAHIMA, BAKOGA, BAKONGO, BAMBUTI, BANGALA, BASHI,
  BATWA, EKONDA‡ 1951-52

DRUM-POT
  QUERSIN, BENOIT J.+ QUERSIN, CHRISTINE M.‡
  NIGERIA‡ ABAKPA-RIGA, AFO, ALAGO, ANGAS, ANKWAI,
  BIROM, BUROM, CHAMBA, EGGON, FULANI, HAUSA, ICHEN,
  IDOMA, JARAWA, JUKUN, KALABARI, KANTANA, KUTEP,
  KWALLA, NUPE, PYEM, RINDRE, TIV, YERGAM, YORUBA‡
  1972-73

DRUM-POTTERY
  WANKLYN, CHRISTOPHER‡ MOROCCO‡ AIT-SIDI-MERRI,
  DEGWANA, MISIWA, OULED-MTAA‡ 1963+ 1969

DRUM-PROVERB
  SMEND, W.A.‡ TOGO‡ HAUSA‡ 1905

  SPEED, FRANCIS E.+ THIEME, DARIUS L.‡ NIGERIA‡
  YORUBA‡ 1966

DRUM-ROYAL-TIMI-OF-EDE
  HARRIS, JOHN REES‡ NIGERIA‡ URHOBO, YORUBA‡ 1965

DRUM-SINGLE-HEADED
  MERRIAM, ALAN P.+ MERRIAM, BARBARA W.‡ ZAIRE‡
  BAHIMA, BAKOGA, BAKONGO, BAMBUTI, BANGALA, BASHI,
  BATWA, EKONDA‡ 1951-52

  QUERSIN, BENOIT J.+ QUERSIN, CHRISTINE M.‡
  CAMEROON‡ BAFIA, BALLOM, BAMILEKE, BAMUM, BULU
  ETON, PEUL, PYGMIES, SANAGA, TIKAR, VUTE‡ 1967

  QUERSIN, BENOIT J.‡ ZAIRE‡ BUSHOCNG, COOFA, IBAAM,
  NGEENDE, PYAANG, SHOOWA‡ 1970

DRUM-SLIT
  AMES, DAVID W.‡ NIGERIA‡ IGBO‡ 1963-64

  BAHMAN, GARY‡ SIERRA LEONE‡ LIMBA, MANDINGO,
  TEMNE‡ 1971

  BIEBUYCK, DANIEL P.‡ ZAIRE‡ LEGA, LUBA, LUNDA,
  MANGBETU, MAYOGO, NANDE, NYANGA, ZAMBE‡ 1952-61

  GANSEMANS, JOS‡ ZAIRE‡ LUBA‡ 1970

  HERZOG, GEORGE‡ LIBERIA‡ GREBO, JABO, KRU‡ 1930

  MERRIAM, ALAN P.+ MERRIAM, BARBARA W.‡ ZAIRE‡
  BAHIMA, BAKOGA, BAKONGO, BAMBUTI, BANGALA, BASHI,
  BATWA, EKONDA‡ 1951-52

  MERRIAM, ALAN P.+ MERRIAM, BARBARA W.‡ ZAIRE‡
  BASONGYE‡ 1959-60

  QUERSIN, BENOIT J.+ QUERSIN, CHRISTINE M.‡
  CAMEROON‡ BAFIA, BALLOM, BAMILEKE, BAMUM, BULU
  ETON, PEUL, PYGMIES, SANAGA, TIKAR, VUTE‡ 1967

  QUERSIN, BENOIT J.+ QUERSIN, CHRISTINE M.‡
  NIGERIA‡ ABAKPA-RIGA, AFO, ALAGO, ANGAS, ANKWAI,
  BIROM, BUROM, CHAMBA, EGGON, FULANI, HAUSA, ICHEN,
  IDOMA, JARAWA, JUKUN, KALABARI, KANTANA, KUTEP,
  KWALLA, NUPE, PYEM, RINDRE, TIV, YERGAM, YORUBA‡
  1972-73

  QUERSIN, BENOIT J.‡ ZAIRE‡ BATWA, EKONDA, NTOMBA‡
  1970

DRUM-SLIT
   QUERSIN, BENOIT J.+ QUERSIN, CHRISTINE M.≠ ZAIRE≠
   BATWA, BOLIA, EKONDA≠ 1971

   SAPIR, J. DAVID≠ SENEGAL≠ DIOLA-FOGNY, DIOLA-KASA≠
   1960-65

   STONE, RUTH M.+ STONE, VERLON L.≠ LIBERIA≠ KPELLE≠
   1970

   VAN OVEN, JACOBA≠ SIERRA LEONE≠ FULA, GALLINAS,
   GOLA, LIMBA, LOKO, MANDINGO, MENDE, SHERBRO, SUSU,
   TEMNE, VAI, YALUNKA≠ 1964-67

DRUM-SLIT-KIYONDO
   MERRIAM, ALAN P.≠ ZAIRE≠ BASONGYE≠ 1973

DRUM-SLIT-LECTURE
   CARRINGTON, JOHN F.+ GORDON, MERYL≠ ZAIRE-U.S.≠ ≠
   1975

DRUM-SLIT-LUNKUFI
   MERRIAM, ALAN P.≠ ZAIRE≠ BASONGYE≠ 1973

DRUM-SNARE
   AMES, DAVID W.≠ NIGERIA≠ HAUSA≠ 1963

DRUM-SOGO
   JONES, ARTHUR M.≠ GHANA-ENGLAND≠ EWE≠ 1956

DRUM-TAMBU
   MERRIAM, ALAN P.+ MERRIAM, BARBARA W.≠ ZAIRE≠
   BAHIMA, BAKUGA, BAKONGO, BAMBUTI, BANGALA, BASHI,
   BATWA, EKONDA≠ 1951-52

DRUM-TUNED
   DEPARTMENT OF THEATRE ARTS, UNIVERSITY OF DAR ES
   SALAAM≠ TANZANIA≠ ≠

DRUM-WATER
   ALBERTS, ARTHUR S.≠ ZAIRE≠ ≠ 1952-54

   BRANDILY, MONIQUE≠ CHAD≠ KANEMBU, KOTOKO, TEDA≠
   1961+ 1963+ 1965

   HOLIDAY, GEOFFREY D.≠ NIGER≠ TUAREG≠ CA1958

   ROUGET, GILBERT≠ GUINEA≠ MALINKE≠ 1952

ENTERTAINMENT
   ZEZURU‡ 1972-73

   LORTAT-JACOB, BERNARD‡ ETHIOPIA‡ DORZE‡ 1974-75

   MASSING, ANDREAS‡ LIBERIA‡ KRU‡ 1971-72

   MOREY, ROBERT H.‡ LIBERIA‡ GBANDE, LOMA, MANDINGO‡
   1935

   OKIE, PACKARD L.‡ LIBERIA‡ BASSA, GBANDE, GOLA,
   KISSI, LOMA, MENDE, VAI‡ 1947-54

   OKIE, PACKARD L.‡ LIBERIA‡ BASSA, BELE, GIO,
   KPELLE, KRU, MANDINGO, VAI‡ 1947-54

   QUERSIN, BENOIT J.+ QUERSIN, CHRISTINE M.‡
   CAMEROON‡ BAFIA, BALLOM, BAMILEKE, BAMUM, BULU
   ETON, PEUL, PYGMIES, SANAGA, TIKAR, VUTE‡ 1967

   QUERSIN, BENOIT J.+ QUERSIN, CHRISTINE M.‡
   NIGERIA‡ ABAKPA-RIGA, AFO, ALAGO, ANGAS, ANKWAI,
   BIROM, BUROM, CHAMBA, EGGON, FULANI, HAUSA, ICHEN,
   IDOMA, JARAWA, JUKUN, KALABARI, KANTANA, KUTEP,
   KWALLA, NUPE, PYEM, RINDRE, TIV, YERGAM, YORUBA‡
   1972-73

   QUERSIN, BENOIT J.+ QUERSIN, CHRISTINE M.‡ ZAIRE‡
   BATWA, BOLIA, EKONDA‡ 1971

   QUERSIN, BENOIT J.+ QUERSIN, CHRISTINE M.‡ ZAIRE‡
   BAKUTU, BOKOTE, BONGANDO, BOSAKA, BOYELA, NKUNDU,
   PYGMIES-BATWA, PYGMIES-NGOMBE‡ 1972

   RICARD, ALAIN J.‡ TOGO‡ EWE‡ 1973

   RUBIN, ARNOLD G.‡ NIGERIA‡ CHAMBA, HAUSA, IBO,
   JUKUN, KUTEP, TIKARI, TIV‡ 1964-65

   SAYAD, ALI‡ ALGERIA‡ KABYLE‡ 1968-70

   SELIGMAN, THOMAS KNOWLES‡ LIBERIA‡ KPELLE‡ 1970

   STONE, RUTH M.+ STONE, VERLON L.‡ LIBERIA‡ KPELLE‡
   1970

   VANVELSEN, J.‡ UGANDA‡ KUMAM‡ 1948-60

   WANKLYN, CHRISTOPHER‡ MOROCCO‡ AIT-SIDI-MERRI,

FARMER
  RHODES, WILLARD‡ NIGERIA‡ FULANI, HAUSA, TIV,
  TUAREG, YORUBA‡ 1973-74

FARMER-PRAISE
  AMES, DAVID W.‡ NIGERIA‡ HAUSA‡ 1963

FEAST-FARMER
  AMES, DAVID W.‡ NIGERIA‡ FULBE, HAUSA, YORUBA‡
  1963-64

FEAST-HARVEST
  ARCHIVES OF ETHNIC MUSIC AND DANCE‡ UPPER VOLTA‡
  BOBO, BWABA, DYULA, FULANI, FULBE, GOUIN,
  GOURMANTCHE, LOBI, MINIANKA, MOSSI, SENUFO,
  YARDSE‡

FEAST-WOMEN
  AMES, DAVID W.‡ NIGERIA‡ FULBE, HAUSA, YORUBA‡
  1963-64

FEET-STAMPING
  BOWLES, PAUL+ WANKLYN, CHRISTOPHER‡ MOROCCO‡ ‡
  CA1959-62

FERTILITY
  MERRIAM, ALAN P.+ MERRIAM, BARBARA W.‡ ZAIRE‡
  BASONGYE‡ 1959-60

FESTIVAL
  D'AZEVEDO, WARREN L.‡ LIBERIA‡ GOLA, KPELLE, VAI‡
  1960

  HANLEY, MARY ANN CSJ‡ GHANA‡ BUILSA, DAGARI, EWE,
  FANTI, FRAFRA, GA, KASSENA, NANKANI, TWI‡ 1972

  LORTAT-JACOB, BERNARD‡ MOROCCO‡ AIT-MGOUN‡ 1970

  OWEN, WILFRED, JR.‡ GHANA‡ ASANTE, BRONG, EWE,
  FANTI, GA, TWI‡ 1970-71

  PEEK, PHILIP M.‡ NIGERIA‡ IGBO-WESTERN, ISOKO‡
  1970-71

  PIRRO, ELLEN B.‡ KENYA‡ ‡ 1969

  ROUGET, GILBERT‡ GUINEA‡ MALINKE‡ 1952

  SMOLEY, R.A.‡ DAHOMEY-U.S.‡ ‡ 1970

FESTIVAL
  THIEME, DARIUS L.‡ NIGERIA‡ YORUBA‡ 1964-66

  WILLIAMSON, KAY‡ NIGERIA‡ IJO‡ 1959

FESTIVAL-ANDALUSIAN
  SPENCER, WILLIAM‡ TUNISIA‡ MALOUF‡ 1966-67

FESTIVAL-APOO
  WARREN, DENNIS M.‡ GHANA‡ BUNO‡ 1969-71

FESTIVAL-DURBAR
  GRAESSER, MARK W.‡ GHANA‡ ASANTE, FRAFRA, HAUSA,
  KANJAGA, KONKOMBA‡ 1968-69

FESTIVAL-EGUNGUN
  AWE, BOLANLE ALAKE‡ NIGERIA‡ YORUBA‡ 1972-74

FESTIVAL-ESA-ODE
  DEPARTMENT OF LINGUISTICS AND NIGERIAN LANGUAGES,
  UNIVERSITY OF IBADAN‡ NIGERIA‡ EDO, IJO, ISOKO,
  ITSEKIRI, OWAN, YORUBA‡ 1967-73

FESTIVAL-IFE
  DEPARTMENT OF LINGUISTICS AND NIGERIAN LANGUAGES,
  UNIVERSITY OF IBADAN‡ NIGERIA‡ EDO, IJO, ISOKO,
  ITSEKIRI, OWAN, YORUBA‡ 1967-73

FESTIVAL-JAZZ
  WARE, NAOMI‡ SIERRA LEONE‡ ‡ 1965

FESTIVAL-OGUN
  BALOGUN, ADISA‡ NIGERIA‡ YORUBA‡ 1964‡ 1970

FESTIVAL-OLOKUN
  BEN-AMOS, DAN‡ NIGERIA‡ EDO‡ 1966

FESTIVAL-PLANTING
  DIETERLEN, GERMAINE‡ MALI‡ DOGON‡ 1953

FESTIVAL-PUBERTY
  COLLEGE OF MUSIC, UNIVERSITY OF NIGERIA‡ NIGERIA‡
  BINI, BOKI, DAKARAWA, EFIK-IBIBIO, EKOI, FULANI,
  HAUSA, IBO, IDOMA, IJAW, JABA, MADA, YALA, YORUBA,
  ZABEBMAWA‡

FESTIVAL-PUBERTY-WOMEN
  ADUAMAH, E.Y.‡ GHANA-TOGO‡ EWE‡ 1968-71

FESTIVAL—SHANGO
  ROUGET, GILBERT‡ DAHOMEY‡ FUN, GUN, HOLI, NAGO‡
  1952

FESTIVAL—STATE
  RHODES, WILLARD‡ NIGERIA‡ FULANI, HAUSA, TIV,
  TUAREG, YORUBA‡ 1973—74

FESTIVAL—TOHOSSOU
  ROUGET, GILBERT‡ DAHOMEY‡ FUN, GUN, HOLI, NAGO‡
  1952

FESTIVAL—YAM
  WARREN, DENNIS M.‡ GHANA‡ BONO‡ 1969—71

  WELCH, DAVID B.‡ NIGERIA‡ YORUBA‡ 1970—71

FESTIVAL—YAM—NEW
  TRAGER, LILLIAN‡ NIGERIA‡ YORUBA‡ 1974

FESTIVAL—YEVE
  ADUAMAH, E.Y.‡ GHANA—TOGO‡ EWE‡ 1968—71

FIRST—FRUIT—CEREMONY
  COPE, TREVOR ANTHONY‡ SOUTH AFRICA‡ ZULU‡ 1965—72

FLUTE
  AFRICANA MUSEUM‡ SOUTH AFRICA‡ HOTTENTOT, SOTHO,
  SWAZI, TSWANA, ZULU‡

  ALBERTS, ARTHUR S.‡ GUINEA‡ KISSI, MALINKE‡
  1949—51

  AMES, DAVID W.‡ NIGERIA‡ FULBE, HAUSA, YORUBA‡
  1963—64

  ANKERMANN, BERNHARD‡ CAMEROON‡ BAMUM‡ 1909

  ARCHIVES OF ETHNIC MUSIC AND DANCE‡ UPPER VOLTA‡
  BOBO, BWABA, DYULA, FULANI, FULBE, GOUIN,
  GOURMANTCHE, LOBI, MINIANKA, MOSSI, SENUFO,
  YARDSE‡

  BAHMAN, GARY‡ SIERRA LEONE‡ LIMBA, MANDINGO,
  TEMNE‡ 1971

  BOWLES, PAUL+ WANKLYN, CHRISTOPHER‡ MOROCCO‡ ‡
  CA1959—62

FLUTE

BYRD, ROBERT OAKES‡ UGANDA‡ ALUR, BAGANDA,
BAGWERE, BAKONJO, BANYANKOLE, BANYOLE, KAKWA,
TESO‡

CALAME, B.‡ MALI‡ BAMBARA, BOZO, DOGON, MARKA,
MINIANKA, PEUL, RYMAYBE, SARAKOLE, SOMONO,
SONGHAY‡ 1956-57+ 1960

CALKINS, HOWARD W.+ RADIO DAHOMEY‡ DAHOMEY‡ DENDI,
DOMPAGO, FON, MAHI, YORUBA‡ CA1967

CAMP, CHARLES M.+ TRACEY, HUGH‡ RHODESIA‡ BUDJA,
CHIKUNDA, FUNGWE, HERA, HUNGWE, KARANGA, NDAU,
NDEBELE, NYANJA, NYASA, PEDI, RAMBA, WEMBA, YAO‡
1948

CHRISTIAN, VALERIE‡ UPPER VOLTA‡ BISSA, BOBO,
BWABA, DAGARA, DYULA, FULANI, FULBE, GOUIN,
GOURMANTCHE, HAUSA, KASSENA, KWO, LOBI, MARKA,
MOSSI, NONDOM, POUGOULIS, SAMO-DU-SUD, YARDSE‡
1973-74

CLAUSS, BERNHARD PETER‡ ZAIRE‡ PYGMIES‡ 1973

COLLEGE OF MUSIC, UNIVERSITY OF NIGERIA‡ NIGERIA‡
BINI, BOKI, DAKARAWA, EFIK-IBIBIO, EKOI, FULANI,
HAUSA, IBO, IDOMA, IJAW, JABA, MADA, YALA, YORUBA,
ZABEBMAWA‡

COURLANDER, HAROLD‡ ETHIOPIA‡ TIGRINYA‡ 1943

FIKRY, MONA‡ GHANA‡ WALA‡ 1966-67

GANSEMANS, JOS‡ ZAIRE‡ LUBA‡ 1970

GARINE, I. DE‡ CHAD‡ KERA, MUSEY‡ 1962-63+ 1965

GRAESSER, MARK W.‡ GHANA‡ ASANTE, FRAFRA, HAUSA,
KANJAGA, KONKOMBA‡ 1968-69

HERSKOVITS, MELVILLE J.+ HERSKOVITS, FRANCES S.‡
DAHOMEY‡ FON‡ 1931

JUILLERAT, B.‡ CAMEROON‡ KIRDI‡ 1966+ 1967-68

KNIGHT, RODERIC COPLEY‡ GAMBIA, THE‡ BALANTA,
BAMBARA, FULA, JOLA, MANDINKA, TEMNE, WOLOF‡
1970-71

FLUTE

LESLAU, WOLF‡ ETHIOPIA‡ AMHARA, GURAGE, HARARI,
SHOA-GALLA, SOMALI, TIGRINYA‡ 1947

MAGYAR TUDOMANYOS AKADEMIA NEPZENEKUTATO CSOPORT‡
EGYPT‡ COPT, FELLAHIN, NUBIAN‡ 1966-67 + 1969

MULDROW, WILLIAM+ MULDROW, ELIZABETH‡ ETHIOPIA‡
TESHENNA‡ 1964-65

NORSK RIKSKRINGKASTING‡ GHANA‡ ‡ 1966

PLOTNICOV, LEONARD‡ NIGERIA‡ BIROM, EFIK, HAUSA,
IBIBIO, IBO, IJAW, KAGORO, KATAM, TIV‡ 1961-62

QUERSIN, BENOIT J.+ QUERSIN, CHRISTINE M.‡
CAMEROON‡ BAFIA, BALLOM, BAMILEKE, BAMUM, BULU
ETON, PEUL, PYGMIES, SANAGA, TIKAR, VUTE‡ 1967

QUERSIN, BENOIT J.+ QUERSIN, CHRISTINE M.‡
NIGERIA‡ ABAKPA-RIGA, AFU, ALAGO, ANGAS, ANKWAI,
BIROM, BUROM, CHAMBA, EGGON, FULANI, HAUSA, ICHEN,
IDOMA, JARAWA, JUKUN, KALABARI, KANTANA, KUTEP,
KWALLA, NUPE, PYEM, RINDRE, TIV, YERGAM, YORUBA‡
1972-73

RHODES, WILLARD‡ NIGERIA‡ FULANI, HAUSA, TIV,
TUAREG, YORUBA‡ 1973-74

ROUGET, GILBERT‡ DAHOMEY‡ FON, GUN, HOLI, NAGO‡
1952

ROUGET, GILBERT+ GESSAIN, R.+ GESSAIN, M.‡
SENEGAL‡ BASSARI, BEDIK‡ 1967

RUBIN, ARNOLD G.‡ NIGERIA‡ CHAMBA, HAUSA, IBO,
JUKUN, KUTEP, TIKARI, TIV‡ 1964-65

SMEND, W.A.‡ TOGO‡ HAUSA‡ 1905

SMITS, LUCAS GERARDUS ALFONSUS‡ ALGERIA‡ TUAREG‡
1968-69

VAN THIEL, PAUL A.H.‡ UGANDA‡ BANTU, BANYANKOLE‡
1964-65+ 1969+ 1970-72

WILLIAMS, CHESTER S.‡ SOMALIA‡ ‡ 1962

FLUTE-VERTICAL
  BATWA, EKONDA‡ 1951-52

  RUBIN, ARNOLD G.‡ NIGERIA‡ CHAMBA, HAUSA, IBO,
  JUKUN, KUTEP, TIKARI, TIV‡ 1964-65

FOLKLORE
  AFRIKA-STUDIECENTRUM‡ TOGO‡ TYOKOSSI‡

  BOUQUIAUX, LUC‡ CENTRAL AFRICAN REPUBLIC‡ BANDA,
  ISONGO, MONZOMBO, NGBAKA-MABO‡

  CENTRE DE RECHERCHES ANTHROPOLOGIQUES
  PREHISTORIQUES ET ETHNOGRAPHIQUES‡ ALGERIA‡ ARAB,
  BERBER, MAGHREB‡

  CHILDS, GLADWYN‡ ANGOLA‡ OVIMBUNDU‡ 1962

  CLAUSS, BERNHARD PETER‡ ANGOLA‡ HIMBA-MUGAMBO‡
  1970-72

  D'HERTEFELT, MARUL‡ RWANDA‡ ‡ 1953-73

  DE HEN, FERDINAND JOSEPH‡ MOROCCO‡ AIT-ATTA,
  AIT-BU-SUEMMEZ, IHANSALEN‡ 1960-61

  DOHERTY, DEBORAH‡ KENYA‡ SAMBURU‡ 1973

  ETHNOMUSICOLOGY CENTRE JAAP KUNST‡ MALAWI‡ LOMWE,
  MANGANJA‡ 1971

  GIBSON, GORDON D.‡ BOTSWANA‡ GCIRIKU, HERERO‡
  1953

  GIBSON, GORDON D.‡ NAMIBIA‡ HERERO, HIMBA, KUVALE‡
  1960-61

  GREENSTEIN, ROBERT CARL‡ MALAWI‡ AMBO, CHEWA,
  LOMWE, MANGANJA, NGONI, TUMBUKA, YAO‡ 1971-75

  HIMMELHEBER, HANS G.‡ MALI‡ BAMBARA‡ 1953

  LOMBARD, JACQUES‡ MALAGASY REPUBLIC‡ SAKALAVA‡
  1969-74

  MAGYAR TUDOMANYOS AKADEMIA NEPZENEKUTATO CSOPORT‡
  ETHIOPIA‡ AMHARA, GALLA, KAFFICHO, KULLO, TIGRE‡

  MCLEOD, NORMA‡ MALAGASY REPUBLIC‡ ‡ 1962-63

FOLKLORE
  MUSEU DO DUNDO‡ ANGOLA‡ LUBA, LUNDA, LWENA,
  CHOKWE‡

  OGIERIRIAIXI, EVINMA‡ NIGERIA‡ EDO‡ 1970-73

  PARKER, CAROLYN ANN‡ KENYA‡ BAJUN, SWAHILI‡
  1971-72

  RADIO CLUBE DE MOCAMBIQUE‡ MOZAMBIQUE‡ CHANGANE,
  CHENGUE, CHOPI, LUBA, MAKONDE, MAKUA, RONGA,
  SWAZI, VACANDA, VANDAU, VATSUA‡

  SAVARY, CLAUDE‡ DAHOMEY‡ FON‡ 1966-67

  SAYAD, ALI‡ ALGERIA‡ KABYLE‡ 1968-70

  SAYAD, ALI‡ ALGERIA‡ CHAOUI‡ 1971-72

  SCHWEEGER-HEFEL, ANNEMARIE‡ UPPER VOLTA‡ DOGON,
  KURUMBA, PEUL‡

  STAHLKE, HERBERT F.W.‡ NIGERIA‡ YATYE‡ 1966-67

  THIEL, JOSEF FRANZ‡ ZAIRE‡ MBALA, TEKE, YANSI‡
  1961-71

  TRADITIONAL MUSIC DOCUMENTATION PROJECT‡
  MOZAMBIQUE‡ CHOPI‡

  TRADITIONAL MUSIC DOCUMENTATION PROJECT‡ NIGERIA‡
  IBIBIO, IBO, KALABARI, TIV, YORUBA‡

  TRADITIONAL MUSIC DOCUMENTATION PROJECT‡ UPPER
  VOLTA‡ ‡

  WESTPHAL, ERNST O.J.‡ BOTSWANA‡ BUSHMEN,
  HOTTENTOT, YEI‡ 1953-74

  WESTPHAL, ERNST O.J.‡ NAMIBIA‡ BUSHMEN, KUANYAMA‡
  1953-74

  WESTPHAL, ERNST O.J.‡ SOUTH AFRICA‡ BUSHMEN‡
  1953-74

  WILLIAMSON, KAY‡ NIGERIA‡ IJO‡ 1959

  WILLIS, ROY GEOFFREY‡ TANZANIA‡ FIPA‡ 1966

FOLKLORE
  WOLLNER, CHAD A.‡ ETHIOPIA‡ ‡ 1972

  WOLLNER, CHAD A.‡ KENYA‡ ‡ 1972

FOLKTALE
  ALLEN, LEONARD E.‡ SIERRA LEONE‡ ‡ 1950

  AMES, DAVID W.‡ GAMBIA, THE‡ WOLOF‡ 1951

  ANIAKOR, CYRIL CHIKE‡ NIGERIA‡ IKWERE‡ 1965

  ARGYLE, WILLIAM JOHNSON‡ ZAMBIA‡ SOLI‡ 1957-59

  ARMISTEAD, SAMUEL G. + KATZ, ISRAEL J. +
  SILVERMAN, JOSEPH H.‡ MOROCCO‡ SEPHARDIC-JEW‡
  1962

  BABALOLA, ADEBOYE‡ NIGERIA‡ YORUBA‡ 1962-74

  BAHMAN, GARY‡ SIERRA LEONE‡ LIMBA, MANDINGO,
  TEMNE‡ 1971

  BEN-AMOS, DAN‡ NIGERIA‡ EDO‡ 1966

  BISELE, MARGUERITE A.‡ BOTSWANA‡ KUNG-BUSHMEN‡
  1971-72

  BOAS, FRANZ‡ ‡ KRU‡ PRE-1935

  BOAS, FRANZ‡ NIGERIA-U.S.‡ YORUBA‡ 1933

  CAMARA, S.‡ SENEGAL‡ MALINKE‡ 1970+ 1971

  CAMP, CHARLES M.+ TRACEY, HUGH‡ RHODESIA‡ BUDJA,
  CHIKUNDA, FUNGWE, HERA, HUNGWE, KARANGA, NDAU,
  NDEBELE, NYANJA, NYASA, PEDI, RAMBA, WEMBA, YAO‡
  1948

  CENTRE FOR THE STUDY OF NIGERIAN LANGUAGES‡
  NIGERIA‡ HAUSA‡

  CHRISTIAN, VALERIE‡ UPPER VOLTA‡ BISSA, BOBO,
  BWABA, DAGARA, DYULA, FULANI, FULBE, GOUIN,
  GOURMANTCHE, HAUSA, KASSENA, KWO, LOBI, MARKA,
  MOSSI, NONDOM, POUGOULIS, SAMO-DU-SUD, YARDSE‡
  1973-74

  COLLEGE OF MUSIC, UNIVERSITY OF NIGERIA‡ NIGERIA‡

FOLKTALE
BINI, BOKI, DAKARAWA, EFIK-IBIBIO, EKOI, FULANI, HAUSA, IBO, IDOMA, IJAW, JABA, MADA, YALA, YORUBA, ZABEBMAWA‡

CROWLEY, DANIEL J.‡ ZAIRE-U.S.‡ ‡ 1961

CURTIN, PHILIP D.‡ SENEGAL‡ ARAB, DIAKHANKE, MALINKE, PULAR‡ 1966

DAVIDSON, MARJORY‡ ZAMBIA‡ NGONI‡ 1967-71

DIAS, MARGOT‡ MOZAMBIQUE‡ MAKONDE‡ 1957-58

DIAS, MARGOT‡ MOZAMBIQUE‡ CHOKWE, CHOPI‡ 1959

DIHOFF, IVAN R.‡ NIGERIA‡ CHORI, HAUSA‡ 1972

EL-SHAMY, HASAN M.‡ EGYPT‡ ARAB, DINKA, NUBIAN‡ 1968-71

EL-SHAMY, HASAN M.‡ EGYPT-U.S.‡ ARAB‡ 1961

ELWA RADIO STATION, LIBERIA‡ LIBERIA‡ ‡ CA1960-1975

ELWA STUDIO, NIGERIA‡ NIGERIA‡ IBO, NUPE, YORUBA‡

FIKRY, MONA‡ GHANA‡ WALA‡ 1966-67

FRY, GLADYS M.‡ EGYPT-U.S.‡ ‡ 1963

FRY, GLADYS M.‡ ETHIOPIA-U.S.‡ ‡ 1963

FRY, GLADYS M.‡ GHANA-U.S.‡ ‡ 1963

FRY, GLADYS M.‡ KENYA-U.S.‡ ‡ 1963

FRY, GLADYS M.‡ MALI-U.S.‡ ‡ 1963

FRY, GLADYS M.‡ NIGERIA-U.S.‡ ‡ 1963

FRY, GLADYS M.‡ RHODESIA-U.S.‡ ‡ 1963

FRY, GLADYS M.‡ SOUTH AFRICA-U.S.‡ ‡ 1963

FRY, GLADYS M.‡ SUDAN-U.S.‡ ‡ 1963

FRY, GLADYS M.‡ TUNISIA-U.S.‡ ‡ 1963

FOLKTALE

GAY, JUDITH S.‡ LIBERIA‡ KPELLE‡ 1971-73

HAMBLY, WILFRED D.‡ ANGOLA‡ OVIMBUNDU‡ 1929-30

HARING, LEE‡ KENYA‡ AKAMBA‡ 1967-68

HARRIES, JEANETTE‡ MOROCCO‡ BERBER‡ 1964-65

HOLSOE, SVEND E.‡ LIBERIA‡ DEI, GBANDE, GOLA, KPELLE, MANDINGO, VAI‡ 1965-70

HURREIZ, SAYED H.‡ SUDAN‡ GAALIIN‡ 1970-71

INNES, GORDON‡ GAMBIA, THE‡ MANDINKA‡ 1968-69

INNES, GORDON‡ SIERRA LEONE‡ MENDE‡ 1963

INSTITUTE OF AFRICAN STUDIES, UNIVERSITY OF IFE‡ NIGERIA‡ IBO, TIV, YORUBA‡

JOHNSON, GERALD T.‡ SIERRA LEONE‡ MENDE, TEMNE‡ 1967-68

KAEMMER, JOHN E.‡ RHODESIA‡ KOREKORE, SHONA, ZEZURU‡ 1972-73

KEIL, CHARLES‡ NIGERIA‡ TIV, YORUBA‡

KILSON, MARION D. DE B.‡ SIERRA LEONE‡ MENDE‡ 1960

KIRK-GREENE, ANTHONY H.M.‡ NIGERIA‡ HAUSA, KAGORO, TIV‡ 1962-65

KNIGHT, RODERIC COPLEY‡ GAMBIA, THE‡ BALANTA, BAMBARA, FULA, JOLA, MANDINKA, TEMNE, WOLOF‡ 1970-71

KRIEL, A.P.‡ RHODESIA‡ KARANGA, SHONA‡ 1966

KRIEL, A.P.‡ SOUTH AFRICA‡ XHOSA, ZULU‡ 1973

LA PIN, DIERDRE A.‡ NIGERIA‡ YORUBA‡ 1972-73

LESLAU, WOLF‡ ETHIOPIA‡ AMHARA, GURAGE, HARARI, SHOA-GALLA, SOMALI, TIGRINYA‡ 1947

MAALU-BUNGI‡ ZAIRE‡ LULUA‡ 1969+ 1972+ 1973

FOLKTALE
  MERRIAM, ALAN P.+ MERRIAM, BARBARA W.‡ ZAIRE‡
  BASONGYE‡ 1959-60

  MISJONSSKOLEN‡ CAMEROON‡ ‡

  MISJONSSKOLEN‡ MALAGASY REPUBLIC‡ ‡

  MISJONSSKOLEN‡ SOUTH AFRICA‡ ZULU‡

  MISSION SOCIOLOGIQUE DU HAUTE-OUBANGUI‡ CENTRAL
  AFRICAN REPUBLIC‡ NZAKARA, ZANDE‡

  NOSS, PHILIP A.‡ CAMEROON‡ GBAYA‡ 1966-67

  OGBU, JOHN U.+ PEEK, PHILIP M.‡ NIGERIA-U.S.‡
  IGBO‡ 1968

  OPLAND, JEFFREY‡ SOUTH AFRICA‡ XHOSA, ZULU‡
  1969-73

  OTTENHEIMER, HARRIET+ OTTENHEIMER, MARTIN‡ COMORO
  ISLANDS‡ ‡ 1967-68

  OWEN, WILFRED, JR.‡ GHANA‡ ASANTE, BRONG, EWE,
  FANTI, GA, TWI‡ 1970-71

  PRUITT, WILLIAM F., JR.‡ ZAIRE‡ KETE, PYGMIES,
  SALAMPASU‡ 1966-67

  RABEN, JOSEPH‡ NIGERIA-U.S.‡ IBO‡ 1950

  ROGERS, HENRY EDWIN‡ SIERRA LEONE‡ SHERBRO‡ 1966

  RUBIN, ARNOLD G.‡ NIGERIA‡ CHAMBA, HAUSA, IBO,
  JUKUN, KUTEP, TIKARI, TIV‡ 1964-65

  SAPIR, J. DAVID‡ SENEGAL‡ DIOLA-FOGNY, DIOLA-KASA‡
  1960-65

  SIGWALT, RICHARD+ SOSNE, ELINOR‡ ZAIRE‡ SHI‡
  1971-73

  SKINNER, A. NEIL+ SKINNER, MARGARET G.‡ NIGERIA‡
  ANGAS, FULA, HAUSA, KABBA, YORUBA‡ 1967-74

  STUDSTILL, JOHN D.‡ ZAIRE‡ LUBA‡ 1972

  STUTTMAN, LEONARD M.‡ LIBERIA‡ GREBO, KRAHN‡ 1956

FOLKTALE
  SUDAN NATIONAL MUSEUM‡ SUDAN‡ BONGO, JALUO,
  NUBIAN‡ 1959-64

  SZCZESNIAK, ANDREW L.‡ NIGERIA-U.S.‡ IBO‡ 1961

  TENRAA, ERIC WILLIAM FREDERICK‡ TANZANIA‡ BURUNGE,
  SANDAWE, SWAHILI‡ 1958-66

  TUCKER, ARCHIBALD NORMAN‡ KENYA‡ LUO‡

  TUCKER, ARCHIBALD NORMAN‡ TANZANIA‡ HADZA, IRAQW,
  NGAZIJA, SANDAWE, SANYE, SWAHILI‡

  TUCKER, ARCHIBALD NORMAN‡ UGANDA‡ ACHOLI, BAGANDA,
  IK, KARAMOJONG, TEPETH, TESO‡

  VERSFELD, BARBARA‡ SOUTH AFRICA‡ XHOSA‡ 1965

  WARNIER, JEAN-PIERRE‡ CAMEROON‡ MANKON‡ 1972-74

  WARREN, DENNIS M.‡ GHANA‡ BONO‡ 1969-71

  WEISSWANGE, KARIN I.S.‡ LIBERIA‡ LOMA, MANDINGO‡
  1963-65+ 1972-73

  WOLFF, HANS‡ NIGERIA‡ BIROM‡ 1953

  WOLFF, HANS‡ NIGERIA‡ IJO, ITSEKIRI‡ 1953

  WOLFF, HANS‡ NIGERIA‡ JUKUN‡ 1953

  WOLFF, HANS‡ NIGERIA-U.S.‡ YORUBA‡ 1960-64

  ZEMPLEIVI, ANDRAS‡ CHAD‡ MOUNDANG‡ 1969

  ZEMPLEIVI, ANDRAS‡ IVORY COAST‡ SENUFO-NA-FAARA‡
  1972-74

FOLKTALE-CYCLE
  HURREIZ, SAYED H.‡ SUDAN‡ GAALIIN‡ 1970-71

FOLKTALE-EDO
  DEPARTMENT OF LINGUISTICS AND NIGERIAN LANGUAGES,
  UNIVERSITY OF IBADAN‡ NIGERIA‡ EDO, IJO, ISOKO,
  ITSEKIRI, OWAN, YORUBA‡ 1967-73

FOLKTALE-HUNTING
  NOSS, PHILIP A.‡ CAMEROON‡ GBAYA‡ 1966-67

FOLKTALE-INTERVIEW
  FRY, GLADYS M.‡ EGYPT-U.S.‡ ‡ 1963

  FRY, GLADYS M.‡ ETHIOPIA-U.S.‡ ‡ 1963

  FRY, GLADYS M.‡ GHANA-U.S.‡ ‡ 1963

  FRY, GLADYS M.‡ KENYA-U.S.‡ ‡ 1963

  FRY, GLADYS M.‡ MALI-U.S.‡ ‡ 1963

  FRY, GLADYS M.‡ NIGERIA-U.S.‡ ‡ 1963

  FRY, GLADYS M.‡ RHODESIA-U.S.‡ ‡ 1963

  FRY, GLADYS M.‡ SOUTH AFRICA-U.S.‡ ‡ 1963

  FRY, GLADYS M.‡ SUDAN-U.S.‡ ‡ 1963

  FRY, GLADYS M.‡ TUNISIA-U.S.‡ ‡ 1963

  HURREIZ, SAYED H.‡ SUDAN‡ GAALIIN‡ 1970-71

  OGBU, JOHN U.+ PEEK, PHILIP M.‡ NIGERIA-U.S.‡
  IGBO‡ 1968

  SZCZESNIAK, ANDREW L.‡ NIGERIA-U.S.‡ IBO‡ 1961

FOLKTALE-OTUO
  DEPARTMENT OF LINGUISTICS AND NIGERIAN LANGUAGES,
  UNIVERSITY OF IBADAN‡ NIGERIA‡ EDO, IJO, ISOKO,
  ITSEKIRI, OWAN, YORUBA‡ 1967-73

GAMBLING
  CLAUSS, BERNHARD PETER‡ BOTSWANA‡ BUSHMEN‡
  1971-72

GAME
  BISELE, MARGUERITE A.‡ BOTSWANA‡ KUNG-BUSHMEN‡
  1971-72

  GANSEMANS, JOS‡ ZAIRE‡ LUBA‡ 1970

  KOIZUMI, FUMIO‡ SENEGAL‡ ‡ 1971

  KOIZUMI, FUMIO‡ TANZANIA‡ ‡ 1971

  RANSBOTYN DE DECKER, DANIEL‡ TOGO‡ BOGO, EWE‡
  1972-74

GAME
   ROUGET, GILBERT‡ GUINEA‡ MALINKE‡ 1952

   ROUGET, GILBERT‡ SENEGAL‡ LEBOU, PEUL, SARAKOLE,
   SOCE, TUKULOR, WOLOF‡ 1952

GENEALOGY
   CURTIN, PHILIP D.‡ SENEGAL‡ ARAB, DIAKHANKE,
   MALINKE, PULAR, SONINKE‡ 1966

   CURTIN, PHILIP D.‡ SENEGAL‡ ARAB, DIAKHANKE,
   MALINKE, PULAR‡ 1966

   FIKRY, MONA‡ GHANA‡ WALA‡ 1966-67

   HURREIZ, SAYED H.‡ SUDAN‡ GAALIIN‡ 1970-71

GONG-METAL-DOUBLE
   MERRIAM, ALAN P.‡ ZAIRE‡ BASONGYE‡ 1973

GONG-ROCK
   AFRICANA MUSEUM‡ SOUTH AFRICA‡ HOTTENTOT, SOTHO,
   SWAZI, TSWANA, ZULU‡

   CALAME, B.‡ MALI‡ BAMBARA, BOZO, DOGON, MARKA,
   MINIANKA, PEUL, RYMAYBE, SARAKOLE, SOMONO,
   SONGHAY‡ 1956-57+ 1960

   RHODES, WILLARD‡ NIGERIA‡ FULANI, HAUSA, TIV,
   TUAREG, YORUBA‡ 1973-74

GOURD
   CHRISTIAN, VALERIE‡ UPPER VOLTA‡ BISSA, BOBO,
   BWABA, DAGARA, DYULA, FULANI, FULBE, GOUIN,
   GOURMANTCHE, HAUSA, KASSENA, KWO, LOBI, MARKA,
   MOSSI, NONDOM, POUGOULIS, SAMO-DU-SUD, YARDSE‡
   1973-74

   CHRISTIAN, VALERIE+ ROSELLINI, JAMES N.‡ UPPER
   VOLTA‡ FULBE, KASSENA, MARKA, MOSSI‡ 1973

   GRAESSER, MARK W.‡ GHANA‡ ASANTE, FRAFRA, HAUSA,
   KANJAGA, KONKOMBA‡ 1968-69

   KNIGHT, RODERIC COPLEY‡ GAMBIA, THE‡ BALANTA,
   BAMBARA, FULA, JOLA, MANDINKA, TEMNE, WOLOF‡
   1970-71

   PLOTNICOV, LEONARD‡ NIGERIA‡ BIROM, EFIK, HAUSA,

GOURD
  IBIBIO, IBO, IJAW, KAGURO, KATAM, TIV‡ 1961-62

  RHODES, WILLARD‡ NIGERIA‡ FULANI, HAUSA, TIV,
  TUAREG, YORUBA‡ 1973-74

GOURD-STRUCK
  QUERSIN, BENOIT J.+ QUERSIN, CHRISTINE M.‡
  NIGERIA‡ ABAKPA-RIGA, AFO, ALAGO, ANGAS, ANKWAI,
  BIROM, BUROM, CHAMBA, EGGON, FULANI, HAUSA, ICHEN,
  IDOMA, JARAWA, JUKUN, KALABARI, KANTANA, KUTEP,
  KWALLA, NUPE, PYEM, RINDRE, TIV, YERGAM, YORUBA‡
  1972-73

  QUERSIN, BENOIT J.‡ ZAIRE‡ BUSHOONG, COOFA, IBAAM,
  NGEENDE, PYAANG, SHOOWA‡ 1970

GRAMMATICAL-DATA
  ANDRADE, MANUEL+ HERZOG, GEORGE‡ ‡ JABO‡ 1931

  BENDER, MARVIN LIONEL‡ ETHIOPIA‡ BERTA, BODI, MAO,
  MUSUJI, SAI, TSAMAY‡ 1964-74

  BOAS, FRANZ‡ ‡ IGANDA-LUGANDA‡ PRE-1935

  BOAS, FRANZ‡ ‡ KRU‡ PRE-1935

  BROWN, HERBERT‡ ‡ FANTI‡ 1954-57

  FRANKEL, GERD‡ ‡ LUHYA‡ 1959

  HALL, JOHN F.‡ UPPER VOLTA‡ MOSSI‡ 1962

  HANLEY, -‡ SOUTH AFRICA‡ ZULU‡

  HICKERSON, NANCY+ HYMES, VIRGINIA+ KELLER, JAMES‡
  -U.S.‡ TIGRINYA‡ 1954

  HOPKINS, JERRY‡ ‡ YORUBA‡ 1956

  KINBADE, M. DALE‡ ‡ TONGA‡ 1960

  LEUSCHEL, DON‡ ‡ NDEBELE, ZULU‡ 1957-58

  MADIGAN, BOB‡ KENYA‡ KAMBA‡ 1957-58

  MARING, JOEL‡ LIBERIA‡ EBURNEO-LIBERIEN, GREBO‡
  1958

GRAMMATICAL-DATA
  ORENT, AMNON‡ ETHIOPIA‡ KAFA‡ 1966-67

  REDDEN, JAMES ERSKINE‡ KENYA‡ LUO‡ 1959

  REDDEN, JAMES ERSKINE‡ -U.S.‡ BAMBARA‡ 1962

  REDDEN, JAMES ERSKINE‡ ZAIRE‡ LINGALA‡ 1962

  REDDEN, JAMES ERSKINE‡ ‡ ITSEKIRI‡ 1958

  REDDEN, JAMES ERSKINE‡ ‡ TONGA‡ 1959-60

  RIGGS, VENDA‡ NIGERIA‡ YORUBA‡ 1949

  SIMPSON, AL‡ ‡ BULU‡ 1958

  TUCKER, ARCHIBALD NORMAN‡ KENYA‡ LUO‡

  TUCKER, ARCHIBALD NORMAN‡ SUDAN‡ BARI, DINKA,
  LOTUKO, SHILLUK, ZANDE‡

  TUCKER, ARCHIBALD NORMAN‡ TANZANIA‡ HADZA, IRAQW,
  NGAZIJA, SANDAWE, SANYE, SWAHILI‡

  TUCKER, ARCHIBALD NORMAN‡ UGANDA‡ ACHOLI, BAGANDA,
  IK, KARAMOJONG, TEPETH, TESO‡

  WOLFF, HANS‡ NIGERIA‡ IGBIRA‡ 1953

  WOLFF, HANS‡ NIGERIA‡ JUKUN‡ 1953

  WOLFF, HANS‡ NIGERIA‡ KAJE‡ 1953

GRAMMATICAL-DATA-EWE
  REDDEN, JAMES ERSKINE‡ GHANA‡ AKIM, AKWAPIM,
  ASANTE, EWE‡ 1958-63

GRAMMATICAL-DATA-FANTI
  WEST, MONTY‡ ‡ FANTI‡ 1957

GRAMMATICAL-DATA-LOKELE
  ARCHIVES OF LANGUAGES OF THE WORLD‡ ‡ KWA‡

GRAMMATICAL-DATA-MEIN
  WOLFF, HANS‡ NIGERIA‡ IJO, IJAW-WESTERN‡ 1953

GRAMMATICAL-DATA-OKRIKA
  WOLFF, HANS‡ NIGERIA‡ IJO, KALABARI‡ 1953

GRAMMATICAL-DATA-SOMALI
  MARING, JOEL‡ SOMALIA‡ SOMALI‡ 1959

GRAMMATICAL-DATA-TARAKIRI
  WOLFF, HANS‡ NIGERIA‡ IJO, IJAW-WESTERN‡ 1953

GRAMMATICAL-DATA-TWI
  BLAIR, BOB‡ GHANA‡ ASANTE‡ 1958

  BOAS, FRANZ‡ GHANA‡ AKWAPIM‡ PRE-1935

  REDDEN, JAMES ERSKINE‡ GHANA‡ AKIM, AKWAPIM,
  ASANTE, EWE‡ 1958-63

GREETING
  ADUAMAH, E.Y.‡ GHANA-TOGO‡ EWE‡ 1968-71

  GLAZE, ANITA‡ IVORY COAST‡ SENUFO‡ 1969-70

  MERRIAM, ALAN P.+ MERRIAM, BARBARA W.‡ BURUNDI‡
  ABATUTSI, BARUNDI, BATWA‡ 1951-52

  MERRIAM, ALAN P.+ MERRIAM, BARBARA W.‡ RWANDA‡
  ABAGOGWE, ABAGOYI, ABAHORORO, ABANYAMBO, ABATUTSI,
  ABAYOVU, BAHIMA, BAHUTU, BAKIGA, BATWA‡ 1951-52

  MERRIAM, ALAN P.‡ ZAIRE‡ BASONGYE‡ 1973

  OWEN, WILFRED, JR.‡ GHANA‡ ASANTE, BRONG, EWE,
  FANTI, GA, TWI‡ 1970-71

  PRESTON, JEROME, JR.‡ KENYA‡ LUO‡ 1966

GUITAR
  ALBERTS, ARTHUR S.‡ GHANA‡ EWE, GA, IBO, TWI‡
  1949-51

  ALBERTS, ARTHUR S.‡ GUINEA‡ KISSI, MALINKE‡
  1949-51

  ARCHIVES OF ETHNIC MUSIC AND DANCE‡ RHODESIA‡ ‡

  ARCHIVES OF ETHNIC MUSIC AND DANCE‡ UPPER VOLTA‡
  BOBO, BWABA, DYULA, FULANI, FULBE, GOUIN,
  GOURMANTCHE, LOBI, MINIANKA, MOSSI, SENUFO,
  YARDSE‡

  BAHMAN, GARY‡ SIERRA LEONE‡ LIMBA, MANDINGO,
  TEMNE‡ 1971

GUITAR
  CAMP, CHARLES M.+ TRACEY, HUGH‡ RHODESIA‡ BUDJA,
  CHIKUNDA, FUNGWE, HERA, HUNGWE, KARANGA, NDAU,
  NDEBELE, NYANJA, NYASA, PEDI, RAMBA, WEMBA, YAO‡
  1948

  CAMP, CHARLES M.+ TRACEY, HUGH‡ SOUTH AFRICA‡
  BHACA, CHOPI, HLUBI, NDAU, NYASA, PONDO, SHANGAAN,
  SOTHO, SWAZI, TSWANA, VENDA, XHOSA‡ 1947-48

  CAMP, CHARLES M.+ TRACEY, HUGH‡ ZAMBIA‡ BEMBA,
  LALA, LOZI, TONGA, ZINZA‡ 1947-48

  CHRISTIAN, VALERIE‡ UPPER VOLTA‡ BISSA, BOBO,
  BWABA, DAGARA, DYULA, FULANI, FULBE, GOUIN,
  GOURMANTCHE, HAUSA, KASSENA, KWO, LOBI, MARKA,
  MOSSI, NONDOM, POUGOULIS, SAMO-DU-SUD, YARDSE‡
  1973-74

  COPLAN, DAVID+ THOMASON, LEE‡ GHANA‡ ASANTE, EWE,
  KROBO‡ 1974

  DOBRIN, ARTHUR‡ KENYA‡ GUSII‡ 1966

  ESTES, RICHARD D.‡ ANGOLA‡ SONGO‡ 1970

  FERNANDEZ, JAMES W.‡ GABON‡ FANG‡ 1960

  HANLEY, MARY ANN CSJ‡ NIGERIA‡ ANGAS, BACHAMA,
  CHAMBA, EFIK, GWANDARA, HAUSA, IBIBIO, IBO, JABA,
  KERI-KERI, YORUBA‡ 1973

  KNIGHT, RODERIC COPLEY‡ GAMBIA, THE‡ BALANTA,
  BAMBARA, FULA, JOLA, MANDINKA, TEMNE, WOLOF‡
  1970-71

  MERRIAM, ALAN P.+ MERRIAM, BARBARA W.‡ ZAIRE‡
  BAHIMA, BAKOGA, BAKONGO, BAMBUTI, BANGALA, BASHI,
  BATWA, EKONDA‡ 1951-52

  OKIE, PACKARD L.‡ LIBERIA‡ BASSA, GBANDE, GOLA,
  KISSI, LOMA, MENDE, VAI‡ 1947-54

  OKIE, PACKARD L.‡ LIBERIA‡ BASSA, BELE, GIO,
  KPELLE, KRU, MANDINGO, VAI‡ 1947-54

GUITAR-ELECTRIC
  HANLEY, MARY ANN CSJ‡ GHANA‡ BUILSA, DAGARI, EWE,
  FANTI, FRAFRA, GA, KASSENA, NANKANI, TWI‡ 1972

HAMMER
  ALBERTS, ARTHUR S.‡ LIBERIA‡ FANTI, LOMA, MANO‡
  1949-51

HANDCLAPPING
  ADUAMAH, E.Y.‡ GHANA-TOGO‡ EWE‡ 1968-71

  ARMSTRONG, ROBERT G.‡ NIGERIA‡ IDOMA‡ 1964

  BOWLES, PAUL+ WANKLYN, CHRISTOPHER‡ MOROCCO‡ ‡
  CA1959-62

  CAMP, CHARLES M.+ TRACEY, HUGH‡ ZAMBIA‡ BEMBA,
  LALA, LOZI, TONGA, ZINZA‡ 1947-48

  HANLEY, MARY ANN CSJ‡ GHANA‡ BUILSA, DAGARI, EWE,
  FANTI, FRAFRA, GA, KASSENA, NANKANI, TWI‡ 1972

  HANLEY, MARY ANN CSJ‡ NIGERIA‡ ANGAS, BACHAMA,
  CHAMBA, EFIK, GWANDARA, HAUSA, IBIBIO, IBO, JABA,
  KERI-KERI, YORUBA‡ 1973

  JONES, ARTHUR M.‡ GHANA-ENGLAND‡ EWE‡ 1956

  JONES, ARTHUR M.‡ ZAMBIA‡ LALA‡ 1944

  LESLAU, WOLF‡ ETHIOPIA‡ AMHARA, GURAGE, HARARI,
  SHOA-GALLA, SOMALI, TIGRINYA‡ 1947

  MERRIAM, ALAN P.‡ ZAIRE‡ BASONGYE‡ 1973

  VAN OVEN, JACOBA‡ SIERRA LEONE‡ FULA, GALLINAS,
  GOLA, LIMBA, LOKO, MANDINGO, MENDE, SHERBRO, SUSU,
  TEMNE, VAI, YALUNKA‡ 1964-67

  WEMAN, HENRY PAUL‡ RHODESIA‡ KARANGA, LEMBA,
  VENDA, ZULU‡ 1957

  WEMAN, HENRY PAUL‡ SOUTH AFRICA‡ VENDA, ZULU‡
  1956-57

  WEMAN, PAUL HENRY‡ TANZANIA‡ HAYA, SUKUMA,
  SWAHILI‡ 1957

HARP
  BIEBUYCK, DANIEL P.‡ ZAIRE‡ LEGA, LUBA, LUNDA,
  MANGBETU, MAYOGO, NANDE, NYANGA, ZAMBE‡ 1952-61

  COLLEGE OF MUSIC, UNIVERSITY OF NIGERIA‡ NIGERIA‡

HARP
  BINI, BOKI, DAKARAWA, EFIK-IBIBIO, EKOI, FULANI,
  HAUSA, IBO, IDOMA, IJAW, JABA, MADA, YALA, YORUBA,
  ZABEBMAWA‡

  COURLANDER, HAROLD‡ ETHIOPIA‡ TIGRINYA‡ 1943

  MERRIAM, ALAN P.+ MERRIAM, BARBARA W.‡ ZAIRE‡
  BAHIMA, BAKOGA, BAKONGO, BAMBUTI, BANGALA, BASHI,
  BATWA, EKONDA‡ 1951-52

  MISSION SOCIOLOGIQUE DU HAUTE-OUBANGUI‡ CENTRAL
  AFRICAN REPUBLIC‡ NZAKARA, ZANDE‡

  ROUGET, GILBERT‡ MAURITANIA‡ ‡ 1952

  WEISSWANGE, KARIN I.S.‡ LIBERIA‡ LOMA, MANDINGO‡
  1963-65+ 1972-73

HARP-ARCHED
  BRANDILY, MONIQUE‡ CHAD‡ KANEMBU, KOTOKO, TEDA‡
  1961+ 1963+ 1965

HARP-BOW-ADEUDEU
  BYRD, ROBERT OAKES‡ UGANDA‡ ALUR, BAGANDA,
  BAGWERE, BAKONJO, BANYANKOLE, BANYOLE, KAKWA,
  TESO‡

HARP-BOW-BOLON-BATA
  VAN OVEN, JACOBA‡ SIERRA LEONE‡ FULA, GALLINAS,
  GOLA, LIMBA, LOKO, MANDINGO, MENDE, SHERBRO, SUSU,
  TEMNE, VAI, YALUNKA‡ 1964-67

HARP-BOW-ENANGA
  BYRD, ROBERT OAKES‡ UGANDA‡ ALUR, BAGANDA,
  BAGWERE, BAKONJO, BANYANKOLE, BANYOLE, KAKWA,
  TESO‡

HARP-BURUNUBA
  ROUGET, GILBERT‡ GUINEA‡ MALINKE‡ 1952

HARP-JAW'S
  AFRICANA MUSEUM‡ SOUTH AFRICA‡ HOTTENTOT, SOTHO,
  SWAZI, TSWANA, ZULU‡

HARP-LUTE
  AMES, DAVID W.‡ NIGERIA‡ IGBO‡ 1963-64

  ARCHIVES OF ETHNIC MUSIC AND DANCE‡ UPPER VOLTA‡

HARP-LUTE
  BOBO, BWABA, DYULA, FULANI, FULBE, GOUIN,
  GOURMANTCHE, LOBI, MINIANKA, MOSSI, SENUFO,
  YARDSE‡

  CHRISTIAN, VALERIE‡ UPPER VOLTA‡ BISSA, BOBO,
  BWABA, DAGARA, DYULA, FULANI, FULBE, GOUIN,
  GOURMANTCHE, HAUSA, KASSENA, KWO, LOBI, MARKA,
  MOSSI, NONDOM, POUGOULIS, SAMO-DU-SUD, YARDSE‡
  1973-74

  GARINE, I. DE‡ CHAD‡ KERA, MUSEY‡ 1962-63+ 1965

  JUILLERAT, B.‡ CAMEROON‡ KIRDI‡ 1966+ 1967-68

HARP-LUTE-BOLON
  KNIGHT, RODERIC COPLEY‡ GAMBIA, THE‡ BALANTA,
  BAMBARA, FULA, JOLA, MANDINKA, TEMNE, WOLOF‡
  1970-71

  ROUGET, GILBERT‡ GUINEA‡ MALINKE‡ 1952

HARP-LUTE-INSTRUCTION
  RUTHERFORD, DOUGLAS I.‡ MALI‡ BAMBARA‡ 1972

HARP-LUTE-KOGBELENU
  ROUGET, GILBERT‡ GUINEA‡ MALINKE‡ 1952

HARP-LUTE-KONDENE
  VAN OVEN, JACOBA‡ SIERRA LEONE‡ FULA, GALLINAS,
  GOLA, LIMBA, LOKO, MANDINGO, MENDE, SHERBRO, SUSU,
  TEMNE, VAI, YALUNKA‡ 1964-67

HARP-LUTE-KORA
  ALBERTS, ARTHUR S.‡ GUINEA‡ KISSI, MALINKE‡
  1949-51

  ARCHIVES OF ETHNIC MUSIC AND DANCE‡ GAMBIA, THE‡
  MANDINKA‡

  ARCHIVES OF ETHNIC MUSIC AND DANCE‡ GUINEA‡ ‡

  ARCHIVES OF ETHNIC MUSIC AND DANCE‡ SENEGAL‡ ‡

  BIRD, CHARLES S.‡ MALI‡ BAMBARA‡ 1967-68

  CAMARA, S.‡ SENEGAL‡ MALINKE‡ 1970+ 1971

  CURTIN, PHILIP D.‡ SENEGAL‡ ARAB, DIAKHANKE,

HARP-LUTE-KORA
  MALINKE, PULAR‡ 1966

  ENGLAND, NICHOLAS M.‡ SENEGAL‡ ‡ 1969-70

  KNIGHT, RODERIC COPLEY‡ GAMBIA, THE‡ BALANTA,
  BAMBARA, FULA, JOLA, MANDINKA, TEMNE, WOLOF‡
  1970-71

  KNIGHT, RODERIC COPLEY‡ SENEGAL‡ FULA, JOLA,
  MANDINKA, WOLOF‡ 1970-71

  PEVAR, MARC DAVID‡ GAMBIA, THE‡ MANDINKA‡ 1972

  ROUGET, GILBERT‡ GUINEA‡ MALINKE‡ 1952

  RUTHERFORD, DOUGLAS I.‡ MALI‡ BAMBARA‡ 1972

  SAPIR, J. DAVID‡ SENEGAL‡ DIOLA-FOGNY, DIOLA-KASA‡
  1960-65

  VAN OVEN, JACOBA‡ SIERRA LEONE‡ FULA, GALLINAS,
  GOLA, LIMBA, LOKO, MANDINGO, MENDE, SHERBRO, SUSU,
  TEMNE, VAI, YALUNKA‡ 1964-67

HARP-SIMBINGO
  CAMARA, S.‡ SENEGAL‡ MALINKE‡ 1970+ 1971

  KNIGHT, RODERIC COPLEY‡ GAMBIA, THE‡ BALANTA,
  BAMBARA, FULA, JOLA, MANDINKA, TEMNE, WOLOF‡
  1970-71

HARP-ZITHER
  CAMP, CHARLES M.+ TRACEY, HUGH‡ SOUTH AFRICA‡
  BHACA, CHOPI, HLUBI, NDAU, NYASA, PONDO, SHANGAAN,
  SOTHO, SWAZI, TSWANA, VENDA, XHOSA‡ 1947-48

  QUERSIN, BENOIT J.+ QUERSIN, CHRISTINE M.‡
  CAMEROON‡ BAFIA, BALLOM, BAMILEKE, BAMUM, BULU
  ETON, PEUL, PYGMIES, SANAGA, TIKAR, VUTE‡ 1967

HARP-ZITHER-MVET
  ARCHIVES OF ETHNIC MUSIC AND DANCE‡ CAMEROON‡ ‡

  PEPPER, HERBERT‡ GABON‡ FANG‡ 1960

HARVEST
  BROADCASTING CORPORATION OF CHINA‡ ETHIOPIA‡ ‡

HARVEST
  MULDROW, WILLIAM+ MULDROW, ELIZABETH‡ ETHIOPIA‡
  TESHENNA‡ 1964-65

HERDING
  CAMP, CHARLES M.+ TRACEY, HUGH‡ ZAMBIA‡ BEMBA,
  LALA, LOZI, TONGA, ZINZA‡ 1947-48

  MADIGAN, BOB‡ KENYA‡ KAMBA‡ 1957-58

  MERRIAM, ALAN P.+ MERRIAM, BARBARA W.‡ BURUNDI‡
  ABATUTSI, BARUNDI, BATWA‡ 1951-52

  MERRIAM, ALAN P.+ MERRIAM, BARBARA W.‡ RWANDA‡
  ABAGOGWE, ABAGOYI, ABAHORORO, ABANYAMBO, ABATUTSI,
  ABAYOVU, BAHIMA, BAHUTU, BAKIGA, BATWA‡ 1951-52

  MERRIAM, ALAN P.+ MERRIAM, BARBARA W.‡ ZAIRE‡
  BAHIMA, BAKOGA, BAKONGO, BAMBUTI, BANGALA, BASHI,
  BATWA, EKONDA‡ 1951-52

  WEMAN, HENRY PAUL‡ RHODESIA‡ KARANGA, LEMBA,
  VENDA, ZULU‡ 1957

HERDING-MILKING
  MERRIAM, ALAN P.+ MERRIAM, BARBARA W.‡ ZAIRE‡
  BAHIMA, BAKOGA, BAKONGO, BAMBUTI, BANGALA, BASHI,
  BATWA, EKONDA‡ 1951-52

HERO-EPIC-LECTURE
  BIRD, CHARLES S.+ KEIM, KAREN R.‡ MALI-U.S.‡
  BAMBARA‡ 1975

HEROIC-RECITATION
  VAN THIEL, PAUL A.H.‡ UGANDA‡ BANTU, BANYANKOLE‡
  1964-65+ 1969+ 1970-72

HIGHLIFE
  AMES, DAVID W.‡ NIGERIA‡ IGBO‡ 1963-64

  ARCHIVES OF ETHNIC MUSIC AND DANCE‡ GHANA‡
  DAGARTI, DAGOMBA, DONNO, EWE, GA, KONKOMBA, LOBI‡

  COPLAN, DAVID+ THOMASON, LEE‡ GHANA‡ ASANTE, EWE,
  KROBO‡ 1974

  HANLEY, MARY ANN CSJ‡ GHANA‡ BUILSA, DAGARI, EWE,
  FANTI, FRAFRA, GA, KASSENA, NANKANI, TWI‡ 1972

HIGHLIFE
  STUTTMAN, LEONARD M.‡ LIBERIA‡ GREBO, KRAHN‡ 1956

  WARREN, DENNIS M.‡ GHANA‡ BONO‡ 1969-71

HISTORICAL-TEXT
  BORGATTI, JEAN M.‡ NIGERIA‡ EDO‡ 1972-73

HISTORY
  AFRIKA-STUDIECENTRUM‡ TOGO‡ TYOKOSSI‡

  ALPERS, EDWARD ALTER‡ TANZANIA‡ DOE, KAMI, KWERE,
  LUGURU, ZARAMO‡ 1972-73

  ANSTEY, ROGER THOMAS‡ ZAIRE‡ BABOMA, BASENGELE,
  BATENDE, BOLIA‡ 1963

  AROM, SIMHA‡ CENTRAL AFRICAN REPUBLIC‡
  AKA-PYGMIES, LINDA-BANDA, NGBAKA-MABO‡ 1964-67+
  1971-73

  AWE, BOLANLE ALAKE‡ NIGERIA‡ YORUBA‡ 1972-74

  BAIRU, TAFLA‡ ETHIOPIA‡ GALLA, OROMO‡ 1973-74

  BELLMAN, BERYL LARRY‡ LIBERIA‡ KPELLE, LOMA‡ 1969

  BEN-AMOS, DAN‡ NIGERIA‡ EDO‡ 1966

  BLOCH, MONICA E.‡ MALAGASY REPUBLIC‡ MERINA,
  TANALA‡ 1964-71

  BRANTLEY, CYNTHIA‡ KENYA‡ GIRYAMA‡ 1970-71

  BROWN, JAMES W.‡ GHANA‡ ASANTE‡ 1970

  BUCHANAN, CAROLE‡ UGANDA‡ BANYORO, BATORO‡
  1968-69

  CENTRE DE RECHERCHES ANTHROPOLOGIQUES
  PREHISTORIQUES ET ETHNOGRAPHIQUES‡ ALGERIA‡ ARAB,
  BERBER, MAGHREB‡

  CHRISTIAN, VALERIE‡ UPPER VOLTA‡ BISSA, BOBO,
  BWABA, DAGARA, DYULA, FULANI, FULBE, GOUIN,
  GOURMANTCHE, HAUSA, KASSENA, KWO, LOBI, MARKA,
  MOSSI, NONDOM, POUGOULIS, SAMO-DU-SUD, YARDSE‡
  1973-74

HISTORY

CIPARISSE, GERARD JEAN‡ ZAIRE‡ BAKONGO, BASUKU,
BAYAKA‡ 1970-71

COHEN, DAVID WILLIAM‡ UGANDA‡ BASOGA‡ 1966-67

COHEN, DAVID WILLIAM‡ UGANDA‡ BASOGA‡ 1971-72

CURTIN, PHILIP D.‡ SENEGAL‡ ARAB, DIAKHANKE,
MALINKE, PULAR, SONINKE‡ 1966

CURTIN, PHILIP D.‡ SENEGAL‡ ARAB, DIAKHANKE,
MALINKE, PULAR‡ 1966

D'HERTEFELT, MARUL‡ RWANDA‡ ‡ 1953-73

DALBY, DAVID+ AFRICAN STUDIES-I.U.‡ AFRICA-U.S.‡ ‡
1969

DEPARTMENT OF AFRICAN LANGUAGES, UNIVERSITY OF
RHODESIA‡ RHODESIA‡ NDEBELE, SHONA‡

DEPLAEN, GUY‡ ZAIRE‡ LUBA, YEKE‡ 1973-74

DIAS, MARGOT‡ MOZAMBIQUE‡ MAKONDE‡ 1957-58

DRAKE, H. MAX‡ MALAWI‡ TUMBUKA, YAO‡ 1967

DUNGER, GEORGE A.‡ CAMEROON‡ BEKOM, DUALA, KAKA,
NSUNGLI‡

DURAN, JAMES JOSEPH‡ KENYA‡ KIPSIGI‡ 1971

ECHENBERG, MYRON J.‡ UPPER VOLTA‡ GURUNSI, MARKA,
SAMO‡ 1967

EKECHI, FELIX K.‡ NIGERIA‡ IGBO‡ 1973

ELWA RADIO STATION, LIBERIA‡ LIBERIA‡ ‡
CA1960-1975

ELWA STUDIO, NIGERIA‡ NIGERIA‡ IBO, NUPE, YORUBA‡

ETHNOMUSICOLOGY CENTRE JAAP KUNST‡ MALAWI‡ LOMWE,
MANGANJA‡ 1971

FEDERAL DEPARTMENT OF ANTIQUITIES, NATIONAL
MUSEUM, KADUNA‡ NIGERIA‡ ELOYI, GEDE‡

HISTORY

FEINBERG, HARVEY‡ GHANA‡ FANTI‡ 1967-68

FIKRY, MONA‡ GHANA‡ WALA‡ 1966-67

FOSS, PERKINS‡ NIGERIA‡ URHOBO‡ 1971-72

GAY, JUDITH S.‡ LIBERIA‡ KPELLE‡ 1971-73

GLAZE, ANITA‡ IVORY COAST‡ SENUFO‡ 1969-70

GREENSTEIN, ROBERT CARL‡ MALAWI‡ AMBO, CHEWA,
LOMWE, MANGANJA, NGONI, TUMBUKA, YAO‡ 1971-75

HAIGHT, BRUCE MARVIN‡ GHANA‡ DYULA, GONJA‡
1972-73

HAIGHT, BRUCE MARVIN‡ SIERRA LEONE‡ LOKO‡ 1967

HAY, MARGARET JEAN‡ KENYA‡ LUO‡ 1968-70+ 1973

HEALD, SWETTE SCOTT‡ UGANDA‡ GISU‡ 1966-69

HIMMELHEBER, HANS G.‡ MALI‡ BAMBARA‡ 1953

HOLSOE, SVEND E.‡ LIBERIA‡ DEI, GBANDE, GOLA,
KPELLE, MANDINGO, VAI‡ 1965-70

HOOVER, JAMES JEFFREY‡ ZAIRE‡ LUNDA‡ 1973-75

HURREIZ, SAYED H.‡ SUDAN‡ GAALIIN‡ 1970-71

IJAGBEMI, ELIJAH A.‡ SIERRA LEONE‡ TEMNE‡ 1965-67

INNES, GORDON‡ GAMBIA, THE‡ MANDINKA‡ 1968-69

INSTITUTE OF AFRICAN STUDIES, UNIVERSITY OF IFE‡
NIGERIA‡ IBO, TIV, YORUBA‡

IRVINE, JUDITH TEMKIN‡ SENEGAL‡ WOLOF‡ 1970-71

JUWAYEYI, YUSUF MCDADDLY‡ MALAWI‡ ‡ 1972-75

KATZ, RICHARD‡ BOTSWANA‡ KUNG-BUSHMEN‡ 1968

KAYE, ALAN S.‡ NIGERIA‡ ARAB-SHUWA‡ 1974

KLEIN, MARTIN A.‡ SENEGAL‡ WOLOF, SERER‡ 1963-64

HISTORY

KOIZUMI, FUMIO‡ ETHIOPIA‡ AMHARA‡ 1971

KOIZUMI, FUMIO‡ SENEGAL‡ ‡ 1971

KUBIK, GERHARD‡ AFRICA-ANGOLA, CAMEROON, CENTRAL AFRICAN REPUBLIC, CONGO-PEOPLE'S REPUBLIC OF THE, EGYPT, GABON, KENYA, MALAWI, MOZAMBIQUE, NIGERIA, SUDAN, TANZANIA, TOGO, UGANDA, ZAIRE, ZAMBIA‡ ‡ 1959-73

LA PIN, DIERDRE A.‡ NIGERIA‡ YORUBA‡ 1972-73

LANGE, WERNER‡ ETHIOPIA‡ BENS, BOSA, CARA, HINNARIO, KAFA, MERU, NA'O, SE, SEKA, SHE, ZARAS‡ 1972-73

LANGWORTHY, HARRY W.‡ ZAMBIA‡ CHEWA‡ 1964

LAUER, JOSEPH JEROME‡ IVORY COAST‡ GUERE‡ 1971

LIMA, AUGUSTO GUILHERME MESQUITELA‡ ANGOLA‡ BUSHMEN, CHOKWE, NGANGELA‡ 1963-70

LISZKA, STANLEY WALTER, JR.‡ KENYA‡ TAITA‡ 1972-74

LIVINGSTONE MUSEUM‡ ZAMBIA‡ LEYA-SUBIYA‡

LLOYD, DAVID TYRRELL‡ ZAIRE‡ AZANDE‡ 1973

LOMBARD, JACQUES‡ MALAGASY REPUBLIC‡ SAKALAVA‡ 1969-74

LORTAT-JACOB, BERNARD‡ ETHIOPIA‡ DORZE‡ 1974-75

LUCKAU, STEPHEN R.‡ LIBERIA‡ GREBO, JABO‡ 1971

MALER, THOMAS A.‡ TANZANIA‡ DIGO, GIRYAMA, MAKONDE, TINDIGA‡ 1967-68

MAPOMA, ISAIAH MWESA‡ ZAMBIA‡ BEMBA‡ 1968-70+ 1973

MARAIRE, DUMISANI ABRAHAM‡ RHODESIA‡ SHONA‡ 1971+ 1974

MARTIN, JANE JACKSON‡ LIBERIA‡ GREBO‡ 1968+ 1972-75

HISTORY

MASSING, ANDREAS‡ LIBERIA‡ KRU‡ 1971-72

MCLEOD, NORMA‡ MALAGASY REPUBLIC‡ ‡ 1962-63

MISSION SOCIOLOGIQUE DU HAUTE-OUBANGUI‡ CENTRAL
AFRICAN REPUBLIC‡ NZAKARA, ZANDE‡

MOULOUD, MAMMERI‡ ALGERIA‡ BERBER‡

MUSEE ROYAL DE L'AFRIQUE CENTRALE‡ ‡ BIRCM, BOLIA,
HOLOHOLO, KANEMBU, KONDA, KONGO, LEGA, MBALA,
MBUUN, MONGO, NANDE, PENDE, RUNDI, RWANDA, SANGA,
SHI, SUKU, TETELA, YEKE‡

NATIONAL MUSEUM OF TANZANIA‡ TANZANIA‡ MAKONDE,
MALILA, MWERA, YAO‡

NOSS, PHILIP A.‡ CAMEROON‡ GBAYA‡ 1966-67

ODED, ARYE‡ UGANDA‡ BAGANDA, BAYUDAYA‡ 1967-68

OFRI, DORITH‡ LIBERIA‡ VAI‡ 1965-72

OLMSTEAD, JUDITH VIRGINIA‡ ETHIOPIA‡ DITA, DORZE‡
1969-71+ 1973

ORENT, AMNON‡ ETHIOPIA‡ KAFA‡ 1966-67

OTTENHEIMER, HARRIET+ OTTENHEIMER, MARTIN‡ COMORO
ISLANDS‡ ‡ 1967-68

OWEN, WILFRED, JR.‡ GHANA‡ ASANTE, BRONG, EWE,
FANTI, GA, TWI‡ 1970-71

PAIRAULT, CLAUDE ALBERT‡ CHAD‡ GULA-IRO‡ 1959-64

PANTALEONI, HEWITT‡ GHANA‡ EWE‡ 1969-71

PEEK, PHILIP M.‡ NIGERIA‡ IGBO-WESTERN, ISOKO‡
1970-71

PRUITT, WILLIAM F., JR.‡ ZAIRE‡ KETE, PYGMIES,
SALAMPASU‡ 1966-67

QUERSIN, BENOIT J.‡ ZAIRE‡ BUSHOONG, COOFA, IBAAM,
NGEENDE, PYAANG, SHOOWA‡ 1970

QUERSIN, BENOIT J.+ QUERSIN, CHRISTINE M.‡ ZAIRE‡

HISTORY
   BAKUTU, BOKOTE, BONGANDO, BOSAKA, BOYELA, NKUNDU,
   PYGMIES-BATWA, PYGMIES-NGOMBE‡ 1972

   RANSBOTYN DE DECKER, DANIEL‡ TOGO‡ BOGO, EWE‡
   1972-74

   RANSBOTYN DE DECKER, DANIEL‡ ZAIRE‡ BAKONGO‡ 1968

   RANUNG, BJORN L.C.‡ NIGERIA‡ IGEDE‡ 1971-72

   RAPHAEL, RONALD P.‡ CAMEROON‡ FULBE, KONDJA, VUTE,
   WAWA‡ 1974

   RAPHAEL, RONALD P.‡ NIGERIA‡ FULBE, MAMBILA‡ 1974

   REEFE, THOMAS Q.‡ ZAIRE‡ LUBA‡ 1972-73

   ROBINSON, DAVID W.‡ SENEGAL‡ PULAR‡ 1968-69

   ROTBERG, ROBERT I.‡ ZAMBIA‡ BISA‡ 1967

   SAPIR, J. DAVID‡ SENEGAL‡ DIOLA-FOGNY, DIOLA-KASA‡
   1960-65

   SAYAD, ALI‡ ALGERIA‡ KABYLE‡ 1968-70

   SCHEUB, HAROLD‡ SOUTH AFRICA‡ XHOSA, ZULU‡
   1967-68

   SHEFFIELD, JAMES‡ DAHOMEY‡ YORUBA‡ 1971+ 1973

   SHEFFIELD, JAMES‡ NIGERIA‡ YORUBA‡ 1971

   SIEGMANN, WILLIAM CHARLES‡ LIBERIA‡ BASSA, GBANDE‡
   1973-74

   SIGWALT, RICHARD+ SOSNE, ELINOR‡ ZAIRE‡ SHI‡
   1971-73

   SKINNER, ELLIOTT P.‡ UPPER VOLTA‡ MOSSI‡ 1955-65

   SPENCER, WILLIAM‡ MOROCCO‡ ‡ 1969

   STUDSTILL, JOHN D.‡ ZAIRE‡ LUBA‡ 1972

   SUDAN NATIONAL MUSEUM‡ SUDAN‡ BONGO, JALUO,
   NUBIAN‡ 1959-64

HISTORY
  SULZMANN, ERIKA‡ ZAIRE‡ BABOMA, BASENGELE, BOLIA,
  EKONDA, NTOMBA‡ 1953-72

  TENRAA, ERIC WILLIAM FREDERICK‡ TANZANIA‡ BURUNGE,
  SANDAWE, SWAHILI‡ 1958-66

  THIEL, JOSEF FRANZ‡ ZAIRE‡ MBALA, TEKE, YANSI‡
  1961-71

  TLOU, THOMAS‡ BOTSWANA‡ HERERO, LOZI, MBUKUSHU,
  ROLONG, TSWANA, YEI‡ 1970

  TRADITIONAL MUSIC DOCUMENTATION PROJECT‡
  MOZAMBIQUE‡ CHOPI‡

  TRADITIONAL MUSIC DOCUMENTATION PROJECT‡ NIGERIA‡
  IBIBIO, IBO, KALABARI, TIV, YORUBA‡

  TRADITIONAL MUSIC DOCUMENTATION PROJECT‡ UPPER
  VOLTA‡ ‡

  TSEHAI, BRHANE SILASSIE‡ ETHIOPIA‡ DARASSA,
  SIDAMO, WOLAMO‡ 1969-73

  VAN ROUVEROY VAN NIEUWAAL, EMILE A.B.‡ TOGO‡
  KOSSI‡ 1969-73

  VAN THIEL, PAUL A.H.‡ UGANDA‡ BANTU, BANYANKOLE‡
  1964-65+ 1969+ 1970-72

  WARNIER, JEAN-PIERRE‡ CAMEROON‡ MANKON‡ 1972-74

  WESTPHAL, ERNST O.J.‡ BOTSWANA‡ BUSHMEN,
  HOTTENTOT, YEI‡ 1953-74

  WESTPHAL, ERNST O.J.‡ NAMIBIA‡ BUSHMEN, KUANYAMA‡
  1953-74

  WESTPHAL, ERNST O.J.‡ SOUTH AFRICA‡ BUSHMEN‡
  1953-74

  WILLIAMSON, KAY‡ NIGERIA‡ IJO‡ 1959

  WOLLNER, CHAD A.‡ ETHIOPIA‡ ‡ 1972

  WOLLNER, CHAD A.‡ KENYA‡ ‡ 1972

  WYLIE, KENNETH CHARLES‡ NIGERIA‡ ‡ 1965-66

HISTORY-KOLOKUMA
DEPARTMENT OF LINGUISTICS AND NIGERIAN LANGUAGES,
UNIVERSITY OF IBADAN‡ NIGERIA‡ EDO, IJO, ISOKO,
ITSEKIRI, OWAN, YORUBA‡ 1967-73

HISTORY-LIFE
ROBERTSON, CLAIRE C.‡ GHANA‡ GA‡ 1972

SHOSTAK, MARJORIE JANET‡ BOTSWANA‡ HERERO,
KUNG-BUSHMEN‡ 1969-71

VAUGHAN, JAMES H.‡ NIGERIA‡ MARGI‡ 1974

HISTORY-MAHMADU-LAMINE
HRBEK, IVAN‡ SENEGAL‡ SONINKE‡

HISTORY-MISSION-CHRISTIAN
SPENCER, LEON P.‡ KENYA‡ KAMBA, KIKUYU, KISII,
LUO‡ 1968-69

HISTORY-NATIONALISM
MACDONALD, RODERICK JAMES‡ MALAWI‡ ‡ 1966-67

HISTORY-NEMBE
DEPARTMENT OF LINGUISTICS AND NIGERIAN LANGUAGES,
UNIVERSITY OF IBADAN‡ NIGERIA‡ EDO, IJO, ISOKO,
ITSEKIRI, OWAN, YORUBA‡ 1967-73

HISTORY-POLITICAL
NEWBURY, M. CATHARINE‡ RWANDA‡ BANYARWANDA‡
1970-72

SANDGREN, DAVID PETER‡ KENYA‡ KIKUYU‡ 1970-71

HISTORY-ROYAL
NEWBURY, DAVID S.‡ ZAIRE‡ BAHAVU‡ 1972-74

HISTORY-SOCIAL
SANDGREN, DAVID PETER‡ KENYA‡ KIKUYU‡ 1970-71

HISTORY-TOWN
WARREN, DENNIS M.‡ GHANA‡ BONO‡ 1969-71

HISTORY-TWENTIETH-CENTURY
PAGE, MELVIN E.‡ MALAWI‡ ‡ 1972-74

HORN
AKPABOT, SAMUEL EKPE‡ NIGERIA‡ BIROM, HAUSA,
IBIBIO, IBO‡ 1964-73

HORN
ARCHIVES OF ETHNIC MUSIC AND DANCE‡ GHANA‡
DAGARTI, DAGOMBA, DONNO, EWE, GA, KONKOMBA, LOBI‡

BRANDILY, MONIQUE‡ CHAD‡ KANEMBU, KOTOKO, TEDA‡
1961+ 1963+ 1965

CALAME, B.‡ MALI‡ BAMBARA, BOZO, DOGON, MARKA,
MINIANKA, PEUL, RYMAYBE, SARAKOLE, SOMONO,
SONGHAY‡ 1956-57+ 1960

CAMP, CHARLES M.+ TRACEY, HUGH‡ RHODESIA‡ BUDJA,
CHIKUNDA, FUNGWE, HERA, HUNGWE, KARANGA, NDAU,
NDEBELE, NYANJA, NYASA, PEDI, RAMBA, WEMBA, YAO‡
1948

CAMP, CHARLES M.+ TRACEY, HUGH‡ ZAMBIA‡ BEMBA,
LALA, LOZI, TONGA, ZINZA‡ 1947-48

NORSK RIKSKRINGKASTING‡ GHANA‡ ‡ 1966

PAASCHE, -‡ TANZANIA‡ KIZIBA‡ 1910

QUERSIN, BENOIT J.+ QUERSIN, CHRISTINE M.‡
CAMEROON‡ BAFIA, BALLOM, BAMILEKE, BAMUM, BULU
ETON, PEUL, PYGMIES, SANAGA, TIKAR, VUTE‡ 1967

QUERSIN, BENOIT J.+ QUERSIN, CHRISTINE M.‡
NIGERIA‡ ABAKPA-RIGA, AFO, ALAGO, ANGAS, ANKWAI,
BIROM, BUROM, CHAMBA, EGGON, FULANI, HAUSA, ICHEN,
IDOMA, JARAWA, JUKUN, KALABARI, KANTANA, KUTEP,
KWALLA, NUPE, PYEM, RINDRE, TIV, YERGAM, YORUBA‡
1972-73

VAN THIEL, PAUL A.H.‡ UGANDA‡ BANTU, BANYANKOLE‡
1964-65+ 1969+ 1970-72

WEMAN, HENRY PAUL‡ RHODESIA‡ KARANGA, LEMBA,
VENDA, ZULU‡ 1957

WEMAN, PAUL HENRY‡ TANZANIA‡ HAYA, SUKUMA,
SWAHILI‡ 1957

HORN-ANIMAL
MULDROW, WILLIAM+ MULDROW, ELIZABETH‡ ETHIOPIA‡
TESHENNA‡ 1964-65

HORN-ANTELOPE
MERRIAM, ALAN P.+ MERRIAM, BARBARA W.‡ BURUNDI‡

HORN-ANTELOPE
  ABATUTSI, BARUNDI, BATWA‡ 1951-52

  QUERSIN, BENOIT J.+ QUERSIN, CHRISTINE M.‡ ZAIRE‡
  BATWA, BOLIA, EKONDA‡ 1971

  QUERSIN, BENOIT J.+ QUERSIN, CHRISTINE M.‡ ZAIRE‡
  BAKUTU, BOKOTE, BONGANDO, BOSAKA, BOYELA, NKUNDU,
  PYGMIES-BATWA, PYGMIES-NGOMBE‡ 1972

  RUBIN, ARNOLD G.‡ NIGERIA‡ CHAMBA, HAUSA, IBO,
  JUKUN, KUTEP, TIKARI, TIV‡ 1964-65

HORN-ELEPHANT
  NORSK RIKSKRINGKASTING‡ GHANA‡ ‡ 1966

  QUERSIN, BENOIT J.+ QUERSIN, CHRISTINE M.‡ ZAIRE‡
  BAKUTU, BOKOTE, BONGANDO, BOSAKA, BOYELA, NKUNDU,
  PYGMIES-BATWA, PYGMIES-NGOMBE‡ 1972

  VAN OVEN, JACOBA‡ SIERRA LEONE‡ FULA, GALLINAS,
  GOLA, LIMBA, LOKO, MANDINGO, MENDE, SHERBRO, SUSU,
  TEMNE, VAI, YALUNKA‡ 1964-67

HORN-GOURD
  CARLISLE, ROXANE C.‡ SUDAN‡ ANUAK, DINKA, GAALIIN,
  NUER, SHILLUK‡ 1963

  MERRIAM, ALAN P.+ MERRIAM, BARBARA W.‡ BURUNDI‡
  ABATUTSI, BARUNDI, BATWA‡ 1951-52

  QUERSIN, BENOIT J.+ QUERSIN, CHRISTINE M.‡ ZAIRE‡
  BATWA, BOLIA, EKONDA‡ 1971

HORN-LANGUAGE
  AMES, DAVID W.‡ NIGERIA‡ HAUSA‡ 1963

  HERZOG, GEORGE‡ LIBERIA‡ GREBO, JABO, KRU‡ 1930

  SAPIR, J. DAVID‡ SENEGAL‡ DIOLA-FOGNY, DIOLA-KASA‡
  1960-65

HORN-TRANSVERSE
  AMES, DAVID W.‡ NIGERIA‡ IGBO‡ 1963-64

  HERZOG, GEORGE‡ LIBERIA‡ GREBO, JABO, KRU‡ 1930

  MERRIAM, ALAN P.+ MERRIAM, BARBARA W.‡ RWANDA‡
  ABAGOGWE, ABAGOYI, ABAHORORO, ABANYAMBO, ABATUTSI,

HORN-TRANSVERSE
  ABAYOVU, BAHIMA, BAHUTU, BAKIGA, BATWA‡ 1951-52

  MERRIAM, ALAN P.+ MERRIAM, BARBARA W.‡ ZAIRE‡
  BAHIMA, BAKOGA, BAKONGO, BAMBUTI, BANGALA, BASHI,
  BATWA, EKONDA‡ 1951-52

  STONE, RUTH M.+ STONE, VERLON L.‡ LIBERIA‡ KPELLE‡
  1970

HORN-VERTICAL
  AMES, DAVID W.‡ NIGERIA‡ HAUSA‡ 1963

HORN-WOODEN
  MULDROW, WILLIAM+ MULDROW, ELIZABETH‡ ETHIOPIA‡
  TESHENNA‡ 1964-65

  OKIE, PACKARD L.‡ LIBERIA‡ BASSA, BELE, GIO,
  KPELLE, KRU, MANDINGO, VAI‡ 1947-54

  STONE, RUTH M.+ STONE, VERLON L.‡ LIBERIA‡ KPELLE‡
  1970

HOUSE-NEW
  MERRIAM, ALAN P.+ MERRIAM, BARBARA W.‡ RWANDA‡
  ABAGOGWE, ABAGOYI, ABAHORORO, ABANYAMBO, ABATUTSI,
  ABAYOVU, BAHIMA, BAHUTU, BAKIGA, BATWA‡ 1951-52

HUMOROUS
  AMES, DAVID W.‡ GAMBIA, THE‡ WOLOF‡ 1951

HUNTER-PRAISE
  AMES, DAVID W.‡ NIGERIA‡ FULBE, HAUSA, YORUBA‡
  1963-64

HUNTING
  ARCHIVES OF ETHNIC MUSIC AND DANCE‡ RHODESIA‡ ‡

  ARCHIVES OF TRADITIONAL MUSIC‡ ‡ YORUBA‡ CA1940

  BROADCASTING CORPORATION OF CHINA‡ ETHIOPIA‡ ‡

  CAMARA, S.‡ SENEGAL‡ MALINKE‡ 1970+ 1971

  CAMP, CHARLES M.+ TRACEY, HUGH‡ ZAMBIA‡ BEMBA,
  LALA, LOZI, TONGA, ZINZA‡ 1947-48

  CURTIS, NATALIE‡ AFRICA-EAST‡ ‡ CA1919

HUNTING
  GANSEMANS, JOS‡ ZAIRE‡ LUBA‡ 1970

  GROHS, ELISABETH‡ TANZANIA‡ NDOROBO, NGURU, ZIGUA‡
  1970

  HERSKOVITS, MELVILLE J.+ HERSKOVITS, FRANCES S.‡
  GHANA‡ ASANTE‡ 1931

  HOLIDAY, GEOFFREY D.‡ NIGER‡ TUAREG‡ CA1958

  KNIGHT, RODERIC COPLEY‡ GAMBIA, THE‡ BALANTA,
  BAMBARA, FULA, JOLA, MANDINKA, TEMNE, WOLOF‡
  1970-71

  MANN, WILLIAM MICHAEL‡ ZAMBIA‡ BEMBA, BISA‡ 1967

  MERRIAM, ALAN P.+ MERRIAM, BARBARA W.‡ ZAIRE‡
  BASONGYE‡ 1959-60

  NOSS, PHILIP A.‡ CAMEROON‡ GBAYA‡ 1966-67

  QUERSIN, BENOIT J.+ QUERSIN, CHRISTINE M.‡ ZAIRE‡
  BATWA, BOLIA, EKONDA‡ 1971

  QUERSIN, BENOIT J.+ QUERSIN, CHRISTINE M.‡ ZAIRE‡
  BAKUTU, BOKOTE, BONGANDO, BOSAKA, BOYELA, NKUNDU,
  PYGMIES-BATWA, PYGMIES-NGOMBE‡ 1972

  RHODES, WILLARD‡ NIGERIA‡ FULANI, HAUSA, TIV,
  TUAREG, YORUBA‡ 1973-74

  SMEND, W.A.‡ TOGO‡ HAUSA‡ 1905

  SPEED, FRANCIS E.+ THIEME, DARIUS L.‡ NIGERIA‡
  YORUBA‡ 1966

  VAN OVEN, JACOBA‡ SIERRA LEONE‡ FULA, GALLINAS,
  GOLA, LIMBA, LOKO, MANDINGO, MENDE, SHERBRO, SUSU,
  TEMNE, VAI, YALUNKA‡ 1964-67

  WEMAN, HENRY PAUL‡ SOUTH AFRICA‡ VENDA, ZULU‡
  1956-57

  WEMAN, PAUL HENRY‡ TANZANIA‡ HAYA, SUKUMA,
  SWAHILI‡ 1957

HUNTING-CEREMONY
  SUDAN NATIONAL MUSEUM‡ SUDAN‡ BONGO, JALUO,

IDIOPHONE-PLUCKED
  HANLEY, MARY ANN CSJ‡ NIGERIA‡ ANGAS, BACHAMA,
  CHAMBA, EFIK, GWANDARA, HAUSA, IBIBIO, IBO, JABA,
  KERI-KERI, YORUBA‡ 1973

  SMITS, LUCAS GERARDUS ALFONSUS‡ BOTSWANA‡
  KUNG-BUSHMEN, SAN‡ 1972

IDIOPHONE-PLUCKED-KASAYI
  MERRIAM, ALAN P.+ MERRIAM, BARBARA W.‡ ZAIRE‡
  BAHIMA, BAKOGA, BAKONGO, BAMBUTI, BANGALA, BASHI,
  BATWA, EKONDA‡ 1951-52

IDIOPHONE-STRUCK
  AMES, DAVID W.‡ NIGERIA‡ HAUSA‡ 1963

  AMES, CAVID W.‡ SENEGAL‡ WOLOF‡ 1950-51

  CURTIN, PHILIP D.‡ SENEGAL‡ ARAB, DIAKHANKE,
  MALINKE, PULAR‡ 1966

  GLAZE, ANITA‡ IVORY COAST‡ SENUFO‡ 1969-70

  HANLEY, MARY ANN CSJ‡ GHANA‡ BUILSA, DAGARI, EWE,
  FANTI, FRAFRA, GA, KASSENA, NANKANI, TWI‡ 1972

  MERRIAM, ALAN P.+ MERRIAM, BARBARA W.‡ ZAIRE‡
  BASONGYE‡ 1959-60

  QUERSIN, BENOIT J.+ QUERSIN, CHRISTINE M.‡ ZAIRE‡
  BATWA, BOLIA, EKONDA‡ 1971

  VAN OVEN, JACOBA‡ SIERRA LEONE‡ FULA, GALLINAS,
  GOLA, LIMBA, LOKO, MANDINGO, MENCE, SHERBRO, SUSU,
  TEMNE, VAI, YALUNKA‡ 1964-67

IDIOPHONE-WOODEN
  AMES, DAVID W.‡ NIGERIA‡ IGBO‡ 1963-64

IMPROVISATION
  OERTLI, PEO‡ DAHOMEY‡ AIZO‡ 1973-74

INAUGURATION-PRESIDENT
  NEWBURY, DOROTHY J.‡ LIBERIA‡ BASSA, LOMA‡
  1969-70+ 1972

INDEPENDENCE-CELEBRATION
  COX, WILLIAM L.‡ BURUNDI‡ ‡ 1962

INHERITANCE
  SNYDER, FRANCIS GREGORY‡ SENEGAL‡ DIOLA‡ 1973

INITIATION
  BUNGER, ROBERT LOUIS‡ KENYA‡ OROMA, POKOMO‡
  1969-70

  DENG, FRANCIS‡ SUDAN‡ DINKA‡ 1971

  GANSEMANS, JOS‡ ZAIRE‡ LUBA‡ 1970

  GARINE, I. DE‡ CHAD‡ KERA, MUSEY‡ 1962-63+ 1965

  GEOFFRION, CHARLES A.‡ MALAWI‡ ACHEWA, MANGANJA,
  NGONI‡ 1971-72

  KNIGHT, RODERIC COPLEY‡ GAMBIA, THE‡ BALANTA,
  BAMBARA, FULA, JOLA, MANDINKA, TEMNE, WOLOF‡
  1970-71

  MALER, THOMAS A.‡ TANZANIA‡ DIGO, GIRYAMA,
  MAKONDE, TINDIGA‡ 1967-68

  NOSS, PHILIP A.‡ CAMEROON‡ GBAYA‡ 1966-67

  QUERSIN, BENOIT J.‡ ZAIRE‡ BUSHOONG, COOFA, IBAAM,
  NGEENDE, PYAANG, SHOOWA‡ 1970

  SIMMONS, W.S.‡ SENEGAL‡ BADYARANKE‡ 1964-66

INITIATION-CEREMONY
  ENGLAND, NICHOLAS M.‡ BOTSWANA‡ TSWANA‡ 1957-61

  ENGLAND, NICHOLAS M.‡ NAMIBIA‡ HERERO‡ 1957-61

INITIATION-FEMALE
  QUERSIN, BENOIT J.‡ ZAIRE‡ BATWA, EKONDA, NTOMBA‡
  1970

  VIDAL, PIERRE ANTOINE‡ CENTRAL AFRICAN REPUBLIC‡
  GBAYA, KARA‡ 1961-74

INITIATION-MALE
  VIDAL, PIERRE ANTOINE‡ CENTRAL AFRICAN REPUBLIC‡
  GBAYA, KARA‡ 1961-74

INITIATION-PORO
  ZEMPLEIVI, ANDRAS‡ IVORY COAST‡ SENUFO-NA-FAARA‡
  1972-74

INSTALLATION
  D'AZEVEDO, WARREN L.‡ LIBERIA‡ GOLA‡ 1967

INSTALLATION-CEREMONY
  COPE, TREVOR ANTHONY‡ SOUTH AFRICA‡ ZULU‡ 1965-72

INSTRUMENTAL
  GANSEMANS, JOS‡ RWANDA‡ HUTU, TUTSI, TWA‡ 1973-74

  GANSEMANS, JOS‡ ZAIRE‡ LUBA, LUNDA, SALAMPASU‡
  1970-73

INSULT
  COLLEGE OF MUSIC, UNIVERSITY OF NIGERIA‡ NIGERIA‡
  BINI, BOKI, DAKARAWA, EFIK-IBIBIO, EKOI, FULANI,
  HAUSA, IBO, IDOMA, IJAW, JABA, MADA, YALA, YORUBA,
  ZABEBMAWA‡

INSULT-AGE-SET
  DENG, FRANCIS‡ SUDAN‡ DINKA‡ 1971

INTERNATIONAL-FOLK-MUSIC-
  NORSK RIKSKRINGKASTING‡ GHANA‡ ‡ 1966

INTERVIEW
  ARCHIVES OF ETHNIC MUSIC AND DANCE‡ SENEGAL‡ ‡

  ARCHIVES OF LANGUAGES OF THE WORLD‡ LIBERIA‡ SUSU‡

  COLEMAN, MILTON‡ UGANDA‡ KARAMOJONG‡ 1967

  NEWBURY, DOROTHY J.‡ LIBERIA‡ BASSA, LOMA‡
  1969-70+ 1972

  ROTBERG, ROBERT I.‡ ZAMBIA‡ BISA‡ 1967

  SKINNER, A. NEIL+ SKINNER, MARGARET G.‡ NIGERIA‡
  ANGAS, FULA, HAUSA, KABBA, YORUBA‡ 1967-74

INTERVIEW-DADIE-BERNARD
  DUMONT, LILLIAN E.‡ IVORY COAST‡ ‡ 1973

INTERVIEW-ENGLISH
  PARKER, CAROLYN ANN‡ KENYA‡ BAJUN, SWAHILI‡
  1971-72

INTERVIEW-IBRAHIM-A.
  SPENCER, WILLIAM‡ MOROCCO‡ ‡ 1965

INTERVIEW-KENYATTA-J.
  MORGENTHAU, HENRY‡ KENYA‡ ‡ 1961

INTERVIEW-LAYE-CAMARA
  DUMONT, LILLIAN E.‡ SENEGAL‡ WOLOF, PEUL‡ 1973

INTERVIEW-MAKANNEU-RAS
  ROMERO, PATRICIA‡ KENYA‡ ‡ 1973

INTERVIEW-MBOYA-T.
  MORGENTHAU, HENRY‡ KENYA‡ ‡ 1961

 N IR ‹I -NK IM-N A
INTERVIEW-NKEM-NWANKO
  ROMERO, PATRICIA‡ NIGERIA‡ IBO‡ 1973

INTERVIEW-OKO-WONODA
  ROMERO, PATRICIA‡ NIGERIA‡ IBO‡ 1973

INTERVIEW-SEMBENE-OUSMANE
  DUMONT, LILLIAN E.‡ SENEGAL‡ WOLOF, PEUL‡ 1973

INTERVIEW-SWAHILI
  PARKER, CAROLYN ANN‡ KENYA‡ BAJUN, SWAHILI‡
  1971-72

INTERVIEW-TRACEY-H.
  GILLIS, FRANK J.+ TRACEY, HUGH‡ SOUTH AFRICA-U.S.‡
  ‡ 1971

INTERVIEW-WORLD-WAR-I
  FETTER, BRUCE‡ ZAIRE‡ SETTLERS-AFRICAN‡ 1972-73

ISLAM-INTERVIEW
  HURREIZ, SAYED H.‡ SUDAN‡ GAALIIN‡ 1970-71

ISLAMIC-ORDER-INTERVIEW
  HURREIZ, SAYED H.‡ SUDAN‡ GAALIIN‡ 1970-71

JAZZ
  WARE, NAOMI‡ SIERRA LEONE‡ ‡ 1969

JUDICIAL
  MUSEE ROYAL DE L'AFRIQUE CENTRALE‡ ‡ BIROM, BOLIA,
  HOLOHOLO, KANEMBU, KONDA, KONGO, LEGA, MBALA,
  MBUUN, MONGO, NANDE, PENDE, RUNDI, RWANDA, SANGA,
  SHI, SUKU, TETELA, YEKE‡

KALIMBA
  DAVIDSON, MARJORY‡ ZAMBIA‡ NGONI‡ 1967-71

KALIMBA
  KRAJEWSKI, F. JOSEPH‡ MALAWI‡ NYANJA‡ 1967

KONGOMA
  BAHMAN, GARY‡ SIERRA LEONE‡ LIMBA, MANDINGO,
  TEMNE‡ 1971

  STONE, RUTH M.+ STONE, VERLON L.‡ LIBERIA‡ KPELLE‡
  1970

  VAN OVEN, JACOBA‡ SIERRA LEONE‡ FULA, GALLINAS,
  GOLA, LIMBA, LOKO, MANDINGO, MENDE, SHERBRO, SUSU,
  TEMNE, VAI, YALUNKA‡ 1964-67

KORAN-CHANT
  ARCHIVES OF ETHNIC MUSIC AND DANCE‡ SENEGAL‡ ‡

  KNIGHT, RODERIC COPLEY‡ GAMBIA, THE‡ BALANTA,
  BAMBARA, FULA, JOLA, MANDINKA, TEMNE, WOLOF‡
  1970-71

KORAN-RECITATION
  LAADE, WOLFGANG KARL‡ TUNISIA‡ ARAB, BERBER, JEW‡
  1960

LAMENT
  CAMP, CHARLES M.+ TRACEY, HUGH‡ RHODESIA‡ BUDJA,
  CHIKUNDA, FUNGWE, HERA, HUNGWE, KARANGA, NDAU,
  NDEBELE, NYANJA, NYASA, PEDI, RAMBA, WEMBA, YAO‡
  1948

  CURTIS, NATALIE‡ SOUTH AFRICA‡ ZULU‡ CA1919

  WEMAN, HENRY PAUL‡ SOUTH AFRICA‡ VENDA, ZULU‡
  1956-57

LAND-TRANSFER
  SNYDER, FRANCIS GREGORY‡ SENEGAL‡ DIOLA‡ 1970

LAND-USE
  SNYDER, FRANCIS GREGORY‡ SENEGAL‡ DIOLA‡ 1970

  SNYDER, FRANCIS GREGORY‡ SENEGAL‡ DIOLA‡ 1973

LANGUAGE
  DURAN, JAMES JOSEPH‡ KENYA‡ KIPSIGI‡ 1971

  SHOSTAK, MARJORIE JANET‡ BOTSWANA‡ HERERO,
  KUNG-BUSHMEN‡ 1969-71

LANGUAGE-AFRICA-INFLUENCE
  DALBY, DAVID+ AFRICAN STUDIES-I.U.‡ AFRICA-U.S.‡ ‡
  1969

LANGUAGE-LUO-CONVERSATION
  KIRWEN, MICHAEL CARL‡ TANZANIA‡ SUBA‡ 1963-69

LANGUAGE-SECRET
  DIETERLEN, GERMAINE‡ MALI‡ DOGON‡ 1969

LANGUAGE-YANSI
  THIEL, JOSEF FRANZ‡ ZAIRE‡ MBALA, TEKE, YANSI‡
  1961-71

LECTURE
  MPHAHLELE, EZEKIEL+ AFRICAN STUDIES-I.U.‡ ‡ ‡
  1968

LECTURE-ADDY-MUSTAPHA
  ARCHIVES OF ETHNIC MUSIC AND DANCE‡ GHANA‡
  DAGARTI, DAGOMBA, DONNO, EWE, GA, KONKOMBA, LOBI‡

LEGAL
  SNYDER, FRANCIS GREGORY‡ SENEGAL‡ DIOLA‡ 1970

  SULZMANN, ERIKA‡ ZAIRE‡ BABOMA, BASENGELE, BOLIA,
  EKONDA, NTOMBA‡ 1953-72

LEGEND
  EL-SHAMY, HASAN M.‡ EGYPT‡ ARAB, DINKA, NUBIAN‡
  1968-71

  HURREIZ, SAYED H.‡ SUDAN‡ GAALIIN‡ 1970-71

  STUDSTILL, JOHN D.‡ ZAIRE‡ LUBA‡ 1972

  YODER, WALTER D.‡ SOUTH AFRICA-U.S.‡ ‡ 1955

LIKEMBE
  LAMBRECHT, FRANK L.+ LAMBRECHT, DORA J.M.‡
  BOTSWANA‡ KUNG-BUSHMEN, YEI‡ 1967-68

  MERRIAM, ALAN P.+ MERRIAM, BARBARA W.‡ ZAIRE‡
  BAHIMA, BAKOGA, BAKONGO, BAMBUTI, BANGALA, BASHI,
  BATWA, EKONDA‡ 1951-52

  MERRIAM, ALAN P.+ MERRIAM, BARBARA W.‡ ZAIRE‡
  BASONGYE‡ 1959-60

LIKEMBE
  QUERSIN, BENOIT J.+ QUERSIN, CHRISTINE M.‡ ZAIRE‡
  BATWA, BOLIA, EKONDA‡ 1971

LINGUISTIC-DATA
  HARRIES, JEANETTE‡ MOROCCO‡ BERBER‡ 1964-65

  WESTPHAL, ERNST O.J.‡ BOTSWANA‡ BUSHMEN,
  HOTTENTOT, YEI‡ 1953-74

  WESTPHAL, ERNST O.J.‡ NAMIBIA‡ BUSHMEN, KUANYAMA‡
  1953-74

  WESTPHAL, ERNST O.J.‡ SOUTH AFRICA‡ BUSHMEN‡
  1953-74

LINGUISTICS-LECTURE
  DALBY, DAVID+ AFRICAN STUDIES-I.U.‡ AFRICA-U.S.‡ ‡
  1969

  DALBY, DAVID+ AFRICAN STUDIES-I.U.‡ AFRICA-U.S.‡ ‡
  1969

LITURGY
  KNAPPERT, JAN D.‡ KENYA‡ SWAHILI‡ 1969+ 1973

  LESLAU, WOLF‡ ETHIOPIA‡ AMHARA, GURAGE, HARARI,
  SHOA-GALLA, SOMALI, TIGRINYA‡ 1947

LITURGY-FALASHA
  SHELEMAY, KAY KAUFMAN‡ ETHIOPIA‡ FALASHA-JEW‡
  1973

LOVE
  AMES, DAVID W.‡ NIGERIA‡ IGBO‡ 1963-64

  ARCHIVES OF TRADITIONAL MUSIC‡ ‡ YORUBA‡ CA1940

  BROADCASTING CORPORATION OF CHINA‡ ETHIOPIA‡ ‡

  BUNGER, ROBERT LOUIS‡ KENYA‡ OROMA, POKOMO‡
  1969-70

  CAMP, CHARLES M.+ TRACEY, HUGH‡ SOUTH AFRICA‡
  BHACA, CHOPI, HLUBI, NDAU, NYASA, PONDO, SHANGAAN,
  SOTHO, SWAZI, TSWANA, VENDA, XHOSA‡ 1947-48

  CAMP, CHARLES M.+ TRACEY, HUGH‡ ZAMBIA‡ BEMBA,
  LALA, LOZI, TONGA, ZINZA‡ 1947-48

LOVE
  COLLEGE OF MUSIC, UNIVERSITY OF NIGERIA‡ NIGERIA‡
  BINI, BOKI, DAKARAWA, EFIK-IBIBIO, EKOI, FULANI,
  HAUSA, IBO, IDOMA, IJAW, JABA, MADA, YALA, YORUBA,
  ZABEBMAWA‡

  CURTIS, NATALIE‡ SOUTH AFRICA‡ ZULU‡ CA1919

  HOLIDAY, GEOFFREY D.‡ ALGERIA‡ TUAREG‡ CA1958

  JUILLERAT, B.‡ CAMEROON‡ KIRDI‡ 1966‡ 1967-68

  MALER, THOMAS A.‡ TANZANIA‡ DIGO, GIRYAMA,
  MAKONDE, TINDIGA‡ 1967-68

  MOREY, ROBERT H.‡ LIBERIA‡ GBANDE, LOMA, MANDINGO‡
  1935

  SEDLAK, PHILIP A.S.‡ KENYA‡ DURUMA, GIRYAMA,
  SWAHILI‡ 1971

  VANVELSEN, J.‡ UGANDA‡ KUMAM‡ 1948-60

  WEMAN, HENRY PAUL‡ SOUTH AFRICA‡ VENDA, ZULU‡
  1956-57

LULLABY
  ARCHIVES OF TRADITIONAL MUSIC‡ ‡ YORUBA‡ CA1940

  CAMP, CHARLES M.‡ TRACEY, HUGH‡ RHODESIA‡ BUDJA,
  CHIKUNDA, FUNGWE, HERA, HUNGWE, KARANGA, NDAU,
  NDEBELE, NYANJA, NYASA, PEDI, RAMBA, WEMBA, YAO‡
  1948

  FERNANDEZ, JAMES W.‡ GABON‡ FANG‡ 1960

  GANSEMANS, JOS‡ ZAIRE‡ LUBA‡ 1970

  HERSKOVITS, MELVILLE J.‡ HERSKOVITS, FRANCES S.‡
  DAHOMEY‡ FON‡ 1931

  HERSKOVITS, MELVILLE J.‡ HERSKOVITS, FRANCES S.‡
  GHANA‡ ASANTE‡ 1931

  LORTAT-JACOB, BERNARD‡ ETHIOPIA‡ DORZE‡ 1974-75

  MERRIAM, ALAN P.‡ MERRIAM, BARBARA W.‡ ZAIRE‡
  BAHIMA, BAKOGA, BAKONGO, BAMBUTI, BANGALA, BASHI,
  BATWA, EKONDA‡ 1951-52

LULLABY

  QUERSIN, BENOIT J.+ QUERSIN, CHRISTINE M.‡ ZAIRE‡
BATWA, BOLIA, EKONDA‡ 1971

  RITZENTHALER, ROBERT + RITZENTHALER, PAT‡
CAMEROON‡ BAFUT‡ 1959

  ROUGET, GILBERT‡ GUINEA‡ MALINKE‡ 1952

  ROUGET, GILBERT+ GESSAIN, R.+ GESSAIN, M.‡
SENEGAL‡ BASSARI, BEDIK‡ 1967

  WEMAN, HENRY PAUL‡ RHODESIA‡ KARANGA, LEMBA,
VENDA, ZULU‡ 1957

LUTE

  AMES, DAVID W.‡ NIGERIA‡ HAUSA‡ 1963

  BRANDILY, MONIQUE‡ CHAD‡ FEZZANAIS, TEDA‡ 1969

  CALAME, B.‡ MALI‡ BAMBARA, BOZO, DOGON, MARKA,
MINIANKA, PEUL, RYMAYBE, SARAKOLE, SOMONO,
SONGHAY‡ 1956-57+ 1960

  CONDOMINAS, G.‡ MALAGASY REPUBLIC‡ ‡ 1959

  MERRIAM, ALAN P.+ MERRIAM, BARBARA W.‡ ZAIRE‡
BAHIMA, BAKOGA, BAKONGO, BAMBUTI, BANGALA, BASHI,
BATWA, EKONDA‡ 1951-52

  ROUGET, GILBERT‡ MAURITANIA‡ ‡ 1952

  SARDAN, J.-P. OLIVIER DE‡ NIGER‡ SONGHAY‡ 1969

  VAN OVEN, JACOBA‡ SIERRA LEONE‡ FULA, GALLINAS,
GOLA, LIMBA, LOKO, MANDINGO, MENDE, SHERBRO, SUSU,
TEMNE, VAI, YALUNKA‡ 1964-67

  WILLIAMS, CHESTER S.‡ SOMALIA‡ ‡ 1962

LUTE-BOWED

  ALBERTS, ARTHUR S.‡ UPPER VOLTA‡ BAMBARA, MOSSI‡
1949-51

  AMES, DAVID W.‡ NIGERIA‡ FULBE, HAUSA, YORUBA‡
1963-64

  ARCHIVES OF ETHNIC MUSIC AND DANCE‡ UPPER VOLTA‡
BOBO, BWABA, DYULA, FULANI, FULBE, GOUIN,

LUTE-BOWED
  GOURMANTCHE, LOBI, MINIANKA, MOSSI, SENUFO,
  YARDSE‡

  BOWLES, PAUL+ WANKLYN, CHRISTOPHER‡ MOROCCO‡ ‡
  CA1959-62

  BRANDILY, MONIQUE‡ CHAD‡ FEZZANAIS, TEDA‡ 1969

  CALAME, B.‡ MALI‡ BAMBARA, BOZO, DOGON, MARKA,
  MINIANKA, PEUL, RYMAYBE, SARAKOLE, SOMONO,
  SONGHAY‡ 1956-57+ 1960

  CHRISTIAN, VALERIE+ ROSELLINI, JAMES N.‡ UPPER
  VOLTA‡ FULBE, KASSENA, MARKA, MOSSI‡ 1973

  COOKE, PETER R.‡ UGANDA‡ BAGANDA‡ 1965-68

  CURTIN, PHILIP D.‡ SENEGAL‡ ARAB, DIAKHANKE,
  MALINKE, PULAR, SONINKE‡ 1966

  CURTIN, PHILIP D.‡ SENEGAL‡ ARAB, DIAKHANKE,
  MALINKE, PULAR‡ 1966

  DOBRIN, ARTHUR‡ KENYA‡ GUSII‡ 1966

  HARTWIG, GERALD W.‡ TANZANIA‡ KEREWE‡ 1968-69

  MERRIAM, ALAN P.+ MERRIAM, BARBARA W.‡ BURUNDI‡
  ABATUTSI, BARUNDI, BATWA‡ 1951-52

  MERRIAM, ALAN P.+ MERRIAM, BARBARA W.‡ ZAIRE‡
  BAHIMA, BAKOGA, BAKONGO, BAMBUTI, BANGALA, BASHI,
  BATWA, EKONDA‡ 1951-52

  QUERSIN, BENOIT J.+ QUERSIN, CHRISTINE M.‡
  NIGERIA‡ ABAKPA-RIGA, AFO, ALAGO, ANGAS, ANKWAI,
  BIROM, BUROM, CHAMBA, EGGON, FULANI, HAUSA, ICHEN,
  IDOMA, JARAWA, JUKUN, KALABARI, KANTANA, KUTEP,
  KWALLA, NUPE, PYEM, RINDRE, TIV, YERGAM, YORUBA‡
  1972-73

  SURUGUE, BERNARD‡ NIGER‡ DJERMA-SONGHAY‡ 1969

  VAN OVEN, JACOBA‡ SIERRA LEONE‡ FULA, GALLINAS,
  GOLA, LIMBA, LOKO, MANDINGO, MENDE, SHERBRO, SUSU,
  TEMNE, VAI, YALUNKA‡ 1964-67

  VAUGHAN, JAMES H.‡ NIGERIA‡ MARGI‡ 1974

LUTE-BOWED
  WOLFF, HANS‡ NIGERIA‡ EFIK, HAUSA, IBIBIO, KAJE,
  SOBO, PABIR, YORUBA‡ 1953-54

LUTE-BOWED-GOGE
  HANLEY, MARY ANN CSJ‡ GHANA‡ BUILSA, DAGARI, EWE,
  FANTI, FRAFRA, GA, KASSENA, NANKANI, TWI‡ 1972

  RHODES, WILLARD‡ NIGERIA‡ FULANI, HAUSA, TIV,
  TUAREG, YORUBA‡ 1973-74

LUTE-BOWED-IMZAD
  CARD, CAROLINE E.‡ ALGERIA‡ TUAREG‡ 1972

  HOLIDAY, GEOFFREY D.‡ NIGER‡ TUAREG‡ CA1958

  PELLIGRA, D.‡ ALGERIA‡ TUAREG‡ 1970

LUTE-BOWED-KAMENJA
  WANKLYN, CHRISTOPHER‡ MOROCCO‡ AIT-SIDI-MERRI,
  DEGWANA, MISIWA, OULED-MTAA‡ 1963+ 1969

LUTE-BOWED-MASENQO
  LEMMA, TESFAYE‡ ETHIOPIA‡ ‡ 1970

  SHELEMAY, KAY KAUFMAN‡ ETHIOPIA‡ FALASHA-JEW‡
  1973

LUTE-BOWED-SARANGI
  UPADHYAYA, HARI S.+ ORI, R.‡ MAURITIUS‡
  UTTAR-PRADESH‡ 1961

LUTE-DYELI-KONU
  ROUGET, GILBERT‡ GUINEA‡ MALINKE‡ 1952

LUTE-MULTIPLE-BOW
  QUERSIN, BENOIT J.‡ ZAIRE‡ BUSHOONG, COOFA, IBAAM,
  NGEENDE, PYAANG, SHOOWA‡ 1970

  QUERSIN, BENOIT J.‡ ZAIRE‡ BATWA, EKONDA, NTOMBA‡
  1970

  QUERSIN, BENOIT J.+ QUERSIN, CHRISTINE M.‡ ZAIRE‡
  BATWA, BOLIA, EKONDA‡ 1971

  QUERSIN, BENOIT J.+ QUERSIN, CHRISTINE M.‡ ZAIRE‡
  BAKUTU, BOKOTE, BONGANDO, BUSAKA, BOYELA, NKUNDU,
  PYGMIES-BATWA, PYGMIES-NGOMBE‡ 1972

LYRE-BOWL-ENDONGO
  BYRD, ROBERT OAKES‡ UGANDA‡ ALUR, BAGANDA,
  BAGWERE, BAKONJO, BANYANKOLE, BANYOLE, KAKWA,
  TESO‡

LYRE-BOWL-ENTONGOLI
  BYRD, ROBERT OAKES‡ UGANDA‡ ALUR, BAGANDA,
  BAGWERE, BAKONJO, BANYANKOLE, BANYOLE, KAKWA,
  TESO‡

LYRE-KRAR
  LEMMA, TESFAYE‡ ETHIOPIA‡ ‡ 1970

MALINKE-LECTURE
  BROOKS, GEORGE+ DALBY, DAVID+ VAUGHAN, JAMES H.‡
  AFRICA-U.S.‡ MALINKE‡ 1969

MANCHESTER-CONFERENCE
  ROMERO, PATRICIA‡ KENYA‡ ‡ 1973

MARABOUT
  AMES, DAVID W.‡ GAMBIA, THE‡ WOLOF‡ 1951

  AMES, DAVID W.‡ SENEGAL‡ WOLOF‡ 1950-51

  FERCHIOU, SOPHIE‡ TUNISIA‡ ‡ 1969

MARIMBA
  ARCHIVES OF ETHNIC MUSIC AND DANCE‡ MOZAMBIQUE‡ ‡

MARKET
  MERRIAM, ALAN P.+ MERRIAM, BARBARA W.‡ ZAIRE‡
  BAHIMA, BAKOGA, BAKONGO, BAMBUTI, BANGALA, BASHI,
  BATWA, EKONDA‡ 1951-52

MARKET-INTERVIEW
  BUCHANAN, CAROLE‡ UGANDA‡ BANYORO, BATORO‡
  1968-69

MARKET-TRADER-INTERVIEW
  ROBERTSON, CLAIRE C.‡ GHANA‡ GA‡ 1972

MARRIAGE
  AMES, DAVID W.‡ GAMBIA, THE‡ WOLOF‡ 1951

  AMES, DAVID W.‡ NIGERIA‡ HAUSA‡ 1963

  AMES, DAVID W.‡ SENEGAL‡ WOLOF‡ 1950-51

MARRIAGE
  ARCHIVES OF ETHNIC MUSIC AND DANCE‡ ETHIOPIA‡
  AMHARA, TIGRINYA‡

  ARCHIVES OF ETHNIC MUSIC AND DANCE‡ UPPER VOLTA‡
  BOBO, BWABA, DYULA, FULANI, FULBE, GOUIN,
  GOURMANTCHE, LOBI, MINIANKA, MOSSI, SENUFO,
  YARDSE‡

  ARMISTEAD, SAMUEL G. + KATZ, ISRAEL J. +
  SILVERMAN, JOSEPH H.‡ MOROCCO‡ SEPHARDIC-JEW‡
  1962

  BRANDILY, MONIQUE‡ CHAD‡ KANEMBU, KOTOKO, TEDA‡
  1961+ 1963+ 1965

  BRANDILY, MONIQUE‡ CHAD‡ FEZZANAIS, TEDA‡ 1969

  BUCHANAN, CAROLE‡ UGANDA‡ BANYORO, BATORO‡
  1968-69

  CAMP, CHARLES M.+ TRACEY, HUGH‡ SOUTH AFRICA‡
  BHACA, CHOPI, HLUBI, NDAU, NYASA, PONDO, SHANGAAN,
  SOTHO, SWAZI, TSWANA, VENDA, XHOSA‡ 1947-48

  CAMPBELL, CAROL‡ KENYA‡ BAJUN, SWAHILI‡ 1972

  CARLISLE, ROXANE C.‡ SUDAN‡ ANUAK, DINKA, GAALIIN,
  NUER, SHILLUK‡ 1963

  CHRISTIAN, VALERIE‡ UPPER VOLTA‡ BISSA, BOBO,
  BWABA, DAGARA, DYULA, FULANI, FULBE, GOUIN,
  GOURMANTCHE, HAUSA, KASSENA, KWO, LOBI, MARKA,
  MOSSI, NONDOM, POUGOULIS, SAMO-DU-SUD, YARDSE‡
  1973-74

  CURTIN, PHILIP D.‡ SENEGAL‡ ARAB, DIAKHANKE,
  MALINKE, PULAR‡ 1966

  EL-SHAMY, HASAN M.‡ EGYPT‡ ARAB, DINKA, NUBIAN‡
  1968-71

  ELLOVICH, RISA SUE‡ IVORY COAST‡ DYULA, MALINKE,
  VOLTAIC‡ 1973-74

  ETHNOMUSICOLOGY CENTRE JAAP KUNST‡ GAMBIA, THE‡
  MANDINKA‡ 1958

  FARSY, MUHAMMED S.‡ TANZANIA-ZANZIBAR‡ ‡ CA1958

MARRIAGE

FIKRY, MONA‡ GHANA‡ WALA‡ 1966-67

GANSEMANS, JOS‡ ZAIRE‡ LUBA‡ 1970

HANLEY, MARY ANN CSJ‡ GHANA‡ BUILSA, DAGARI, EWE,
FANTI, FRAFRA, GA, KASSENA, NANKANI, TWI‡ 1972

HANLEY, MARY ANN CSJ‡ GHANA‡ AKAN, EWE, TWI‡ 1973

HARRIES, JEANETTE‡ MOROCCO‡ BERBER‡ 1971-72

HERSKOVITS, MELVILLE J.+ HERSKOVITS, FRANCES S.‡
DAHOMEY‡ FON‡ 1931

HESS, ROBERT A.‡ NIGERIA‡ BURA‡ 1969

KIRWEN, MICHAEL CARL‡ TANZANIA‡ SUBA‡ 1963-69

KNIGHT, RODERIC COPLEY‡ GAMBIA, THE‡ BALANTA,
BAMBARA, FULA, JOLA, MANDINKA, TEMNE, WOLOF‡
1970-71

LAADE, WOLFGANG KARL‡ TUNISIA‡ ARAB, BERBER, JEW‡
1960

LANGE, WERNER‡ ETHIOPIA‡ BENS, BOSA, CARA,
HINNARIO, KAFA, MERU, NA'O, SE, SEKA, SHE, ZARAS‡
1972-73

LEMMA, TESFAYE‡ ETHIOPIA‡ ‡ 1970

LORTAT-JACOB, BERNARD‡ MOROCCO‡ AIT-MGOUN‡ 1969

MERRIAM, ALAN P.+ MERRIAM, BARBARA W.‡ BURUNDI‡
ABATUTSI, BARUNDI, BATWA‡ 1951-52

MERRIAM, ALAN P.+ MERRIAM, BARBARA W.‡ RWANDA‡
ABAGOGWE, ABAGOYI, ABAHORORO, ABANYAMBO, ABATUTSI,
ABAYOVU, BAHIMA, BAHUTU, BAKIGA, BATWA‡ 1951-52

MERRIAM, ALAN P.+ MERRIAM, BARBARA W.‡ ZAIRE‡
BAHIMA, BAKOGA, BAKONGO, BAMBUTI, BANGALA, BASHI,
BATWA, EKONDA‡ 1951-52

OTTENHEIMER, HARRIET+ OTTENHEIMER, MARTIN‡ COMORO
ISLANDS‡ ‡ 1967-68

QUERSIN, BENOIT J.+ QUERSIN, CHRISTINE M.‡

MARRIAGE
  NIGERIA‡ ABAKPA-RIGA, AFO, ALAGO, ANGAS, ANKWAI,
  BIROM, BUROM, CHAMBA, EGGON, FULANI, HAUSA, ICHEN,
  IDOMA, JARAWA, JUKUN, KALABARI, KANTANA, KUTEP,
  KWALLA, NUPE, PYEM, RINDRE, TIV, YERGAM, YORUBA‡
  1972-73

  RHODES, WILLARD‡ NIGERIA‡ FULANI, HAUSA, TIV,
  TUAREG, YORUBA‡ 1973-74

  ROUGET, GILBERT‡ SENEGAL‡ LEBOU, PEUL, SARAKOLE,
  SOCE, TUKULOR, WOLOF‡ 1952

  RUBIN, ARNOLD G.‡ NIGERIA‡ CHAMBA, HAUSA, IBO,
  JUKUN, KUTEP, TIKARI, TIV‡ 1964-65

  SIGWALT, RICHARD+ SOSNE, ELINOR‡ ZAIRE‡ SHI‡
  1971-73

  WANKLYN, CHRISTOPHER‡ MOROCCO‡ AIT-SIDI-MERRI,
  DEGWANA, MISIWA, OULED-MTAA‡ 1963+ 1969

  WEMAN, HENRY PAUL‡ SOUTH AFRICA‡ VENDA, ZULU‡
  1956-57

  WEMAN, PAUL HENRY‡ TANZANIA‡ HAYA, SUKUMA,
  SWAHILI‡ 1957

  ZEMP, HUGO‡ MOROCCO‡ ‡ 1960

MARRIAGE-INTERVIEW
  ROBERTSON, CLAIRE C.‡ GHANA‡ GA‡ 1972

MARRIAGE-ISLAMIC
  SAPIR, J. DAVID‡ SENEGAL‡ DIOLA-FOGNY, DIOLA-KASA‡
  1960-65

MASK-VOICE
  ROUGET, GILBERT+ GESSAIN, R.+ GESSAIN, M.‡
  SENEGAL‡ BASSARI, BEDIK‡ 1967

MASS-CATHOLIC
  HANLEY, MARY ANN CSJ‡ GHANA‡ BUILSA, DAGARI, EWE,
  FANTI, FRAFRA, GA, KASSENA, NANKANI, TWI‡ 1972

  HANLEY, MARY ANN CSJ‡ NIGERIA‡ ANGAS, BACHAMA,
  CHAMBA, EFIK, GWANDARA, HAUSA, IBIBIO, IBO, JABA,
  KERI-KERI, YORUBA‡ 1973

MASS-CATHOLIC
  HANLEY, MARY ANN CSJ‡ UPPER VOLTA‡ ‡ 1972

MASS-YORUBA
  WILLETT, FRANK‡ NIGERIA‡ YORUBA‡ 1972

MBIRA
  ARCHIVES OF ETHNIC MUSIC AND DANCE‡ RHODESIA‡ ‡

  CAMP, CHARLES M.+ TRACEY, HUGH‡ RHODESIA‡ BUDJA,
  CHIKUNDA, FUNGWE, HERA, HUNGWE, KARANGA, NDAU,
  NDEBELE, NYANJA, NYASA, PEDI, RAMBA, WEMBA, YAO‡
  1948

  CAMP, CHARLES M.+ TRACEY, HUGH‡ SOUTH AFRICA‡
  BHACA, CHOPI, HLUBI, NDAU, NYASA, PONDO, SHANGAAN,
  SOTHO, SWAZI, TSWANA, VENDA, XHOSA‡ 1947-48

  CAMP, CHARLES M.+ TRACEY, HUGH‡ ZAMBIA‡ BEMBA,
  LALA, LOZI, TONGA, ZINZA‡ 1947-48

  KAEMMER, JOHN E.‡ RHODESIA‡ KOREKORE, SHONA,
  ZEZURU‡ 1972-73

  TRADITIONAL MUSIC DOCUMENTATION PROJECT‡ RHODESIA‡
  KARANGA, MANYIKE-BOCHA, NDAU, NJANJA, SENA-TONGA,
  ZEZURU‡

  WEMAN, HENRY PAUL‡ RHODESIA‡ KARANGA, LEMBA,
  VENDA, ZULU‡ 1957

MBIRA-BONGO
  KNIGHT, RODERIC COPLEY‡ GAMBIA, THE‡ BALANTA,
  BAMBARA, FULA, JOLA, MANDINKA, TEMNE, WOLOF‡
  1970-71

MBIRA-TUNING
  WEMAN, HENRY PAUL‡ RHODESIA‡ KARANGA, LEMBA,
  VENDA, ZULU‡ 1957

MEDICAL-PRACTICE
  HAWTHORNE, RICHARD‡ LIBERIA‡ MANO‡ 1970

MEMBRANOPHONE
  FEDERAL DEPARTMENT OF ANTIQUITIES, NATIONAL
  MUSEUM, KADUNA‡ NIGERIA‡ ELOYI, GEDE‡

MERCHANT-INTERVIEW
  BAIER, STEPHEN B.‡ NIGER‡ HAUSA, KANURI, TUAREG‡

MERCHANT-INTERVIEW
  1972

MILIKIT
  SHELEMAY, KAY KAUFMAN‡ ETHIOPIA‡ FALASHA-JEW‡
  1973

MILITARY
  PAGE, MELVIN E.‡ MALAWI‡ ‡ 1972-74

  WEMAN, HENRY PAUL‡ SOUTH AFRICA‡ VENDA, ZULU‡
  1956-57

MIRLITON
  BIEBUYCK, DANIEL P.‡ ZAIRE‡ LEGA, LUBA, LUNDA,
  MANGBETU, MAYOGO, NANDE, NYANGA, ZAMBE‡ 1952-61

MISSION-PRESBYTERIAN
  PRUITT, WILLIAM F., SR.‡ ZAIRE‡ LUBA, LULUA‡
  1945-49

MONOCHORD
  KNIGHT, RODERIC COPLEY‡ GAMBIA, THE‡ BALANTA,
  BAMBARA, FULA, JOLA, MANDINKA, TEMNE, WOLOF‡
  1970-71

MUSIC
  AFRIKA-STUDIECENTRUM‡ TOGO‡ TYOKOSSI‡

  ARCHIVES OF LANGUAGES OF THE WORLD‡ SOUTH AFRICA‡
  DUMA-KARANGA‡ 1954

  BOUQUIAUX, LUC‡ CENTRAL AFRICAN REPUBLIC‡ BANDA,
  ISONGO, MONZOMBU, NGBAKA-MABO‡

  BROEKHUYSE, JAN T.‡ UPPER VOLTA‡ SAMO‡ 1969

  BRYAN, SAM‡ SENEGAL‡ ‡ 1969

  CENTRE DE RECHERCHES ANTHROPOLOGIQUES
  PREHISTORIQUES ET ETHNOGRAPHIQUES‡ ALGERIA‡ ARAB,
  BERBER, MAGHREB‡

  CENTRE FOR THE STUDY OF NIGERIAN LANGUAGES‡
  NIGERIA‡ HAUSA‡

  COLEMAN, MILTON‡ UGANDA‡ KARAMOJONG‡ 1967

  DEVITT, PAUL C.S.‡ BOTSWANA‡ ‡ 1971-72

MUSIC

DIAS, MARGOT‡ ANGOLA‡ MUSSEQUES‡ 1960

DIAS, MARGOT‡ MOZAMBIQUE‡ MAKONDE‡ 1957-58

DIAS, MARGOT‡ MOZAMBIQUE‡ CHOKWE, CHOPI‡ 1959

DUNGER, GEORGE A.‡ CAMEROON‡ BEKOM, DUALA, KAKA,
NSUNGLI‡

ELWA RADIO STATION, LIBERIA‡ LIBERIA‡ ‡
CA1960-1975

ELWA STUDIO, NIGERIA‡ NIGERIA‡ IBO, NUPE, YORUBA‡

GUIGNARD, AUDE‡ SENEGAL‡ BEDIK, MALINKE, PEUL‡
1968

HOHENWART-GERLACHSTEIN, ANNA‡ EGYPT‡ ABABDA, BEJA,
FADIDJA, FELLAHIN‡ 1960+ 1962-63

HOLSOE, SVEND E.‡ LIBERIA‡ DEI, GBANDE, GOLA,
KPELLE, MANDINGO, VAI‡ 1965-70

INSTITUT D'ETHNOLOGIE DE L'UNIVERSITE DE
STRASBOURG‡ MALI‡ BAMBARA‡

INSTITUT D'ETHNOLOGIE DE L'UNIVERSITE DE
STRASBOURG‡ MOROCCO‡ GNAWA‡

INSTITUTO NACIONAL DE FOLKLORE, VENEZUELA‡
BURUNDI‡ ‡ 1961

INSTITUTO NACIONAL DE FOLKLORE, VENEZUELA‡
TANZANIA‡ ‡ 1961

JENKINS, JEAN‡ ETHIOPIA‡ ‡ 1962-70

JOHNSTON, THOMAS FREDERICK‡ MOZAMBIQUE‡ TSONGA‡
1968-70

JOHNSTON, THOMAS FREDERICK‡ SOUTH AFRICA‡ TSONGA‡
1968-70

KAEMMER, JOHN E.‡ RHODESIA‡ GARWE, MANYIKA‡ 1971

KAUFFMAN, ROBERT A.‡ RHODESIA‡ SHONA‡ 1960-65,
1971

MUSIC
  KEIL, CHARLES‡ NIGERIA‡ TIV, YORUBA‡

  MARTIN, JANE JACKSON‡ LIBERIA‡ GREBO‡ 1968+
  1972-75

  MISJONSSKOLEN‡ CAMERCON‡ ‡

  MISJONSSKOLEN‡ MALAGASY REPUBLIC‡ ‡

  MISJONSSKOLEN‡ SOUTH AFRICA‡ ZULU‡

  MOORE, BAI T.‡ LIBERIA‡ BASSA, DEI, GBANDE, GIO,
  GOLA, KISSI, KPELLE, LOMA, MANDINGO, MANO, MENDE,
  VAI‡ 1962-73

  MURPHY, ROBERT‡ NIGER‡ TUAREG‡ 1959-60

  MURPHY, ROBERT‡ NIGERIA‡ TUAREG‡ 1959-60

  MUSEU DO DUNDO‡ ANGOLA‡ LUBA, LUNDA, LWENA,
  CHOKWE‡

  PAIRAULT, CLAUDE ALBERT‡ CHAD‡ GULA-IRO‡ 1959-64

  PARKER, CAROLYN ANN‡ KENYA‡ BAJUN, SWAHILI‡
  1971-72

  REEFE, THOMAS Q.‡ ZAIRE‡ LUBA‡ 1972-73

  ROUGET, GILBERT‡ CONGO, PEOPLE'S REPUBLIC OF THE‡
  PYGMIES-NGOUNDI‡ 1948

  ROUGET, GILBERT‡ DAHOMEY‡ FON, GUN, YORUBA‡
  1952-71

  ROUGET, GILBERT‡ GUINEA‡ MALINKE‡ 1952

  SCHWEEGER-HEFEL, ANNEMARIE‡ UPPER VOLTA‡ DOGON,
  KURUMBA, PEUL‡

  SIGWALT, RICHARD+ SOSNE, ELINOR‡ ZAIRE‡ SHI‡
  1971-73

  SKINNER, A. NEIL+ SKINNER, MARGARET G.‡ NIGERIA‡
  ANGAS, FULA, HAUSA, KABBA, YORUBA‡ 1967-74

  SOLANO, ROBERT P.‡ GHANA‡ ‡ 1970-71

MUSIC
  SOLANO, ROBERT P.‡ UPPER VOLTA‡ ‡ 1970-71

  VAUGHAN, JAMES H.‡ NIGERIA‡ MARGI, VENGO‡ 1960

  VIVELO, FRANK ROBERT‡ BOTSWANA‡ HERERO‡ 1973

  WALLMAN, SANDRA‡ LESOTHO‡ BASUTO‡ 1963

  WESTPHAL, ERNST O.J.‡ BOTSWANA‡ BUSHMEN,
  HOTTENTOT, YEI‡ 1953-74

  WESTPHAL, ERNST O.J.‡ NAMIBIA‡ BUSHMEN, KUANYAMA‡
  1953-74

  WESTPHAL, ERNST O.J.‡ SOUTH AFRICA‡ BUSHMEN‡
  1953-74

  WIDSTRAND, CARL G.‡ ‡ SWAHILI‡

  WILLIS, ROY GEOFFREY‡ TANZANIA‡ FIPA‡ 1966

  WILSON, VIVIAN J.‡ RHODESIA‡ TONGA‡ 1970

MUSIC-ART
  CHERKI, SALAH‡ MOROCCO‡ ARAB‡ CA1960

  HANLEY, MARY ANN CSJ‡ GHANA‡ BUILSA, DAGARI, EWE,
  FANTI, FRAFRA, GA, KASSENA, NANKANI, TWI‡ 1972

  LORTAT-JACOB, BERNARD‡ MOROCCO‡ BERBER, TAMAZIGT,
  TASLHIT‡ 1969-73

MUSIC-ART-ANDALUSIAN
  ARCHIVES OF ETHNIC MUSIC AND DANCE‡ MOROCCO‡ ARAB‡

MUSIC-ART-ARAB-ANDALUSIAN
  LAADE, WOLFGANG KARL‡ TUNISIA‡ ARAB, BERBER, JEW‡
  1960

MUSIC-LECTURE
  MENSAH, ATTAH‡ GILLIS, FRANK J.‡ ZAMBIA-U.S.‡ ‡
  1970

MUSIC-MANINKA-ORIGIN
  KNIGHT, RODERIC COPLEY‡ GAMBIA, THE‡ BALANTA,
  BAMBARA, FULA, JOLA, MANDINKA, TEMNE, WOLOF‡
  1970-71

MUSIC-POPULAR
  ALBERTS, ARTHUR S.‡ LIBERIA‡ ‡ 1949-51

MUSIC-POPULAR-CONGOLESE
  KNIGHT, RODERIC COPLEY‡ ZAIRE‡ ‡ 1970-71

MUSIC-URBAN
  KAUFFMAN, ROBERT A.‡ RHODESIA‡ SHONA‡ 1960-65,
  1971

MUSICIAN
  LORTAT-JACOB, BERNARD‡ MOROCCO‡ AIT-BOUGMEZ‡
  FTOUKA‡ 1971

  MANN, WILLIAM MICHAEL‡ ZAMBIA‡ BEMBA, BISA‡ 1967

  MERRIAM, ALAN P.+ MERRIAM, BARBARA W.‡ ZAIRE‡
  BASONGYE‡ 1959-60

  TARDITS, CLAUDE‡ DAHOMEY‡ GUN‡ 1955

  TENRAA, ERIC WILLIAM FREDERICK‡ TANZANIA‡ BURUNGE,
  SANDAWE, SWAHILI‡ 1958-66

  VAN OVEN, JACOBA‡ SIERRA LEONE‡ FULA, GALLINAS,
  GOLA, LIMBA, LOKO, MANDINGO, MENDE, SHERBRO, SUSU,
  TEMNE, VAI, YALUNKA‡ 1964-67

MUSICIAN-GRIOT
  AMES, DAVID W.‡ SENEGAL‡ WOLOF‡ 1950-51

  BIRD, CHARLES S.‡ MALI‡ BAMBARA‡ 1967-68

  CAMARA, S.‡ SENEGAL‡ MALINKE‡ 1970+ 1971

  CURTIN, PHILIP D.‡ SENEGAL‡ ARAB, DIAKHANKE,
  MALINKE, PULAR, SONINKE‡ 1966

  ERNOULT, CLAUDE+ ROUGET, GILBERT‡ MAURITANIA‡ ‡

  ROUGET, GILBERT‡ GUINEA‡ MALINKE‡ 1952

  ROUGET, GILBERT‡ SENEGAL‡ LEBOU, PEUL, SARAKOLE,
  SOCE, TUKULOR, WOLOF‡ 1952

MUSICIANS-AKAN-LECTURE
  NKETIA, J.H. KWABENA+ WARE, NAOMI‡ GHANA-U.S.‡
  AKAN‡ 1965

MYTH
  KATZ, RICHARD‡ BOTSWANA‡ KUNG-BUSHMEN‡ 1968

  KAYE, ALAN S.‡ CHAD‡ ARAB‡ 1970

  STUDSTILL, JOHN D.‡ ZAIRE‡ LUBA‡ 1972

  WILLIS, ROY GEOFFREY‡ TANZANIA‡ FIPA‡ 1966

MYTH-ORIGIN
  STUDSTILL, JOHN D.‡ ZAIRE‡ LUBA‡ 1972

NAMING
  LINENBRUEGGE, GERTRUDE R.I.‡ NIGERIA‡ IBO‡ 1966

NAMING-CEREMONY
  COLLEGE OF MUSIC, UNIVERSITY OF NIGERIA‡ NIGERIA‡
  BINI, BOKI, DAKARAWA, EFIK-IBIBIO, EKOI, FULANI,
  HAUSA, IBO, IDOMA, IJAW, JABA, MADA, YALA, YORUBA,
  ZABEBMAWA‡

NARRATIVE
  BEN-AMOS, DAN‡ NIGERIA‡ HAUSA‡ 1966

  BLAIR, BOB‡ GHANA‡ ASANTE‡ 1958

  DEPARTMENT OF AFRICAN LANGUAGES, UNIVERSITY OF
  RHODESIA‡ RHODESIA‡ NDEBELE, SHONA‡

  KAYE, ALAN S.‡ CHAD‡ ARAB‡ 1970

  KAYE, ALAN S.‡ SUDAN‡ ARAB‡ 1970

  MURPHY, ROBERT‡ NIGER‡ TUAREG‡ 1959-60

  MURPHY, ROBERT‡ NIGERIA‡ TUAREG‡ 1959-60

  NANCARROW, OWEN T.‡ RHODESIA‡ NDEBELE‡ 1970-71

NARRATIVE-IFE
  DEPARTMENT OF LINGUISTICS AND NIGERIAN LANGUAGES,
  UNIVERSITY OF IBADAN‡ NIGERIA‡ EDO, IJO, ISOKO,
  ITSEKIRI, OWAN, YORUBA‡ 1967-73

NARRATIVE-IINTSOMI
  SCHEUB, HAROLD‡ SOUTH AFRICA‡ XHOSA, ZULU‡
  1967-68

  SCHEUB, HAROLD‡ SOUTH AFRICA‡ NDEBELE, XHOSA,

NARRATIVE-IINTSOMI
   ZULU‡ 1972-73

NARRATIVE-IJEBU
   DEPARTMENT OF LINGUISTICS AND NIGERIAN LANGUAGES,
   UNIVERSITY OF IBADAN‡ NIGERIA‡ EDO, IJO, ISOKO,
   ITSEKIRI, OWAN, YORUBA‡ 1967-73

NARRATIVE-IKALE
   DEPARTMENT OF LINGUISTICS AND NIGERIAN LANGUAGES,
   UNIVERSITY OF IBADAN‡ NIGERIA‡ EDO, IJO, ISOKO,
   ITSEKIRI, OWAN, YORUBA‡ 1967-73

NARRATIVE-IZINGANEKWANE
   SCHEUB, HAROLD‡ SOUTH AFRICA‡ XHOSA, ZULU‡
   1967-68

   SCHEUB, HAROLD‡ SOUTH AFRICA‡ NDEBELE, XHOSA,
   ZULU‡ 1972-73

NARRATIVE-IZINGANU
   SCHEUB, HAROLD‡ SOUTH AFRICA‡ NDEBELE, XHOSA,
   ZULU‡ 1972-73

NARRATIVE-MIGRATION
   ELLOVICH, RISA SUE‡ IVORY COAST‡ DYULA, MALINKE,
   VOLTAIC‡ 1973-74

NARRATIVE-PROSE
   PIA, JOSEPH J.‡ SOMALIA‡ SOMALI‡ 1962

NARRATIVE-TINSIMU
   SCHEUB, HAROLD‡ SWAZILAND‡ SWAZI‡ 1972-73

NDONGO-ENSEMBLE
   ARCHIVES OF ETHNIC MUSIC AND DANCE‡ UGANDA‡
   BASOGA‡

NYERERE-PRESIDENT-SPEECH
   MORGENTHAU, HENRY‡ TANZANIA‡ ‡ 1965

OBOE
   BOWLES, PAUL＋ WANKLYN, CHRISTOPHER‡ MOROCCO‡ ‡
   CA1959-62

   QUERSIN, BENOIT J.＋ QUERSIN, CHRISTINE M.‡
   NIGERIA‡ ABAKPA-RIGA, AFO, ALAGO, ANGAS, ANKWAI,
   BIROM, BUROM, CHAMBA, EGGON, FULANI, HAUSA, ICHEN,
   IDOMA, JARAWA, JUKUN, KALABARI, KANTANA, KUTEP,

OBOE
  KWALLA, NUPE, PYEM, RINDRE, TIV, YERGAM, YORUBA‡
  1972-73

  ZEMP, HUGO‡ MOROCCO‡ ‡ 1960

OCARINA
  MERRIAM, ALAN P.+ MERRIAM, BARBARA W.‡ ZAIRE‡
  BASONGYE‡ 1959-60

  STARR, FREDERICK A.‡ ZAIRE‡ BAKUBA, BALUBA‡ 1906

OLATUNJI-B.-PERFORMANCE
  CAZDEN, NORMAN‡ NIGERIA-U.S.‡ ‡ 1960

ORAL-DATA
  CENTRE DE RECHERCHES ANTHROPOLOGIQUES‡ SENEGAL‡
  BASSARI, BEDIK, CONIAGUI, MALINKE, TENDA‡

  HOHENWART-GERLACHSTEIN, ANNA‡ EGYPT‡ ABABDA, BEJA,
  FADIDJA, FELLAHIN‡ 1960+ 1962-63

  KOIZUMI, FUMIO‡ ETHIOPIA‡ AMHARA‡ 1971

  KOIZUMI, FUMIO‡ NIGERIA‡ YORUBA‡ 1971

  KOIZUMI, FUMIO‡ SENEGAL‡ ‡ 1971

  KOIZUMI, FUMIO‡ TANZANIA‡ ‡ 1971

  MOORE, BAI T.‡ LIBERIA‡ BASSA, DEI, GBANDE, GIO,
  GOLA, KISSI, KPELLE, LOMA, MANDINGO, MANO, MENDE,
  VAI‡ 1962-73

  PENCHOEN, THOMAS GOODENOUGH‡ MOROCCO‡
  BERBER-AYT-NDIR‡ 1969-74

  PENCHOEN, THOMAS GOODENOUGH‡ TUNISIA‡
  BERBER-DJERBA‡ 1969

  STENNES, LESLIE H.‡ CAMEROON‡ FULANI, GIDDER‡
  1956-73

  WILSON, VIVIAN J.‡ RHODESIA‡ TONGA‡ 1970

ORAL-DATA-ART
  AKYEA, E. OFORI‡ GHANA‡ ASANTE‡ 1967

ORAL-DATA-COLONIAL
  DORSON, RICHARD M.‡ NIGERIA-U.S.‡ BRITISH, HAUSA‡
  1967

ORAL-DATA-INTERVIEW
  DORSON, RICHARD M.‡ NIGERIA-U.S.‡ BRITISH, HAUSA‡
  1967

ORAL-DATA-LINGALA
  VALLEE, ROGER P.‡ CONGO, PEOPLE'S REPUBLIC OF THE‡
  ‡ 1967

ORCHESTRA-ROYAL
  QUERSIN, BENOIT J.+ QUERSIN, CHRISTINE M.‡
  NIGERIA‡ ABAKPA-RIGA, AFO, ALAGO, ANGAS, ANKWAI,
  BIROM, BUROM, CHAMBA, EGGON, FULANI, HAUSA, ICHEN,
  IDOMA, JARAWA, JUKUN, KALABARI, KANTANA, KUTEP,
  KWALLA, NUPE, PYEM, RINDRE, TIV, YERGAM, YORUBA‡
  1972-73

ORGAN
  HANLEY, MARY ANN CSJ‡ GHANA‡ BUILSA, DAGARI, EWE,
  FANTI, FRAFRA, GA, KASSENA, NANKANI, TWI‡ 1972

  HANLEY, MARY ANN CSJ‡ NIGERIA‡ ANGAS, BACHAMA,
  CHAMBA, EFIK, GWANDARA, HAUSA, IBIBIO, IBO, JABA,
  KERI-KERI, YORUBA‡ 1973

  WEMAN, PAUL HENRY‡ NIGERIA‡ YORUBA‡ 1957

PADDLING
  MERRIAM, ALAN P.+ MERRIAM, BARBARA W.‡ ZAIRE‡
  BAHIMA, BAKOGA, BAKONGO, BAMBUTI, BANGALA, BASHI,
  BATWA, EKONDA‡ 1951-52

  QUERSIN, BENOIT J.+ QUERSIN, CHRISTINE M.‡ ZAIRE‡
  BAKUTU, BOKOTE, BONGANDO, BOSAKA, BOYELA, NKUNDU,
  PYGMIES-BATWA, PYGMIES-NGOMBE‡ 1972

PANPIPES
  ARCHIVES OF ETHNIC MUSIC AND DANCE‡ RHODESIA‡ ‡

  CAMP, CHARLES M.+ TRACEY, HUGH‡ RHODESIA‡ BUDJA,
  CHIKUNDA, FUNGWE, HERA, HUNGWE, KARANGA, NDAU,
  NDEBELE, NYANJA, NYASA, PEDI, RAMBA, WEMBA, YAO‡
  1948

  COOKE, PETER R.‡ UGANDA‡ BAGANDA‡ 1965-68

PARABLE
  NOSS, PHILIP A.‡ CAMEROON‡ GBAYA‡ 1966-67

PHONETICS
  TUCKER, ARCHIBALD NORMAN‡ SOUTH AFRICA‡ PEDI,
  SOTHO, TSWANA, XHOSA, ZULU‡

PIPE
  VAN THIEL, PAUL A.H.‡ UGANDA‡ BANTU, BANYANKOLE‡
  1964-65‡ 1969‡ 1970-72

PIPE-ENSEMBLE
  KAEMMER, JOHN E.‡ RHODESIA‡ KOREKORE, SHONA,
  ZEZURU‡ 1972-73

POETRY
  ANDERSON, LOIS ANN‡ MOROCCO‡ BERBER‡ 1971

  BABALOLA, ADEBOYE‡ NIGERIA‡ YORUBA‡ 1962-74

  BAKER, CATHRYN ANITA‡ TUNISIA‡ ‡ 1972-73

  BERLINER, PAUL FRANKLIN‡ RHODESIA‡ SHONA‡ 1972

  BRUTUS, DENNIS‡ SNYDER, EMILE‡ SOUTH AFRICA-U.S.‡
  ‡ 1966

  CAMPBELL, CAROL‡ KENYA‡ BAJUN, SWAHILI‡ 1972

  CARLISLE, ROXANE C.‡ SUDAN‡ ANUAK, DINKA, GAALIIN,
  NUER, SHILLUK‡ 1963

  CENTRE DE RECHERCHES ANTHROPOLOGIQUES
  PREHISTORIQUES ET ETHNOGRAPHIQUES‡ ALGERIA‡ ARAB,
  BERBER, MAGHREB‡

  D'HERTEFELT, MARUL‡ RWANDA‡ ‡ 1953-73

  DIETERLEN, GERMAINE‡ MALI‡ PEUL‡ 1960

  DUMONT, LILLIAN E.‡ IVORY COAST‡ ‡ 1973

  HARRIES, JEANETTE‡ MOROCCO‡ BERBER‡ 1971-72

  JOHNSON, JOHN W. ‡ SOMALIA‡ SOMALI‡ 1966-69

  KAYE, ALAN S.‡ NIGERIA‡ ARAB-SHUWA‡ 1974

  LAADE, WOLFGANG KARL ‡ TUNISIA‡ ARAB, BERBER, JEW‡

POETRY
  1960

  LOMBARD, JACQUES‡ MALAGASY REPUBLIC‡ SAKALAVA‡
  1969-74

  LORTAT-JACOB, BERNARD‡ MOROCCO‡ AIT-BOUGMEZ,
  FTOUKA‡ 1971

  MOULOUD, MAMMERI‡ ALGERIA‡ BERBER‡

  OPLAND, JEFFREY‡ SOUTH AFRICA‡ XHOSA, ZULU‡
  1969-73

  SKINNER, A. NEIL+ SKINNER, MARGARET G.‡ NIGERIA‡
  ANGAS, FULA, HAUSA, KABBA, YORUBA‡ 1967-74

  VAN ROUVEROY VAN NIEUWAAL, EMILE A.B.‡ TOGO‡
  KOSSI‡ 1969-73

POETRY-ELEGIAC
  OGBU, JOHN U.‡ NIGERIA‡ IBO‡ 1972

POETRY-HEELLO
  JOHNSON, JOHN W. ‡ SOMALIA‡ SOMALI‡ 1966-69

POETRY-HEROIC
  KABEMBA, MUFUTA KABANDANYI‡ ZAIRE‡ KUBA, LUBA‡
  1965+ 1972

POETRY-INSULT
  IRVINE, JUDITH TEMKIN‡ SENEGAL‡ WOLOF‡ 1970-71

POETRY-INTERVIEW
  BRUTUS, DENNIS+ SNYDER, EMILE‡ SOUTH AFRICA-U.S.‡
  ‡ 1966

  JOHNSON, JOHN W. ‡ SOMALIA‡ SOMALI‡ 1966-69

POETRY-ITU-AFA
  OGBU, JOHN U.‡ NIGERIA‡ IBO‡ 1972

POETRY-NARRATIVE
  KIRK-GREENE, ANTHONY H.M.‡ NIGERIA‡ HAUSA, KAGORO,
  TIV‡ 1962-65

POETRY-RITUAL
  OGBU, JOHN U.‡ NIGERIA‡ IBO‡ 1972

POETRY-SOCIAL-ETIYERI
  ISOLA, AKINWUMI‡ NIGERIA‡ YORUBA‡ 1968-74

POETRY-WIGLO
  JOHNSON, JOHN W. ‡ SOMALIA‡ SOMALI‡ 1966-69

POLITICAL
  BARNES, SANDRA THEIS‡ NIGERIA‡ YORUBA‡ 1972

  GEOFFRION, CHARLES A.‡ SIERRA LEONE‡ TEMNE,
  MANDINGO‡ 1966-67

  GERHART, GAIL M.‡ SOUTH AFRICA‡ ‡ 1964

  LEVINE, WILLIAM J.‡ SOMALIA‡ SOMALI‡ 1962

  MERRIAM, ALAN P.+ MERRIAM, BARBARA W.‡ ZAIRE‡
  BAHIMA, BAKOGA, BAKONGO, BAMBUTI, BANGALA, BASHI,
  BATWA, EKONDA‡ 1951-52

  MERRIAM, ALAN P.‡ ZAIRE‡ BASONGYE‡ 1973

  RHODES, WILLARD‡ ZAMBIA‡ SHONA‡ 1958-59

  SULZMANN, ERIKA‡ CONGO, PEOPLE'S REPUBLIC OF THE‡
  ATYO‡ 1962

  SULZMANN, ERIKA‡ ZAIRE‡ BABOMA, BASENGELE, BOLIA,
  EKONDA, NTOMBA‡ 1953-72

  VANVELSEN, J.‡ MALAWI‡ TONGA‡ 1960

  WALLMAN, SANDRA‡ LESOTHO‡ BASUTO‡ 1963

POLITICAL-EMERGENCY
  ROSS, MARC HOWARD‡ KENYA‡ KIKUYU‡ 1967

POLITICAL-INTERVIEW
  MORGENTHAU, HENRY+ MONDOLANE, EDUARDO‡ MOZAMBIQUE‡
  ‡ 1965

POLITICAL-ORAL-DATA
  MORGENTHAU, HENRY‡ SOUTH AFRICA‡ ‡ CA1961

POLITICS-DISCUSSION
  MORGENTHAU, HENRY‡ KENYA‡ ‡ 1961

POLITICS-INTERVIEW
  MORGENTHAU, HENRY‡ TANZANIA‡ ‡ 1965

POLITICS—SPEECH
  BRUTUS, DENNIS≠ SNYDER, EMILE≠ SOUTH AFRICA-U.S.≠
  ≠ 1966

  OFONAGURO, W. IBEKWE≠ IRWIN, GRAHAM≠ NIGERIA-U.S.≠
  ≠ 1967

POLITICS—1930—1950
  VAILLANT, JANET G.≠ SENEGAL≠ SERER≠ 1973

POSSESSION
  BOURGEOT, A.≠ ALGERIA≠ TUAREG≠ 1970

  CAMP, CHARLES M.≠ TRACEY, HUGH≠ ZAMBIA≠ BEMBA,
  LALA, LOZI, TONGA, ZINZA≠ 1947—48

  CARLISLE, ROXANE C.≠ SUDAN≠ ANUAK, DINKA, GAALIIN,
  NUER, SHILLUK≠ 1963

  GARINE, I. DE≠ CHAD≠ KERA, MUSEY≠ 1962-63≠ 1965

  KOECHLIN, B.≠ MALAGASY REPUBLIC≠ MAHAFALY,
  MASIKORO, VEZO≠ 1967—69

  VANVELSEN, J.≠ UGANDA≠ KUMAM≠ 1948—60

  WARREN, DENNIS M.≠ GHANA≠ BONO≠ 1969—71

  YOUSSEF, AIT≠ MOROCCO≠ ≠ 1966

POT—CLAY
  HANLEY, MARY ANN CSJ≠ NIGERIA≠ ANGAS, BACHAMA,
  CHAMBA, EFIK, GWANDARA, HAUSA, IBIBIO, IBO, JABA,
  KERI-KERI, YORUBA≠ 1973

POTTER—INTERVIEW
  BUCHANAN, CAROLE≠ UGANDA≠ BANYORO, BATORO≠
  1968—69

PRAISE
  ABDULKADIR, DATTI≠ NIGERIA≠ HAUSA-FULANI≠ 1973

  ADAMS, CHARLES R.≠ LESOTHO≠ BASOTHO≠ 1969—70

  AMES, DAVID W.≠ GAMBIA, THE≠ WOLOF≠ 1951

  AMES, DAVID W.≠ SENEGAL≠ WOLOF≠ 1950—51

  ARMSTRONG, ROBERT G.≠ UNDOGWU, PATRICK≠ NIGERIA≠

PRAISE
  IDOMA‡ 1961

  BEN-AMOS, DAN‡ NIGERIA‡ EDO‡ 1966

  BESMER, FREMONT E.‡ NIGERIA‡ HAUSA‡ 1968-70

  BIRD, CHARLES S.‡ MALI‡ BAMBARA‡ 1967-68

  CAMP, CHARLES M.+ TRACEY, HUGH‡ ZAMBIA‡ BEMBA,
  LALA, LOZI, TONGA, ZINZA‡ 1947-48

  CENTRE FOR THE STUDY OF NIGERIAN LANGUAGES‡
  NIGERIA‡ HAUSA‡

  CHRISTIAN, VALERIE‡ UPPER VOLTA‡ BISSA, BOBO,
  BWABA, DAGARA, DYULA, FULANI, FULBE, GOUIN,
  GOURMANTCHE, HAUSA, KASSENA, KWO, LOBI, MARKA,
  MOSSI, NONDOM, POUGOULIS, SAMO-DU-SUD, YARDSE‡
  1973-74

  CHRISTIAN, VALERIE+ ROSELLINI, JAMES N.‡ UPPER
  VOLTA‡ FULBE, KASSENA, MARKA, MOSSI‡ 1973

  CIPARISSE, GERARD JEAN‡ ZAIRE‡ BAKONGO, BASUKU,
  BAYAKA‡ 1970-71

  COHEN, DAVID WILLIAM‡ UGANDA‡ BASOGA‡ 1971-72

  COHEN, RONALD‡ NIGERIA‡ KANURI‡ 1956

  COLLEGE OF MUSIC, UNIVERSITY OF NIGERIA‡ NIGERIA‡
  BINI, BOKI, DAKARAWA, EFIK-IBIBIO, EKOI, FULANI,
  HAUSA, IBO, IDOMA, IJAW, JABA, MADA, YALA, YORUBA,
  ZABEBMAWA‡

  COPE, TREVOR ANTHONY‡ SOUTH AFRICA‡ ZULU‡ 1965-72

  CRAVEN, ANNA‡ NIGERIA‡ AFO, GEDE‡ 1969-70

  CURTIN, PHILIP D.‡ SENEGAL‡ ARAB, DIAKHANKE,
  MALINKE, PULAR‡ 1966

  DAVIDSON, MARJORY‡ ZAMBIA‡ NGONI‡ 1967-71

  DOBRIN, ARTHUR‡ KENYA‡ GUSII‡ 1966

  GANSEMANS, JOS‡ ZAIRE‡ LUBA‡ 1970

PRAISE

GIBSON, GORDON D.‡ ANGOLA‡ CHAVIKWA, HAKAWONA, HIMBA, KEPE, KUVALE, VATWA, ZIMBA‡ 1971-73

GIBSON, GORDON D.‡ NAMIBIA‡ HERERO, HIMBA, KUVALE‡ 1960-61

GLAZE, ANITA‡ IVORY COAST‡ SENUFO‡ 1969-70

GRAESSER, MARK W.‡ GHANA‡ ASANTE, FRAFRA, HAUSA, KANJAGA, KONKOMBA‡ 1968-69

HANLEY, MARY ANN CSJ‡ NIGERIA‡ ANGAS, BACHAMA, CHAMBA, EFIK, GWANDARA, HAUSA, IBIBIO, IBO, JABA, KERI-KERI, YORUBA‡ 1973

HIMMELHEBER, HANS G.‡ MALI‡ BAMBARA‡ 1953

HURREIZ, SAYED H.‡ SUDAN‡ GAALIIN‡ 1970-71

JUILLERAT, B.‡ CAMEROON‡ KIRDI‡ 1966+ 1967-68

LESLAU, WOLF‡ ETHIOPIA‡ AMHARA, GURAGE, HARARI, SHOA-GALLA, SOMALI, TIGRINYA‡ 1947

LEWIS, HERBERT S.‡ ETHIOPIA‡ GALLA‡ 1965-66

MAPOMA, ISAIAH MWESA‡ ZAMBIA‡ BEMBA‡ 1968-70+ 1973

MERRIAM, ALAN P.+ MERRIAM, BARBARA W.‡ BURUNDI‡ ABATUTSI, BARUNDI, BATWA‡ 1951-52

MERRIAM, ALAN P.+ MERRIAM, BARBARA W.‡ RWANDA‡ ABAGOGWE, ABAGOYI, ABAHORORO, ABANYAMBO, ABATUTSI, ABAYOVU, BAHIMA, BAHUTU, BAKIGA, BATWA‡ 1951-52

ORENT, AMNON‡ ETHIOPIA‡ KAFA‡ 1966-67

PEVAR, MARC DAVID‡ GAMBIA, THE‡ MANDINKA‡ 1972

QUERSIN, BENOIT J.+ QUERSIN, CHRISTINE M.‡ ZAIRE‡ BATWA, BOLIA, EKONDA‡ 1971

RANUNG, BJORN L.C.‡ NIGERIA‡ IGEDE‡ 1971-72

REID, MARLENE B.‡ TANZANIA‡ BASUKUMA‡ 1966+ 1969

RITZENTHALER, ROBERT + RITZENTHALER, PAT‡

PRAISE
  CAMEROON‡ BAFUT‡ 1959

  SAPIR, J. DAVID‡ SENEGAL‡ DIOLA-FOGNY, DIOLA-KASA‡
  1960-65

  STRUMPF, MITCHEL‡ GHANA‡ DAGARTI, EWE, KONKOMBA‡
  1969-72

  SULZMANN, ERIKA‡ CONGO, PEOPLE'S REPUBLIC OF THE‡
  ATYO‡ 1962

  VAN OVEN, JACOBA‡ SIERRA LEONE‡ FULA, GALLINAS,
  GOLA, LIMBA, LOKO, MANDINGO, MENDE, SHERBRO, SUSU,
  TEMNE, VAI, YALUNKA‡ 1964-67

  WARREN, DENNIS M.‡ GHANA‡ BONO‡ 1969-71

  WELCH, DAVID B.‡ NIGERIA‡ YORUBA‡ 1970-71

  WOLFF, HANS‡ NIGERIA‡ EFIK, HAUSA, IBIBIO, KAJE,
  SOBO, PABIR, YORUBA‡ 1953-54

PRAISE-ANCESTOR
  RANUNG, BJORN L.C.‡ NIGERIA‡ IGEDE‡ 1971-72

PRAISE-CATTLE
  CARLISLE, ROXANE C.‡ SUDAN‡ ANUAK, DINKA, GAALIIN,
  NUER, SHILLUK‡ 1963

PRAISE-CULT
  BUCHANAN, CAROLE‡ UGANDA‡ BANYORO, BATORO‡
  1968-69

PRAISE-DIVINITY
  BEN-AMOS, DAN‡ NIGERIA‡ EDO‡ 1966

PRAISE-DIVINITY-ESHU
  ABIMBOLA, WANDE‡ NIGERIA‡ YORUBA‡ 1971

PRAISE-DIVINITY-IJALA
  ABIMBOLA, WANDE‡ NIGERIA‡ YORUBA‡ 1971

  BALOGUN, ADISA‡ NIGERIA‡ YORUBA‡ 1964+ 1970

PRAISE-DIVINITY-SHANGO
  ISOLA, AKINWUMI‡ NIGERIA‡ YORUBA‡ 1968-74

PRAISE-GERES
  BUNGER, ROBERT LOUIS‡ KENYA‡ OROMA, POKOMO‡
  1969-70

PRAISE-HUSBAND
  DENG, FRANCIS‡ SUDAN‡ DINKA‡ 1971

PRAISE-IJALA
  DEPARTMENT OF LINGUISTICS AND NIGERIAN LANGUAGES,
  UNIVERSITY OF IBADAN‡ NIGERIA‡ EDO, IJO, ISOKO,
  ITSEKIRI, OWAN, YORUBA‡ 1967-73

PRAISE-IZIBONGO
  SCHEUB, HAROLD‡ SOUTH AFRICA‡ XHOSA, ZULU‡
  1967-68

PRAISE-MERCHANT
  BAIER, STEPHEN B.‡ NIGER‡ HAUSA, KANURI, TUAREG‡
  1972

PRAISE-NAME
  HOOVER, JAMES JEFFREY‡ ZAIRE‡ LUNDA‡ 1973-75

  MERRIAM, ALAN P.+ MERRIAM, BARBARA W.‡ ZAIRE‡
  BASONGYE‡ 1959-60

  WOLFF, HANS‡ NIGERIA-U.S.‡ YORUBA‡ 1960-64

PRAISE-NESE
  BUNGER, ROBERT LOUIS‡ KENYA‡ OROMA, POKOMO‡
  1969-70

PRAISE-ORIKI
  BALOGUN, ADISA‡ NIGERIA‡ YORUBA‡ 1967

  WELCH, DAVID B.‡ NIGERIA‡ YORUBA‡ 1970-71

PRAISE-OXEN
  DENG, FRANCIS‡ SUDAN‡ DINKA‡ 1971

PRAISE-POETRY
  AFRICANA MUSEUM‡ SOUTH AFRICA‡ HOTTENTOT, SOTHO,
  SWAZI, TSWANA, ZULU‡

  AFRIKA-STUDIECENTRUM‡ TOGO‡ TYOKOSSI‡

  ALIGWEKWE, EVALYN R.‡ NIGERIA‡ IBO‡ 1960

  AMES, DAVID W.‡ NIGERIA‡ FULBE, HAUSA, YORUBA‡

PRAISE-POETRY
 1963-64

 AWE, BOLANLE ALAKE‡ NIGERIA‡ YORUBA‡ 1972-74

 BUNGER, ROBERT LOUIS‡ KENYA‡ OROMA, POKOMO‡
 1969-70

 DE HEN, FERDINAND JOSEPH‡ MOROCCO‡ AIT-ATTA,
 AIT-BU-SUEMMEZ, IHANSALEN‡ 1960-61

 DEPARTMENT OF AFRICAN LANGUAGES, UNIVERSITY OF
 RHODESIA‡ RHODESIA‡ NDEBELE, SHONA‡

 DES FORGES, ALISON LIEBHAFSKY‡ RWANDA‡ BATUTSI‡
 1968

 ELWA STUDIO, NIGERIA‡ NIGERIA‡ IBO, NUPE, YORUBA‡

 ETHNOMUSICOLOGY CENTRE JAAP KUNST‡ MALAWI‡ LOMWE,
 MANGANJA‡ 1971

 FOSS, PERKINS‡ NIGERIA‡ URHOBO‡ 1971-72

 INSTITUTE OF AFRICAN STUDIES, UNIVERSITY OF IFE‡
 NIGERIA‡ IBO, TIV, YORUBA‡

 IRVINE, JUDITH TEMKIN‡ SENEGAL‡ WOLOF‡ 1970-71

 KABEMBA, MUFUTA KABANCANYI‡ ZAIRE‡ KUBA, LUBA‡
 1965+ 1972

 MARAIRE, DUMISANI ABRAHAM‡ RHODESIA‡ SHONA‡ 1971+
 1974

 MCLEOD, NORMA‡ MALAGASY REPUBLIC‡ ‡ 1962-63

 MISSION SOCIOLOGIQUE DU HAUTE-OUBANGUI‡ CENTRAL
 AFRICAN REPUBLIC‡ NZAKARA, ZANDE‡

 OFRI, DORITH‡ LIBERIA‡ VAI‡ 1965-72

 OGBU, JOHN U.‡ NIGERIA‡ IBO‡ 1972

 PRUITT, WILLIAM F., JR.‡ ZAIRE‡ KETE, PYGMIES,
 SALAMPASU‡ 1966-67

 TRADITIONAL MUSIC DOCUMENTATION PROJECT‡
 MOZAMBIQUE‡ CHOPI‡

PRAISE-POETRY
   TRADITIONAL MUSIC DOCUMENTATION PROJECT‡ NIGERIA‡
   IBIBIO, IBO, KALABARI, TIV, YORUBA‡

   TRADITIONAL MUSIC DOCUMENTATION PROJECT‡ UPPER
   VOLTA‡ ‡

   WOLLNER, CHAD A.‡ ETHIOPIA‡ ‡ 1972

   WOLLNER, CHAD A.‡ KENYA‡ ‡ 1972

PRAISE-POETRY-ESA-EGUN
   DEPARTMENT OF LINGUISTICS AND NIGERIAN LANGUAGES,
   UNIVERSITY OF IBADAN‡ NIGERIA‡ EDO, IJO, ISOKO,
   ITSEKIRI, OWAN, YORUBA‡ 1967-73

PRAISE-POETRY-ESA-ODE
   DEPARTMENT OF LINGUISTICS AND NIGERIAN LANGUAGES,
   UNIVERSITY OF IBADAN‡ NIGERIA‡ EDO, IJO, ISOKO,
   ITSEKIRI, OWAN, YORUBA‡ 1967-73

PRAISE-POETRY-IGEDE-IBI
   DEPARTMENT OF LINGUISTICS AND NIGERIAN LANGUAGES,
   UNIVERSITY OF IBADAN‡ NIGERIA‡ EDO, IJO, ISOKO,
   ITSEKIRI, OWAN, YORUBA‡ 1967-73

PRAISE-POETRY-IGEDE-IRE
   DEPARTMENT OF LINGUISTICS AND NIGERIAN LANGUAGES,
   UNIVERSITY OF IBADAN‡ NIGERIA‡ EDO, IJO, ISOKO,
   ITSEKIRI, OWAN, YORUBA‡ 1967-73

PRAISE-POETRY-OFO
   DEPARTMENT OF LINGUISTICS AND NIGERIAN LANGUAGES,
   UNIVERSITY OF IBADAN‡ NIGERIA‡ EDO, IJO, ISOKO,
   ITSEKIRI, OWAN, YORUBA‡ 1967-73

PRAISE-RULER
   AMES, DAVID W.‡ NIGERIA‡ HAUSA‡ 1963

   AMES, DAVID W.‡ NIGERIA‡ FULBE, HAUSA, YORUBA‡
   1963-64

   AMES, DAVID W.‡ NIGERIA‡ IGBO‡ 1963-64

   BESMER, FREMONT E.‡ NIGERIA‡ HAUSA‡ 1968-70

   BIRD, CHARLES S.‡ MALI‡ BAMBARA‡ 1967-68

   CARLISLE, ROXANE C.‡ SUDAN‡ ANUAK, DINKA, GAALIIN,

PRAISE-RULER
  NUER, SHILLUK‡ 1963

  CURTIN, PHILIP D.‡ SENEGAL‡ ARAB, DIAKHANKE,
  MALINKE, PULAR‡ 1966

  FIKRY, MONA‡ GHANA‡ WALA‡ 1966-67

  GANSEMANS, JOS‡ ZAIRE‡ LUBA‡ 1970

  HERSKOVITS, MELVILLE J.+ HERSKOVITS, FRANCES S.‡
  DAHOMEY‡ FON‡ 1931

  HERSKOVITS, MELVILLE J.+ HERSKOVITS, FRANCES S.‡
  GHANA‡ ASANTE‡ 1931

  OWEN, WILFRED, JR.‡ GHANA‡ ASANTE, BRONG, EWE,
  FANTI, GA, TWI‡ 1970-71

  QUERSIN, BENOIT J.+ QUERSIN, CHRISTINE M.‡
  CAMEROON‡ BAFIA, BALLOM, BAMILEKE, BAMUM, BULU
  ETON, PEUL, PYGMIES, SANAGA, TIKAR, VUTE‡ 1967

  QUERSIN, BENOIT J.+ QUERSIN, CHRISTINE M.‡
  NIGERIA‡ ABAKPA-RIGA, AFO, ALAGO, ANGAS, ANKWAI,
  BIROM, BUROM, CHAMBA, EGGON, FULANI, HAUSA, ICHEN,
  IDOMA, JARAWA, JUKUN, KALABARI, KANTANA, KUTEP,
  KWALLA, NUPE, PYEM, RINDRE, TIV, YERGAM, YORUBA‡
  1972-73

  QUERSIN, BENOIT J.‡ ZAIRE‡ BUSHOONG, COOFA, IBAAM,
  NGEENDE, PYAANG, SHOOWA‡ 1970

  VAN OVEN, JACOBA‡ SIERRA LEONE‡ FULA, GALLINAS,
  GOLA, LIMBA, LOKO, MANDINGO, MENDE, SHERBRO, SUSU,
  TEMNE, VAI, YALUNKA‡ 1964-67

PRAISE-SHANGO
  WELCH, DAVID B.‡ NIGERIA‡ YORUBA‡ 1970-71

PRAYER
  AFRIKA-STUDIECENTRUM‡ TOGO‡ TYOKOSSI‡

  FERNANDEZ, JAMES W.‡ GABON‡ FANG‡ 1960

  FIKRY, MONA‡ GHANA‡ WALA‡ 1966-67

  LEWIS, HERBERT S.‡ ETHIOPIA‡ GALLA‡ 1965-66

PRAYER
  NEWBURY, DOROTHY J.‡ LIBERIA‡ BASSA, LOMA‡
  1969-70+ 1972

  PRESTON, JEROME, JR.‡ KENYA‡ LUO‡ 1966

PRAYER-CALL
  BOWLES, PAUL+ WANKLYN, CHRISTOPHER‡ MOROCCO‡ ‡
  CA1959-62

PRAYER-CHANT-ISLAMIC
  ARCHIVES OF ETHNIC MUSIC AND DANCE‡ UPPER VOLTA‡
  BOBO, BWABA, DYULA, FULANI, FULBE, GOUIN,
  GOURMANTCHE, LOBI, MINIANKA, MOSSI, SENUFO,
  YARDSE‡

PRAYER-CHRISTIAN
  VAN ROUVEROY VAN NIEUWAAL, EMILE A.B.‡ TOGO‡
  KOSSI‡ 1969-73

PRAYER-ISLAMIC
  AFRIKA-STUDIECENTRUM‡ TOGO‡ TYOKOSSI‡

  VAN ROUVEROY VAN NIEUWAAL, EMILE A.B.‡ TOGO‡
  KOSSI‡ 1969-73

PRAYER-LIBATION
  ADUAMAH, E.Y.‡ GHANA-TOGO‡ EWE‡ 1968-71

PRAYER-SABBATH
  ODED, ARYE‡ UGANDA‡ BAGANDA, BAYUDAYA‡ 1967-68

PREACHING
  HANLEY, MARY ANN CSJ‡ GHANA‡ BUILSA, DAGARI, EWE,
  FANTI, FRAFRA, GA, KASSENA, NANKANI, TWI‡ 1972

PRIEST-FALASHA-INTERVIEW
  SHELEMAY, KAY KAUFMAN‡ ETHIOPIA‡ FALASHA-JEW‡
  1973

PROCESSION
  BOWLES, PAUL+ WANKLYN, CHRISTOPHER‡ MOROCCO‡ ‡
  CA1959-62

PROSE
  BAKER, CATHRYN ANITA‡ TUNISIA‡ ‡ 1972-73

  D'HERTEFELT, MARUL‡ RWANDA‡ ‡ 1953-73

PROVERB
  ANDRADE, MANUEL+ HERZOG, GEORGE‡ ‡ JABO‡ 1931

  BEN-AMOS, DAN‡ NIGERIA‡ EDO‡ 1966

  BEN-AMOS, DAN‡ NIGERIA‡ HAUSA‡ 1966

  COLLEGE OF MUSIC, UNIVERSITY OF NIGERIA‡ NIGERIA‡
  BINI, BOKI, DAKARAWA, EFIK-IBIBIO, EKOI, FULANI,
  HAUSA, IBO, IDOMA, IJAW, JABA, MADA, YALA, YORUBA,
  ZABEBMAWA‡

  HERSKOVITS, MELVILLE J.+ HERSKOVITS, FRANCES S.‡
  NIGERIA‡ YORUBA‡ 1931

  HERZOG, GEORGE‡ LIBERIA‡ GREBO, JABO, KRU‡ 1930

  LUCKAU, STEPHEN R.‡ LIBERIA‡ GREBO, JABO‡ 1971

  NOSS, PHILIP A.‡ CAMEROON‡ GBAYA‡ 1966-67

  OERTLI, PEO‡ DAHOMEY‡ AIZO‡ 1973-74

  PLOTNICOV, LEONARD‡ NIGERIA‡ BIRCM, EFIK, HAUSA,
  IBIBIO, IBO, IJAW, KAGORO, KATAM, TIV‡ 1961-62

  QUERSIN, BENOIT J.+ QUERSIN, CHRISTINE M.‡ ZAIRE‡
  BATWA, BOLIA, EKONDA‡ 1971

  RANSBOTYN DE DECKER, DANIEL‡ TOGO‡ BOGO, EWE‡
  1972-74

  WOLFF, HANS‡ NIGERIA‡ AGBADU, URHOBO‡ 1953

  WOLFF, HANS‡ NIGERIA‡ EDO-BINI‡ 1953

  WOLFF, HANS‡ NIGERIA‡ JUKUN‡ 1953

  WOLFF, HANS‡ NIGERIA-U.S.‡ YORUBA‡ 1960-64

PROVERB-BICA
  WOLFF, HANS‡ NIGERIA‡ NUPE‡ 1953

PROVERB-DRUM
  SMEND, W.A.‡ TOGO‡ HAUSA‡ 1905

  SPEED, FRANCIS E.+ THIEME, DARIUS L.‡ NIGERIA‡
  YORUBA‡ 1966

RATTLE
  HANLEY, MARY ANN CSJ‡ GHANA‡ BUILSA, DAGARI, EWE,
  FANTI, FRAFRA, GA, KASSENA, NANKANI, TWI‡ 1972

  MERRIAM, ALAN P.+ MERRIAM, BARBARA W.‡ ZAIRE‡
  BAHIMA, BAKOGA, BAKONGO, BAMBUTI, BANGALA, BASHI,
  BATWA, EKONDA‡ 1951-52

  NATIONAL MUSEUM OF TANZANIA‡ TANZANIA‡ MAKONDE,
  MALILA, MWERA, YAO‡

  NORSK RIKSKRINGKASTING‡ GHANA‡ ‡ 1966

  PLOTNICOV, LEONARD‡ NIGERIA‡ BIRCM, EFIK, HAUSA,
  IBIBIO, IBO, IJAW, KAGORO, KATAM, TIV‡ 1961-62

  QUERSIN, BENOIT J.+ QUERSIN, CHRISTINE M.‡
  CAMEROON‡ BAFIA, BALLOM, BAMILEKE, BAMUM, BULU
  ETON, PEUL, PYGMIES, SANAGA, TIKAR, VUTE‡ 1967

  QUERSIN, BENOIT J.+ QUERSIN, CHRISTINE M.‡ ZAIRE‡
  BATWA, BOLIA, EKONDA‡ 1971

  SEYFRIED, CAPTAIN‡ TANZANIA‡ ‡ 1906-09

  SMEND, W.A.‡ TOGO‡ HAUSA‡ 1905

  STARR, FREDERICK A.‡ ZAIRE‡ BAKUBA, BALUBA‡ 1906

  WELCH, DAVID B.‡ NIGERIA‡ YORUBA‡ 1970-71

  WEMAN, HENRY PAUL‡ RHODESIA‡ KARANGA, LEMBA,
  VENDA, ZULU‡ 1957

  WILLETT, FRANK‡ NIGERIA‡ YORUBA‡ 1972

RATTLE-ANKLE
  AMES, DAVID W.‡ NIGERIA‡ IGBO‡ 1963-64

RATTLE-BASKET
  AMES, DAVID W.‡ NIGERIA‡ IGBO‡ 1963-64

  MERRIAM, ALAN P.+ MERRIAM, BARBARA W.‡ ZAIRE‡
  BASONGYE‡ 1959-60

  MERRIAM, ALAN P.‡ ZAIRE‡ BASONGYE‡ 1973

  NETTL, BRUNO +RABEN, JOSEPH‡ NIGERIA-U.S.‡ IBO‡
  1950-51

RATTLE-CONTAINER
  MERRIAM, ALAN P.‡ ZAIRE‡ BASONGYE‡ 1973

  STONE, RUTH M.+ STONE, VERLON L.‡ LIBERIA‡ KPELLE‡
  1970

  VAN OVEN, JACOBA‡ SIERRA LEONE‡ FULA, GALLINAS,
  GOLA, LIMBA, LOKO, MANDINGO, MENDE, SHERBRO, SUSU,
  TEMNE, VAI, YALUNKA‡ 1964-67

RATTLE-GOURD
  ADUAMAH, E.Y.‡ GHANA-TOGO‡ EWE‡ 1968-71

  AMES, DAVID W.‡ NIGERIA‡ IGBO‡ 1963-64

  BUCHANAN, CAROLE‡ UGANDA‡ BANYORO, BATORO‡
  1968-69

  GANSEMANS, JOS‡ ZAIRE‡ LUBA‡ 1970

  GLAZE, ANITA‡ IVORY COAST‡ SENUFO‡ 1969-70

  HANLEY, MARY ANN CSJ‡ GHANA‡ AKAN, EWE, TWI‡ 1973

  HANLEY, MARY ANN CSJ‡ NIGERIA‡ ANGAS, BACHAMA,
  CHAMBA, EFIK, GWANDARA, HAUSA, IBIBIO, IBO, JABA,
  KERI-KERI, YORUBA‡ 1973

  JONES, ARTHUR M.‡ GHANA-ENGLAND‡ EWE‡ 1956

  NEWBURY, DOROTHY J.‡ LIBERIA‡ BASSA, LOMA‡
  1969-70+ 1972

  OKIE, PACKARD L.‡ LIBERIA‡ BASSA, BELE, GIO,
  KPELLE, KRU, MANDINGO, VAI‡ 1947-54

  QUERSIN, BENOIT J.+ QUERSIN, CHRISTINE M.‡
  NIGERIA‡ ABAKPA-RIGA, AFO, ALAGO, ANGAS, ANKWAI,
  BIROM, BUROM, CHAMBA, EGGON, FULANI, HAUSA, ICHEN,
  IDOMA, JARAWA, JUKUN, KALABARI, KANTANA, KUTEP,
  KWALLA, NUPE, PYEM, RINDRE, TIV, YERGAM, YORUBA‡
  1972-73

  RHODES, WILLARD‡ NIGERIA‡ FULANI, HAUSA, TIV,
  TUAREG, YORUBA‡ 1973-74

  RUBIN, ARNOLD G.‡ NIGERIA‡ CHAMBA, HAUSA, IBO,
  JUKUN, KUTEP, TIKARI, TIV‡ 1964-65

RATTLE-GOURD
  STONE, RUTH M.+ STONE, VERLON L.‡ LIBERIA‡ KPELLE‡
  1970

  VAN OVEN, JACOBA‡ SIERRA LEONE‡ FULA, GALLINAS,
  GOLA, LIMBA, LOKO, MANDINGO, MENDE, SHERBRO, SUSU,
  TEMNE, VAI, YALUNKA‡ 1964-67

RATTLE-IRON
  ADUAMAH, E.Y.‡ GHANA-TOGO‡ EWE‡ 1968-71

READING-ARABIC-CLASSICAL
  HALE, KEN‡ EGYPT‡ ARAB‡

RECREATION
  WARNIER, JEAN-PIERRE‡ CAMEROON‡ MANKON‡ 1972-74

RELIGIOUS
  ABUZAHRA, NADIA‡ TUNISIA‡ SAHEL‡ 1966

  AMES, DAVID W.‡ NIGERIA‡ IGBO‡ 1963-64

  ANDREWS, LORETTA K.‡ ZAMBIA‡ ‡ 1971

  ARCHIVES OF ETHNIC MUSIC AND DANCE‡ ANGOLA‡ ‡

  BELLMAN, BERYL LARRY‡ LIBERIA‡ KPELLE, LOMA‡ 1969

  DENG, FRANCIS‡ SUDAN‡ DINKA‡ 1971

  DEPARTMENT OF ANTHROPOLOGY, UNIVERSITY OF BRITISH
  COLUMBIA‡ TUNISIA‡ ‡

  DUNGER, GEORGE A.‡ CAMEROON‡ BEKOM, DUALA, KAKA,
  NSUNGLI‡

  EDWARDS, BETTY‡ SIERRA LEONE‡ ‡ 1969

  EL-SHAMY, HASAN M.‡ EGYPT‡ ARAB, DINKA, NUBIAN‡
  1968-71

  ELWA RADIO STATION, LIBERIA‡ LIBERIA‡ ‡
  CA1960-1975

  HERSKOVITS, MELVILLE J.+ HERSKOVITS, FRANCES S.‡
  NIGERIA‡ YORUBA‡ 1931

  JOHNSON, GERALD T.‡ SIERRA LEONE‡ MENDE, TEMNE‡
  1967-68

RELIGIOUS
  KATZ, RICHARD‡ BOTSWANA‡ KUNG-BUSHMEN‡ 1968

  KULP, PHILIP M.‡ NIGERIA‡ BURA‡ 1973

  LESLAU, WOLF‡ ETHIOPIA‡ FALASHA‡ CA1947

  LEWIS, HERBERT S.‡ ETHIOPIA‡ GALLA‡ 1965-66

  MACGAFFEY, WYATT‡ ZAIRE‡ KONGO‡ 1970

  MISJONSSKOLEN‡ CAMEROON‡ ‡

  MISJONSSKOLEN‡ MALAGASY REPUBLIC‡ ‡

  MISJONSSKOLEN‡ SOUTH AFRICA‡ ZULU‡

  MUSEE ROYAL DE L'AFRIQUE CENTRALE‡ ‡ BIROM, BOLIA,
  HOLOHOLO, KANEMBU, KONDA, KONGO, LEGA, MBALA,
  MBUUN, MONGO, NANDE, PENDE, RUNDI, RWANDA, SANGA,
  SHI, SUKU, TETELA, YEKE‡

  NEWBURY, DAVID S.‡ ZAIRE‡ BAHAVU‡ 1972-74

  OERTLI, PEO‡ DAHOMEY‡ AIZO‡ 1973-74

  OTTENHEIMER, HARRIET‡ OTTENHEIMER, MARTIN‡ COMORO
  ISLANDS‡ ‡ 1967-68

  PEEK, PHILIP M.‡ NIGERIA‡ IGBO-WESTERN, ISOKO‡
  1970-71

  RADIO CLUBE DE MOCAMBIQUE‡ MOZAMBIQUE‡ CHANGANE,
  CHENGUE, CHOPI, LUBA, MAKONDE, MAKUA, RONGA,
  SWAZI, VADANDA, VANDAU, VATSUA‡

  SULZMANN, ERIKA‡ ZAIRE‡ BABOMA, BASENGELE, BOLIA,
  EKONDA, NTOMBA‡ 1953-72

  UPADHYAYA, HARI S.‡ ORI, R.‡ MAURITIUS‡
  UTTAR-PRADESH‡ 1961

RELIGIOUS-AFRICAN-JEWISH
  ODED, ARYE‡ UGANDA‡ BAGANDA, BAYUDAYA‡ 1967-68

RELIGIOUS-CATHOLIC
  NJAKA, MAZI E.N.‡ NIGERIA‡ ‡ 1972

RELIGIOUS-CHRISTIAN
  ALBERTS, ARTHUR S.‡ AFRICA-WEST‡ BAULE, MANO,
  MOSSI‡ 1949

  AMES, DAVID W.‡ NIGERIA‡ IGBO‡ 1963-64

  GELZER, DAVID G.‡ CAMEROON‡ ‡

  HAMBLY, WILFRED D.‡ ANGOLA‡ OVIMBUNDU‡ 1929-30

  HANLEY, MARY ANN CSJ‡ GHANA‡ BUILSA, DAGARI, EWE,
  FANTI, FRAFRA, GA, KASSENA, NANKANI, TWI‡ 1972

  HANLEY, MARY ANN CSJ‡ GHANA‡ AKAN, EWE, TWI‡ 1973

  HANLEY, MARY ANN CSJ‡ NIGERIA‡ ANGAS, BACHAMA,
  CHAMBA, EFIK, GWANDARA, HAUSA, IBIBIO, IBO, JABA,
  KERI-KERI, YORUBA‡ 1973

  HANLEY, MARY ANN CSJ‡ UPPER VOLTA‡ ‡ 1972

  MASSING, ANDREAS‡ LIBERIA‡ KRU‡ 1971-72

  MERRIAM, ALAN P.‡ ZAIRE‡ BASONGYE‡ 1973

  MISHLER, ROBERT E.‡ NIGERIA‡ MARGI‡ 1971-72

  OKIE, PACKARD L.‡ LIBERIA‡ BASSA, KRU‡ 1947-54

  STUTTMAN, LEONARD M.‡ LIBERIA‡ GREBO, KRAHN‡ 1956

  WEMAN, PAUL HENRY‡ NIGERIA‡ YORUBA‡ 1957

  WEMAN, HENRY PAUL‡ RHODESIA‡ KARANGA, LEMBA,
  VENDA, ZULU‡ 1957

  WEMAN, PAUL HENRY‡ TANZANIA‡ HAYA, SUKUMA,
  SWAHILI‡ 1957

  WEMAN, PAUL HENRY‡ ZAIRE‡ LUBA‡ 1957

  WEMAN, PAUL HENRY‡ ZAMBIA‡ ‡ 1957

  WOLFF, HANS‡ NIGERIA‡ EFIK, HAUSA, IBIBIO, KAJE,
  SOBO, PABIR, YORUBA‡ 1953-54

RELIGIOUS-COPTIC
  DAVIS, GORDON‡ ETHIOPIA‡ COPT‡ 1968

RELIGIOUS-COPTIC
  MAGYAR TUDOMANYOS AKADEMIA NEPZENEKUTATO CSOPORT‡
  EGYPT‡ COPT, FELLAHIN, NUBIAN‡ 1966-67 + 1969

RELIGIOUS-CULT
  COLLEGE OF MUSIC, UNIVERSITY OF NIGERIA‡ NIGERIA‡
  BINI, BOKI, DAKARAWA, EFIK-IBIBIO, EKOI, FULANI,
  HAUSA, IBO, IDOMA, IJAW, JABA, MADA, YALA, YORUBA,
  ZABEBMAWA‡

RELIGIOUS-ISLAMIC
  CURTIN, PHILIP D.‡ SENEGAL‡ ARAB, DIAKHANKE,
  MALINKE, PULAR‡ 1966

  FIKRY, MONA‡ GHANA‡ WALA‡ 1966-67

  GEOFFRION, CHARLES A.‡ SIERRA LEONE‡ TEMNE,
  MANDINGO‡ 1966-67

  LAADE, WOLFGANG KARL‡ TUNISIA‡ ARAB, BERBER, JEW‡
  1960

  LESLAU, WOLF‡ ETHIOPIA‡ AMHARA, GURAGE, HARARI,
  SHOA-GALLA, SOMALI, TIGRINYA‡ 1947

  ODED, ARYE‡ UGANDA‡ BAGANDA, BAYUDAYA‡ 1967-68

  OKIE, PACKARD L.‡ LIBERIA‡ BASSA, BELE, GIO,
  KPELLE, KRU, MANDINGO, VAI‡ 1947-54

  VAN OVEN, JACOBA‡ SIERRA LEONE‡ FULA, GALLINAS,
  GOLA, LIMBA, LOKO, MANDINGO, MENDE, SHERBRO, SUSU,
  TEMNE, VAI, YALUNKA‡ 1964-67

  WOLFF, HANS‡ NIGERIA‡ EFIK, HAUSA, IBIBIO, KAJE,
  SOBO, PABIR, YORUBA‡ 1953-54

RELIGIOUS-JEWISH
  LAADE, WOLFGANG KARL‡ TUNISIA‡ ARAB, BERBER, JEW‡
  1960

RELIGIOUS-PRAISE
  ABIMBOLA, WANDE‡ NIGERIA‡ YORUBA‡ 1971

  HERSKOVITS, MELVILLE J.+ HERSKOVITS, FRANCES S.‡
  DAHOMEY‡ FON‡ 1931

  HERSKOVITS, MELVILLE J.+ HERSKOVITS, FRANCES S.‡
  GHANA‡ ASANTE‡ 1931

RHYME
  ABUZAHRA, NADIA‡ TUNISIA‡ SAHEL‡ 1966

RIDDLE
  AMES, DAVID W.‡ GAMBIA, THE‡ WOLOF‡ 1951

  ANDERSON, LOIS ANN‡ MOROCCO‡ BERBER‡ 1971

  BEN-AMOS, DAN‡ NIGERIA‡ EDO‡ 1966

  BEN-AMOS, DAN‡ NIGERIA‡ HAUSA‡ 1966

  BOAS, FRANZ‡ SIERRA LEONE‡ BOLUM‡ PRE-1935

  EL-SHAMY, HASAN M.‡ EGYPT‡ ARAB, DINKA, NUBIAN‡
  1968-71

  FIKRY, MONA‡ GHANA‡ WALA‡ 1966-67

  GAY, JUDITH S.‡ LIBERIA‡ KPELLE‡ 1971-73

  HARRIES, JEANETTE‡ MOROCCO‡ BERBER‡ 1964-65

  KUBIK, GERHARD‡ AFRICA-ANGOLA, CAMEROON, CENTRAL
  AFRICAN REPUBLIC, CONGO-PEOPLE'S REPUBLIC OF THE,
  EGYPT, GABON, KENYA, MALAWI, MOZAMBIQUE, NIGERIA,
  SUDAN, TANZANIA, TOGO, UGANDA, ZAIRE, ZAMBIA‡ ‡
  1959-73

  NOSS, PHILIP A.‡ CAMEROON‡ GBAYA‡ 1966-67

  TENRAA, ERIC WILLIAM FREDERICK‡ TANZANIA‡ BURUNGE,
  SANDAWE, SWAHILI‡ 1958-66

RIDICULE
  HERSKOVITS, MELVILLE J.+ HERSKOVITS, FRANCES S.‡
  DAHOMEY‡ FON‡ 1931

RITUAL
  AFRIKA-STUDIECENTRUM‡ TOGO‡ TYOKOSSI‡

  AKPABOT, SAMUEL EKPE‡ NIGERIA‡ BIROM, HAUSA,
  IBIBIO, IBO‡ 1964-73

  ARGYLE, WILLIAM JOHNSON‡ ZAMBIA‡ SOLI‡ 1957-59

  AROM, SIMHA‡ CENTRAL AFRICAN REPUBLIC‡
  AKA-PYGMIES, LINDA-BANDA, NGBAKA-MABO‡ 1964-67+
  1971-73

RITUAL
    STRASBOURG‡ MOROCCO‡ GNAWA‡

    INSTITUTE OF AFRICAN STUDIES, UNIVERSITY OF IFE‡
    NIGERIA‡ IBO, TIV, YORUBA‡

    IRVINE, JUDITH TEMKIN‡ SENEGAL‡ WOLOF‡ 1970-71

    KABEMBA, MUFUTA KABANDANYI‡ ZAIRE‡ KUBA, LUBA‡
    1965+ 1972

    KAEMMER, JOHN E.‡ RHODESIA‡ KOREKORE, SHONA,
    ZEZURU‡ 1972-73

    KATZ, RICHARD‡ BOTSWANA‡ KUNG-BUSHMEN‡ 1968

    KILSON, MARION D. DE B.‡ GHANA‡ GA‡ 1964-65+ 1968

    KOIZUMI, FUMIO‡ ETHIOPIA‡ AMHARA‡ 1971

    KOIZUMI, FUMIO‡ NIGERIA‡ YORUBA‡ 1971

    LARSON, THOMAS J.‡ BOTSWANA‡ HAMBUKUSU‡ 1972

    LEWIS, HERBERT S.‡ ETHIOPIA‡ GALLA‡ 1965-66

    LIMA, AUGUSTO GUILHERME MESQUITELA‡ ANGOLA‡
    BUSHMEN, CHOKWE, NGANGELA‡ 1963-70

    LOMBARD, JACQUES‡ MALAGASY REPUBLIC‡ SAKALAVA‡
    1969-74

    LORTAT-JACOB, BERNARD‡ ETHIOPIA‡ DORZE‡ 1974-75

    MAGYAR TUDOMANYOS AKADEMIA NEPZENEKUTATO CSOPORT‡
    EGYPT‡ COPT, FELLAHIN, NUBIAN‡ 1966-67 + 1969

    MAPOMA, ISAIAH MWESA‡ ZAMBIA‡ BEMBA‡ 1968-70+
    1973

    MARAIRE, DUMISANI ABRAHAM‡ RHODESIA‡ SHONA‡ 1971+
    1974

    MCLEOD, NORMA‡ MALAGASY REPUBLIC‡ ‡ 1962-63

    MISSION SOCIOLOGIQUE DU HAUTE-OUBANGUI‡ CENTRAL
    AFRICAN REPUBLIC‡ NZAKARA, ZANDE‡

    NATIONAL MUSEUM OF TANZANIA‡ TANZANIA‡ MAKONDE,

RITUAL
  MALILA, MWERA, YAO‡

  OERTLI, PEO‡ DAHOMEY‡ AIZO‡ 1973-74

  PAIRAULT, CLAUDE ALBERT‡ CHAD‡ GULA-IRO‡ 1959-64

  RADIO CLUBE DE MOCAMBIQUE‡ MOZAMBIQUE‡ CHANGANE,
  CHENGUE, CHOPI, LUBA, MAKONDE, MAKUA, RONGA,
  SWAZI, VACANDA, VANDAU, VATSUA‡

  RANSBOTYN DE DECKER, DANIEL‡ TOGO‡ BOGO, ÉWE‡
  1972-74

  REID, MARLENE B.‡ TANZANIA‡ BASUKUMA‡ 1966‡ 1969

  ROMERO, PATRICIA‡ GHANA‡ ASANTE‡ 1972

  SHEFFIELD, JAMES‡ DAHOMEY‡ YORUBA‡ 1971‡ 1973

  SHEFFIELD, JAMES‡ NIGERIA‡ YORUBA‡ 1971

  SIEGMANN, WILLIAM CHARLES‡ LIBERIA‡ BASSA, GBANDE‡
  1973-74

  SKINNER, ELLIOTT P.‡ UPPER VOLTA‡ MOSSI‡ 1955-65

  SUDAN NATIONAL MUSEUM‡ SUDAN‡ BONGO, JALUO,
  NUBIAN‡ 1959-64

  SULZMANN, ERIKA‡ CONGO, PEOPLE'S REPUBLIC OF THE‡
  ATYO‡ 1962

  TARDITS, CLAUDE‡ DAHOMEY‡ GUN‡

  TENRAA, ERIC WILLIAM FREDERICK‡ TANZANIA‡ BURUNGE,
  SANDAWE, SWAHILI‡ 1958-66

  THIEME, DARIUS L.‡ NIGERIA‡ YORUBA‡ 1964-66

  TRADITIONAL MUSIC DOCUMENTATION PROJECT‡
  MOZAMBIQUE‡ CHOPI‡

  TRADITIONAL MUSIC DOCUMENTATION PROJECT‡ NIGERIA‡
  IBIBIO, IBO, KALABARI, TIV, YORUBA‡

  TRADITIONAL MUSIC DOCUMENTATION PROJECT‡ UPPER
  VOLTA‡ ‡

RITUAL
  TURNER, VICTOR WITTER‡ UGANDA‡ BAGISU‡ 1966

  VAN THIEL, PAUL A.H.‡ UGANDA‡ BANTU, BANYANKOLE‡
  1964-65+ 1969+ 1970-72

  WOLLNER, CHAD A.‡ ETHIOPIA‡ ‡ 1972

  WOLLNER, CHAD A.‡ KENYA‡ ‡ 1972

RITUAL-BANA
  VIDAL, PIERRE ANTOINE‡ CENTRAL AFRICAN REPUBLIC‡
  GBAYA, KARA‡ 1961-74

RITUAL-COPTIC
  ABDELSAYED, FR. GABRIEL H.A.‡ EGYPT‡ COPT‡
  1965-69

RITUAL-EXORCISM
  CARLISLE, ROXANE C.‡ SUDAN‡ ANUAK, DINKA, GAALIIN,
  NUER, SHILLUK‡ 1963

RITUAL-HEALING-HYPNOSIS
  MALER, THOMAS A.‡ TANZANIA‡ DIGO, GIRYAMA,
  MAKONDE, TINDIGA‡ 1967-68

RITUAL-HUNTING
  GROHS, ELISABETH‡ TANZANIA‡ NDOROBO, NGURU, ZIGUA‡
  1970

RITUAL-ISLAMIC-FEAST
  OFRI, DORITH‡ LIBERIA‡ VAI‡ 1965-72

RITUAL-LABI
  VIDAL, PIERRE ANTOINE‡ CENTRAL AFRICAN REPUBLIC‡
  GBAYA, KARA‡ 1961-74

RITUAL-MAGIC
  SULZMANN, ERIKA‡ ZAIRE‡ BABOMA, BASENGELE, BOLIA,
  EKONDA, NTOMBA‡ 1953-72

RITUAL-METALLURGY
  VIDAL, PIERRE ANTOINE‡ CENTRAL AFRICAN REPUBLIC‡
  GBAYA, KARA‡ 1961-74

RITUAL-OBJECT-INTERVIEW
  HEALD, SWETTE SCOTT‡ UGANDA‡ GISU‡ 1966-69

RITUAL—ONDO
  DREWAL, HENRY JOHN‡ DAHOMEY‡ YORUBA‡ 1973

RITUAL—SACRED—FOREST
  ZEMPLEIVI, ANDRAS‡ IVORY COAST‡ SENUFO—NA—FAARA‡
  1972—74

RITUAL—SHANGO
  ENGLAND, NICHOLAS M.‡ NIGERIA‡ YORUBA‡ 1969—70+
  1972

RITUAL—SHRINE
  BORGATTI, JEAN M.‡ NIGERIA‡ EDO‡ 1972—73

RITUAL—SPIRIT—POSSESSION
  ZEMPLEIVI, ANDRAS‡ CHAD‡ MOUNDANG‡ 1969

RITUAL—TITLE—TAKING
  BORGATTI, JEAN M.‡ NIGERIA‡ EDO‡ 1972—73

RITUAL—VODUN
  SAVARY, CLAUDE‡ DAHOMEY‡ FON‡ 1966—67

ROYAL
  BAY, EDNA GRACE‡ DAHOMEY‡ FON‡ 1972.

  MAPOMA, ISAIAH MWESA‡ ZAMBIA‡ BEMBA‡ 1968—70+
  1973

  ROUGET, GILBERT‡ DAHOMEY‡ FON, GUN, HOLI, NAGO‡
  1952

  TARDITS, CLAUDE‡ DAHOMEY‡ GUN‡ 1955

  VAN THIEL, PAUL A.H.‡ UGANDA‡ BANTU, BANYANKOLE‡
  1964—65+ 1969+ 1970—72

ROYAL—ORCHESTRA
  QUERSIN, BENOIT J.+ QUERSIN, CHRISTINE M.‡
  NIGERIA‡ ABAKPA—RIGA, AFO, ALAGO, ANGAS, ANKWAI,
  BIROM, BUROM, CHAMBA, EGGON, FULANI, HAUSA, ICHEN,
  IDOMA, JARAWA, JUKUN, KALABARI, KANTANA, KUTEP,
  KWALLA, NUPE, PYEM, RINDRE, TIV, YERGAM, YORUBA‡
  1972—73

RULER
  QUERSIN, BENOIT J.‡ ZAIRE‡ BUSHOCNG, COOFA, IBAAM,
  NGEENDE, PYAANG, SHOOWA‡ 1970

RULER-INTERVIEW
  VAUGHAN, JAMES H.‡ NIGERIA‡ MARGI‡ 1974

SANZA
  BYRD, ROBERT OAKES‡ UGANDA‡ ALUR, BAGANDA,
  BAGWERE, BAKONJO, BANYANKOLE, BANYOLE, KAKWA,
  TESO‡

  QUERSIN, BENOIT J.+ QUERSIN, CHRISTINE M.‡
  NIGERIA‡ ABAKPA-RIGA, AFO, ALAGO, ANGAS, ANKWAI,
  BIROM, BUROM, CHAMBA, EGGON, FULANI, HAUSA, ICHEN,
  IDOMA, JARAWA, JUKUN, KALABARI, KANTANA, KUTEP,
  KWALLA, NUPE, PYEM, RINDRE, TIV, YERGAM, YORUBA‡
  1972-73

  QUERSIN, BENOIT J.‡ ZAIRE‡ BUSHOONG, COOFA, IBAAM,
  NGEENDE, PYAANG, SHOOWA‡ 1970

  QUERSIN, BENOIT J.‡ ZAIRE‡ BATWA, EKONDA, NTOMBA‡
  1970

  QUERSIN, BENOIT J.+ QUERSIN, CHRISTINE M.‡ ZAIRE‡
  BAKUTU, BOKOTE, BONGANDO, BOSAKA, BOYELA, NKUNDU,
  PYGMIES-BATWA, PYGMIES-NGOMBE‡ 1972

  ROUGET, GILBERT‡ DAHOMEY‡ FON, GUN, HOLI, NAGO‡
  1952

  STONE, RUTH M.+ STONE, VERLON L.‡ LIBERIA‡ KPELLE‡
  1970

  VAN OVEN, JACOBA‡ SIERRA LEONE‡ FULA, GALLINAS,
  GOLA, LIMBA, LOKO, MANDINGO, MENDE, SHERBRO, SUSU,
  TEMNE, VAI, YALUNKA‡ 1964-67

SATIRE
  ABDULKADIR, DATTI‡ NIGERIA‡ HAUSA-FULANI‡ 1973

SCHOOL
  DENG, FRANCIS‡ SUDAN‡ DINKA‡ 1971

  JOHNSON, GERALD T.‡ SIERRA LEONE‡ MENDE, TEMNE‡
  1967-68

SCRIPT-KPELLE-INTERVIEW
  STONE, RUTH M.+ STONE, VERLON L.‡ LIBERIA‡ KPELLE‡
  1970

SCRIPT-VAI
  HOLSOE, SVEND E.‡ LIBERIA‡ DEI, GBANDE, GOLA,
  KPELLE, MANDINGO, VAI‡ 1965-70

SECRET-SOCIETY
  GEOFFRION, CHARLES A.‡ SIERRA LEONE‡ TEMNE,
  MANDINGO‡ 1966-67

  GLAZE, ANITA‡ IVORY COAST‡ SENUFO‡ 1969-70

  HERSKOVITS, MELVILLE J.+ HERSKOVITS, FRANCES S.‡
  DAHOMEY‡ FON‡ 1931

  HERSKOVITS, MELVILLE J.+ HERSKOVITS, FRANCES S.‡
  NIGERIA‡ YORUBA‡ 1931

  OKIE, PACKARD L.‡ LIBERIA‡ BASSA, GBANDE, GOLA,
  KISSI, LOMA, MENDE, VAI‡ 1947-54

  OKIE, PACKARD L.‡ LIBERIA‡ BASSA, BELE, GIO,
  KPELLE, KRU, MANDINGO, VAI‡ 1947-54

  RANUNG, BJORN L.C.‡ NIGERIA‡ IGEDE‡ 1971-72

  ROUGET, GILBERT‡ DAHOMEY‡ FON, GUN, HOLI, NAGO‡
  1952

  VAN OVEN, JACOBA‡ SIERRA LEONE‡ FULA, GALLINAS,
  GOLA, LIMBA, LOKO, MANDINGO, MENDE, SHERBRO, SUSU,
  TEMNE, VAI, YALUNKA‡ 1964-67

  WOLFF, HANS‡ NIGERIA‡ EFIK, HAUSA, IBIBIO, KAJE,
  SOBO, PABIR, YORUBA‡ 1953-54

SECRET-SOCIETY-LEADER
  D'AZEVEDO, WARREN L.‡ LIBERIA‡ GOLA‡ 1967

SECRET-SOCIETY-MALE-IDION
  PLOTNICOV, LEONARD‡ NIGERIA‡ BIRCM, EFIK, HAUSA,
  IBIBIO, IBO, IJAW, KAGORO, KATAM, TIV‡ 1961-62

SECRET-SOCIETY-MALE-OGBON
  PLOTNICOV, LEONARD‡ NIGERIA‡ BIRCM, EFIK, HAUSA,
  IBIBIO, IBO, IJAW, KAGORO, KATAM, TIV‡ 1961-62

SECRET-SOCIETY-NJAU
  GEOFFRION, CHARLES A.‡ MALAWI‡ ACHEWA, MANGANJA,
  NGONI‡ 1971-72

SECRET-SOCIETY-SANDE
  JOHNSON, GERALD T.‡ SIERRA LEONE‡ MENDE, TEMNE‡
  1967-68

SECT-DERVISH
  HEAD, SYDNEY W.‡ SUDAN‡ DERVISH‡ 1962

SENTENCE
  REDDEN, JAMES ERSKINE‡ CAMEROON‡ BANTU‡ 1971

  REDDEN, JAMES ERSKINE‡ KENYA‡ LUO‡ 1960-65

  REDDEN, JAMES ERSKINE‡ UPPER VOLTA‡ MOSSI‡
  1962-63

SERENADE
  MERRIAM, ALAN P.+ MERRIAM, BARBARA W.‡ ZAIRE‡
  BAHIMA, BAKOGA, BAKONGO, BAMBUTI, BANGALA, BASHI,
  BATWA, EKONDA‡ 1951-52

SHAMAN
  QUERSIN, BENOIT J.+ QUERSIN, CHRISTINE M.‡ ZAIRE‡
  BATWA, BOLIA, EKONDA‡ 1971

SHEEP-SHEARING
  LORTAT-JACOB, BERNARD‡ MOROCCO‡ AIT-MGOUN‡ 1970

SHRINE-OSHUN
  QUERSIN, BENOIT J.+ QUERSIN, CHRISTINE M.‡
  NIGERIA‡ ABAKPA-RIGA, AFO, ALAGO, ANGAS, ANKWAI,
  BIROM, BUROM, CHAMBA, EGGON, FULANI, HAUSA, ICHEN,
  IDOMA, JARAWA, JUKUN, KALABARI, KANTANA, KUTEP,
  KWALLA, NUPE, PYEM, RINDRE, TIV, YERGAM, YORUBA‡
  1972-73

SLAVE
  BOWLES, PAUL+ WANKLYN, CHRISTOPHER‡ MOROCCO‡ ‡
  CA1959-62

SOCIAL
  ADAMS, CHARLES R.‡ LESOTHO‡ BASOTHO‡ 1969-70

  AFRIKA-STUDIECENTRUM‡ TOGO‡ TYOKOSSI‡

  AKPABOT, SAMUEL EKPE‡ NIGERIA‡ BIROM, HAUSA,
  IBIBIO, IBO‡ 1964-73

  ARGYLE, WILLIAM JOHNSON‡ ZAMBIA‡ SOLI‡ 1957-59

SOCIAL

 AROM, SIMHA‡ CENTRAL AFRICAN REPUBLIC‡
AKA-PYGMIES, LINDA-BANDA, NGBAKA-MABO‡ 1964-67+
1971-73

BARNES, SANDRA THEIS‡ NIGERIA‡ YORUBA‡ 1972

BELLMAN, BERYL LARRY‡ LIBERIA‡ KPELLE, LOMA‡ 1969

BERLINER, PAUL FRANKLIN‡ RHODESIA‡ SHONA‡ 1972

BLACKING, JOHN A.R.‡ UGANDA‡ BAGANDA, BATORO,
KARAMOJONG‡ 1965

BLOCH, MONICA E.‡ MALAGASY REPUBLIC‡ MERINA,
TANALA‡ 1964-71

BLOUNT, BEN G.‡ KENYA‡ LUO‡ 1971

BORGATTI, JEAN M.‡ NIGERIA‡ EDO‡ 1972-73

BRANDILY, MONIQUE‡ CHAD‡ KANEMBU, KOTOKO, TEDA‡
1961+ 1963+ 1965

BRANDILY, MONIQUE‡ LIBYA‡ FEZZANAIS, TEDA‡ 1969

CHRISTIAN, VALERIE‡ UPPER VOLTA‡ BISSA, BOBO,
BWABA, DAGARA, DYULA, FULANI, FULBE, GOUIN,
GOURMANTCHE, HAUSA, KASSENA, KWO, LOBI, MARKA,
MOSSI, NONDOM, POUGOULIS, SAMO-DU-SUD, YARDSE‡
1973-74

CIPARISSE, GERARD JEAN‡ ZAIRE‡ BAKONGO, BASUKU,
BAYAKA‡ 1970-71

ELWA STUDIO, NIGERIA‡ NIGERIA‡ IBO, NUPE, YORUBA‡

ETHNOMUSICOLOGY CENTRE JAAP KUNST‡ MALAWI‡ LOMWE,
MANGANJA‡ 1971

ETHNOMUSICOLOGY CENTRE JAAP KUNST‡ SIERRA LEONE‡ ‡
1974

EULENBERG, JOHN BRYSON‡ NIGERIA‡ HAUSA‡ 1972

GIBSON, GORDON D.‡ BOTSWANA‡ GCIRIKU, HERERO‡
1953

HATFIELD, COLBY R.‡ TANZANIA‡ SUKUMA‡ 1971

SOCIAL

HIMMELHEBER, HANS G.‡ MALI‡ BAMBARA‡ 1953

INSTITUTE OF AFRICAN STUDIES, UNIVERSITY OF IFE‡ NIGERIA‡ IBO, TIV, YORUBA‡

IRVINE, JUDITH TEMKIN‡ SENEGAL‡ WOLOF‡ 1970-71

KAEMMER, JOHN E.‡ RHODESIA‡ KOREKORE, SHONA, ZEZURU‡ 1972-73

KAYE, ALAN S.‡ CHAD‡ ARAB‡ 1970

KAYE, ALAN S.‡ NIGERIA‡ ARAB-SHUWA‡ 1974

KIRK-GREENE, ANTHONY H.M.‡ NIGERIA‡ HAUSA, KAGORO, TIV‡ 1962-65

KOIZUMI, FUMIO‡ NIGERIA‡ YORUBA‡ 1971

KOIZUMI, FUMIO‡ TANZANIA‡ ‡ 1971

KUBIK, GERHARD‡ AFRICA-ANGOLA, CAMEROON, CENTRAL AFRICAN REPUBLIC, CONGO-PEOPLE'S REPUBLIC OF THE, EGYPT, GABON, KENYA, MALAWI, MOZAMBIQUE, NIGERIA, SUDAN, TANZANIA, TOGO, UGANDA, ZAIRE, ZAMBIA‡ ‡ 1959-73

LARSON, THOMAS J.‡ BOTSWANA‡ HAMBUKUSU‡ 1972

LIMA, AUGUSTO GUILHERME MESQUITELA‡ ANGOLA‡ BUSHMEN, CHOKWE, NGANGELA‡ 1963-70

LORTAT-JACOB, BERNARD‡ MOROCCO‡ BERBER, TAMAZIGT, TASLHIT‡ 1969-73

LOUDON, JOSEPH BUIST‡ SOUTH AFRICA‡ ZULU‡ 1952

LOUDON, JOSEPH BUIST‡ TRISTAN DA CUNHA‡ ‡ 1963-64

MANN, WILLIAM MICHAEL‡ ZAMBIA‡ BEMBA, BISA‡ 1967

MAPOMA, ISAIAH MWESA‡ ZAMBIA‡ BEMBA‡ 1968-70+ 1973

MAKAIRE, DUMISANI ABRAHAM‡ RHODESIA‡ SHONA‡ 1971+ 1974

MCLEOD, NORMA‡ MALAGASY REPUBLIC‡ ‡ 1962-63

SOCIAL

MERRIAM, ALAN P.+ MERRIAM, BARBARA W.‡ BURUNDI‡
ABATUTSI, BARUNDI, BATWA‡ 1951-52

MERRIAM, ALAN P.+ MERRIAM, BARBARA W.‡ RWANDA‡
ABAGOGWE, ABAGOYI, ABAHORORO, ABANYAMBO, ABATUTSI,
ABAYOVU, BAHIMA, BAHUTU, BAKIGA, BATWA‡ 1951-52

MERRIAM, ALAN P.+ MERRIAM, BARBARA W.‡ ZAIRE‡
BAHIMA, BAKOGA, BAKONGO, BAMBUTI, BANGALA, BASHI,
BATWA, EKONDA‡ 1951-52

MERRIAM, ALAN P.+ MERRIAM, BARBARA W.‡ ZAIRE‡
BASONGYE‡ 1959-60

ONWUKA, RALPH I.‡ NIGERIA‡ IBO‡

PLOTNICOV, LEONARD‡ NIGERIA‡ BIRCM, EFIK, HAUSA,
IBIBIO, IBO, IJAW, KAGORO, KATAM, TIV‡ 1961-62

QUERSIN, BENOIT J.+ QUERSIN, CHRISTINE M.‡
NIGERIA‡ ABAKPA-RIGA, AFO, ALAGO, ANGAS, ANKWAI,
BIROM, BUROM, CHAMBA, EGGON, FULANI, HAUSA, ICHEN,
IDOMA, JARAWA, JUKUN, KALABARI, KANTANA, KUTEP,
KWALLA, NUPE, PYEM, RINDRE, TIV, YERGAM, YORUBA‡
1972-73

QUERSIN, BENOIT J.‡ ZAIRE‡ BUSHOCNG, COOFA, IBAAM,
NGEENDE, PYAANG, SHOOWA‡ 1970

RANSBOTYN DE DECKER, DANIEL‡ TOGO‡ BOGO, EWE‡
1972-74

REID, MARLENE B.‡ TANZANIA‡ BASUKUMA‡ 1966+ 1969

RHODES, WILLARD‡ RHODESIA‡ SHONA‡ 1958-59

RITZENTHALER, ROBERT + RITZENTHALER, PAT‡
CAMEROON‡ BAFUT‡ 1959

ROBBINS, MICHAEL COOK‡ UGANDA‡ BAGANDA‡ 1967-72

SAYAD, ALI‡ ALGERIA‡ KABYLE‡ 1968-70

SIEGMANN, WILLIAM CHARLES‡ LIBERIA‡ BASSA, GBANDE‡
1973-74

SKINNER, ELLIOTT P.‡ UPPER VOLTA‡ MOSSI‡ 1955-65

SOCIAL

SMITS, LUCAS GERARDUS ALFONSUS‡ ALGERIA‡ TUAREG‡ 1968-69

SMITS, LUCAS GERARDUS ALFONSUS‡ BOTSWANA‡ KUNG-BUSHMEN, SAN‡ 1972

SMITS, LUCAS GERARDUS ALFONSUS‡ LESOTHO‡ BASOTHO‡ 1969+ 1974-75

SMOCK, DAVID R.‡ NIGERIA‡ IBO‡ 1962-63

SNYDER, FRANCIS GREGORY‡ SENEGAL‡ DIOLA‡ 1970

SNYDER, FRANCIS GREGORY‡ SENEGAL‡ DIOLA‡ 1973

SPAIN, DAVID H.‡ NIGERIA‡ KANURI‡ 1966-67

SPENCER, WILLIAM‡ TUNISIA‡ MALOUF‡ 1966-67

SUDAN NATIONAL MUSEUM‡ SUDAN‡ BONGO, JALUO, NUBIAN‡ 1959-64

SULZMANN, ERIKA‡ ZAIRE‡ BABOMA, BASENGELE, BOLIA, EKUNDA, NTOMBA‡ 1953-72

TARDITS, CLAUDE‡ DAHOMEY‡ GUN‡

TRADITIONAL MUSIC DOCUMENTATION PROJECT‡ MOZAMBIQUE‡ CHOPI‡

TRADITIONAL MUSIC DOCUMENTATION PROJECT‡ NIGERIA‡ IBIBIO, IBO, KALABARI, TIV, YORUBA‡

TRADITIONAL MUSIC DOCUMENTATION PROJECT‡ UPPER VOLTA‡ ‡

VAN THIEL, PAUL A.H.‡ UGANDA‡ BANTU, BANYANKOLE‡ 1964-65+ 1969+ 1970-72

VELLENGA, DOROTHY DEE‡ GHANA‡ ‡ 1969

WOLLNER, CHAD A.‡ ETHIOPIA‡ ‡ 1972

WOLLNER, CHAD A.‡ KENYA‡ ‡ 1972

ZEMP, HUGO‡ IVORY COAST‡ BAULE, DAN, GUERE, MALINKE, SENUFO‡ 1962+ 1964-67

SOCIAL-CELEBRATION
  KNIGHT, RODERIC COPLEY‡ SENEGAL‡ FULA, JOLA,
  MANDINKA, WOLOF‡ 1970-71

SOCIAL-CONDITIONS
  UPADHYAYA, HARI S.+ ORI, R.‡ MAURITIUS‡
  UTTAR-PRADESH‡ 1961

SOCIAL-CRITICISM
  SEDLAK, PHILIP A.S.‡ KENYA‡ DURUMA, GIRYAMA,
  SWAHILI‡ 1971

SOCIAL-DANCE
  ADAMS, CHARLES R.‡ SWAZILAND‡ SWAZI‡ 1969-70

SOCIAL-FAMILY-LIFE
  MADIGAN, BOB‡ KENYA‡ KAMBA‡ 1957-58

SOCIAL-MEN
  HERSKOVITS, MELVILLE J.+ HERSKOVITS, FRANCES S.‡
  GHANA‡ ASANTE‡ 1931

  HERZOG, GEORGE‡ LIBERIA‡ GREBO, JABO, KRU‡ 1930

SOCIAL-ORAL-DATA
  MORGENTHAU, HENRY‡ SOUTH AFRICA‡ ‡ CA1961

SOCIAL-RALLY
  KNIGHT, RODERIC COPLEY‡ GAMBIA, THE‡ BALANTA,
  BAMBARA, FULA, JOLA, MANDINKA, TEMNE, WOLOF‡
  1970-71

SOCIAL-REFORM
  THIEL, JOSEF FRANZ‡ ZAIRE‡ MBALA, TEKE, YANSI‡
  1961-71

SOCIAL-WOMEN
  HERZOG, GEORGE‡ LIBERIA‡ GREBO, JABO, KRU‡ 1930

SOCIAL-WOMEN-INSULT
  HERSKOVITS, MELVILLE J.+ HERSKOVITS, FRANCES S.‡
  GHANA‡ ASANTE‡ 1931

SOCIETY-CURING
  RUBIN, ARNOLD G.‡ NIGERIA‡ CHAMBA, HAUSA, IBO,
  JUKUN, KUTEP, TIKARI, TIV‡ 1964-65

SOCIETY-MEN
  WARNIER, JEAN-PIERRE‡ CAMEROON‡ MANKON‡ 1972-74

SONG-CYCLE-BOBONGO
   QUERSIN, BENOIT J.+ QUERSIN, CHRISTINE M.‡ ZAIRE‡
   BATWA, BOLIA, EKONDA‡ 1971

SONG-IBIRIIMBO
   DES FORGES, ALISON LIEBHAFSKY‡ RWANDA‡ BATUTSI‡
   1968

SORCERER
   MERRIAM, ALAN P.+ MERRIAM, BARBARA W.‡ ZAIRE‡
   BAHIMA, BAKOGA, BAKONGO, BAMBUTI, BANGALA, BASHI,
   BATWA, EKONDA‡ 1951-52

SPEECH
   LUCKAU, STEPHEN R.‡ LIBERIA‡ GREBO, JABO‡ 1971

SPEECH-OJUNWU-C.O.
   OFONAGURO, W. IBEKWE+ IRWIN, GRAHAM‡ NIGERIA-U.S.‡
   ‡ 1967

SPIRIT
   FAIK-NZUJI, MADIYA‡ ZAIRE‡ LUBA‡ 1974

   ROUGET, GILBERT‡ DAHOMEY‡ FON, GUN, HOLI, NAGO‡
   1952

SPIRIT-POSSESSION
   ARCHIVES OF ETHNIC MUSIC AND DANCE‡ RHODESIA‡ ‡

   BROGGER, JAN C.‡ ETHIOPIA‡ SIDAMO‡

   GERLACH, LUTHER PAUL‡ KENYA-TANZANIA‡ ARAB, DIGO,
   DURUMA‡ 1958-60

SPIRIT-POSSESSION-SHINKI
   ZEMPLEIVI, ANDRAS‡ CHAD‡ MOUNDANG‡ 1969

SPIRIT-SOCIETY
   HERZOG, GEORGE‡ LIBERIA‡ GREBO, JABO, KRU‡ 1930

SPIRIT-SUPPLICATION
   MERRIAM, ALAN P.+ MERRIAM, BARBARA W.‡ ZAIRE‡
   BAHIMA, BAKOGA, BAKONGO, BAMBUTI, BANGALA, BASHI,
   BATWA, EKONDA‡ 1951-52

SPIRITUAL
   VELLENGA, DOROTHY DEE‡ GHANA‡ ‡ 1969

SPORTS
  OWEN, WILFRED, JR.‡ GHANA‡ ASANTE, BRONG, EWE,
  FANTI, GA, TWI‡ 1970-71

STAMPING-TUBE-BAMBOO
  COPLAN, DAVID+ THOMASON, LEE‡ GHANA‡ ASANTE, EWE,
  KROBO‡ 1974

STICK
  NORSK RIKSKRINGKASTING‡ GHANA‡ ‡ 1966

  PLOTNICOV, LEONARD‡ NIGERIA‡ BIRCM, EFIK, HÁUSA,
  IBIBIO, IBO, IJAW, KAGORO, KATAM, TIV‡ 1961-62

STICK-PERCUSSION
  BIEBUYCK, DANIEL P.‡ ZAIRE‡ LEGA, LUBA, LUNDA,
  MANGBETU, MAYOGO, NANDE, NYANGA, ZAMBE‡ 1952-61

STICK-SCRAPED
  LAMBRECHT, FRANK L.+ LAMBRECHT, DORA J.M.‡
  BOTSWANA‡ KUNG-BUSHMEN, YEI‡ 1967-68

  MERRIAM, ALAN P.+ MERRIAM, BARBARA W.‡ ZAIRE‡
  BAHIMA, BAKOGA, BAKONGO, BAMBUTI, BANGALA, BASHI,
  BATWA, EKONDA‡ 1951-52

  QUERSIN, BENOIT J.+ QUERSIN, CHRISTINE M.‡
  CAMEROON‡ BAFIA, BALLOM, BAMILEKE, BAMUM, BULU
  ETON, PEUL, PYGMIES, SANAGA, TIKAR, VUTE‡ 1967

  QUERSIN, BENOIT J.‡ ZAIRE‡ BATWA, EKONDA, NTOMBA‡
  1970

  QUERSIN, BENOIT J.+ QUERSIN, CHRISTINE M.‡ ZAIRE‡
  BATWA, BOLIA, EKONDA‡ 1971

STONE-CUTTING
  ALBERTS, ARTHUR S.‡ LIBERIA‡ FANTI, LOMA, MANO‡
  1949-51

SWAHILI-ORAL-CLASSROOM
  MOSES, RAE A.‡ TANZANIA‡ ‡ 1966

TAMBOURINE
  BOWLES, PAUL+ WANKLYN, CHRISTOPHER‡ MOROCCO‡ ‡
  CA1959-62

  DEPARTMENT OF ANTHROPOLOGY, UNIVERSITY OF BRITISH
  COLUMBIA‡ TUNISIA‡ ‡

TAMBOURINE
  FARSY, MUHAMMED S.‡ TANZANIA-ZANZIBAR‡ ‡ CA1958

  HANLEY, MARY ANN CSJ‡ GHANA‡ AKAN, EWE, TWI‡ 1973

  WILLIAMS, CHESTER S.‡ SOMALIA‡ ‡ 1962

TATOOING
  AMES, DAVID W.‡ NIGERIA‡ FULBE, HAUSA, YORUBA‡
  1963-64

TITLE-TAKING-RITUAL
  BORGATTI, JEAN M.‡ NIGERIA‡ EDO‡ 1972-73

TOPICAL
  QUERSIN, BENOIT J.+ QUERSIN, CHRISTINE M.‡
  CAMEROON‡ BAFIA, BALLOM, BAMILEKE, BAMUM, BULU
  ETON, PEUL, PYGMIES, SANAGA, TIKAR, VUTE‡ 1967

  QUERSIN, BENOIT J.+ QUERSIN, CHRISTINE M.‡ ZAIRE‡
  BATWA, BOLIA, EKONDA‡ 1971

  STONE, RUTH M.+ STONE, VERLON L.‡ LIBERIA‡ KPELLE‡
  1970

TOTEM
  HERSKOVITS, MELVILLE J.+ HERSKOVITS, FRANCES S.‡
  GHANA‡ ASANTE‡ 1931

TRADE-VILLAGE
  MADIGAN, BOB‡ KENYA‡ KAMBA‡ 1957-58

TRANCE-SUFI
  WANKLYN, CHRISTOPHER‡ MOROCCO‡ AIT-SIDI-MERRI,
  DEGWANA, MISIWA, OULED-MTAA‡ 1963+ 1969

TRANSLATION-HAYA-HAYA-CIC
  REINING, PRISCILLA‡ TANZANIA‡ HAYA‡

TRANSLATION-KU-KW-VERBS
  REINING, PRISCILLA‡ TANZANIA‡ HAYA‡

TRANSLATION-MU-BA-CLASS-N
  REINING, PRISCILLA‡ TANZANIA‡ HAYA‡

TRAPPING
  NOSS, PHILIP A.‡ CAMEROON‡ GBAYA‡ 1966-67

TRUE-WHIG-PARTY
  NEWBURY, DOROTHY J.‡ LIBERIA‡ BASSA, LOMA‡
  1969-70+ 1972

TRUMPET
  ARCHIVES OF ETHNIC MUSIC AND DANCE‡ ETHIOPIA‡
  AMHARA, TIGRINYA‡

ULULATION
  BOWLES, PAUL+ WANKLYN, CHRISTOPHER‡ MOROCCO‡ ‡
  CA1959-62

  CAMP, CHARLES M.+ TRACEY, HUGH‡ RHODESIA‡ BUDJA,
  CHIKUNDA, FUNGWE, HERA, HUNGWE, KARANGA, NDAU,
  NDEBELE, NYANJA, NYASA, PEDI, RAMBA, WEMBA, YAO‡
  1948

  HANLEY, MARY ANN CSJ‡ GHANA‡ BUILSA, DAGARI, EWE,
  FANTI, FRAFRA, GA, KASSENA, NANKANI, TWI‡ 1972

  VAUGHAN, JAMES H.‡ NIGERIA‡ MARGI‡ 1974

URBAN-BAR
  BRAVMANN, RENE A.‡ UPPER VOLTA‡ BOBO, DYULA‡
  1972-74

URBAN-NIGHTCLUB
  BRAVMANN, RENE A.‡ UPPER VOLTA‡ BOBO, DYULA‡
  1972-74

VICTORY
  ARCHIVES OF TRADITIONAL MUSIC‡ ‡ YORUBA‡ CA1940

VOCABULARY
  GIBSON, GORDON D.‡ ANGOLA‡ CHAVIKWA, HAKAWONA,
  HIMBA, KEPE, KUVALE, VATWA, ZIMBA‡ 1971-73

VOICE-DISGUISE
  ARMSTRONG, ROBERT G. +WITTIG, R. CURT‡ NIGERIA‡
  IDUMA‡ 1964

  STONE, RUTH M.+ STONE, VERLON L.‡ LIBERIA‡ KPELLE‡
  1970

WAR
  ADUAMAH, E.Y.‡ GHANA-TOGO‡ EWE‡ 1968-71

  AGUDZE, BERNARD‡ TOGO‡ EWE‡ 1965-67

WAR

ARCHIVES OF TRADITIONAL MUSIC‡ ‡ YORUBA‡ CA1940

BAHMAN, GARY‡ SIERRA LEONE‡ LIMBI, MANDINGO, TEMNE‡ 1971

BERLIN PHONOGRAMM-ARCHIV‡ AFRICA-GERMANY‡ BULE‡ 1909

BROADCASTING CORPORATION OF CHINA‡ ETHIOPIA‡ ‡

CALAME, B.‡ MALI‡ BAMBARA, BOZO, DOGON, MARKA, MINIANKA, PEUL, RYMAYBE, SARAKOLE, SOMONO, SONGHAY‡ 1956-57‡ 1960

CAMP, CHARLES M.+ TRACEY, HUGH‡ RHODESIA‡ BUDJA, CHIKUNDA, FUNGWE, HERA, HUNGWE, KARANGA, NDAU, NDEBELE, NYANJA, NYASA, PEDI, RAMBA, WEMBA, YAO‡ 1948

CARLISLE, ROXANE C.‡ SUDAN‡ ANUAK, DINKA, GAALIIN, NUER, SHILLUK‡ 1963

CURTIN, PHILIP D.‡ SENEGAL‡ ARAB, DIAKHANKE, MALINKE, PULAR‡ 1966

DENG, FRANCIS‡ SUDAN‡ DINKA‡ 1971

DOBRIN, ARTHUR‡ KENYA‡ GUSII‡ 1966

HERSKOVITS, MELVILLE J.+ HERSKOVITS, FRANCES S.‡ DAHOMEY‡ FON‡ 1931

HERZOG, GEORGE‡ LIBERIA‡ GREBO, JABO, KRU‡ 1930

LESLAU, WOLF‡ ETHIOPIA‡ AMHARA, GURAGE, HARARI, SHOA-GALLA, SOMALI, TIGRINYA‡ 1947

MERRIAM, ALAN P.+ MERRIAM, BARBARA W.‡ ZAIRE‡ BAHIMA, BAKOGA, BAKONGO, BAMBUTI, BANGALA, BASHI, BATWA, EKONDA‡ 1951-52

MOREY, ROBERT H.‡ LIBERIA‡ GBANDE, LOMA, MANDINGO‡ 1935

NETTL, BRUNO +RABEN, JOSEPH‡ NIGERIA-U.S.‡ IBO‡ 1950-51

PLOTNICOV, LEONARD‡ NIGERIA‡ BIRCM, EFIK, HAUSA,

WHISTLE-LANGUAGE
   FAIK-NZUJI, MADIYA‡ ZAIRE‡ LUBA‡ 1974

WOMEN
   DRAKE, H. MAX‡ MALAWI‡ TUMBUKA, YAO‡ 1967

   ELLOVICH, RISA SUE‡ IVORY COAST‡ DYULA, MALINKE,
   VOLTAIC‡ 1973-74

   SARDAN, J.-P. OLIVIER DE‡ NIGER‡ SONGHAY‡ 1969

   SHAMAY, M.‡ ALGERIA‡ ‡ 1968

WOMEN-INTERVIEW
   ROBERTSON, CLAIRE C.‡ GHANA‡ GA‡ 1972

WORD-LIST
   BISELE, MARGUERITE A.‡ BOTSWANA‡ KUNG-BUSHMEN‡
   1971-72

   HAMBLY, WILFRED D.‡ ANGOLA‡ OVIMBUNDU‡ 1929-30

   LONG, RONALD W.‡ GHANA‡ MANDE‡ 1968

   LONG, RONALD W.‡ UPPER VOLTA‡ MANDE‡ 1968

   MASSING, ANDREAS‡ LIBERIA‡ KRU‡ 1971-72

   PEEK, PHILIP M.‡ NIGERIA‡ IGBO-WESTERN, ISOKO‡
   1970-71

   REDDEN, JAMES ERSKINE‡ CAMEROON‡ BANTU‡ 1971

   REDDEN, JAMES ERSKINE‡ KENYA‡ LUO‡ 1960-65

   REDDEN, JAMES ERSKINE‡ UPPER VOLTA‡ MOSSI‡
   1962-63

   SAPIR, J. DAVID‡ SENEGAL‡ DIOLA-FOGNY, DIOLA-KASA‡
   1960-65

   VAUGHAN, JAMES H.‡ NIGERIA‡ MARGI‡ 1974

WORD-LIST-AMHARIC
   LESLAU, WOLF‡ ETHIOPIA‡ AMHARA, GURAGE, HARARI,
   SHOA-GALLA, SOMALI, TIGRINYA‡ 1947

WORD-LIST-HARARI
   LESLAU, WOLF‡ ETHIOPIA‡ AMHARA, GURAGE, HARARI,

WORK
  BATWA, BOLIA, EKONDA‡ 1971

  QUERSIN, BENOIT J.+ QUERSIN, CHRISTINE M.‡ ZAIRE‡
  BAKUTU, BOKOTE, BONGANDO, BOSAKA, BOYELA, NKUNDU,
  PYGMIES-BATWA, PYGMIES-NGOMBE‡ 1972

  RITZENTHALER, ROBERT + RITZENTHALER, PAT‡
  CAMEROON‡ BAFUT‡ 1959

  ROUGET, GILBERT‡ SENEGAL‡ LEBOU, PEUL, SARAKOLE,
  SOCE, TUKULOR, WOLOF‡ 1952

  UNITED CHRISTIAN MISSIONARY SOCIETY, DISCIPLES OF
  CHRIST‡ ZAIRE‡ LINGALA, LONKUNDO‡

  WEISSWANGE, KARIN I.S.‡ LIBERIA‡ LOMA, MANDINGO‡
  1963-65+ 1972-73

WORK-COOPERATIVE
  OFRI, DORITH‡ LIBERIA‡ VAI‡ 1965-72

WORK-FIELD
  AMES, DAVID W.‡ GAMBIA, THE‡ WOLOF‡ 1951

  AMES, DAVID W.‡ NIGERIA‡ FULBE, HAUSA, YORUBA‡
  1963-64

  BAHMAN, GARY‡ SIERRA LEONE‡ LIMBA, MANDINGO,
  TEMNE‡ 1971

  GLAZE, ANITA‡ IVORY COAST‡ SENUFO‡ 1969-70

  HANLEY, MARY ANN CSJ‡ GHANA‡ BUILSA, DAGARI, EWE,
  FANTI, FRAFRA, GA, KASSENA, NANKANI, TWI‡ 1972

  HERSKOVITS, MELVILLE J.+ HERSKOVITS, FRANCES S.‡
  DAHOMEY‡ FON‡ 1931

  LAMAN, K.E.‡ ZAIRE‡ BAKONGO‡ 1911

  MASSING, ANDREAS‡ LIBERIA‡ KRU‡ 1971-72

  OKIE, PACKARD L.‡ LIBERIA‡ BASSA, BELE, GIO,
  KPELLE, KRU, MANDINGO, VAI‡ 1947-54

  ROUGET, GILBERT+ GESSAIN, R.+ GESSAIN, M.‡
  SENEGAL‡ BASSARI, BEDIK‡ 1967

WORK-FIELD
  SAPIR, J. DAVID‡ SENEGAL‡ DIOLA-FOGNY, DIOLA-KASA‡
  1960-65

  WEMAN, HENRY PAUL‡ RHODESIA‡ KARANGA, LEMBA,
  VENDA, ZULU‡ 1957

  WEMAN, PAUL HENRY‡ TANZANIA‡ HAYA, SUKUMA,
  SWAHILI‡ 1957

WORK-FIELD-CLEARING
  STONE, RUTH M.+ STONE, VERLON L.‡ LIBERIA‡ KPELLE‡
  1970

WORK-GRINDING
  AMES, DAVID W.‡ NIGERIA‡ FULBE, HAUSA, YORUBA‡
  1963-64

  CURTIS, NATALIE‡ MOZAMBIQUE‡ NDAL‡ CA1919

  LORTAT-JACOB, BERNARD‡ MOROCCO‡ AIT-MGOUN‡ 1970

  RUBIN, ARNOLD G.‡ NIGERIA‡ CHAMBA, HAUSA, IBO,
  JUKUN, KUTEP, TIKARI, TIV‡ 1964-65

WORK-HARVEST
  ARCHIVES OF ETHNIC MUSIC AND DANCE‡ UPPER VOLTA‡
  BOBO, BWABA, DYULA, FULANI, FULBE, GOUIN,
  GOURMANTCHE, LOBI, MINIANKA, MOSSI, SENUFO,
  YARDSE‡

  DOBRIN, ARTHUR‡ KENYA‡ GUSII‡ 1966

  LORTAT-JACOB, BERNARD‡ MOROCCO‡ AIT-MGOUN‡ 1970

  SAPIR, J. DAVID‡ SENEGAL‡ DIOLA-FOGNY, DIOLA-KASA‡
  1960-65

WORK-HOEING
  ETHNOMUSICOLOGY CENTRE JAAP KUNST‡ GAMBIA, THE‡
  MANDINKA‡ 1958

WORK-HOUSE-BUILDING
  GLAZE, ANITA‡ IVORY COAST‡ SENUFO‡ 1969-70

WORK-PLANTING
  STONE, RUTH M.+ STONE, VERLON L.‡ LIBERIA‡ KPELLE‡
  1970

WORK-POUNDING
  SARDAN, J.-P. OLIVIER DE‡ NIGER‡ SONGHAY‡ 1969

WORK-THRESHING
  CAMP, CHARLES M.+ TRACEY, HUGH‡ RHODESIA‡ BUDJA,
  CHIKUNDA, FUNGWE, HERA, HUNGWE, KARANGA, NDAU,
  NDEBELE, NYANJA, NYASA, PEDI, RAMBA, WEMBA, YAO‡
  1948

  WEMAN, HENRY PAUL‡ RHODESIA‡ KARANGA, LEMBA,
  VENDA, ZULU‡ 1957

WORK-THRESHING-MILLET
  ARCHIVES OF ETHNIC MUSIC AND DANCE‡ UPPER VOLTA‡
  BOBO, BWABA, DYULA, FULANI, FULBE, GOUIN,
  GOURMANTCHE, LOBI, MINIANKA, MOSSI, SENUFO,
  YARDSE‡

WORK-WOMEN
  HARRIES, JEANETTE‡ MOROCCO‡ BERBER‡ 1964-65

WRESTLING
  AMES, DAVID W.‡ GAMBIA, THE‡ WOLOF‡ 1951

  AMES, DAVID W.‡ NIGERIA‡ FULBE, HAUSA, YORUBA‡
  1963-64

  AMES, DAVID W.‡ NIGERIA‡ IGBO‡ 1963-64

  QUERSIN, BENOIT J.+ QUERSIN, CHRISTINE M.‡ ZAIRE‡
  BAKUTU, BOKOTE, BONGANDO, BOSAKA, BOYELA, NKUNDU,
  PYGMIES-BATWA, PYGMIES-NGOMBE‡ 1972

  SAPIR, J. DAVID‡ SENEGAL‡ DIOLA-FOGNY, DIOLA-KASA‡
  1960-65

XYLOPHONE
  AKPABOT, SAMUEL EKPE‡ NIGERIA‡ BIROM, HAUSA,
  IBIBIO, IBO‡ 1964-73

  ALBERTS, ARTHUR S.‡ GHANA‡ EWE, GA, IBO, TWI‡
  1949-51

  ALBERTS, ARTHUR S.‡ GUINEA‡ KISSI, MALINKE‡
  1949-51

  ALBERTS, ARTHUR S.‡ MALI‡ BAMBARA‡ 1949-51

  ALBERTS, ARTHUR S.‡ UPPER VOLTA‡ BAMBARA, MOSSI‡

XYLOPHONE
  1949-51

  AMES, DAVID W.‡ NIGERIA‡ IGBO‡ 1963-64

  ANDERSON, LOIS ANN‡ UGANDA‡ ‡ 1964-66+ 1969

  ARCHIVES OF ETHNIC MUSIC AND DANCE‡ CAMEROON‡ ‡

  ARCHIVES OF ETHNIC MUSIC AND DANCE‡ GHANA‡
  DAGARTI, DAGOMBA, DONNO, EWE, GA, KONKOMBA, LOBI‡

  ARCHIVES OF ETHNIC MUSIC AND DANCE‡ GUINEA‡ ‡

  ARCHIVES OF ETHNIC MUSIC AND DANCE‡ UPPER VOLTA‡
  BOBO, BWABA, DYULA, FULANI, FULBE, GOUIN,
  GOURMANTCHE, LOBI, MINIANKA, MOSSI, SENUFO,
  YARDSE‡

  ARCHIVES OF ETHNIC MUSIC AND DANCE‡ ZAMBIA‡ LOZI,
  LUCHAZI‡

  ARNOTT, D.‡ UPPER VOLTA‡ MALINKE‡ 1956

  BAHMAN, GARY‡ SIERRA LEONE‡ LIMBA, MANDINGO,
  TEMNE‡ 1971

  BIRD, CHARLES S.‡ MALI‡ BAMBARA‡ 1967-68

  CALAME, B.‡ MALI‡ BAMBARA, BOZO, DOGON, MARKA,
  MINIANKA, PEUL, RYMAYBE, SARAKOLE, SOMONO,
  SONGHAY‡ 1956-57+ 1960

  CAMP, CHARLES M.+ TRACEY, HUGH‡ SOUTH AFRICA‡
  BHACA, CHOPI, HLUBI, NDAU, NYASA, PONDO, SHANGAAN,
  SOTHO, SWAZI, TSWANA, VENDA, XHOSA‡ 1947-48

  CAMP, CHARLES M.+ TRACEY, HUGH‡ ZAMBIA‡ BEMBA,
  LALA, LOZI, TONGA, ZINZA‡ 1947-48

  CLAUSS, BERNHARD PETER‡ MALI‡ BAMBARA, TAMACHECK‡
  1973

  COOKE, PETER R.‡ UGANDA‡ BAGANDA‡ 1965-68

  DEPARTMENT OF THEATRE ARTS, UNIVERSITY OF DAR ES
  SALAAM‡ TANZANIA‡ ‡

  ELLOVICH, RISA SUE‡ IVORY COAST‡ DYULA, MALINKE,

XYLOPHONE
  VOLTAIC‡ 1973-74

  ENGLAND, NICHOLAS M.‡ SENEGAL‡ ‡ 1969-70

  FERNANDEZ, JAMES W.‡ GABON‡ FANG‡ 1960

  FIKRY, MONA‡ GHANA‡ WALA‡ 1966-67

  GANSEMANS, JOS‡ ZAIRE‡ LUBA‡ 1970

  GLAZE, ANITA‡ IVORY COAST‡ SENUFO‡ 1969-70

  HANLEY, MARY ANN CSJ‡ GHANA‡ BUILSA, DAGARI, EWE,
  FANTI, FRAFRA, GA, KASSENA, NANKANI, TWI‡ 1972

  HASSENPFLUG, EARL C.‡ MALI‡ BOZO, DOGON‡ 1970

  HERZOG, GEORGE‡ LIBERIA‡ GREBO, JABO, KRU‡ 1930

  KOECHLIN, B.‡ MALAGASY REPUBLIC‡ MAHAFALY,
  MASIKORO, VEZO‡ 1967-69

  LESLAU, WOLF‡ ETHIOPIA‡ AMHARA, GURAGE, HARARI,
  SHOA-GALLA, SOMALI, TIGRINYA‡ 1947

  MEINHOF, CARL‡ TANZANIA‡ BONDEI‡ 1902-03

  MERRIAM, ALAN P.+ MERRIAM, BARBARA W.‡ ZAIRE‡
  BASONGYE‡ 1959-60

  MERRIAM, ALAN P.‡ ZAIRE‡ BASONGYE‡ 1973

  MULDROW, WILLIAM+ MULDROW, ELIZABETH‡ ETHIOPIA‡
  TESHENNA‡ 1964-65

  OKIE, PACKARD L.‡ LIBERIA‡ BASSA, BELE, GIO,
  KPELLE, KRU, MANDINGO, VAI‡ 1947-54

  PLOTNICOV, LEONARD‡ NIGERIA‡ BIROM, EFIK, HAUSA,
  IBIBIO, IBO, IJAW, KAGORO, KATAM, TIV‡ 1961-62

  QUERSIN, BENOIT J.+ QUERSIN, CHRISTINE M.‡
  NIGERIA‡ ABAKPA-RIGA, AFO, ALAGO, ANGAS, ANKWAI,
  BIROM, BUROM, CHAMBA, EGGON, FULANI, HAUSA, ICHEN,
  IDOMA, JARAWA, JUKUN, KALABARI, KANTANA, KUTEP,
  KWALLA, NUPE, PYEM, RINDRE, TIV, YERGAM, YORUBA‡
  1972-73

XYLOPHONE
  RHODES, WILLARD‡ NIGERIA‡ FULANI, HAUSA, TIV,
  TUAREG, YORUBA‡ 1973-74

  RUBIN, ARNOLD G.‡ NIGERIA‡ CHAMBA, HAUSA, IBO,
  JUKUN, KUTEP, TIKARI, TIV‡ 1964-65

  STONE, RUTH M.+ STONE, VERLON L.‡ LIBERIA‡ KPELLE‡
  1970

  TESSMAN, GUNTHER‡ CAMEROON‡ FANG-PANGWE‡ 1907

  VAN OVEN, JACOBA‡ SIERRA LEONE‡ FULA, GALLINAS,
  GOLA, LIMBA, LOKO, MANDINGO, MENDE, SHERBRO, SUSU,
  TEMNE, VAI, YALUNKA‡ 1964-67

  WEMAN, PAUL HENRY‡ ZAIRE‡ LUBA‡ 1957

XYLOPHONE-AMADINDA
  BYRD, ROBERT OAKES‡ UGANDA‡ ALUR, BAGANDA,
  BAGWERE, BAKONJO, BANYANKOLE, BANYOLE, KAKWA,
  TESO‡

XYLOPHONE-BALA
  ROUGET, GILBERT‡ GUINEA‡ MALINKE‡ 1952

XYLOPHONE-BALO
  KNIGHT, RODERIC COPLEY‡ GAMBIA, THE‡ BALANTA,
  BAMBARA, FULA, JOLA, MANDINKA, TEMNE, WOLOF‡
  1970-71

XYLOPHONE-BIRIFOR
  ARCHIVES OF ETHNIC MUSIC AND DANCE‡ UPPER VOLTA‡
  BOBO, BWABA, DYULA, FULANI, FULBE, GOUIN,
  GOURMANTCHE, LOBI, MINIANKA, MOSSI, SENUFO,
  YARDSE‡

XYLOPHONE-DUET
  ARCHIVES OF ETHNIC MUSIC AND DANCE‡ GHANA‡
  DAGARTI, DAGOMBA, DONNO, EWE, GA, KONKOMBA, LOBI‡

XYLOPHONE-EMBAIRE
  BYRD, ROBERT OAKES‡ UGANDA‡ ALUR, BAGANDA,
  BAGWERE, BAKONJO, BANYANKOLE, BANYOLE, KAKWA,
  TESO‡

XYLOPHONE-ENDIGA
  BYRD, ROBERT OAKES‡ UGANDA‡ ALUR, BAGANDA,
  BAGWERE, BAKONJO, BANYANKOLE, BANYOLE, KAKWA,

XYLOPHONE-ENDIGA
  TESO‡

XYLOPHONE-ENSEMBLE
  ARCHIVES OF ETHNIC MUSIC AND DANCE‡ UPPER VOLTA‡
  BOBO, BWABA, DYULA, FULANI, FULBE, GOUIN,
  GOURMANTCHE, LOBI, MINIANKA, MOSSI, SENUFO,
  YARDSE‡

XYLOPHONE-MIRULI
  BYRD, ROBERT OAKES‡ UGANDA‡ ALUR, BAGANDA,
  BAGWERE, BAKONJO, BANYANKOLE, BANYOLE, KAKWA,
  TESO‡

XYLOPHONE-TUNING
  MERRIAM, ALAN P.‡ ZAIRE‡ BASONGYE‡ 1973

YODEL
  CAMP, CHARLES M.+ TRACEY, HUGH‡ RHODESIA‡ BUDJA,
  CHIKUNDA, FUNGWE, HERA, HUNGWE, KARANGA, NDAU,
  NDEBELE, NYANJA, NYASA, PEDI, RAMBA, WEMBA, YAO‡
  1948

ZITHER
  BIEBUYCK, DANIEL P.‡ ZAIRE‡ LEGA, LUBA, LUNDA,
  MANGBETU, MAYOGO, NANDE, NYANGA, ZAMBE‡ 1952-61

  CAMP, CHARLES M.+ TRACEY, HUGH‡ SOUTH AFRICA‡
  BHACA, CHOPI, HLUBI, NDAU, NYASA, PONDO, SHANGAAN,
  SOTHO, SWAZI, TSWANA, VENDA, XHOSA‡ 1947-48

  COOKE, PETER R.‡ UGANDA‡ BAGANDA‡ 1965-68

  KOECHLIN, B.‡ MALAGASY REPUBLIC‡ MAHAFALY,
  MASIKORO, VEZO‡ 1967-69

  PLOTNICOV, LEONARD‡ NIGERIA‡ BIRCM, EFIK, HAUSA,
  IBIBIO, IBO, IJAW, KAGORO, KATAM, TIV‡ 1961-62

  QUERSIN, BENOIT J.+ QUERSIN, CHRISTINE M.‡
  NIGERIA‡ ABAKPA-RIGA, AFO, ALAGO, ANGAS, ANKWAI,
  BIROM, BUROM, CHAMBA, EGGON, FULANI, HAUSA, ICHEN,
  IDOMA, JARAWA, JUKUN, KALABARI, KANTANA, KUTEP,
  KWALLA, NUPE, PYEM, RINDRE, TIV, YERGAM, YORUBA‡
  1972-73

  QUERSIN, BENOIT J.‡ ZAIRE‡ BATWA, EKONDA, NTOMBA‡
  1970

ZITHER
  ROUGET, GILBERT‡ DAHOMEY‡ FON, GUN, HOLI, NAGO‡
  1952

ZITHER-RAFT
  AMES, DAVID W.‡ NIGERIA‡ IGBO‡ 1963-64

  QUERSIN, BENOIT J.+ QUERSIN, CHRISTINE M.‡
  NIGERIA‡ ABAKPA-RIGA, AFO, ALAGO, ANGAS, ANKWAI,
  BIROM, BUROM, CHAMBA, EGGON, FULANI, HAUSA, ICHEN,
  IDOMA, JARAWA, JUKUN, KALABARI, KANTANA, KUTEP,
  KWALLA, NUPE, PYEM, RINDRE, TIV, YERGAM, YORUBA‡
  1972-73

  RHODES, WILLARD‡ NIGERIA‡ FULANI, HAUSA, TIV,
  TUAREG, YORUBA‡ 1973-74

  RUBIN, ARNOLD G.‡ NIGERIA‡ CHAMBA, HAUSA, IBO,
  JUKUN, KUTEP, TIKARI, TIV‡ 1964-65

ZITHER-STICK
  MERRIAM, ALAN P.+ MERRIAM, BARBARA W.‡ ZAIRE‡
  BAHIMA, BAKOGA, BAKONGO, BAMBUTI, BANGALA, BASHI,
  BATWA, EKONDA‡ 1951-52

ZITHER-TRIANGULAR-FRAME
  OKIE, PACKARD L.‡ LIBERIA‡ BASSA, BELE, GIO,
  KPELLE, KRU, MANDINGO, VAI‡ 1947-54

  STONE, RUTH M.+ STONE, VERLON L.‡ LIBERIA‡ KPELLE‡
  1970

  VAN OVEN, JACOBA‡ SIERRA LEONE‡ FULA, GALLINAS,
  GOLA, LIMBA, LOKO, MANDINGO, MENDE, SHERBRO, SUSU,
  TEMNE, VAI, YALUNKA‡ 1964-67

ZITHER-TROUGH
  HARTWIG, GERALD W.‡ TANZANIA‡ KEREWE‡ 1968-69

  MERRIAM, ALAN P.+ MERRIAM, BARBARA W.‡ BURUNDI‡
  ABATUTSI, BARUNDI, BATWA‡ 1951-52

  MERRIAM, ALAN P.+ MERRIAM, BARBARA W.‡ RWANDA‡
  ABAGOGWE, ABAGOYI, ABAHORORO, ABANYAMBO, ABATUTSI,
  ABAYOVU, BAHIMA, BAHUTU, BAKIGA, BATWA‡ 1951-52

  MERRIAM, ALAN P.+ MERRIAM, BARBARA W.‡ ZAIRE‡
  BAHIMA, BAKOGA, BAKONGO, BAMBUTI, BANGALA, BASHI,
  BATWA, EKONDA‡ 1951-52

ZITHER-TROUGH
  WEMAN, PAUL HENRY‡ TANZANIA‡ HAYA, SUKUMA,
  SWAHILI‡ 1957

ZITHER-TROUGH-INANGA
  DES FORGES, ALISON LIEBHAFSKY‡ RWANDA‡ BATUTSI‡
  1968